Advanced
C# Programming

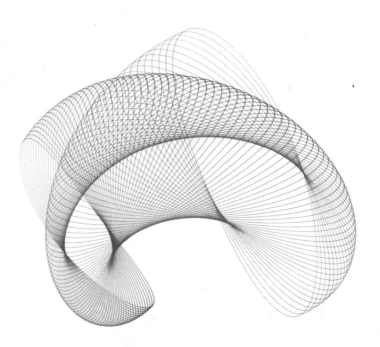

About the Author

Paul Kimmel founded Software Conceptions, Inc., in Okemos, Michigan in 1990. Paul specializes in object-oriented architecture and software design. He is the frameworks columnist for *Windows Developer Magazine,* a bimonthly columnist for *codeguru.com,* and a contributing columnist to *InformIT*. Paul has written several books on object-oriented programming. He is currently the lead architect for a C# and ASP.NET enterprise application for managing the corrections division of the sherrif's office in Oregon, and he has successfully implemented dozens of corporate and commercial applications in the telecom, insurance, and financial industries and for law enforcement and government agencies, with customers throughout the United States, Canada, and Puerto Rico.

Advanced
C# Programming

Paul Kimmel

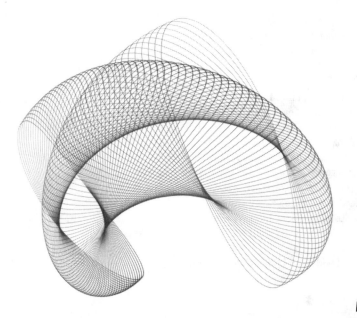

McGraw-Hill/Osborne

New York Chicago San Francisco
Lisbon London Madrid Mexico City
Milan New Delhi San Juan Seoul
Singapore Sydney Toronto

McGraw-Hill/Osborne
2600 Tenth Street
Berkeley, California 94710
U.S.A.

To arrange bulk purchase discounts for sales promotions, premiums, or fund-raisers, please contact **McGraw-Hill/**Osborne at the above address. For information on translations or book distributors outside the U.S.A., please see the International Contact Information page immediately following the index of this book.

Advanced C# Programming

1234567890 CUS CUS 0198765432

ISBN 0-07-222417-7

Publisher	Brandon A. Nordin
Vice President & Associate Publisher	Scott Rogers
Editorial Director	Wendy Rinaldi
Project Editor	Katie Conley
Acquisitions Coordinator	Tim Madrid
Technical Editors	Kevin Feige, Rob Howard, Roger Stanev
Copy Editor	Carl Wikander
Proofreader	Linda Medoff
Indexer	Irv Hershman
Computer Designers	George Toma Charbak, Tara Davis
Illustrators	Michael Mueller, Lyssa Wald
Cover Series Design	Greg Scott
Cover Illustration	Akira Inoue/Photonica

This book was composed with Corel VENTURA™ Publisher.

For Trevor, Douglas, and Noah,
I love you for the good-natured, loving boys that you are
and the fine men I know you will be.
Love, Fat Daddy

Contents at a Glance

Contents

Acknowledgments

I would like to thank Wendy Rinaldi and Katie Conley at McGraw-Hill/Osborne. There is a tremendous amount of work that goes into a book, and even more that goes into books with lots of code. Without their vision and efforts, I wouldn't have had the opportunity to write this book. I hope I gave as much as I got.

Thanks to David Fugate at Waterside for proactive stewardship and for taking care of the nuts-and-bolts stuff that makes it possible for me to write. Special thanks to Mary Bonnici who has taken professional care of all financial matters without fail for many years now.

Special thanks to Susan Warren and Rob Howard at Microsoft. Susan and Rob provided invaluable assistance by reviewing the outline, providing timely and proactive assistance on the tough questions, and coordinating all of the IBUYSPY coverage. Thank you Susan and Rob.

Thanks to Steve Balmer, who has made it a policy for all of the busy Microsoft employees to drop what they are doing to help customers and authors. Clearly, the program managers and developers take Steve seriously. As far as I know, no one was directly compensated for helping me with technical questions, and my total experience demonstrates Microsoft's clear commitment to developers, to Microsoft .NET, and to the authors and publishers trying to bring developers the highest quality of information possible. Thanks to all of the program managers and developers who answered dozens of questions cheerfully and quickly.

I would like to thank Lewis Gouge. Mr. Gouge played matchmaker between me and Multnomah County ISD. Building an enterprise system using .NET for the corrections department was a rewarding challenge. Thanks to Steve "Mr. Ed" Chennault, Mark "Ploki" Davis, Bill Arnold, Joe "Bilbo" Shook, Robert Phillips, Brook Riddick, Yvette Yutze, Jeff Braunstein, Peggy Duerscherl, Richard "Jelly" Augelli, Eric "Hank Hill" Cotter, John "Ballpeen" Armitage, Kathy Erwin, Geoff Caylor, and Karen Britton. I enjoyed working with and learning from so many smart people in one place.

Thanks to Yonnie, Erin, and Larinda at Wynne's in Portland, Oregon for food and adult beverages.

Finally, thank you to my family—Lori, Alex, Douglas, Noah, and Trevor. The only thing I enjoy more than building software and writing is spending time with you guys. Home truly is where my heart is.

Introduction

*A*dvanced C# Programming is about programmers and code. This book was conceived around the idea of providing a lot of code listings for programmers who need to solve problems now.

In each chapter you will find a brief introduction presenting the program showcased in the chapter and describing the kinds of problems that you may encounter and how the code presented will help you tackle them. From there, you can go right to the complete code listing to find the solutions, then read the explanations that follow describing the technology that supports the code listing.

Because each code listing is a complete application, you will find several applications that demonstrate both primary and secondary capabilities of C# and Microsoft .NET.

Advanced C# Programming was written for developers who have an intermediate to advanced level of experience with similar languages, such as C++, Delphi, or Visual Basic .NET, or who have read an introductory-level book explaining the fundamentals of object-oriented programming with C#.

As a special feature, Chapters 12 through 16 demonstrate the advanced aspects of ASP.NET programming for the Web with C#. I am pleased to tell you that these chapters of *Advanced C# Programming* showcase the IBUYSPY.COM Web site as the application for demonstrating software development concepts for the Web. We could not have done this without the blessing and able assistance of Microsoft and Susan Warren, program manager for ASP.NET.

The code examples in this book will demonstrate how to use the most beneficial and powerful aspects of C# programming for Windows and the Web. Everything you need to know about Reflection, Assemblies, object-oriented programming, security and authentication, and Web Services and Web applications for e-commerce sites can be found within this book. All you have to do is open it up and begin exploring.

Windows Applications

OBJECTIVES

► Learn advanced idioms in C#

► Learn fundamental Windows programming
  skills for .NET

► Learn about custom control creation, including
  topics on shaped forms, control transparency,
  GraphicsPath objects, and linear gradient brushes

► Learn Peer-To-Peer programming and Web
  Services by participating in the .NET
  Terrarium game

► Learn all about ADO.NET

Language Foundations

IN THIS CHAPTER:

Object-Oriented Basics

Operator Overloading

Attributes

Reflection

Summary

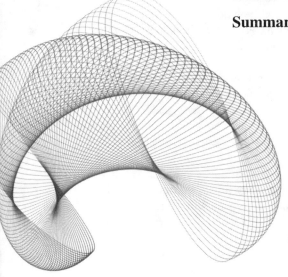

This is the only chapter of its kind in *C# Developer's Guide*. It provides a general review of advanced idioms before we embark on the journey of exploring code listings. These advanced idioms are essential to implementing solutions used in C#, and this review will help get us all on the same footing.

For senior programmers with many years of experience in object-oriented programming, this chapter may be a good review for you. For everyone, there are important aspects of C# programming and .NET programming in general that will be new because they were introduced in .NET. Discussions of what is meant by "delegates," by "Reflection," and by "an assembly" will provide important foundations for building advanced applications in C#. Every chapter after this one builds on these advanced general concepts.

Object-Oriented Basics

Object-oriented basics are far from basic. Every object-oriented language implements a subset of those things that make a good object-oriented language. And C#, distinct from C++, Delphi, or Visual Basic 6 or Visual Basic.NET, has its own unique way of implementing these aspects of an object-oriented programming language (OOPL).

The tenets of object-oriented programming are *encapsulation, inheritance, aggregation,* and *polymorphism.* Languages that support these basic tenets are considered object-oriented languages. There is a diverse set of idioms and constructs that facilitate each of these tenets, including things like templates, operator overloading, interfaces, multithreading, multiple inheritance, exception handling, pointers, and garbage collection. C# is a powerful OOPL that supports the tenets of object-oriented programming by providing operator overloading, inheritance, interfaces, exception handling, garbage collection, multiple interface inheritance, reflection, and multithreading. C# does not support templates, raw pointers, or multiple class inheritance. There is a lot of debate over whether or not these latter three features introduce more problems than they solve; for this reason they were left out of C#.

Instead of multiple inheritance, pointers, and templates, you do get additional new features that will help you build Web applications and Web services. C# supports COM Interop, multilanguage programming, and rapid application development. There are a few trade-offs.

C# is *managed* code. The benefit is that you don't have to worry about the slicing problem caused by bad pointers, and the garbage collector will help you avoid memory leaks. The trade-off is the relinquishment of raw pointers. Pointers support some advanced idioms, like reference-counted objects and access to all memory. This same access to any memory address provides ultimate control and responsibility. With power comes responsibility. (For raw pointers, you can still use unmanaged C++ code.)

C# is most like C++ in its grammar. Most of the everyday idioms you will use regularly in C# have the same syntax as C++, making the learning curve for C++ programmers the shallowest. Delphi and Java programmers will also find the transition to C# relatively easy, and even VB programmers will find a transition from VB to C# easier than from VB to C++.

C++ and Java programmers will feel right at home with the C# syntax, and Visual C++ programmers will appreciate the Visual Basic–like rapid application development supported by C# for Windows and the Web.

Defining Classes

The class construct has the same basic elements found in C++. To define a class in C#, you need to add the following construct to a code unit.

```
Access-modifier class name
{
}
```

TIP

C# is case-sensitive. Keywords are typed in the same case you will need to use in your code. C++ is also case-sensitive; other languages, like Delphi and Visual Basic .NET, are case-insensitive.

Access modifier describes the accessibility of the class. Classes for general consumption will be *public*. The *name* is any name that is unique by characters and case in the same namespace. (We'll get back to namespaces in a moment.)

Applying these basic rules to defining classes, the following example demonstrates a class defined in C#.

```
public class MyFirstClass
{
}
```

By default, classes have public access in C#; and by convention, class names are initial-capped, as demonstrated. The *M* in "My," the *F* in "First," and the *C* in "Class" are all capitalized, a convention referred to as *Pascal casing*. (Conventions are there to breed consistency, but are elections that you can choose to adopt or not. We will stick with conventions in this book.)

Implementing a Class in a Console Application

A *console application* is one that runs at a command prompt without a graphical user interface, or at least without the Windows Forms graphical user interface.

When you create a console application from the New Project dialog, you will get the basic code shown here:

```
using System;
namespace HelloWorld
{
    /// <summary>
    /// Summary description for Class1.
    /// </summary>
```

```
class Class1
{
  /// <summary>
  /// The main entry point for the application.
  /// </summary>
  [STAThread]
  static void Main(string[] args)
  {
    //
    // TODO: Add code to start application here
    //
  }
}
}
```

The *using* statement at the beginning of the listing indicates that the console application is using the System.dll assembly installed with the Microsoft.NET framework. The System assembly contains the most fundamental elements of the Common Language Runtime. For now, think of an assembly as an application or DLL, and the *using* statement as an "include" in C++ or a "uses" in Delphi.

The namespace construct comes next. Namespaces are a higher level of conceptualization than classes. A namespace is a convenient way to organize elements together and to uniquely identify them. Two separate namespaces can contain the same class. By default, the namespace given to the console application will be the name given to the project in the New Project dialog.

The three slash marks (///) is a special comment used to support automatic documentation generation, and the // and /* */ comment styles are supported in C# too. The class definition is provided next. By default, auto-generated code constructs are given the name *type number*—for example, Class1, where Class is derived from the type of construct, a class, and the number is appended as a suffix to ensure a unique name. You are encouraged to provide a descriptive name for your classes.

Inside the basic console application, we have the startup procedure Main. Main is defined as a *static member*, which means we do not have to have an instance of the enclosing class to call the method. The argument **string[] args** indicates that Main is passed an array of strings representing the command line arguments.

Finally, note that all constructs have an opening and closing bracket pair, { }, using the same level of block indentation to facilitate readability.

Hello World   Using our simple console application we can display some text to the console by adding the statement Console.WriteLine("Hello World!"); the modified application follows.

```
using System;
namespace HelloWorld
{
```

```
/// <summary>
/// Summary description for Class1.
/// </summary>
class Class1
{
  /// <summary>
  /// The main entry point for the application.
  /// </summary>
  [STAThread]
  static void Main(string[] args)
  {
    Console.WriteLine("Hello World!");
    Console.ReadLine();
  }
}
}
```

Using the Visual Studio 6 keyboard scheme—modifiable in My Profile in Visual Studio .NET—we can press F5 to run the application. Both WriteLine and ReadLine are static members in the Console class, so we do not need to create an instance of a Console object to call these methods.

Console.WriteLine writes a line to the command prompt, appending a new line to the end of the text, and the statement Console.ReadLine waits for a carriage return before continuing. Also, note that statements in C# are terminated with a semicolon.

Reading from the Command Prompt   If you want to read arguments passed from the command prompt, then you can get them out of the array of strings represented by the parameter *args*. By modifying the code as follows, we can echo the text entered at the command prompt instead of "Hello World".

```
using System;
namespace HelloWorld
{
  /// <summary>
  /// Summary description for Class1.
  /// </summary>
  class Class1
  {
    /// <summary>
    /// The main entry point for the application.
    /// </summary>
    [STAThread]
    static void Main(string[] args)
    {
      Console.WriteLine(args[0]);
```

```
        Console.ReadLine();
    }
  }
}
```

The preceding code writes the value of the first argument passed on the command prompt to the console.

To supply a command line argument, run the assembly from the command prompt or follow these steps to supply a command line argument in the Visual Studio .NET IDE.

1. In Visual Studio .NET, click View | Solution Explorer.

2. In Solution Explorer, right-click over the project name and select the Properties context menu.

3. In the Property Pages dialog, select the Configuration Properties folder followed by the Debugging page.

4. Enter a value for the Command Line Arguments (see Figure 1-1) in the Start Options section.

5. Press F5 to re-run the application in the VS.NET IDE. You will see the value you entered in the Command Line Arguments field in Step 4.

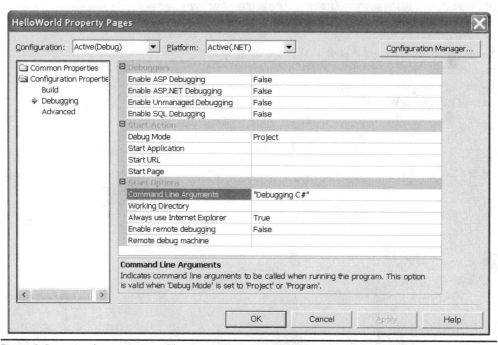

Figure 1-1 *Supplying command line arguments in the HelloWorld Property Pages*

Implementing Fields and Properties

Fields are data in classes. By convention, fields are private; if you need to provide access to consumers then you are encouraged to do so through property methods. Property methods, or properties, look and act like data from the perspective of the consumer but act like methods from the perspective of the producer.

NOTE

Consumers *are programmers who use the classes, and* producers *are programmers who create the classes. The same programmer can be both a producer and consumer of the same class.*

The benefit of data, of course, is that it provides a way to maintain the state of an object. The benefit of properties is that they allow you to constrain the way data is accessed with code, just as if access were limited to access via methods, but from the perspective of the consumer the properties are used like data.

Defining Fields   Fields can be any kind of data. By convention, fields use the private access modifier, allowing only the producer to manipulate the field directly. Consumers must manipulate fields using property methods.

NOTE

By convention, you should name fields using camel-casing. In camel-casing, the first letter of the first word is lowercase and the first letter of subsequent words are uppercase. Do not use the Hungarian notation.

If fields are complex data types, then you can create instances of those types in the constructor (see the section "Implementing Methods") or upon demand. The following listing demonstrates a simple field type that stores the value of *args[0]* as a string type.

```
using System;
namespace HelloWorld
{
  /// <summary>
  /// Summary description for Class1.
  /// </summary>
  class Class1
  {
    private static string arg0 = null;
    /// <summary>
    /// The main entry point for the application.
    /// </summary>
    [STAThread]
    static void Main(string[] args)
    {
      arg0 = args[0];
```

```
      Console.WriteLine(arg0);
      Console.ReadLine();
    }
  }
}
```

The statement in boldface defines a static field. Because we are assigning the value of *args[0]* to the private field *arg0*, and there is no instance of Class1.

The Main method is a starting point for a console application. We could use it for that purpose only and revise the class accordingly to perform the same task but while using an instance of the class. The code so revised follows:

```
using System;
namespace HelloWorld
{
  /// <summary>
  /// Summary description for Class1.
  /// </summary>
  class Class1
  {
    private string arg0 = null;

    public void WriteCommandLine( string arg )
    {
      Console.WriteLine(arg);
      Console.ReadLine();
    }
    /// <summary>
    /// The main entry point for the application.
    /// </summary>
    [STAThread]
    static void Main(string[] args)
    {
      Class1 class1 = new Class1();
      class1.arg0 = args[0];
      class1.WriteCommandLine(class1.arg0);
    }
  }
}
```

In the preceding example, the Main method plays the role of startup method only, and an instance of the class is used to perform the work. The Main method creates an instance of

Class1. The value of *args[0]* is assigned to the private field *arg0*; we can do this because Main is also a member of Class1. The statement

```
class1.WriteCommandLine(class1.arg0)
```

writes the contents of the command line to the console.

Defining Properties   If you are reasonably comfortable with console applications, static members, and creating objects, then this code is ultra trivial. Let's step it up a little bit. We'll leave the example and look at the mechanics of using properties.

Properties are effectively methods. Properties can have a getter and a setter. The *getter* is the property method that is called when a property is used as a right-hand-side value. The *setter* is called when the property is used as a left-hand-side value.

TIP

You do not have to have an underlying field associated with a property. The value of the property can be derived rather than stored in a field.

Properties, like any member, can have access modifiers, which are usually public for properties. The basic syntax of a readable and writable property follows.

```
Access-Modifier Type Property-Name
{
  get
  {
    return field;
  }
  set
  {
    field = value;
  }
}
```

The *Access-Modifier* is usually public but can be any of the allowable access modifiers (see the section "Using Modifiers"). *Type* is the type of the field that the property represents. The *Property-Name* is any valid name. Usually there is a relationship between a property and its underlying field. One convention is to name the field with an underscore prefix and the property without the underscore. For example, a field *myValue* would be associated with a property MyValue. This convention is used to make it easy to associate properties with their field values. You don't want to spend your time fishing for fields.

The getter is defined by the get{} part of the property. This is a code block, and you can put as much or as little code as you'd like to in this code block. Ultimately, you want to return the value that represents the property value.

The setter is defined by the set{ } part of the property. This is a code block, too, and you can put as much code as you'd like in the setter. The part that is not intuitive is that the value passed to the setter is represented by the argument value. The argument is implicit; you will just have to know it is there.

Property Naming Conventions

Microsoft offers some naming guidelines. Instead of inventing your own, you are gently encouraged to adopt these guidelines for consistency. Consistency among disparate developers is the reason to have guidelines. The bulleted list reflects the naming conventions proposed by Microsoft.

▶ Use a descriptive noun to name your property.

▶ Use the Pascal case naming convention. As mentioned earlier, Pascal case names have the initial letters of each word in the name uppercased. For example, MyProperty shows the *M* in "My" and the *P* in "Property" uppercased.

▶ Do not use Hungarian notation (surprise!).

▶ Name the property with the same name as its underlying field. Use camel-casing for the field and Pascal casing for the property. (Camel-casing lowercases the first letter of the first word and uppercases the first letter of subsequent words. For example, "camelCased" demonstrates camel-casing.)

Read-Only Properties

Read-only properties are those property statements that only have a getter. Use read-only properties when the consumer cannot change the value of the property. Suppose we have a temperature class. The temperature class has two modes—Celsius and Fahrenheit. Based on the temperature mode, we will return one of two possible values for the temperature value. The listing demonstrates the read-only temperature property Value.

```
public enum TemperatureMode
{
  fahrenheit, celsius
}

class Temperature
{
  private TemperatureMode mode = TemperatureMode.fahrenheit;
  private double celsius = 0;
  private double fahrenheit = 0;

  public Temperature( double aTemperature, TemperatureMode aMode )
  {
    mode = aMode;
    SetTemperature(aTemperature, aMode);
  }
```

```
private void SetTemperature(double aTemperature, TemperatureMode aMode)
{
  if( aMode == TemperatureMode.fahrenheit )
  {
    fahrenheit = aTemperature;
    celsius = FahrenheitToCelsius(aTemperature);
  }
  else
  {
    celsius = aTemperature;
    fahrenheit = CelsiusToFahrenheit(aTemperature);
  }
}

public static double CelsiusToFahrenheit(double celsius)
{
  return celsius * (9.0/5) + 32;
}

public static double FahrenheitToCelsius(double fahrenheit)
{
  return (fahrenheit - 32) * 5.0/9;
}

public TemperatureMode Mode
{
  get
  {
    return mode;
  }
  set
  {
    mode = value;
  }
}

public double Value
  {
    get
    {
      return mode == TemperatureMode.fahrenheit ?
        fahrenheit : celsius;
    }
  }

public bool Test()
```

```
  {
    return fahrenheit == CelsiusToFahrenheit(celsius)
       && celsius == FahrenheitToCelsius(fahrenheit);
  }
}
```

The code listing defines an enumeration to represent the mode that the temperature will be displayed in when it is requested through the read-only property Value. (The Value property is shown in boldface font.)

There are a couple of other interesting highlights in the preceding listing. The Value property demonstrates the ternary operator (? :) found in C, C++, and C#. The test precedes the question mark (?). The true value follows the question mark (?), and the false value follows the colon (:). The test in the temperature property is

```
mode == TemperatureMode.fahrenheit
```

and the true result will be the fahrenheit field. False will yield the celsius field value. The mode property demonstrates a readable and writable property statement. CelsiusToFahrenheit and FahrenheitToCelsius were implemented as static methods, since it is reasonable to assume that these two methods will be useful to other elements of code without a Temperature object.

Write-Only Properties

A write-only property statement would have a setter only. Write-only properties are less common than read-only properties because it is more difficult to cause harm by reading a property than it is by writing a property.

One instance where you may want to use writable properties is when you query for a password. You may not want to let consumers ask what password was supplied after the password is supplied. Presumably, some mischievous programmer could snoop objects containing passwords.

The help documentation in Visual Studio .NET states not to use write-only properties. Semantically, write-only properties are methods that modify an object without a method to read the modified value. You might contrive an idiom for write-only properties that is useful. There is no technical prohibition against write-only properties.

Indexed Properties

An indexed property is used to represent a list of items contained in a class. Indexed properties support the notation *object[index]*, where the object looks like an array to the consumer. Indexed properties have a special notation and some guidelines for their use.

▶   Use one indexed property per class, making it the default indexed property.

▶   Avoid nondefault indexed properties.

▶   Name the indexed property "Item" as a general rule.

▶   Use indexed properties for classes that contain an array of elements.

▶   Do not use an indexed property and method that are semantically equivalent. Use one
     or the other.

The following code demonstrates a class named IndexedProperty. IndexedProperty
contains a cached copy of the command line arguments (or any array of strings) and allows
consumers to index any element in the underlying array. For all intents and purposes,
instances of the class IndexedProperty can be used just like an array.

```csharp
class IndexedProperty
{
  private string[] args = null;

  public IndexedProperty(string[] args)
  {
    this.args = new string[args.Length];
    args.CopyTo(this.args, 0);
  }

  [System.Runtime.CompilerServices.IndexerName("Command")]
  public string this [int index]
  {
    get
    {
      return args[index];
    }
    set
    {
      args[index] = value;
    }
  }
}
```

The indexed property begins on the line containing "this[int index]." Except for the property
method header, the getter and setter are implemented as are any other property. Indexed
properties are not referred to by name in C#; the indexer is implicit, and you simply add
the [] index operator after the object name. For example, if we created an instance of the
IndexedProperty class, then we can index the field represented by the indexer.

In the preceding example, the indexer represents the *args* field. The following code fragment
demonstrates creating an instance of the IndexedProperty object and indexing the *args* field.

```csharp
IndexedProperty obj = new IndexedProperty(args);
Console.WriteLine( obj[0] );
Console.ReadLine();
```

The first statement creates an instance of the IndexedProperty class, and the second line demonstrates using the indexer as if obj were an array.

TIP

You can use "this." to get Intellisense to display a list of members of an object internally while you are programming in the code editor in Visual Studio .NET.

There are a couple of other points of interest in IndexedProperty. The constructor demonstrates how to distinguish between a field and a parameter that have the same name. Note that the parameter *args* and the field *args* are identical in the constructor. (You might want to rename the field of the parameter if this happens.) You can use the implicit reference to self, "this", to indicate when you are referring to the object's field versus a parameter with the same name when a name collision occurs.

TIP

You can insert an indexed property from the Class View window by right-clicking the class and clicking Add | Add Indexer from the class' context menu. Complete the wizard (shown in Figure 1-2) to insert the indexer.

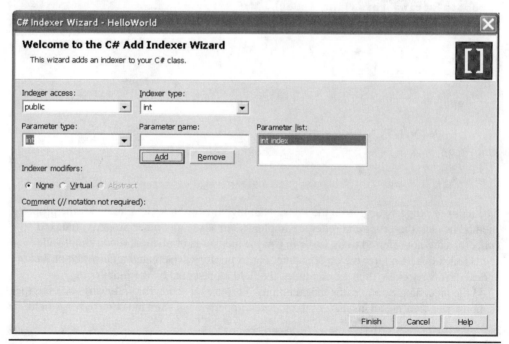

Figure 1-2   *The C# Indexer Wizard filled out to add the indexer for the IndexedProperty class*

The IndexerNameAttribute applied to the indexed property is used to provide a friendly name for languages that don't support indexers.

```
[System.Runtime.CompilerServices.IndexerName("Command")]
```

(Refer to the section "Attributes" for more information about attributes.)

If we were to use the IndexedProperty class defined in C# in a Visual Basic .NET program, then we could create an instance of the class and access the indexed property through the name Command. Assuming we named the instance "obj," as in the preceding example, then **obj.Command(0)** would invoke the indexed property and return the 0th element of *args*.

Implementing Methods

Methods in C# always have the same method heading options. The following grammar example demonstrates all of the possible information you can supply when adding a method to a class.

[Attribute][Modifiers]Return-Type Name([parameters])

All grammatical features in [] are optional. You do not have to use attributes when implementing methods (or other members); when you understand them, you will know when and why to use attributes. Modifiers, such as public, describe accessibility. Modifiers relate to the information hiding. All methods require a return type. The equivalent of a procedure is a method that returns void, and functions return a non-void data type. The *Name* of a method should be a verb of a verb phrase. You can supply zero or more parameters. The signature of a parameter is *type name*, followed by a comma if more than one parameter is used. The bulleted list paraphrases the method name guidelines as suggested by Microsoft.

► Use verbs or phrases beginning with a verb for method names.

► Use Pascal case naming.

► Don't use the Hungarian notation. (I threw this one in for consistency.)

► Provide a descriptive name that states the behavior the method performs (for example, CalculateBalance).

NOTE

If it isn't clear by now, let me state that Microsoft is moving away from using the Hungarian notation. The Hungarian notation was adopted for the weakly typed C programming language and propagated to the VB language. Strongly typed languages like C# do not need prefix notations. The compiler makes sure that you don't mix types inappropriately.

Several examples of methods have been demonstrated already in this chapter, and you will see hundreds more throughout the book. Let's continue with the next topic.

Constructors   There are two special methods, the constructor and the destructor. Constructors have exactly the same name as the class. No other members may have the same name—where *same* applies to case, too—as the class, other than the constructor. Constructors can have zero or more parameters and do not have return types. (We'll talk about the destructor in the next section.)

Constructors are overloaded simply by adding additional constructors with distinct arguments. The following bulleted list provides an overview of constructor guidelines.

▶ If a class has all static members, then implement a private constructor to prevent instances from being created.

▶ Keep constructors short, performing only simple tasks like parameter-to-field assignment in the constructor. This approach allows objects to be created very quickly.

▶ Provide a protected constructor for use by child classes.

▶ As a recommendation, do not implement an empty constructor for structs. If you don't provide the empty parameter constructor for structs, the compiler adds a default constructor that initializes all members to their null equivalents.

▶ Use constructor parameters to set properties. Constructing classes with parameters or creating objects with the default constructing and assigning values to properties should produce the same result.

▶ Be consistent when naming parameters. A common technique is to add an increasing number of parameters for each overloaded constructor.

Destructors   Destructors have the same name as constructors with the addition of the complement operator (~) affixed as the first character of the destructor name.

NOTE

The ~ character is used as the 2s complement operator in C++. It was someone's clever idea to use the complement operator for destructors, implying the relationship between constructor and destructor. That is, destructors are the complement of constructors.

Implement a destructor when you have resources in your class that need to be cleaned up, as when closing a file. When implementing constructors, keep in mind that the name of the constructor is constrained by the name of the class. Destructors cannot be overloaded or inherited. Destructors are invoked automatically, and destructors are never called directly. The CLR garbage collector invokes destructors. When a destructor is called, it implicitly calls the Object.Finalize method. Finally, destructors have no modifiers or parameters.

Non-Deterministic Destruction and Garbage Collection

C# uses non-deterministic destruction. The CLR implements a garbage collector that cleans up memory when objects are no longer used. This means that you don't have to worry as much about destructors in C# as you do in C++ or Delphi.

The garbage collector will call the destructor for your objects when they are no longer needed. The destructor will call any Finalize method. You can force garbage collection by calling GC.Collect, but this is not a recommended process. The garbage collector suspends any running threads, which can cause performance problems. Besides, the garbage collector will do a good job of determining when to run.

Implementing a Dispose Method

If you have unmanaged resources in your classes, then you can implement a Dispose method to support deterministic cleanup. By allowing consumers to call a Dispose method, you can let the consumer decide when they have finished with files or network connections.

Use a technique similar to the following to implement a Dispose method.

```
private bool disposed = false;
public void Dispose()
{
  if (disposed) return;
  // cleanup code here
  GC.SuppressFinalize(this);
  disposed = true;
}
```

First, you declare a private field, *disposed*, to be used to track whether the Dispose method has been called previously, initializing *disposed* to False. In the Dispose method, check to see if Dispose has already been called and return if it has. Perform the cleanup and then call the GC.SupressFinalize( ) method, passing the reference to the object whose Finalize you want to suppress. Finally, set the field disposed to True.

Much of the time you will not need to implement a destructor or a Dispose method. Managed objects in the CLR will be garbage collected automatically. Implement a destructor and Dispose method if you are sure you need them.

Implementing Events

Events form the pinnacle of the Windows object-oriented triad, with properties and methods forming the base. Events were designed to respond to occurrences in code. As with properties and methods, there are two perspectives from which events can be viewed, that of the consumer and that of the producer.

When you are writing classes, you will want to anticipate internal occurrences that you want to let consumers respond to. For those occurrences, you will want to introduce an event and raise that event when the occurrence happens. When you are consuming classes, you will want to write event handlers, wire them up to an object's events, and write the code that actually responds when the event is raised. (*Wiring up* an event simply means associating a method with an event.)

In C++ we use the function pointer idiom and in Delphi we use the procedural type idiom to implement events and event handlers. C# has evolved what are effectively raw function pointers. C# implements the Delegate idiom. *Delegates* are special classes that store the function pointer. The difference between a raw function pointer and a delegate is that a delegate can maintain more than one function pointer. Delegates containing more than one function pointer are referred to as *multicast delegates*.

Technically, the delegate statement describes the signature of a procedure as a type. Any method with a signature matching the signature of the delegate can be added to the invocation list of a delegate object. Describing a delegate signature is consistent with describing a function pointer in C++ or a procedural type in Delphi. The following three statements demonstrate the similarities.

```
typedef void (*func)();      // Visual C++ 6.0 function pointer definition
type TProc = procedure;      // Delphi (Object Pascal) procedural type
delegate void Delegate();    // C# delegate
```

Each statement roughly demonstrates a function pointer declaration in the respective languages. The difference is that only the C# delegate (or any .NET language delegate) can store more than one address. Function pointers in C++ and procedural types in Delphi can refer only to one function address. You would need to create an array of pointer types in C++ and Delphi to refer to multiple function addresses. C# effectively contains the array in the type, allowing one delegate to store multiple addresses. That is the big difference.

Of course, if you are a VB6 programmer, then you have to learn what a function pointer is and then learn what is different about a delegate. For C++ and Delphi professionals, think array of function pointers with a single signature. Unfortunately, if you do not learn what a function pointer is and how to use delegates, then you will be writing code that is the equivalent of two-legged stools.

Declaring Events Using Existing Delegates   Event declarations are straightforward. For the most part, events are destined to be used by class consumers, so they are generally declared as public members. A syntax example is demonstrated next.

```
Access-Modifier event Delegate-Type event-name
```

The *Access-Modifier* is generally public. The *event* keyword is a literal that indicates this member is an event. The *Delegate-Type* is a class that is described by a method signature and uses the keyword *delegate*. An example of an existing delegate is the EventHandler delegate. *Event-name* is the member name of the event; this is what consumers will use to refer to the event in code. The following statement demonstrates an event using the EventHandler delegate.

```
public event EventHandler Changed;
```

The signature of EventHandler is a procedure that returns void and has two parameters, *object* and *System.EventArgs*. The declaration of the EventHandler delegate exists in the CLR as

```
public delegate void EventHandler(object sender, System.EventArgs e);
```

(This delegate already exists; thus, you do not have to define it yourself.) EventHandler is the delegate used for many Windows Forms controls, like the Button control's Click event.

Declaring New Delegate Types   If you want to define a custom delegate, you can follow the basic example provided in the previous section demonstrating the EventHandler delegate.

A delegate definition is exactly the same as a procedure header with the keyword *delegate* added between the access modifier and the return type. The following example defines a new delegate for a procedure that returns void and takes no arguments.

```
public delegate void Delegate();
```

Recall that C# is case-sensitive and note that the preceding example introduces a delegate named "Delegate." Any procedure that returns void and takes no arguments can be assigned to events or fields that are declared as Delegate types.

Raising Events as a Producer   Producers raise events. Raising an event in C# is performed by calling a procedure using the event name. By convention, events are raised by protected members with the same name as the event with "On" as a prefix.

Returning to our original example of the Changed event defined as an EventHandler type, we can pair the event with a protected method that raises the event.

```
public event EventHandler Changed;
protected void OnChanged()
{
  if(Changed == null) return;
  Changed(this, System.EventArgs.Empty);
}
```

The event is named "Changed." Consumers can assign any number of methods that match the signature of the EventHandler delegate to this one event member. Inside the class containing the code, you would call OnChanged anywhere that you want to raise the Change event. OnChanged checks to make sure that Changed has been assigned to at least one delegate; if it hasn't, then OnChanged returns. Otherwise, Changed is treated like a method by the producer and is called, with the producer passing it the necessary arguments.

When a producer raises an event with a *sender* parameter, that value is always satisfied with the internal reference to self: this. In our simple example, we pass a null *System.EventArgs* parameter because we are not using that value. If you need to pass specific values to a consumer's event handler, then you can create an instance of *System.EventArgs* or create a delegate that takes a specific subclass of EventArgs.

Handling Events as a Consumer   Consumers handle events by wiring an event handler to an event member of an object. The example program EventsDemo.sln contains the classes EventChanged and Form1. For our scenario, we assume that Form1 contains an EventChanged object and wants to handle the EventChanged.Changed event. For this to work Form1 needs to create an instance of EventChanged and assign a method to EventChanged.Changed. The following example demonstrates code in Form1 that wires an event handler to EventChanged.Changed.

```
private void button1_Click(object sender, System.EventArgs e)
{
  MessageBox.Show(sender.ToString());
}
```

```
private EventChanged obj = new EventChanged();
private void Form1_Load(object sender, System.EventArgs e)
{
  obj.Changed += new System.EventHandler(button1_Click);
  obj.Value = 5;
}
```

The EventChanged object is named "obj" and instantiated as a field in the form. Form1_Load (an event itself) wires the EventChanged.Changed event to Form1's button1_click method. (The button click method was already available and happens to have the same signature as the Changed event.) The += operator is used to assign the new System.EventHandler object to Changed. Doing this will append the event handler to the invocation list.

Only the += and −= operators are overloaded to append and remove event handlers from an events invocation list. You cannot use the assignment operator to assign a delegate to an event.

How Does Multicasting Work?   Think of an event declaration as a field whose type is an aggregate type: a delegate. When you assign a delegate to the event, you are inserting the delegate into a list that is a member of the delegate type. When you raise the event by invoking the event as a method call, you are actually interacting with an object. When the event method is called internally, it iterates through all of the delegates appended to the internal list and calls each one of them.

Returning to our example containing the public event EventHandler Changed, when we raise the event by calling Changed, every delegate assigned to Changed is called. This is referred to as *multicasting*. Delegates can be bound to a single method or to multiple methods.

It is possible to layer several pieces of an entire solution into one event by assigning several delegates to a single event. What you should not do is rely on delegates being called in any specific order.

Creating Instances of Classes

Objects are instantiated by invoking the constructor using the new operator. You can create instances of objects and assign them to variables whose type is the same type as the object instantiated or a type in the object's ancestry. That is, instances of child types can be assigned to variables declared as a type of the object's parent. The reverse is not true. (See the upcoming section "Inheritance" for more information.)

Keep in mind that constructors have the same name as the class, can have public or non-public access modifiers, and may have zero or more parameters. Constructors can be overloaded. So, there may be more than one constructor that is suitable for you to call. Here are several examples demonstrating object instantiation.

```
// simple object creation
FileStream fs = new FileStream("c:\\temp\\killme.txt", FileMode.CreateNew);
fs.Write(new Byte[]{65, 66, 67, 68, 69}, 0, 5);
fs.Close();

// array examples
string[] strings = new string[10];
strings[0] = "Some Text!";
int[] integers = new int[]{0,1,2,3,4,5};
```

The first statement creates an instance of the FileStream class. (You will need to add the System.IO namespace to your application with a using statement to use the FileStream class.) FileStream objects have several constructors. The example used takes a file path and a FileMode. Keep in mind that C# strings use the backslash (\) as an escape character; you will need to use the \\ backslash pair when you mean backslash within a string. The second statement demonstrates an inline construction of an array of bytes with an initializer list.

The first array example demonstrates constructing an array of strings with storage room for 10 strings. Valid indexes for arrays in C# are 0 to $n - 1$, where n represents the number of elements in the array. The second example constructs an array of integers using an initializer list. The initializer list provides the values for the array and the extent. The size of integers is 6, and valid indexes are 0 to 5. In C# you can specify both the number of elements and an initializer list for arrays, but you don't need both.

Defining Interfaces

Interfaces allow you to define an adapter to your classes. In the object-oriented world, we have inheritance, aggregation, and association. Inheritance describes a relationship where a new thing is a generalization of an existing thing. For example, a Jeep is a generalization of an automobile and can be described using inheritance. Jeeps have transmissions, demonstrating an aggregation relationship. A Jeep may also have a driver, which is an example of an association relationship. The transmission belongs to the Jeep, but the driver does not.

Interfaces describe relationships that can sometimes be defined in other ways, like inheritance, aggregation, or association, but may best be described as *supporting capabilities*. For example, stereo equipment in a car may have knobs that allow you to tune radio stations or pick tracks on a CD. But, what if that same stereo equipment allows you to tune an FM station without touching the knobs directly on the device? We could say that stereo equipment that supports tuning in general has a tuning interface. As a result we can affix other controls that tap into the stereo interface. Perhaps an infrared device or controls on the steering column could use the interface to perform the same function as the controls physically on the stereo equipment.

The knob on the stereo is a *physical* control on the stereo. The volume is an *attribute*. The ability to change the volume can be implemented as a method or property method, either of which in turn could be used to support an interface for changing volume. Other devices could implement the same interface, which we'll call Audio. Other unrelated devices could support the Audio interface: televisions, CB radios, cell phones, telephone, stereo, or communications equipment in an airplane. Suppose we create a universal remote control that can talk to any device that implements the Audio interface. Any device that supported the audio interface could be adjusted—made louder or quieter—with the same remote control. Now, your surround sound, big screen TV, and tuner could be controlled by the same device.

The basic syntax for defining an interface is similar to that for defining a class. The next code fragment demonstrates the basic syntax by implementing the Audio interface. (By convention we will name the interface with an *I* prefix.)

```
public interface IAudio
{
  void AdjustVolume( int value );
}
```

The interface definition has an access modifier; in the example the access modifier is public. The keyword interface follows the access modifier, and the name of the interface completes the interface header. Members of an interface do not use an access modifier but have a procedure heading for each member of the interface. Every class that implements an interface will have to implement all of the methods defined by the interface.

Implementing Interfaces

Suppose you have defined an interface or want to implement an existing interface. You will need to indicate that the class will implement the interface. The following listing demonstrates an interface and a partially complete class that implements the interface.

```
public interface IAudio
{
  void AdjustVolume(int value );
}

public class Radio : IAudio
{
  private int volume = 0;

  void IAudio.AdjustVolume(int value)
  {
    volume += value;
  }
}
```

The class Radio indicates that it is implementing the IAudio interface using the inheritance syntax in the class header. (The syntax for inheritance and implementing interfaces is the same: add a colon and the name of the interface in the class header.) When you indicate that you are implementing an interface, you are entering a contract that states that you will add methods defined by the interface. The notable difference between methods and methods that implement an interface is that you must include the interface name and member-of operator in the procedure header for all interface methods. The procedure header void IAudio.AdjustVolume(int value) indicates that this implementation of AdjustVolume is satisfying the contract between the IAudio interface and the Radio class.

If you are implementing more than one interface, then add the additional interfaces to the class heading, delimiting each additional interface with a comma.

It is important to remember that when you implement an interface you aren't getting any methods or data from the interface. Also, keep in mind that only methods can be described in an interface; you may not describe fields or properties in interfaces.

Inheritance

When you define an inheritance relationship there are two classes involved at a minimum. One class is the parent and the second is the child. (The relationship between parent and child is also called *superclass* and *subclass*, where superclass is synonymous with parent and subclass is synonymous with child.) Such a parent-child relationship is referred to as an *IsA* relationship. For example, I am the offspring of my father (and mother), so I am a Kimmel (and Symons), inheriting the DNA goop that comes from Kimmel's (and Symons').

When you define an inheritance relationship in C#, the child class gets all of the members defined in the parent class. When you inherit, you get all of the fields, properties, and methods defined in the parent. Unlike chromosomal inheritance, object-oriented inheritance means you get everything.

I think most of you understand inheritance, but there is one more description that I'd like to introduce because inheritance is an important concept. If class B inherits from class A, then, logically, A intersection B would be class A.

The notation for inheritance is identical to that for interface inheritance. To indicate that class B inherits from class A, you would write the class header as follows:

```
Public class B : A
```

Unlike with interface inheritance, when you inherit from a class, you do not have to implement any methods from the parent class because they are already implemented in the parent class.

Inheritance Terminology

There are a lot of terms associated with inheritance relationships. Since you will encounter them in this book, I will review several of them here briefly.

▶ If class B inherits from A, then A is the *parent* and B is the *child*.

▶ If class B inherits from A, then A is also referred to as the *superclass* and B is the *subclass*.

▶ Inheritance relationships satisfy the *IsA* test. In our example we would say that B IsA A (although it is grammatically horrendous).

▶ Inheriting is also referred to as *generalizing*.

▶ *Siblings* are classes that inherit from the same parent.

▶ Very seldom, but occasionally, you will hear people refer to *grandparents, ancestors,* and *offspring* when talking about inheritance relationships.

It is possible that all of these ways of referring to the same thing, inheritance, can lead to confusion.

As far as I know, no one has referred to second cousins or great aunts when talking object inheritance relationships, but these terms could be used and should be used in such a way as to describe the same relationships as when the terms are used to describe human kinship. For example, a cousin would be the child of your parent's sibling.

General Guidelines for Inheritance

You're the boss when it comes to inheritance. From experience, I have included some guidelines for using inheritance relationships, but ultimately you will have to decide on a case-by-case basis.

▶ If you define a class and later decide that it needs to be modified, then consider inheriting from the original class to add the new code.

▶ Try to keep your inheritance relationships shallow and broad. There is no perfect ratio between the numbers of siblings to children, but there usually are more siblings than offspring in established frameworks.

▶ Investigate *Refactoring*. Refactoring is the best way invented so far to guide programmers in simplifying existing code. Essentially, Refactoring is an organized approach to factoring out common code. (Unfortunately, we cannot elaborate on Refactoring here, but Refactorings will be used to produce the code listings in this book.)

▶ Don't be afraid to experiment and change your mind.

▶ Explore existing frameworks to get a sense of proportion. (Excellent frameworks to explore include Delphi's VCL and the .Net Framework.)

Inheritance Example

You will find dozens of examples of inheritance throughout this book, and you can look in the CLR for many more examples. To be thorough, we will continue with our radio example to demonstrate the basic technical aspects of inheritance. The next listing demonstrates several classes that all have the same root, our Radio class.

```csharp
public interface IAudio
{
   void AdjustVolume(int value );
}


public class Radio : IAudio
{
```

```csharp
    private int volume = 0;

    void IAudio.AdjustVolume(int value)
    {
      volume += value;
    }

    public int Volume
    {
      get
      {
        return volume;
      }
      set
      {
        volume = value;
      }
    }

    private double station = 94.1;

    public double Station
    {
      get
      {
        return station;
      }
      set
      {
        station = value;
      }
    }

    public void Receive()
    {
    }
}

public enum RadioBand
{
  AM, FM
}

public class AMFMRadio : Radio
{
```

```
    private RadioBand band = RadioBand.AM;
    public RadioBand Band
    {
      get
      {
        return band;
      }
      set
      {
        band = value;
      }
    }
}

public class CommunicationsRadio : Radio
{
  public void Transmit()
  {
  }
}
```

The code listing provides a couple of examples of inheritance. CommunicationsRadio and AMFMRadio inherits from Radio. AMFMRadio introduces the notion of an AM and FM band, and the CommunicationsRadio introduces the ability to transmit as well as the inherited ability to receive.

Encapsulation and Aggregation

Encapsulation and aggregation refer to the ability of classes to contain members. More specifically, *aggregation* refers to the ability of classes (and structures) to contain members whose types are also classes (or structures).

My favorite example of encapsulation is the relationship between the human body and the bladder. Thankfully, the bladder is encapsulated inside of the human body. Could you imagine a world where people could express their displeasure with you by squeezing your bladder? "Ouch, that's me foot!" Squeeze.

What a mess.

Clearly, the bladder is a class. It performs a function and has state. We know what the function is, and we often feel the state at the most inopportune times. Thankfully, the bladder is encapsulated behind skin and bone and an in-born sense of personal space.

This is how you should view encapsulation and aggregation. Encapsulation allows you to put data safely inside of classes, limiting access and avoiding embarrassing situations. Aggregation allows you to put complex types safely inside of classes, again limiting access and avoiding embarrassing situations.

Figure out where a particular data element should go by its semantic meaning and place that data inside of an appropriate class. A good way to think about where to put data is by thinking about whose job it is to own and protect the data. (Don't let your neighbor have your bladder.) Think of aggregation as adding complex types—read classes—to new types. The bladder is a complex type, and the human body has a member that is a bladder.

In an expert medical system, implementing a class that represents the human body and the bladder might be appropriate. However, for convenience, we will expand our Radio example to demonstrate aggregation and encapsulation. The listing demonstrates a new class BoomBox that has an AMFMRadio. The AMFMRadio demonstrates encapsulation and aggregation.

```
public class BoomBox
{
  private AMFMRadio radio;

  public AMFMRadio Radio
  {
    get
    {
      return radio;
    }
  }

  BoomBox()
  {
    radio = new AMFMRadio();
  }
}
```

Polymorphism

Polymorphism has been described in many ways. Several times I have seen reference to its Greek roots, given as "many forms," and sometimes the descriptions are long and complex. I am going to try something a little different. I am going to use an analogy that I hope makes sense to you.

Suppose you have a household chore that is suitable for a child to do. I have four children. We start them on chores at eighteen months. Yes, a toddler can empty wastebaskets at eighteen months. Cruel, perhaps, but functional. Here is the analogy.

You are watching the Superbowl. It is the fourth quarter with two minutes to go, and your team has the ball but is down by 8 points. Not only do they have to make the touchdown, but your team has to get the two-point conversion. To sweeten the tension, you have $500 bet with a bookie for your team to win. Now, you're out of beer. You need a beer, but you can't leave the game because by the time you get back, the game will be over. You need a kid to make the beer run, and any kid will do.

That's polymorphism.

When you have a general problem that can be solved by any provider within a common set of providers, then you need polymorphism.

If beer and football analogies don't make sense to you, don't worry; they don't make much sense to me either. Let's try a more technical approach (for people who watch TLC instead of Monday Night Football).

Remember that I said that inheritance is also referred to as generalization? Well, if you declare something as the general (or parent) type and instantiate—create instances of—specific types, then you have more options regarding the specific type that you create. A good example of this is demonstrated by the EventHandler delegate. The EventHandler delegate is defined to take an object as the first parameter. The object class is the root of all classes. Effectively, this means that any object can be passed to satisfy the sender parameter of an EventHandler method. This is polymorphism: declare general types and actually use specific types.

Using Modifiers

Modifiers address *information hiding*. Information hiding exemplifies the cliché "out of sight, out of mind." That is, as a producer, if you can conceal something from a consumer, then they don't have to worry about it. Hence, out of mind.

Access modifiers allow you to put things out of mind when you are programming. When producing classes, make only those things public that consumers need to interact with to use the class. By limiting what you expose in the public interface, you are making it easier to consume your classes. This is true even if you are the first consumer of the classes you produce.

There are several access modifiers to choose from. C# supports public, protected, internal, protected internal, private, and read-only for fields. The bulleted list briefly describes the purpose of each access modifier.

▶ The *public* access modifier provides unrestricted access to types and members.

▶ The *protected* access modifier provides unrestricted access internally and to child classes and restricted access to consumers. The protected access modifier can be applied to nested types.

▶ The *private* access modifier provides the most restricted access. Only the producer of a class may use its private members. Consumers and children have no access to private members. The private access modifier can be applied to nested types.

▶ The *internal* access modifier means that types and members are accessible only within the same assembly. The internal modifier is used to allow code to cooperate internally across class boundaries without exposing those elements to consumers outside of the assembly.

▶ The *protected internal* modifier limits access to the same assembly for nested types.

When you are declaring top-level types, you must use the public or internal access modifier. You may use private and protected access for types only when those types are nested. A *nested type* is a type definition that contains a type definition.

You may not combine access modifiers, except for the protected internal modifier. You may not use access modifiers on namespaces. If you don't specify an access modifier, then a default access level will be used. It is best to specifically indicate the level of access rather than relying on a default access.

Using Class Modifiers

When you define classes and the enclosing element is a namespace, then the class can be defined to have public or internal access. If you don't specify a modifier for a top-level class, then the class will have public access.

Nested classes can be defined with any access modifier, but you may only use protected, protected internal, and private access modifiers on nested classes.

Class access modifier rules apply to any struct and enum types, too.

Using Member Modifiers

You may use any access modifier on members of types, too. If you define members without an access modifier, then members are private by default.

Operator Overloading

Operators are tokens that perform an operation on data. Data are referred to as *operands* when they are the subject of an operation. Common operators, like the addition operator, +, exist for value types. An example of a value type is an integer, like 5. It is intuitive to perform operations like 5 + 4 on integer types.

Unfortunately, all of the possible types that may exist cannot be anticipated; but when types are invented, it may also be intuitive to perform simple operations on those types, too. An example is demonstrated by the string concatenation operator. When you encounter code like

```
string s = "overloaded operators " + "are cool"
```

it is intuitively understood that the statement is performing string concatenation.

Overloaded operators are methods. Specifically, they are methods with a special syntax. You can understand operators by thinking of overloaded operators as two parts. The first part implements a regular named method that performs the task that the operator would perform. The second part defines the operator method using the special syntax and calls the named method inside of the operator. (Of course, you could always skip overloading operators, but that would be no fun.)

Coding Operator Methods

The procedure heading for operator methods is very similar to regular methods. Specify a return type and argument types and names; but, instead of a method name, you use the keyword *operator* and the operator token where you would have used the method name.

Borrowing from the help file examples, we could implement a complex number class. (Complex numbers have a real and imaginary part.) We could implement an overloaded addition operator that adds the real parts and the imaginary parts of two complex numbers, yielding a new complex number that is the sum of the two added complex numbers.

```
public static Complex operator +(Complex c1, Complex c2)
{
  return new Complex(c1.real + c2.real, c1.imaginary + c2.imaginary);
}
```

The code listing is extracted from a struct that defines a complex number as a number that is initialized with a real number and scalar part of the imaginary number. For example, if you construct a complex number with 2 for the real argument and 3 for the imaginary part, then you get the complex number 2 + 3i. The overloaded operator in the preceding example defines the + operator for Complex types as a static type that takes two Complex objects and returns a new Complex object that is the sum of the two arguments. In the example, you would invoke this operator+ method by writing a statement that adds two complex numbers.

```
Complex c = new Complex(4, 3);
Complex d = new Complex(1, 2);
Complex e = c + d;
```

The first two statements create instances of two complex numbers. The final statement invokes the operator+ method, returning a new object to the variable *e*. The best way to get a handle on overloaded operators is to write some simple examples and place breakpoints on the statements that invoke the operator and in the operator method. You will quickly see that the operation results in a method invocation.

Overloading Operator Guidelines and Limitations

Be circumspect about defining overloaded operators. The most important thing to avoid doing is creating operators that are counterintuitive. For example, overloading the addition operator to perform subtraction. Don't do this. Following these basic guidelines for overloading operators will keep you out of trouble:

▶ Define methods that perform the operation using the op_ prefix followed by the name of the operator to support languages like Visual Basic .NET that don't support operator overloading.

▶ Implement the overloaded operator by calling the named method. (Why codify the operator behavior twice?)

▶ Overload an operator only in the class the operator applies to.

▶ Use operator overloading when the operation is intuitive and the result seems logical.

▶ Overload operators symmetrically. If you implement addition, then implement subtraction.

Table 1-1 lists operators and indicates whether they can be overloaded or not. Not all operators can be overloaded.

Operator	Overloadable
+, −, !, ~, ++, − −, True, False	Unary operators that can be overloaded.
+, −, *, /, %, &, |, ^, <<, >>	Binary operators that can be overloaded.
==, !=, <, >, <=, >=	Comparison operators that can be overloaded but must be overloaded in pairs. (You will get a compiler indicating what the pair operator is and reminding you that you need to overload the pair.)
&&, ||	These conditional logic operators cannot be overloaded.
[]	The array operator cannot be overloaded, but you can define an indexer. (Refer to the section "Indexed Properties" for more information.)
+=, −=, *=, /=, %=, &=, |=, ^=,	Assignment operators cannot be overloaded.
<<=, >>=	The left-shift and right-shift operators cannot be overloaded.
=, ., ?:, new, is, sizeof, typeof	These operators cannot be overloaded.

Table 1-1   *The Overloadability of Operators*

Overloaded operators allow you to define special methods that make code simpler to write and more intuitive. You will not need to write overloaded operators frequently, but you will be using them as a consumer of CLR code quite frequently.

Attributes

It is idioms like interface and attributes that get us into trouble as programmers. The reason is that these terms do double duty. For years, "interface" meant simply the members declared in a class. When COM was introduced, interface took on another meaning; interface became a construct—a lot like a class. (For VB programmers, interfaces and classes blur a great deal.)

The same problem exists for the word "attribute" and the idiom Attribute. In the general sense, "attribute" is synonymous with "property." An attribute is a property of a type. The .NET Attribute itself is actually a class. (There are likely to be as many confusing discussions surrounding attributes as there are about parent and child, superclass and subclass, and object and class.)

In C# an Attribute with a capital *A* is a class that adds metadata to your assembly. Metadata, or additional data, was added to help eradicate "DLL Hell." Historically external data that an application needed was stored in a registry or INI file. Attributes allow this supporting cast of data to travel with the assembly. Attribute classes allow you to add the metadata to your assemblies, and Reflection allows you to extract that metadata when you need it. This is analogous to reading and writing from the registry. As a result of having the metadata cleverly folded into the assembly, deploying .NET applications is simpler than deploying COM-based applications.

Examples of attributes can be found in the AssemblyInfo.cs module. An example is the AssemblyTitleAttribute class.

```
[assembly: AssemblyTitle("")]
```

By adding text between the parentheses in the AssemblyTitleAttribute, you can add a title for your assembly that will show up in the Properties dialog. By convention, attribute classes have an Attribute suffix, but the suffix is left off when the attribute is used. The assembly: tag indicates that this is an assembly-level attribute.

Because attributes are implemented as classes, you generalize existing Attribute classes to create new attributes for new uses. Attributes are used for many things, from providing hints for component properties to requesting security permissions. Many new attributes will be created, but the rhythm for using Attributes is similar to that for constructing an object. Place the name of the Attribute class immediately before the entity the Attribute describes and pass the arguments defined by the Attribute's constructor. Constructor arguments are referred to as *positional arguments*. You can also initialize properties in an Attribute object by passing named arguments.

Reflection

Reflection is a capability implemented in .NET that allows you to dynamically discover information, such as the namespaces, interfaces, classes, methods, properties, and fields in an assembly. In addition to providing a way to request the value of metadata described by attributes, Reflection allows you to find out about the types and members in types defined in an assembly, and Reflection allows you to emit Intermediate Language (IL) code at run-time. IL is similar in intent to Java byte code. IL is the code before it is compiled into machine-readable code.

Reflection is powerful mojo. We will explore it in detail in this book. Chapter 2 demonstrates how to discover information about assemblies using Reflection, and Chapter 10 demonstrates how to create custom attributes that can be read using Reflection.

Summary

This chapter has provided an overview of core language foundations that you will need in almost every application that you create. There will be 16 chapters and their attendant applications that demonstrate these concepts in context. While the examples are brief in this chapter, the topics are central to all C# programming and you will find many examples of them in upcoming chapters.

Assembly Viewer

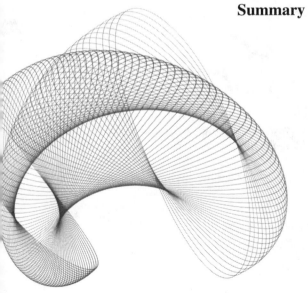

This chapter demonstrates how to load assemblies dynamically and explore those assemblies using Reflection. Working with assemblies and Reflection in just the second chapter is a pretty tall order, but the assembly viewer will help you master these subjects as well as build Windows applications using controls in the Windows Forms namespace and GDI+.

Demonstrated Topics

This chapter's primary topic is using dynamic discovery to explore assemblies using Reflection. If you are able to dynamically load and use assemblies, you can take advantage of thin client programming by loading assemblies over HTTP connections, which supports automatic deployment and updates of Windows Forms–based applications. There will also be ample examples of the following topics:

▶ Working with value types

▶ Using the StringBuilder class

▶ Defining static methods

▶ Defining classes and inheritance

▶ Defining and implementing interfaces

▶ Using the IEnumerator interface

▶ Multithreading safely in Windows Forms

▶ Programming with the Graphics object

▶ Debugging with System.Diagnostics

▶ Loading information from a resource, which facilitates internationalization

▶ Basic printing using PrintDocument

Code Listing for the Assembly Manager

In this chapter we will be discussing at length the code for AssemblyViewer.sln, which is available on the McGraw-Hill/Osborne web site, **www.osborne.com**. The complete code requires 43 pages to list completely, so to avoid padding the book, we will reproduce here in Listing 2-1 just the salient portions. Fortunately, you will be able to easily copy the classes and methods that are listed, or you can cut and paste them from the source code posted on **www.osborne.com**.

The AssemblyManager.cs module contains the AssemblyManager class. This class demonstrates how to load and explore assemblies using Reflection.

Listing 2-1 *AssemblyManager.cs manages loading and reading the assembly.*

```
1:  using System;
2:  using System.Reflection;
3:  using System.Diagnostics;
4:  using Diag = System.Diagnostics;
5:  using System.IO;
6:  using System.Collections;
7:  using System.Text;
8:  using System.Windows.Forms;
9:
10: namespace AssemblyViewer
11: {
12:   /// <summary>
13:   /// Summary description for AssemblyManager.
14:   /// </summary>
15:   public class AssemblyManager
16:   {
17:     private string name = "";
18:     private Assembly assembly;
19:
20:     public AssemblyManager(string assemblyName)
21:     {
22:       Debug.Assert(File.Exists(assemblyName));
23:       Name = assemblyName;
24:     }
25:
26:     public Assembly Assembly
27:     {
28:       get
29:       {
30:         return assembly;
31:       }
32:     }
33:
34:     public string Name
35:     {
36:       get
37:       {
```

```
38:              return name;
39:          }
40:          set
41:          {
42:            if(name.Equals(value)) return;
43:            name = value;
44:            Changed();
45:          }
46:        }
47:
48:        private void Changed()
49:        {
50:          Debug.Assert(File.Exists(name));
51:          assembly = null;
52:          assembly = Assembly.LoadFrom(name);
53:        }
54:
55:        private string Formatted(Type type)
56:        {
57:          const string mask = "{0} \r\n";
58:          string result = string.Format(mask, type.Name);
59:          Broadcaster.Broadcast(result);
60:          return result;
61:        }
62:
63:        private string Formatted(MemberInfo info)
64:        {
65:          const string mask = "\t{0} {1}\r\n";
66:          string result = string.Format( mask,
67:            info.MemberType.ToString(), info.Name );
68:          Broadcaster.Broadcast(result);
69:          return result;
70:        }
71:
72:        private string Load()
73:        {
74:          StringBuilder str = new StringBuilder();
75:          IEnumerator outer = assembly.GetTypes().GetEnumerator();
76:
77:          while(outer.MoveNext())
78:          {
79:            Type type = (Type)outer.Current;
```

```
 80:            str.Append(Formatted(type));
 81:
 82:            IEnumerator inner = type.GetMembers().GetEnumerator();
 83:
 84:            while(inner.MoveNext())
 85:            {
 86:              str.Append(Formatted((MemberInfo)inner.Current));
 87:              Application.DoEvents();
 88:            }
 89:          }
 90:
 91:       return str.ToString();
 92:     }
 93:
 94:     public string Text
 95:     {
 96:       get
 97:       {
 98:         return GetText();
 99:       }
100:     }
101:
102:     public string GetText()
103:     {
104:       return Load();
105:     }
106:
107: }
108:}
```

using Statements

There are two places you will see the *using* keyword. The *using* statement is employed to import namespaces and as a block statement for managing objects.

Listing 2-1 demonstrates how to use namespaces. Think of a *using* statement as adding a reference to a DLL. Assemblies in the framework are actually contained in DLL files; thus

```
using System.Reflection;
```

refers to a DLL that begins with the word system.

Assemblies can contain multiple namespaces. For example, System.Reflection is contained in the System.dll assembly. However, System.Windows.Forms is actually the name of the assembly containing the Windows Forms controls. You can explore assemblies in the .NET framework by navigating to C:\WINNT\Microsoft.NET\Framework\v1.0.3705\.

Creating an Alias with the using Directive

You can create an alias for namespaces with the *using* directive. Changing

```
using System.Diagnostics;
```

to

```
using Diag = System.Diagnostics;
```

creates an alias Diag for the System.Diagnostics namespace. Wherever you might use the fully qualified System.Diagnostics namespace, you can replace it with the alias Diag.

Defining a using Scope

The second way *using* is used is similar to the with statement in VB.NET. When you employ the *using* statement in code with an object, you are defining a scope that will implicitly dispose of the object at the end of the *using* block. The object will be disposed of even if an exception is thrown before the end of the *using* block, as long as the object created in the *using* block implements the IDisposable interface.

IDisposable is an interface that has a single method, the Dispose method. Implement IDisposable if you need deterministic cleanup. For example, when you open a file, you will want to close it as soon as you are finished with the file. The following fragment demonstrates how to use a *using* block to define a block that will dispose of an object at the end of the block.

```
using (FormAbout form = new FormAbout())
{
   form.ShowDialog();
}
```

The *using* statement declares and creates an instance of the object. The instance name referenced in the *using* statement is used in the block, and when the block exits, the form's Dispose method is called. (To verify this, overload the inherited Dispose method and place a breakpoint in the Dispose method. If you are not sure how to overload methods, refer to the section "Defining the Interface" later in this chapter.)

Defining Your Namespace Name

A few years ago classes were the highest level of abstraction. Namespaces provide a way to organize classes in higher level relationships and to create unique names. Namespaces are housekeeping tools.

NOTE

ProgIds are used for purposes similar to those of namespaces. However, ProgIds are limited to 39 characters and are not guaranteed to be unique. ProgIds, which may contain no punctuation except a period, are still supported for COM Interop.

When you create an application, the name you give it will be used as the default namespace name. Every module you add to that project will be given the same namespace as defined by the project. If you add a new project to the solution, the new project will get a namespace name identical to the project name.

Namespaces are public, and you may not add an access modifier to namespaces. You can declare class, interface, struct, enum, delegate, and other namespace types inside of a namespace.

Line 11 of Listing 2-1 indicates that the AssemblyManager is defined in the AssemblyViewer namespace. If you don't specify a namespace, the default namespace is used. You can modify the default namespace in the General Property Pages for the AssemblyViewer project (see Figure 2-1).

Defining Classes

Line 15 of Listing 2-1 contains the class header for the AssemblyManager class. AssemblyManager is defined as a public class and is the only class in the listing. Most of the time the classes you define will have public access. Line 108 defines the closing block for the AssemblyManager. (Refer to Chapter 1 for general information on classes.)

```
15:    public class AssemblyManager
108:}
```

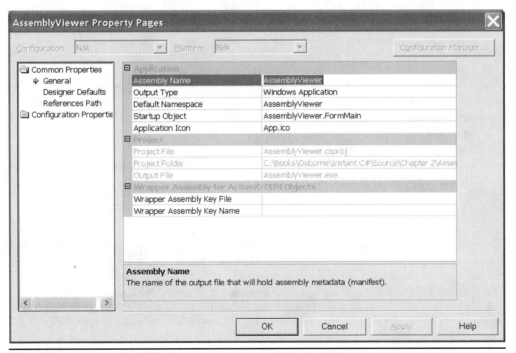

Figure 2-1   *Viewing the default namespace in Visual Studio .NET*

Implementing Constructors

Constructors are the only members of a class that can have the same name and case as the class. Constructors use an access modifier and can have arguments to initialize an instance but do not define a return type. As a general rule, keep constructors short and to the point.

Lines 19 through 23 of Listing 2-1 implement the constructor for the AssemblyManager. Line 21 ensures that the assembly file exists, and line 22 assigns the assemblyName argument to the Name property. Two strategies you can employ to make your constructors behave reliably, just as we did in the AssemblyManager constructor, are discussed in the following sub-sections.

Guarding Your Code with Assert   Line 21 calls the static method File.Exists, returning a Boolean value indicating whether the file represented by assemblyName exists. The static method Debug.Assert is defined in the System.Diagnostics namespace. Assert is a development tool that you can use as a sentinel. While the conditional compilation constant DEBUG is used, the Assert method is turned on. This means that you can leave debug code in place and use conditional compilation to toggle debug code.

When the condition evaluated in the Assert method fails, the Call Stack is displayed in a dialog box, enabling you to continue to run the application or abort. The purpose of the Assert method is to provide the developer with an early warning that an assumption made about the state of the system failed. (Write a simple program that calls System .Diagnostics.Debug.Assert (false) to see the Call Stack Trace dialog.)

Initializing Object Properties   The purpose of a constructor is to initialize the state of an object. The constructor on lines 19 through 23 of Listing 2-1 initializes the AssemblyManager. Line 22 does a bit more than it seems to do. If you look closely, you will notice that Name is an attribute of the AssemblyManager class. If convention is followed, then we know that the uppercase attribute is a property.

Name = assemblyName invokes the property setter for the Name property on lines 33 to 44. If you look at the setter method, you will see that if the underlying field equals the *value* parameter, then we exit the setter. The parameter *value* is implicit; you just need to know *value* is the name of the parameter passed to setters and has the data type of the property. Because the setter does more than change the field value, we use the if-conditional as a sentinel to prevent unnecessary work.

If *value* is different—that is, if *value* represents a different assembly—then we invoke the Changed method. Instead of actually performing the work in the setter, we use a method. When a new assembly name is provided, the Changed method loads the assembly.

The Changed method is defined on lines 47 to 52 of Listing 2-1. Again, we check to see if the assembly exists. We might change the name after the AssemblyManager is created. (We could get rid of the original check in the constructor, if we choose to.) The old assembly is assigned to null, and the new name is used to load the assembly. Assembly.LoadFrom is a static method that returns an initialized instance of the assembly.

Walking the Assembly Using Reflection

The workhorse of the AssemblyManager class is the Load function. Load uses enumerators to walk all of the types defined in the assembly and an enumerator for each of the types to walk the members of that type. Using the nested loops, we get all of the types and all of those types' members. This information is formatted and returned as a string, which allows us to create a simplified interface for the class (see the Text property and the GetText method in Listing 2-1).

Load is defined on lines 69 to 90 in Listing 2-1. Line 70 instantiates a StringBuilder object. (StringBuilder is defined in the System.Text namespace.) StringBuilder is used to facilitate adding a lot of formatted string information into a single string buffer. You could use the string value type, but some simple comparative trials indicate the StringBuffer works faster for many string operations.

The reason StringBuilder is faster than String for many string concatenation operations is that StringBuilder is mutable and String is immutable. That is, StringBuilder is designed for concatenation, but when you concatenate a string, a new string object is created for each operation. Hence, the following

```
string str += "Hello, World!";
```

performs a String.Concat (static) operation that returns a new string instance, whereas the StringBuilder is just packing the additional string information into the StringBuilder buffer. No new StringBuilder objects are created.

What Is Reflection?

Reflection is the ability of .NET to discover Run Time Type Information about classes. However, it is significantly much more than that. With Reflection, you can discover everything about the types and members defined in assemblies, as well as load and run those assemblies dynamically. On top of all of this, you can use the System.Reflection.Emit namespace to emit Intermediate Language (IL) to build types at runtime.

Reflection is a capability whose flexibility and power have not been truly absorbed by the IT community at large. There will likely be many tools built on this technology when it is completely understood. For now, let's leave the definition of Reflection to the description provided in the preceding paragraph and Chapter 1. Reflection will also be discussed in Chapters 5 and 10.

Using Reflection

When you have an instance of an assembly object, you use Reflection by asking the assembly for collections that contain the members defined in an assembly. When you have an instance of a type, you ask the type for collections representing the Method, Field, Event, Property, Constructor, and Parameter information. Each of these types—like FieldInfo—describes the element of the type referred to.

There are two straightforward ways to get an instance of an assembly object. The first is to call Assembly.LoadFrom, passing the name of an assembly, and the second is by calling the static method Reflection.Assembly.GetCallingAssembly. An example of the first method can be found in the Changed method in Listing 2-1, and the second method returns the assembly containing the call GetCallingAssembly.

After you have a reference to the assembly you want to explore, you need to invoke the method that contains the information you want to obtain. For example, if I want to get all of the types defined by an assembly, then I declare an array of Type and invoke *assembly*.GetTypes(), where *assembly* refers to any instance of an assembly. The AssemblyViewer application uses an enumerator to walk these types.

What Are Enumerators?   It is important to understand what enumerators are and why you might use them. When you write code that iterates over data in a collection, list, or array, you might usually use a *for* or *while* loop. However, neither the *for* or *while* construct is an object; these are statements. Statements cannot be passed as parameters to methods, but enumerators, which are objects, can be passed as parameters to methods. Ah!

Implementing enumerators for things that are iterated—like the characters in a string, the rows in a DataSet, or the members of an array—provides you with a single common way of just iterating. Using enumerators also means that you can pass an enumerator to a method. When might you want to pass an enumerator to a method, you ask? A very insightful question, grasshopper. When you write an algorithm that is the same regardless of the data type.

Examples of algorithms that are the same regardless of data type are things like sorting algorithms. If I pass an enumerator that allows me to iterate over data rather than an array of a specific type, then I write the algorithm once and pass various instances of enumerators. Using an enumerator is useful for more than just sorting algorithms. You can and should define any method to take enumerators when the implementation of that method is data independent.

The .NET framework defines the IEnumerator interface. Any class that supports enumerating its elements can implement the IEnumerator interface. IEnumerator requires that the consumer implement MoveNext, Reset, and Current. MoveNext can be used as the loop control method, returning a Boolean, and the Current property returns the currently referenced object. Reset moves the internal reference index to the first element.

Using Enumerators to Walk the Assembly Information   Types that implement the IEnumerator interface usually have a GetEnumerator method. For example, Assembly.GetTypes returns an array of Type. The System.Array implements IEnumerator and System.Array .GetEnumerator returns an IEnumerator.

To enumerate each type in an assembly, you would write code similar to the following:

```
IEnumerator enumerator = assembly.GetEnumerator();
While(enumerator.MoveNext())
{
   // do something with enumerator.Current;
}
```

The Load method in Listing 2-1 demonstrates how an enumerator for the Types and MemberInfo array is returned by Type.GetMembers.

GetMembers returns an array of MemberInfo. Elements in the MemberInfo array include properties, fields, methods, and events. If you want to get an array of just the methods, then you could invoke Type.GetMethods. The same is true for other member types.

Executing Code Discovered by Reflection   The power provided by Reflection is more than an ability to find out what assemblies contain. You can actually invoke the types and members defined in assemblies and discovered by Reflection. The next listing is an example of dynamically loading an assembly and invoking a static method by Reflection.

```
const string s =
  "c:\\winnt\\Microsoft.NET\\Framework" +
  "\\v1.0.3705\\System.Windows.Forms.dll";
  Assembly assembly = Assembly.LoadFrom(s);
  Type type = assembly.GetType(
    "System.Windows.Forms.MessageBox", true);
  type.InvokeMember("Show", BindingFlags.Public |
    BindingFlags.InvokeMethod |
    BindingFlags.Static, null, null,
    new object[] {"Invoked by Reflection"});
```

The first statement defines a constant path to the System.Windows.Forms.dll assembly defined by the framework. The second statement uses the Assembly.LoadFrom method to load the assembly—Listing 2-1 provides another example of this. The third retrieves the meta type of the MessageBox class, and the final statement invokes a member in the MessageBox class. The first argument is the name of the member to refer to. The third member *Ors* three enumerated values together, indicating that Show is a Public, Static method that we want to invoke. The first null argument can be replaced with a subclass that describes how to bind the method, and the second null is an instance of the type that you want to invoke the method on. For example, if Show were a non-static method, then we would need to create an instance of the MessageBox class and pass it for this argument value. The final argument is an array of parameters that will be passed to the invoked method.

Broadcasting Operations

Listing 2-1 contains a statement Broadcaster.Broadcast. This is a technique I derived for sending internal information to a single location, allowing listeners who want to know what is going on to tune into the broadcaster. As an example of this, we could designate the main form as a listener and display the status of operations on the main form. The AssemblyViewer does exactly this; the main form has a status bar that is used to display the progress of the AssemblyManager during a load operation.

NOTE

There are existing facilities for writing to the Event Log using debug and trace listeners. However, these tools are not shipped with an application when the conditional compilation directives DEBUG and TRACE are not defined in the application. Usually you do not ship applications with these constants defined. (You can and should write critical information to the EventLog in a shipped application; you just won't use trace listeners to do so. Use the EventLog class for deployed event logging.)

Listing 2-2 shows the Broadcaster class and the IListener interface.

Listing 2-2   *The implementation of the Broadcaster class and the IListener interface.*

```
1:   using System;
2:   using System.Collections;
3:
4:   namespace AssemblyViewer
5:   {
6:     /// <summary>
7:     /// Summary description for Broadcaster.
8:     /// </summary>
9:     public class Broadcaster
10:    {
11:      private static Broadcaster instance = null;
12:      private ArrayList listeners = null;
13:      protected Broadcaster()
14:      {
15:        listeners = new ArrayList();
16:      }
17:
18:      static private Broadcaster Instance
19:      {
20:        get
21:        {
22:          if( instance == null )
23:            instance = new Broadcaster();
24:          return instance;
25:        }
26:      }
27:
28:      public static void Add(IListener listener)
29:      {
30:        Instance.listeners.Add(listener);
31:      }
32:
33:      public static void Remove(IListener listener)
```

```
34:      {
35:         Instance.listeners.Remove(listener);
36:      }
37:
38:      public static void Broadcast(string message)
39:      {
40:         IEnumerator enumerator = Instance.listeners.GetEnumerator();
41:         while(enumerator.MoveNext())
42:         {
43:            if(((IListener)enumerator.Current).Listening())
44:               ((IListener)enumerator.Current).Listen(message);
45:         }
46:      }
47:   }
48:
49:   public interface IListener
50:   {
51:      bool Listening();
52:      void Listen(string message);
53:   }
54: }
```

The Broadcaster class and the IListener interface shown in Listing 2-2 are used to centralize the sharing of information between objects and the GUI. Based on the implementation of the Broadcaster, any class that implements IListener and registers with the Broadcaster is capable of receiving string data sent to the Broadcaster. The class and the interface demonstrate a few salient techniques, so we will examine each.

Implementing the Broadcaster

The Broadcaster demonstrates the Singleton pattern. A *Singleton* is a class that you want to ensure has only one instance. Often, this pattern is used to reflect the existence of a single resource, like a single printer. A Singleton class is created by making the constructor protected or private and providing access only through a static member. The Broadcaster does this through the internal, private Instance property.

Every public method in Broadcaster is static. When you invoke a public member in the Broadcaster (or any Singleton), the method references the read only Instance property. Instance checks to see if the single instance of the Broadcaster has been created. If the Singleton doesn't exist, then one instance is created and assigned to the private field *instance*. The Singleton object is then returned. The result is that the Broadcaster contains a reference to an instance of itself.

If you add an IListener to the ArrayList of listeners, then every time the static method Broadcast is called, all listeners who are listening will receive the string content. This strategy can be employed to display internal status information, write to a log file, trace your deployed application, or to perform some combination of these tasks. (It is recommended that you use Debug and Trace listeners in conjunction with the Broadcaster idiom.) Also, notice that the IEnumerator is used to iterate the ArrayList of listeners.

Defining the Interface

The IListener interface defines two methods: Listening and Listen. Listening is a function that returns a Boolean indicating whether the object implementing the IListener interface wants to receive messages. This allows the object to metaphorically plug its ears without unregistering from the Broadcaster. The Listen method is the method that will receive the string content when listening.

You can use the Broadcaster by implementing the IListener interface. The FormMain class implements IListener to display broadcasted messages in the status bar. In the example of the main form, you can add the form to the list of listeners in the Form's Load. Another good place to add a control to the list of listeners is in the constructor of a class. Consider implementing IDisposable and Dispose to remove the object from the Broadcaster's listeners list when the object is disposed of.

The following code fragment demonstrates the pieces you might encounter in a class that implements the IListener interface and receives messages from the Broadcaster.

```csharp
public class FormMain : System.Windows.Forms.Form, IListener
{

  private void FormMain_Load(object sender, System.EventArgs e)
  {
    Broadcaster.Add(this);

  }
  protected override void Dispose( bool disposing )
  {
    if( disposing )
    {
      if(components != null)
      {
        components.Dispose();
      }
    }
    Broadcaster.Remove(this);
    base.Dispose( disposing );
  }

  void IListener.Listen(string message)
  {
    ChangeStatus(message.Trim());
  }
```

```
bool IListener.Listening()
{
  return true;
}
}
```

In the example, we inserted the code to remove the form from the Broadcaster's listeners list in the protected Dispose method already provided for us when the form was added to the project in Visual Studio .NET.

Secondary Topics

The AssemblyManager contains code that loaded and walked the types and members of an assembly. There was a lot of additional code in the AssemblyManager class, as there will be in any application, and this code was described, too. We will now move on to secondary topics for this chapter.

In this section, let's take a look at the kinds of things you will commonly find in Windows Forms–based applications.

Value Types Versus Reference Types

Whether you use a string type or the StringBuilder class, you are using objects. Every thing, including what appear to be native types, is a class in .NET, and every class has the same root: Object.

To easily demonstrate that types like the string type are classes in .NET, declare a string variable and begin typing a line of code using the string variable and the member of an operator. Intellisense will display the list of members that you can invoke on the string type (see Figure 2-2). Only types can have members; hence, the list of members clearly indicates that what appear to be native types are actually aggregate types.

There is a difference between types that appear to be native types, like int and string, and types that are obviously classes, like StringBuilder and the AssemblyManager. Types that you use like native types are descended from the ValueType class. Classes that are not value types are called *reference types*.

There are some notable differences between value types and reference types. Types like string and int that inherit from ValueType are allocated on the stack, and reference types are allocated on the heap. Allocating value types on the stack allows them to be created faster than if they were created on the heap. Value types are not garbage collected, reducing the amount of workload on the garbage collector. When you need to invoke members on value types, a heap-allocated object is created behind the scenes, and the internal value of the value type is copied to the heap-allocated object. When you are finished invoking members on a value type, the values in the heap-allocated object are copied back to the value type and the heap allocated object is destroyed. These internal operations of copying and copying back are referred to as *boxing* and *unboxing*, respectively.

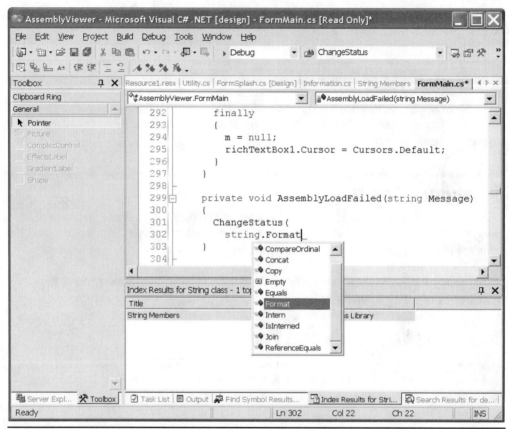

Figure 2-2   *Intellisense illustrates that types like string are classes.*

NOTE

Think of stack memory as the memory made available to methods, and think of heap memory as the global memory pool. Stack memory is literally a chunk of memory referred to by your CPUs stack register, and heap memory is referred to by your CPUs data register.

The BoxingDemo.sln is a console application that demonstrates a scenario where boxing occurs. It is easy to pick out when boxing occurs if you look at the Intermediate Language (IL) code. There is an IL instruction called "box" that is invoked. You can see the IL (in Figure 2-3) for the console application listed next.

```
using System;
namespace BoxingDemo
{
   /// <summary>
```

```
/// Summary description for Class1.
/// </summary>
class Class1
{
  /// <summary>
  /// The main entry point for the application.
  /// </summary>
  [STAThread]
  static void Main(string[] args)
  {
    int I = 5;
    string s = I.GetType().Name;
    Console.WriteLine(s);
  }
}
}
```

ValueType objects like int types do not carry their type information around with them. This is one of the reasons they are lightweight with respect to reference types. When the I.GetType method is invoked, boxing occurs and the type information is available as requested. Notice that no special code was required; boxing occurred automatically behind the scenes as a function of the CLR.

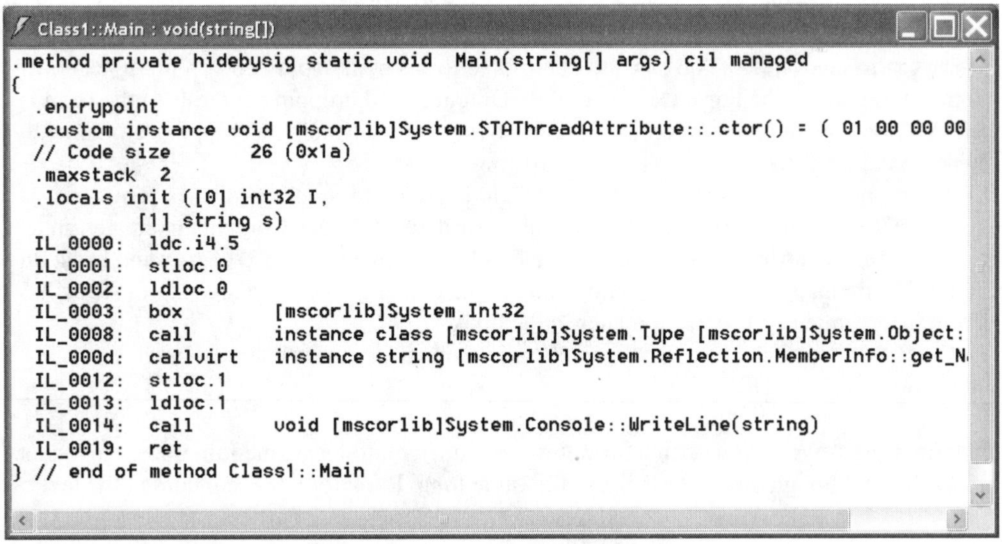

```
Class1::Main : void(string[])
.method private hidebysig static void  Main(string[] args) cil managed
{
  .entrypoint
  .custom instance void [mscorlib]System.STAThreadAttribute::.ctor() = ( 01 00 00 00
  // Code size       26 (0x1a)
  .maxstack  2
  .locals init ([0] int32 I,
           [1] string s)
  IL_0000:  ldc.i4.5
  IL_0001:  stloc.0
  IL_0002:  ldloc.0
  IL_0003:  box        [mscorlib]System.Int32
  IL_0008:  call       instance class [mscorlib]System.Type [mscorlib]System.Object:
  IL_000d:  callvirt   instance string [mscorlib]System.Reflection.MemberInfo::get_N
  IL_0012:  stloc.1
  IL_0013:  ldloc.1
  IL_0014:  call       void [mscorlib]System.Console::WriteLine(string)
  IL_0019:  ret
} // end of method Class1::Main
```

Figure 2-3   *Intermediate Language code for the BoxingDemo.exe.*

Windows Forms Controls

The AssemblyViewer demonstrates several Windows Forms Controls. (It is important to note, though, that because the AssemblyManager exists, we could wrap another presentation layer around the AssemblyManager and create a console application or Web application.) The main form demonstrates the Form, StatusBar, MainMenu, OpenFileDialog, and RichTextBox controls. We'll take a look at the FormMain module next.

The FormMain.cs contains 400 lines of code. To prevent chapter bloat we will refer to excerpts from the code listing rather than provide the whole listing for FormMain.cs here.

Working with the Form Control

When you add a form to your project, the default namespace is wrapped around the class defining the form. The class heading follows the namespace in the file that contains the definition of the form. The class heading for a Windows Form will demonstrate the syntax for inheritance, as each form you create will inherit from System.Windows.Forms.Form. The class heading is shown next.

```
public class FormMain : System.Windows.Forms.Form, IListener
```

The statement is understood to mean that FormMain inherits from System.Windows.Forms.Form and, since IListener is an interface, implements the IListener interface.

When you work with a form, you already have all of the members inherited from the base Form class, and the Visual Studio .NET IDE presents two views for forms. There is the *code designer view* where you write and edit code, and there is the *form designer view* where you visually design your graphical user interface. This dual view of graphic designer and code view is what makes the combination of C# and Visual Studio .NET a rapid-application environment.

Adding Controls to Forms   You can add controls to forms by dragging and dropping a control from the toolbox to the Form Designer view. Dragging and dropping controls to the form is referred to as "painting the interface." Alternatively, you can add controls programmatically by declaring a reference to a control and creating an instance.

When you paint a control on a form, a field is added to the form's class. The InitializeComponent method is called by the constructor. InitializeComponent creates an instance of the control. All of this code is added for you by the Form Designer and is useful for demonstrating the steps you would need to take to add controls dynamically. (We will return to dynamic control creation later in the book.)

The RAD part of all of this is that the Form Designer is generating code based on your interaction with the IDE.

Code Outlining   When you open a form it may be difficult to locate the InitializeComponent method, even though this method is usually quite long. Look for a box containing the text "Windows Form Designer Generated Code." The IDE uses code outlining to allow you to collapse and expand regions of code. Since the Form Designer code is managed by the designer, this block of code is collapsed by default.

The collapsed state of the Form Designer code is suggesting that you should leave this code alone. Of course, you are welcome to expand the code and examine how controls are created and managed.

Region Directive   Code outlining introduces the new region directive. The region directive allows you to manually create logical code blocks that can be expanded and collapsed to facilitate code housekeeping. The region directive uses the pragma operator # and is a block statement.

```
#region some text
#endregion
```

Code between the #region and #endregion can be collapsed and expanded to organize your code. For example, you could place all of your private methods inside of a region directive and collapse the lines of code containing the private members. The value of *some text* is a statement indicating what is inside the region, providing a hint to readers when the region is collapsed.

Use the + and − symbols in the code view or the Edit | Outlining menu item to expand and collapse code regions.

Implementing Event Handlers in Forms   The easiest way to implement event handlers for a Windows Form is to select the control of interest in the Form Designer view. Press F4 to focus the Properties window, and click the button with the lightning bolt in the Properties window. Clicking the lightning bolt switches the Properties window view so that it shows the events for the selected object. To select another object, click a control on the Form Designer or select the alternate control from the list of objects at the top of the Properties window.

To allow the Form Designer to generate the event handler for you, double-click the editable space adjacent to the name of the event that you want to generate code for.

When you double-click on the editable part of the Properties window, an event handler with the correct signature is generated for you. Additionally, the code that wires the event to the delegate property is inserted in the designer-managed region of the form's code, the InitializeComponent method.

FormMain implements the Load event. The code for the Load event—both the wire-up code and the event handler—is shown next.

```
private void InitializeComponent()
{
  // an excerpt from InitializeComponent
  this.Load += new System.EventHandler(this.FormMain_Load);
}
private void FormMain_Load(object sender, System.EventArgs e)
{
  Initialize();
}
```

The InitializeComponent method adds the Form_Load method generated by the Form Designer to the invocation list of the Load delegate. (Remember: delegates are multicast, which means that more than one handler can be assigned to a delegate like Load.) The FormMain_Load handler is generated by the designer, too. Again, the RAD part of all of this is that double-clicking on the event in the Properties window is a lot faster than writing the preceding code from scratch. Of course, you can write this code from scratch too, and there will be times that you want to.

A good strategy is to create a simple method named Initialize to perform your initialization code. This keeps the Load handler concise. In fact, this is a good strategy for event handlers in general: write a well-named method to perform the work for the handler. Doing so results in self-documenting code.

Writing Code   When it comes to writing code there is no difference between writing code in a class and writing code in a form class. A class is a class. Add fields, properties, methods, and events based on need rather than the type of the class.

Using the StatusBar

The StatusBar control is used to display the status of an application, usually at the bottom of a form. In the AssemblyViewer application, we target the StatusBar as the display control for broadcasted messages. (Remember that FormMain implements the IListener interface.)

```
private void Initialize()
{
  openFileDialog1.InitialDirectory = GetInitialDirectory();
  Broadcaster.Add(this);
}
private void ChangeStatus(string status)
{
  statusBar1.Text = status;
  statusBar1.Refresh();
}
void IListener.Listen(string message)
{
  ChangeStatus(message.Trim());
}
```

In AssemblyViewer, we registered MainForm as a listener with the Broadcaster, as shown in the Initialize method. The IListener.Listen method implements the Listen method of the IListener interface. When the Broadcaster invokes Listen for registered listeners, FormMain displays the information on the status bar by calling the ChangeStatus method.

Of course, you could wire the main form directly to the AssemblyManager, but I prefer not to have classes wired directly to GUIs. By not having a reference to FormMain in the AssemblyManager, it is easier to use the AssemblyManager in a new context, like a console application. You can also achieve a similar result using events. Either of these techniques illustrates the concept of *loose coupling*.

Using the MainMenu

Menus are comprised of MainMenu and MenuItem objects. When you paint a main menu onto a form, the MainMenu control is added to the component tray (underneath the gray form canvas). The presentation of the main menu is drawn on the form itself.

When you want to add MenuItem objects to the main menu, you do so by typing the name of the menu item directly into the location where you want that menu item to be displayed. Available MenuItem locations are indicated by a dotted outline with the text "Type Here" in it. When you type the caption for the menu, the Form Designer generates the field and code necessary to wire the menu.

The most common event for menu items is the Click event. To generate a Click event handler, double-click on the menu item or use the Properties window technique described earlier.

Remember, MainMenu and MenuItem objects are controls. They receive the focus and are interacted with just like any other control.

Using the OpenFileDialog

The OpenFileDialog control displays a Windows Explorer–style dialog, enabling the user to select a file based on a programmer-described file mask. The OpenFileDialog supports a programmer-configurable InitialDirectory and Title. The following method taken from the FormMain module demonstrates how to display the dialog and retrieve the selected FileName.

```
public void OpenAssembly()
{
  if( openFileDialog1.ShowDialog() == DialogResult.OK)
    OpenAssembly(openFileDialog1.FileName);
}
```

The call to OpenAssembly loads the selected assembly into the AssemblyViewer.

If you wanted to specify a filter mask that is suitable for selecting assemblies, then you could specify the mask using the Properties window or with the following statement:

```
openFileDialog1.Filter = "Class Library(*.dll)|*.dll|Executables
(*.exe)|*.exe";
```

Filter masks are specified in pairs. The first half is the displayed mask that is selectable from the File of type combobox, and the second half is the actual mask. For example, "Class Library (*.dll)|*.dll" will display "Class Library (*.dll)" in the File of type combobox, and when you select this filter, only files matching *.dll will be displayed in the dialog.

Using RichTextBox

Rich Text is a kind of markup language. Known as Rich Text Format, or RTF, Rich Text supports embedded tags that describe the format of the text. The RichTextBox is similar to the TextBox, but supports embedded RTF formatting. The primary purpose of the RichTextBox is to display formatted text, but the RichTextBox can display plain text and has built-in capabilities that support loading and saving the content of the text property to a file.

Putting Text in the RichTextBox   The Text can be plain text or Rich Text. To programmatically assign string data to a RichTextBox control, assign a string variable to the Text property.

```
richTextBox1.Text = "C# Developer's Guide";
```

Loading a Text File   Load text from an external text file by calling the LoadFile method. LoadFile takes three forms, the easiest of which specifies the file name of a file containing RTF formatting:

```
richTextBox1.LoadFile("file.rtf");
```

A second form of the RichTextBox has the RichTextBoxStreamType enumeration that allows you to express the type of formatting the file contains. For example, to load plain text, you could rewrite the LoadFile statement:

```
richTextBox1.LoadFile("file.rtf", RichTextBoxStreamType.PlainText );
```

RichTextBoxStreamType is an enumeration defined in the System.Windows.Forms namespace. You will need to use the fully qualified name or ensure there is a *using* statement that refers to the System.Windows.Forms namespace.

Saving a Text File   RichTextBox.SaveFile performs the symmetric operation to LoadFile. SaveFile writes the contents of the RichTextBox control to an RTF or TXT file by calling SaveFile and passing a file name.

Using the ZoomFactor   RichTextBox.ZoomFactor is an interesting property. With ZoomFactor you can express a percentage increase in the size of the text. Setting ZoomFactor to 2 will double the size of the text, and .64 will reduce the size of the text by approximately half. Acceptable values are from .64 to 64, the latter being 64 times the normal size. This property is an excellent feature for applications supporting people with disabilities and for presentations. Suppose, for example, that you are displaying the content of the RichTextBox on an overhead projector. Setting the ZoomFactor to increase text size will make it easier for your audience to see the content in the RichTextBox control.

Using the LinkLabel

The LinkLabel control represents a Windows Forms hyperlink, further blurring the lines between Windows and Web applications. Enter an URL in the LinkLabel.Text property and, when a user clicks on the LinkLabel control, the value of the Text property can be used to open IE, for example.

The code listing that follows is taken from the About form in the AssemblyViewer. The URL of the author of the application is expressed in a LinkLabel. When the user clicks the link label, IE is started and the default page of **www.softconcepts.com** is opened.

```
private void linkLabel1_LinkClicked(object sender,
  LinkLabelLinkClickedEventArgs e)
{
```

```
(sender as LinkLabel).LinkVisited = true;
Process.Start( (sender as LinkLabel).Text );
}
```

The Process class is defined in the System.Diagnostics namespace, and Start is a static method. The Process class is useful for starting, stopping, controlling, and monitoring applications. In this example, the http// moniker implicitly instructs Process.Start to start a new instance of IE, given the association between URLs and Internet Explorer.

Basic Printing

Crystal Reports, which is a popular tool from Seagate Software, is now Crystal Decisions. For advanced printing and reporting, you can integrate Crystal Decisions–based controls into your application, but basic printing is supported by the PrintDocument control.

To implement basic printing add a PrintDocument control to your application and invoke the Print method. When you call PrintDocument.Print, the PrintPage event is fired. PrintPage is passed a PrintPageEventArgs object that contains a Graphics object representing the Device Context (DC) of the printer. With this Graphics object, you have the methods supported by the Graphics class, like DrawString. The following code is taken from the FormMain module and writes the contents of the RichTextBox to the printer.

```
public void printDocument1_PrintPage(
  object sender, PrintPageEventArgs e)
{
  e.Graphics.DrawString(richTextBox1.Text,
    richTextBox1.Font, Brushes.Black, 0, 0);
}
```

You could use the exact same code to write the text content of the RichTextBox control to some other Device Context, like a form itself.

If you want to support Printer Setup, then use the PageSetupDialog. The PageSetupDialog allows the user to modify the PageSettings and PrinterSettings for a given document. To use the PageSetupDialog control, click and drag a PageSetupDialog control to the application and set the PageSetupDialog.Document property to a PrintDocument control, printDocument1 in the AssemblyViewer.

To display the PageSetupDialog, invoke the ShowDialog method. The changes you make will be applied to the PrintDocument associated with the PageSetupDialog. (Refer to the MainForm.cs module in the AssemblyViewer for an example that demonstrates these two controls.)

Embedded Resource File Management

Resource files are used to externalize content such as string data. By placing your string data in a resource file, you can provide different language versions of your resource files and thereby more easily internationalize text.

To add a resource file to your application, right-click the project in the Solution Explorer. From the project context menu, select Add | Add New Item. Within the Add New Item dialog, select the Assembly Resource File template, as shown in Figure 2-4.

When you select the resource file from the Solution Explorer, a resource editor is displayed, as shown in Figure 2-5. You can add resource content to the resource file using the editor. As shown in the figure, string resource entries are presented as a table of name, value, comment, type, and mimetype information. This is similar to resource files. The biggest distinction is that resource files in .NET are stored as XML files, rather than plain text. You can view the XML by clicking the XML tab (shown in Figure 2-5).

The Utility.cs module demonstrates how to use a ResourceManager to read data from the resource (.resx) file. To read string information from a resource file, create an instance of the ResourceManager class defined in the System.Resources namespace and invoke the GetString method. The next code listing demonstrates using the ResourceManager as it is implemented in the Utility.cs module.

```
public class Utility
{
  public static string GetResourceString(string resourceName)
  {
    ResourceManager manager = new
      ResourceManager("AssemblyViewer.Resource1",
      Assembly.GetExecutingAssembly());
    return manager.GetString(resourceName);
  }
}
```

The ResourceManager needs to know the resource file that you want to load and the assembly that contains that resource file. In the example, we are getting the default-named resource file in the executing assembly.

Multithreading

Finally, we come to multithreading. Multithreading is a complex subject. There are several facets to multithreading, so we will limit our discussion to multithreading in this chapter to the way it was used to help implement the AssemblyViewer.

The AssemblyViewer uses a separate thread to display the Splash screen while the application is loaded. A luxury to be sure, but what is the point of a splash screen if it is executed in a linear fashion? That is, while the splash screen is loading, no real initialization occurs, and I never liked letting the splash screen contain the initialization code. (You are likely to find, however, that many splash screens do actually contain initialization code.)

In our sample application, the splash screen is splashed on its own thread. There are four ways to contrive seemingly asynchronous behavior in .NET. The Timer control and Application.Idle event provide event-driven synchronous behavior. Controls support the asynchronous BeginInvoke and EndInvoke. The ThreadPool class provides a pool of available threads, and the Thread class allows you to spin up and manage threads yourself.

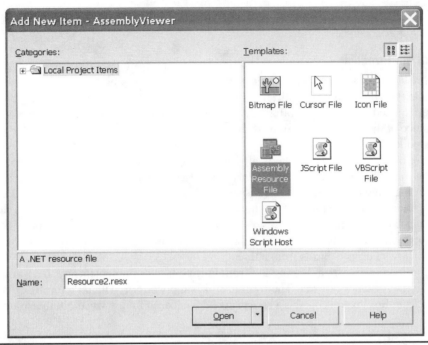

Figure 2-4   *Add New Item dialog allows you to add items to your project from the templates list.*

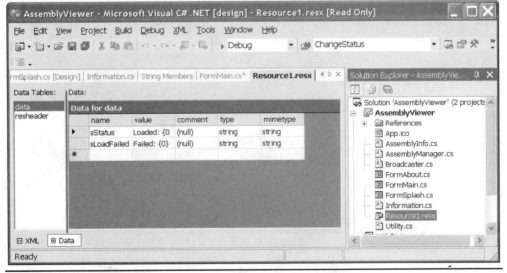

Figure 2-5   *Use the string resource editor to externalize text information, facilitating application internationalization.*

The AssemblyViewer uses a thread from the ThreadPool class; hence, that is the facet of threading introduced here.

ThreadPool Threading

The ThreadPool is a class that manages a pool of threads for you. Multithreading using threads in the ThreadPool is no different than creating a Thread object. However, your work load is lightened a bit, and grabbing a thread from the pool is often a bit faster than creating an instance of the Thread class because the pool most likely has a thread waiting for you to give it work.

To use a thread in the ThreadPool, all you have to do is give the ThreadPool some work to do in the form of a Delegate. In this instance, the Delegate will act as a procedure representing work for the thread to do. Every other aspect of threading is identical to spinning a Thread object yourself. The most important thing to remember is that ThreadPool threads require just as much care as Thread instances, especially when it comes to Windows Forms controls. Windows Forms controls are not thread-safe; thus, you must take extra care when interacting with Windows Forms controls from a thread.

The following excerpt in Listing 2-3 from FormSplash.cs implements the fade-in splash screen in the AssemblyViewer. The form itself is simply a form with a PictureBox control on it. The PictureBox control contains a cool picture downloaded from **www.digitalblasphemy.com**.

Listing 2-3   *FormSplash.cs (excerpt) demonstrates the multithreaded code that implements the fade-in splash screen.*

```
1:   bool done = false;
2:   private void Increment()
3:   {
4:     Opacity += .05;
5:     lock(this)
6:     {
7:       done = Opacity >= 1;
8:     }
9:   }
10:
11:  private void Show(Object state)
12:  {
13:    try
14:    {
15:      while(!done)
16:      {
17:        this.Invoke(new MethodInvoker(Increment));
18:        Thread.Sleep(100);
19:      }
20:      Thread.Sleep(1500);
```

```
21:    }
22:    finally
23:    {
24:      Close();
25:    }
26: }
27:
28: public static void Splash()
29: {
30: #if !DEBUG
31:    FormSplash form = new FormSplash();
32:    form.Opacity = 0;
33:    form.Show();
34:    ThreadPool.QueueUserWorkItem(
35:      new WaitCallback(form.Show));
36: #endif
37: }
```

The remainder of this chapter and section will refer to the code in Listing 2-3.

Queuing a Work Item in the ThreadPool

Delegates are so important that event handlers do not work without them, and you cannot use multithreading in any .NET language unless you understand delegates. To recap, a delegate contains the address of one or more methods. Threading works by giving a thread a delegate containing procedures representing work to be done by the thread.

In Listing 2-3, the static method Splash creates the Splash form with an Opacity of 0. When Form.Opacity is 0, the form is transparent; 1 represents an opaque form. With an Opacity percentage between 0 and 1, you have a semi-transparent form. The Splash form is shown transparently, and the thread will slowly increase the Opacity value until the form is Opaque, at which point the thread is finished.

Lines 34 and 35 in Listing 2-3 demonstrate how to multithread using the ThreadPool class. The ThreadPool is defined in the System.Threading namespace, and QueueUserWorkItem is a static method.

QueueUserWorkItem takes a WaitCallback delegate. The signature of a WaitCallback delegate is a method that has a single object argument. (We won't use the state object in this example, but we still have to provide the argument. The state argument facilitates passing information to worker methods.)

QueueUserWorkItem adds the method Show to a Queue in the ThreadPool, which will in turn use or create a thread to perform the work. You can assure yourself that multithreading is occurring by opening the Threads window from the Debug | Window | Threads menu item. When a thread is assigned, it will invoke the Show method—the WaitCallback delegate—on that thread.

Windows Forms Synchronous Method Invocation

The Show method is defined on lines 11 through 26 in Listing 2-3. This Show method slowly fades in the form by adjusting the Opacity. Unfortunately, because Windows Forms controls are not thread-safe, the Opacity must be changed on the same thread as the one it resides on. The Show method is not on that thread.

The way that we actually update the Opacity value is by calling the form's Invoke method. Invoke is thread-safe; Invoke marshals the delegate argument into the same thread as the thread that the calling object is on. (Again, without delegates safe threading would not be possible.)

Invoke requires a MethodInvoker delegate and executes the code inside the method used to initialize the delegate. The Increment method updates the Opacity value. The *done* field is used to indicate that the form is opaque. We lock the Done method while we are updating it, blocking the thread running Show from examining the Done value until it has been updated.

Finally, Show uses the *try finally* construct to catch exceptions and close the form. For example, if a user closed the application before the Splash form was completely Opaque, Show would refer to a disposed form (this is on line 17 in Listing 2-3) and raise an exception. The exception handler responds to an immediate application shut-down.

Summary

Perhaps the reason many books do not show complete applications is that there are dozens of skills necessary to create even basic applications. As this chapter demonstrated, simple applications can draw on a wide range of programming skills.

This chapter demonstrated Windows Forms programming, multithreading, Reflection, enumerators, delegates, and resource file management. Chapter 3 implements a video kiosk and explores GDI+ programming in further detail.

CHAPTER 3

Video Kiosk

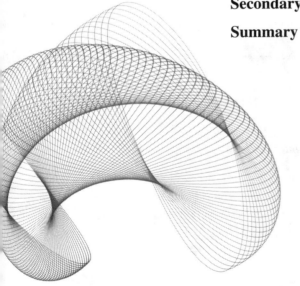

T he power of graphics programming in Windows has, thankfully, been encapsulated in an object-oriented framework. A substantial measure of graphics programming support has existed in Windows for some time, but it has been challenging to get at. The Video Kiosk example program in this chapter demonstrates how to use the new framework, dubbed "GDI+." Many clever and engaging applications use non-standard user interfaces to convey meaning or encourage people to play with them. This chapter demonstrates some of the fundamental skills you will need to use GDI+. The skills demonstrated in this chapter will help you create professional applications that use graphics in traditional ways and perhaps clever new ways.

Demonstrated Topics

From the examples in this chapter you will be able to master the intricacies of GDI+ and find code that demonstrates the following topics:

▶   Creating custom controls (an introduction)

▶   Creating a control library

▶   Using the ControlPaint class to paint standard controls

▶   Working with virtual methods

▶   Overriding events

▶   Exception handling, including catching specific exceptions

▶   Employing COM Interop (demonstrated by using the ActiveX Media Player)

▶   Implementing interfaces

▶   Adding items to your TODO lists with the TODO comments

▶   Working with the MessageBox and TimeSpan classes

What Is GDI+?

In keeping with the spirit of .NET, perhaps GDI+ should be redubbed GDI.NET. The name is not relevant to the technology though. (The asymmetry just bugs me.)

Windows has always supported pretty advanced graphics programming. This basic technology is referred to as *GDI* (*graphics device interface*). The problem with GDI is that it is not approachable.

Windows visual programming may be thought of, metaphorically, as painting on a canvas. If you think about it, with a steady hand and a bit of diligence you could draw a Windows application form in a program like Paint. The painting-on-canvas metaphor is precisely like that, except you have standardized chunks of code that do the drawing for you.

In Windows, a canvas is referred to as a *device context* (*DC*). If you have programmed with GDI (pre-.NET Windows programming), then you have used API methods that required a handle to a device context, usually abbreviated hDC. What makes GDI unapproachable is that GDI is comprised of a disparate bunch of structures and API methods that are unorganized and uncategorized; that is to say, GDI is procedural.

GDI+ is an organized and categorized object-oriented version of GDI. By encapsulating the notion of the canvas and other drawing capabilities into an object-oriented framework, we get the same benefits we get with any other object-oriented framework. We get reusable classes and components that are more approachable and comprehensible. In short, GDI+ wraps GDI into an object-oriented framework. Now, instead of hunting and pecking, we only have to look in a general area—the namespaces that make up GDI+—and learn something about the organization of the types and classes in those namespaces.

NOTE

It is important to note that the Microsoft developers were the first developers to benefit from the classification of basic, disparate API graphics methods when they came up with new graphics features. New features found in GDI+ include gradient brushes, cardinal splines, independent path objects, scalable regions, and alpha blending as well as support for a wide variety of image formats. You will get an opportunity to work with gradient brushes, path objects, and scalable regions directly in this chapter.

GDI+ Namespaces

GDI+ is comprised of classes in the System.Drawing.dll, which includes the System.Drawing, System.Drawing.Design, System.Drawing.Drawing2D, System.Drawing.Imaging, System .Drawing.Printing, and System.Drawing.Text namespaces. These contain classes and types that support three broad categories of managing graphics: 2D vector graphics, imaging, and typography.

Vector graphics include basic line, shape, and curve drawing capabilities defined by points. *Imaging* includes support for displaying graphics that are difficult to render using vector graphics, like digital photographs, bitmaps, and icons. And, *typography* supports drawing text using a variety of fonts, sizes, and styles. This broad spectrum of support provides you with tremendous flexibility for rendering graphics-based images, vector graphics, and text.

Understanding the GDI+ Programming Model

The Internet is a stateless environment. In the Internet era, many things seem to be trending toward statelessness. *Statelessness* means simply that each time code interacts, it must be reminded of what it needs to know. (Sort of like wearing name tags at a meeting where everyone is working together but are strangers. A stateless environment means your code is always a stranger to other code.)

Statelessness is necessary for the Internet because it makes it very difficult to support tracking state information for millions of connected users. My assumption is that what is believed to work for the potentially huge scale of the Internet could also benefit the demands of graphics programming.

In practical terms, what statelessness means is that every time you want to display some text on a canvas, you have to remind GDI+ what font and brush to use. Like a doddering old grandfather, GDI+ just can't seem to remember. (We'll come back to fonts and brushes later.) This means you have to remember for GDI+. That is to say, each time you draw some text, you will have to tell GDI+ what font and brush to draw the text with. Not only will GDI+ forget what font and brush you just used, but it won't keep track of the last location you wrote the text at, and it will even forget the screen size. That's right. GDI+ will not update information about the size of the canvas if that size changes between the last time you requested a Graphics object (think DC) and the next time you use that Graphics object.

Statelessness means the programmer has to explicitly indicate information like the font, brush, pen, color, and location each time the code interacts with a device context. You must not cache the DC in .NET either. Code such as the following is a no-no.

```csharp
public class CacheGraphics : System.Windows.Forms.Form
{
  Graphics graphics;
  public CacheGraphics()
  {
    graphics = new Graphics();
  }
}
```

The preceding code defines a class CacheGraphics that inherits from Form. The constructor creates a new Graphics object and stores it in the *graphics* field.

While the Graphics object is the name of the class that contains the DC, doing both of the things shown in the listing—creating a Graphics object directly and caching that Graphics object—are mistakes. Since GDI+ is stateless, changes to the DC will not be propagated to your cached Graphics object. For example, if you resize the form, then your Graphics object represents a region that does not accurately reflect your DC. Additionally, you must invoke the factory method CreateGraphics to get an instance of a Graphics object.

TIP

You can compel consumers of your code to use a factory method by making the constructor of a class protected or private and invoking that method through a public static method in the same class.

The factory method CreateGraphics is required because there is a lot of work that goes on behind the scenes to instantiate a Graphics object. Using a factory method ensures that all of that required initialization occurs properly every time. This technique also allows the producers of the Graphics class to perform some behind-the-scenes optimization. (We would know what that is if we had access to the Common Language Runtime source code.)

As you will see in this chapter, you should not cache a Graphics object; request it using CreateGraphics each time you need it. You must use the factory method CreateGraphics (or get the Graphics object argument from an event handler) each time you need it, and you will have to pass in state information, like fonts and brushes, each time you perform a graphics operation.

Examining the PlayControl

The PlayControl shown in Figure 3-1 shows the custom graphical user interface. From the figure you may be able to discern that the control is in a form with slightly rounded edges and no title bar. More pronounced are the elliptical buttons. It may be difficult to detect in black and white, but in addition to the buttons being round or oval, they also use a gradient brush to enhance the 3D effect.

You might also notice that some controls display basic images, like the triangular play button, and other controls display images, like the open button displaying the folder.

Other effects include the background appearance, the VK (Video Kiosk trademark logo in base relief), and the custom slider at the top of the PlayControl. I will describe the code that creates these effects, as well as provide the source code to allow you to experiment further or solve any problem you might have.

Implementing the PlayControl

The PlayControl is composed of buttons. Like standard buttons, these buttons respond to a Click event. In that regard, the control is very simple: click a button, a Click event handler is invoked, and some code is run.

There are two issues that make the player control reusable in a general sense rather than a single-use form for one application. The buttons are implemented as separate controls, and the PlayControl doesn't do anything. Each Button Click event simply invokes an equivalent operation on another class that implements the IPlayer interface. (We haven't discussed the IPlayer interface yet; we'll get to it next.) For example, if you click Play, then the Play method of the player associated with the PlayControl is invoked—as long as it implements the IPlayer interface. Hence, classes allow us to reuse individual controls, and interfaces allow us to reuse the whole component. Perhaps the equivalent of a radio, VCR, or cassette player could use this generic component. The IPlayer interface is shown in Listing 3-1.

Figure 3-1   *A custom graphical user interface implemented using GDI+*

Listing 3-1   *The IPlayer interface allows us to separate the graphical user interface of the PlayControl from any particular implementation, creating a truly thin client.*

```
using System;

namespace VideoKiosk
{
  public interface IPlayer
  {
    void Close();
    void Play();
    void Pause();
    void Stop();
    void FastForward();
    void FastReverse();
    void VolumeUp();
    void VolumeDown();
    bool Open();
    double Duration();
    bool Mute();
    void Mute(bool state);
    double Elapsed();
  }
}
```

From the listing we can determine that the IPlayer interface is quite generic and possibly suited for many modern devices that we might choose to emulate on a computer.

In the Video Kiosk, the main form, Form1.cs, implements the IPlayer interface. This means that the contract between IPlayer and Form1 is that Form1 must implement all of the methods defined by the interface. Subsequently, based on our implementation, Form1 can be associated as a player with the PlayControl. This can be accomplished by passing to the form a reference to an instance of the PlayControl in the PlayControl's constructor. Here is the call to create and associate the PlayControl with Form1 in Form1's Load event.

```
private PlayControl control = null;
private void Form1_Load(object sender, System.EventArgs e)
{
  control = new PlayControl(this);
  control.Show();
}
```

And here is the constructor for the PlayControl. The PlayControl instances keep track of the player it is associated with.

```
private IPlayer player;
public PlayControl()
```

```
{
  InitializeComponent();
}

public PlayControl(IPlayer player) : this()
{
  this.player = player;
}
```

Since Form1 owns the PlayControl, we know that when Form1 is closed, the PlayControl will be, too. The PlayControl constructor demonstrates how to invoke the default constructor. The default constructor is the PlayControl method that takes no arguments. Invoking the default constructor is critical because the default constructor contains the call to InitializeComponent. Without the InitializeComponent statement, none of the controls will be created and the form won't be displayed or work correctly.

NOTE

If you are having difficulty following the code, you can run the sample VideoKiosk.sln to step through the code. From the two fragments, Form1_Load is invoked first. The statement containing new PlayControl(this) invokes the PlayControl constructor that takes an IPlayer interface. The default constructor is invoked due to the presence of the : this() clause in the constructor. In the default constructor InitializeComponent is called, and when the default constructor returns, this.player = player is executed. (It is important to understand how constructor invocation works.)

It is the : this() clause that invokes the default constructor. After the default constructor returns, the player arguments are cached into the *player* field. Our PlayControl now has a player to control.

NOTE

A sane person might reasonably argue "Why not use the default controls provided with the ActiveX Media Player?" or "Why not implement the play control right in the form that contains the Media Player?" The simple answer is "Then what would we talk about?" The better answer is that we could do that. However, for a little more work, we have a new component, the PlayControl, that is a separate component that can be used for something else later (and we also have something to talk about).

Now when the user clicks the play button (we all know which one that is), the code in the PlayControl is very simple.

```
player.Play();
```

This statement runs code in Form1. In our example program, the code in Form1 contains the following.

```
void IPlayer.Play()
{
  axMediaPlayer1.Play();
}
```

Of course, if we used something besides the ActiveX Media Player, the code in IPlayer.Play would be a little different. (I introduced interfaces in Chapter 1. You can review that material if you need a reminder about implementing interfaces.)

In a real application, we need more than the simple statement invoking the Play method. An application would include the event invocation and some sanity checking. The VideoKiosk implements Play, as shown in Listing 3-2.

Listing 3-2   *Implementing the PlayControl.Play method.*

```
private void Play()
{
  if(player==null) return;
  try
  {
    player.Play();
    PlayerState = PlayerState.playing;
  }
  catch
  {
    PlayError();
    PlayerState = PlayerState.stopped;
  }
}

private void playButton1_Click(
  object sender, System.EventArgs e)
{
  Play();
}
```

As a general rule, it is bad form to write code directly into an event handler. Instead we use a well-named method, Play, that in conjunction with the PlayControl context indicates exactly what is going on. The Play method uses a sentinel that checks to make sure the internal reference to the player is not null. (Some people like positive *if-conditional* checks and block statements. I prefer the sentinel. No admittance if the conditional fails.)

In an exception-handling block, the player's Play method is invoked. Using an interface ensures that there is a Play method, and using the exception-handling block ensures that our program won't explode if something goes wrong on the player. (Think of your infrared remote control. You can push the button on the remote control even if the television is unplugged and nothing bad happens. Same concept here.) If we get past the call to player.Play, then we change the state of the player. (This is used to update the enabled buttons.)

NOTE

Could you imagine if hardware devices ran like some software? Press the On button on your remote control, and, if you haven't paid your cable bill, the remote control electrocutes you. Thinking about reasonable fail states is how we code exception handlers. No BSDs! (That is, No Blue Screen of Death!)

If an error does occur, such as having no media file, then the catch block takes over. The PlayError method is called, and the PlayControl state is returned to stop.

You can look up PlayError. PlayError uses the MessageBox class you learned about in Chapter 1 to display a message indicating that the media file could not be played. Using a separate PlayError method affords the opportunity to add something more helpful at a later date if we need to, while stubbing out a solution now. Perhaps we could write code that diagnoses the problem more closely and provides a reasonable way to solve the problem.

TIP

Notice that I did not handle actually changing button states in the Play method. This would be doing too much. Actually changing the PlayerState property provides us with a convenient place to do that. Because the PlayerState setter is a method, we can run some code in the setter. For example, we can update the button states to reflect the new value of the PlayerState.

Creating the Graphical User Interface for the PlayControl

Creating technically advanced graphical user interfaces is challenging. Creating graphical user interfaces that are attractive and professional is both technically challenging and requires artistic skill at a level that artists are more likely than computer scientists to possess. Of course, it is possible that good programmers are also talented artists, and that is the combination needed to create interfaces like the Headspace skin of the Windows Media Player shown in Figure 3-2.

There are a few ways to create advanced interfaces, including using digital photography, claymation, vector graphics, and drawing. A great strategy for implementing artistically appealing interfaces is to hire artists to do the artistic part. Hire a professional artist to draw, paint, or photograph a graphical user interface, and then charge your programmers with turning the image into an application.

To create the PlayControl, I borrowed the background of the Intervideo WinDVD control that shipped with my Dell laptop. The buttons, tracker, and the elapsed time text were added to the basic background image.

Adding the Background Image to the PlayControl

Form classes have a BackgroundImage property. If you need something other than the basic gray background for your Windows applications, then you can create a custom image or use an existing graphic and assign that image to the BackgroundImage property of the form. Doing this will eliminate the need to create advanced appearances with controls only.

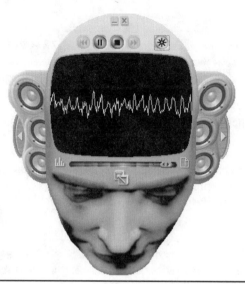

Figure 3-2   *The Headspace skin for the Windows Media Player demonstrates exceptional artistry.*

Everything is colored pixels in Windows applications. You are encouraged to use background images to speed up development. It is much easier (once you have an image) to create advanced custom effects with images than it is to create those effects using controls; additionally, your applications will be lighter and faster with fewer controls. For any visual effect that does not respond to user feedback, consider using a background image. Figure 3-3 shows the PlayControl without the benefit of the background image.

Clearly we could use Windows Forms controls to create various regions for the tracker, buttons, and progress time indicator, but Windows Forms controls are rectilinear. The result would not be especially appealing. Simply by adding the background image, we get a visually appealing backdrop for the PlayControl (see Figure 3-4).

Now that we have a nice backdrop for our application, we can layer the controls that provide dynamic feedback and accept input from the user to complete the PlayControl.

Adding Custom Controls to the PlayControl

Rectangular buttons would look out of place on our ergonomic PlayControl. To create buttons that look at home in our PlayControl, we will have to delve into our GDI+ toolbox.

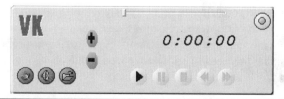

Figure 3-3   *The PlayControl without the background image*

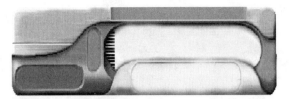

Figure 3-4   *The background image provides a visually appealing backdrop for our application without code or customized controls.*

The round shapes in the PlayControl suggest that softer-edged, elliptical buttons would look more at home. Unfortunately, these controls are not part of the standard toolbox; hence, we will have to create custom buttons.

An excellent way to quickly create new controls is to add a custom control to your project. The custom control provides a class that has all of the methods and properties you will need to create a wide variety of controls. Listing 3-3 demonstrates a custom control–based round button that provides the basis for all of the buttons shown on the PlayControl in Figure 3-1.

Listing 3-3   *The source code that is the basis for the round buttons on the PlayControl*

```
1:     public class RoundButton :
2:        System.Windows.Forms.Control
3:     {
4:       private bool hasOutline = false;
5:
6:       protected bool down = false;
7:
8:       protected virtual Color GetColor()
9:       {
10:        Color[] colors = {Color.Silver, Color.Gray};
11:        return colors[Convert.ToInt32(down)];
12:      }
13:
14:      protected virtual Brush GetBrush(bool buttonState)
15:      {
16:        return new LinearGradientBrush(
17:          new Point(2,2), new Point(Width -1 , Height - 1),
18:          Color.White, GetColor());
19:      }
20:
21:      private int GetPenWidth()
22:      {
23:        // use button state to adjust pen width
24:        return 1 + Convert.ToInt32(down);
25:      }
```

```
26:
27:     private Pen GetPen()
28:     {
29:       return new Pen(Brushes.Black, GetPenWidth());
30:     }
31:
32:     public bool HasOutline
33:     {
34:       get
35:       {
36:         return hasOutline;
37:       }
38:       set
39:       {
40:         hasOutline = value;
41:         Invalidate();
42:       }
43:     }
44:
45:     private void DrawButtonOutline(Graphics graphics)
46:     {
47:       graphics.DrawEllipse(GetPen(), 1, 1,
48:         Bounds.Width - 2, Bounds.Height - 2);
49:     }
50:
51:     private void DrawButton(Graphics graphics)
52:     {
53:       graphics.FillEllipse(GetBrush(down), 0, 0,
54:         Width, Height);
55:       if(hasOutline)DrawButtonOutline(graphics);
56:     }
57:
58:     protected override void OnPaint(
59:        System.Windows.Forms.PaintEventArgs e)
60:     {
61:       base.OnPaint(e);
62:       DrawButton(e.Graphics);
63:       DrawGraphic(e.Graphics);
64:     }
65:
66:     protected override void OnResize(System.EventArgs e)
67:     {
68:       GraphicsPath path = new GraphicsPath();
69:       path.AddEllipse(0, 0, Bounds.Width, Bounds.Height);
```

```
70:        Region = new Region(path);
71:        Invalidate();
72:        base.OnResize(e);
73:      }
74:
75:    protected override void OnMouseDown(
76:       System.Windows.Forms.MouseEventArgs e)
77:      {
78:        base.OnMouseDown(e);
79:        down = true;
80:        Invalidate();
81:      }
82:
83:    protected override void OnMouseUp(
84:       System.Windows.Forms.MouseEventArgs e)
85:      {
86:        base.OnMouseUp(e);
87:        down = false;
88:        Invalidate();
89:      }
90:
91:    protected virtual void DrawDownGraphic(
92:      Graphics graphics)
93:      {
94:        Matrix m = new Matrix();
95:        m.Scale(1.03F,1.03F);
96:        graphics.Transform = m;
97:
98:      }
99:
100:    protected virtual void DrawGraphic(
101:       Graphics graphics)
102:      {
103:        if(down) DrawDownGraphic(graphics);
104:      }
105:
106:    protected virtual Brush GraphicBrush()
107:      {
108:        return Enabled ? Brushes.Black: Brushes.Silver;
109:      }
110:    }
```

The code demonstrates several aspects of GDI+. We will decompose the code extracted from the RoundButton.cs module in separate sections, describing the techniques demonstrated.

Constructors, Destructors, and Dispose Method

Because a control is a class, you may encounter things in a control that you are likely to find in any class. There are three common methods that you are likely to find in any class, including a control—these are constructors, destructors, and a Dispose method.

The RoundButton doesn't implement a constructor, a destructor, or a Dispose method. In this particular instance we do not need them. In this particular instance we do not perform any of the actions that require their presence. Other classes in the Controls.dll—part of the VideoKiosk.sln—demonstrate examples of constructors and the Dispose method.

Control Constructors   The purpose of constructors is to initialize objects defined in your classes. This holds true for Control classes. If your controls do not contain members that need to be created with the new operator, or your classes do not need to perform any special initialization, then you do not need a constructor.

Constructors are usually public, define no return type, and have the same name as the class that contains them. In our RoundButton class, we don't use a constructor because we do not need to perform any special initialization.

Constructors can be overloaded by defining additional methods with the same name as the class, but you do not have to specifically indicate that a constructor is overloaded by using a modifier. Two methods—including constructors and destructors—with the same name as the class will automatically be overloaded, and calls to that constructor will be resolved, based on unique argument types.

A good strategy demonstrated by the Form class is to call an intializer method from the constructor, rather than cluttering the constructor. Form1 calls the InitializeComponent method. The reason for this is that the Form has controls painted on it that must be initialized.

Control Dispose Methods   C# is a .NET language. I state the obvious as a way to segue into a subject that may not be obvious. Languages like Object Pascal or C++ use deterministic construction and destruction. This means that the programmer is responsible for both creating and destroying objects.

.NET employs non-deterministic destruction. This means that the programmer is not responsible for destroying objects. The garbage collector will clean up objects for you. As a result, you will write code that invokes the new operator, but there is no equivalent free operator. Inconveniently, sometimes you will be writing code that uses resources that need deterministic cleanup. This is where the Dispose method comes in.

NOTE

You can invoke the garbage collector explicitly by calling GC.Collect, but this is not a recommended practice.

The result of all this is that you are likely to see more classes that implement a Dispose method rather than a destructor. Because Dispose is a public method, a consumer can invoke it explicitly, but you cannot rely on when a destructor is called in .NET. If you need deterministic cleanup, then implement a Dispose method.

Where Is the Destructor?   Where is the destructor in the control? That is a reasonable question. As mentioned in the preceding section, C# uses non-deterministic cleanup, so you will encounter the destructor less often than in languages that use deterministic cleanup. However, you should know what a constructor looks like and the rules that are applied to constructors.

```
~RoundButton()
{
}
```

There are other rules that apply to destructors, too. Classes can have only one destructor, and that destructor cannot be defined to take any arguments. Destructors cannot be overloaded or inherited, and destructors cannot be called. Destructors are called automatically by the garbage collector. Users have no control over when destructors are invoked.

Using Arrays for Conditional Logic

I learned the technique I'm about to describe from Danny Thorpe, another talented developer who helped build Borland's Delphi. In Object Pascal, using an array instead of conditional logic resulted in significantly more optimized code. If you compare conditional logic to array-indexing in C#, you might be surprised that using conditional logic results in shorter IL code than indexing an array. The following fragment demonstrates two variations that return a color based on the value of the *down* field.

```
protected virtual Color GetColor()
{
   Color[] colors = {Color.Silver, Color.Gray};
   return colors[Convert.ToInt32(down)];
}
protected virtual Color GetColor()
{
  if( down )
    return Color.Gray;
  else
    return Color.Silver;
}
```

The first example uses an array and results in a concise code listing. The second example uses *if-conditional* logic and is a bit easier to understand. As I mentioned, the second example produces shorter IL code. The reason for this is that C# does not allow typed arrays; as a result, we must convert the Boolean down to an integer to index the array.

For very simple evaluations we can use the ternary (?:) operator. The next example demonstrates using the ternary operator to evaluate the *down* state.

```
protected virtual Color GetColor()
{
```

```
    return down ? Color.Gray : Color.Silver;
}
```

The ternary operator is understood as follows. Immediately after the *return* keyword, a value that results in a Boolean is evaluated. If the evaluation—in the example *down*—is true, then the expression after the question mark symbol (?) is returned. If the evaluation is false, then the expression after the colon (:) is evaluated and returned. In the example, if *down* is true, then the color Gray is returned.

The third implementation produces the least amount of IL code. Unfortunately, it becomes difficult to perform multi-choice evaluations using the ternary operator, and if you must evaluate more than two possible choices you might want to use a case statement. However, the Boolean evaluation demonstrated by the GetColor implementation actually used in the RoundButton produces concise code and is a favorite of mine. Finally, because the array-indexing is contained within a well-named function, GetColor, it is okay to use code that is a bit more esoteric than you might normally prefer.

Regardless of the technique you use you should be aware of the general implications:

▶ Indexing an array of choices produces concise, esoteric code.

▶ Using *if-conditional* code is pretty straightforward and easily understood, but becomes difficult to manage if you have too many choices or nest *if* conditionals.

▶ Case statements are helpful for organizing multiple choices.

▶ The ternary operator is excellent for simple Boolean evaluations.

Choose whatever technique suits your needs, but try to avoid complicated *if-conditional* logic or convoluted case statements.

Color Structure   The Color structure contains a long list of predefined colors. You can use one of the predefined colors when you need a color, or you can specify a color by expressing the color as a name. The GetColor method demonstrates using existing colors.

You can also specify custom colors by expressing alpha blend, red, green, and blue values from 0 to 255. The alpha component of the color represents transparency; a value of 127 represents a color that will be approximately 50 percent transparent. The statement Color.FromArgb(255, 0, 0, 255) creates a color that is a nice tone of blue.

Convert Class Functions   The Convert class used in GetColor contains static methods that will convert values from one type to a specific type. Convert.ToInt32 will convert the argument value to a 32-bit integer. Convert.ToInt32(down) converts the Boolean field *down* to an integer representation.

TIP

The Convert class demonstrates an example of a class with only methods. Because Convert does not need to maintain state, all of the methods can be static, which means you will not have to create an instance of the Convert class to use it.

Methods in the Convert class are overloaded and defined to accept a wide variety of data types. If the Convert method is unable to convert the value you passed to the type requested, an InvalidCastException will be thrown.

Using Graphics Objects

Instances of the Graphics class represent the canvas in GDI+. You will need to request a Graphics object each time you want to perform custom drawing. There are a couple of ways to get a Graphics object. You can invoke the CreateGraphics method on controls that have a canvas, like forms, and you can get a Graphics object as a property of the PaintEventArgs argument passed to the Paint event handler.

Regardless of how you obtained a Graphics object, once you have a Graphics object, you can invoke any methods defined by the Graphics class. Because GDI+ is stateless, you should not cache the Graphics object, nor should you use the same Graphics object between calls to a method.

Listing 3-3, lines 58 to 64, demonstrates how to use the Graphics object passed to the Paint event handler in the PaintEventArgs parameter. Listing 3-4 demonstrates how to request a Graphics object each time a paint operation is performed.

Implementing a Paint Event Handler   The Paint event handler receives two arguments. The first argument is an object, and the second argument is an instance of the PaintEventArgs class.

When you need to perform custom painting, you can implement a Paint event handler. For the purposes of our discussion, there are two custom effects that are applied directly to the PlayControl. The Paint event handler for the PlayControl follows:

```
private void PlayControl_Paint(
   object sender, System.Windows.Forms.PaintEventArgs e)
{
   OutlineControl(e.Graphics);
   DrawTrademark(e.Graphics);
}
```

The Refactored methods describe the task each performs. The first statement outlines the PlayControl to provide a nice clean edge. This is necessary because we are not using the standard form shape. The second statement draws the "VK" trademark in base relief. Listing 3-4 contains the code to support OutlineControl and DrawTrademark.

Listing 3-4   *Code to support the Paint event handler for custom drawing on the PlayControl*

```
1:   private Point[] GetPoints(int shift)
2:   {
3:     return new Point[]
4:     {
5:       new Point(3 + shift, 0 + shift),
6:       new Point(Bounds.Width - 3 + shift, 0 + shift),
```

```
 7:        new Point(Bounds.Width + shift, 3),
 8:        new Point(Bounds.Width + shift, Bounds.Height - 3 + shift),
 9:        new Point(Bounds.Width - 3 + shift, Bounds.Height + shift),
10:        new Point(3 + shift, Bounds.Height + shift),
11:        new Point(0 + shift, Bounds.Height - 3 + shift),
12:        new Point(0 + shift, 3 + shift),
13:        new Point(3 + shift, 0 + shift)
14:    };
15: }
16:
17: private void OutlineControl(Graphics graphics)
18: {
19:   graphics.SmoothingMode = SmoothingMode.AntiAlias;
20:   graphics.DrawPolygon(new Pen(Brushes.Black, 2),
21:   GetPoints(-1));
22:   graphics.DrawPolygon(new Pen(Brushes.White, 2),
23:   GetPoints(1));
24: }
25:
26: private void DrawShadowText(Graphics graphics,
27:   string s, Font font, Brush foreBrush, Brush backBrush, int x, int y)
28: {
29:   graphics.DrawString(s, font, backBrush, new Point(x, y));
30:   graphics.DrawString(s, font, foreBrush, new Point(x-1, y-1));
31: }
32:
33: private void DrawTrademark(Graphics graphics)
34: {
35:   Font font = new Font("Haettenschweiler", 24,
36:   FontStyle.Bold);
37:   DrawShadowText(graphics, "VK", font,
38:      Brushes.DarkSlateBlue, Brushes.White, 5, 5);
39: }
```

OutlineControl on lines 17 to 24 uses the Graphics object passed to the PlayControl's Paint event handler and sets the SmoothingMode to AntiAlias. Anti-aliasing will help create a smoother line by overlapping some of the pixels in the polygon to blend pixels, resulting in a smoother-looking appearance. Drawing the polygon with the same points—returned by GetPoints—used to define the shape of the form results in a clean, outlined edge for the form.

DrawTrademark employs a second method that I named DrawShadowText. DrawShadowText draws the text twice using two brushes. By offsetting the text slightly one way or another, you can create different shadow effects. By offsetting the text by –1 and drawing the text with a brighter color, an inset effect (base relief) is created. By varying the offsettiung values on line 30, you can create various text effects.

Overloading the OnPaint Method   If you create custom effects on a form, then you will need to re-create those effects each time the form is repainted. However, if you create custom controls, and those controls have custom effects, then you will want to overload the OnPaint method of the custom control. It is by overloading the OnPaint method that you ensure that customizations to a control's appearance are re-created each time the control is painted. This is the strategy employed in the RoundButton class, shown on lines 58 through 64 of Listing 3-3.

Referring to Listing 3-3 now, the overloaded OnPaint method is not an event handler. The method is internal to the class that is performing custom painting, so the sender argument is not needed. The OnPaint method does get a PaintEventArgs object containing the Graphics object used to perform the custom drawing. If you want the default drawing performed, then you should call the inherited OnPaint method, as is shown on line 92; by calling the inherited OnPaint method in the base class, you will ensure that the event handler is raised, too.

After the inherited drawing is performed, you can add the code that performs your custom drawing. In Listing 3-3, DrawButton and DrawGraphic are called. Together, these two additional methods create the round button. We will look at some of the GDI+ methods that support creating the round buttons in a moment.

Invalidating a Control   When you want a control to be repainted, you call the Invalidate method. Invalidate will force the control to be painted by calling the OnPaint method, which, in turn, will raise the Paint event. Invalidating a control is demonstrated in the HasOutline property. When HasOutline is changed, the hasOutline field is changed and the control is invalidated, on line 72, to repaint the control with an outline.

Drawing and Filling Shapes   The Graphics class defines several methods for drawing and filling shapes. The DrawEllipse and FillEllipse methods are used to create the custom buttons. For example, FillEllipse draws and fills the basic button, and DrawEllipse draws the outline of the button when HasOutline is True.

Drawing methods use a Pen object to draw the line representing the shape. The shapes are expressed as a region constrained by a bounding rectangle. FillEllipse works almost identically to DrawEllipse; however, instead of a Pen, you need to pass a Brush to FillEllipse because the fill method paints the interior of a region.

There are two flavors of fill and draw methods. One flavor takes integer arguments defining the rectangular region, and the second flavor accepts floating-point numbers representing the rectangular region. The benefit of having a floating-point version of shape-drawing methods is that you can perform arithmetic operations that return floating-point numbers without having to truncate those numbers to integers.

The specific drawing or filling method invoked depends on the type of the arguments. Polymorphism helps here. There are several overloaded versions for each of the drawing and filling methods, and the compiler determines, based on the argument types, which specific method to call.

In addition to defining the rectangular region by expressing four points, you can express the rectangular regions as a pair of Point structures or a Rectangle structure. If you use points or rectangles, then you will need to use Point or Rectangle if the initial values are integers, and PointF and RectangleF if the initial values are floating-point values. Several examples demonstrating using the Point and Rectangle structures can be found in the RoundButton.cs module.

Applying Transforms to Graphics Objects

GDI+ uses world, page, and device coordinates. When you make a call to a Graphics method, the positions you express are in world coordinate space. GDI+ transforms the world coordinate arguments through two transformations, from world coordinates to page coordinates and then device coordinates.

GDI+ takes care of these transformations behind the scenes. The benefit to us as programmers is that we can change the origin, change the PageUnit from the default pixel to some other unit of measure, and perform operations like scaling images.

These capabilities were employed to create the visual effect of the button changing position when RoundButton objects are clicked by the user. If the button doesn't change appearance, however slight, when the user clicks the button, then the illusion is lost. The following excerpt from the RoundButton class applies a scaled Matrix transform to the Graphics object before drawing the button graphic, resulting in the illusion that the button has moved slightly when the user has clicked the button.

```
protected virtual void DrawDownGraphic(Graphics graphics)
{
  Matrix m = new Matrix();
  m.Scale(1.03F,1.03F);
  graphics.Transform = m;
}


protected virtual void DrawGraphic(Graphics graphics)
{
  if(down) DrawDownGraphic(graphics);
}


protected override void DrawGraphic(Graphics graphics)
{
  base.DrawGraphic(graphics);
  graphics.FillPolygon(GraphicBrush(), GetPoints());
}
protected override void OnPaint(System.Windows.Forms.PaintEventArgs e)
{
  base.OnPaint(e);
  DrawButton(e.Graphics);
  DrawGraphic(e.Graphics);
}


protected override void OnMouseDown(System.Windows.Forms.MouseEventArgs e)
```

```
{
    base.OnMouseDown(e);
    down = true;
    Invalidate();
}
```

When the user clicks an instance of the RoundButton control, the OnMouseDown method is fired. From the listing we can determine that the base class OnMouseDown method is called. This will allow users to intercept that event; that is, we aren't disrupting the default behavior. Then, the *down* field is set to True and the control is invalidated. Calling the Invalidate method forces a repaint to occur. At this point, the overloaded OnPaint method is called. Again, we perform the base.OnPaint behavior followed by the custom behavior.

The custom Paint behavior draws the button, and then draws the graphic. If *down* is True—which in our scenario, it is—the DrawDownGraphic method is invoked. (This is where the transform comes into play.) DrawDownGraphic creates a Matrix object. Matrix.Scale is called to scale the Matrix object, and that Matrix object is applied to the graphics.Transform property. The end result is a graphic that looks as if it has moved slightly when the button is depressed.

When you understand the mechanics, you will find them to be quite straightforward. The artistry is finding the right combination of brushes, colors, and shadings to make the illusion as realistic as possible. You will have to judge for yourself how realistic the button appears to be by running the VideoKiosk.sln sample application. The better the artistry, the higher quality the application.

Using the GraphicsPath Object to Create Shaped Forms

The GraphicsPath class is defined in the System.Drawing.Drawing2D namespace. GraphicsPath objects are used to represent a series of connected lines and curves. You have heard of shaped Windows Forms. Well, GraphicsPath objects are how you create shaped Windows Forms.

GraphicsPath objects allow you to create shaped forms by adding lines and curves to the GraphicsPath object, and then using the object to define the clipping region for a form. The PlayControl has rounded edges, demonstrating a subtly shaped form. The following excerpt from the PlayControl demonstrates code that subtly shapes the PlayControl by rounding the corners. (A second example demonstrating the GraphicsPath object is defined in the OnResize method on lines 66 to 73 of Listing 3-3.)

```
private void ShapeForm()
{
    GraphicsPath path = new GraphicsPath();
    path.AddPolygon(GetPoints(0));
    Region = new Region(path);
}
```

A GraphicsPath object is created. A polygon defined by GetPoints is added to the GraphicsPath, and that GraphicsPath object is used to define the clipping region of the

PlayControl form. Region = new Region(path) demonstrates the code that modifies the form's clipping region.

The code fragment demonstrates a bare-bones example of creating a shaped Windows Form. The example is beneficial to the PlayControl because it is appropriate, but as a stand-alone example it is not very compelling. The next section demonstrates a more-advanced shaped form.

Defining Clipping Regions   System.Windows.Forms controls have a Region property. The Region property is a class that represents the clipping region of a control. Regions are scalable because they are expressed in word coordinates. When you define a clipping region, you are not just drawing a shape—the clipped region is the form.

Listing 3-5 is taken from the ShapedForm.sln. The code redefines the form's clipping region to appear as shown in Figure 3-5. The form is clipped to include the form's frame. You can click on the top part of the clipped form shown in Figure 3-5 and drag the form around, and the form will respond to input from the user just as if it were the normally shaped rectangular form.

Listing 3-5   *A shaped form based on a string added to a GraphicsPath object*

```
private void Form1_Load(object sender, System.EventArgs e)
{
  BackColor = Color.Red;
  GraphicsPath path = new GraphicsPath();
  path.AddString("C#", Font.FontFamily, 1, 75,
    new Point(0, 0), new StringFormat());
  Region = new Region(path);
}


private void Form1_Click(object sender, System.EventArgs e)
{
  MessageBox.Show("Clicked!");
}
```

TIP

Remember to add a using statement to include the System.Drawing.Drawing2D namespace.

The code changes the background color in the Form Load event. A GraphicsPath object is created, and a string is added to that path, using the form's Font and some basic position and size information. A new clipping Region is constructed and assigned to the form's Region property. The result is shown in Figure 3-1. If you look closely you can see the Form.Text

Figure 3-5   *A shaped form created by a string, "C#", added to a GraphicsPath object*

property, and when you run the application you will be able to discern the form header and client regions. (The header is blue and the client region is red.) Click on the client region and the Form1_Click method will be invoked.

Linear Gradient Brushes

Brushes are used to fill the interiors of shapes. There are several kinds of brushes, including the HatchBrush, LinearGradientBrush, PathGradientBrush, SolidBrush, and TextureBrush. These brush types produce a specific kind of result when you use them to fill graphic shapes. When you need a brush, you can create an instance of one of these brush types or use the Brushes class, which contains predefined solid brushes.

If this book were produced in color, what you would be able to discern from Figure 3-1 is that the custom round buttons are using a LinearGradientBrush to enhance the 3D effect. A LinearGradientBrush is a brush whose color transitions from a starting color to an ending color over the space painted by the brush. You have probably seen this technique used most often in splash screens or on older-style install programs.

The LinearGradientBrush has several overloaded constructors. The version used on lines 45 to 50 of Listing 3-3 takes two points and two colors. The points describe the starting and ending points of the gradient, and the colors describe the beginning and color of the gradient. In the example, by using a White starting color and a darker ending color, we get the appearance of light reflecting on the button, which enhances the 3D appearance.

You can specify a wide variety of properties that refine the gradient effect. The Blend property is a class that describes what percentages of the starting and ending colors to use at positions along the gradient. The GammaCorrection property is a Boolean that indicates whether gamma correction is applied to the gradient. The InterpolationColors property allows you to specify a ColorBlend that supports displaying multi-color linear gradients. The LinearColors property is an array of colors containing the starting and ending colors for the gradient. The Transform property defines a Matrix that allows you to translate, scale, rotate, or skew gradients. Finally, the Rectangle property defines the starting and ending points of the gradient brush.

The LinearGradientBrush is used to paint the interior of RoundButtons. The colors used to produce the gradients are based on the value of the *down* field. Up buttons are light and down buttons are darker.

Listing 3-6 demonstrates the LinearGradientBrush RotateTransform and SetTriangularShape methods. You will have to run the code to see the neat visual effect. There is no way to reproduce it in black and white.

Listing 3-6   *The GradientBrush.sln demo program demonstrates some advanced features of the LinearGradientBrush class.*

```
1:  using System;
2:  using System.Drawing;
3:  using System.Drawing.Drawing2D;
4:  using System.Collections;
5:  using System.ComponentModel;
6:  using System.Windows.Forms;
7:  using System.Data;
8:
9:  namespace GradientBrushDemo
10: {
11:   public class Form1 : System.Windows.Forms.Form
12:   {
13:
14:     [ Chopped out code that was generated by the forms designer]
15:     private System.Windows.Forms.Timer timer1;
16:
17:     private float angle = 0;
18:
19:     private LinearGradientBrush GetBrush()
20:     {
21:       return new LinearGradientBrush(
22:         new Rectangle( 20, 20, 200, 100),
23:         Color.Orange,
24:         Color.Yellow,
25:         0.0F,
26:         true);
27:     }
28:
29:     private void Rotate( Graphics graphics,
30:       LinearGradientBrush brush )
31:     {
32:       brush.RotateTransform(angle);
33:       brush.SetBlendTriangularShape(.5F);
34:       graphics.FillEllipse(brush, brush.Rectangle);
35:     }
36:
37:     private void Rotate(Graphics graphics)
38:     {
39:       angle += 5 % 360;
40:       Rotate(graphics, GetBrush());
41:     }
42:
```

```
43:    private void timer1_Tick(object sender, System.EventArgs e)
44:    {
45:      Rotate(CreateGraphics());
46:    }
47:
48:    private void Form1_Paint(object sender,
49:      System.Windows.Forms.PaintEventArgs e)
50:    {
51:      Rotate(e.Graphics);
52:    }
53:  }
54: }
```

The example uses a Timer control to paint an ellipse at regular intervals. The gradient brush uses Yellow and Orange. Each time the Rotate method is called, a floating-point value is incremented by 5. Modulo arithmetic is used to keep the angle between 0 and 360. The angle represents degrees. The RotateTransform method rotates the gradient brush on line 32. SetBlendTriangularShape uses the ending color as a center focal point, and FillEllipse draws a filled elliptical shape using the gradient brush.

Pens

When you draw filled-in areas, you need a Brush. When you draw lines, you will need a Pen. You can get a basic Pen from the Pens object, or you can create an instance of a Pen from scratch and specify the PenAlignment, Width, Color, and DashStyle.

The following example creates a Pen object initialized with a LinearGradientBrush and draws an ellipse using the Pen.

```
LinearGradientBrush brush =
  new LinearGradientBrush(new Rectangle(0, 0, 2, 2),
  Color.White, Color.Green, LinearGradientMode.ForwardDiagonal);

Pen p = new Pen(brush, 10F);
e.Graphics.DrawEllipse( p, 5, 5, 100, 200);
```

(The code is contained in the ShapedForm.sln example for convenience.)

Implementing the Tracker Control

The RoundButton was derived from the Control class. When you are creating custom controls, an easier technique is to find a control that is close to the new control that you want to make, and inherit from that control. In the case of the RoundButton, we might improve the control, or simplify its construction, by inheriting from the ButtonBase class.

Another strategy to keep in mind is that, if you want to use a control in your own application, then creating the control in your application is reasonable. If you want to redistribute your controls, then you will want to create a Control Class Library, which will package your controls into a tidy, redistributable package. (Refer to Chapter 9 for more on creating custom controls.)

Sometimes you will find that there is no good control to inherit from. This means you will have to derive your control higher up the control food chain and inherit from the System.Windows.Forms.Control class.

NOTE

For our purposes here, we will continue to use the Control as the base class for our controls in this chapter—you can read Chapters 8 and 9 for more information on creating controls in general. In general, you will need to know how to create Control Class libraries, how to implement and test control classes and custom controls, and how to place those controls in the Toolbox. You will also learn how to associate a custom icon with your control in the Toolbox in later chapters.

Defining the Tracker Control

For our purposes, it is reasonable to implement the Tracker as a custom control. The Tracker is shown as the little slider at the top of the PlayControl in Figure 3-1. The Tracker behaves just like the ProgressBar control you are probably already familiar with.

Like the ProgressBar, the Tracker uses a graphic to indicate relative progress. The Tracker allows the user to express a minimum, maximum, and position value. If position is closer to the minimum value, then the graphic progress indicator is closer to the left side of the control; if the position is closer to the maximum value, then the progress indicator approaches the right side of the control.

Implementing the Tracker control will allow you to explore GDI+ in greater detail. The complete source listing for the Tracker is defined in Tracker.cs in the Controls.dll project as part of the VideoKiosk.sln. Minimum defines the relative left side of the Tracker, and Maximum defines the relative right side. The progress indicator is painted along a horizontal groove relative to the value of the Position property. For an experienced programmer, figuring out where the progress indicator is painted is a simple matter of multiplying the percentage of the position by the difference between the minimum and maximum values.

Suppose the range of values is between 0 and 1,000. To avoid invalidating the control and repainting a possible 1,000 times, an arbitrary number of subdivisions are defined to paint the progress indicator at regular intervals when the change is significant.

Using the SetStyle Method

The PlayControl simulates an occasion where we invested considerable effort in creating the interface. The background image represents this investment. It would be a shame to cover the background image up with controls. By allowing the background image to peek through controls, we are able to sustain the visually appealing background.

Unfortunately, controls do not support a transparent background by default. Hence, we would either have to make controls like the Tracker look like our background image or let the background image show through. The second choice is likely to yield the most seamless result and is actually cheaper to implement.

To allow the background image to show through, a control requires that you set the ControlStyles.SupportsTransparentBackColor attribute. This is accomplished by calling the Control.SetStyle method in the control's constructor.

```
public Tracker()
{
  this.SetStyle(ControlStyles.SupportsTransparentBackColor, true);
}
```

When you paint the Tracker control onto the PlayControl, you can set the BackColor to Transparent, which will allow the background image on the form to show through. The effective result is that the Tracker control blends into the PlayControl.

Using the ControlPaint Class

With GDI, if you wanted to draw beveled controls that had a 3D appearance, you could use the API procedure DrawEdge. GDI+ implements a ControlPaint class that has several static methods that support drawing 3D bordered shapes and shapes that look like standard controls, such as a Button.

The ControlPaint class is defined in the Systems.Windows.Forms namespace. ControlPaint has static methods for drawing buttons, checkboxes, combo buttons, grids, menu glyphs, radio buttons, and size grips, among other things. Instead of trying to figure out how to draw what looks like a groove for the progress indicator, I used the ControlPaint class to create the visual appearance of the Tracker.

Drawing a 3D Border   The Tracker class has a method DrawBar that draws the groove that the progress indicator appears to track along. DrawBar takes a graphics object argument and calls the DrawBorder3D method.

```
protected virtual void DrawBar(Graphics graphics)
{
  ControlPaint.DrawBorder3D(graphics, GetX(), GetY(),
    GetWidth(), GetHeight(), Border3DStyle.Etched, Border3DSide.All);
}
```

DrawBorder3D is a static method, so we do not need to create a ControlPaint object to invoke this method. As with many drawing methods, we express the region as the boundaries of a rectangle. GetX(), GetY(), GetWidth(), and GetHeight() were implemented by me to return calculated offsets for the groove based on the size of the Tracker. The final two arguments are enumerated values chosen from those available based on the desired result. I wanted the progress indicator to look as if it were tracking along the groove, and the Etched border style and All sides of the border created this effect.

Drawing a Button Control   There are several ways to create the tracker button. You could load a graphic image, then scale the image based on the size of the Tracker. For convenience,

the shape of a button seemed suitable. The Tracker.DrawTracker method uses the
ControlPaint.DrawButton method to create the progress indicator.

```
protected virtual void DrawTracker(Graphics graphics)
{
  ControlPaint.DrawButton(graphics,
    TrackPosition(), (Height-8)/2, 5, 10, ButtonState.Normal);
}
```

I implemented the TrackPosition method to determine where to position the progress
indicator along the horizontal axis. The vertical offset is determined by the (Height-8)/2
calculation, which will work reasonably well unless the Tracker is too small to be functional.
The ButtonState.Normal enumerated value draws the button in its normal up-state appearance.

Calling the Graphics.DrawImage Method

There are several buttons implemented for the PlayButton. The biggest difference between
all of the buttons is the image that is displayed on the button. Before we distribute the
control, we should take advantage of this knowledge.

If the big difference is the graphic drawn, then we should be able to extract the capability
of drawing the graphic and consolidate all of the buttons to one button. The RoundButton.cs
module contains several button classes. While I implemented a control named ImageButton,
I did not consolidate all of the button classes. If you were to create the image for the
other buttons, then you could fairly easily consolidate the button classes and get rid of
the other buttons.

The code listing that follows is derived from the DarkButton control, which in turn is
derived from the RoundButton control. DarkButton demonstrates how to overload some
methods that change the gradient brush. Again, this is code that can be generalized by adding
the two brush colors used to create the gradient as properties of the RoundButton class.
Listing 3-7 takes the next leap, which externalizes the graphic aspect of the button.

Listing 3-7   *This code implements an ImageButton that is derived from the RoundButton in
Listing 3-3.*

```
1:  public class ImageButton : DarkButton
2:    {
3:       // TODO: Make sure that the image can be deleted!
4:       private Image graphic = null;
5:
6:       public ImageButton()
7:       {
8:
9:       }
10:
```

```
11:     protected override Color GetColor()
12:     {
13:       Color[] colors = {Color.MidnightBlue, Color.Black};
14:       return colors[Convert.ToInt32(down)];
15:     }
16:
17:     private int GetX()
18:     {
19:       return (Width - graphic.Size.Width) / 2;
20:     }
21:
22:     private int GetY()
23:     {
24:       return (Height - graphic.Size.Height) / 2;
25:     }
26:
27:     private ImageAttributes GetImageAttribute()
28:     {
29:       ImageAttributes attribute = new ImageAttributes();
30:       attribute.SetColorKey(Color.White, Color.White,
31:         ColorAdjustType.Default);
32:       return attribute;
33:     }
34:
35:     private Rectangle GetRectangle()
36:     {
37:       return new Rectangle(GetX() + 1, GetY() + 1,
38:         graphic.Size.Width, graphic.Size.Height);
39:     }
40:
41:     protected override void DrawGraphic(Graphics graphics)
42:     {
43:       base.DrawGraphic(graphics);
44:       if( graphic == null ) return;
45:
46:       graphics.DrawImage(graphic,
47:         GetRectangle(), 0, 0,
48:         graphic.Size.Width, graphic.Size.Height,
49:         GraphicsUnit.Pixel,
50:         GetImageAttribute());
51:     }
52:
```

```
53:    — public Image Graphic
54:      {
55:        get
56:        {
57:          return graphic;
58:        }
59:        set
60:        {
61:          graphic = value;
62:          Invalidate();
63:        }
64:      }
65:  }
```

The key to painting the image on the button is to allow the surrounding part of the image to be masked out of the display. For example, if you have a 16×16-pixel image but the image doesn't take up all of the pixels, then there will be part of the image that you don't want to display. To define the pixels that you don't want to display—that you want to screen out—you will need to create an ImageAttributes object that defines the color of the pixels that you want to screen.

Shown on line 46, DrawImage has many overloaded versions to accommodate a variety of arguments designed to precisely manage the incorporation of a graphics image. The version used takes an Image argument, a Rectangle that specifies the bounding region for the image, the four coordinates of the portion of the image to draw—allowing you to subdivide images—the GraphicsUnit that the coordinates describe, and the ImageAttributes object described earlier.

TIP

You can write code that reads a specific pixel. For example, you might read the top/left-most pixel and use the color of that pixel as the color to screen out.

The ImageButton uses an ImageAttributes object with color keys of White. The result is that White is screened from the displayed image. If you want to conceal part of the image, then in this case make the part of the image you want to conceal White. Figure 3-6 shows the result of trying to display the image without screening the extra pixels using the ImageAttributes object.

Figure 3-6   *This is what happens (zoomed) if you forget to screen out the extra pixels.*

Secondary Topics

We have covered a lot of ground in this chapter. The total listing for the VideoKiosk.sln, including the Controls.dll class library, contains several hundred lines of code. As we have discussed, some of the code can be consolidated. With a little effort, you could reduce the number of buttons to a single round image button. If I were to do this for you, then you might miss all of the various code fragments and techniques that demonstrate the power of GDI+, such as shape drawing.

There are several other facets of .NET that were employed to complete the VideoKiosk.sln sample program. While these topics are secondary to programming with GDI+, you will find them helpful. Let's take a couple more pages to examine some of these aspects of .NET.

Implementing the Elapsed Time Clock

The elapsed time clock is updated on a Timer tick. Using the Timer control is a convenient way to perform lightweight background processing. Clearly, using the Timer is not multithreading, but for such a simple task as updating a clock, the Timer is reasonable and sufficient.

The Timer control works by raising an event when an interval expressed in milliseconds elapses. When the Timer.Interval elapses, the SetPosition method uses the Player.Elapsed value to update the position of the Tracker. A side effect of updating the progress indicator of the Tracker is the updating of the display label containing the elapsed time displayed as a digital clock.

The position value is expressed as seconds; thus, the position value can be used to create the time value for the clock display. This is done by creating an instance of the TimeSpan structure, initialized with the elapsed seconds. The code to create the clock is shown next.

```
private TimeSpan GetSpan(int position)
{
  return new TimeSpan(0,0,0,position, 0);
}

private string GetMask()
{
  return "{0}:{1,2:0#}:{2,2:0#}";
}

private string GetFormatted(TimeSpan span)
{
  return string.Format(GetMask(), span.Hours,
    span.Minutes, span.Seconds);
}
private void ChangePosition()
{
```

```
    labelElapsed.Text = GetFormatted(GetSpan(Position));
}
```

The TimeSpan structure knows how to convert the elapsed seconds represented by the position to hours, minutes, and seconds. Every 60 seconds will be converted to another minute, and 60 minutes to an hour, automatically. The GetMask method returns a formatting string used to control the appearance of the TimeSpan, and that formatted string is used to update the digital clock.

Using TimeSpan to Evaluate Time Differences

The TimeSpan structure is used to measure time periods as short as 100 nanoseconds, which are represented as one tick in a TimeSpan. TimeSpan values can be represented as positive and negatives spans of time measured in terms of days, hours, minutes, seconds, and fractions of seconds. The string format d.hh:mm:ss.ff would display the days, hours, minutes, seconds, and fractions of a second represented by a single TimeSpan. The largest unit of time represented by the TimeSpan is the day.

If the default string value of the TimeSpan were acceptable, then we could use the TimeSpan.ToString() method, which would return the TimeSpan in hh:mm:ss format by default.

If you perform an arithmetic operation on DateTime values, for instance subtracting one time from another, the operation will return a TimeSpan object.

Formatting Strings

For our purposes we elected not to use the default TimeSpan.ToString method. This is an arbitrary decision that allows us to take a closer look at the string.Format method and formatting masks. (In a production system, it would be cheaper to use the TimeSpan.ToString method.)

GetMask returns a formatting mask. The mask is "{0}:{1,2:0#}:{2,2:0#}". Characters in the brackets {} represent replaceable format characters, and everything else represents a literal value. Inspecting {1,2:0#}, we understand this replaceable parameter to be replaceable parameter 1, which is zero-filled and can be up to two numeric characters in length.

In general, the first value in brackets represents the zero-based argument to be formatted. The second argument—if present, it is delimited by a comma—represents the width of the formatted value. If you add a negative sign, then the value is left-justified, and a plus sign will right-justify the value. By default, the width will pad the formatted value with spaces. The optional formatting string follows the colon. Our 0# formatting string means that the formatted output will be padded with a 0 and a number. If the number takes both spaces, then the 0 will not be displayed.

Using the ToolTip Control

Windows Forms provides a ToolTip component. When you add the ToolTip component to your application, it is added to the Component Tray, rather than directly on the form. Components in the Component Tray are nonvisible components; that is, they do not show up at run-time.

When you add the ToolTip to the Component Tray for a specific Form, the controls on that form will have the ToolTip property added to their list of properties. If you provide text for the ToolTip property, then the tip will be displayed when a user hovers the mouse over the control.

NOTE

Components are added to the Component Tray by dragging and dropping them onto the form. However, nonvisible components are dropped over a form but actually displayed in the Component Tray. This strategy was probably adopted to help eliminate form clutter.

The ToolTip control's relationship to other controls is not immediately intuitive. If you examine Windows Forms controls initially, you might suspect that .NET does not support ToolTips. All you need to do is add the ToolTip component to a form by dropping the component into the Component Tray.

Adding Controls to the Toolbox

Generally, you create a user control to add several controls to a common container. When you add a control to your project, that control is automatically added to the Windows Forms tab of the Toolbox.

If you want to add controls in a Control Class Library to the Toolbox, then you will need to create a Control Class Library, select Customize Toolbox from the Toolbox context menu, and use the Customize Toolbox dialog to add the Control Class Library to the list of those that you want to display in the Toolbox. Chapters 8 and 9 will elaborate more on this subject.

Catching and Handling Specific Exceptions

Chapter 2 introduced the subject of exception handling by demonstrating the resource protection block, implemented with the *try finally* construct. The VideoKiosk demonstrates the *try catch* construct and how to catch specific instances of exceptions.

To catch any exception in a method, use the *try catch* construct, placing the code to try in the brackets immediately after the *try* keyword and the error-handling code in the brackets immediately after the *catch* keyword. The following fragment demonstrates the basic syntax of the *try catch* exception-handling block.

```
try
{
  // code to try
}
catch
{
  // code to run if an error occurs
}
```

The example demonstrates a catch-all exception handler. If any exception occurs in the *try* block in the preceding code, then the code in the *catch* block runs. Not every procedure should have an exception-handling block. If you have an idea of how to reconcile the error, then you will want to implement an exception handler. If the code might cause the program to crash, then you might want to implement an exception handler to shut down in an organized manner and record the error. But blanket, do-nothing exception handling should be avoided. The latter is the default behavior of .NET applications.

If you want to handle a specific exception and ignore all others, then you can indicate the class of the exceptions you want to handle by implementing one or more *catch* blocks. The following SetMaximum method demonstrates how to catch the OverflowException that might occur if the duration is greater than a 32-bit integer.

```
private void SetMaximum(double duration)
{
  try
  {
    tracker1.Minimum = 0;
    tracker1.Maximum = Convert.ToInt32(duration);
  }
  catch(OverflowException e)
  {
    MessageBox.Show(e.Message, "Media Error!",
      MessageBoxButtons.OK, MessageBoxIcon.Exclamation);
  }
}
```

The Convert.ToInt32 method would raise an exception if duration is greater than the maximum value for a 32-bit integer. If this were to happen, then the *catch* block would catch the OverflowException in the object e, which in turn can be used to aid in resolving the error. The example simply displays the error to the user with the idea that they might elect to pick another file.

If an exception other than the OverflowException occurs, then the *catch* block implemented in SetMaximum will not be notified of the exception.

Adding TODO Items to the Task List

Visual Studio .NET supports comment tokens. Comment tokens are special keywords, including TODO, and those that you define. When these keywords appear immediately after the whack whack (//) comment token, those comments are added as tasks to the Task List.

You can view comment tokens in the Task List by selecting View | Show Tasks | All or View Show Tasks | Comment in Visual Studio. If there is something you want to be reminded to do, add a TODO comment in your code at the point where you want to perform the task. Include text that reminds you what the problem is. To add custom comment tokens, define those custom comments in the Options Dialog on the Environment | Task List page (see Figure 3-7).

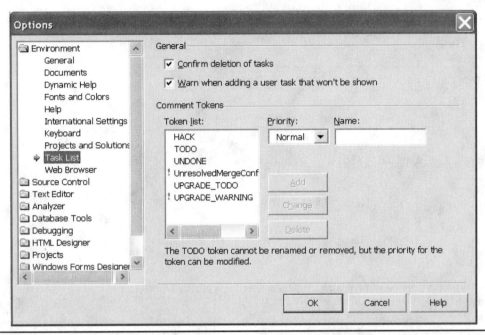

Figure 3-7   *Defining custom comment tokens in the Task List page of the Options dialog*

Listing 3-7 demonstrates a TODO item on line 3 in the ImageButton class. The TODO comment reminds me that I have to make sure that I can delete an Image property. If you have an Image property, then the Image editor, which is automatically associated with an Image property, will allow you to select an Image using an Open dialog. Unfortunately, you cannot automatically delete the Image by setting the Image back to (None). You have to add a DefaultValueAttribute to the Image property to support deleting the image. The DefaultValueAttribute provides an initial value and a substitute value if you remove a provided value in the Properties window. Listing 3-8 demonstrates a revision to the ImageButton class that allows me to delete the Image property.

Listing 3-8   *Revising the ImageButton class and resolving the TODO reminder from Listing 3-7*

```
1:  public class ImageButton : DarkButton
2:    {
3:      private Image graphic = null;
4:
5:      public ImageButton()
6:      {
7:
8:      }
```

```
 9:
10:    protected override Color GetColor()
11:    {
12:      Color[] colors = {Color.MidnightBlue, Color.Black};
13:      return colors[Convert.ToInt32(down)];
14:    }
15:
16:    private int GetX()
17:    {
18:      return (Width - graphic.Size.Width) / 2;
19:    }
20:
21:    private int GetY()
22:    {
23:      return (Height - graphic.Size.Height) / 2;
24:    }
25:
26:    private ImageAttributes GetImageAttribute()
27:    {
28:      ImageAttributes attribute = new ImageAttributes();
29:      attribute.SetColorKey(Color.White, Color.White,
30:        ColorAdjustType.Default);
31:      return attribute;
32:    }
33:
34:    private Rectangle GetRectangle()
35:    {
36:      return new Rectangle(GetX() + 1, GetY() + 1,
37:        graphic.Size.Width, graphic.Size.Height);
38:    }
39:
40:    protected override void DrawGraphic(Graphics graphics)
41:    {
42:      base.DrawGraphic(graphics);
43:      if( graphic == null ) return;
44:
45:      graphics.DrawImage(graphic,
46:        GetRectangle(), 0, 0,
47:        graphic.Size.Width, graphic.Size.Height,
48:        GraphicsUnit.Pixel,
49:        GetImageAttribute());
50:    }
51:
52:    [DefaultValue(null)]
53:    public Image Graphic
```

```
54:        {
55:          get
56:          {
57:            return graphic;
58:          }
59:          set
60:          {
61:            graphic = value;
62:            Invalidate();
63:          }
64:        }
65:
66:    }
```

The DefaultValueAttribute on line 52 in Listing 3-8 resolves the TODO problem. When you fix a TODO problem, remove the TODO comment and the reminder is removed from the Task List.

A good strategy is to define Comment Tokens that will help you organize and track outstanding issues. You can simply use the TODO comment token or define custom tokens that have special meaning for you or your team.

Using the Process Class

Chapter 2 introduced the Process class. The Process.Start static method is associated with the Click event handler of the leftmost ImageButton on the PlayControl. Click this button and write the following code

```
Process.Start("http://www.softconcepts.com");
```

COM Interop

There is a concept in .NET referred to as "COM Interop" (for interoperability). COM uses type libraries to describe interfaces, and .NET eliminates the type library by introducing Reflection and by embedding metadata into .NET assemblies. Chapter 2 explains Reflection, assemblies, and metadata.

A perfect example of this is the ActiveX MediaPlayer used in the VideoKiosk. The ActiveX MediaPlayer is a COM-based control. When you want to use COM (also referred to as ActiveX) controls in .NET, you can import those controls by selecting Customize Toolbox from the Toolbox context menu. Visual Studio .NET will import the type library for that COM control, allowing you to use COM-based controls in .NET applications.

Unfortunately, when you use COM controls in .NET assemblies, you are reverting to the "DLL Hell" zone. You will have to create an installation program that distributes and registers those COM controls, just as you would if you were developing and deploying an application developed before .NET.

Summary

GDI+ is an evolutionary stage of GDI. All of the great graphics programming you could do with GDI before .NET is much easier to do now that we have .NET. It is easier to do because we now have great methods and capabilities that are organized into classes that make these capabilities easier to find and employ.

Remember that GDI+ is stateless. You will have to pass information like colors, brushes, and fonts every time you invoke a GDI+ method. Remember also that you should not cache Graphics objects. Request Graphics objects with the factory method CreateGraphics or use the Graphics object passed to Paint event handlers.

Finally, GDI+ supports vector graphics, imaging, and typography. Vector graphics supports line and curve drawing. Imaging supports managing complex images like bitmap, GIF, or JPEG files, and typography supports advanced typesetting and fonts. Like GDI, GDI+ is a big fish—just better organized and more approachable.

Terrarium

IN THIS CHAPTER:

Demonstrated Topics

Downloading, Installing, and Configuring
Terrarium

Playing Terrarium

Reviewing the Terrarium Framework

Creating Plants and Critters

Introducing Plants and Critters to the Terrarium

Secondary Topics

Serializing Objects

Summary

C hildren are motivated by fun. Many adults in our field are motivated by fun too. Perhaps some mature, older programmers have lost touch with their inner Peter Pan, but a recent experience with a development team in Oregon illustrated that creative adults are motivated by fun too.

While working on a project in Oregon, several contract developers and I had the unenviable position of helping mainframe programmers learn C#. These programmers had no prior Windows programming experience, only nominal PC skills, and no prior C or C++ experience. The question was how do we go about making learning a new language, paradigm, and complex subject matter fun. We found the answer in Terrarium.

In 2001, I was visiting Microsoft, and Tom Kaiser mentioned this peer-to-peer game developed with .NET. He was very excited about the technology and the Terrarium game. The next year, I fortunately recalled that discussion when facing the training dilemma. Searching the Web I discovered to my delight that Terrarium was available on the **www.gotdotnet.com** website. I downloaded Terrarium from the site, and a few minutes later had a Terrarium up and running with some critters and plants. I had created a small ecosystem in a few minutes. Fogies and management might scoff at the notion, but creative people *are* motivated by fun.

What is Terrarium?

Terrarium is a game developed in .NET. Terrarium is a virtual ecosystem with plants, herbivores, and carnivores. The plants grow and reproduce. The herbivores eat plants, grow, and reproduce, and the carnivores eat the herbivores and grow and reproduce. Herbivores hunt plants and consume them, and carnivores hunt herbivores and consume them. All of this happens visually on your PC. There are rules that describe the patterns of growth, consumption, and reproduction. The trick is that you and other programmers get to define these rules writing .NET code. The real trick is to either create a balance in the ecosystem or take over, consuming everything in sight.

Terrarium is fun. Your code interacts with other programmer's code, and this interaction provides a powerful way to learn how to program with .NET.

Demonstrated Topics

Aside from having fun, it is important that we learn. (This is true unless you are independently wealthy and have no boss looking over your shoulder.) Creating plants and animals can teach you a lot about programming, and especially a lot about programming in C#.

Terrarium uses the peer-to-peer model. Instead of a client-server model—also referred to as a spoke-and-hub model—Terrarium demonstrates an application that is composed of peers intercommunicating to work in a concerted way. In the Terrarium, the clients (PCs) interact to create an ecosystem. Your PC and other PCs (peers) are all part of a bigger ecosystem. Plants and animals are moving between your PC and other PCs in your slice of the ecosystem. To be precise, code that you write gets transported to other peers that make up your ecosystem, and that code runs safely on those other peers.

Plants and animals are teleported, in the vernacular of the Terrarium game. A Terrarium server stores a peer IP address list. When the teleporter—represented by a blue ball—encounters an organism, a peer is selected at random from your peer list, and the organism is sent to that peer's IP address. Transporting the organism occurs on the PC and is accomplished by serializing the organism's state and sending a copy of the organism assembly to the peer. The sent assembly is examined for security violations and breaches of game etiquette—for example, Reflection and File IO are not allowed. If the organism is safe and doesn't have code that would effectively allow cheating then an instance of the organism is created and the state is deserialized.

What can be learned by participating in a Terrarium ecosystem? That is the subject of this chapter. By reading this chapter and completing the examples herein, you will have an opportunity (to have fun and) to learn about

- ▶ Smart client updates for Windows Forms applications
- ▶ A graphics-based application using DirectX and COM Interop
- ▶ Regular expressions
- ▶ Reflection
- ▶ XML Web Services
- ▶ Peer-to-peer networked applications
- ▶ Code access security
- ▶ Inheritance
- ▶ Applying attributes to define behavior
- ▶ Implementing event handlers

Downloading, Installing, and Configuring Terrarium

The first thing you will need to do is download the Terrarium client application (shown in Figure 4-1) from **www.gotdotnet.com**. You can also download a Terrarium server from the same site if you want to host your own Terrarium. (You don't have to download the Terrarium server; the client application will do.) Terrarium is free after you agree to an online customer agreement.

TIP

Everyone who wants to participate in your ecosystem will need to download a copy of the Terrarium client.

After you download the Terrarium client (and, optionally, the server), you will need to perform some basic configuration steps to implement how you want to run the Terrarium. There are a couple of ways that you can run Terrarium; each of those and the configuration settings you will need to make are discussed next.

Figure 4-1   *A Terrarium ecosystem running on my laptop with the plants and animals defined in this chapter*

Configuring the Terrarium Client

You can configure the Terrarium client application to interact with other peers in the great wide world. This option registers your PC with a Terrarium server, so other peers know where to find you. The Terrarium server will place your PC in a slice of the global ecosystem; your PC may interact with a couple of dozen or as many as a couple of hundred other PCs.

You can also create your own Terrarium for testing and debugging purposes, create a serverless peer-to-peer ecosystem (this is a good option if your network administrator won't let your PC interact outside of the firewall), or install the Terrarium server for a more robust internal ecosystem. For our purposes, you will need at least one PC with one instance of the Terrarium client running its own ecosystem, a .ter file.

If you elect to run the Terrarium server behind your company's firewall, then you will need to install the Terrarium server on a machine with MS SQL Server. (I have found that MSDE—the desktop SQL Server version—will run the Terrarium server reliably, although this is not recommended by Microsoft.)

Let's examine the steps for configuring the Terrarium client for screensaver mode, Terrarium mode with or without peers, and ecosystem mode. We will follow this up with a quick review, describing how to install and configure the Terrarium server.

Running the Terrarium Client

Terrarium makes an interesting screensaver. You can configure Terrarium to run as your screensaver, in addition to several other configuration options. Let's review these quickly, so we can get to the programming.

Configuring Screen Saver Mode

When you install the Terrarium client, you can indicate that you want Terrarium to run as your screensaver. If you elect not to run Terrarium as your screensaver, you can always select the .NET Terrarium from the Screen Saver tab of the Display applet at any time if you change your mind.

If your co-workers have never seen Terrarium, expect to attract some attention when plants and bugs are being actively pursued and consumed on your screen.

Configuring Terrarium Mode

Terrarium mode can be used for debugging and testing your bugs before putting them into an ecosystem. You will need to create a Terrarium to run in Terrarium mode. Follow these steps to create a Terrarium:

1. To run in Terrarium mode, click the Show Terrarium Mode Controls button, shown in Figure 4-2. (The button icon is represented by the fish tank icon in the lower-left corner, and the text is visible as a hint when you hover the mouse.)

2. Click Create a New Terrarium and provide a file name in the New Terrarium dialog. Terrarium will restart in Terrarium mode after you click Save.

3. If you want other players to be able to participate in this Terrarium, provide a name for the Peer Channel (also shown in Figure 4-2).

You are ready to introduce plants and animals into the Terrarium. At the top right of the Terrarium client are status indicators, the number of Animals in your client instance, and the number of peers in your slice of the ecosystem. Green status indicators mean that everything is all right, and red status indicators mean that a particular aspect of the Terrarium is not

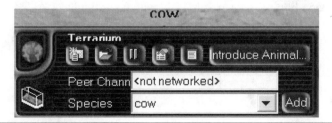

Figure 4-2   *Terrarium mode controls*

operating correctly. You can hover the mouse cursor over the status indicator for information or click the Help link at the top center of the client for more information (see Figure 4-3).

Configuring Ecosystem Mode

Ecosystem mode is where you are playing with others in the larger ecosystem. (You can install your own instance of the Terrarium server from **www.gotodotnet.com**.) To play in ecosystem mode, you will need to modify some game settings. Right-click the Terrarium client to configure your Terrarium client. You will need to make a few changes to participate in the ecosystem:

1. In the Terrarium Game Settings dialog, click the Registration button and enter an e-mail address. This information is used to send you status information.

2. Click the Community button and select your Country and State (you can leave this information blank).

3. You can click the Performance button and adjust the CPU usage slider to experiment with performance.

4. Finally, click the Server button and enter the URL to the Terrarium server you are participating in. For example, the default path is **http://www.terrariumgame.net/ terrarium/**. If you install the Terrarium server on a computer at your location, then you will need to enter that URL. For example, running the server on my laptop, I changed the Server URL to **http://lap800/terrarium/**—that is, the location in which I installed the Terrarium server.

5. Click Accept Changes to update the Game Settings. (You will need to stop and restart the client for Server URL game settings to take effect.)

You will need to visit the **www.gotdotnet.com** website to check for available server locations.

Configuring the Terrarium Server

You do not need to install and configure a Terrarium server to run the examples defined in this chapter. For that reason, I won't elaborate on configuring the Terrarium server. I will tell you that one has been running behind a firewall at the location I am writing this, and there has been no difficulty.

   Follow the instructions for configuring the Terrarium server, including installing SQL Server. We have been successfully running the Terrarium server using the Microsoft SQL Server Desktop Engine, known as MSDE, with no difficulty.

Figure 4-3   *Status indicators, animals, and peers*

Playing Terrarium

To play Terrarium, you will need to participate in an ecosystem or run in Terrarium mode and add plants, herbivores, and carnivores. Aside from the various creatures making for more lively interactions, the ecosystem must have some balance. No plants, and the herbivores will starve to death. No carnivores, and the herbivores will consume all of the available plant life and die off. Too many carnivores, and the herbivores are quickly devoured, and then the carnivores starve, too.

Running in Terrarium mode successfully encourages you to find a balance. In general, plenty of plants, and your herbivores thrive. The ecosystem seems to seek a balance of about ten herbivores for every carnivore. There is a catch: introduce too many varieties of carnivores, and your carnivores will consume both carnivores and herbivores. Creating either a harmonious ecosystem or killer bugs is fun; it depends on your perspective. (Some people on our team like to create the best offensive herbivores and "win" by creating the largest population.)

Environment Reporting Every Six Minutes

Terrarium gathers statistics approximately every six minutes when you are running Terrarium. You can view this information to determine which critters are dominating and the relative health of the plants and animals in your Terrarium. Clicking Show Trace Window shows a Trace Window and a Population Statistics window. To view the trace information about the critters in your ecosystem and the relative populations of the organisms in your Terrarium, select a specific instance of a critter and open the Trace Window (a Deer trace is shown in Figure 4-4).

If you are running in ecosystem mode and running your own server, then you can obtain broad server statistics directly from the server via a Web Service. These statistics are accessible by navigating your browser to the Web application installed with the Terrarium server. The server statistics are self-explanatory.

Understanding XML Web Services in Terrarium

Terrarium is a peer-to-peer application. The server is used for gathering information like ecosystem statistics. XML Web Services are employed to allow participants to access those statistics and find out about the welfare of their creations.

Programming an XML Web Service

Let's take a moment to look at XML Web Services.

Computer software needs a straightforward and reliable way to exchange data. Microsoft offered Distributed COM (DCOM) based on a proprietary implementation. For a variety of reasons—and partially based on its proprietary nature—DCOM does not satisfy the real need of customers. XML Web Services is a new way to think of an existing problem: how do we get software implemented on different computers and languages to interoperate?

Microsoft believes the answer is XML Web Services. XML, or eXtensible Markup Language, is a standardized markup language, like WML and HTML. XML is simple text composed of tags that have inferred meanings and support user-defined extensions. Because

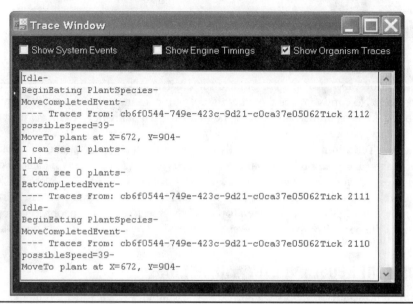

Figure 4-4   *Output from the WriteTrace command showing the internal operation of the Deer trace (code available online)*

XML is text, it can easily be passed over a TCP/IP network, such as the Internet. Examining the whole picture, we have a user-definable, text-based language that can describe things and pass easily over the Internet. Data can be represented in XML, and, more important, objects can be represented as XML text. The result is that complex objects can be transported over the Internet as simple XML text. XML Web Services is the name of the part of the .NET framework that implements these capabilities.

To implement a Web Service, select the ASP.NET Web Service template from the New Projects dialog. The template will create a DLL-targeted solution that contains a class that inherits from System.Web.Services.WebService. A Web Service contains code like any other assembly. The difference is that methods marked with the WebMethodAttribute can be invoked directly by consumers. (A Web Service may talk to other services, but let's set that aside for a moment.)

Web Services is a technology based on XML that supports transferring information across the Internet—any TCP/IP connection—using open standards rather than proprietary standards. The Web Service provider and the consumer are not implemented by the same entity. Code that is implemented by the same producer and that exists within the same infrastructure is accessible to that producer. Web Services address problems like operating system interoperability and providing access to data to external consumers.

Suppose you work for a tools vendor, and your company has elected to provide a library of regular expressions that perform complex string searching capabilities. You could expose these regular expressions as XML Web Services and allow consumers to use your regular expressions for a fee. Regular expressions are implemented as a terse language that can perform some very powerful string searching and replacing operations. For example, ^[0-9a-zA-Z]+$

can be used to determine whether a string contains at least one or more alpha or numeric characters. We could expose our regular expressions as a named XML Web Service as part of a tool library. (Regular expressions are implemented in the System.Text.RegularExpressions namespace in the .NET framework.) Listing 4-1 implements a Web Service with the alphanumeric string test WebMethod.

Listing 4-1   *A Web Service that represents a tool vendor publishing regular expressions*

```
1:   using System;
2:   using System.Collections;
3:   using System.ComponentModel;
4:   using System.Data;
5:   using System.Diagnostics;
6:   using System.Web;
7:   using System.Web.Services;
8:   using System.Text.RegularExpressions;
9:
10:  namespace Expressions
11:  {
12:    /// <summary>
13:    /// Summary description for Expressions.
14:    /// </summary>
15:    public class Expressions : System.Web.Services.WebService
16:    {
17:      public Service1()
18:      {
19:        //CODEGEN: This call is required by the
20:        //ASP.NET Web Services Designer
21:        InitializeComponent();
22:      }
23:
24:      #region Component Designer generated code
25:
26:      //Required by the Web Services Designer
27:      private IContainer components = null;
28:
29:      /// <summary>
30:      /// Required method for Designer support - do not modify
31:      /// the contents of this method with the code editor.
32:      /// </summary>
33:      private void InitializeComponent()
34:      {
35:      }
36:
```

```
37:      /// <summary>
38:      /// Clean up any resources being used.
39:      /// </summary>
40:      protected override void Dispose( bool disposing )
41:      {
42:         if(disposing && components != null)
43:         {
44:            components.Dispose();
45:         }
46:         base.Dispose(disposing);
47:      }
48:
49:      #endregion
50:
51:      [WebMethod()]
52:      public bool IsAlphaNumeric(string input)
53:      {
54:         return Regex.IsMatch(input, "^[0-9a-zA-Z]+$");
55:      }
56:
57:   }
58: }
```

The only code that was generated by the ASP.NET Web Service template is the WebMethod defined on lines 51 through 55. Notice that the method looks like any other method, except for the WebMethod attribute on line 51. The .NET Framework takes care of a lot of the work for us. The solution Expressions.sln contains the Web Service shown in Listing 4-1, and the TestExpressions.sln contains a Windows Forms application that invokes the Web Service.

To implement the Web Service represented by the code in Listing 4-1, follow these numbered steps.

1. Create a new ASP.NET Web Service project. Name the project **Expressions**.

2. Add the method from lines 51 through 55 to the WebService class you created in step 1.

3. Add a *using* System.Text.RegularExpressions; statement to the top of the .cs module containing the code from step 2.

4. Compile and run the Web Service application by selecting Debug, Start. (This step will open Internet Explorer and the .asmx page (see Figure 4-5) created by the template. You can use this page to test the Web Service.)

You can write a test application by creating a second project. A Windows Forms application will suffice. Add a Web Reference to the test application in the Solution Explorer. You can create an instance of the object defined in the Web Service. For example, suppose you named the Web Service "Expressions" and installed it on your PC. After adding a Web reference to

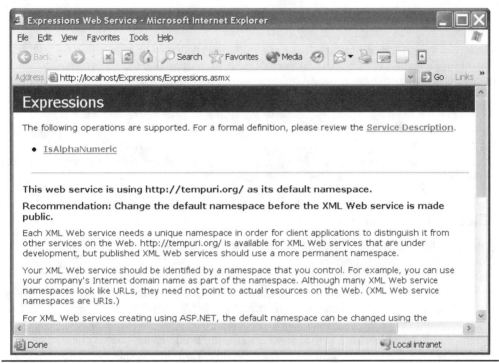

Figure 4-5   *An .asmx page that you can use to test Web Services*

the Web Service in a second project, you can create an instance of the service, as demonstrated next.

```
localhost.Expressions expressions = new localhost.Expressions();
expressions.IsAlphaNumeric("test123");
```

The first statement creates an instance of the Web Service. After we have an instance of the Web Service object, we can use that object as if it were defined within the same project.

The example in this section is pretty basic. Read Chapter 12 for more examples of Web Services.

Critter Timing

When the Terrarium is running, every organism in the Terrarium is provided with a small slice of CPU time, about 2 to 5 milliseconds. Each organism has that modest interval in which to perform actions like resting, searching for food, defending, and procreating.

When you create animals, you will need to keep the amount of time you have available in mind as you implement your strategy. Unfortunately, we can learn the mechanics of programming organisms, but good strategies are highly subjective and ecosystem dependent. It will be up to you to experiment with strategy.

Teleporter

While you are playing, a blue ball floats around the ecosystem. The blue ball is the teleporter (shown in Figure 4-6), which transports plants and animals around the ecosystem. The teleporter is responsible for cross-pollinating peers with organisms from other peers in the system. The end result is that you never know what is going to show up in your terrarium. (When playing in ecosystem mode, some of the carnivores can be devastating.)

The teleporter makes Terrarium interesting. Check out the **www.gotodotnet.com** website for advanced strategies, which include tracking the location of the teleporter. The teleporter can be used as an escape route, a convergence point, or a means of spreading your organisms to the greatest number of peers.

Smart Client Updates

Another sample application that ships with Terrarium is the Application Updater (AppUpdater.dll). The Application Updater is installed in the \Program Files\Terrarium\ bin directory.

When you start Terrarium and at regular intervals while it is running, the Terrarium client contacts the master server application and requests updates for the application. The client contacts an XML Web Service on the master server. A comparison between the version of your client and the latest version is made. If the server contains updated versions of the client, then the updates are loaded into a new directory. The next time Terrarium is started the new version is run. At least one old version is kept around in case there is a problem.

.NET supports a revised concept of *thin client programming*. The Application Updater demonstrates this model. The concept is simple: an application seamlessly and automatically grabs updated components across a network—a small application starter could be downloaded or deployed, and that application's whole *raison d'être* is to download the rest of the application and constantly grab updated assemblies across a network. That network could be the Internet.

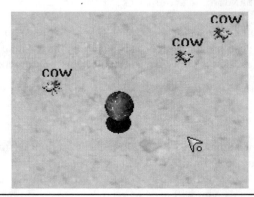

Figure 4-6   *The blue ball is the teleporter, which is responsible for moving organisms between peers in the ecosystem.*

Dynamically Updating Assemblies

The Assembly class has a method named LoadFrom. Assembly.LoadFrom accepts an assembly name. The argument **assembly** can be on the local file system or at the other end of the world on some Web server. When you have an Assembly, you can compare manifest information, like version numbers, conditionally updating the assembly or not. The benefit is that this can occur without the user's intercession.

Let's return to our regular expressions subscription service. Suppose instead of dynamically invoking a Web method that tests a finite set of regular expressions, we elect to allow our customers to dynamically load the regular expressions across the Internet. We can accomplish this by loading an assembly across the Web, reading all of the expressions from the assembly, and continuing to process. The user is pleasantly surprised when the available expressions get better and better. Listing 4-2 implements the assembly that provides regular expressions to subscribers.

Listing 4-2   *A Class Library assembly that can be loaded dynamically across the Web*

```
using System;
using System.Collections;

namespace Expressions
{
  public class Expressions
  {
    public Hashtable GetExpressions()
    {
      Hashtable hashtable = new Hashtable();
      hashtable.Add("Numeric", @"^\d+$");
      hashtable.Add("Social Security Number",
        @"^(\d\d\d)-(\d\d)-(\d\d\d\d)$" );
      return hashtable;

    }
  }
}
```

TIP

The "at" (@) symbol prevents the backslashes from being treated like escape characters.

Following our original concept, we don't want to provide the expressions directly to the user. If they had the expressions, which are the same as the source code, why would they need our service? The example program fills a hash table with keys and values. We can show the consumer the keys and apply the values. All the user selects is "Social Security Number," and internally we apply the regular expressions @"^(\d\d\d)-(\d\d)-(\d\d\d\d)$". (The regular expression is understood to mean match strings that have three digits, a hyphen, two more digits, a hyphen, and four digits. The expressions restrict extra characters at the beginning and end of the string with ^ and $, respectively.)

The consumer application supports complex string matching. To retrieve updated regular expressions, our consumer application loads the assembly containing the expressions into our consumer application. Listing 4-3 demonstrates how to request, load, and get the information out of the assembly.

Listing 4-3   *Loading an assembly from a Web server*

```
private void UpdateExpressions()
{
  try
  {
    Assembly assembly =
      Assembly.LoadFrom("http://localhost/regex/expressions.dll");

    Type type = assembly.GetType("Expressions.Expressions");
    Object instance = Activator.CreateInstance(type);

    Hashtable newtable = (Hashtable) type.InvokeMember("GetExpressions",
      BindingFlags.Instance | BindingFlags.InvokeMethod |
      BindingFlags.Public, null, instance, new object[]{});

    foreach(object key in newtable.Keys)
    {
      comboBox1.Items.Add(key.ToString());
    }

    hashtable = newtable;
  }
  catch(Exception e)
  {
    MessageBox.Show(e.Message, "Update Error",
      MessageBoxButtons.OK, MessageBoxIcon.Error);
  }
}
```

The code loads the assembly using the http:// moniker. The namespace and class are passed—"Expressions.Expressions"—as a string to load the type from the assembly. An instance of the object is created using an Activator class; and the method GetExpressions, which returns a Hashtable, is invoked. We read all of the keys representing our expressions into a combo box. If all of the preceding code succeeds, then a field named hashtable is assigned to the local Hashtable, newtable. The user sees our well-named expressions but never the expressions, representing our intellectual property and the reason we get paid.

A complete working sample is demonstrated in Client.sln. You will need to compile both projects—client.csproj and expressions.csproj—to test the example. The expressions.dll assembly will need to be copied to a Web server. Your PC will work as long as you are running Internet Information Services. Our example demonstrates using the PC as a test platform, but it works just as well using any other Web server.

Peer-to-Peer Computing

Each Terrarium client is an equal peer in the Terrarium game. When you are running in ecosystem mode, the server associates several logically close peers to your peer list. (This is the role of the server in Terrarium: tracking peers.) All of the peer groups have some overlap, so every peer in Terrarium is ultimately part of one big ecosystem.

When the blue ball teleporter encounters an organism, a random peer from your peer list is selected. Terrarium uses System.IO to stream the state of the organism to a file. The assembly containing the organism selected by the teleporter and the selected organism's stream state information are sent to the selected peer using a NetworkStream class in the System.Net.Sockets namespace.

The receiving peer checks the organism assembly for references to assemblies that might represent cheating in the context of Terrarium, like Reflection. If the organism assembly passes the evaluation, the organism is loaded into the receiving Terrarium client, and System.Runtime.Serialization is used to read the organism's state. As a result, a duplicate organism is re-created on the receiver and removed from the sender. (*Teleportation*—perhaps this is how we will get Star Trek transporters to work. Scan your brain. Create a clone at the new location. E-mail the brain scan of the transportee, load the brain scan into the clone, and kill the original.)

Support for Multiple Programming Languages

Terrarium is an excellent place for programmers to experiment with multi-language programming support. (We won't go into multi-language programming here.) It is, however, practical to anticipate that in the near future programming teams will be comprised of programmers with skills in more than one .NET programming language.

Code Access Security

Running in ecosystem Terrarium means sending and receiving assemblies across a network constantly, with compiled code moving to and fro at random. This might make managers, network administrators, and even developers a bit squeamish.

One of the compelling facets of Terrarium is that it demonstrates that compiled code can move safely between computers if the security model is employed. Refer to the later section "Introducing Code Access Security" for a brief example of code access security and to Chapter 16 for a more comprehensive discussion on security.

Reviewing the Terrarium Framework

Any reasonable application is likely to be described by its architecture. Terrarium is a peer-to-peer application that you interact with by creating plant and animal organisms. You can't create just any organism. You create organisms by inheriting from existing types—Plant or Animal—defined in the OrganismBase.dll assembly. How well your organism fares is a product of how well you program your strategy within the context of the Terrarium architecture.

The Terrarium architecture is too big to cover here in detail. (Someone will probably write a book on Terrarium soon.) You can find a cross-referenced architectural overview on the **www.gotodotnet.com** website. Although you will be able to create new organisms without having explored that information, the organisms will be disadvantaged. The top-level classes in Terrarium are Action, AnimalState, DefendAction, EngineSettings, MoveToAction, OrganismState, PlantState, Vector, Animal, AttackAction, EatAction, MovementVector, Organism, Plant, and ReproduceAction. From the top-level types, you might infer that interplay in Terrarium can be quite complex. You would be correct.

There are also several events, event arguments, attributes, exceptions, and interfaces in Terrarium. All of these members in the Terrarium framework are used to describe the behavior of your organism. The basic idea is that you create an organism by inheriting from a Plant or Animal. You apply attributes to describe the characteristics of your organism, and you implement event handlers to codify the organism's contextual responses. To be successful, plants have to grow and seed. More important, animals have to hunt, feed, breed, and possibly attack, defend, and evade.

I will provide basic examples of a plant, an herbivore, and a carnivore. However, if you are going to compete in the larger ecosystem, then be forewarned that there are some serious bugs out there.

Creating Plants and Critters

The graphics in Terrarium are fun, but they are not nearly as good as the conceptual and competitive aspect of coding plants and animals. Plants grow and reproduce by spreading seeds. Your plants will thrive if there is more seeding and growing than there is being eaten. Unfortunately, where plants are concerned, once you release a plant you are at the mercy of the Herbivores directly and the Carnivores indirectly. In general, plants are easy to implement and do reasonably well. Conversely, plants aren't very fun to watch.

Animals are different. Animals move and actively participate in the ecosystem. How well an animal does is more dependent on the clever strategy implemented by the programmer. (Don't feel bad if your animals get chomped. Being a good programmer and a good strategist are not the same thing. Good code might actually be counterproductive in Terrarium because object-oriented code may run slower than hack code.) In this next section we will take a look at some basic plants and animals.

Creating a Plant

Plants are boring but an important part of the ecosystem. Plants provide us with a convenient and easy way to introduce an organism into the ecosystem. The basic steps for creating an organism are as follows:

1. Create a Class Library project.
2. Include a reference to organismbase.dll, which is installed with the Terrarium client.
3. Include a reference to system.drawing.dll, the GDI+ assembly that ships with the .NET framework.
4. Define a class that inherits from the Plant class (or Animal to create an animal).
5. Define some required attributes.
6. Code your organism (see Listing 4-4).

Listing 4-4   *An implementation for a Plant*

```
1:   using System;
2:   using System.Collections;
3:   using System.Drawing;
4:   using System.Reflection;
5:   using System.IO;
6:
7:   [assembly: OrganismClass("AloeVera")]
8:   [assembly: AuthorInformation("Paul Kimmel", "pkimmel@softconcepts.com")]
9:
10:  [MaximumEnergyPoints(10)]
11:  [MatureSize(26)]
12:  [SeedSpreadDistance(50)]
13:
14:  public class AloeVera : Plant
15:  {
16:   public override void SerializePlant(MemoryStream m)
17:   {}
18:
19:   public override void DeserializePlant(MemoryStream m)
20:   {}
21:
22:  }
```

The assembly attribute OrganismClass names the class we will be introducing into the ecosystem. You will need to define a class with the same name as the one used to initialize the OrganismClass attribute. (Lines 14 through 22 implement the AloeVera plant.) The assembly-level attribute AuthorInformation is required; this information is used to indicate ownership and provide contact information in case something is awry in the ecosystem.

The MaximumEnergyPoints, MatureSize, and SeedSpreadDistance are values that work like the plant's DNA, describing the plant. You can experiment with these attribute values to create plants that thrive, grow, and germinate.

Lines 16 and 19 implement empty serialization and deserialization methods. These methods are abstract methods that you must implement; they have more meaning for animals. You can store knowledge about an organism's ecosystem when that organism is teleported. You may want to implement these methods for animals. (Refer to the later section "Serializing Objects" for more information on implementing serialization in Terrarium.)

Creating Critters

Animals are substantially more challenging to implement than plants. There are some aspects of programming animals that are the same whether you are programming an herbivore or a carnivore. We'll examine the common aspects of implementing animals before we implement an herbivore and a carnivore.

To implement an animal, whether a plant eater or meat eater, you will need to perform these steps:

1. Create a Class Library project.
2. Add references to organismbase.dll and system.drawing.dll.
3. Create a class that inherits from Animal and has the same name as the one you will provide to the OrganismClass assembly-level attribute.
4. Implement a suite of attributes that approximately describe the conceptual DNA of your organism. These attributes are MatureSize, Carnivore, AnimalSkin, MarkingColor, MaximumEnergyPoints, EatingSpeedPoints, AttackDamagePoints, DefendDamagePoints, MaximumSpeedPoints, CamouflagePoints, and EyesightPoints.
5. Provide code to describe the behavior of your organism. (This is the tricky part.)

Rules in Common for Animals

You have 100 points that you can distribute among the MaximumEnergyPoints, EatingSpeedPoints, AttackDamagePoints, DefendDamagePoints, MaximumSpeedPoints, CamouflagePoints, and EyesightPoints. For herbivores you will likely want to emphasize things like MaximumSpeedPoints and EatingSpeedPoints. You might also want to emphasize DefendDamagePoints—think rhinoceros and cape buffalo. CamouflagePoints, hiding, might be a good attribute for small fast animals, and DefendDamagePoints might be a good attribute for large, slow animals. If you are creating a carnivore, then you might want to have huge AttackDamagePoints, EyesightPoints, and MaximumSpeedPoints but to de-emphasize things like camouflage. I'm not a zoologist, but I can think of reasonable combinations that make sense for various attributes. Lions are reasonably successful because they have some speed, use camouflage, and inflict maximum damage. On the other hand, hyenas hunt in packs and scavenge. (I think of the carnivores and herbivores as a particular kind of animal and emphasize the characteristics those animals have.)

If you test your critter in Terrarium mode—as opposed to ecosystem mode—you might get a warning based on attribute settings. Arbitrarily, it seems, DefendDamagePoints should be in increments of 4 and EyesightPoints should be in increments of 10 (see Figure 4-7).

Animals have their attribute characteristics, which enhance or detract from the success of a species. More important is the code you write for these animals. A clever strategist might write code to create collaborative hunting behavior or aggressive predator-avoidance responses.

Certain things will rush your creature's demise. If your creature throws an unhandled exception, then that instance of your critter will be destroyed and removed from the ecosystem. Terrarium promotes writing code that is proactive about exception handling. If your critter takes too long to do its thing, then it will be destroyed too. You have about 2 milliseconds per turn to squeeze in all of the activity your creature needs to initiate or complete. Complicated code might cause your creature to die simply because the code is constipated.

You can use WriteTrace to send messages to the trace window in Terrarium mode. Use WriteTrace to debug your critters before introducing them into the ecosystem.

After you have created your organism, you can add your critters to a local Terrarium. This will provide you with the greatest opportunity to debug…well, your bug. You can view trace messages to see how your bug is actually behaving and view statistics about the success of your critter. Once you have introduced your organism into an ecosystem, you may not reintroduce the same critter. You can add more copies of the existing critter, but not revised copies. If you change the same bug and want to reintroduce that bug, then you will need to create a new local Terrarium.

When your bug is ready for prime time, introduce it into a larger ecosystem. As a side note, there are some Terrarium contests at the time of this writing, and you can win cool things like an Xbox if your bug is the most successful. To see some really successful critters, you are encouraged to participate in a larger ecosystem and obtain a copy of the leading bugs. You can use the .NET IL disassembler (ILDASM.EXE) to view the elements of these critters. Some of the leaders have been programmed to exhibit very complex behaviors.

Creating a Herbivore

I will start by demonstrating an herbivore. Herbivores are easier to program and tend to be about ten times more successful than carnivores, although even herbivore behavior can become quite complex.

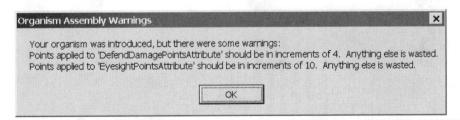

Figure 4-7   *A hint you will receive providing guidance on the application of attribute points*

I picked a cow. It seems that the reason cows survive at all is because we keep them in pens and bring food to them. Based on my understanding of cow behavior, I programmed the cow to look around. If the cow sees any food, then the cow moves toward the food. If the cow bumps into anything, it tries to eat it. The cow has no concept of predators and has only simple food-searching behavior; the cow probably will not do very well in an ecosystem (see Listing 4-5).

Listing 4-5   *The Terrarium equivalent of a cow*

```
1:   using System;
2:   using System.Drawing;
3:   using System.Collections;
4:   using System.Reflection;
5:   using System.IO;
6:
7:   [assembly: AuthorInformation("Paul Kimmel",
8:     "pkimmel@softconcepts.com")]
9:   [assembly: OrganismClass("Cow")]
10:
11:  [MatureSize(30)]
12:  [Carnivore(false)]
13:  [AnimalSkin(AnimalSkinFamilyEnum.Beetle)]
14:  [MarkingColor(KnownColor.Blue)]
15:  [MaximumEnergyPoints(10)]
16:  [EatingSpeedPoints(10)]
17:  [AttackDamagePoints(0)]
18:  [DefendDamagePoints(10)]
19:  [MaximumSpeedPoints(30)]
20:  [CamouflagePoints(15)]
21:  [EyesightPoints(25)]
22:
23:  public class Cow : Animal
24:  {
25:    PlantState target = null;
26:
27:    protected override void Initialize()
28:    {
29:      Idle += new IdleEventHandler(IdleEvent);
30:      MoveCompleted +=
31:        new MoveCompletedEventHandler(MoveCompletedEvent);
32:    }
33:
34:    private void IdleEvent(object sender, IdleEventArgs e)
35:    {
36:      WriteTrace("Idle");
37:      if(CanReproduce)
38:        BeginReproduction(null);
39:
```

```
40:      if( IsMoving || IsReproducing || IsEating )
41:        return;
42:
43:      SearchForFood();
44:    }
45:
46:    private void SearchForFood()
47:    {
48:      ArrayList organisms = Scan();
49:      foreach(OrganismState organism in organisms)
50:      {
51:        if( organism is PlantState )
52:        {
53:          MoveTo( (PlantState)organism );
54:          return;
55:        }
56:      }
57:    }
58:
59:    private int PossibleSpeed()
60:    {
61:      int possibleSpeed = Species.MaximumSpeed;
62:      while( possibleSpeed > 2 &&
63:        State.EnergyRequiredToMove(possibleSpeed,
64:          possibleSpeed) > (State.StoredEnergy / 2))
65:      {
66:        possibleSpeed /= 2;
67:      }
68:
69:      if( possibleSpeed < 2) possibleSpeed = 2;
70:      return possibleSpeed;
71:    }
72:
73:    private void MoveCompletedEvent(object sender,
74:      MoveCompletedEventArgs e)
75:    {
76:
77:      try
78:      {
79:        if(WithinEatingRange(target)
80:          && (State.EnergyState < EnergyState.Full))
81:          BeginEating(target);
82:      }
83:      catch
84:      {}
85:    }
86:
87:
88:    private void MoveTo(PlantState plant)
89:    {
```

```
90:      target = plant;
91:      BeginMoving(new MovementVector(plant.Position, PossibleSpeed()));
92:    }
93:
94:    public override void SerializeAnimal(MemoryStream m)
95:    {}
96:
97:    public override void DeserializeAnimal(MemoryStream m)
98:    {}
99: }
```

Cows are reasonably large, as indicated by their MatureSize attribute of 30 (the largest animals can have a mature size of 48). The larger the size to maturity, the longer it will be before the animal can reproduce. However, large animals can be intimidating; hence, size might be a good quality for a super predator.

Setting the Carnivore attribute to False indicates that the animal is a herbivore (line 12). You have to pick from one of the existing skins. You may be describing the equivalent of a cow, but all critters in Terrarium visually appear to be one of the bugs defined in the AnimalSkinFamilyEnum value. Use the AnimalSkin attribute to describe the appearance of your organism. The MarkingColor attribute will be used to describe colorful bugs. (The MarkingColor attribute was not implemented in earlier versions of Terrarium.)

The cow attributes defined on lines 15 through 21 are pretty weak. The Cow has low energy points, eats very slowly, has almost no DefendDamagePoints, is slow, and has poor eyesight. (Does it sound like an animal that can only thrive in captivity?)

The Cow is defined on lines 23 through 96. Critter behaviors are implemented as event handlers. These handlers are established in the overridden Initialize method (see lines 27 through 32). The Cow implements an IdleEventHandler and a MoveCompletedEventHandler. (There are several more behaviors that can be described, including attacking and defending behaviors.) Event handlers are associated with events using the overloaded += operator, as demonstrated on lines 29 through 31.

When our Cow gets an idle slice of CPU time—a turn—it checks to see if it can reproduce (lines 37 through 38). Methods that have a Begin prefix are asynchronous. This means that when line 38 is invoked it returns immediately. Line 40 checks to see if we are reproducing or moving—perhaps searching for food or eating. If the Cow is doing any of these things, as codified on lines 40 and 41, then we return immediately. Finally, if none of the conditions on line 40 exists, then we begin searching for food.

Lines 46 through 57 implement the food-searching behavior. The Scan method on line 48 returns all of the organisms that the Cow can see, as defined by the EyesightPoints field-of-vision attribute. Each organism is evaluated. When a plant is discovered, the Cow moves toward the plant, represented by the PlantState check on line 51.

We move at a rate that consumes up to half of our available energy. The MoveTo method is defined on lines 88 to 92. BeginMoving is an asynchronous method that puts our bug on the move. MovementVector takes a Point structure argument and a speed. We calculate the speed in the PossibleSpeed method.

PossibleSpeed is a popular algorithm that I borrowed from some code samples on the **www.gotdotnet** website. By trial and error, I discovered that running a bug at top speed is a good way to commit suicide. PossibleSpeed (on lines 59 through 71) evaluates the critter's maximum speed, defined by the MaximumSpeedPoints. The PossibleSpeed value is used to determine a speed and distance the critter can travel based on the energy stored and the energy required to move a specific distance at a specific speed. Running at maximum speed will likely cause your critter to race at a startling rate and then seemingly die of a heart attack.

The MoveCompletedEvent might be called for a variety of reasons. Recall that BeginMoving is asynchronous. Our bug may stop moving due to its arrival at the food source or running into something else. Our bug—lines 73 through 85—simply assumes that we have arrived at our food destination. If we are WithinEatingRange and hungry—represented by the State.EnergyState value on line 80—then we begin eating. A successful bug might detect the presence of a predator or an obstacle and do something else, like run.

Finally, we must implement overridden SerializeAnimal and DeserializeAnimal methods. In the case of the Cow, these are empty methods. (See "Serializing Objects" later in this chapter for more information.)

Iterating a Collection of Objects   Lines 49 through 56 of Listing 4-5 demonstrates the *foreach* construct. In Chapter 2, I demonstrated the IEnumerator interface. You can request an enumerator from a class, like ArrayList, that implements IEnumerable to iterate through a collection of objects. An easier means of iterating objects is the *foreach* construct.

Foreach supports declaring a variable and iterating through a collection containing objects defined by the collection, as demonstrated in Listing 4-5. This is easier than using an enumerator, although it is dependent on the IEnumerable interface. You can create strongly typed collections that can be iterated with a *foreach* by implementing IEnumerable. There is an easy way to implement strongly typed collections, as you'll see next.

Inheriting from CollectionBase and ReadOnlyCollectionBase   A strongly typed collection is a collection of a specific kind of type, for example, a collection of organisms or contacts. The most direct means of creating a strongly typed collection is to inherit from ReadOnlyCollectionBase or CollectionBase. ReadOnlyCollectionBase will facilitate creating a readable collection of strongly typed objects, and CollectionBase will facilitate creating a readable and writable collection of strongly typed objects. Listing 4-6 demonstrates how to create a strongly typed collection of customer objects.

Listing 4-6   *This code demonstrates a strongly typed collection of Customer objects, created by inheriting from ReadOnlyCollectionBase.*

```
1:  public class Customers : ReadOnlyCollectionBase
2:  {
3:    public Customers()
4:    {
5:      ReadCustomers();
6:    }
```

```
 7:
 8:    public Customer this[int index]
 9:    {
10:      get
11:      {
12:        return (Customer)InnerList[index];
13:      }
14:    }
15:
16:
17:    public Customer this[string name]
18:    {
19:      get
20:      {
21:        return (Customer)this[Find(name)];
22:      }
23:    }
24:
25:    private int Find(string name)
26:    {
27:      for( int i = 0; i < Count - 1; i++)
28:      {
29:        if( this[i].Name.Equals(name) ) return i;
30:      }
31:      return -1;
32:    }
33:
34:    private void ReadCustomers()
35:    {
36:      InnerList.Add(
37:        new Customer("Robert Golieb", "(617) 555-1212"));
38:      InnerList.Add(
39:        new Customer("Mark Davis", "(503) 555-1212"));
40:    }
41: }
42:
43: public class Customer
44: {
45:   private string name;
46:   private string phone;
47:
48:   public Customer(string name, string phone)
49:   {
50:     this.name = name;
51:     this.phone = phone;
```

```
52:    }
53:
54:    public string Name
55:    {
56:      get
57:      {
58:        return name;
59:      }
60:      set
61:      {
62:        name = value;
63:      }
64:    }
65:
66:    public string Phone
67:    {
68:      get
69:      {
70:        return phone;
71:      }
72:
73:      set
74:      {
75:        phone = value;
76:      }
77:    }
78: }
```

The ReadOnlyCollectionBase class implements ICollection and IEnumerable. ICollection is designed to provide a Count, copying elements to an array, and synchronized access to the underlying elements. IEnumerable has one method, GetEnumerator. IEnumerable is the interface that *foreach* requires to iterate over the elements in a collection or array.

The code in Listing 4-6 implements a Customer class and a collection of Customer objects, named Customers. By inheriting from ReadOnlyCollectionBase, we get an underlying structure to store elements in and code that implements ICollection and IEnumerable. By implementing the indexer, *this*, we can treat instances of Customers just like a typed array. For example, customers[0], where customers is an instance of the Customers class, would return the Customer object at the 0th index position. An indexer is implemented on lines 8 through 14. We can also implement an indexer that takes a string (see lines 17 through 23). The string indexer and the Find method collaborate to accept a string and find the object containing a Name field that contains the index value. For example, Customers["Robert Golieb"] would return the object containing the Name initialized to Robert Golieb.

Only producers can initialize the elements of a ReadOnlyCollectionBase. The ReadCustomers method on lines 34 to 40 demonstrates a means of initializing the collection.

You could just as easily initialize the collection by reading from an XML file or a database. Inherit from the CollectionBase class for a readable and writable, strongly typed collection.

Improving the Cow

We can improve the Cow herbivore by adding some intelligent behavior. We can add event handlers to respond to attacks and exhibit defensive behavior, and I have demonstrated how to find food already. The Deer.sln provides an improvement over the Cow. The deer keeps track of food using a ReadOnlyCollectionBase and looks for the closest food to eat. You can see the code for the deer by opening the Deer.sln, available on the **www.osborne.com** website. Listing 4-7 demonstrates a collection used to track plants for the deer.

Listing 4-7   *Implementing a food-tracking collection for an herbivore*

```
public class Plants : ReadOnlyCollectionBase
{
  private Animal animal;

  public PlantState ClosestPlant()
  {
    PlantState closest = null;
    foreach(PlantState plant in this)
    {
      if((closest == null) ||
        ( animal.DistanceTo(plant) < animal.DistanceTo(closest)))
        closest = plant;
    }

    InnerList.Remove(closest);
    return closest;
  }

  public Plants(Animal animal)
  {
    this.animal = animal;

    ArrayList organisms = animal.Scan();
    foreach(OrganismState organism in organisms)
    {
      if( organism is PlantState )
        InnerList.Add(organism);
    }
  }

  public PlantState this[int index]
```

```
   {
     get
     {
       return (PlantState)InnerList[index];
     }
   }
 }
}
```

NOTE

You can create savage herbivores by setting the AttackDamagePoints attribute and invoking the BeginAttacking method on plant eaters. Perhaps you can kill all of the plant-eating competitors or destroy weaker carnivores.

When the Deer is hungry, it requests a collection of plants within range. The Plants collection removes animals from the scan. The Plants.ClosestPlant method returns the plant that is closest to an individual Deer's position and removes that plant from the collection. The closest plant is returned, and the Deer can eat with the least amount of expended energy. The Cow as provided in Listing 4-5 dies from lack of initiative. The Deer (solution available for download), using the plant tracking strategy, is much more productive than the Cow and destroyed so many plants that it eventually starved itself out.

Creating a Carnivore

Carnivores are a bit trickier to create. Their food source moves and might even fight back. Carnivores can be eaten. Observations of some carnivores in a few ecosystems indicate that there seems to be a ratio of 1 carnivore for every 10 herbivores. This is probably codified behavior in the Terrarium game itself. Without carnivores, it may be difficult to achieve balance in a Terrarium.

The code for a slightly modified carnivore required ten pages. Instead of padding this book with a huge code listing, I am not reproducing the code here, but I do encourage you to download the sample Lion.sln code and examine the complete listing. I will cover some basic points from Lion.sln that will help you build a carnivore.

Setting Carnivore Attributes   Carnivores and herbivores use the same attributes. You may want to balance them differently for carnivores. To create a meat eater, you will have to initialize the Carnivore attribute with True, or your critter won't be able to eat animals. (There are no omnivores.) You can increase attributes like AttackDamagePoints to inflict great injury on your prey or like MaximumSpeedPoints to create the equivalent of a Lion or Cheetah.

Some attributes arbitrarily have to be even multiples of some value. The EatingSpeedPoints attribute needs to be multiples of 4. (Hungry carnivores like Lions can eat at their leisure, unless there are hyenas roaming about.) Testing your organism in Terrarium mode will provide you with hints about wasted DNA points.

Programming Hunting Behavior   The Scan method will return an ArrayList of organism that your critter can see. Scan returns plants and animals. You can filter the list to only animals or only plants, as demonstrated in Listing 4-6. For example, a carnivore might care only about animals; you might also program advanced behaviors, such as heading toward plants hoping hungry herbivores might show up.

Introducing Plants and Critters to the Terrarium

When you have completed your plant or animal, you can introduce it into the ecosystem. If your code has defects, like unhandled exceptions, then you will not be able to modify it and reintroduce the same organism. For this reason, it is preferable to test the organism in Terrarium mode before submitting it to a larger ecosystem.

An overly aggressive exception handling approach will prevent your organisms from being annihilated by the Terrarium application. The following fragment demonstrates an AttackCompletedEvent handler for the Lion.

```
private void AttackCompletedEvent(object sender, AttackCompletedEventArgs e)
{
  try
  {
    if(e.Killed)
    {
      if(CanEat)
      {
        BeginEating(e.AttackAction.TargetAnimal);
      }
    }
  }
  catch(Exception x)
  {
    WriteTrace(x.Message);
  }
}
```

When the AttackCompletedEvent is raised, we can check the AttackCompletedEventArgs, which will indicate whether the attackee is dead. If it is, then we can check whether we can eat— State.EnergyState < EnergyState.Full—and, if so, call the asynchronous BeginEating method to begin eating the prey.

When a new assembly is introduced to each client, the assembly is examined for code that may be deemed as cheating in the context of the game. If your organism passes muster, then ten copies of the organism are added to the Terrarium when you first introduce the organism.

If your organism becomes extinct, then you can add the original critter from the extinct species list. You cannot modify the species and reintroduce modified code. As a result, a species that has become extinct is likely to die again for the same reasons.

Introducing Code Access Security

Terrarium typifies code that is arriving from a variety of destinations. In ecosystem mode, code may be coming from anywhere in the world—recall that there are no isolated slices of the ecosystem. Terrarium is a good way for Microsoft to introduce the new Code Access Security model

Any code that uses the Common Language Runtime must interact with the security model. The fundamental premise is that code using the CLR must produce verifiably type-safe code, and you cannot presume that code will be granted any permissions. For example, if you produce a Web Service for general consumption, you should not presume that your code will be granted specific permissions, and you must handle errors resulting from denied permissions. (Refer to Chapter 16 for more information on Code Access Security and Imperative and Declarative security.)

Secondary Topics

Terrarium supports the notion of serializing object state. Serializing object state simply means writing the state information of an object to another form—for example, a binary file. Writing the state of an object to a file promotes moving that state information across a network. The symmetric deserializing method knows exactly the order and type of data to read from the serialized file.

Terrarium provides you with a suitable opportunity to experiment with serialization. When the Teleporter bumps into an instance of your organism, a peer is selected from your peer list. The organism is removed from your Terrarium, and a copy of the DLL is sent to the peer selected from the list. State information is sent too. If you provide an implementation for the SerializePlant or SerializeAnimal, and DeserializePlant or DeserializeAnimal, as the case may be, then that additional state information is also sent. The remaining section in this chapter demonstrates serialization by implementing Serialize and Deserialize methods for the Lion carnivore.

Serializing Objects

Earlier in the chapter, I mentioned how Terrarium uses the System.IO namespace. The Serialize and Deserialize methods in organisms use the MemoryStream class. A *stream* is simply a contiguous collection of bytes. Simply representing data as contiguous bytes is how your computer sees the data, and a contiguous block of bytes can be easily ported in a variety of ways, including across the Internet. A MemoryStream is simply a stream that is stored in memory—as opposed to a FileStream, which is a file represented as a stream.

A conceptual level of programming is the class. By representing data as various streams with a common interface, it becomes possible for data in various forms to be treated consistently and polymorphically. Implement a method that takes a stream, and the specific operations you perform are the same, whether you are dealing with a MemoryStream or a FileStream. There are minor differences between stream types. For example, you don't express a file name with a MemoryStream, but FileStreams represent files as contiguous blocks of bytes, and it is intuitive that you actually need a file for this purpose.

You can track additional state information for organisms in Terrarium by implementing the Serialize and Deserialize methods. You are required only to stub out these methods, but the code in Listing 4-8 demonstrates how to serialize state information as an organism is being teleported and deserialize state information after the organism is teleported.

Serializing Organisms Using MemoryStream Objects

Methods marked with the abstract modifier must be overridden and implemented in child classes, even if that implementation is simply an empty method call. This is what we have done with the implementations of the organisms thus far. We didn't implement the serialization methods because there wasn't a practical reason to do so. However, you could contrive a reason. Perhaps your critter tracks the number of successful kills and the kind of species that frequently attacks it. You might elect to stream the most offensive critter and the easiest prey and choose to avoid the former and seek out the latter to help make your organisms more successful. This is an issue of strategy. Listing 4-8 demonstrates serialization and deserialization by streaming those activities that the Lion was participating in prior to being teleported.

Listing 4-8   *Serializing and deserializing state information using a MemoryStream*

```csharp
public override void SerializeAnimal(MemoryStream m)
{
  try
  {
    byte[] buffer = new Byte[]{
      Convert.ToByte(IsDefending), Convert.ToByte(IsAttacking),
      Convert.ToByte(IsEating), Convert.ToByte(IsMoving)};
    m.Write(buffer, 0, buffer.Length);
    WriteTrace("SerializeAnimal");
  }
  catch(Exception e)
  {
    WriteTrace(e.Message);
  }
}

public override void DeserializeAnimal(MemoryStream m)
{
  try
  {
    byte[] buffer = new Byte[4];
    m.Read(buffer, 0, buffer.Length);
    WriteTrace("WasDefending: " + Convert.ToBoolean(buffer[0]));
```

```
      WriteTrace("WasAttacking: " + Convert.ToBoolean(buffer[1]));
      WriteTrace("WasEating: " + Convert.ToBoolean(buffer[2]));
      WriteTrace("WasMoving: " + Convert.ToBoolean(buffer[3]));
      WriteTrace("DeserializeAnimal");
  }
  catch(Exception e)
  {
      WriteTrace(e.Message);
  }
}
```

TIP

Indicate the type of the Exception you want to catch in the catch predicate of an exception handler to obtain an instance of the exception object, as demonstrated in Listing 4-8.

The SerializeAnimal method writes the IsDefending, IsAttacking, IsEating, and IsMoving properties of the animal containing the code in Listing 4-8. To demonstrate that we can retrieve the state information, the DeserializeAnimal method reads the exact same data in the same quantity as was written in the SerializeAnimal method.

Writing to a FileStream

A FileStream represents the kind of code you cannot add to your organism. When an organism is loaded into Terrarium, one of the things Terrarium looks for is code that tries to perform file IO. File IO is not permitted in Terrarium because this might allow malicious code to be transported between Peers. This prohibition is one example of the security model in action in .NET. If you try the code in Listing 4-9, you will receive an error and your organism will fail, but the code will demonstrate how to obtain a temporary file name and to write information to a file.

Listing 4-9   *This code demonstrates file IO using the FileStream class.*

```
string filename = Path.GetTempFileName();
FileStream file = new FileStream(filename, FileMode.CreateNew);
m.WriteTo(file);
file.Close();
```

The first statement in Listing 4-9 demonstrates how to request a temporary file name in .NET. (You might recall that GetTempFileName used to be a Windows API method. Now GetTempFileName is a static method in the Path class defined in the System.IO namespace.) The second statement demonstrates how to create a new FileStream and file, passing the .tmp file name created in the first statement. The m.WriteTo statement demonstrates how to write information from one stream to another. The object *m* is representative of a MemoryStream passed to SerializeAnimal. Any instance of a MemoryStream will do. Finally, we close the FileStream, returning the file handle to the operating system.

Summary

Terrarium provides an excellent opportunity to learn a great detail about C# programming. Terrarium is also a bit addictive if you have a bit of imagination. An addiction to learning is a good thing. Hopefully, you will have an opportunity to install the Terrarium client—perhaps even the server—and create several organisms to add to an ecosystem. In the process of experimenting with Terrarium, you will get a crash course in inheritance, implementing event handlers and using attributes, exception handlers, regular expressions, Reflection, implementing strongly typed collections, and how streams and serialization work in .NET. These topics are all demonstrated at length in this chapter and the code that is available from the **www.osborne.com** and **www.softconcepts.com** websites.

This chapter also introduced Code Access Security. Security is demonstrated at length in Chapter 16.

Building Database Applications with ADO.NET

IN THIS CHAPTER:

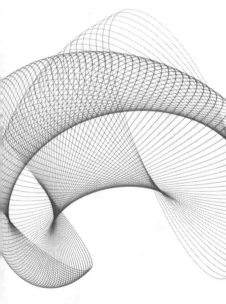

Demonstrated Topics

A Quick Review of ADO.NET Namespaces

Connecting to DataSources

Understanding the Role of the Adapter

Working with the DataSet

Using the DataTable

Using the DataView

Using the DataReader for Read-Only Data

Displaying Information in the DataGrid

Using the Command Object

Generating SQL with the CommandBuilder

Summary

T he current version of ADO incorporates revisions designed to accommodate the world we live in today. In the 21st century, information is big business. Speedy access to mountains of data by thousands or even millions of simultaneous users is the reality. ADO.NET was revised to mirror this reality.

Previous versions of ADO were based largely on a *connected* model. Each user held a connection to a data source while interacting with the data. The result were bottlenecks caused by the large number of possible physical connections. Assuming clients are PCs connected to the Internet and the servers are web servers, then database problems can be exacerbated by distance and bandwidth.

Generally, the number of transactions per interval of time can be used to determine total throughput. At one completed transaction per minute, an application could support 1,440 transactions per day. One transaction per second and an application could support 86,400 transactions per day. Clearly, these numbers are not in the millions. ADO.NET was revised to address the problem of limited physical connections to a data source, to increase reliability, and to work in the world as it exists today—a connected world.

The current ADO.NET is based on a disconnected model and centers around the DataSet and XML. In short, the ADO.NET model follows the pattern of connecting to the data source, performing a short transaction, and disconnecting from the data source. There are some new capabilities and classes that were introduced with ADO.NET. This chapter will demonstrate how to use ADO.NET to write database applications.

Demonstrated Topics

Chapter 2 introduced the subject of Reflection by demonstrating how to explore the CLR. A tools provider could use such a utility to completely document the CLR and provide a reference application that associated specific aspects of the CLR with example code. For this concept to work, we would need to write the information we discovered by Reflection to a database and then add code examples to that database.

Based on a discussion I had with a Microsoft program manager, Microsoft has an internal application that fills the role of a resource tool for developers internally working with .NET. Fortunately, Microsoft has released Rotor, which is the shared source code for the common language infrastructure (CLI), a significant part of the base classes for .NET. Rotor is available for download from Microsoft.

We can create our own reference application as a reasonable means of demonstrating ADO.NET. The demonstrated topics in this chapter are set against the backdrop of a CLR reference application and will show you how to

- ► Use connections
- ► Use adapters
- ► Program with the new DataSet class
- ► Fill and interact with the DataTable
- ► Use the DataView class

▶ Speed up database access with the DataReader

▶ Execute SQL commands using the Command object

▶ Automatically generate SQL statements with the CommandBuilder

▶ Create data bound graphical user interfaces with the DataGrid

The Secondary Topics section will borrow from the demonstrated topics and describe how to use the DataSet as a return type for an XML Web Service, binding data to controls on Web Pages and inheriting the TraceListener to facilitate debugging and testing.

A Quick Review of ADO.NET Namespaces

ADO.NET is comprised of assemblies, namespaces, and classes that are part of the bigger .NET Framework. The main namespace for ADO.NET is the System.Data namespace. System.Data contains classes like the DataSet and DataTable. Within the System.Data namespace is System.Data.Common, System.Data.OleDb, System.Data.SqlClient, and System.Data.SQLTypes. Additionally, System.XML is fundamental to ADO.NET and to .NET in general.

The System.Data.Common namespace contains classes that are shared by ADO.NET providers. For example, both the System.Data.OleDb and System.Data.SQLClient namespaces contain adapters that inherit from a common adapter in the System.Data.Common namespace.

System.Data.OleDb and System.Data.SQLClient are namespaces that contain symmetric capabilities. The SQLClient namespace contains classes for working with MS SQL Server 7.0 or higher databases, and the OleDb namespace contains classes for working with all other OleDb-compatible databases, including MS Access.

System.Data.SQLTypes contains classes that represent native SQL data types.

Last but not least is System.XML. XML is used to describe data. For example, if you specify the DataSet as a return type for a Web Service, then the DataSet will be serialized as XML to facilitate transporting the DataSet. XML is used to define data schemas (XSD schemas).

As we proceed with the examples in this chapter, I will indicate where specific classes come from, and you can use this short section as a resource to explore additional information about ADO.NET.

Let's approach ADO.NET systematically, beginning with the first thing we must do: create a connection to a data source.

Connecting to DataSources

Programmers experienced with prior versions of ADO know that ADO supported a disconnected database model. However, ADO prior to .NET was fundamentally a connected model and was not based on XML. The disconnected ADO.NET will not hold connections—we say it is disconnected—and uses XML, which makes it easy to move data across networks because XML is just hypertext.

However, you will need to create and use a connection to get at the data. You can create an SqlConnection for MS SQL Server 7.0 data sources or higher or an OleDbConnection for any other data source that supports OLE DB.

To optimize connection usage, you will want to take advantage of connection pooling. Connection pooling is a collection, or pool, of connections that applications can share. An OleDbConnection uses connection pooling automatically. An SqlConnection manages connection pooling implicitly. An SqlConnection that uses the same connection string can be pooled. You must close connections to take advantage of connection pooling.

Connecting to an OLE DB Data Store

ADO.NET creates an environment where the conditions of working with various data sources are similar from the perspective of the code you write. To learn how to program using ADO.NET, you can use any data source that is available. One such data source that supports OLE DB is the Microsoft Access Jet Engine. (MS Access ships with Microsoft Office Professional.) We'll use Access as our OLE DB example.

To connect to an OLE DB provider you will need to provide a specific connection string. There are a couple of good strategies that you can employ to obtain a working connection string. If you are adding the connection in the presentation layer, then you can drag an OleDbConnection right out of Server Explorer onto the Windows Form or Web Form (see Figure 5-1). Another good strategy for creating a second string has to do with creating a Microsoft Data Link file.

If you create a text file with a .UDL extension (for example, in Windows Explorer) and double-click that file, then you can use the Data Link Properties applet (see Figure 5-2) to configure a connection. The Data Link Properties applet provides you with a visual interface to create the connection. Complete the information on each tab and the .UDL file will contain a valid connection string. To create a connection to a Microsoft Access 2000 or 2002 database, follow these steps:

1. Create a blank text file with a .UDL extension. Double-click the file to open the file with the Data Link Properties applet.

2. On the Provider tab, select the Microsoft Jet 4.0 OLE DB Provider. Click the Next button, shown in Figure 5-2.

3. On the Connection tab, use the browse button—a button with an ellipses caption—to browse to your database file. Access databases have an .MDB extension. (You can use Windows Explorer to search for an Access database.) You can ignore item 2, leaving the default user name "Admin" in the user name field unless you know this isn't valid for the database you selected.

4. You can use the Test Connection button to determine if you have a valid connection.

5. If the Test succeeds, then you can click OK to save the configuration changes.

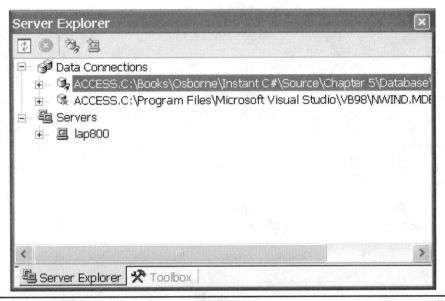

Figure 5-1   *Drag a connection from the Data Connections in Server Explorer to automatically add an OleDbConnection component to your project.*

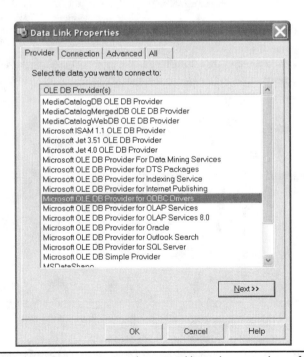

Figure 5-2   *Use the Data Link Properties applet to quickly and accurately configure a connection string.*

The Advanced tab of the Data Link Properties applet allows you to specify access permissions. The default is shared, read-write access to the database through this connection. The All tab contains name and value pairs that allow you to modify every connection value. Generally, the defaults will do, unless you have a specific reason for modifying initialization values, such as Jet OLEDB: Encrypt Database.

After you close the Data Link Properties applet, you open the .UDL file with Notepad and copy the connection string created by the applet. Here is an example of the connection string value created by the UDL applet for the Reference.mdb sample database available with the source code for this book.

```
Provider=Microsoft.Jet.OLEDB.4.0;DataSource=C:\Temp\Reference.mdb;
Persist Security Info=False
```

Wrap the preceding statement in quotes and you can use it to initialize an OleDbConnection object without having to remember the provider name, Microsoft.Jet.OLEDB.4.0. Listing 5-1 demonstrates how to write code that will open the database described by our example connection string.

Listing 5-1   *The following demonstrates how to open an OleDbConnection and ensure it is closed using a resource protection block.*

```csharp
public static void TestConnection()
{
  OleDbConnection connection = new OleDbConnection();
  connection.ConnectionString =
    @"Provider=Microsoft.Jet.OLEDB.4.0;" +
    @"Data Source=C:\Temp\Reference.mdb;" +
    @"Persist Security Info=False";

  connection.Open();
  try
  {
    Console.WriteLine(connection.State.ToString());
    Console.ReadLine();
  }
  finally
  {
    connection.Close();
  }
}
```

TIP

Strings in C# can be @-quoted or quoted. A quoted string will treat a single backslash as an escape character and a double backslash as a backslash. An @-quoted string will prevent escape characters from being processed.

Add a *using* statement to refer to the System.Data.OleDb namespace to use the OleDb providers in Listing 5-1. You can create the OleDbConnection object passing the connection string to the constructor or assigning the connection string to the ConnectionString property after the object is created. Invoke the Open method to open the connection. The code in the *try* part of the *try finally* handler—also referred to as a *resource protection block*—represents work. In Listing 5-1, we are simply writing the state of the connection object to the console. The *finally* block is always invoked, which is what we want. We always want to close the connection, and the *finally* block will ensure that the connection is closed even in the event of an exception.

Connecting to an MS SQL Server Data Store

From the perspective of the code needed to connect an SQL database, the code is almost identical to Listing 5-1. The biggest difference resides in the connection string. The connection string will need to contain information that is relevant to an MS SQL Server database. You can use the same two techniques described in the previous section—drag a connection from Server Explorer or create a .UDL file and use the Data Link Properties applet—to define a connection string to an SQL Server database.

We can use almost the identical code to that found in Listing 5-1 to open a connection to an SQL Server database. (The Microsoft Desktop Engine [MSDE] is a good SQL Sever database to use in a development environment, because you can perform initial software writing on a disconnected PC. This is especially useful when you are programming at the beach or in a hammock.) When connecting to an SQL Server database, you will need to include the System.Data.SqlClient namespace and create an instance of the SqlConnection object.

```
SqlConnection connection = new SqlConnection();
connection.ConnectionString =
   @"data source=LAP800\VSDOTNET;initial catalog=master;" +
   @"integrated security=SSPI;persist security info=False;" +
   @"workstation id=LAP800;packet size=4096";
```

There are huge benefits to be reaped when using a well-architected framework. Let's take a moment to look at one such benefit that is offered to us in ADO.NET.

Using ADO.NET Interfaces to Declare Types

A reasonable thing you may want to do is to make it easy to switch between data providers. There are several scenarios where this is likely, and I will describe one next.

Working on a project in Portland, Oregon, we were building an enterprise solution in C# to IBM's Universal Database. Residing in Michigan, I found it nice to occasionally go home and telecommute. (It helps me get caught up on yard work.) I want to work from the home office—for the multi-processor workstations with flat screens, a great library, a huge office chair, and, best of all, family—but I don't want to install every database a customer may be using. Instead, I will write my applications to allow me to quickly and simply switch to an alternate data provider. Combine ADO.NET with CASE tools for databases and you can easily replicate a production database in a non-production environment. Of course, if your employer doesn't buy my arguments, then you could present the alternate database scenario as a flexibility issue.

The basic idea is that you define methods that return ADO.NET interfaces (instead of specific provider classes) and then construct a specific provider class. You can combine CASE tools to replicate a production database with ADO.NET interfaces rather than classes and a Boolean switch managed with an external XML file, and you have a versatile application-development environment and database heterogeneity.

Switching Between Databases Using an IDbConnection

Listing 5-2 demonstrates how we can declare variables as interfaces realized by the ADO.NET providers and create an instance of a specific provider based on dynamic criterion. Listing 5-2 uses a conditional compiler directive to switch between databases. This solution requires a recompile. In a moment, I will demonstrate how to achieve the same result without recompiling.

Listing 5-2   *Use the IDbConnection interface to declare your types and you can assign any ADO.NET connection that realizes the interface.*

```
1:  public class MultiConnection
2:  {
3:    private static string GetConnectionString()
4:    {
5:      #if DEBUG
6:      return @"Provider=Microsoft.Jet.OLEDB.4.0;" +
7:             @"Data Source=C:\Temp\Refernce.mdb;" +
8:             @"Persist Security Info=False";
9:      #else
10:     return @"data source=LAP800\VSDOTNET;initial catalog=master;" +
11:            @"integrated security=SSPI;persist security info=False;" +
12:            @"workstation id=LAP800;packet size=4096";
13:     #endif
14: }
15:   private static IDbConnection GetConnection()
16:   {
17:     #if DEBUG
18:     return new OleDbConnection(GetConnectionString());
19:     #else
20:     return new SqlConnection(GetConnectionString());
21:     #endif
22:   }
23:
24:   public static void Test()
25:   {
26:     IDbConnection connection = GetConnection();
```

```
27:      connection.Open();
28:      try
29:      {
30:        Console.WriteLine(connection.State.ToString());
31:        Console.ReadLine();
32:      }
33:      finally
34:      {
35:        connection.Close();
36:      }
37:    }
38: }
```

The only real change made to the code is to declare the connection as an IDbConnection instead of an SqlConnection or an OleDbConnection. The balance of the code is consistent with the previous example in Listing 5-1. You can toggle the conditional compiler statements on lines 5 and 17 of Listing 5-2 to switch between the SQL and OLE databases.

A common framework makes it possible to write code once, and switch between something as significant as a database without writing multiple versions of the code for each database. A great framework puts this kind of flexibility at your fingertips. The .NET framework is a superlative framework. We can use a BooleanSwitch to externalize switching databases without recompiling.

Switching Between Data Providers with a BooleanSwitch

A second scenario where it may be beneficial to allow a user to switch between databases is when you are writing a consumer product, and you don't want to force your customer to use a specific database provider. Suppose you write a consumer application and want to allow the customer to choose between databases. By the time the customer has the application, it is too late to recompile. You can use a BooleanSwitch internally and an XML file externally to support switching between data providers (as well as supporting any kind of externalized dynamic switching).

Listing 5-3 is a revision of Listing 5-2. The revision demonstrates the addition of a BooleanSwitch, and Listing 5-4 provides the listing for the XML file that defines the switch.

Listing 5-3   *This code (a revision of Listing 5-2) demonstrates using a BooleanSwitch.*

```
1:  public class SwitchedMultiConnection
2:  {
3:    private static BooleanSwitch Switch =
4:      new BooleanSwitch("Provider",
5:      "Supports switching between data providers");
6:
7:    private static string GetConnectionString()
8:    {
9:      if( Switch.Enabled )
```

```
10:     {
11:         return @"Provider=Microsoft.Jet.OLEDB.4.0;" +
12:             @"Data Source=C:\Books\Osborne\Instant C#" +
13:             @"\Source\Chapter 5\Database\Reference.mdb;" +
14:             @"Persist Security Info=False";
15:     }
16:     else
17:     {
18:         return @"data source=LAP800\VSDOTNET;initial catalog=master;" +
19:             @"integrated security=SSPI;persist security info=False;" +
20:             @"workstation id=LAP800;packet size=4096";
21:     }
22:   }
23:
24:   private static IDbConnection GetConnection()
25:   {
26:     if (Switch.Enabled)
27:     {
28:       return new OleDbConnection(GetConnectionString());
29:     }
30:     else
31:     {
32:       return new SqlConnection(GetConnectionString());
33:     }
34:   }
35:
36:   public static void Test()
37:   {
39:     IDbConnection connection = GetConnection();
40:     connection.Open();
41:     try
42:     {
43:       Console.WriteLine(connection.State.ToString());
44:       Console.ReadLine();
45:     }
46:     finally
47:     {
48:       connection.Close();
49:     }
48:   }
49: }
```

Lines 3 through 5 of Listing 5-3 declare and initialize a BooleanSwitch as a static member. Making the switch static means that we will only instantiate one BooleanSwitch and share it between all instances of the class using the switch. Lines 9 and 26 use the BooleanSwitch in place of the conditional compiler directive to determine whether we should use the OleDb or SqlClient connection.

There are a few differences between a BooleanSwitch and conditional compiler directives. The conditional compiler directive must be changed and recompiled. The code that fails evaluation is excluded from the compiled assembly. Code in both parts of the BooleanSwitch code block is written to the compiled assembly, and to switch between different versions of the code we change the external definition of the switch in an XML file without recompiling. The .config file containing the switch definition is provided in Listing 5-4.

Listing 5-4   *This code defines the .config file containing the BooleanSwitch.*

```
<configuration>
  <system.diagnostics>
    <switches>
      <add name="Provider" value="1" />
    </switches>
  </system.diagnostics>
</configuration>
```

Name the configuration file the same name as the assembly that will use it, adding a .config extension. For example, if your assembly is named myapp.exe, then your configuration file will be myapp.exe.config. Create the configuration file in the same directory as the one containing the assembly. A complete description of the contents of a BooleanSwitch defined in a configuration file is provided in Chapter 7, in the section entitled "Using Switches."

Combining provider interfaces with BooleanSwitch objects provides us with a convenient way to switch between providers without recompiling our code. The next piece of the ADO.NET puzzle is the adapter.

Understanding the Role of the Adapter

ADO.NET separates data access from data manipulation. Adapters are part of the data access layer of ADO.NET. Adapters are used to move data between a connection and classes that store cached data for manipulation, including the DataSet and DataTable. To read data from a connection to a data source, you can use the Fill method. To read the schema only, you can invoke the FillSchema method, and Update will accept the modified revisions to data in a DataTable or DataSet and update the data source with the revisions.

There is an OleDbDataAdapter for OLE DB providers, an SqlDataAdapter for MS SQL Server providers, and an IDbAdapter interface that allows you to write provider-independent code, as we did with IDbConnection in the preceding section.

Adapters are initialized with SQL and connection objects. The adapter provides the bridge from the connection to the data manipulation objects. In this section, I will demonstrate the Fill, FillSchema, and Update methods of an adapter.

Initializing an Adapter

Adapters are initialized with an SQL SELECT command and a connection object of the same provider type. Use an OleDbDataAdapter with an OleDbConnection and a SqlDataAdapter with a SqlConnection. (I won't repeat this information. Assume that, if one or the other of the OleDb provider or SqlClient provider has a specific class, there is a symmetric class for the other provider type.)

To initialize an adapter, create an instance of the adapter with an SQL SELECT command and a like connection. Here is an example of an adapter object being created with an OleDbConnection referring to the Reference.mdb MS Access database available with this book.

```
OleDbConnection connection = new OleDbConnection();
connection.ConnectionString =
  @"Provider=Microsoft.Jet.OLEDB.4.0;" +
  @"Data Source=C:\Temp\Reference.mdb;" +
  @"Persist Security Info=False";

OleDbDataAdapter adapter = new OleDbDataAdapter(
  "SELECT * FROM METHOD", connection);
```

The last statement demonstrates one of the four possible ways to initialize an adapter object. The other three overloaded constructors for the adapter are variations of the one shown; you can use the Visual Studio help documentation for examples of the other variations.

Connection Pooling Strategy

If you recall, we spoke about connection pooling earlier. Connection pooling is implicitly based on the connection string. To take advantage of the more optimal use of connections via connection pooling, you can use a simple technique for ensuring that your code isn't littered with literal connection strings. Listing 5-5 provides an example of a factored class that supports maintaining only one instance of a connection string.

Listing 5-5   *This code demonstrates how to use a class to ensure that you have only one instance of a connection string.*

```
1:  public class FactoredConnection
2:  {
3:    private static BooleanSwitch booleanSwitch =
4:      new BooleanSwitch("PKimmel",
5:      "Used to switch between connection strings");
6:
7:    public static string GetOleDbConnectionString()
8:    {
9:      if(booleanSwitch.Enabled)
10:     {
11:       return @"Provider=Microsoft.Jet.OLEDB.4.0;" +
```

```
12:                      @"Data Source=C:\Books\Osborne\Instant C#" +
13:                      @"\Source\Chapter 5\Database\Reference.mdb;" +
14:                      @"Persist Security Info=False";
15:      }
16:    else
17:    {
18:        return @"Provider=Microsoft.Jet.OLEDB.4.0;" +
19:                      @"Data Source=C:\Temp\Reference.mdb;" +
20:                      @"Persist Security Info=False";
21:      }
22: }
23:
24:    public static string GetSqlConnectionString()
25:    {
26:      if(booleanSwitch.Enabled)
27:      {
28:        return @"data source=LAP800\VSDOTNET;initial catalog=master;" +
29:                    @"integrated security=SSPI;persist security info=False;" +
30:                    @"workstation id=LAP800;packet size=4096";
31:      }
32:    else
33:    {
34:      throw new Exception(
35:        "Make sure you have a MS SQL Server instance available.");
36:      }
37:    }
39:    public static OleDbConnection GetOleDbConnection()
40:    {
41:      return new OleDbConnection(GetOleDbConnectionString());
42:    }
43:
44:    public static SqlConnection GetSqlConnection()
45:    {
46:      return new SqlConnection(GetSqlConnectionString());
47:    }
48: }
```

Again, in Listing 5-5 we use a BooleanSwitch—on lines 9 and 26—to support easy switching between versions of the connection string. This is consistent with an approach we might take for a connected versus a disconnected development environment. Notice that the *else* condition for GetSqlConnectionString throws an exception. You will need to ensure that you have access to MS SQL Server or MSDE installed on your desktop and have an instance accessible to your application.

Using the approach demonstrated in Listing 5-5, we can be sure that we are facilitating connection pooling by using the same connection string. This approach does not prohibit you from creating a new instance of a connection without the FactoredConnection class.

General Programming Strategy

The preceding section demonstrated a FactoredConnection class that facilitates connection pooling by creating a separate class containing the connection string. There is another strategic reason to write code like that demonstrated. I refer to it as *Kimmel's Theory of Convergent Code.*

NOTE

Kimmel's Theory of Convergent Code: *Code that converges on a single instance of an algorithm or class is good because it promotes reuse, consistency, and a high degree of re-orchestrated dynamic behavior.*

The basic idea behind convergent versus divergent code is that the smallest piece of code that can be reused without replicating the code is the *method.* Anything below a method must be duplicated to be reused. That is, lines of code must be copied and pasted to be reused. Copied and pasted code is divergent code for the simple reason that there is more than one instance of an algorithm. The negative result of divergent code is that for each instance of the divergent code, a programmer must replicate, individually test, and separately maintain the individuated lines of code. The result is that divergent code tends to decay over time according to the number of times the code is copied and pasted. The result is that divergent code tends toward semantically similar operations diverging in behavior, yielding the perception of unreliable performance.

To summarize: relative to our FactoredConnection class, we have only one instance of the connection string to maintain. If the connection changes, we propagate the change in one place. If we want the behavior of the FactoredConnection to change then, we again only need to change the code in place. Consider the case where we want to read the connection string from an external resource like the registry. Again, we only need change the code in one place.

Convergent code in the form of methods yields the following good rule of thumb: prefer singular, short, well-named, highly reusable methods to lines of code, which represent plural, monolithic, non-reusable methods. William Opdikes' doctoral dissertation from 1990 was the impetus for the subject of *refactoring,* which supports my theory of convergence. You can read about refactoring in Martin Fowler's superlative *Refactoring: Improving the Design of Existing Code* (Addison-Wesley).

Invoking the Adapter Fill Method

The Fill method is used to move data between a connection and a DataSet. To fill a DataSet, you will need to create a connection and an adapter and invoke the adapter's Fill method. A DataSet object is passed as an argument to the Fill method. You do not need to specifically create an instance of a connection to use an adapter. You may pass a connection string instead of a connection object to the adapter, and the adapter will internally create an instance of a connection and then open and close the connection automatically. Here are a couple of examples that demonstrate using the Fill command.

```
public static void TestFill()
{
  OleDbConnection connection = FactoredConnection.GetOleDbConnection();
  OleDbDataAdapter adapter = new OleDbDataAdapter(
    "SELECT * FROM METHOD", connection);

  DataSet dataSet = new DataSet();
  connection.Open();
  try
  {
    adapter.Fill( dataSet );
  }
  finally
  {
    connection.Close();
  }

  WalkDataSet( dataSet );
}
```

The preceding example verbosely creates an OlDbConnection, OleDbDataAdapter, and a DataSet, opens the connection and then fills the DataSet. WalkDataSet represents a method that performs useful work. (You can find the code for WalkDataSet in the ADOSampleCode.sln available online at **www.osborne.com**.)

The second example, which follows, demonstrates a concise version that passes a connection string to the OleDbDataAdapter constructor, and the adapter will be responsible for opening and closing the connection.

```
private static void TestFill2()
{
  OleDbDataAdapter adapter = new OleDbDataAdapter(
    "SELECT * FROM METHOD",
    FactoredConnection.GetOleDbConnectionString());

  DataSet dataSet = new DataSet();
  adapter.Fill( dataSet );
  WalkDataSet( dataSet );
}
```

(The FactoredConnection class was introduced in the earlier section "Connection Pooling Strategy.") The preceding example demonstrates a concise way to fill a DataSet. More important, notice that in both instances we are operating on the DataSet after the connection is closed. (The first example closes the DataSet explicitly, and the second example closes the DataSet after the Fill operation.) This demonstrates the connectionless mode of operation in ADO.NET. The data has been cached in the DataSet and is available completely independent of the connection and adapter.

Invoking the Adapter FillSchema Method

If you are performing a large number of insert statements and aren't interested in existing rows of data, then you can request the schema only. To read schema—a description of a table—into a DataSet only, employ the FillSchema method.

As is true with the Fill method, you can actually fill a single DataTable or add a table to a DataSet. The DataSet is a collection of tables and optional relationships between those tables. (Refer to the later sections "Working with the DataSet" and "Using the DataTable" for more information.) FillSchema takes a DataSet or DataTable argument and a SchemaType enumerated value, either Mapped or Source. Here is an example of a method that reads the description of a table only into a DataSet.

```
public static void TestFillSchema()
{
  OleDbDataAdapter adapter = new OleDbDataAdapter(
    "SELECT * FROM METHOD",
    FactoredConnection.GetOleDbConnectionString());

  DataSet dataSet = new DataSet();
  adapter.FillSchema(dataSet, SchemaType.Source);
}
```

The DataSet in the preceding fragment will contain a single table with columns only; the columns represent the schema information. The enumerated value SchemaType.Source—of two possible values, the other being SchemaType.Mapped—instructs the adapter to use the schema described by the source table. The alternative is to use the schema transformed by column mappings. (Refer to the section "Working with the DataSet" later in the chapter for more information on column mappings.)

Updating Changes to Data

An adapter plays the role of bridge between a connection and a DataSet. Just as we used an adapter to read data from a data source via a connection into a DataSet, we use the adapter to update changes made to the data. Updating includes SQL UPDATE, SQL INSERT, and SQL DELETE operations.

The means by which we instruct the adapter to update data is to provide SQL commands for the operations we want to perform. For example, if we have added new rows, then we need to provide an INSERT command to the adapter before we call the Update method. The basic steps for updating data are to open a connection, create an adapter providing an SQL SELECT statement and the connection as initial values, fill a DataSet with data, modify the data, create SQL commands that describe how to perform updates, and invoke the adapter Update method. One version of these steps is demonstrated in Listing 5-6.

Listing 5-6   *This code demonstrates how to update a DataSet using an adapter.*

```
1:   public static void TestUpdate()
2:   {
3:     OleDbConnection connection =
4:       FactoredConnection.GetOleDbConnection();
5:
6:     OleDbDataAdapter adapter = new OleDbDataAdapter(
7:       "SELECT * FROM METHOD", connection);
8:
9:     DataSet dataSet = new DataSet();
10:    connection.Open();
11:    adapter.Fill(dataSet);
12:    connection.Close();
13:
14:    DataRow row = dataSet.Tables[0].NewRow();
15:    row["Name"] = "TestUpdate";
16:    dataSet.Tables[0].Rows.Add(row);
17:
18:    OleDbCommandBuilder commandBuilder =
19:      new OleDbCommandBuilder(adapter);
20:
21:    connection.Open();
22:    adapter.Update(dataSet);
23:    connection.Close();
24: }
```

Lines 3 and 4 of Listing 5-6 create a connection object. Lines 6 and 7 use the connection object to create the adapter. Line 9 creates an instance of a DataSet. Line 10 opens the connection, line 11 fills the DataSet, and line 12 closes the connection. We don't need an open connection to manage the DataSet, and it is better if we close the connection immediately. In a real application, it is unlikely that the code actually adding data will be this simple.

Lines 14 through 16 of Listing 5-6 demonstrate how to add a new row to the tables in a DataSet. Line 14 adds the row. Line 15 updates one field in the row, and line 16 adds the row to the table's collection of Rows using the Rows.Add command.

Line 18 of Listing 5-6 uses the adapter to construct an OleDbCommandBuilder. The command builder automatically uses the schema information for a table to generate INSERT, DELETE, and UPDATE SQL commands. Refer to the section "Generating SQL with the CommandBuilder" later in this chapter for more information on the OleDbCommandBuilder.

Lines 21 through 22 of Listing 5-6 opens the connection, updates the database, and closes the connection. The DataSet knows that we inserted a new row; hence, the adapter knows to use the adapter's InsertCommand property to write the row of data we added on lines 14 through 16.

Working with the DataSet

The DataSet is an evolution of the ADO RecordSet. The DataSet is a connectionless repository for ADO.NET, and you can use DataSet objects without ever connecting to a data source. We have only briefly introduced the DataColumn, DataRow, and DataTable, but these objects can exist and you can programmatically interact with them without ever connecting to a data source.

In general, the DataSet model is consistent with how we think about a relational database. The DataSet contains a DataRelationCollection and a DataTableCollection. The DataTableCollection contains a DataRowCollection, DataColumnCollection, ChildRelations, ParentRelations, and ExtendedProperties. The DataRowCollection contains instances of DataRow objects, and the DataColumnCollection contains DataColumn objects. There is also a view of data represented by the DataView class.

You can use the DataSet and contained objects in the traditional way by connecting to data providers as demonstrated earlier in this chapter, or you can use the DataSet as an in-memory repository to store data in an organized way. This next section demonstrates how to employ aspects of the DataSet.

Adding DataTable Objects to a DataSet

When you create a DataSet object and fill it from a DataAdapter based on a single SQL SELECT statement, what really happens is that a DataTable is created and is added to the DataSet's DataTableCollection. The premise is that for ADO.NET to support a connectionless model for database management, it must support storing and managing data in relations that are likely to exist.

The most common relationship is the simple master-detail relationship. One table plays the role of the master table and the other table plays the role of detail table. In a typical master-detail relationship, you will need a master table, a detail table, and a DataRelation. The AssemblyViewer.sln for this chapter available for download demonstrates one such relationship between a table containing CLR TypeInfo objects and ConstructorInfo objects. Listing 5-7 demonstrates how to fill DataTable objects and add those objects to a DataSet.

Listing 5-7 *This code demonstrates how to add DataTable objects to a DataSet.*

```
1:   OleDbConnection connection = new OleDbConnection(connectionString);
2:   OleDbDataAdapter adapter = new OleDbDataAdapter(
3:     "SELECT * FROM TYPE", connection);
4:   DataSet dataSet = new DataSet();
5:
6:   DataTable typeTable = new DataTable("TYPE");
7:   adapter.Fill( dataTable );
8:   dataSet.Tables.Add(typeTable);
9:
10:  DataTable constructorTable = new DataTable("CONSTRUCTOR");
```

```
11: adapter = new OleDbDataAdapter(
12:    "SELECT * FROM CONSTRUCTOR", connection);
13: adapter.Fill( constructorTable );
14:
15: dataSet.Tables.Add(constructorTable);
```

Line 1 of Listing 5-7 creates a connection object. Because we don't explicitly open the connection, the adapter will take care of opening and closing the connection for us. (You have seen several examples of a connection string to the Reference.mdb database. The variable connectionString was used to represent the actual connection string.) The second statement creates an OleDbDataAdapter to bridge between the connection and a DataTable.

Line 4 of Listing 5-7 creates a DataSet. When we want to represent a collection of tables, we use the DataSet, although it is acceptable and possible to use a single DataTable if we only need one table. Line 6 creates a new DataTable object, and line 7 demonstrates how easy it is to fill a DataTable directly without using a DataSet. Line 8 adds the DataTable to our DataSet object. Lines 10 through 15 repeat the process for the CONSTRUCTOR table.

When the last statement in line 15 of Listing 5-7 finishes executing, the DataSet contains two tables. There is no relationship between the tables yet. We need to define the relationship as a separate object and add it to the DataSet.

Creating Master-Detail Relationships

In the preceding section, we added two tables to a DataSet. To logically join those tables, we need to create a DataRelation object and add that to the table. Listing 5-8 demonstrates the code that, when combined with the code in Listing 5-7, defines a master-detail relationship within the DataSet.

Listing 5-8   *Add a DataRelation to a DataSet.*

```
DataColumn parent =
  dataSet.Tables["TYPE"].Columns["UnderlyingSystemType"];
DataColumn child =
  dataSet.Tables["CONSTRUCTOR"].Columns["DeclaringType"];
DataRelation relation = new DataRelation(
  "TypesAndConstructors", parent, child);
dataSet.Relations.Add(relation);
```

NOTE

Generally, I prefer to name my related columns identically to facilitate identifying relationships between tables in the same database. However, the Reference.mdb database represents the types defined in the CLR, and the columns are created from the names of actual properties in the CLR. For example, UnderlyingSystemType is a property in the TypeInfo type defined in the CLR.

Just as with JOIN statements in SQL, a DataRelation relies on columns. In Listing 5-8 we initialize two DataColumn objects by selecting a column from each DataTable that represents a logical relationship between two disparate tables. In the Common Language Runtime, a TypeInfo object has an UnderlyingSystemType property that is logically related to the ConstructorInfo's DeclaringType property. We use the TYPE table's UnderlyingSystem Type column and the CONSTRUCTOR table's DeclaringType column to initialize a new DataRelation, providing a name and the two logically related columns as arguments to the DataRelation constructor.

When the last statement—dataSet.Relations.Add(relation)—runs in Listing 5-8, you have a logical master-detail relationship in the DataSet. This relationship is depicted Figure 5-3.

Figure 5-3 was created from the Relationships dialog in MS Access 2002 but is an accurate visualization of the DataSet after the code in Listing 5-7 and Listing 5-8 runs. Each table shown represents a DataTable, and the line between the tables represents the DataRelation object.

You can bind the DataSet to a Windows Forms or Web Forms DataGrid, and the DataGrid will accurately manage the master-detail aspects by presenting the data in a hierarchical relationship. You can explore the AssemblyViewer.sln for an example. The code to bind the DataSet to a DataGrid requires a single statement:

```
dataGrid1.DataSource = dataSet;
```

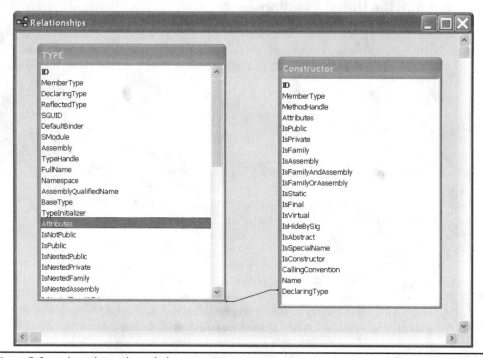

Figure 5-3 *The Relationships dialog in MS Access is an accurate depiction of the two DataTables related by a single DataRelation.*

Creating Data Column Mappings

Another common thing that you might want to do is clean up unsightly column names. I have encountered a large number of databases with obscure column names, like the NAME_SEQ_TS. It is often very difficult to figure out the role of such columns after the original DBA has left the project. Unfortunately, you may not always be in a position to re-design a database.

NOTE

Documenting and managing databases are good reasons for using CASE tools. ERwin, DataArchitect, and Select are all good CASE tools that make it easy to design, document, and maintain databases.

One such instance where we elected not to re-design the database was where the customer's motivation for re-implementing the system was not dissatisfaction with the existing implementation. The customer simply no longer wanted to be held hostage by a hardware vendor that charged exorbitant rent. Our mission statement was to provide a new system with behavior that duplicated the behavior of the existing system. There were supposed to be no new features. The existing system was implemented in Natural and Adabas, and we were porting it to C#, ASP.NET, and UDB. In essence, we were porting a non-object–oriented system implemented as a terminal application to a thin client Web application. Our charter did not really permit re-engineering the database, so we did the next best thing. We used column mappings to more clearly name older legacy columns that had obscure names. Listing 5-9 demonstrates how we can use DataTableMapping and DataColumnMapping objects in concert to support providing alternate names for columns.

Listing 5-9 *Using DataTableMapping and DataColumnMapping objects*

```
OleDbConnection connection = new OleDbConnection(connectionString);
OleDbDataAdapter adapter = new OleDbDataAdapter(
  "SELECT * FROM PARAMETER_TABLE", connection);
DataSet dataSet = new DataSet();

DataTableMapping tableMapping =
  adapter.TableMappings.Add("Parameter", "PARAMETER_TABLE");

tableMapping.ColumnMappings.Add("ParameterType", "Parameter Type");
adapter.Fill(dataSet, "Parameter");

dataGrid1.DataSource = dataSet.Tables[0];
```

Listing 5-9 creates a table mapping named Parameter that maps to the Reference.mdb PARAMETER_TABLE table. The DataColumnMapping is implicitly created when we invoke the DataTableMapping.ColumnMappings.Add method. The source table column ParameterType is mapped to the reader-friendly "Parameter Type" column. Invoking the

Fill method on adapter and using the DataTableMapping name will fill the data table with the columns from the source table, PARAMETER_TABLE, using the mapped column names.

Of course, you can accomplish this much with SQL statements that describe column aliases—usually with an *As* clause in the SELECT statement. The DataTableMapping and DataColumnMappings can be used for updates too. Listing 5-10 demonstrates how to use the mapped table and column to perform an update using the mapped values.

Listing 5-10   *A revised version of Listing 5-9 demonstrates how to perform an update against the mapped table and column.*

```
OleDbConnection connection = new OleDbConnection(connectionString);
OleDbDataAdapter adapter = new OleDbDataAdapter(
  "SELECT * FROM PARAMETER_TABLE", connection);
  DataSet dataSet = new DataSet();

DataTableMapping tableMapping =
  adapter.TableMappings.Add("Parameter", "PARAMETER_TABLE");

tableMapping.ColumnMappings.Add("ParameterType", "Parameter Type");
  adapter.Fill(dataSet, "Parameter");

// Demonstrates updating using the mapped objects
DataRow dataRow = dataSet.Tables[0].NewRow();
dataRow["Parameter Type"] = "Test";
dataSet.Tables[0].Rows.Add(dataRow);
adapter.InsertCommand = (new
  OleDbCommandBuilder(adapter)).GetInsertCommand();
adapter.Update(dataSet, "Parameter");

dataGrid1.DataSource = dataSet.Tables[0];
```

TIP

It is perfectly acceptable to create an inline object to avoid littering your code with temporary variables, as demonstrated by the OleDbCommandBuilder created inline in Listing 5-10. Use an inline object if you don't need a reference to that object later in the same code.

The comment beginning with the word "Demonstrates" is where the new code has been inserted to revise Listing 5-9. This code is very similar to performing an update without mappings. We request a new DataRow. We use the indexer for the DataRow to modify a single field by referring to the mapped column name. We add the modified row to the Rows collection and wrap it up by creating an OleDbCommandBuilder to write our SQL for us and invoking the OleDbDataAdapter.Update command. Remember to use the mapped table name for the update just as we did with the Fill operation.

Using the DataTable

The DataTable maps to a table in a database. You can also use a DataTable as an in-memory data store for data that will never see the inside of a database. As my good and smart friend Eric Cotter says, "Think of a DataTable as just a convenient way to store data."

Although you are not required to limit the use of a DataTable to database applications, the DataTable was primarily defined for this purpose. DataTable objects are primarily composed of DataRowCollection and DataColumnCollection objects. Logically, a DataTable looks like a single spreadsheet where the intersection of a column and row represents a field. Operations you are likely to want to perform on a DataTable include filling a table from a data source and updating that data source after you modify the data in the table. We have already looked at several examples demonstrating this use of the DataTable, and the AssemblyViewer.sln for this chapter has several more. Another task you may want to perform is to create and define a DataTable programmatically, including creating keyed and incremented columns.

The AssemblyViewer.sln defines several types that inherit from the DataTable. Each of these types is capable of creating an in-memory DataTable or a table in an Access database that represents a type object. For example, the PropertyTable defined in Database.cs is capable of reading all of the properties from a PropertyInfo object, defining a DataTable, and adding all of the PropertyInfo details to the DataTable. (For discussions on Reflection, see Chapter 2 and Chapter 11.)

The basic idea is that a type is passed to the PropertyTable's CreateNew method. Reflection is used to get all of the PropertyInfo—the property descriptions—objects for that type. A table is dynamically created using the property names and types of the PropertyInfo object, then each of the PropertyInfo objects representing the properties of the type passed to CreateNew is iterated, and the values of each of the PropertyInfo objects is added to the dynamic table. (I'd like to add the complete listing here for the AssemblyViewer.sln, but the Refactored Database module alone is 728 lines of code. You will have to download the example solution and step through the application to explore all of the code.) To facilitate your understanding, the following bulleted list describes the Reflection algorithm used with all of the members of a type.

- ▶ Determine the elements of the type you want to explore. In this instance, we will explore the Properties of a type only.

- ▶ Properties are described by the System.Reflection.PropertyInfo class.

- ▶ Iterate all of the properties of a PropertyInfo class, adding a column to a DataTable for each property defined by the PropertyInfo class. Every property will itself be described by the same properties.

- ▶ Iterate all of the properties of the type you want to explore, writing the value associated with each property's PropertyInfo.

A property is described by the PropertyInfo object. A PropertyInfo object has several properties that describe a property. (A bit of a tongue twister.) A property is described by MemberType, PropertyType, Attributes, IsSpecialName, CanRead, CanWrite, Name, DeclaringType, and ReflectedType. Every property in a type is initialized with a value for each of these elements of its type record, if you will. To create a table that describes a class relative to its properties, we can store the value for each property of the PropertyInfo object. When adding this data to a table it is helpful to add a keyed column and columns for each of the PropertyInfo properties. This is what the AssemblyViewer.sln does. We'll examine each part of this process in the sections that follow by walking through the code that creates the Property table in the Reference.mdb database.

Creating a DataTable Object

Creating the DataTable is easy. Ensure that you have the System.Data.dll assembly referenced, which it is by default in new projects. Add a *using* statement that refers to the System.Data namespace to the module that you will be declaring a DataTable in. Construct a new instance of a DataTable providing a name for the DataTable.

```
DataTable table = new DataTable("PROPERTY");
```

Recall that I said that you can use a DataTable independent of providers and DataSets. The preceding code is all you need to create a new DataTable.

Creating a Primary Key, Auto-Incremented Column

For our purposes, we can use a simple auto-increment column as the primary key for our property table. We add a DataColumn to the table created in the preceding section and provide some specific information for that data column. The updated code follows in Listing 5-11.

Listing 5-11   *This code demonstrates how to create an auto-incremented primary key column in a DataTable.*

```
DataTable table = new DataTable("PROPERTY");
DataColumn column = table.Columns.Add();
column.ColumnName = columnName;
column.AutoIncrement = true;
column.AutoIncrementSeed = 1;
column.AutoIncrementStep = 1;
column.Unique = true;
table.PrimaryKey = new DataColumn[]{column};
```

After we create the DataTable, we create a new column by invoking the DataTable.Columns.Add method. Provide a ColumnName as demonstrated, indicate that this column is auto- incremented by setting the DataColumn.AutoIncrement property to True. You can optionally set the DataColumn.AutoIncrementSeed and DataColumn.AutoIncrementStep properties or use the default value 1 for each. The AutoIncrementSeed value is the starting number for the automatically incremented column, and the AutoIncrementStep value defines the value added to each increment. Indicate that the column must be unique, as demonstrated in the preceding fragment.

Finally, a DataTable's primary key can be composed of multiple columns. For this reason we must initialize the DataTable.PrimaryKey property with an array of DataColumn objects. In our example—on the last line of code in Listing 5-11—the array of columns that make up the key is composed of our single column.

Walking the Properties of the PropertyInfo Class

Adding your basic vanilla column is much easier than adding keyed and incremented columns. All we need to do is create a DataColumn object by requesting it from the DataTable and provide a name and data type for the column. Following this logic, we can create a DataTable that maps to a PropertyInfo record with the code in Listing 5-12.

Listing 5-12   *This code demonstrates how to create a table that mirrors the PropertyInfo class.*

```
DataTable table = new DataTable("PROPERTY");
DataColumn column = table.Columns.Add();
column.ColumnName = columnName;
column.AutoIncrement = true;
column.AutoIncrementSeed = 1;
column.AutoIncrementStep = 1;
column.Unique = true;
table.PrimaryKey = new DataColumn[]{column};

PropertyInfo[] infos = typeof(PropertyInfo).GetProperties(
  BindingFlags.Public | BindingFlags.NonPublic |
  BindingFlags.Instance | BindingFlags.Static);

foreach(PropertyInfo info in infos)
{
  column = table.Columns.Add();
  column.ColumnName = info.Name;
  column.DataType = typeof(string);
  column.ReadOnly = true;
}
```

The new code retrieves the array of PropertyInfo objects for a PropertyInfo class itself. The BindingFlags indicate that we should get both public and non-public as well as instance and static members of the type. The *foreach* statement works under the covers by requesting an Enumerator from a type. The implication is that the type must implement the IEnumerable interface. System.Array types—anything declared with the [ ] array operator—implicitly implement the IEnumerable interface. For each PropertyInfo, a DataColumn is requested from the DataTable; the ColumnName, DataType, and ReadOnly properties are set. (The ReadOnly property is set because we can't really change the implementation of a type by modifying our database; hence, it makes no sense to allow users to modify PropertyInfo values.)

When we are all finished, we have a table whose schema mirrors the properties of a PropertyInfo class. A similar approach can be used to add rows of data to the DataTable. Refer to Listings 5-6 and 5-10 for examples of adding rows of data to a DataTable. You can also refer to the AssemblyViewer.sln for several examples of adding data to a DataTable.

Using the DataView

A DataView is by default a read-only view of data in a DataTable. You can enable modifying a DataView by changing the AllowNew, AllowEdit, and AllowDelete properties of the DataView to True. A DataView is initialized with a DataTable and can be used to sort, filter, and modify data.

We can create a DataView that shows read-only properties by filtering the CanWrite field of our Property table. Listing 5-13 demonstrates how to create a DataView and apply a row filter using syntax roughly equivalent to a predicate in a *Where* clause.

Listing 5-13   *This code demonstrates how to create a DataView and apply a row filter.*

```
OleDbConnection connection = new OleDbConnection(connectionString);
OleDbDataAdapter adapter =
  new OleDbDataAdapter("SELECT * FROM PROPERTY", connection);
DataTable table = new DataTable();
adapter.Fill(table);
DataView dataView = new DataView(table);
dataView.RowFilter = "CanWrite = 'False'";

dataGrid1.DataSource = dataView;
```

The big difference between Listing 5-13 and earlier listings is the creation of the DataView. As mentioned, we initialize a DataView with a DataTable. Optionally, we can filter and sort the DataView without requerying the data source. The example demonstrates a DataView.RowFilter that filters rows in the PROPERTY table by the string value of 'False' for CanWrite.

The last step demonstrates how to bind the DataView to a Windows Forms DataGrid. Refer to the AssemblyViewer.sln for a complete code listing. Check out the section "Binding a DataSet to a DataGrid" later in this chapter for more on using ADO.NET with controls.

Using the DataReader for Read-Only Data

A DataReader can be used to obtain a forward-only and read-only view of data without the overhead of a DataSet. A DataReader requires a connection and a command and is initialized by invoking a command object's ExecuteReader method. Listing 5-14 provides a brief example of using an OleDbDataReader.

Listing 5-14   *Using an OleDbDataReader to read all of the rows returned by an SQL command*

```
OleDbConnection connection = new OleDbConnection(connectionString);
OleDbCommand command =
  new OleDbCommand("SELECT * FROM FIELD", connection);
connection.Open();
OleDbDataReader reader = command.ExecuteReader();
while( reader.Read())
{
  Debug.WriteLine(reader.GetValue(0));
}
reader.Close();
connection.Close();
```

We can't bind the DataReader to the grid because a DataReader does not implement the IList or IListSource interfaces. That is the technical reason. The logical reason is that a grid can be scrolled forward and backward, and a DataReader is forward-only.

You must maintain an open connection while a DataReader is active, as demonstrated by the code. Ensure that you call Close on the reader when you have finished with it, because the connection cannot be reused until the reader has been closed. The benefit of using a DataReader is that it performs very fast read operations.

Displaying Information in the DataGrid

Object-oriented frameworks tend to be very flexible because there is a certain amount of commonality throughout the framework. One example is the Windows Forms DataGrid control. The DataGrid control has a DataSource property. You can assign a variety of objects to a DataSource because the DataSource is implemented to work with any object that implements the IList or IListSource interfaces. (IListSource has two members, one of which returns an object that implements IList.) As a result, there is a tremendous flexibility when it comes to binding to the DataSource property.

In general, the DataSource property can be assigned to a DataTable, DataSet, DataView, DataViewManager, and any object that implements IList or IListSource. The net effect of the generic implementation of the DataSource is that you can obviously bind to objects defined in ADO.NET, but you can also bind to a list of any kind of object.

Recall that in Listing 5-12 we invoked the GetProperties method. GetProperties returned an array of PropertyInfo objects, represented in code as PropertyInfo[ ]. An array's underlying type is System.Array. Interestingly enough, System.Array implements the IList interface. The implication, then, is that we should be able to bind the DataGrid.DataSource property directly to the PropertyInfo[ ] returned by GetProperties. In fact, if you write the following code, you will get almost an identical result to the one you would get if you assigned the DataTable in Listing 5-12 to a DataGrid's DataSource property.

```
dataGrid1.DataSource = this.GetType().GetProperties();
```

The preceding single statement produces the view shown in the DataGrid in Figure 5-4. Try binding to the arrays returned by invoking GetMembers, GetFields, and GetMethods.

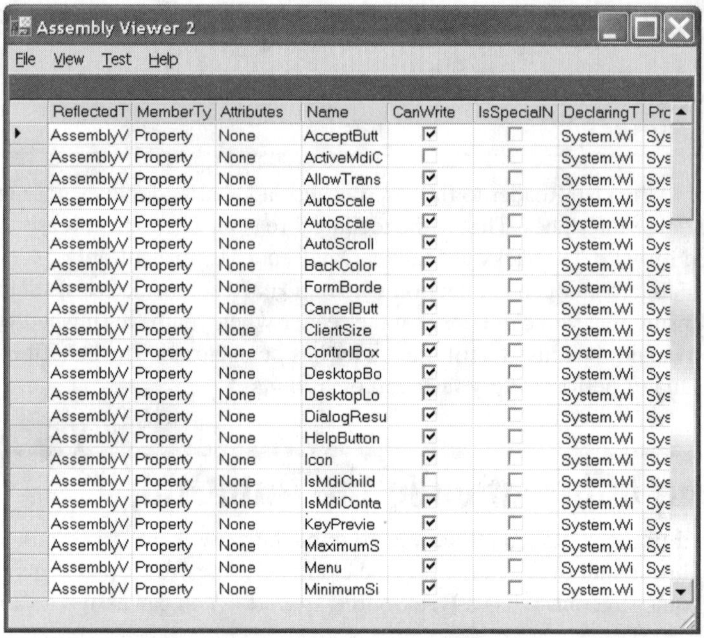

Figure 5-4   *A DataGrid that has been bound directly to an array of PropertyInfo objects*

Using the Command Object

Command objects are used to encapsulate SQL commands in an object. Use the SqlCommand for MS SQL Server providers and the OleDbCommand for OLE DB providers. Command objects store the SQL text that represents SELECT, UPDATE, INSERT, and DELETE statements, as well as provide you with an object for other SQL commands for particular providers. Examples of other commands include CREATE TABLE, ALTER TABLE, and DROP TABLE.

To create an OleDbCommand object, we can construct an instance of the object by passing the SQL text and an instance of an OleDbConnection object. The OleDbCommand object can be used as an instruction to an OleDbDataAdapter or directly to execute SQL commands that don't return a result set. Listing 15-4 provides an example of creating an OleDbCommand used to request a DataReader. You can look at that example and OleDbCommand objects created in the AssemblyViewer.sln for more examples.

One kind of command that we haven't looked at yet are commands used to create entities in a database. We can use an OleDbCommand and an SQL CREATE TABLE statement to add a new table to a database. The code in Listing 5-15 demonstrates how to create a table in an Access database. (You will need to vary the SQL slightly to match the syntax of the provider that you are using; the provider's user's guide is the best resource for specific SQL syntax.)

Listing 5-15   *This code demonstrates how to create a table in an OLE DB provider.*

```
const string connectionString =
  @"Provider=Microsoft.Jet.OLEDB.4.0;Password=;" +
  @"User ID=;Data Source=C:Temp\Reference.mdb;";
OleDbConnection connection = new OleDbConnection();
const string SQL =
  @"CREATE TABLE Constructor ([ID] COUNTER (1,1), " +
  @"[MemberType] string,[MethodHandle] string, " +
  @"[Attributes] string,[IsPublic] string, " +
  @"[IsPrivate] string,[IsFamily] string, " +
  @"[IsAssembly] string,[IsFamilyAndAssembly] string, " +
  @"[IsFamilyOrAssembly] string,[IsStatic] string, " +
  @[IsFinal] string,[IsVirtual] string,[IsHideBySig] string, " +
  @"[IsAbstract] string,[IsSpecialName] string, " +
  @"[IsConstructor] string,[CallingConvention] string, " +
  @"[Name] string,[DeclaringType] string, " +
  @"CONSTRAINT [Index1] PRIMARY KEY ([ID]))";
OleDbCommand command = new OleDbCommand(SQL, connection);
command.ExecuteNonQuery();
```

Most of the code in Listing 5-15 is the SQL text. (We'll see a better way to manage SQL statements in a moment.) The first statement is a literal connection string for the Jet OLE DB provider, including the Provider, Password, User ID, and Data Source clauses. The second statement creates an instance of an OleDbConnection. The third statement is a literal CREATE TABLE SQL statement that is appropriate for a Jet OLE DB provider. (Jet is the name of MS Access' database engine.) The OleDbCommand object is created by initializing an instance with the SQL text and the connection object. Finally, we send the query to the database engine with the command object.

The CREATE TABLE statement is specific to the database we are sending the SQL text to. The basic syntax is CREATE TABLE (*tablename fielddefinitions [fielddefinition1, ... fielddefinition(n)] constraints),* where the table name is a valid name, and the field definitions indicate the field name and data type and any constraints such as a primary key.

The CREATE TABLE statement demonstrates how to create an auto-increment column. The ID column described as [ID] COUNTER (1,1) defines an auto-increment column that uses a seed value of 1 and an increment value of 1. The CONSTRAINT [Index1] PRIMARY KEY ([ID]) defines an index named Index1 as the primary key based on the ID column.

Generating SQL with the CommandBuilder

Writing SQL statements can be a little tedious. There is an easier way to generate SQL with ADO.NET. Construct an instance of an OleDbCommandBuilder and initialize the command builder with an adapter that was initialized with a SELECT statement. The schema returned by the SELECT statement can be used to generate SQL INSERT, DELETE, and UPDATE statements.

Lines 18 and 19 of Listing 5-6 constructs an OleDbCommandBuilder with an OleDbDataAdapter instance. The command text used to initialize the OleDbDataAdapter was "SELECT * FROM METHOD". From the schema that can be read from the METHOD table, verbose instances of SQL commands can be generated. When you invoke the OleDbDataAdapter.Update command, the SQL created by the OleDbCommandBuilder is necessary to update the data source based on changes made to the tables in the DataSet.

Secondary Topics

You know how to create connections and use adapters to bridge data read via a connection into a DataTable or DataSet. These objects are seldom used in isolation. In your average application, you will be using ADO.NET objects in conjunction with visual controls, applications, and perhaps Web Services.

This part of the chapter introduces contextual ways in which you will use ADO.NET, including returning a DataSet from a Web Service. You can use the examples in this part of the chapter as a brief introduction to these subjects and explore the rest of the book for additional examples. Explore the sample applications that ship with Visual Studio .NET and the **www.gotdotnet.com** and **www.codeguru.com** websites as additional resources for more code examples.

Binding a DataSet to a DataGrid

You can bind data directly to a System.Web.UI.WebControls.DataGrid. The requirement is that the data must implement the IEnumerable interface. Data can be bound to a System.Windows.Forms.DataGrid control if the data object implements the IList or IListSource interfaces. The DataSet class implements IEnumerable, IList, and IListSource, which means that you can quickly create a user interface to bind a DataSet to DataGrids in Windows Forms or Web Forms.

These two fragments demonstrate how to bind a DataSet to a Windows Forms and Web Forms DataGrid.

```
DataGrid.DataSource = DataSet;
```

The preceding statement is all you need to bind a DataSet to a Windows Forms DataGrid.

```
DataGrid.DataSource = DataSet;
DataGrid.DataBind();
```

The preceding are the basic two statements necessary to bind a DataSet to a Web Forms DataGrid.

The DataGrid represents a specific instance of a DataGrid, and the DataSet represents a specific instance of a DataSet object. Additionally, you can bind a DataTable or any other collection that implements one of the necessary interfaces. For example, System.Array—which is the underlying type when you declare an array of any type—implements the IList interface. Hence, as demonstrated earlier in "Displaying Information in the DataGrid," any array of types can be displayed in a DataGrid. The public properties of the type of the object in the array will be used to create columns in the DataGrid.

Returning a DataSet from a Web Service

XML is an integral part of the .NET Framework. ADO.NET employs XML to manage data. The DataSet was defined with the SerializableAttribute. It is the SerializableAttribute and XML that support returning a DataSet from a Web Service. Listing 5-16 contains a monolithic Web Method (defined in the Reference.sln available for download from **www.osborne.com**) that dynamically explores the methods of the type passed to the Web Method.

Listing 5-16   *This code demonstrates a Web Method that returns a DataSet.*

```
[WebMethod, ReflectionPermission(SecurityAction.Demand)]
public DataSet GetMethods(string type)
{
  DataTable table = new DataTable("METHOD");
  MethodInfo[] methods = Type.GetType(type).GetMethods();
```

```
DataColumn column;
foreach(PropertyInfo propertyInfo
  in typeof(MethodInfo).GetProperties())
{
  column = table.Columns.Add();
  column.ColumnName = propertyInfo.Name;
  column.DataType = typeof(string);
}

DataRow dataRow;
foreach(MethodInfo methodInfo in methods)
{
  dataRow = table.NewRow();
  foreach(PropertyInfo propertyInfo
    in methodInfo.GetType().GetProperties())
  {
    dataRow[propertyInfo.Name] =
      propertyInfo.GetValue(methodInfo, null);
  }

  table.Rows.Add(dataRow);
}
DataSet dataSet = new DataSet();
dataSet.Tables.Add(table);
return dataSet;
}
```

Pass in the full namespace of a type, and the GetMethods Web Method will create a table based on the properties of the MethodInfo type. The properties become the columns of the DataTable. Each method's properties become the rows for the DataTable. Add the DataTable to a DataSet, and we can return the dynamically reflected type's methods.

It is necessary to Demand ReflectionPermission if we are going to use Reflection from a Web Service. Any code that is downloaded from a network is not guaranteed to be granted Reflection permission.

Implementing a TraceListener

The AssemblyViewer.sln defines a nested class that inherits from TraceListener. By inheriting from TraceListener, we can register an instance of our custom TraceListener

listener with the System.Diagnostics.Trace class's Listeners collection. The result is that our custom listener can catch Trace messages and display them as part of our presentation layer. (This is consistent with the Trace window provided with Terrarium. Refer to Chapter 4 for information on Terrarium.)

Listing 15-17 demonstrates a private nested TraceListener class added to the main form of the AssemblyViewer.sln, and we can use the main form as a TraceListener window to display Trace information while we are testing our application.

Listing 15-17   *Implementation of a custom TraceListener*

```
private class Listener : TraceListener
{
  private StatusBar statusBar;
  public Listener(StatusBar statusBar) : base()
  {
    this.statusBar = statusBar;
  }

  public override void Write(string text)
  {
    statusBar.Text = text;
    Application.DoEvents();
  }

  public override void WriteLine(string text)
  {
    statusBar.Text = text;
    Application.DoEvents();
  }
}
```

To implement a custom TraceListener, you need to override the Write and WriteLine methods. When we add an instance of our TraceListener, Listener, to the System.Diagnostics .Trace.Listeners collection, messages written with the Trace object are sent to our listener too. Based on the implementation of our listener, we store a reference to a StatusBar and display trace information on the StatusBar control. In effect, the owning form's StatusBar control becomes a visual Trace Window.

Rather than inventing new classes, we can find new ways to use existing classes. The .NET Framework is well organized but extensive. Before you write a significant amount of new code, leverage as much of the existing framework as you can.

Summary

Consistent with the general approach of this book, this chapter demonstrated several topics that you are likely to find in a single application. A large number of applications are database applications. ADO.NET provides advancements in database programming that are intended to promote scalability. You can use an older version of ADO with COM Interop—but once you get used to ADO.NET you will not want to go back in time.

This chapter provided an AssemblyViewer.sln that builds on your knowledge of Reflection to demonstrate how to create dynamic databases. Reflected properties were a convenient mechanism for accomplishing this.

After completing this chapter, you should have a good understanding of ADO.NET and an improved understanding of Reflection; you should also know how to bind data to the DataGrid control for Windows Forms and Web Forms and how to implement a custom TraceListener. This chapter also further introduced Web Services. You will find these skills beneficial in simple Windows applications, as well as in complex enterprise solutions.

PART
II

Tools and Components

OBJECTIVES

► Learn about the Visual Studio .NET extensibility model, including the Common Object Model

► Create Visual Studio .NET project templates

► Learn how to write bullet-proof applications with the System.Diagnostics namespace

► Use PerformanceCounters to track your application's behavior

► Create user and custom controls, including surface constituent controls

► Learn to use the ThreadPool for optimal control behavior

► Create a TypeConverter, a TypeDescriptor, and a TypeEditor, and implement an extender provider and IConvertible

► Add metadata to your application using attributes and create custom attributes

► Learn how to add controls to the Toolbox, including how to associate a custom image with your control

► Explore the .NET framework using Reflection

CHAPTER 6

Customizing Visual Studio .NET

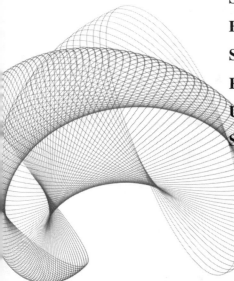

Microsoft has made a considerable effort in providing an automation and extensibility model for Visual Studio .NET. Automating and extending Visual Studio .NET to support common tasks is an optimal way to facilitate rapid application development. Tedious, highly repetitive, or monotonous tasks can be automated by creating wizards, add-ins, macros, or project templates to speed up development.

Macros are based on the Visual Basic language and are supported by a large extensibility model that lets you control every facet of Visual Studio .NET. Instead of trying to provide a reference manual for the extensibility interface, which needs its own book, I will demonstrate how to create wizards, create a custom project template, and write macros. As a result, you will have a practical tool for creating your own wizards—extensions to Visual Studio .NET—and a good introduction to the extensibility model for .NET.

Demonstrated Topics

If you find yourself performing the same tasks repeatedly, then you are ready for this chapter. An obvious task you and I perform regularly is to create a new project. Whether we are implementing a Web Service, ASP.NET, Windows, or Console application, we use the File | New Project applet to create a project based on an existing project template. One of the things you can do with Visual Studio .NET is create your own custom project templates. The steps for creating a project template are a bit involved, but in this chapter I will provide you with examples that demonstrate how to

- ▶ Create a custom wizard by implementing the IDTWizard interface
- ▶ Create a custom project template
- ▶ Register and test wizards
- ▶ Write macros in the Macros IDE

The secondary topics in the second part of this chapter demonstrate supporting topics. I will introduce Jscript.NET and how it is employed by the wizard engine that ships with Visual Studio .NET and how to use the regasm utility, which is necessary for registering assemblies in the global assembly cache.

Creating a Custom Wizard

Microsoft made wizards ubiquitous. Almost everyone that has used a computer has used a wizard. The term *wizard* as it is generally used refers to a linear series of dialogs that require feedback to create a desired result. Wizards are essentially linear subprograms. Prior to the early 1990s many programs were linear. When the Windows operating system and programming languages for Windows became commonplace developers began writing applications that behaved in a spatial way. Interestingly, we have returned to linear subprograms—wizards—because it is easier to limit user interaction to a series of linear steps in some instances. This is especially true when performing outcome-based, new, or difficult tasks.

For professional programmers, a *wizard* refers to writing an application or subprogram that supports a linear series of steps toward completion of a specific goal. Specifically, we accomplish this by implementing the IDTWizard interface. For a user, the mechanics of operating a wizard are simple, and for the most part involve clicking Next. For developers, creating a wizard involves some specific mechanics and requires a moderate amount of effort to synthesize the choices to simple inputs in order to get the wizard user to the Next button as quickly as possible. Fortunately, the Microsoft developers have made the mechanics of implementing a wizard simple, but, as always, the creative part is left to the individual development effort. Listing 6-1 provides a vanilla Hello World–style wizard as an introduction. Refer to the section "Extending Visual Studio .NET with Wizards," later in this chapter, for an example of a practical wizard.

Listing 6-1   *Inheriting the IDTWizard interface to create a wizard for Visual Studio .NET*

```
using System;
using EnvDTE;
using System.Windows.Forms;

namespace HelloWizard
{
  public class HelloWizard : IDTWizard
  {
    public void Execute(object Application,
      int hwndOwner, ref object[] ContextParams,
      ref object[] CustomParams,  ref wizardResult retval)
    {
      MessageBox.Show("Hello Wizard");
      retval = EnvDTE.wizardResult.wizardResultSuccess;
    }

  }
}
```

Superficially, a wizard is a class that implements the IDTWizard interface defined in EnvDTE. There is only one wizard method, the Execute method. Execute starts the wizard. What your code does from that point depends on the task you are walking the user through. Our wizard displays a message box and returns the enumerated value that indicates success. There are some more steps that we have to perform to test the wizard, which we'll discuss next.

Creating the Wizard Project

Wizards are created as class library projects. Use the New Project dialog (shown in Figure 6-1) and select the Class Library project template. Provide a name for the wizard and click OK. There are no special steps you need to take to create the wizard project.

Implementing the IDTWizard Interface

To implement the IDTWizard interface, you will need to add a reference to the envdte.dll assembly in the project references section. The EnvDTE represents the design time environment, that is, Visual Studio .NET's extensibility model. Add a *using* statement to refer to the EnvDTE namespace and indicate that your class realizes the IDTWizard interface. (Implementing interfaces and inheritance use the same notation, as demonstrated in the class header of Listing 6-1.)

TIP

Type **using** and then press CTRL -SPACEBAR to get a drop-down list of available namespaces.

IDTWizard has a single method that you must implement. The wizard will be initialized with the handle of an owner, an array of context, an array of custom parameters, and a return value. The return value uses the pass-by-reference parameter modifier.

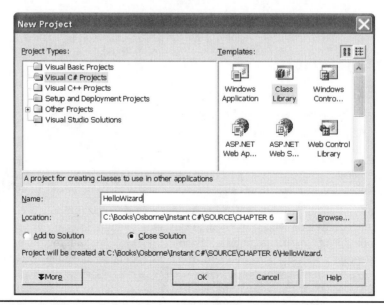

Figure 6-1   *The New Project dialog with the Class Library template selected*

Passing Arguments by Reference

If you want to return a single value from a method, then define and implement a method that is referred to as a function. Functions are methods that have a return type other than void. You can also use the ref modifier for parameters to return multiple values. Arguments defined with the ref modifier reflect changes made to those arguments by the caller. The ref modifier is equivalent to passing a pointer in C++, a **ByRef** argument in Visual Basic .NET, or a **var** argument in Delphi. See Listing 6-1 for the proper placement of the ref modifier.

Testing the Wizard

An easy way to test your wizards is to create a Macro that invokes the wizard. The Singleton object DTE contains a method, LaunchWizard, that will load and run a wizard. Refer to "Writing a Macro" and "Testing the Wizard with a Macro" later in this chapter, for an explanation of macros and wizard launch files. Listing 6-2 contains the macro code that tests HelloWizard, and Listing 6-3 contains text that you can put in a wizard launch file. (These listings are provided for reference. The rest of the chapter will describe the relationships and steps you need to complete to use these files.)

Listing 6-2   *A Visual Basic macro to test HelloWizard*

```
Imports System
Imports EnvDTE
Imports System.Diagnostics

Public Module Module1

  Public Sub Test()

    Const Path As String = _
         "C:\Temp\HelloWizard.vsz"

    Debug.WriteLine("This is running!")
    Dim ContextParams(1) As Object
    ContextParams(0) = Nothing
    DTE.LaunchWizard(Path, ContextParams)

  End Sub

End Module
```

The macro can be created by opening the Macro IDE. Select Tools | Macros | Macros IDE to open the Macros IDE (shown in Figure 6-2, with the code shown in Listing 6-2). From

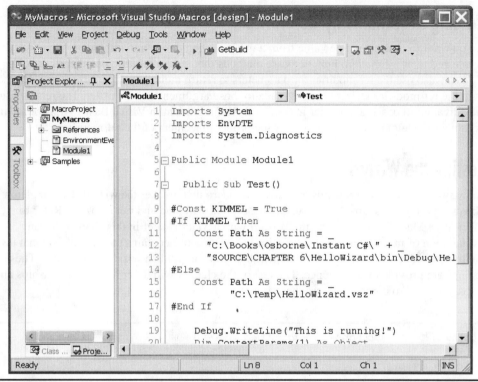

Figure 6-2   *The Macros IDE can be used to automate repetitive tasks without creating add-ins or wizards.*

Listing 6-2 it should be evident that you need to create a wizard launch file. Wizard launch files have a .vsz extension and are named identically to the class library containing the wizard that the launch file is associated with. Listing 6-3 contains the wizard launch file for HelloWizard.dll.

Listing 6-3   *An example wizard launch file for the HelloWizard.dll class library*

```
VSWIZARD 7.0
Wizard=HelloWizard.HelloWizard
Param=<Nothing>
```

The text shown in Listing 6-3 should be placed in a file named HelloWizard.vsz that is placed in the same directory as the one containing the HelloWorld.dll that has been registered with regasm.exe. Regasm is a utility that ships with Visual Studio .NET. Refer to "Registering Wizards" later in this chapter for more information.

Creating a Project Template for Visual Studio .NET Wizards

There are several project templates that ship with Visual Studio .NET that allow you to create projects like the Class Library project, Windows and Web applications, Web Services, controls, and add-ins. There is no specific project template for creating a wizard. As an introduction to project templates, we will walk through creating a project template that will show up in the New Project dialog.

There is a wizard—VsWizard.dll, in C:\Program Files\Microsoft Visual Studio .NET\ Common7\IDE\VsWizard.dll—that provides a basic engine for project templates. This generic engine uses specific sample files, scripts, and other input files to create a new project from a project template. Accordingly, we do not have to write a custom engine to create a project template, but we do have to create some specific files that the engine uses as inputs and some sample files used as templates to create a new wizard project. Our goal, stated as simply as possible, is to *create a new project template for Visual Studio .NET wizards*. Here are the steps we will need to complete to create a wizard project template, which I will refer to as a Wizard Library henceforth:

▶ Copy an existing template that is close to the new template we want to create. We will use the existing Class Library template because a wizard project is a class library or DLL.

▶ Add new template files to our template project based on the kind of template we are creating. To create a wizard, we need a .cs file containing a class that implements IDTWizard. We can use Listing 6-1 without the MessageBox as a template.

▶ Modify the templates.inf file that contains the list of files contained in our template project.

▶ Modify the common.js (Jscript .NET) source code that contains generic methods invoked by the vsWizard engine. We need to add code to create a specific class library project that contains a reference to the envdte.dll assembly.

▶ Modify the default.js script file that contains methods that are generic to our template project.

▶ Add an icon file to our project template.

▶ Modify the wizard launch file to make sure the vsWizard engine wizard is associated with our template.

▶ Modify the VSDir file to add our project template to the New Project dialog.

These steps do not have to be completed in any specific order, but we will approach them as defined. As you can see, this is an involved process (which I would like to see become much easier). However, this is an extensible solution and a generic one that supports any project template. Each of the remaining subsections will, in turn, describe each part of the overall process as listed, with explanatory details.

Copying an Existing Project Template

Project templates are represented by the icons you see in the New Project dialog (see Figure 6-2). They are much easier to use than creating a project from scratch using a text editor, although you could create a project from scratch with any text editor.

CAUTION

Different versions of Visual Studio will provide different project templates. Check your help documentation for the features available with your version of Visual Studio .NET. Professional developers should have the Enterprise Architect version.

The easiest way to create a new project template is to copy an existing one that is close to the new one you want to create. The closest one available is the Class Library template. By default, these files are installed in C:\Program Files\Microsoft Visual Studio .NET\VC#\ VC#Wizards. The Class Library template is represented by CSharpDLLWiz. To create the new derivative project template, follow these numbered steps:

1. Copy the C:\Program Files\Microsoft Visual Studio .NET\VC#\VC#Wizards\ CSharpDLLWiz folder and paste the copy into the same directory. (If you did not use the default installation directories then you will need to make the necessary adjustments.)

2. The copy will be named "Copy of CSharpDLLWiz" by default. Using Windows Explorer rename this file to CSharpDLLWizWiz to stay relatively close to the convention exhibited.

These wizard folders contain a Scripts and Templates subdirectory, each containing a language identifier. In the version I have, the language identifier is 1033. (I believe the language identifier is an identifier that represents English; non-English users will have a different identifier.)

The Scripts\1033 folder contains the Jscript default.js file containing script specific to our project template. Refer to "Modifying the Default.js Script" later in this section. The Templates\1033 folder contains actual files containing code that will be copied by the Wizard engine to create our new project. Refer to the next section, "Adding Files for the Wizard Library Template," for more information on this part of the process.

If you have a new folder that looks like the following example, then we are ready to continue.

```
C:\Program Files\Microsoft Visual Studio .NET\VC#\VC#Wizards
  CSharpDLLWizWiz\Scripts\1033
    default.js
  CSharpDLLWizWiz\Templates\1033
    assemblyinfo.cs
    file1.cs
    Templates.inf
```

Remember, these files were all copied from the CSharpDLLWiz, which represents the Class Library project template.

Adding Files for the Wizard Library Template

The Templates\1033 folder needs to be updated to contain files that we want in our Wizard Library template. We don't need to change the file names in use; hence, we don't need to change the contents of the Templates.inf . However, we do need to change the file1.cs file to contain code that describes a wizard template. Listing 6-4 provides the code for the modified file1.cs file.

TIP

Make sure you use the same file names. These are used by the Jscript functions, and your project template will not work if you change the file names without updating the script to conform to the new file names.

Listing 6-4   *Modify the template source file, file1.cs, to describe a class that contains an implementation of IDTWizard*

```
using System;
using EnvDTE;

namespace [!output SAFE_NAMESPACE_NAME]
{
  /// <summary>
  /// Summary description for [!output SAFE_CLASS_NAME].
  /// </summary>
  public class [!output SAFE_CLASS_NAME] : IDTWizard
  {
    public [!output SAFE_CLASS_NAME]()
    {
      //
      // TODO: Add constructor logic here
      //
}

  public void Execute(object Application, int hwndOwner,
    ref object[] ContextParams,
    ref object[] CustomParams,  ref wizardResult retval)
  {
    //
    // TODO: Add your custom code here
    //
```

```
        retval = EnvDTE.wizardResult.wizardResultSuccess;
    }
  }
}
```

The code looks almost identical to our example in Listing 6-1, except for the addition of replaceable tokens represented by SAFE_CLASS_NAME. Again, don't change these unless you are prepared to change the script files that refer to these values. I won't demonstrate this process, but you can probably figure it out by closely examining the supporting Jscript code.

Modifying the default.js Script

The default.js script file is defined in Scripts\1033. We only have to make a small change, but it is an important change. As you know, wizard projects need a reference to the envdte.dll assembly. We will need to load a reference to this assembly in new Wizard Library projects, so we will have to modify our script accordingly to ensure that this happens. This is a change that must be coordinated with changes in the common.js script file to work properly—and is one of the reasons I think project templates could use some work. (Refer to the next section, "Modifying the common.js Script," for information on coordinating changes.) Listing 6-5 provides the modified default.js script file.

Listing 6-5 *Modify the copied default.js file, making the small change indicated in bold face font*

```
1:   // (c) 2001 Microsoft Corporation
2:
3:   function OnFinish(selProj, selObj)
4:   {
5:     var oldSuppressUIValue = true;
6:     try
7:     {
8:       oldSuppressUIValue = dte.SuppressUI;
9:         var strProjectPath = wizard.FindSymbol("PROJECT_PATH");
10:        var strProjectName = wizard.FindSymbol("PROJECT_NAME");
11:        var strSafeProjectName = CreateSafeName(strProjectName);
12:        wizard.AddSymbol("SAFE_PROJECT_NAME", strSafeProjectName);
13:
14:        var bEmptyProject = 0; //wizard.FindSymbol("EMPTY_PROJECT");
15:
16:        var proj = CreateCSharpProject(strProjectName,
17:          strProjectPath, "defaultDll.csproj");
18:
```

```
19:          var InfFile = CreateInfFile();
20:          if (!bEmptyProject)
21:          {
22:            AddReferencesForWizard(proj);
23:            AddFilesToCSharpProject(proj,
24:               strProjectName, strProjectPath, InfFile, false);
25:          }
26:          proj.Save();
28:        }
29:    catch(e)
30:        {
31:          if( e.description.length > 0 )
32:            SetErrorInfo(e);
33:          return e.number;
34:        }
35:    finally
36:        {
37:          dte.SuppressUI = oldSuppressUIValue;
38:          if( InfFile )
39:            InfFile.Delete();
40:        }
41: }
42:
43: function GetCSharpTargetName(strName, strProjectName)
44: {
45:    var strTarget = strName;
46:
47:    switch (strName)
48:    {
49:      case "readme.txt":
50:        strTarget = "ReadMe.txt";
51:        break;
52:      case "File1.cs":
53:        strTarget = "Class1.cs";
54:        break;
55:      case "assemblyinfo.cs":
56:        strTarget = "AssemblyInfo.cs";
57:        break;
58:    }
59:    return strTarget;
60: }
61:
```

```
62: function DoOpenFile(strName)
63: {
64:   var bOpen = false;
65:
66:   switch (strName)
67:   {
68:     case "Class1.cs":
69:     bOpen = true;
70:     break;
71:   }
72:   return bOpen;
73: }
74:
75: function SetFileProperties(oFileItem, strFileName)
76: {
77:   if(strFileName == "File1.cs" || strFileName == "assemblyinfo.cs")
78:   {
79:     oFileItem.Properties("SubType").Value = "Code";
80:   }
81: }
```

The wizard engine was designed to use external Jscript functions, which is certainly a discretionary choice of the innovator. If you know Jscript, then the code is self-evident. There are four functions: OnFinish, GetCSharpTargetName, DoOpenFile, and SetFileProperties. These methods are invoked specifically when the Wizard Library project template is requested.

SetFileProperties sets a property to indicate that the two .cs files contain code. DoOpenFile is used to open the class module inside Visual Studio .NET, which is the file you will be interested in modifying, as it contains the implementation of the custom wizard. GetCSharpTargetName performs simple file name substitution. The only relevant change in our template is that file1.cs is created as class1.cs. OnFinish performs the substitutions for replaceable parameters in file1.cs and puts the project together, including adding references. The only change we needed to make was to substitute a call to AddReferencesForWizard on line 22. The original script file contained a call to AddReferencesForClass(proj),which is defined in common.js. We need to implement AddReferencesForWizard; we'll complete this step in the next section.

Modifying the common.js Script

Project Templates are separated into various pieces based on the shared wizard engine, a pre-determined folder structure, some pre-existing template files, and two Jscript files that interplay to create a new project template. I found this convolution of folders and scripts a bit unapproachable and not at all intuitive. As a programmer, I would prefer a unified approach that involved more programming and less interaction with external directory structures; this is one of the reasons I am describing it for you. I thought you might need a bit of help.

In the C:\Program Files\Microsoft Visual Studio .NET\VC#\VC#Wizards\1033 folder, there is a common.js Jscript file that contains script common to all project templates. We will need to modify this file to ensure that our project has the correct references. Listing 6-6 provides that the revised common.js file contains AddReferencesForWizard. (I didn't provide the entire listing because it is very long. Just add the code in Listing 6-6 to common.js.)

TIP

You are modifying files that are installed by Visual Studio .NET. It is a good idea to back up these files before proceeding.

Listing 6-6   *The revised common.js file containing AddReferenceFor Wizard*

```
/***********************************************************
Description:
        oProj: Project object
***********************************************************/
function AddReferencesForWizard(oProj)
{
  var refmanager = GetCSharpReferenceManager(oProj);
  var bExpanded = IsReferencesNodeExpanded(oProj)
  refmanager.Add("System");
  refmanager.Add("System.Data");
  refmanager.Add("System.XML");
  refmanager.Add("envdte");

  if(!bExpanded)
    CollapseReferencesNode(oProj);
}
```

The key is old-fashioned reuse: copy and paste. Copy and paste AddReferencesForClass and add the single statement that will include a reference to envdte, as shown in boldface. Our Wizard Library is very close to the Class Library template, which provides us with an opportunity for copy-and-paste reuse. Of course, if you are making an as-yet unheard of template, then you might have guessed that you have your work cut out for you. The final two steps are to create our wizard launch file and a VSDir file.

Creating the Wizard Launch File

We have already discussed the wizard launch file in the earlier section "Creating a Custom Wizard." In this instance, the wizard already exists, so we will be instructing the New Project dialog which wizard to use. The wizard launch files for project templates are contained in the

C:\program Files\Microsoft Visual Studio .NET\VC#\CSharpProjects folder when you use the default installation.

The Class Library project template wizard launching file is contained in CSharpDLL.vsz. In keeping with the exhibited extension, we will name our wizard launch file CSharpDLLWiz.vsz. You can start by copying the CShaprDLL.vsz file and pasting it to the same directory. Rename the file CSharpDLLWiz.vsz and modify it to point to our template directory, as shown in Listing 6-7.

Listing 6-7   *The wizard launch file for our Wizard Library project template*

```
VSWIZARD 7.0
Wizard=VsWizard.VsWizardEngine
Param="WIZARD_NAME = CSharpDLLWizWiz"
Param="WIZARD_UI = FALSE"
Param="PROJECT_TYPE = CSPROJ"
```

The only change made was to change the first parameter to refer to our Wizard Library folder. The first parameter is a relative path, and the other parameters provide conditional values for the wizard engine.

We are almost finished. The final step is to create the VSDir and test the project template by creating a new wizard project.

Creating the VSDir File

VSDir files are used to provide information to the Add Item and New Project dialogs to describe how items are displayed. From visual observation, you can get a reasonable idea of the contents of these files. In general, you need to indicate an icon and a name and specify the association between the applet in the Add Item and New Project dialogs and which operation is invoked. The VSDir file is provided in Listing 6-8. An explanation of the cryptic looking entries is provided after the listing.

Listing 6-8   *The VSDir file for our project template wizard*

```
CSharpDLLWiz.vsz|{FAE04EC1-301F-11d3-BF4B-00C04F79EFBC}|Wizard Library|
20|#2323|{FAE04EC1-301F-11d3-BF4B-00C04F79EFBC}|4547|  |WizardLibrary
```

The entry is made as a single line of text in the VSDir file that contains existing project templates items. By default, this file is C:\Program Files\Microsoft Visual Studio .NET\VC#\CShaprProjects\CSharpEx.vsdir. This is the same folder as the one that will contain your wizard launch file.

The entry is broken into fields by the pipe (|) symbol. Each pipe delimits a field. Table 6-1 describes the name and entry for each field in the VSDir file.

Relative Path Name	CSharpDLLWiz.vsz	Specifies the wizard launch file using a relative path. Store the .vsz file in the same directory as the .vsdir file.
{FAE04EC1-301F-11d3-BF4B-00C04F79EFBC}	CLSID package	A GUID representing a resource DLL. This particular GUID refers to something named the C Sharp Editor Factory.
Wizard Library	Localized name	This is the localized name of the template and the name that appears in the dialog (see Figure 6-3).
20	Sort priority	Determines the order in which elements are listed. A sort priority of 1 is the highest.
#2323	Description	A string or resource identifier containing a localized text description of the template. (The description appears in the New Project dialog—again, refer to Figure 6-3.)
{FAE04EC1-301F-11d3-BF4B-00C04F79EFBC}	DLLPath or CLSID package	Contains a GUID that refers to an EXE or DLL resource that contains icons for the template.
4547	Icon resource ID	Combined with the preceding entry, indicates which icon to use from the resource file. (We'll use the same one as the Class Library.)
<blank>	Flags	Bitwise flags, not used by our template. You can refer to the Visual Studio .NET help for VSDir files for individual flag values.
WizardLibrary	Suggested base name	Specifies the default name for the template. Our entry represents a project; therefore, the root name for Wizard Library projects will be WizardLibrary. The first new project will be WizardLibrary1, and so on.

Table 6-1   *Fields Used to Describe Entries in the Add Item or New Project Dialog*

The examples shown in Table 6-1 were used to describe our Wizard Library project template as it is shown in Figure 6-3.

To test the Wizard Library project template, select File | New | Project and pick the Wizard Library template, as shown in Figure 6-3. When you click OK, you should have a new Class Library project containing an assemblyinfo.cs file and a file named Class1.cs that provides a basic implementation for an IDTWizard. Make sure that a reference to the envdte.dll assembly has been added too. Now all you will need to focus on is the code that performs the automated task.

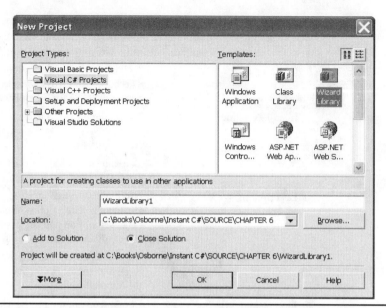

Figure 6-3   *The Wizard Library project template as described by our VSDir entry in Listing 6-8*

You might wonder where the project template comes from. I haven't mentioned it. Consistent with the entire process, there are several files that are shared. One of these is the DefaultDLL.csproj file. This file is shared by DLL project templates and is located in the C:\Program Files\Microsoft Visual Studio .NET\VC#\VC#Wizards folder, named DefaultDLL.csproj.

Creating project templates is more of a copy-and-paste and file management process than a programming process. However, if you want to automate repetitive tasks or simplify difficult tasks, then create a project template.

Extending Visual Studio .NET with Wizards

The benefits of wizards are that you can provide an easy way to do something that may be difficult for beginner-to-intermediate developers and you can automate certain tasks. By creating a wizard, you can make advanced aspects of .NET programming available to everyone on your team.

In this section I will demonstrate a practical wizard that automatically creates a strongly typed collection. A strongly typed collection inherits from either of the abstract classes ReadOnlyCollectionBase or CollectionBase. These classes implement IList, IListSource, and IEnumerable. The result is that you can create a collection that behaves like an array, can be bound to controls such as a DataGrid, and can serialize the collection into an ADO.NET DataSet.

The TypedCollectionWizard automates creating a strongly typed collection based on the System.Collections.CollectionBase class; creating a new module, a class that inherits from CollectionBase; and adding an indexer and an Add method to support serialization for Web Services. I will walk you through creating the TypedCollectionWizard, which demonstrates Visual Studio .NET extensibility. You will learn how to write macros and how to program against the Common Environment Object Model.

Writing a Macro

The steps for creating, registering, and testing wizards are the same as those described in "Creating a Custom Wizard." The skills that will be helpful include writing and running macros, general programming in C#, creating Windows Forms user interfaces, registering assemblies with regasm.exe, and writing a wizard launch file. For no particular reason, we'll start with writing macros.

Part of the automation and extensibility model is the support for macros. The Macros IDE is a separate project-based development environment. Macros are written using Visual Basic .NET. You can record interaction with Visual Studio .NET or write macros from scratch. You start the Macros IDE from the Tools | Macros | Macros IDE menu item in Visual Studio .NET. You already know how to use Visual Studio .NET, and the Macros IDE is very similar.

Open the Macros IDE. From the View menu select Project Explorer. The Macros IDE is project-centric, and macro projects are stored in files with a .vsmacro extension. However, you can import and export modules containing Visual Basic .NET code. To create a macro, select an existing or create a new module—source code file—and open it. Add a simple subroutine. (*Subroutine* is the VB vernacular for a method.) Place the cursor in the text editor on your subroutine and select Debug | Start from the Macros IDE menu. Listing 6-9 demonstrates a HelloWorld macro.

Listing 6-9   *A HelloWorld macro written in the Macros IDE in the Visual Basic .NET language*

```
Sub HelloWorld()
  MsgBox("Hello World!")
End Sub
```

As you might have guessed, this macro displays a message box and is equivalent to the static C# method invocation MessageBox.Show("Hello World!"). All of the macros from this chapter are available for download in a file named Module1.vb.

Such macros are useful for introduction only. A more useful macro might be one that adds a new class to an existing project. This is similar in nature to what we will be doing with the TypedCollectionWizard.

The macro in Listing 6-10 adds a new class to the active project in Visual Studio .NET. The argument "Local Project Items\Class" is literally a path in the Add New Item dialog if you string the command—AddNewItem—to the folder Local Project Items and the item Class. This might be obvious from Figure 6-4.

Listing 6-10   *A macro that adds a new class to an existing project*

```
Sub TestNewFile()
  DTE.ItemOperations.AddNewItem( _
    "Local Project Items\Class", "")
End Sub
```

The second argument to AddNewItem is the name of the file to add. If you leave this option blank or pass an empty string, then a unique and appropriately named file will be created. If you write code equivalent to that in Listing 6-10 in C#, you will need to pass an empty string. *Great.* The big question is what is the DTE? I will take a moment to answer that next.

A Brief Introduction to the Common Environment Object Model

I think of the DTE as an object representing the design-time environment. In the help literature, the design-time environment is referred to as the *Common Environment Object Model*, the automation model, or the extensibility model. A single, good name would be helpful. We'll just use DTE when referring to Visual Studio .NET extensibility.

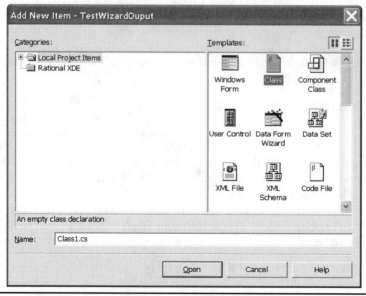

Figure 6-4   *The AddNewItem method requires the logical path to the item you want to add.*

The DTE is the root object that represents an object model that exposes the capabilities of Visual Studio .NET. (Visual SourceSafe has something similar, and so do many other Microsoft applications.) The DTE provides object-oriented accessibility to Visual Studio .NET using interfaces. This is commonly referred to as *automation*. You can get an idea of how extensive the Common Environment Object Model—the DTE—is by looking at the visual reference accessible by following the help link ms-help://MS.VSCC/MS.MSDNVS/ vsintro7/html/vxgrfautomationobjectmodelchart.htm in Visual Studio .Net. It is extensive.

Unfortunately, the DTE is so big that we would have a hard time scratching the surface without writing another whole book. (If enough letters get sent to my publisher, then such a book might get published.) Instead, we'll use a target approach to solve our particular problem and at the same time provide you with an introduction. The sections that follow demonstrate how to use the DTE from macros and C# code, which will provide you with a reasonable start. A good conceptual vision of the DTE is to think of interfaces that act as a façade that allows you to interact with Visual Studio .NET, including menus, documents, projects, macros, and the rest.

Writing Code with Macros

Earlier in the chapter, I demonstrated how to use project templates to effectively generate code. The wizard engine essentially uses existing code as a template and fills in the part that changes, like class names. However, you can use the DTE to dynamically generate new code on-the-fly. Writing code on-the-fly in a macro was a good way to test my approach to creating a C# code generator for the TypedCollectionWizard. Listing 6-11 demonstrates the macro I used to test the DTE's ability to generate code.

Listing 6-11   *Generating code using a macro*

```
1:   Public Sub TestWriteCode()
2:     Try
3:       Dim item As ProjectItem = _
4:         DTE.ItemOperations.AddNewItem( _
5:         "Local Project Items\Code File")
6:
7:       Dim defaultNamespace = _
8:         item.ContainingProject.Properties. _
9:         Item("DefaultNamespace").Value
10:
11:       Dim code As CodeNamespace = _
12:         item.FileCodeModel.AddNamespace(defaultNamespace)
13:
14:       Dim editPoint As EditPoint = _
15:         code.StartPoint.CreateEditPoint
16:
17:       editPoint.LineDown(2)
```

```
18:
19:        editPoint.Insert(DateTime.Now.ToString() + vbCrLf)
20:
21:     Catch e As Exception
22:        MsgBox(e.Message, MsgBoxStyle.OKOnly, "Error")
23:     End Try
24: End Sub
```

In summary, the code in Listing 6-11 creates a new C# code file, adds a namespace to it, and inserts some text into the namespace. Listing 6-12 provides an example of the output from running the macro in Listing 6-11.

Lines 3 through 5 of Listing 6-11 create a new C# source code file that contains no code and obtains a reference to the ProjectItem representing the file. (This is similar to the macro in Listing 6-10.) This source code file will be added to whatever project has the focus in Visual Studio .NET, but won't create a project. Lines 7 through 10 determine what the default namespace is for the project containing our new file, and lines 11 and 12 create a formatted namespace element (see Listing 6-12). Notice that we retain a reference to the CodeNamespace object. Just as if we were writing code manually, everything is context dependent. The objects returned represent the context.

Lines 14 and 15 of Listing 6-11 create an edit point at the start of the namespace. An edit point can be used to insert code manually, or we can use other Add methods (explore the FileCodeModel for available methods). Line 17 moves the edit point down two lines, and line 19 inserts some text representing our code. The result is shown in Listing 6-12.

Listing 6-12 *Code generated by the macro in Listing 6-11*

```
namespace TestWizardOuput
{
5/9/2002 5:12:23 PM
}
```

Clearly, if we can create a file, add a namespace and other elements, and write text directly, then it is possible to write code in this manner. The TypedCollectionWizard uses a partial template and the DTE to generate a complete strongly typed collection class.

Creating the Code Generator

A code generator can be created by factoring out elements of code that never change and using replaceable string parameters for elements that will change. This is the approach used by the wizard engine that creates code from templates, and it is the approach used to generate the code for the TypedCollectionWizard. Listing 6-13 contains the class that represents the template.

Listing 6-13   *The Wizard class represents the template code for the wizard-created typed collection.*

```
1:   using System;
2:
3:   namespace TypedCollectionWizard
4:   {
5:      /// <summary>
6:      /// Summary description for Wizard.
7:      /// </summary>
8:      public class Wizard
9:      {
10:        /// <summary>
11:        /// Parameter 0 is the class name; parameter 1 is the type name;
12:        /// parameter 2 is the optional setter; parameter 3 is the comment.
13:        /// </summary>
14:        private const string template =
15:          "  // Code generator by pkimmel@softconcepts.com\r\n" +
16:          "  {3}\r\n" +
17:          "  public class {0} : System.Collections.CollectionBase\r\n" +
18:          "  {{\r\n" +
19:          "    public {1} this[int index]\r\n" +
20:          "    {{\r\n" +
21:          "      get{{ return ({1})InnerList[index]; }}\r\n" +
22:          "      {2}" +
23:          "    }}\r\n\r\n" +
24:          "    public int Add({1} value)\r\n" +
25:          "    {{\r\n" +
26:          "      return InnerList.Add(value);\r\n" +
27:          "    }}\r\n" +
28:          "  }}\r\n";
29:
30:        private const string setter =
31:          "set{ InnerList[index] = value; }\r\n";
32:
33:        private string name;
34:        private string typeName;
35:        private bool hasGetter = true;
36:        private bool hasSetter = true;
37:        private string comment;
38:
```

```
39:      public Wizard(string name, string typeName, bool hasGetter,
40:        bool hasSetter, string comment)
41:      {
42:        this.name = name;
43:        this.typeName = typeName;
44:        this.hasGetter = hasGetter;
45:        this.hasSetter = hasSetter;
46:        this.comment = comment;
47:      }
48:
49:      private string GetSetter()
50:      {
51:        return hasSetter ? setter : "\r\n";
52:      }
53:
54:      private string GetCode()
55:      {
56:        return
57:          string.Format(template, name, typeName,
58:          GetSetter(), comment );
59:      }
60:
61:      public string GetTemplate
62:      { get{ return template; } }
63:
64:      public string Code
65:      { get{ return GetCode(); }}
66:
67: }
68: }
```

The code for the wizard is easy to follow. I will summarize. Lines 14 through 28 of Listing 6-13 represent the template code using parameterized values for parts that will vary from class to class. The balance of the code accepts the parameters as arguments and substitutes those values for the parameters on request—that is, when GetCode is called.

More important is strategy. By using a class for the wizard, I can test the generator without completing the wizard, making sure that the generated code is accurate. TestWizardCode.csproj, available for download, does exactly that. Assuming the name of the typed collection is Customers and it represents a collection of Customer objects, the wizard generates the class shown in Listing 6-14.

Listing 6-14   *Wizard-generated code*

```
public class Customers : System.Collections.CollectionBase
{
  public Customer this[int index]
  {
    get{ return (Customer)InnerList[index]; }
    set{ InnerList[index] = value; }
  }

  public int Add(Customer value)
  {
    return InnerList.Add(value);
  }
}
```

Listing 6-14 is, in fact, syntactically accurate code. Assuming you have implemented a class that describes Customer, then this code will compile and work correctly. The inherited code from the collection class allows us to bind typed collections to controls, enumerate the elements using the *foreach* construct, serialize Customers to a DataSet, and return Customers from Web Services. A pretty powerful combination and a common design pattern that the reader should become accustomed to.

The next step is to create a user interface that will allow the consumer to enter the values representing the collection and collected object type.

Implementing the Wizard User Interface

I shamelessly copied the Add Indexer Wizard from Visual Studio .NET. (In reality, I wanted the TypedCollectionWizard to look as if it belonged with similar wizards.) The graphical user interface is shown in Figure 6-5.

The code for the user interface is available for download in a file named FormWizard.cs. I will tell you about a couple of strategies I employ to make working with dialog forms easier.

User Interface Strategies

In general, I use property methods to access the value of controls. As a result, I refer to the data rather than the control; if I change the control, then I only have to change the reference to the control in one place. For example, here is the code representing the typed collection name entered in the TextBox.

```
private string ClassName
{ get{ return textBoxClassName.Text; }}
```

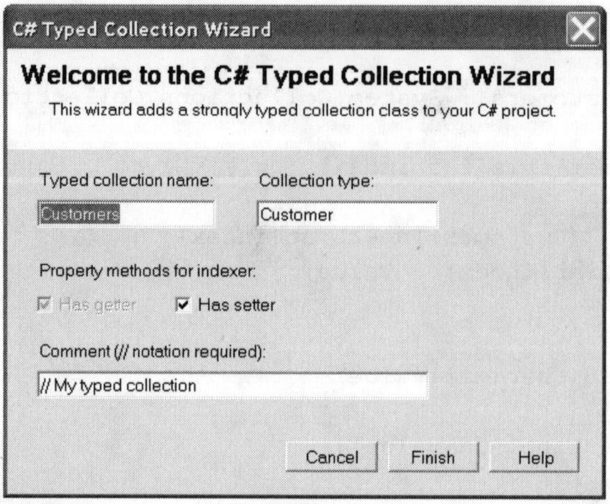

Figure 6-5   *The TypedCollectionWizard user interface*

If I changed the underlying control from a TextBox to something else, then I only have to change GUI code that refers to the value of the TextBox in this one location.

Another strategy I employ is to validate field input at the user interface and in the class too. This is based on the concept *G.I.G.O.*, or *garbage in, garbage out*, one of the first acronyms I learned in computer science. I employed regular expressions to validate input. A class name must be a contiguous string of alphanumeric characters, beginning with an alphabetic character. The following code confirms that this is the case:

```
private void DoValidateField(Control control, string value,
  string expression, string errorText)
{
  if( !Regex.IsMatch(value, expression))
  {
    control.Focus();
    throw new Exception(errorText);
  }
}
private void ValidateClassName()
{
  DoValidateField(textBoxClassName,
    ClassName, @"^\w$|^\w[A-Za-z0-9]+$",
    "Valid class name is required");
}
```

TIP

Refactoring is a methodical approach to improving the design of existing code, named by William Opdike and popularized when XP (Extreme Programming) was introduced.

The method ValidateClassName invokes a refactored method that accepts a control and three string arguments. The third argument is a regular expression. If the Text content of the control does not match the regular expression, then the control is given the focus and an exception is thrown. (Refer to Chapter 4 for more on regular expressions.)

Dialog Form Strategies

The FormWizard is employed as a dialog form. A strategy I use for dialog forms is to create a static method named Execute. The static method accepts the inputs and returns the outputs for the form. The form consumer does not need to worry about creating and destroying the form, only the inputs and outputs. The following short listing demonstrates how the FormWizard provides this service to a consumer.

```
public static bool Execute(ref string generatedCode)
{
  using(Form1 form = new Form1())
  {
    if( form.ShowDialog() == DialogResult.OK)
    {
      generatedCode = form.Code;
      return true;
    }
    else
      return false;
  }
}
```

The consumer ultimately will be the TypedCollectionWizard. The class that implements IDTWizard simply needs to invoke this static method, evaluate the Boolean return value, and work with the generated code.

If you are writing a Windows Forms–based application, you can use the same approach as shown in the preceding fragment. The alternative is that consumers of your dialog forms have to construct the forms, evaluate the DialogResult, and concern themselves with specific properties of the form. Essentially, you will have to duplicate the preceding code everywhere you interact with the form, which will make it at least twice as long as the code needs to be. Here is how you show the form based on the static Execute method.

```
string generatedCode = string.Empty;
If(FormWizard.Execute(generatedCode))
  // do something
```

The preceding is a very simple interaction between the form and the form consumer.

Implementing the Wizard

Because we have implemented the generator as a class and the form with a simple Execute method interaction, implementing the wizard is a snap.

If you will recall from the earlier section "Creating a Custom Wizard," all we must do is implement the IDTWizard.Execute method. Additionally, our wizard must take the code returned by the form and write it to a code file. Listing 6-15 demonstrates a means of implementing the wizard.

Listing 6-15   *Implementing the ITDWizard interface and completing the wizard*

```
1:   using System;
2:   using System.IO;
3:   using EnvDTE;
4:   using System.Windows.Forms;
5:
6:   namespace TypedCollectionWizard
7:   {
8:     /// <summary>
9:     /// Summary description for Class1.
10:    /// </summary>
11:    public class CollectionWizard : IDTWizard
12:    {
13:      // Implements IDTWizard.Execute
14:      public void Execute(object Application,
15:        int hwndOwner, ref object[] ContextParams,
16:        ref object[] CustomParams,  ref wizardResult retval)
17:      {
18:
19:        string generatedCode = string.Empty;
20:        if( FormWizard.Execute(ref generatedCode))
21:        {
22:          WriteCode((DTE)Application, generatedCode);
23:          retval = EnvDTE.wizardResult.wizardResultSuccess;
24:        }
```

```
25:        else
26:        {
27:           retval = EnvDTE.wizardResult.wizardResultCancel;
28:        }
29:     }
30:
31:     private void WriteCode(DTE dte, string generatedCode)
32:     {
33:       try
34:       {
35:          DoWriteCode(dte, generatedCode);
36:       }
37:       catch(Exception e)
38:       {
39:         MessageBox.Show(e.Message, "Error Writing Code",
40:            MessageBoxButtons.OK, MessageBoxIcon.Error);
41:       }
42:     }
43:
44:
45:     private void DoWriteCode(DTE dte, string generatedCode)
46:     {
47:        ProjectItem item = dte.ItemOperations.AddNewItem(
48:           @"Local Project Items\Code File", "" );
49:
50:        string defaultNamespace =
51:          (string)item.ContainingProject.Properties.Item(
52:          "DefaultNamespace").Value;
53:
54:         CodeNamespace code =
55:            item.FileCodeModel.AddNamespace(defaultNamespace, 0);
56:
57:        EditPoint editPoint = code.StartPoint.CreateEditPoint();
58:        editPoint.LineDown(2);
59:        editPoint.Insert(generatedCode);
60:       }
61:     }
62: }
```

By now most of this code should look familiar. Lines 14 through 29 of Listing 6-15 satisfy the IDTWizard contract. Instead of displaying "Hello Wizard," we display the form and write the code if Execute returns True. WriteCode manages the error handling using a *try catch* exception handler, and DoWriteCode generates the code file.

What may not be obvious is that the DTE object is passed as the first parameter to the Execute method; we cast the *Application* object parameter to a DTE object on line 22 of Listing 6-15 and use that DTE instance to create the source code file. DoWriteCode on lines 45 through 60 is almost identical to the macro code in Listing 6-11 and the explanation that follows. Instead of writing the date and time, we write the generated code returned by the Wizard class on line 59.

The automation model in Visual Studio .NET is powerful and vast. It is one of the aspects of Visual Studio .NET that make .NET a compelling choice for software developers and software development. Next, we need to test the wizard. We'll start by creating a wizard launch file.

Completing the Sample Wizard Launch File

The wizard launch file has a .vsz extension and is read when the wizard is loaded and run. The launch file for the TypedCollectionWizard is straightforward. We only have to provide a name for the wizard and indicate that there are no parameters expected. The following text is added to a file named TypedCollectionWizard.vsz and copied to the same folder containing the TypedCollectionWizard.dll.

```
VSWIZARD 7.0
Wizard=TypedCollectionWizard.CollectionWizard
Param=<Nothing>
```

The wizard engine does not require that you have the .vsz file in the same folder as the wizard DLL. However placing the wizard and the launch file in the same directory works easily.

The first statement is required and must be added as is. The second statement describes the assembly and the class in that assembly that contains the IDTWizard implementation. Subsequent statements are used to describe parameters that are passed to the wizard. Our wizard takes no parameters, which is what the Param statement in the launch file indicates. The next listing is the C# indexer wizard launch file, which works with the wizard engine. This file shows two parameter arguments.

```
VSWIZARD 7.0
Wizard=VsWizard.VsWizardEngine
Param="WIZARD_NAME = CSharpIndexerWiz"
Param="PROJECT_TYPE = CSPROJ"
```

You can pass whatever parameters your wizard needs. The style demonstrated describes values for the names WIZARD_NAME and PROJECT_TYPE.

Registering Wizards

Assemblies that are not added to the global assembly cache—the GAC, pronounced *gak*—but need registry information can be registered with the regasm utility that ships with .NET. To register the TypedCollectionWizard, enter the following command:

```
c:\winnt\Microsoft.NET\v1.0.3705\regasm
c:\temp\TypedCollectionWizard.dll /codebase
```

The path described is the default path for the .NET framework, specifically for version 1.0.3705. The directory c:\temp assumes that you are registering the wizard from the c:\temp directory. If you are using another directory, then substitute that directory in place of c:\temp. The /codebase switch stores the complete path using the file:// moniker in the registry. The wizard is not a COM component; it is the Visual Studio .NET application that is using the registry information to load the assembly. (Refer to "Using the regasm Utility" at the end of this chapter for more on regasm.)

I mentioned the global assembly cache in the beginning of this section. The GAC is a machine-wide cache for assemblies that are shared by many applications. Wizards are used only by Visual Studio .NET; hence, we don't need to add wizards to the GAC. The GAC is literally a folder-like repository that uses assembly metadata to ascertain differences between assemblies, thereby helping to avoid conflicts that commonly occurred with COM. You can learn more about the GAC from the Visual Studio .NET help documentation. .NET ships with GACutil.exe, a utility for adding assemblies to the GAC.

Testing the Wizard with a Macro

Having created a test application for the wizard user interface and wizard class, created the wizard, and created the launch file, we can use the macro from Listing 6-2 to test the wizard. After the *const Path* variable is replaced with the path information for the TypedCollectionWizard.vsz wizard launch file, the wizard can be run using a macro.

Visual Studio .NET supports adding a menu item or some other metaphor to Visual Studio .NET. You can create an Add-In that implements the IDTExtensibility2 interface and combine the IDTWizard interface to create a menu item in Visual Studio .NET. Refer to the "Creating an Add-In" help topic in Visual Studio .NET for more on Add-Ins and IDTExtensibility2. The IDTCommandTarget interface will let you run the wizard from the command window as an alternative option.

Running the Wizard from the Command Window

Now that we have a macro that launches our wizard, we can run the TypedCollectionWizard from the command window. Select View | Other Windows | Command Window to open the command window. If you created the test macro—borrowing the code from Listing 6-2— then you should see a list of macros as soon as you type **M** in the command window. I created my test macro in the MyMacros project, in a module named Module1, and named the subroutine TestCollectionWizard. Referring to the Macros object, the whole command becomes

```
Macros.MyMacros.Module1.TestCollectionWizard
```

Intellisense will provide a list of available commands, as shown in Figure 6-6, as I begin typing the word **Macros**.

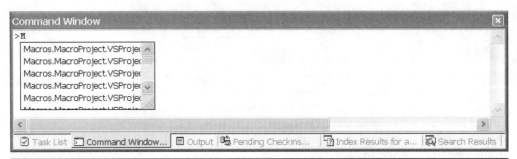

Figure 6-6   *Intellisense shows the list of available commands in the Command Window.*

TIP

*You can use the command window to access the automation model in Visual Studio .NET and initiate commands directly. For example, type **File.NewFile** in the command window to open the New File dialog.*

Secondary Topics

As you might have determined by now, there are several languages and utilities that professional programmers will have to become familiar with to make the most of .NET. This chapter introduced gacutil.exe, regasm.exe, Jscript.NET, macros, and Visual Basic .NET. We can't learn them all here. I learned how to use them over a dozen or so years of reading and experimenting. However, I can introduce subjects and point you in the right direction to help you pursue further interests (and sell more books for my publisher). To wrap up this chapter, I want to briefly return to Jscript .NET and the regasm.exe utility.

Returning to Jscript .NET

I briefly mentioned Jscript in the beginning of this chapter. Jscript plays a secondary role in the implementation of template projects. There is an external compiler that can be used to compile Jscript .NET code. However, Jscript is a complete language like C# and Visual Basic .NET. There is a tremendous amount of information on Jscript in Visual Studio .NET, and you can use the command-line compiler jsc.exe to compile Jscript code. Refer to the **www.osborne.com** and **www.amazon.com** websites for books on Jscript if you are interested.

Places you are likely to encounter script (besides when creating template projects) are client-side code for Web pages and ACT. ACT, or Microsoft Application Center Test, is an application that ships with the enterprise version of Visual Studio .NET. ACT is used to automate testing for Web client applications. You can write custom script or modify recorded script in ACT to test your Web pages.

Follow the numbered steps to write and compile a Jscript .NET application. (Jscript .NET applications must be compiled from a command prompt.)

1. Open Notepad.

2. Type **print("Hello World!")**.

3. Save the text as Hello.js, keeping track of where you save the Hello.js file, and close Notepad.

4. Open the command prompt (for old-timers, a DOS window).

5. At the command prompt, type **c:\winnt\Microsoft.NET\Framework\V1.0.3705\ jsc Hello.js**, including the path to Hello.js, if necessary

The jsc.exe compiler will convert the Hello.js source into an executable assembly Hello.exe. Enter **Hello** to run the Hello.exe application. The output should simply be the text "Hello World!"

Using the regasm Utility

Wizards are DLL assemblies that are integrated into Visual Studio .NET using COM. The most reliable way to register a wizard is to use the regasm.exe utility that ships with the .NET framework. The two forms of regasm.exe that seem to work the best are

```
regasm assemblyname /codebase
```

and

```
regasm assemblyname /unregister
```

The regasm part of the statement refers to the utility. The italicized *assemblyname* is the DLL assembly containing the wizard, and the /codebase switch adds the code base to the registry. Technically, the /codebase switch equates to the complete path information.

The second statement unregisters the wizard assembly. Before you modify and recompile a wizard assembly, you will need to run the second statement, passing the name of your wizard in place of the *assemblyname* value.

The wizard itself is not using COM. Visual Studio .NET extensibility relies on COM. Registering the wizard assembly allows Visual Studio .NET to load it. When you register an assembly with /codebase, you will get a warning indicating that you should add a strong name to the assembly. This will help avoid version problems. You can use the strong name utility—sn.exe—that ships with .NET to add a strong name to your assembly. This is a good idea if you are going to share the wizard.

To view the entries that will be written to the registry, run regasm with the /regfile switch as follows:

```
regasm assemblyname /regfile:regfile
```

Replace *assemblyname* with the name of your assembly and the second instance of *regfile* with the name of a file with a .reg extension. If you generate a registry file, then the entries are not written to the registry. If you experiment with and without the /codebase switch, you will see that the file:// moniker and path information are used when you specify the /codebase switch. Without the /codebase switch, Visual Studio cannot find the wizard.

Summary

So many great technologies and so little time. Just ten short years ago I recall writing my own interrupt handler for the hard error interrupt 0x24. This system error occurs when, for example, a user takes a floppy disk out of the drive while the disk is being read from or written to. Exception handling has supplanted writing interrupt handlers as a way to catch serious errors.

Technology is growing so rapidly that professional programmers will ultimately have to specialize. Like plumbers, electricians, roofers, carpenters, architects, general contractors, sheet rock hangers, roofers (and whatever other jobs there are for home builders), programmers will have to specialize too. In this one chapter we touched on three programming languages— Visual Basic .NET, Jscript, and C#—and a couple of utility programs—GACutil.exe and regasm.exe. Just as with other industries that have been around a while, our industry will lead to specialization. We are still dominated by a programmer-centric world, but specialties have been identified, and the complexity of software tools and the demands of customers will ultimately require our industry to train specialists. I specialize in object-oriented architecture using UML and OOP languages.

Interestingly enough, the need for specialists was well documented in Adam Smith's "The Wealth of Nations." Smith simply describes how specializing roles for pin makers—little pieces of wire with a point, used by tailors—allowed pin manufacturers to produce thousands of pins per day instead of hundreds. Smith's description is probably a major impetus behind the modern assembly line. Software tool complexity will ultimately force specialization and perhaps a form of assembly-line software development. Specialization is long overdue, but, fortunately, assembly-line software development is still a long way off.

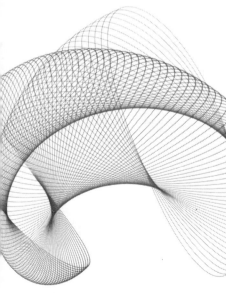

CHAPTER
7

Event Logger

Planning how you will test and debug your code is almost as important as how and what you write. A good UML model and design without an equally good testing-and-debugging strategy is like Batman without Robin. "Dynamic Solo" does not have the same ring as "Dynamic Duo."

When you are building applications you will need unit testing, white box and black box testing, a pinch of automated testing, and a good quality-assurance process. The first step is to adopt some basic strategies that will ensure your code will be great before it leaves your workstation. When a programmer tests his own code, this is referred to as *unit testing*. By incorporating test code into your production code, you can reduce the amount of time you actually spend testing because your code will automatically tell you when something is wrong. Including the ability to turn your test code off and on with a compiler switch is the hallmark of professionalism. Making it easy to incorporate self-diagnosing or tracking capabilities for you and others is how programming legends are born.

One of the first, best books I read on debugging and testing strategies for the C programming language is Dave Thielen's *No Bugs!* (Addison-Wesley, 1992). Thielen's strategies were instrumental to Microsoft in shipping MS-DOS 5.0. (DOS 5.0 is ancient history now.) Many of the techniques introduced by Thielen and others, like Gerald Weinberg, are still prevalent. Just a couple of years ago programmers had to contrive several good techniques because suitable ones weren't readily available. We no longer have to build debugging and testing code from scratch. The Common Language Runtime introduces a battalion of proofing capabilities in the Systems.Diagnostics namespace. When moderately employed, you can wipe out bugs. If you diligently and consistently employ some basic strategies, the bugs don't have much of a chance.

This chapter demonstrates several of the capabilities directly supported by the .NET Framework that will help you minimize the number of bugs that make it off your workstation.

Demonstrated Topics

There are many facets to the .NET Framework. .NET represents a phenomenal commitment by Microsoft to make a coherent and powerful framework for all of their development tools. If you explore any part of .NET you will quickly find that you could explore it for days. The System.Diagnostics namespace is one of these areas, and I encourage you to spend a lot of time in it.

This chapter begins by showing you some basic capabilities that you may be familiar with in concept, but that may be new to you in implementation. We will progress to capabilities that are brand new in .NET.

From the examples in this chapter you will be able to build better applications by mastering

- ▶ Using the EventLog component
- ▶ Logging to a remote computer
- ▶ Employing tracing as a debugging strategy
- ▶ Dumping and viewing the stack frame

▶ Managing debug code automatically using the BooleanSwitch and ConditionalAttribute

▶ Eliciting and responding to user input using custom dialogs

▶ Accessing FileVersion information

▶ Writing debug information to the Output window and asserting program invariants

▶ And, using the PerformanceCounter to keep track of your applications' use of resources

Exploring System.Diagnostics Namespace

You can easily find all of the classes, namespaces, and members of the System.Diagnostics namespace, so I won't list them here. (We would need another 500 pages if we started going down that road.) What I will tell you is that the Diagnostics namespace contains many more classes than the Debug class.

The System.Diagnostics namespace contains a complement of classes that allow you to attack risks to application efficacy on a broad scale. Like the Debug class, the Diagnostics namespace contains classes for tracing code behind the scenes and writing to the event log; debug attributes; switches that read from external configuration files and allow you to turn code on and off without rebuilding your application; and an army of performance counters. (The number and variety of performance counters alone could fill a book. Look at the performance counters in the Server Explorer for evidence.)

I will use specific capabilities of the Diagnostics namespace that allow you to provide a safety net for both Windows and Web applications. I will demonstrate how the Debug class writes information about what your program is doing behind the scenes, and how it ensures that basic assumptions about the state of a program are inviolate. We will use the BooleanSwitch class to read external configuration information that will turn our debug code off and on without rebuilding our application. We will use the ConditionalAttribute to let the compiler turn code off and on at compile time by automatically stripping out capabilities before emitting Intermediate Language (IL). We will review the PerfMon.sln that demonstrates how to use PerformanceCounters to track any application's use of resources. And, we will use the EventLog to provide a convenient place to store information about our application in a custom event log while building, as well as after deploying, applications.

Using the EventLog Component

The Components tab of the Toolbox contains several useful components. A particularly useful one is the EventLog component. The EventLog component can be dragged from the Toolbox into the Component Tray. By modifying the properties of the EventLog component you can quickly specify the name of the log you want to write to, the Source that log entries will be entered under, and the computer containing the log you will write to. The default log names are Application, System, and Security. Generally you will write log entries to a custom log or the Application log. If you enter a unique name in the EventLog.Log property, you can create a custom log file. (You can find the physical log files on your computer by searching for files with a .evt file extension. Generally, log files are found in the c:\winnt\system32\config directory.) Use the custom log if you will be writing a lot of entries to the log during testing. When you deploy your application, write to the Application log listed under a Source that identifies your application.

NOTE

Logs and Sources are listed in the registry under the key HKEY_LOCAL_MACHINE\SYSTEM\ControlSet001\ Services\Eventlog. You can modify keys directly, but if EventLog keys are incorrectly modified then some applications, likely important ones, may stop working. If you are going to modify the registry, it's a good idea to export a complete copy of the registry before you modify it.

The Source is a unique name that identifies the source of the log entries. When you specify the Source name, it must be unique across all logs. This means that if you specify a Source named "Demo" in the Application log, you may not define a Demo Source in any other log. If you want to use a Source in a new log, you will need to delete the Source from an existing log.

Writing to the EventLog

When you are building and testing your application, create a custom log and write as much information as possible to ensure that you are able to diagnose problems that might arise later. When you deploy your application, you will want to be more selective, logging only critical information. Remember, event logs are stored in files on your hard drive and both disks and files fill up.

TIP

The EventLog class has several static WriteEntry methods. It is possible to write text to a log by passing the Source and message to one of the static EventLog.WriteEntry methods without an instance of an EventLog component.

Whether you are writing to a custom log during development or to the application log after deployment, the process of writing to the log is identical. Set the Log, Source, and MachineName and invoke one of the overloaded WriteEntry methods. At a minimum, you can simply pass a string message containing the text you want to log. Supposing we have an EventLog component named eventLog1, we could write an entry to the event log with the following statement:

```
eventLog1.WriteEntry("test");
```

Assuming the component eventLog1.Source is set to the Application source, the preceding statement would create an event log entry that is very similar to the one shown in Figure 7-1. (Results will vary slightly according to the operating system, date and time, computer name, and other factors particular to the computer you are writing event log entries to.)

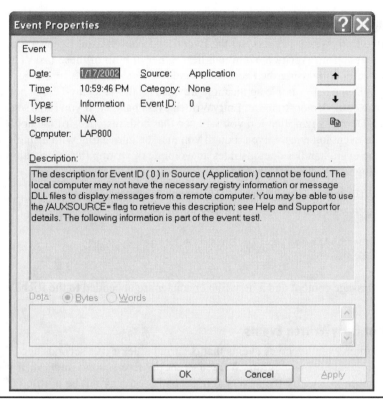

Figure 7-1   *An EventLog EntryWritten, specifying only the message "test".*

Handling EntryWritten Events

The EventLog component defines one event, EntryWritten. The EntryWritten event handler allows your program to respond to events written by your application or other applications as long as the event log entry is written on the local host. Events written to a remote computer will not be received by the EntryWritten event. This feature of the EventLog component supports writing a utility application that monitors the behavior of other applications.

The EntryWritten event is a delegate that receives two arguments: an object and a System.Diagnostics.EntryWrittenEventArgs. The EntryWrittenEventArgs argument contains an Entry property. The EntryWrittenEventArgs.Entry property is an EventLogEntry object that contains the information that describes the event. The EventLogEntry class contains information about the time an event was generated and written, the event message, the event source, and the machine name. You can use this information to monitor the health of an application.

Responding to Event Entries

To respond to EntryWritten events, set the EventLog.EnableRaisingEvents property to True and implement an EntryWritten event handler. Either or both of these tasks can be done programmatically or by using the Properties window.

The DebugDemo.sln example application provided on the McGraw-Hill/Osborne web site, **www.osborne.com**, demonstrates an EntryWritten event handler. If you run a second instance of the DebugDemo.exe application you will see that both instances of the application are responding to event log entries even though you may be interacting with a single instance. The following event handler demonstrates an example of writing the information being sent to the event log to a RichTextBox control.

```
private void eventLog1_EntryWritten(object sender,
System.Diagnostics.EntryWrittenEventArgs e)
{
  richTextBox1.AppendText(e.Entry.Message +  "\n");
}
```

The string Message content and a new-line character are appended to the RichTextBox text value.

Frequency of EntryWritten Events

The EntryWritten event receives events that occurred at least five seconds ago. This means that you will receive only one EntryWritten event per five-second interval. If you invoke WriteEntry more frequently than every five seconds you may not be notified of recent, written events.

It is my experience that you may receive several entries written at very close intervals, but not all of them. For example, suppose you write a *for* loop that writes 100 entries in succession. You are likely to get only a dozen or so the first time the loop executes and get the rest of the events written in the first loop the next time the log is written to.

TIP

To run the EventViewer on a Windows XP machine, open the Control Panel, click to open the Administrative Tools applet, and double-click the Event Viewer shortcut. You can also run an instance of the Microsoft Management Console (mmc.exe) and snap in the Event Viewer.

Of course you can use the EntryWritten handler for early notification of a problem with your system and query the event log for detailed information. You can use the EventViewer to find out more about the behavior of applications or use the EventLog component to write a custom querying tool.

Logging Events to a Remote Machine

The ability to log events to a remote machine can be an excellent way to look over the shoulder of a mission-critical application.

Suppose you are in a skunk works project—like a recent project I was working on in Oregon. You develop an application and hand it off to a testing group after you diligently unit-test your efforts. The testing group deploys the application in the test lab and begins running the application using automated tests, as well as letting users occasionally tinker with the beta product. By implementing the application using the EventLog component and remote machine logging, you can look in on your application from time to time without going to the test lab. If something does go wrong, you will appear clairvoyant when the testers call. More important, you will have an accurate picture of what was going on because this picture will have been illustrated by the entries written to the log on your machine.

By default, when you call EventLog.WriteEntry the entry is written to the local machine. The local machine is the default value, represented by a period (.) in the EventLog.MachineName property. To write to a specific machine, modify the EventLog.MachineName property to the name of the logging device; for example, FORD-4PBWU would instruct the event log control to write entries to the machine named FORD-4PBWU.

Tracing as a Debugging Strategy

For as long as I can remember, programmers have been using functions like printf (in C) to write debug information to a console to track what is going on internally in an application. This strategy is still an excellent technique to use to keep track of the internal operation of your application (kind of like cutting a portal in a cow's stomach to peek in on its digestive process).

With the wide adoption of GUI interfaces and Web applications it is often no longer convenient to write output to a console. The general strategy of tracing the internal digestive process of your application is still valid. Fortunately, the tools that support tracing the internal operation of your application have improved to keep pace with the kinds of applications we are building.

To this end, .NET has implemented a Trace class in the System.Diagnostics namespace. The Trace class writes output to a TraceListener, the Output window in Visual Studio .NET by default. You may also create an instance of other classes that inherit the abstract TraceListener class and instruct the Trace class to send traced messages to those listeners. (This is an excellent example of object-oriented techniques: the capability to Trace is separated from the recipient of the TraceListener.)

TIP

Write Trace information when you write your production code. This is when you will know the most about the exhibited behavior you are interested in.

One of the convenient places you can send Trace information is the EventLog. The EventLogTraceListener is subclassed from TraceListener and facilitates sending Trace information to an event log. Instead of contriving a mechanism for writing trace details, you can combine event logs with the tracing capability to follow your applications execution path down to the minutest detail.

Tracing to the Event Log

Tracing is the equivalent of writing a print statement that tells you something about your application's innards while the program is running. You can use a custom event log if you want to keep a record of trace information.

To use a custom event log to capture a record of trace information you will need an EventLog object, an EventLogTraceListener initialized with the EventLog object, and statements invoking the Trace.WriteLine method, for example.

Creating an EventLogTraceListener

The EventLogTraceListener interacts with an EventLog object to send trace information to an event log. To create an instance of an EventLogTraceListener you can write a statement like the following:

```
System.Diagnostics.EventLogTraceListener listener = new
   System.Diagnostics.EventLogTraceListener(eventLog1);
```

The preceding example assumes the existence of an EventLog component named eventLog1, and that, at a minimum, the EventLog.Source property has been set. Assuming you include the Systems.Diagnostics namespace in a *using* statement, you could shorten the preceding code to simply include the class name, as demonstrated next.

```
Using System.Diagnostics;
...
EventLogTraceListener listener = new EventLogTraceListener(eventLog1);
```

Registering Trace Listeners

The EventLogTraceListener is defined in the Systems.Diagnostics namespace. If you want to trace to an EventLog, the following code example demonstrates how to set up this relationship. (You can find the example code in the DebugDemo.sln sample application provided with this book.)

```
private void MenuForm_Load(object sender, System.EventArgs e)
{
   eventLog1.Source = "Trace";
   Trace.Listeners.Add( new EventLogTraceListener(eventLog1));
   Trace.WriteLine("Test!");
}
```

The preceding code assumes there is an EventLog component named eventLog1. The component only has the default information defined when you drag it from the Components tab of the Toolbox—that is, there is no Source or Log name, and logging will be done to the local machine. You must establish the name of a Source. If the Source does not exist, then the component will create it for you. The Trace class has a static property called Listeners. Listeners is a static read-only property whose type is defined as a TraceListenerCollection. To make eventLog1 a listener for the Trace class we can pass a new instance of an

EventLogTraceListener initialized with eventLog1 as demonstrated in the preceding code listing. The last statement demonstrates a Trace statement that writes the text "Test!" to the Output window and the application event log.

Dumping the Stack

Two more classes defined in the System.Diagnostics namespace are the StackFrame and StackTrace classes. These classes are used for a variety of purposes that include diagnosing your application. For example, an instance of the StackTrace class is defined as part of an Exception.

Using the StackTrace as a Diagnostic Tool

You may want to Trace and write unexpected exceptions to a custom event log. For further diagnosis, it might be helpful to figure out the order of processing that actually occurred in the event that something goes wrong. The Exception.StackTrace object can help you accomplish this.

To refresh your memory: When your program is running, the address of each method invoked is pushed onto the stack memory. When the method returns, the information is pulled from the stack memory. In this manner, the stack winds and unwinds perhaps millions of times when your application is running. At any point there are some number of frames on the stack that indicate the order of method invocation. You can use this information to diagnose your application.

The DebugDemo.sln contains a menu item Tools | Stack Trace that intentionally winds up the stack by forcing an infinite recursion—although we know it's there, so we catch the recursion before it overflows the stack frame—and catching the recursion by showing the stack trace (see Listing 7-1).

Listing 7-1   *This code simulates an infinite loop scenario and dumps the stack trace on an exception.*

```
private int i = 0;
private void StackWinder()
{
  i += 1;
  if( i > 50 ) throw(new Exception("StackWinder"));

    StackWinder(); // intentionally wind up the stack!
}

private void menuItem16_Click(object sender, System.EventArgs e)
{
  try
```

```
  {
    StackWinder();
  }
  catch(Exception x)
  {
    richTextBox1.Clear();
    richTextBox1.AppendText(x.StackTrace.ToString());
  }
}
```

When the Tools | Stack Trace menu item is clicked in DebugDemo.sln, the event handler in Listing 7-1 is invoked. The handler calls StackWinder, which intentionally winds up the stack by invoking itself 50 times. After the fiftieth call to StackWinder an exception is thrown, as shown in Figure 7-2. The catch block in the menu item click handler catches the exception into the object "x" and writes the stack trace to the RichTextBox. (This final step simulates tracing the stack trace.)

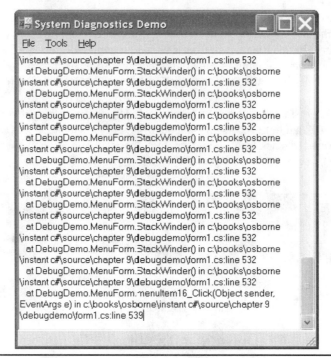

Figure 7-2   *The StackWinder StackTrace after the exception is thrown*

Using the StackFrame as a Diagnostic Tool

The following code fragment demonstrates how to create an instance of a StackFrame object for the current file and displays the file, line, and column information. (This output is consistent with each line of information found in a StackTrace.)

```
StackFrame f = new StackFrame(true);
richTextBox1.AppendText(f.ToString  () + "\n");
```

You can view the text contents of a StackFrame object to see the exact order of your code's execution.

Managing Debug Code Automatically

Tracing and diagnostic capabilities would be a pain in the neck if you had to write the diagnostic code, delete it before you deployed your application, and then rewrite it when your application goes into maintenance mode. For years, most programmers have been familiar with conditional preprocessor directives.

For example, wrap a conditional directive around code. If the directive evaluates to false, the code is removed by the compiler. C# implements preprocessor directives; thus the following directive would only allow the StackFrame example from the preceding section if the preprocessor conditional constant were defined.

```
#if DEBUG
    StackFrame f = new StackFrame(true);
    richTextBox1.AppendText(f.ToString  () + "\n");
#endif
```

If the constant DEBUG is defined, the preprocessor includes the code. If not, then the code is excluded. Visual Studio .NET provides you with a hint. If the code will be included then the code will be in color. If the compiler directive evaluates to False, then the code is grayed out. (The fact that this coloration occurs while you are coding suggests that the preprocessor is running while you are coding. Of course, the truth is that the VS.NET IDE is formatting code and providing Intellisense information while you are coding.)

The Visual Studio .NET IDE provides improvements over conditional compiler directives. The drawback with compiler directives is that you have to put them everywhere you want to conditionally chop out code, and you will have to recompile each time you change the value of the conditional constant. .NET supports an improved form of conditional compilation and switches, maintained in an external XML file. Using the switch class in an XML file means that you are able to turn debugging code off or on without recompiling your source code. We'll explore conditional compilation and XML switches in this section.

Conditional Compilation

Conditional compilation is managed by compiler directives. A compiler directive is a pragma followed by a value that is evaluated as a Boolean. For example, *#if* is the preprocessor conditional *if* statement. If token after the *#if* pragma evaluates to true, then the compiler includes the code between the *#if* and the *#endif*. If the conditional compiler variable evaluates to false, then the code is not included in the output assembly. The following code demonstrates littered conditional code.

```
#if DEBUG
   EventLog.WriteEntry("conditionally written debug information");
#endif
// ... Some more code
#if DEBUG
   EventLog.WriteEntry("some more conditionally written debug information");
#endif
```

TIP

Conditional compiler directives are case sensitive in C#. For example, DEBUG and debug represent two separate constants.

By wrapping the EventLog.WriteEntry statement inside a method, you can reduce the number of occurrences of preprocessor directives to one for each conditionally compiled block of code. Here is the revision.

```
Private void DebugWrite(string message)
{
#if DEBUG
   EventLog.WriteEntry(message);
#endif
}
DebugWrite("conditionally written debug information");
// ... Some more code
DebugWrite("some more conditionally written debug information");
```

Now you see that the conditional code exists in just one place: the wrapper function. Although this is a better solution, there is still a problem. Can you infer the deficiency?

Even when you deploy your application and undefine the DEBUG compiler constant, all of those calls to DebugWrite still occur. DebugWrite is now an empty procedure, but it still exists in the application. Microsoft has invented a better way of managing conditional code using attributes.

The ConditionalAttribute class will evaluate a constant. If the constant exists, the procedure remains. If the constant is undefined, the procedure is stripped from the IL and every invocation of the procedure is automatically stripped from the IL.

The ConditionalAttribute applies to methods. You precede each method with the ConditionalAttribute that should conditionally be emitted to IL and construct the attribute with a case-sensitive string to evaluate. If the string is defined then all invocations of the conditional method are emitted to IL. Undefine the string used to initialize the ConditionalAttribute and the invocations and the conditional methods are automatically removed from the assembly. Listing 7-2 contains an example that demonstrates the ConditionalAttribute. Figures 7-3 and 7-4 show the emitted IL before and after the conditional directive has been undefined.

Listing 7-2   *Using the ConditionalAttribute*

```
using System;

namespace ConditionalDemo
{
  class Class1
  {
    [STAThread]
    static void Main(string[] args)
    {
      HelloWorld();
    }

    [System.Diagnostics.Conditional("DEBUG")]
    static void HelloWorld()
    {
      Console.WriteLine("Hello World");
      Console.ReadLine();
    }
  }
}
```

You can clearly see the HelloWorld method and its invocation in the Main method in the IL disassembly. When you deploy an application, you change the Configuration Manager to reflect that you are releasing your code. This is accomplished by changing the Active Solution Configuration from Debug to Release in the Configuration Manager. One effect of changing the Active Solution Configuration is that the compiler conditional DEBUG is not defined in the Release configuration. Figure 7-4 shows the emitted IL when DEBUG is no longer defined.

TIP

CLS-compliant languages are allowed to ignore the ConditionalAttribute.

What's important here is that you can write all of the testing code you want without worrying that your assembly will suffer from bloat or method fatigue. Calls to conditional methods are removed by the compiler.

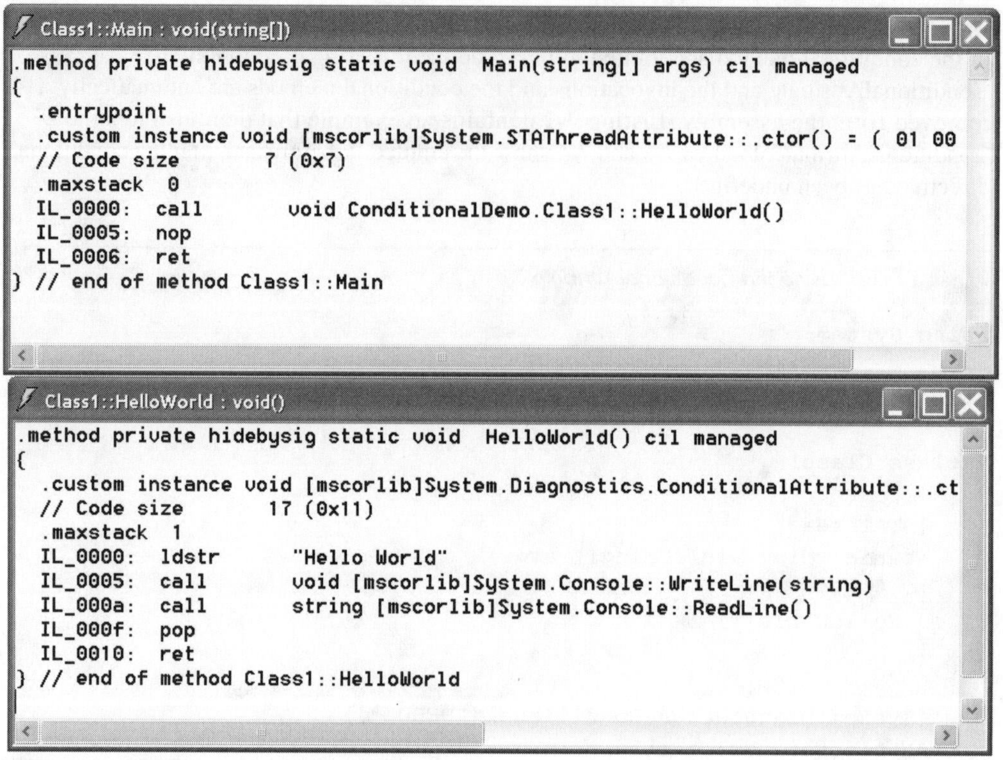

```
  Class1::Main : void(string[])                                         _ □ X
.method private hidebysig static void  Main(string[] args) cil managed
{
  .entrypoint
  .custom instance void [mscorlib]System.STAThreadAttribute::.ctor() = ( 01 00
  // Code size       7 (0x7)
  .maxstack  0
  IL_0000:  call          void ConditionalDemo.Class1::HelloWorld()
  IL_0005:  nop
  IL_0006:  ret
} // end of method Class1::Main
```

```
  Class1::HelloWorld : void()                                          _ □ X
.method private hidebysig static void  HelloWorld() cil managed
{
  .custom instance void [mscorlib]System.Diagnostics.ConditionalAttribute::.ct
  // Code size      17 (0x11)
  .maxstack  1
  IL_0000:  ldstr         "Hello World"
  IL_0005:  call          void [mscorlib]System.Console::WriteLine(string)
  IL_000a:  call          string [mscorlib]System.Console::ReadLine()
  IL_000f:  pop
  IL_0010:  ret
} // end of method Class1::HelloWorld
```

Figure 7-3   The IL as shown in ildasm.exe (an IL disassembler utility), showing the IL in the ConditionalDemo.exe

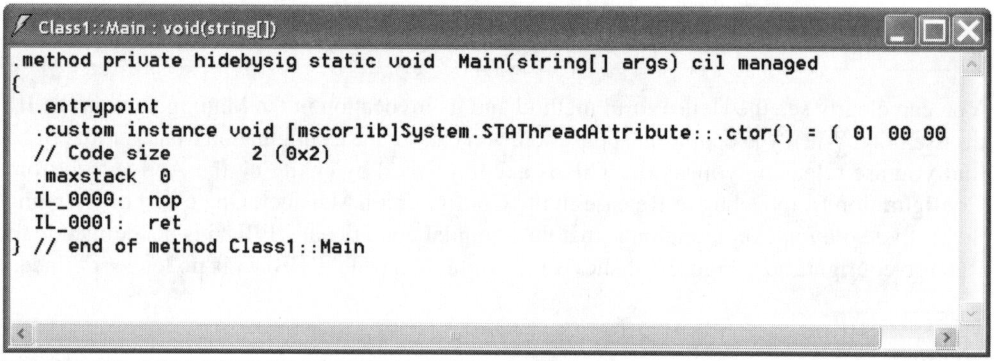

```
  Class1::Main : void(string[])                                        _ □ X
.method private hidebysig static void  Main(string[] args) cil managed
{
  .entrypoint
  .custom instance void [mscorlib]System.STAThreadAttribute::.ctor() = ( 01 00 00
  // Code size       2 (0x2)
  .maxstack  0
  IL_0000:  nop
  IL_0001:  ret
} // end of method Class1::Main
```

Figure 7-4   The IL as shown in ildasme.exe for ConditionalDemo.exe when DEBUG is not defined

Using Switches

The ConditionalAttribute is an improvement over plain preprocessor directives, but you still have to recompile your application to include or exclude conditional methods. There is a third choice, the BooleanSwitch.

A BooleanSwitch Example

The DebugDemo.exe sample application demonstrates using a BooleanSwitch to determine whether an EventLogTraceListener is created or not. Here is the code.

```
static BooleanSwitch booleanSwitch =
  new BooleanSwitch("MySwitch", "Test Switch");

private void MenuForm_Load(object sender, System.EventArgs e)
{
  if( booleanSwitch.Enabled)
  {
    eventLog1.Source = "Trace";
    Trace.Listeners.Add( new EventLogTraceListener(eventLog1));
    Trace.WriteLine("Test!");
  }
}
```

The first statement defines a static BooleanSwitch object, initializing it with the switch MySwitch. The BooleanSwitch in the example will look for a switch named MySwitch defined in the .config file associated with this assembly.

The Load event handler evaluates the BooleanSwitch. If the XML .config file defines a non-zero value for the switch, then BooleanSwitch.Enabled is True and the code in the example will run. The name of the switch is not case-sensitive. Any non-zero value for the switch will be treated as a True value.

Defining the BooleanSwitch in the .config File

You can define a .config file for every assembly. The configuration file is named the same as the assembly with a .config tacked onto the end of the file name. For example, our DebugDemo.exe application will evaluate a DebugDemo.exe.config file in the same folder as the assembly. Listing 7-3 shows the .config file that describes the BooleanSwitch MySwitch.

Listing 7-3   *Describing a BooleanSwitch in an XML .config file*

```
<configuration>
  <system.diagnostics>
  <switches>
```

```
<add name="MySwitch" value="0" />
</switches>
</system.diagnostics>
</configuration>
```

Similar to HTML, XML uses tag pairs. The opening tag is defined inside of a greater-than and less-than (<>) pair of tokens, and the closing tags include a forward whack </>. The <configuration></configuration> tags define the content of the configuration file. Configuration files can contain only one pair of configuration tags.

Implementing the Logger

Of course you can create instances of EventLog objects or use the static methods any time you need event logging. However, speed and robustness are achieved by building collectively easier and more useful chunks of code. For instance, we can wrap up the EventLog class and make a utility that is even easier to use than creating instances and defining sources. We will create the TestLog class library that has an easy-to-use interface and automatically creates and manages event sources. We can plug this class library into any application for which we want to create a custom log during testing.

NOTE

There is another motivation for wrapping up classes and components that are part of a specific framework. By putting a wrapper, or façade, around an existing component you can make it easier to use or exchange the code that implements the façade without adversely affecting clients. Façade is the name of a pattern that supports the concept of simplifying interfaces to classes.

The complete listing for the Logger class defined in the TestLog class library is provided in Listing 7-4. The code adds a façade to an EventLog object. Because the Logger class does not completely conceal the underlying EventLog object, it might be difficult to exchange the underlying implementation—that is, the EventLog. The EventLog is easier to use, though.

Listing 7-4   *The Logger class shown uses a façade to make using an EventLog easier.*

```
1:  using System;
2:  using System.Diagnostics;
3:
4:  namespace TestLog
5:  {
6:    public class Logger
7:    {
8:    #region Private Members
9:      private static EventLog log = null;
```

```
10:       private static EventLogTraceListener listener = null;
11:       private static string source = "";
12:       private static string logName = "";
13:       private static string machineName = "";
14:
15:       private Logger(string source, string logName, string machineName)
16:       {
17:         Logger.source = source;
18:         Logger.logName = logName;
19:         Logger.machineName = machineName;
20:         Initialize();
21:       }
22:
23:       private void Initialize()
24:       {
25:         Check();
26:         CheckListener();
27:         log = new EventLog(logName, machineName, source);
28:         listener = new EventLogTraceListener(log);
29:         Trace.Listeners.Add(listener);
30:       }
31:
32:       private void Check()
33:       {
34:         if(SourceExists() && !LogNamesEqual())
35:         {
36:           string name =
37:             EventLog.LogNameFromSourceName(source, machineName);
38:           CheckLog(name);
39:           EventLog.DeleteEventSource(source, machineName);
40:           EventLog.Delete(name, machineName);
41:         }
42:       }
43:       private void CheckLog(string log)
44:       {
45:         const string Mask = "Do not delete default log {0}";
46:         if( log.ToUpper() == "APPLICATION"
47:           || log.ToUpper() == "SYSTEM"
48:           || log.ToUpper() == "SECURITY" )
49:           throw(new Exception(string.Format(Mask, source)));
50:       }
51:
52:       private void CheckListener()
53:       {
```

```
54:        Trace.Listeners.Remove(listener);
55:    }
56:
57:    private bool SourceExists()
58:    {
59:      return EventLog.SourceExists(source, machineName);
60:    }
61:
62:    private bool LogNamesEqual()
63:    {
64:      return EventLog.LogNameFromSourceName(
65:        source, machineName).ToUpper() == logName.ToUpper();
66:          }
67:
68:    private static EventLog CreateDefault()
69:    {
70:      CreateNew("Logger", "Test", ".");
71:      return log;
72:    }
73:      #endregion
74:
75:    public static void CreateNew(string source,
76:      string logName, string machineName)
77:    {
78:      Logger drop = new Logger(source, logName, machineName);
79:    }
80:
81:    public static EventLog Log
82:    {
83:      get
84:      {
85:        return log != null ? log : CreateDefault();
86:      }
87:    }
88:
89:    [Conditional("DEBUG")]
90:    public static void WriteEntry(string message)
91:    {
92:      Log.WriteEntry(message);
93:    }
94:
95:    [Conditional("DEBUG")]
96:    public static void WriterEntry(string message,
97:      EventLogEntryType type)
```

```
98:      {
99:         Log.WriteEntry(message, type);
100:     }
101:
102:     public static EventLogEntryCollection Entries
103:     {
104:       get
105:       {
106:         return Log.Entries;
107:       }
108:     }
109:
110:         }
111: }
```

The Logger class makes the EventLog easier to use based on pretty simple reasoning. When you are building your application you are encouraged to write as much information about your application as necessary to help you eradicate bugs. When you ship your application, you will want to write critical information to the Application log. Otherwise, you might fill up the event log, which creates problems of its own.

A good strategy is to create a custom log during testing and write anything and everything that will help you hunt down bugs. The TestLog.Logger class was implemented with building and testing in mind. When I am building an application I simply want to log my trace information but not worry about creating unique source names or specifying a custom log. By writing the Logger I can automate creating and managing a custom log and ensure that the Source is unique across all logs. Each time I use the Logger, it will take care of this process for me.

The following sections define the steps necessary to managing a custom event log, and explain the things that are managed automatically by the Logger.

Creating an Event Source

When you create an instance of an EventLog, you need to specify the event source. The Source must be unique across all logs on a single machine. If you want to manually create an event source, you can invoke the static method CreateEventSource passing the source and log name or the source, log, and machine name. Here is an example demonstrating the method invocation.

```
EventLog.CreateEventSource("MyApp", "Application");
```

The preceding example creates the source MyApp in the Application log.

If you look at the Logger, you will see that we do not explicitly create the event source. (We do explicitly delete an event source, though.) The reason we don't create the event source is because the WriteEntry method will create a source that doesn't automatically exist. If the source already exists in another log then an exception will be raised. We do get rid of a conflicting source if one exists.

Determining if a Source Exists

SourceExists is a static method defined in the EventLog. Pass the name of a source to the method and you get a Boolean response indicating if the source exists. This method checks all event logs on the machine. EventLog.SourceExists is demonstrated on line 50 of Listing 7-4.

CAUTION

Don't delete the default Application, System, or Security logs. Deleting these logs may cause your computer to stop running. Another benefit of wrapping the EventLog into the Logger class is that I can codify the check to ensure that one of the default logs is not accidentally deleted. The CheckLog method plays this role.

If the source exists we use the EventLog.LogNameFromSourceName method to determine which log contains the source name we want to use and then delete the source from that log. The Check method on lines 32 through 42 in Listing 7-4 implements the source name conflict resolution code. If the source exists and the log name I want to use is not identical to the log name the source exists in, then the source and log are deleted.

Deleting an Event Source

You can delete an event source when you have finished with it or remove a conflicting source by calling the static method EventLog.DeleteEventSource. Pass the Source and MachineName, and the source will be removed from the Log containing this source. Line 39 of Listing 7-4 demonstrates how to delete an event source.

Deleting a Custom Log

When you have finished with a custom event log, you may want to delete it. Don't delete any of the default logs, including the Application, System, or Security logs. You may have a very difficult time recreating these log entries in the registry, and, as a result of their deletion, your computer may stop working correctly.

NOTE

If recollection serves, I invoked delete on the Application log to see if the EventLog would let me do it. EventLog.Delete removed the Application log. Fortunately, I had exported this branch of the registry and was able to recover it. It is not something I would recommend doing unless you are willing to scrap a machine configuration and start over. But Microsoft may have implemented safeguards into the EventLog since then.

The Logger deletes the log containing our source on line 40 of Listing 7-4 as long as the log isn't one of the big three.

Adding a Trace Listener

The Logger class automatically establishes my custom event log as a Trace listener, too. This occurs on lines 28 and 29 of Listing 7-4.

The net result of the Logger class is that by simply invoking one of the two static Logger.WriteEntry methods, a custom log and trace listener are established. If you carefully look at Listing 7-4 again, you will also see that the number of methods necessary for a consumer to use the Logger class is constrained to a couple.

The Logger class makes it easy to create and use a custom log while building an application and writing Trace information to it.

Secondary Topics

Explore the DebugDemo.sln example program and you will find several other features of the Diagnostics namespace demonstrated. The DebugDemo.sln demonstrates how to

▶ Implement custom dialog boxes

▶ Implement private constructors and when to do it

▶ Pass arguments by reference

▶ Use the FileVersion class (instead of Reflection) to create an AboutBox dialog

▶ Use the Debug class (along with a review of the Assert method)

Finally, we will look at PerformanceCounter objects. PerformanceCounters facilitate measuring your system's performance and use of resources. This can be an invaluable tool to have in your arsenal.

Creating Dialog Boxes

Dialog boxes are forms that are displayed modally to prompt users for information. Visual Basic .NET has the InputBox method, which is nothing more than a function wrapped around a form. The benefit of emulating this function-around-a-form behavior is to make it easy for consumers to perform basic operations.

The DebugDemo.sln implements an InputBox class that displays a single input TextBox. This form (shown in Figure 7-5) is used to query information from the user. The InputBox accepts a title, caption, and default value that describe the content shown. (The InputBox is modeled after the VB.NET InputBox function.)

If the user clicks OK, the form returns DialogResult.OK. If the user clicks Cancel, the form returns DialogResult.Cancel.

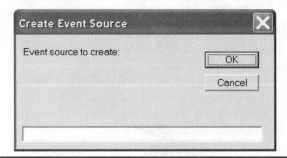

Figure 7-5 *A custom dialog modeled after the VB.NET InputBox function*

Dialogs Return a DialogResult

Dialogs return one of the DialogResult enumerated values. When you are creating custom dialog boxes you should enforce this convention. The Form.ShowDialog function returns a DialogResult value. All you have to do is ensure that the ShowDialog method is invoked and use a control that returns one of the DialogResult values.

The System.Windows.Forms.Button control has a DialogResult property. To create an OK button, type **OK** in a button's Text property and set the DialogResult value to OK. When the user clicks the OK button it will close the form and set the return value of the ShowDialog method to DialogResult.OK. The same procedure will work for a Cancel button.

Private Constructors for Dialogs

To make the dialog easier to use, you want to ensure that consumers invoke the dialog in a constrained way through the InputBox.Show static method. In this instance, Show is a factory method. To make it the only way to construct the form, apply the access modifier *private* to the form's constructor. As a result, only member methods can construct instances of the form. The following code fragment demonstrates this technique.

```
private InputBox()
{
  InitializeComponent();
}

private InputBox( string title, string caption,
  string defaultValue) : this()
{
  Text = title;
  label1.Text = caption;
  textBox1.Text = defaultValue;
}

public static DialogResult Show( string title, string caption,
```

```
      ref string defaultValue )
{
   using(InputBox form = new InputBox(title, caption, defaultValue))
   {
     DialogResult result = form.ShowDialog();
     if( result == DialogResult.OK )
       defaultValue = form.textBox1.Text;

     return result;
   }
}
```

TIP

The using statement demonstrated in the listing will ensure that the form's Dispose method will be called. Objects constructed in a using statement will be Disposed automatically at the end of the using block.

From the listing we can determine that there are two constructors, both having the same name as the class. The default constructor calls InitializeComponents. Without this constructor the controls on our form don't get created. The second constructor, also private, accepts our title, caption, and defaultValue arguments. The : this() clause instructs the compiler to invoke the default constructor, too.

Because both constructors are private, the only way we can create an instance of our form is through the public factory method, Show. This is exactly what we want. Because we want to test the DialogResult value for our Show method, we will need an alternative way to get the input value back from the method. We can accomplish this feat by passing the defaultValue by reference.

Passing Arguments by Reference in C#

If you need to get more than one return value from a method in C#, you can define arguments as reference arguments. The result is that changes to the reference argument will be reflected back to the caller. (Passing arguments by reference is similar to passing a pointer in C++, ByRef in VB, and var in Pascal.)

TIP

Two methods whose argument lists differ only by the ref keyword will be overloaded. Note that you cannot pass a property by ref.

The Show method shown in the listing in the previous section defines the defaultValue as an argument that will be changed by adding the *ref* keyword preceding the argument type (string) in the Show method. You also must specify the *ref* keyword when invoking the method. From the DebugDemo.sln MenuForm we can see how to invoke the InputBox.Show method.

```
if( InputBox.Show(title, caption, ref log) == DialogResult.OK)
```

Note the use of the *ref* keyword preceding the variable log. Methods can be overloaded by the presence or absence of the *ref* keyword.

Changes to arguments passed without the *ref* or *out* keyword area will not be reflected to the caller. Use of the *ref* keyword and changes will be reflected to the caller, and the *ref* argument must be assigned some value. Use of the *out* keyword and changes will be reflected to the caller, but the *out* argument is not guaranteed to be initialized. If you pass an Array by *ref* or by *out*, you are indicating that the array itself will be changed, rather than the values in the array. If you only want to change the values in an array, you do not need to use either the *ref* or *out* keywords.

FileVersion Information

The About form in Chapter 2 demonstrates how to get file version information from the Assembly class by using Reflection. Retrieving version information using Reflection gave us a convenient opportunity to introduce the Assembly class and Reflection. Fortunately, there is a much easier way to retrieve version information.

The System.Diagnostics namespace contains a FileVersion class that has properties that represent all of the values we might use in an About form. The FormAbout defined in the DebugDemo.sln demonstrates how easy it is to retrieve application information. (Of course you will still need to specify this information in the assembly attributes in the AssemblyInfo.cs module contained in your project.)

```
FileVersionInfo info =
   FileVersionInfo.GetVersionInfo(Application.ExecutablePath);
label1.Text = info.ProductName;
label2.Text = "Version: " + info.ProductVersion;
label3.Text = info.FileDescription;
label4.Text = info.LegalCopyright;
label5.Text = info.Comments;
```

The FileVersionInfo.GetVersionInfo static method retrieves a FileVersionInfo object from the file name passed to the method. As demonstrated in the preceding fragment, if you want to get the file information for the executing application, you can pass the Application .ExecutablePath property. When you have the FileVersionInfo object, it is simply a matter of querying the properties for the information you want.

One drawback to the FileVersionInfo class is having to match the assembly attributes to the FileVersionInfo properties. The FileVersionInfo names are not identical to the assembly attribute names. Table 7-1 demonstrates the pairings that you may find useful for creating an About form.

The AssemblyCopyright attribute embeds the © symbol into the attribute text. You can embed special symbols into strings by using literal values. The literal value for the copyright symbol is \xA9, the hexadecimal value A9.

AssemblyVersion information is generated automatically if you use an asterisk for the minor, build, and revision values. For example, [assembly: AssemblyVersion("1.0.0.*")]

Assembly Attribute	FileVersionInfo Property
AssemblyProduct	FileVersionInfo.ProductName
AssemblyVersion	FileVersioninfo.ProductVersion
AssemblyTitle	FileVersioninfo.FileDescription
AssemblyCopyright	FileVersionInfo.LegalCopyright

Table 7-1   *Correspondences Between Assembly Attributes and FileVersionInfo Properties*

will generate a version number 1.0.0 with the last value, the revision number, being generated by the compiler.

Using the Debug Class

The Debug class is defined in the System.Diagnostics namespace. Debug contains all static methods that facilitate finding and resolving defects in your application. The WriteLine method is used to write text to the Output window about the internal operation of applications, and the Assert method is used to enforce application invariants.

Writing information that shows the internal state of your application combined with asserting that predetermined assumptions remain true is invaluable to building error-free applications.

Writing Debug Information to the Output Window

Debug.WriteLine is used to write text to the Output window by default. You can combine Debug .Indent and Debug.Unindent to write formatted, hierarchical information to the Output window .Debug.WriteLineIf works similarly to WriteLine, but only writes information if a Boolean evaluation is True. The following demonstrates the WriteLine and WriteLineIf methods:

```
Debug.WriteLine("source deleted");
Debug.WriteLinfIf( EventLog.SourceExists("MySource"), "Deleting MySource");
```

If you call the Debug.Indent method, then debug information will be written with a tab preceding the text for each time you invoke Indent. Unindent will reduce the indentation by one tab each time it is invoked.

Assert Everything

The Debug.Assert class is used to enforce assumptions about the state of your program while you are building it. Assert enforces assumptions by suspending your application and alerting you whenever an assumption is broken. It does this simply by evaluating a Boolean expression. For example, if you write a conditional test to determine if an event log name is not "APPLICATION" then you can use the same test for the assertion. The *if* conditional check is to make sure your code behaves correctly, and the assertion is combined to tell you, the developer, while you are unit testing if the test ever fails.

```
Debug.Assert( log.ToUpper() != "APPLICATION");
```

The technique is to combine assertions with your conditional logic. The conditional logic is for deployment and the assertion that matches is for debugging. For example, if you as the programmer want to be notified whenever the Logger attempts to delete one of the default logs, then you could write an assertion that makes sure that you are notified. Modifying the Logger.CheckLog method we could add an assertion that tells us if the log is the Application log.

```
private void CheckLog(string log)
{
  const string Mask = "Do not delete default log {0}";

  Debug.Assert(log.ToUpper() != "APPLICATION");
  if( log.ToUpper() == "APPLICATION"
    || log.ToUpper() == "SYSTEM"
    || log.ToUpper() == "SECURITY" )
    throw(new Exception(string.Format(Mask, source)));
}
```

A Brief History of Debugging Tools

The Assert capability is one of the oldest and best programmer tricks around. Capabilities like asserting are built into the operating system. The operating system BIOS loads functions that provide basic system capabilities. These capabilities—such as printing to the screen, writing to the video buffer, or managing mouse behavior—are referred to as *interrupts*.

One of the lowest numbered interrupts—presumably one of the first—is the interrupt 3, the debug or "soft-ice" interrupt. Interrupt 3 suspends an application's execution, putting the application in debug mode. The earliest programmers—in the case of MS-DOS Tim Paterson, Bill Gates, and Paul Allen—needed debugging tools.

You can still use assembly language and the debug interrupt with tools that support assembly language programming. The following script is an assembly language version of the Hello World! application. The program can be written using the debug.exe program at the command line and following each instruction below at a command window.

```
debug
a100
jmp 110
db "Hello, World$"
mov dx,102
mov ah,9
int 3
```

```
int 21
int 20
<return>
rcx
1a
w
g
```

The lines between the instruction a100 and the <return> constitute the assembly code. The instruction a100 means assemble at offset 100 (hexadecimal). The instruction jmp 110 is like a goto statement, db is string pointer, mov dx,102 points the data register dx at the string "Hello, World!$", and $ is the string terminator. Mov ah,9 moves function 9 into the ah register, and interrupt 21 (function 9) runs the print string function loaded by the operating system. If you run this program with the g(go) instruction inside the debugger, then the program will stop at the instruction int 3, the debug interrupt and dump the state of the CPU up to that point.

The hello.com program is included with this book's source code on the McGraw-Hill/Osborne web site, **www.osborne.com**. The point of this discourse is that debugging tools are among the oldest and most long-lived—and for good reason.

If the log names the Application log, then execution will slow way down, allowing you to assess this potentially critical situation. The dialog in Figure 7-6 will be displayed, providing you with an opportunity to Abort, Retry, or Ignore the assertion failure. In this particular instance, you can step through the method and make sure that the exception will be thrown.

If you click Abort, execution will terminate. If you click Retry, the application will break at the next line after the assertion, and you can slowly step through the code or evaluate why things went awry. The Ignore button will instruct the application to continue processing and ignore the assertion.

Enabling and Disabling the Debug Class

If you had to add and remove the Debug code each time the application was modified and deployed, using the Debug class would require a lot of extra work. However, if you write your debug code when you are writing the production code, you will have the greatest awareness about assumptions you are making about the state of your application at a given moment.

When the Configuration Manager is configured for a Debug release the DEBUG conditional compiler constant will be defined and the Debug code will run. When you change the configuration to Release, the DEBUG constant will be undefined and the Debug code will become noop code—that is, the Debug code will automatically be disabled.

Leave your Debug code in place even when you ship your application and use the conditional compiler constant DEBUG to toggle the Debug code off and on.

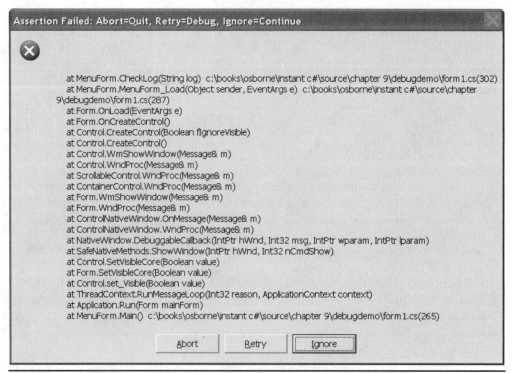

Figure 7-6   *The Abort, Retry, Ignore dialog is displayed when an assertion fails.*

Measuring Performance

The PerformanceCounter class is defined in the System.Diagnostics namespace. Performance counters are associated with performance objects by category. PerformanceCounters allow you to track resource usage, including things like memory, physical disks, CPUs, and threads. (If you look in the Server Explorer—not available in the standard edition of Visual Studio .NET—you will see that there are hundreds of performance objects that can be measured.)

You can use PerformanceCounters by dragging a counter from the Server Explorer onto your application. Just as the Server Explorer can list multiple servers you can select PerformanceCounters from other servers.

The following steps will demonstrate one example of using a LogicalDisk PerformanceCounter to track and display the available disk space on the C: drive.

1. In Visual Studio .NET select the View | Server Explorer menu option.
2. Select the server name representing your PC and expand the server tree node.
3. Expand the PerformanceCounters node until and find the LogicalDisk tree node. (The performance counters are listed by category in alphabetical order.)
4. Expand the LogicalDisk node and the subordinate FreeSpace node (see Figure 7-7).

5. Drag the C: drive performance object onto the Component Tray for the form that you
    want to contain the reference to the counter.

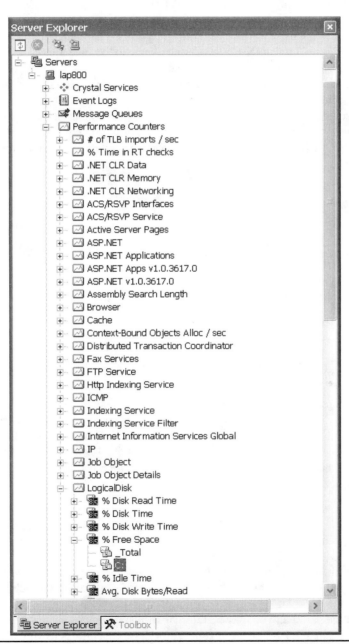

Figure 7-7   *The Server Explorer expanded to the C: drive performance object*

Dragging the performance object from the Server Explorer configures the performance object correctly. Of course, you can create an instance of the PerformanceCounter programmatically and initialize the properties to indicate the performance object you want to track. You will need to manually create a PerformanceCounter if you are creating an assembly that does not have a form. To configure this PerformanceCounter manually set the CategoryName to "LogicalDisk", the CounterName to "% Free Space", the InstanceName to "C:", and the MachineName to your computer's name.

When the PerformanceCounter is configured we can query the counter for present measured values. The DebugDemo.sln demonstrates the percent free space counter by querying the available space on the Application.Idle event. (Application.Idle is an event that fires when your application isn't actively doing anything.) The Form_Load event is used to attach an OnIdle event handler to the Application.Idle event. The code listing to read the free space value and display it in a StatusBar follows.

```
private float GetFreeSpace()
{
  return (float)performanceCounter1.RawValue / 1024;
}

private string GetFreeSpaceString()
{
  const string Mask = "Free Space C: {0:f} GB";
  return string.Format(Mask, GetFreeSpace());
}

private void OnIdle(object sender, System.EventArgs e)
{
  statusBar1.Text = GetFreeSpaceString();
}
```

The PerformanceCounter value is read from the RawValue property. GetFreeSpace converts the value to a decimal representing a multiple of kilobytes. GetFreeSpaceString formats the value, embedding the decimal in a string, and appends the correct scalar. The RawValue for the LogicalDisk category is thousands, and the multiple is millions. By dividing the raw value by 1,024, the multiple becomes 1,024×1,000,000, or a gigabyte.

For an advanced example demonstrating the capabilities of PerformanceCounters, check out the PerfMon.sln that ships with the .NET samples.

Summary

This chapter demonstrates how to use classes in the System.Diagnostics to write debug information, employ assertions, and trace and write information about the vitality of your application to the event log. If you have programmed with VB6 or the Windows API extensively in the past then you may be familiar with some of these capabilities.

A new feature in .NET is enhanced support for these capabilities as well as the ability to view a stack trace or peek in on information in the stack frame at any particular time. Combine all of these capabilities with FileVersion information and the hundreds of PerformanceCounters, and you can obtain a detailed picture of your application and its use of resources.

Creating UserControls

IN THIS CHAPTER:

Extending the .NET framework by creating new classes and custom controls is one of the most effective and enjoyable activities that programmers can participate in.

The UserControl class is a control that contains a drawing surface, like a form, that allows you to design composite controls in the Forms Designer for Windows Forms and ASP.NET. Rather than using code to design a control based on a graphical user interface, you can use the same RAD approach that has existed in Visual Basic for years and visually design reusable controls.

When designing UserControls, you perform the same activities that you would perform when designing a form. Drag and drop controls onto the form, generate the event handlers, modify properties, and implement new methods. The only noteworthy difference between designing forms and UserControls is that forms are generally designed for end users and UserControls are designed for both end users and other developers—that is, your UserControls will appear on forms and in the Toolbox. The last bit of information suggests that if we want to build reusable UserControls then we need to make them general enough so they are not too dependent on a specific application.

This chapter will demonstrate how to use the Forms Designer to design UserControls for Windows Forms applications and how to make those controls reusable.

Demonstrated Topics

There are several aspects that you need to know about to build usable UserControls. As mentioned, UserControls are very similar to forms in design and use. This means that your user controls will contain constituent controls, and those constituent controls will have properties and events that you may want to expose to UserControl consumers. Additionally, you may want to perform custom painting and binding data to UserControls.

From examples in this chapter, you will be able to do the following:

▶   Implement UserControls

▶   Surface constituent control properties and events

▶   Perform custom painting in user controls

▶   Bind data to UserControls using ADO.NET and objects that implement
    the IList interface

Understanding UserControls

There are three basic strategies for implementing custom controls in C#. You can inherit from the Control class to have the ultimate flexibility but the most amount of work. You can implement from a control that is closer to the new one that you want to make, resulting in less flexibility and less work. For instance, if you want to make a label control that has special effects, you could inherit from System.Windows.Forms.Label. Finally, if you want to make a control that is composed of several visual elements, then the best way to do it is to create a UserControl.

This chapter will demonstrate how to create UserControls, and Chapter 9 will demonstrate how to build custom controls from scratch.

What Is a UserControl?

In the .NET Framework, UserControls are defined in the System.Windows.Forms and System.Web.UI namespaces. For our purposes, we are referring to the System.Windows.Forms.UserControl. UserControls inherit from ContainerControl, which in turn inherits from ScrollableControl, which itself inherits from the Control Class. If you look at the .NET Framework, you will note that this is exactly the same ancestry as a Windows Form.

When you are designing a UserControl you will perform the same activities that you perform when designing a Form. Like Forms, UserControls contain other controls referred to as *constituent controls*. A UserControl has a graphical user interface, as do Forms, and usually contains many constituent controls to make up part of a whole solution. For example, you might implement a UserControl with basic contact information and incorporate that control into a contact management form. (Refer to the section "Defining a Data Bound UserControl" later in this chapter.)

GUI Is King

I mean this in the best possible way: the more I see Windows application GUIs implemented by programmers, the more I am convinced graphics artists should render them first and then the programmers should figure out the technological challenges. (Alan Cooper refers to the problems arising from left-brained programmers designing software for a right-brained world in *The Inmates are Running the Asylum*. We programmers are the inmates he is referring to.)

There are several strategies that you can employ when designing the visual aspect of UserControls:

▶ You can get great background graphics and make your controls semi-transparent.

▶ You can get a right-brained person or graphic artist to design some basic visuals for you, and then you can create a standard set of UserControls that you can use over and over again.

▶ You can layer controls to create the effect of both depth and richness, mirroring some of the better-looking software that exists. (There are some good-looking applications that you can borrow from to get you started.)

Unfortunately, I have not been very successful at getting customers to hire artists to design interfaces and have had to rely on the last method more than I would have liked. (I am hopeful that, by writing here that GUIs could be rendered nicely by real artists, someone will adopt that approach.)

Assuming you must rely on *trichromacy*—three colors—and symmetry to create your graphical user interfaces, then at least you can depend on UserControls to facilitate consistency. Trichromatic, symmetric, and consistent isn't art, but it won't be garish either. Now you need a place to begin building your UserControls.

Creating a Control Library

The Windows Control Library template in the New Project dialog is a good way to begin building UserControls. The Windows Control Library will yield an assembly with a DLL extension, and the project will be created with a single UserControl. (You can start with a Class Library and add UserControls manually, but there is no reason not to take reasonable shortcuts if they are available.)

When you create a Windows Control Library, the output type will be Class Library (read DLL), and the template will add the System, System.Data, System.Drawing, System.Windows.Forms, and System.XML namespace references. The template will also add AssemblyInfo.cs and UserControl1.cs modules. The AssemblyInfo file is provided for adding metadata, and the UserControl module contains a class, which inherits from UserControl, that you can use to begin implementing your first UserControl.

You can add as many UserControls to a control library as you would like. You are not limited to a single class per module, but you do want to limit each module to a single UserControl because a .resx file will be associated with the UserControl by file name.

A recommended approach to building UserControls at this point is to build the control with a general solution in mind and to use a generic application to test the UserControl. When the control has the general properties, methods, events, and constituent controls that you have determined are needed, you can incorporate the new UserControl into your application. We will use this approach to build UserControls. The first control is a stack of four buttons that are automatically resized on the basis of the size of the UserControl. The second control incorporates the buttons to make a UserControl with two listboxes, with the buttons serving as a visual metaphor for moving elements between the two listboxes. (After we build these two controls we will explore some additional kinds of controls.)

Creating a ButtonCluster Control

The ButtonCluster uses four standard Button controls on a UserControl container. The ButtonCluster control is shown at the center of the form in Figure 8-1. The text on the buttons suggests that clicking a particular button will move the elements in the direction indicated by the arrow (see Figure 8-1).

NOTE

It is worth noting that the behavior of these buttons may seem intuitive to those familiar with Windows applications, but may not be at all intuitive to non-Windows users. This is a difficulty that every new software application presents.

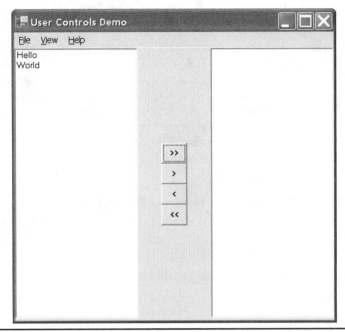

Figure 8-1   *The ButtonCluster user control is located between the two listboxes.*

The status quo is that software developers have to know a little about their audience, and if Windows applications deviate from the Windows look and feel too much, then even experienced computer users will be lost. The current approach is to have custom-tailored training for users of new applications when needed.

From Figure 8-1 we can determine that the UserControl is composed of four buttons. To keep the buttons aligned, we will need to respond to Resize events sent to the UserControl, we will need to modify the Text property for the buttons, and we will need to surface the individual Button Click events in order to allow users to respond to Click events.

TIP

Controls on a UserControl (or Form) are referred to as constituent controls. You will encounter the term surfacing in such uses as "surfacing properties of constituent controls." Other texts refer to this as interface promotion. When you expose the member of an aggregate in the containing control, both "surfacing the member" and "interface promotion" are OK. We will use "surfacing" to be consistent with the .NET help you are likely to encounter.

Designing the UserControl Visual Interface

The visual appearance of our first user control is composed of four equally-sized buttons lined up in a vertical stack. To make the control as generic as possible, we might want to allow the buttons to be aligned horizontally. We may also want to allow the actual buttons to be rendered using other kinds of buttons (like the VideoKiosk buttons in Chapter 2), but we'll keep the button cluster simple.

To create the button cluster class, create a new Windows Control Library project. Drop four buttons on the UserControl container. Use the Visual Studio .NET Format | Make Same Size | Both menu to make the buttons the exact same size. (Make the buttons roughly square.) Use the Format | Align | Centers menu item to align the buttons along a center vertical axis. Resize the UserControl to approximately the same width as a single button and the height to that of all four buttons (an example can be seen in Figure 8-1). Don't worry about precise visual sizing, as we will write the code to make the control visually perfect. The next thing we need to do is write the code to resize each of the buttons proportionately to the size of the containing control.

Implementing the UserControl Resize Event Handler

When the UserControl is resized, we want our buttons to occupy and fully consume exactly one-fourth of the available space. Fortunately, the UserControl can be designed like a form. To generate the Resize event handler, we can use the Event view of the Properties window.

```
private void UserControlButtons_Resize(object sender,
  System.EventArgs e)
{
  ResizeButtons();
}
```

Following a good convention, we simply implement the event handler by calling a well-named method. The well-named method mitigates the need for a comment, and the name indicates precisely what the code will do. As an alternative, we can override the OnResize method. If you choose to override OnResize, make sure you call the base class method. By convention, .NET uses the On prefix for event methods; hence, the Resize event would have an OnResize method that invokes it. (You can look this information up or simply rely on convention.)

If you elect to override the OnResize method, then the overridden method might be implemented as follows:

```
protected override void OnResize(System.EventArgs e)
{
  base.OnResize(e);
  ResizeButtons();
}
```

We can use an overridden OnResize method to implement the constituent resize behavior. We do not need both the event handler and the overridden event handler; although either approach works, usually I prefer to override the method.

It is important to understand why you might have to override the OnResize method, rather than implement an event handler, if we were working in something else besides .NET.

Other languages implement procedural types and function pointers—both are really the same thing. However, your basic function pointer can point to only one function at a time.

Thus, if you were to use a function pointer to implement the resize behavior and consumers were to implement this event, your event handler would be lost. This is because a function pointer event handler can point to only one function at a time.

Delegates are different. Delegates maintain an internal invocation list. This internal invocation list allows delegates—events in .NET—to point to multiple event handlers and notify each of those handlers every time an event is fired. This is referred to as *multicasting*. Since delegates can multicast, we can implement the Resize behavior using an event handler and not worry about some other developer coming along and stomping all over our resize event-handling behavior. Multicast delegates allow us to use event handlers or overridden methods to extend the behavior of UserControls.

Determining Equal Subdivisions for the Buttons

Now that we have an event handler, our UserControl is notified when it is resized. From this point, we can implement the code that sizes each button equally.

When we are coding, it is useful to determine when a solution is generic enough to make sense in some other context. Determining the fractional part of a rectangle is generally useful, and experience suggests that I can reuse this behavior. When code may be generally useful, it is a good idea to create a new class and implement the behavior in the new class. Listing 8-1 implements a Rectangle class that can calculate a new top and new bottom for a rectangle that is a fractional subdivision of a bounding rectangle.

Listing 8-1   *The Rectangles class contains static methods for determining subdivisions of bounding rectangles.*

```
using System;
using System.Drawing;

namespace UserControlsExamples
{
  public class Rectangles
  {
    private Rectangles(){}

    public static Rectangle GetVerticalRectangle(
      Rectangle rectangle, int index, int segments )
    {
      Rectangle r = rectangle;
      r.Size = new Size( r.Width,
        NewBottom(rectangle, index, segments));

      r.Location = new Point(0,
        NewTop(rectangle, index, segments));
      return r;
    }
```

```
    public static int NewTop( Rectangle rectangle,
      int index, int segments )
    {
      return (int)((float)index / segments *
        rectangle.Height);
    }

    public static int NewBottom( Rectangle rectangle,
      int index, int segments)
    {
      return rectangle.Height / segments;
    }
  }
}
```

The class is pretty straightforward: calculate a new top based on the number of subdivisions and the actual division you want, and calculate the bottom by making the height an equal subdivision. More important is how we are able to determine when we have a new class. Simplistically, we provide a good name for a method and then ask ourselves whether this method sounds like a behavior of this particular thing, this class. I named the method GetVerticleRectangle. Thus, the question is "Does ButtonCluster.GetVerticalRectangle— that is, GetVerticalRectangle—sound like a good method for a button cluster?" The clue is in the name of the method, GetVerticalRectangle. The noun *Rectangle* provides a reasonable clue as to the kind of thing this method probably should belong to. This is not a perfect science, but experience and experimentation will help.

TIP

How do we determine that the Rectangles class does not need to be created? The answer: there is no state information. That is, there are no fields. If a class only has methods, then those methods can be static, and we don't need instances of the class.

Now that we have some general methods for determining rectangular subdivisions, we can resize the buttons in the cluster quite easily.

```
private void Initialize()
{
  buttons = new Button[]{buttonAllRight, buttonRight,
    buttonLeft, buttonAllLeft};
}

private void ResizeButtons()
{
  if( buttons == null ) return;
  for( int i=0; i<buttons.Length; i++)
  {
```

```
    buttons[i].Bounds = Rectangles.GetVerticalRectangle(
      this.Bounds, i, buttons.Length);
  }
}
```

The ButtonCluster class was implemented to store a reference to each button in an array (see the preceding listing). Storing the buttons in an array field facilitates iterating over each button and invoking the Rectangles.GetVerticalRectangle method on each rectangle. The argument this.Bounds is the rectangle for the user control. The index *i* is used as the rectangular subdivision, and the Length of the array indicates the number of subdivisions. This approach actually makes the code quite extensible, since we are not relying on literal values to determine the index or number of buttons.

A final word on strategy is in order. You could, of course, use the UserControl's Controls array to access the buttons; however, if you go this route, then you will be more inclined to write code that checks the Type information of each Control in the Controls array. Either approach works reasonably well. If you use the Controls array, then you might run into difficulty if the UserControl contains controls of a similar type, but you don't want to perform a uniform operation on all controls of the same type.

Surfacing Constituent Events

When it comes to the visual aspects of our button cluster, all we need to do is modify the Text property and we are finished. For a more refined look, use the Button.Image property and provide a graphic arrow.

Programmatically, however, we are not quite finished. The purpose of buttons is to respond to Click events. As the event handler is implemented so far, consumers will not be able to get at the Click events for the buttons contained on this control. This presents a slightly sticky problem. A solution—albeit not the best one—is that we must surface the events of the constituent controls. Surfacing constituent control events is not as difficult as it may seem. But there is the question of why we have to do it?

I will answer the "how" first and then we will look at the "why." Understanding why we have to surface constituent control members, and what the alternative is, will help us anticipate what is likely to come in the very near future. (You are learning what is and what is likely to be.)

Promoting Events in Constituent Controls

When you add controls to a UserControl, the new controls are added as fields in the UserControl. The properties of the controls on the UserControl are encapsulated two layers deep. Assume you have an instance of a UserControl, userControl1. Further assume that userControl1 contains a Button control. To get at the Text property of the button, a consumer would have to write some code like **userControl1.Button.Text.** Counting the number of member-of operators— there are two—we know that the Text property is two layers deep. As a result, the button's Text property is not going to show up in the Properties window.

Assuming that Button is public, a consumer could programmatically modify the properties of the Button contained in the UserControl. However, if you want to modify those properties and events in the Properties window, then you will have to surface the properties and events of constituent controls. We want to enable consumers to write code that responds to the individual button clicks, so we'll need to surface the Button Click events.

To surface constituent control events, we need to write event handlers for the controls. Then we need to implement new events in the UserControl. When the constituent control events are raised, we pass the raised events up to the new UserControl events. Effectively, we bubble the events from the contained controls up to the interface level of the UserControl. Listing 8-2 demonstrates the necessary steps.

Listing 8-2 *Surfacing constituent control events*

```
1:   private void Initialize()
2:   {
3:     buttons = new Button[]{buttonAllRight, buttonRight,
4:       buttonLeft, buttonAllLeft};
5:
6:     buttonAllRight.Click += new EventHandler(OnAllRightClick);
7:     buttonRight.Click += new EventHandler(OnRightClick);
8:     buttonAllLeft.Click += new EventHandler(OnAllLeftClick);
9:     buttonLeft.Click += new EventHandler(OnLeftClick);
10: }
11:
12: private bool IsValidIndex(int index)
13: {
14:    return (index >= buttons.GetLowerBound(0) &&
15:      index <= buttons.GetUpperBound(0));
16: }
17:
18: public Button this[int index]
19: {
20:   get
21:   {
22:     Debug.Assert(IsValidIndex(index));
23:     return buttons[index];
24:   }
25: }
26:
27: public event EventHandler AllRightClick;
28: public event EventHandler RightClick;
29: public event EventHandler AllLeftClick;
30: public event EventHandler LeftClick;
31:
32: private void OnAllRightClick(object sender, System.EventArgs e)
33: {
34:   if(AllRightClick != null)
```

```
35:         AllRightClick(sender, e);
36: }
37:
38: private void OnRightClick(object sender, System.EventArgs e)
39: {
40:   if(RightClick != null)
41:      RightClick(sender, e);
42: }
43:
44: private void OnAllLeftClick(object sender, System.EventArgs e)
45: {
46:   if(AllLeftClick != null)
47:      AllLeftClick(sender, e);
48: }
49:
50: private void OnLeftClick(object sender, System.EventArgs e)
51: {
52:   if(LeftClick != null)
53:      LeftClick(sender, e);
54: }
```

Lines 27 through 30 in Listing 8-2 declare four public events. These events will show up in the Event view of the Properties window as AllRightClick, RightClick, AllLeftClick, and LeftClick. Consumers can add event handlers to these event properties. Following convention, lines 6 through 9 in Listing 8-2 add private event handlers to the Click event for our constituent button controls. When the Button Click events are raised, our internal events check to see if consumers have associated event handlers with our public events. If the UserControl's public events have handlers assigned to them, then the events are bubbled up to the surface of the UserControl. Figure 8-2 shows the Call Stack view with the events in the order they were called.

TIP

The operator for events is the += (and – =), as demonstrated in Listing 8-2. Delegates do not even support the assignment operator =. Assignment implies a single value, as in a single delegate. However all delegates are multicast delegates. You may add or remove delegates from the invocation list, but you may not assign only one event handler to an event property.

We could have used the Forms Designer to generate the event handlers for the constituent button controls in Listing 8-2, but the result is the same whether we write the event handlers or the Forms Designer generates them. The real question is why we have to surface constituent control properties and events at all.

Viable Alternatives to Member Promotion

You might assume that you could declare a constituent control, like the buttons in the ButtonCluster, as public. Once the constituent control is public, consumers could access

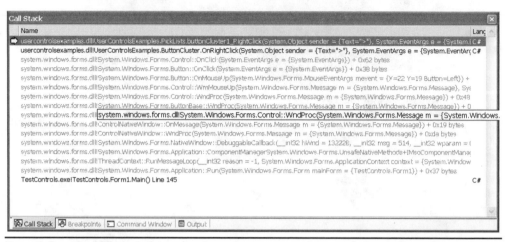

Figure 8-2 *The Call Stack shows that the constituent control responded to the event first and that the event is bubbled up to the containing control.*

its properties and events directly. In fact, the Visual Studio .NET IDE will allow you to do this (see Figure 8-3).

Figure 8-3 shows the AllRightButton as a nested reference property. You can modify property values, but you may not modify events for nested reference type properties; they don't even show up in the Properties window. Of course, when you do modify properties of nested reference types, those properties are not persisted correctly to the resource file. The result is that nested properties are not maintained when you close the IDE, nor are they maintained when you compile and run the application. Technically, this is a bug.

NOTE

Making constituent object fields public does not work correctly in the Properties window, either. Only properties and events will show up in the Properties window; public fields will not.

If you know a little bit about the history of C#, you can draw some conclusions. The first is that what we are trying to do, as shown in Figure 8-2, seems intuitive. If you can modify nested properties programmatically, then you should be able to modify them at design time, too. Second, C# is partly the brainchild of the same guy who built Borland's Delphi, Anders Hejlsberg. Delphi is built on the Object Pascal language, and Delphi in its recent versions supports design-time nested objects. My intuition tells me that you will not have to surface constituent control properties and events for long. Look for nested objects to work properly in the IDE in the near future. For now, public nested object properties do not persist state correctly at design time.

The second thing you might try to do is surface constituent events directly. Consider the following code:

```
public EventHandler AllRightClick
{
```

```
  get
  {
    return buttonAllRight.Click;
  }
}
```

To surface a constituent event directly, you might assume that you can do something like return the event property as demonstrated. This declaration would allow the event property to be the right-hand side value for an assignment statement, but assignment (=) is not defined for events. (The addition-assignment (+=) and the subtraction-assignment (– =) operators are defined for events, but not plain-old assignment.)

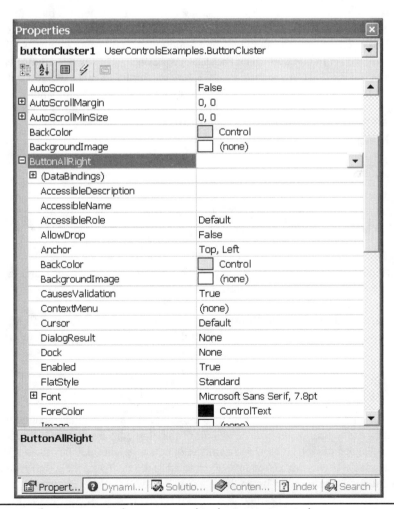

Figure 8-3   *A reference type—a button—nested in the Properties window*

Further, you might try to subclass a delegate class and overload the assignment (=) operator. However, delegate classes are declared with the sealed modifier, which means you may not subclass delegates. You may only declare new delegates based on a method signature.

Creating a PickList Control

We have the ButtonCluster. We can use it in any application by referencing the DLL assembly that contains the ButtonCluster. We can also use the ButtonCluster as a control in another UserControl. By layering complexity, rather than building a single, monolithic control, we end with more individual controls and controls that are easier to manage.

The next control we will build is a UserControl with two ListBox controls and one ButtonCluster. As the ButtonCluster is a separate UserControl, when we build the PickList control, we are acting as a consumer of the ButtonCluster and only have to focus on the new behavior. This is clearly simpler than building a monolithic control that defines the Button and ListBox behavior in one class. The PickList UserControl is shown in Figure 8-1.

Implement the PickList by creating a new UserControl. Paint two ListBox controls on the UserControl, place a panel in between, and add a ButtonCluster to the panel. To maintain the relative position of the ListBoxes and the panel containing the ButtonCluster, change the left ListBox's Dock property to Left, the right ListBox's Dock property to Right, and the center panel to Fill. When the UserControl is resized, the ListBoxes and ButtonClusters will maintain the appearance shown in Figure 8-1. The ButtonCluster's position can be maintained with the following statement:

```
buttonCluster1.Location = new Point(
  panel1.Left + (panel1.Width - buttonCluster1.Width) / 2,
  panel1.Top +  (panel1.Height - buttonCluster1.Height) / 2);
```

The horizontal location of the ButtonCluster is offset from the left edge of the panel by half the difference of the containing panel and the ButtonCluster. The vertical location of the ButtonCluster is offset from the top of the panel by half the difference of the height of the panel and height of the ButtonCluster.

The visual effects are finished. Now we need to implement the behavior that moves elements between the two ListBoxes. We can stub this behavior out by using the Properties window to generate the event handler for each button.

Adding and Removing Elements from ListBoxes

There are four buttons, and we can implement the individual behavior of each button in a handful of ways. Click the >> (all right) button, and all of the elements are moved from the left list to the right list. The << (all left) button performs the opposite operation. Click the > (right) button, and only the selected items are moved from the left list to the right, and the < (left) button moves the selected items from the right list to the left list.

The items in a ListBox are defined as a nested type, ObjectCollection. Listing 8-3 demonstrates methods that will handle moving elements between ListBox controls.

Listing 8-3   *Moving items between ListBox controls*

```
1:   private void SourceToTarget(ListBox.ObjectCollection source,
2:     ListBox.ObjectCollection target)
3:     {
4:       target.AddRange(source);
5:       source.Clear();
6:     }
7:
8:    private void MoveAllLeft()
9:    {
10:      SourceToTarget(listBoxRight.Items, listBoxLeft.Items);
11:   }
12:
13:   private void MoveAllRight()
14:   {
15:     SourceToTarget(listBoxLeft.Items, listBoxRight.Items);
16:   }
17:
18:   private void SourceToTarget(ListBox.SelectedObjectCollection
19:     source, ListBox.ObjectCollection target)
20:   {
21:     IEnumerator e = source.GetEnumerator();
22:     while(e.MoveNext())
23:     {
24:       target.Add(e.Current);
25:     }
26:   }
27:
28:   private void RemoveSelected(ListBox listBox)
29:   {
30:     for( int i=listBox.Items.Count - 1; i>=0; i--)
31:       if(listBox.GetSelected(i))
32:         listBox.Items.RemoveAt(i);
33:   }
34:
35:   private void MoveLeft()
36:   {
37:     SourceToTarget(listBoxRight.SelectedItems,
38:       listBoxLeft.Items);
39:     RemoveSelected(listBoxRight);
40:   }
41:
```

```
42:    private void MoveRight()
43:    {
44:      SourceToTarget(listBoxLeft.SelectedItems,
45:        listBoxRight.Items);
46:        RemoveSelected(listBoxLeft);
47:    }
```

MoveAllRight and MoveAllLeft call the SourceToTarget method, which takes two ListBox.ObjectCollection objects. The lists are transposed according to which direction we are moving the items. ListBox.ObjectCollection represents all of the items in the list. After we invoke AddRange on line 4 in Listing 8-3, we clear all of the elements in the source list, line 5. To move only the selected items, we invoke the SourceToTarget method that takes a ListBox.SelectedObjectCollection as the first argument and a ListBox.ObjectCollection as the second argument. We transpose the arguments according to the direction we are moving elements. We copy only selected items by using an enumerator; interestingly enough, AddRange is not defined for the ListBox.SelectedObjectCollection. After we enumerate all selected items and copy the selected items to the target—lines 18 to 26—we invoke RemoveSelected. RemoveSelected uses an integer, because GetSelected and RemoveAt—lines 31 and 32— are defined to take an integer.

It is a bit unfortunate that ListBox uses a special collection to store objects in the list. This probably facilitates memory optimization, but it makes it more difficult to write a general-purpose utility that manages inter-list item movements.

BeginUpdate and EndUpdate

Sometimes you will need to move a large number of items into a ListBox. If you allow the ListBox to update the list view each time you add an element, the ListBox will take longer to load. To load a large number of items, call ListBox.BeginUpdate before you begin loading the list, and call ListBox.EndUpdate when you have finished loading the list. BeginUpdate will prevent the listing from drawing the new items until you call EndUpdate. The following code fragment demonstrates the technique:

```
listBox1.BeginUpdate();
// load the list. For example, add the code on lines 21 to 25 of listing 3
listBox1.EndUpdate();
```

Implementing an AboutBox Control

The AboutBox is a form that you will find in most Windows applications. This is a great candidate for building once and using many times. This section demonstrates how to implement an AboutBox UserControl. The About properties are read from the assembly metadata using the System.Diagnostics.FileVersionInfo class we learned about in Chapter 7. I won't repeat that information here (see the section "FileVersion Information" in Chapter 7). In this section, we'll focus on surfacing constituent properties like the About Image property.

Drawing and Coding the AboutBox

You can copy and paste the controls from the AboutBox referred to in Chapter 7 onto a UserControl. (You will need to download the source code from the **www.osborne.com** web site.) You can also copy the FormAbout_Load code from the FormAbout.cs form in Chapter 7's DebugDemo to the UserControl Load event. (I won't repeat that code here.)

The FileVersionInfo dynamically reads the assembly metadata to fill in the values displayed on the AboutBox form; hence, moving the code from the form to the UserControl makes it reusable as long as the controls are the same. Of course, you could elect to leave the AboutBox code in a form and import a copy of the form every time you want About information, but the UserControl version gives you added flexibility.

Surfacing Constituent Properties

Surfacing constituent properties is easier than surfacing constituent events. To surface a property of a control contained in your UserControl, declare a public property that has the same type as the control's property you want to surface. Return and set the value of the constituent control's property in the newly defined UserControl property.

For example, we have defined the AboutBoxInfo UserControl. To allow users to change the PictureBox.Image property, we need to surface the Image property. Assuming that our PictureBox control were allowed to use the default name, then adding the next property statement to our user control would suitably surface the constituent image property.

```
public Image Image
{
  get
  {
    return pictureBox1.Image;
  }
  set
  {
    pictureBox1.Image = value;
  }
}
```

From the outside looking in, the UserControl now has an Image property.

I'd like to mention a note on style here. Notice that I used the default name of the PictureBox, "pictureBox1." Previously, I mentioned that you should provide good, descriptive names for methods, properties, events, and fields. Learning when to worry about such things is important too. In the case of the UserControl AboutBoxInfo, there is only one PictureBox and it is a private member of the UserControl. Since consumers can't interact with the PictureBox directly and there is only one, pictureBox1 is as good a name as any. This is a subjective judgment, of course, but software development is as much about knowing what to do as knowing what not to do or worry about.

It would be great if we could simply make constituent controls public and manipulate them directly. You can make constituent controls public, but they will not work correctly in the Properties window. You can modify the values of public constituent properties at design time in the Properties window, but those values will not be maintained when you close Visual Studio .NET or when you compile the application. I suspect this feature will be supported in the next release or two, and you will not have to surface constituent properties and events. (As mentioned, I feel comfortable in making this supposition because public constituent controls seem intuitive and because Anders Hejlsberg is participating in the development of .NET.)

Defining a Data Bound UserControl

The Control class introduces a DataBindings property that is a ControlBindingsCollection. You can bind controls to any class that implements the IBindingList, ITypedList, or IList interfaces. The obvious classes are the ArrayList and Hashtable and the ADO.NET DataSet DataTable, DataView, and DataViewManager classes. Additionally, you can bind to lists of strongly typed objects of the same type. This means that you can bind controls to arrays of user-defined objects.

Chapter 5 focuses on ADO.NET, so we will look at binding arrays of custom types to our UserControl. The first thing we need to do is fabricate a UserControl that contains constituent controls we want to bind to. We will define a UserControl that displays contact information. Next, we'll need to define a class that is capable of containing the information we want to manage, and then add some instances of that class to an array. Finally, we'll bind our custom objects to the UserControl and provide a way to navigate over the elements in the array.

Implementing the UserControl

Create a UserControl named ContactInformation. Add three Labels and three TextBox controls to ContactInformation. Change the Text property of the Labels to "First Name:", "Last Name", and "Phone Number:". Define three public properties named FirstName, LastName, and PhoneNumber. Define the properties as string types. The completed example is shown in Figure 8-4. Use the figure as a visual guide.

The only code you have to write for the ContactInformation control is code that surfaces the three constituent TextBox control's Text properties:

```csharp
public string FirstName
{
  get
  {
    return textBox1.Text;
  }
  set
  {
    textBox1.Text = value;
  }
}
```

```
public string LastName
{
  get
  {
    return textBox2.Text;
  }
  set
  {
    textBox2.Text = value;
  }
}

public string PhoneNumber
{
  get
  {
    return textBox3.Text;
  }
  set
  {
    textBox3.Text = value;
  }
}
```

Figure 8-4   *A form with the data bound ContactInformation UserControl*

Consumers will never see the TextBox controls themselves, so you do not have to rename the TextBox controls. From a consumer's perspective, you have a UserControl named ContactInformation, and the properties are ContactInformation.FirstName, ContactInformation.LastName, and ContactInformation.PhoneNumber.

Implementing the ContactInformation Class

It is convenient and easy to define a class that has properties that match the ContactInformation UserControl. It is helpful to define a plurally named class that contains a collection of our custom class. (These classes represent what are commonly referred to as *business objects*.) Listing 8-4 defines the Contact class and the container, Contacts.

Listing 8-4   *The Contact and Contacts classes*

```
1:   public class Contacts
2:   {
3:     private ArrayList items;
4:
5:     public Contacts()
6:     {
7:       items = new ArrayList();
8:     }
9:
10:    public ArrayList Items
11:    {
12:      get
13:      {
14:        return items;
15:      }
16:    }
17: }
18:
19: public class Contact
20: {
21:        private string firstName;
22:        private string lastName;
23:        private string phoneNumber;
24:
25:        public Contact( string firstName, string lastName, string phoneNumber)
26:        {
27:          this.firstName = firstName;
28:          this.lastName = lastName;
29:          this.phoneNumber = phoneNumber;
```

```
30:        }
31:
32:        public string FirstName
33:        {
34:          get
35:          {
36:            return firstName;
37:          }
38:          set
39:          {
40:            firstName = value;
41:          }
42:        }
43:
44:        public string LastName
45:        {
46:          get
47:          {
48:            return lastName;
49:          }
50:          set
51:          {
52:            lastName = value;
53:          }
54:        }
55:
56:        public string PhoneNumber
57:        {
58:          get
59:          {
60:            return phoneNumber;
61:          }
62:          set
63:          {
64:            phoneNumber = value;
65:          }
66:        }
67: }
```

Listing 8-4 implements a class that has three fields and three matching properties. The constructor is defined to initialize these three fields: firstName, lastName, and phoneNumber. The Contacts class on lines 1 through 17 contains a single ArrayList field, *items*. The Items property is defined as a read-only property (because we only implemented a getter method).

We want consumers to be able to change the elements of the ArrayList but not the ArrayList itself. Making the ArrayList property read-only is how we accomplish this.

If we look in Visual Studio .NET help, we can determine that ArrayList implements IList and is a suitable property to bind to our UserControl properties.

Binding and Navigating

We will need to create some test data to exercise our UserControl. Listing 8-5 creates a couple of instances of Contact and a Contacts object to store them in. Every control, including UserControls, has a DataBindings property. We'll use the ContactInformation DataBindings property to express the bindings between Contact objects and the UserControl. We will wrap the example up by using the UserControl's BindingContext property to support navigating the Contacts.

Listing 8-5   *A form that contains the ContactInformation UserControl and the code that binds the homogeneous objects in an ArrayList to that UserControl*

```
1:  Contacts c = new Contacts();
2:
3:  private void FormDataBound_Load(object sender, System.EventArgs e)
4:  {
5:    c.Items.Add( new Contact("Paul", "Kimmel", "(517) 555-1212"));
6:    c.Items.Add( new Contact("Trevor", "MacDonald", "(517) 555-1212"));
7:
8:    contactInformation1.DataBindings.Add(
9:      new Binding("FirstName", c.Items, "FirstName"));
10:
11:   contactInformation1.DataBindings.Add(
12:     new Binding("LastName", c.Items, "LastName"));
13:
14:   contactInformation1.DataBindings.Add(
15:     new Binding("PhoneNumber", c.Items, "PhoneNumber"));
16: }
17:
18: private void buttonNext_Click(object sender, System.EventArgs e)
19: {
20:   ((CurrencyManager)contactInformation1.
21:       BindingContext[c.Items]).Position -= 1;
22: }
23:
24: private void buttonPrevious_Click(object sender, System.EventArgs e)
25: {
26:   ((CurrencyManager)contactInformation1.
```

```
27:        BindingContext[c.Items]).Position += 1;
28: }
```

TIP

You can add line breaks at the member-of operator for readability without adding any special line-break character.

The code in Listing 8-5 can be found in the TestControls.sln example program and is contained in the FormDataBound.cs Form module. The Form_Load event creates two Contact objects and a Contacts object. The DataBindings.Add takes a Binding object. The Binding object is initialized with a property to bind to, a data source to bind from, and a data member in that source to bind to. The first argument is the property in our UserControl. The data source is represented by the ArrayList Items, and the data member is a named property of one of the objects in the ArrayList, specifically Contact.FirstName, Contact.LastName, and Contact.PhoneNumber.

Because I was the author of the UserControl and the business classes, I named the properties in both identically. This was done precisely for ease of use and convenience.

To navigate the elements in the Contacts object, we have to get synchronize the data source, Contacts.Items, with the UserControl, contactInformation1. The BindingContext property returns a specific child class of the BindingManagerBase. If the data source returns a single property, then BindingContext returns a PropertyManager, and our example returns a collection; hence, BindingContext returns a CurrencyManager. CurrencyManager allows us to iterate over the elements by incrementing or decrementing the Position property.

The CurrencyManager handles the beginning and end of collection management automatically. For that reason, there is no special exception handling code when the position property is modified.

After binding the control to an array of objects, you do not need to write any special code to modify the data. Change the data in the TextBox and the bound field is modified; this is exactly the behavior that you get when you bind to ADO objects, too.

Custom Painting in UserControls

When you add constituent controls to a custom UserControl, you will have to provide custom painting for the constituent controls in each particular control's Paint event handler.

Suppose we wanted to make the labels for our ContactInformation UserControl appear embossed. (Embossing is an effect that makes the text appear to have depth.) Using a System.Windows.Forms.Label control painted on the UserControl, we would need to implement an event handler to handle the Label's Paint event, as the following code demonstrates:

```
this.label1.Paint += new
   System.Windows.Forms.PaintEventHandler(this.label1_Paint);
private void label1_Paint(object sender,
   System.Windows.Forms.PaintEventArgs e)
```

```
{
  // Demonstrates text customization
  Label l = (sender as Label);
  e.Graphics.DrawString(l.Text, l.Font, Brushes.White, new PointF(2,0));
}
```

The first statement adds the event handler for label1's Paint event. You can use the Properties window to generate this statement and the event handler method body. The two lines of code create a temporary variable by typecasting the sender argument to a Label and using the Graphics object to paint the text. It just happens that text in a label is printed at offset 2, 2. By offsetting the second drawing of the text and using a brighter color, we can create an embossed effect.

There are a couple of problems with this simplistic approach. If the text wraps or the alignment changes, then this code won't work. We can fix that by writing some more code to examine the properties of the label, and compensating for wrapped text or alternate text alignment.

Assuming that you have resolved any problems regarding the layout of the text, you should avoid deploying an application containing UserControls that have custom painting behavior (or any custom behavior) implemented as an event handler. If you want custom text effects for labels, then subclass the label type and use the new class in the UserControl. When you write code, consider the question of what class is responsible for this behavior. When you determine the answer, put the behavior in that class. Read Chapter 9 for examples of creating custom controls, and inheriting and customizing existing controls.

Transparent UserControl Background

Chapter 2 proposed that you could create a high-quality graphic background and paint your controls over this background. Blending transparent controls into a graphic background will allow you to create rich user interfaces.

To allow your custom UserControls to be transparent, you will need to set the control style to support a transparent background. This is easily accomplished by calling the SetStyle method in the UserControl's constructor, as demonstrated here:

```
SetStyle(ControlStyles.SupportsTransparentBackColor, true);
```

Because a UserControl does not support the Color.Transparent BackColor value, you can set the BackColor to be Transparent after you invoke SetStyle or when you drop the UserControl onto a form. The TransparentForm Form in the TestControls example project demonstrates a transparent UserControl with a balloon in a picture box, floating seamlessly over a watery surface.

Extending UserControls Through Inheritance

You can extend existing UserControls through inheritance. From the Project menu, select Add Inherited Control. The Add New Items dialog will open, with the Inherited User Control template selected. After you click OK, the Inheritance Picker dialog (see Figure 8-5) will be

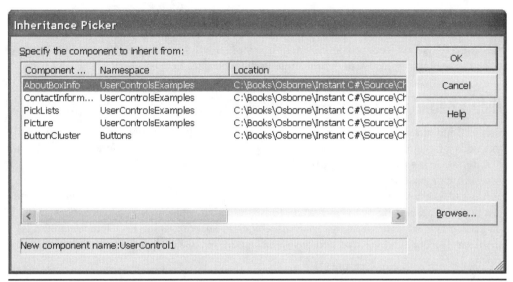

Figure 8-5   *Pick a component to inherit from the Inheritance Picker.*

displayed. Select one of the controls from the current solution or browse for an additional DLL assembly. Add the new behavior and state information, and then compile and test your custom control.

You can implement a class from scratch and express the UserControl inheritance relationship. Visual Studio .NET will generate the resource file automatically, but it is easier to use the Inheritance Picker as just described.

Secondary Topics

There are some additional capabilities that we relied on to build some of the user controls in this chapter. We'll cover these in this section. You will find these topics useful for general programming or for creating custom controls. The two major topics we'll cover are

▶   Using BeginUpdate and EndUpdate while loading list controls

▶   Dynamically positioning and sizing controls

Loading ListBoxes

The strategies that you pick for large tasks can have an impact on the performance of your application. If you load thousands of items in ListBoxes, then users may be caught waiting while your application updates. If you load those items one at a time, then the result may be even worse.

There are a couple of strategies you can use when it comes to loading ListBoxes that will make your application seem more responsive. You can use BeginUpdate and EndUpdate to prevent the ListBox from repainting each time an item is added, or you can use a background thread to load the items. I will demonstrate both techniques here.

Using BeginUpdate and EndUpdate

Earlier, I introduced ListBox.BeginUpdate and ListBox.EndUpdate methods. If you write code that adds a large number of elements to a ListBox, each added item will force the ListBox to update, incurring the overhead of repainting the list each time an element is added. For big lists, this can result in very poor performance.

Instead, every time you load items to a ListBox (or ComboBox) one element at a time, you can precede loading the items with a call to BeginUpdate and follow the load process with an EndUpdate. You can include a *try finally* block to ensure that the EndUpdate method is invoked. The code that follows demonstrates loading 100,000 integer objects to a ListBox.

```
private void LoadListBox()
{
  listBox1.BeginUpdate();
  try
  {
    for(int i=0; i<100000; i++)
      listBox1.Items.Add(i);
  }
  finally
  {
    listBox1.EndUpdate();
  }
}
```

If this code were to run when a form is being loaded, the user would have to wait on the items to be loaded. Another alternative is to use a separate thread to load the items. If the user won't need all of the items before being allowed to interact with the form containing the ListBox, then we can load the ListBox on a background process.

Using the ThreadPool to Load a ListBox

There are several ways to use threads in .NET. One of the easiest is to use a thread available in the ThreadPool. The ThreadPool class contains a pool of threads that you can send work to in the form of a delegate. Define the delegate to perform the work of loading the ListBox and send the delegate to the ThreadPool.QueueUserWorkItem. Additionally, Windows Forms are not directly thread-safe. You must call the control's Invoke method to interact with a Windows Forms control on the same thread on which it was created. Listing 8-6 is a bit more complex, so line numbers were added for reference.

Listing 8-6   *Using the ThreadPool to perform background tasks*

```
1:   private delegate void Add(int i);
2:
3:   private void AddItem(int i)
4:   {
5:     listBox1.Items.Add(i);
6:     Application.DoEvents();
7:   }
8:
9:   private void LoadListBox(object state)
10:  {
11:    for( int i=0; i<100000; i++)
12:       listBox1.Invoke(new Add(AddItem), new object[]{i});
13:  }
14:
15:  private void Form1_Load(object sender, System.EventArgs e)
16:  {
17:    System.Threading.ThreadPool.QueueUserWorkItem(
18:       new System.Threading.WaitCallback(LoadListBox));
19:  }
```

To load the ListBox using the ThreadPool class, we need to complete several steps. The first step is to define a delegate type that reflects a procedure we will use to interact with the Form's thread. Line 1 defines a new delegate, Add, using a method signature that takes an integer and returns void. In Listing 8-6, lines 3 through 7 define a method that will interact with the ListBox directly. AddItem inserts a single item at a time and calls DoEvents to help flush the message queue of the Form's thread. Lines 9 through 13 represent the method that will run on its own thread. LoadListBox takes a single argument, an object. A method that returns void and takes an object has the same signature as a WaitCallback delegate. LoadListBox iterates through a loop and invokes the AddItem method. We use listBox1.Invoke—Invoke is thread-safe—to ensure that items are actually added to the list on the same thread that the ListBox lives on.

Lines 15 through 19 ask the ThreadPool to perform some work. ThreadPool .QueueUserWorkItem places work in the form of a WaitCallback delegate in the ThreadPool queue. The ThreadPool invokes the delegate method using an available Thread or spins up a new one. Either way, we only care that the ThreadPool does its job.

Place a breakpoint on line 12 and start the application. You can open the Threads window— by clicking Debug | Windows | Threads in the IDE—and see that the LoadListBox is running on a different thread than the Form is running on (see Figure 8-6). If you step through the application, you can determine that listBox1.Invoke causes the application to jump to the thread that the Form and ListBox reside on to add items. Most important, the form loads and

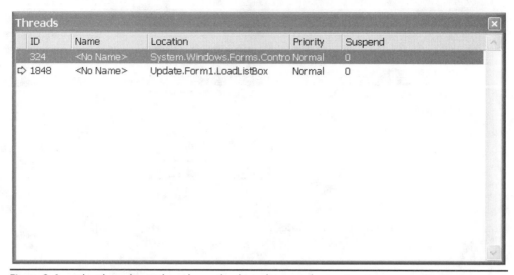

ID	Name	Location	Priority	Suspend	
324	<No Name>	System.Windows.Forms.Contro	Normal	0	
⇨ 1848	<No Name>	Update.Form1.LoadListBox	Normal	0	

Figure 8-6   *The Threads window shows the threads currently running in your application.*

displays very quickly, and the list completes its initialization in the background, making your application appear to be very responsive.

Dynamically Positioning and Sizing Controls

Control extents are defined in two ways. Controls have Top, Left, Width, and Height properties, as well as Location and Size properties. You can modify the extent of a control by directly changing the Top, Left, Width, or Height property, but you may not modify Location.X and Location.Y and the Size.Width and Size.Height properties. Location and Size are immutable.

If you want to change the Location.X and Location.Y (the Left-Top) corner of a control at once, or the Size.Width and Size.Height (which, combined with the Left-Top, describe the Bottom-Right), then you will have to create a new instance of a Location or Size structure.

The Location property of a control is a Point structure, and the Size property is actually a structure named "Size." You construct instances of Location by using the new operator and passing X and Y values. You construct an instance of the Size structure by using the new operator and expressing a new value for the Width and Height values. The Rectangles class in the UserControlsExamples.sln demonstrates how to construct an instance of Size and Location.

To change the upper-left position of the ListBox, you could write the following code:

```
listBox1.Location = new Point(5,5);
```

If you modify Left, Top, Width, or Height values one at a time, then the control will be repainted for each adjustment. By modifying the Top and Left values at the same time, you will reduce the number of times the control is repainted.

Summary

Implementing custom UserControls is a great way to build new controls that are composed of many existing controls. UserControls are ideal for building what are commonly referred to as business controls. An example of a business control, the ContactInformation UserControl, was demonstrated in this chapter.

In this chapter, you learned how to implement custom UserControls, how to surface constituent properties and events, how to perform custom painting, and how to bind business objects to custom UserControls. You also saw that any class that implements the IList interface can be bound to controls, and you learned to use the BindingContext to navigate arrays of those objects.

Combining custom painting, transparency, aggregation, and inheritance will allow you to layer in effects, resulting in a diverse toolset of UserControls. For added performance, you can roll in an extra worker thread, as we did to load a large number of items in a ListBox. It is the combination of these techniques that yields flexible and powerful UserControls that can be used many times.

Special Effects Text

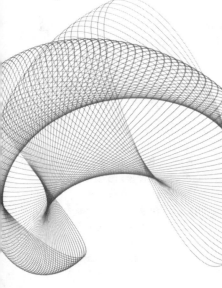

IN THIS CHAPTER:

There is a tremendous amount of support for building custom controls in C#. This chapter continues our discussion of control building in C#. In Chapter 8 we explored the UserControl. Now we will explore in detail those aspects you will need to build, test, and register custom controls.

We'll begin our discussion by building a special effects Label control for Windows Forms, as this will exercise most of the aspects of control building. In addition, we will explore C#'s support for serializing components, creating designers, type converters, and type editors. These skills will allow you to use the full range of support for building professional controls in C# that will interact well with Windows Forms applications. (If you are interested in building controls for ASP.NET, then check out Chapter 14.)

Demonstrated Topics

The primary purpose of this chapter will be to demonstrate most of what you need to know about building, testing, and deploying professional custom controls in an assembly. From the examples in this chapter, you will be able to do the following:

▶ Prototype components

▶ Create a library project for your control

▶ Use attributes from the ComponentModel namespace

▶ Test your controls

▶ Add your controls to the Toolbox

▶ Create a Merge Module project to share your controls

All of these skills will be demonstrated by building an EffectsLabel control that renders various shadow effects. (If what you are looking for is not listed in these topics, make sure you check the "Secondary Topics" section later in the chapter. There are several advanced capabilities demonstrated in that part of the chapter; I just didn't need them to implement the EffectsLabel.)

Rapid Control Prototyping

A convenient way to begin building controls is to prototype them in a Windows Forms application. Pick a control that is close to the control you want to customize. Drop that control onto the form and use the events of the form and the control to rapidly prototype your custom control. (Rapid Application Design (RAD) applies to controls too. Controls are defined in a DLL assembly, which is an application. RAD techniques are valid for controls too.)

In Chapter 3 we implemented a DrawShadowText method to create an embossed effect for the PlayControl. It is likely that we might want to use special text effects in the future. Thus, we will prototype a more permanent solution, and when we have the kinks worked out, we'll capture our solution in a custom control that can be reused without any future coding after the control is finished.

The first step is to pick a control that is similar to the control we ultimately want to create. Picking a close ancestor to inherit from means that we will have to write only a little additional code. If we pick too generic an ancestor, then we will have more work to do. The Label control is perfect for displaying text, so we will use the System.Windows.Forms.Label control as the basis for our custom control. Paint a Label control on a Form in a Windows Application. (Remember, we are prototyping here. Refer to the TestLabel.sln for a completed example of the prototype solution.)

Implement a PaintEventHandler for Custom Painting

The label has most of the solution captured. If we paint the text for the label a second time and slightly offset the text when we paint the second time, we can create various effects. We can perform custom painting in the label's PaintEventHandler.

TIP

To create a PaintEventHandler for a label, select the label and click the Events button (the small lightning bolt icon) in the Properties window to switch to the Events view. Double-click the Paint event to generate the handler.

The label's Paint handler has a PaintEventArgs argument that is initialized with the Graphics object representing the label's device context. We can use GDI+—represented by the Graphics object—to draw the string the second time at an offset to create the effects. (You already know how to do this, to a limited extent, because it was demonstrated in Chapter 3. There are additional considerations for a robust solution, which we will discuss in a moment.)

Pass an Instance of the Control to Methods

When we are prototyping, pass the instance of the control you will be inheriting from to any methods we might need to define. Until the new control is actually created, we will need an instance of the control we are prototyping with. By passing the control around, rather than relying on its existence in the containing form, we can copy the code from the prototype verbatim, and it should work with relatively minor changes.

Thus far we have a Windows application with a label to prototype our solution. You can draw the Text property a second time using Graphics.DrawString to create the initial effect. It won't take long before you realize that there is more to it than just writing the text. Let's proceed by examining the considerations involved in creating a robust solution.

Examining the Problem

Our problem is to create a Label control with special text effects. Here is a complete breakdown of the problems we have to tackle to create a robust solution:

▶   Text in a label can wrap if the length of the text exceeds the width of the control bounds.

▶ The ampersand is the mnemonic that represents the hotkey prefix. If we are using the mnemonic, then we have to display the mnemonic rather than the literal ampersand.

▶ The text can be aligned in several different ways. Our text will have to be displayed with consideration for the TextAlign property.

▶ We will have to accommodate special display and layout information.

▶ We will need a second color and an X and Y offset to create the visual effects.

That should do it.

As you can see, there is quite a bit to writing the text that appears in a label. The end result is worth the effort, as long as we have to pay for that effort only once. The sub-sections that follow solve each of the problems described in the preceding list.

Drawing the Text

To draw the string, we can use the Graphics object passed to the Label's PaintEventHandler, named Paint. We must use the Label's Text and Font, and we'll need to determine the Brush, Rectangle, and StringFormat object. Here is the Label's PaintEventHandler and the supporting Draw method as they are implemented in the TestLabel.csproj.

```
private void Draw(Label label, Graphics g)
{
  Rectangle r = label.ClientRectangle;
  r.X -= 1;
  r.Y -= 1;
  g.DrawString(label.Text, label.Font, Brushes.Black, r, GetFormat(label));
}
private void label1_Paint(object sender,
  System.Windows.Forms.PaintEventArgs e)
{
  Draw((Label)sender, e.Graphics);
}
```

(Remember to avoid implementing behaviors directly in event handlers. Writing well-named methods facilitates reuse and supports self-documenting code.) What we cannot determine from the listing is how the Brush, the Rectangle, and the StringFormat objects are created.

The code looks pretty simple so far. When the code looks simple, it means that we are getting an appropriate amount of detail in our solution. We'll spend the rest of this section describing how to implement the unknown elements: Brush, Rectangle, and StringFormat.

Creating the Brush

For the prototype we can use a Brush from the Brushes class. Brushes contain dozens of properties that define a suite of brushes and colors. For the prototype we can use one of these standard brushes. When we implement the actual control we can let the user specify a color. From the color we can construct a brush as follows:

```
Brush brush = new SolidBrush(color);
```

The SolidBrush class is defined in the System.Drawing namespace. You will need to add a reference to the System.Drawing.dll assembly and a *using* statement to the module containing a reference to a brush. The *using* statement follows:

```
using System.Drawing;
```

Creating the Rectangle

To ensure that the second time the text is written it is written in the same rectangular region as the original text, we can use the ClientRectangle of the Label itself. To create a specific text effect, we need to slightly offset the text the second time it is drawn. A shallow shadow effect can be created by offsetting the text the second time by X–1 and Y–1, where X and Y represent the upper-left position of the ClientRectangle.

Other effects can be created changing the text offset values. Implementing a truly flexible solution means that we ultimately let the consumer specify the offsetting values. While prototyping, it is sufficient to use literal values.

Creating the StringFormat Object

The StringFormat object is the most challenging value we have to derive. The GetFormat function called in the fragment (in the earlier section "Drawing the Text") conceals the hoops we have to jump through to derive the StringFormat object.

From the bulleted list at the beginning of this section, we have to solve the mnemonic—or hotkey—problem, the text alignment problem, and the layout problem. When we derive solutions to these problems, we can test the prototype. Assuming everything works correctly, we can create the control.

I believe in the caveat *divide et impera,* or divide and conquer. The implementation of the GetFormat method contains named methods that describe all of the steps we need to complete to create the StringFormat object. This is essential in ensuring that the second time the text is drawn, it looks precisely like the first time except for the brush color and the offset appearance.

```
private StringFormat GetFormat( Label label )
{
  StringFormat format = new StringFormat();
  SetLineAlignment(label.TextAlign, format);
  SetAlignment(label.TextAlign, format);
  SetFlags(label.RightToLeft, format);
  SetMnemonic(label.UseMnemonic, format);
  return format;
}
```

From the code we can determine that we need to create a StringFormat object. To ensure that the text is aligned properly, we need to set the StringFormat.LineAlignment and the StringFormat.Alignment properties. This is accomplished by converting the Label.TextAlign—a ContentAlignment enumerated value—to a StringAlignment enumerated value. Unfortunately, StringFormat needs StringAlignment values, but the Label uses ContentAlignment properties. The TextALign property needs to be transposed. Next, we need to set the StringFormat.FormatFlags property and determine whether we are using the ampersand (&) as a mnemonic (a hotkey indicator). Listing 9-1 contains the four formatting methods described in GetFormat in the preceding listing.

Listing 9-1   *A numbered listing for SetLineAlignment, SetAlignment, SetFlags, and SetMnemonic*

```
1:   private StringFormat GetFormat( Label label )
2:   {
3:     StringFormat format = new StringFormat();
4:     SetLineAlignment(label.TextAlign, format);
5:     SetAlignment(label, format);
6:     SetFlags(label.RightToLeft, format);
7:     SetMnemonic(label.UseMnemonic, format);
8:     return format;
9:   }
10:
11:
12:  private void SetLineAlignment(ContentAlignment TextAlign,
13:    StringFormat format)
14:  {
15:    switch(TextAlign)
16:    {
17:      case ContentAlignment.BottomLeft:
18:        format.LineAlignment = StringAlignment.Far;
19:        break;
20:      case ContentAlignment.MiddleLeft:
21:        format.LineAlignment = StringAlignment.Center;
22:        break;
23:
24:      case ContentAlignment.TopLeft:
25:        format.LineAlignment = StringAlignment.Near;
26:        break;
27:
28:      case ContentAlignment.BottomCenter:
29:        format.LineAlignment = StringAlignment.Far;
30:        break;
31:
32:      case ContentAlignment.MiddleCenter:
33:        format.LineAlignment = StringAlignment.Center;
34:        break;
35:
36:      case ContentAlignment.TopCenter:
37:        format.LineAlignment = StringAlignment.Near;
38:        break;
39:
```

```
40:      case ContentAlignment.BottomRight:
41:        format.LineAlignment = StringAlignment.Far;
42:        break;
43:
44:      case ContentAlignment.MiddleRight:
45:        format.LineAlignment = StringAlignment.Center;
46:        break;
47:
48:      case ContentAlignment.TopRight:
49:        format.LineAlignment = StringAlignment.Near;
50:        break;
51:    }
52: }
53:
54: private void SetAlignment(Label label, StringFormat format)
55: {
56:   switch(label.TextAlign)
57:   {
58:     case ContentAlignment.BottomLeft:
59:        format.Alignment = StringAlignment.Near;
60:        break;
61:     case ContentAlignment.MiddleLeft:
62:        format.Alignment = StringAlignment.Near;
63:        break;
64:
65:     case ContentAlignment.TopLeft:
66:        format.Alignment = StringAlignment.Near;
67:        break;
68:
69:     case ContentAlignment.BottomCenter:
70:        format.Alignment = StringAlignment.Center;
71:        break;
72:
73:     case ContentAlignment.MiddleCenter:
74:        format.Alignment = StringAlignment.Center;
75:        break;
76:
77:     case ContentAlignment.TopCenter:
78:        format.Alignment = StringAlignment.Center;
79:        break;
80:
81:     case ContentAlignment.BottomRight:
82:        format.Alignment = StringAlignment.Far;
83:        break;
84:
```

```
85:     case ContentAlignment.MiddleRight:
86:        format.Alignment = StringAlignment.Far;
87:        break;
88:
89:     case ContentAlignment.TopRight:
90:        format.Alignment = StringAlignment.Far;
91:        break;
92:   }
93: }
94:
95: private void SetFlags(RightToLeft rightToLeft, StringFormat format)
96: {
97:   if(rightToLeft == RightToLeft.Yes)
98:      format.FormatFlags |= StringFormatFlags.DirectionRightToLeft;
99: }
100:
101: private void SetMnemonic(bool UseMnemonic, StringFormat format)
102: {
103:   if(UseMnemonic )
104:      format.HotkeyPrefix = HotkeyPrefix.Show;
105: }
106:
```

The code in Listing 9-1 contains two methods that are longer than what I normally prefer. SetAlignment and SetLineAlignment employ long switch statements to map ContentAlignment to StringAlignment values. StringFormat.Alignment relies on the StringAlignment enumerated values rather than ContentAlignment values. We could try to algorithmically convert between ContentAlignment and StringAlignment by manipulating the underlying bits, but the result is fragile code. For example, if the CLR is modified to change the underlying bits, then our code would break. By referring to the enumerated names, the resultant code is ungainly but more robust.

SetFlags and SetMnemonic are straightforward methods—although SetMnemonic is a mouthful—that demonstrate self-describing code. Instead of writing a comment that describes what we are doing, we can employ a well-named method that both performs the action and describes it. As a general rule, prefer well-named methods over comments.

Creating a Class Library

Having prototyped the control, we are ready to create the class library and convert our prototype code into a custom control. There are several steps that we need to complete to finish the control and get the most mileage out of our code.

To achieve additional benefits from our code, we can abstract generic behavior from behavior that is useful only for the control. This part of the process is highly subjective, but it is worth the effort to find code that might be reusable and to separate it from the custom control. Code that is abstracted will need to be passed an instance of the control, and code that becomes part of the custom control does not need a reference to the control. We can remove any Label arguments for methods that are added to the control itself.

Abstract Generic Behavior

You might easily imagine scenarios where printing that wraps and uses mnemonics can be used. To avoid having to write those switch statements again, it will be worthwhile to place SetAlignment and SetLineAlignment in a separate utility class. I also chose to place SetFlags, SetMnemonic, the GetFormat factory method, and DrawText in a class by themselves. All of this code can be reused in other contexts.

Because I have described only methods and not fields, all of these methods can be implemented as static methods. When a class does not need to maintain state, you can use static methods—such as described for our utility class—and you won't have to create an instance of the class to use the methods.

As the methods that were prototyped in the Windows application will be placed in a class, separate from the custom control itself, we will have to pass in an instance of the Label control. I have provided a partial listing for the TextEffects utility class, showing the change to SetMnemonic. (The rest of the code can be found in the EffectsLabel.cs module on **www.osborne.com**.)

```
public class TextEffects
{
  public static void SetMnemonic(Label label, StringFormat format)
  {
    if(label.UseMnemonic)
      format.HotkeyPrefix = HotkeyPrefix.Show;
  }
}
```

The rest of the methods that we said would be part of the preceding utility class need the same changes. Pass in any data the method needs to run, and make the method static.

Define a New Control

Defining a Custom Control is straightforward. When you create a class library project, the Class Library template will add a class module. By default there will be a class in the module; rename the class to the name we will use for our control and express the inheritance relationship in the class header.

You can inherit from the Control class if you want to create a completely new control. In our example, we are building a custom effects label based on the System.Windows.Forms.Label control, so we will inherit from the Label control. We can indicate that we are inheriting from the Label using the namespaces, or we can add a *using* statement to the module and shorten the class header. Here are both forms. The first example uses the namespace names in the class header, and the second demonstrates the *using* statement and the shortened class header.

```
public class EffectsLabel : System.Windows.Forms.Label
```

or

```
using System.Windows.Forms;
public class EffectsLabel : Label
```

NOTE

If we reference a namespace, then we need to add a reference to the assembly that contains that namespace. Class libraries do not reference System.Windows.Forms.Dll by default; hence we'll need to add a reference to it for our custom control.

Either form works—namespaces are used for organization, but become ungainly in code if you need to write them many times. If you have two identical names, then you can use the namespaces to clarify the membership of those names.

After we have defined the inheritance relationship, we need to add fields, properties, events, methods, and any other necessary members to our custom control. The complete code is provided in Listing 9-2. For now we will explore the individual elements.

Invoking Base Class Constructor

If we provide a constructor for our control, then we need to invoke the inherited base class constructor. The EffectsLabel has several styles that we will define; thus, we will use the constructor to set the default label style and invoke the base class constructor.

```
public EffectsLabel() : base()
{
   Style = DrawStyle.Shadowed;
}
```

Constructors have no return type and have the same name as the class. The base class constructor is invoked by adding a colon followed by the keyword *base* in the constructor header. Then, we can add any additional code to initialize our class. The Style property was introduced as part of the custom behavior, so I will demonstrate the code that supports changing the style next.

Adding Properties and Methods

Controls are just classes. They just happen to be classes that inherit some fundamental capabilities that allow them to be displayed in Windows Forms or Web Forms and to respond to user inputs. This basic capability is inherited from the Control class. For the most part, all we do is add members to describe the class' behavior and appearance with fields, properties, methods, and events.

To support the notion of a Style for the EffectsLabel, we can implement an enumeration that describes the style with text rather than integers; enumerations are more expressive. And, we need to implement a field to store the Style in and a property so that the Properties window can display the Style at design time. Here is the additional code:

```csharp
public class EffectsLabel : Label
{
  public enum DrawStyle{Custom, Shadowed, Engraved, Embossed};
  private DrawStyle style;
  private Point offset;

  public EffectsLabel() : base()
  {
    Style = DrawStyle.Shadowed;
  }

  public DrawStyle Style
  {
    get
    {
      return style;
    }
    set
    {
      style = value;
      DrawStyleChanged();
      Invalidate();
    }
  }
  protected virtual void DrawStyleChanged()
  {
    switch(style)
    {
      case DrawStyle.Shadowed:
        offset = new Point(-1, -1);
        break;
      case DrawStyle.Embossed:
        offset = new Point(-1, -2);
        break;
      case DrawStyle.Engraved:
        offset = new Point(1, 2);
        break;
      case DrawStyle.Custom:
        offset = new Point(0, 0);
        break;
    }
  }
}
```

The enumeration DrawStyle will let the user pick from named styles. The underlying field that stores the style is listed after the numerator. The constructor follows the enumeration and the field. The public property Style (note the use of the convention of camel-casing fields and Pascal-casing properties) will let the user change the style at design time. The getter simply returns the underlying field value, and the setter performs the steps necessary to update the control.

The setter changes the field value and calls DrawStyleChanged. DrawStyleChanged uses a case statement to define the offsetting values based on the DrawStyle selected. Finally, the control is invalidated, causing the OnPaint method to be invoked. Use Invalidate instead of calling OnPaint directly to repaint the control. Using Invalidate will help avoid flickering by sending a message to the control to paint changed regions of the control, and the message queue can manage the number of times the control is actually repainted.

Adding the Finishing Touch

There are several attributes we can use to add fit and finish to our custom control. This section provides the complete listing for the EffectsLabel control, and we will describe the attributes incorporated into the code, as well as other details that yield the finished control.

Listing 9-2   *The complete listing for the EffectsLabel control*

```
1:  /// <summary>
2:  /// Custom text effects for Windows Forms
3:  /// </summary>
4:  [ToolboxBitmap(
5:    @"EffectsLabel2.bmp")]
6:  //[ToolboxBitmap(typeof(Label))]
7:  public class EffectsLabel : Label
8:  {
9:     public enum DrawStyle{Custom, Shadowed, Engraved, Embossed};
10:    private DrawStyle style;
11:    private Point offset;
12:    private Color overlayColor = Color.Black;
13:
14:    public EffectsLabel() : base()
15:    {
16:    Style = DrawStyle.Shadowed;
17:    }
18:
19:    [Description("Describes the appearance of the label's text."),
20:    Category("Appearance")]
21:    public DrawStyle Style
22:    {
23:      get
24:      {
25:        return style;
26:      }
```

```
27:      set
28:      {
29:        style = value;
30:        DrawStyleChanged();
31:        Invalidate();
32:      }
33:    }
34:
35:    [Description(
36:    "The ForeColor to create the shadow effect."),
37:    Category("Appearance")]
38:    public Color OverlayColor
39:    {
40:      get
41:      {
42:         return overlayColor;
43:      }
44:      set
45:      {
46:        overlayColor = value;
47:        Invalidate();
48:      }
49:    }
50:
51:    [Description("Change this value directly to create a custom effect.)"),
52:    Category("Appearance")]
53:    public Point Offset
54:    {
55:      get
56:      {
57:        return offset;
58:      }
59:      set
60:      {
61:        Style = DrawStyle.Custom;
62:        offset = value;
63:        Invalidate();
64:      }
65:    }
66:
67:    protected virtual void DrawStyleChanged()
68:    {
69:      switch(style)
70:      {
71:        case DrawStyle.Shadowed:
72:          offset = new Point(-1, -1);
73:          break;
74:        case DrawStyle.Embossed:
75:          offset = new Point(-1, -2);
76:          break;
```

```
77:          case DrawStyle.Engraved:
78:            offset = new Point(1, 2);
79:            break;
80:          case DrawStyle.Custom:
81:            offset = new Point(0, 0);
82:            break;
83:        }
84: }
85:
86:   protected override void OnPaint(PaintEventArgs e)
87:   {
88:     base.OnPaint(e);
89:     Draw(e.Graphics);
90:   }
91:
92:   private void Draw(Graphics g)
93:   {
94:     TextEffects.DrawText(this, g, new SolidBrush(overlayColor),
95:     offset.X, offset.Y);
96:   }
97:
98: }
```

Auto Documentation Feature

Lines 1 through 3 in Listing 9-2 demonstrate the three hash mark (///) comments that can be used to generate documentation for your code. The Tools | Build Comment Web Pages menu option will incorporate comments tagged with three hash marks into HTML help documentation. Figure 9-1 shows the comment on line 2 of Listing 9-2 incorporated into the help documentation for the EffectsLabel.

In addition to using the three hash marks for documenting your code, you can use special XML tags to create other documentation features. Table 9-1 lists the comment tags for generating documentation.

Defining the Category

The Properties window organizes properties either alphabetically or by category. This is to help consumers find properties at design time. The CategoryAttribute is demonstrated several places in Listing 9-2. Line 20 demonstrates the CategoryAttribute. We are indicating that the DrawStyle is categorized as an Appearance property. If you click the Categorized button in the Properties window, then the properties for the selected control will be displayed by category, as shown in Figure 9-2.

If the string used to initialize the CategoryAttribute is unique, then a new category will be created in the Properties window.

Providing a Description

At the bottom of the Properties window is a description of the selected property. This value didn't get there by accident. The DescriptionAttribute takes a string argument. The text used

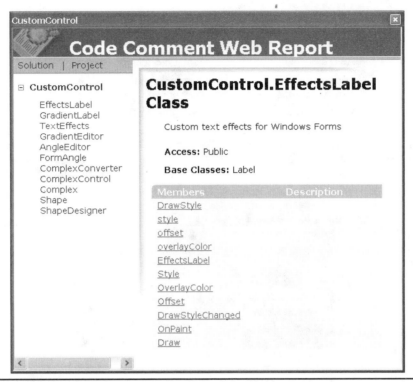

Figure 9-1 *The generated documentation, created in part by reading the comments tagged with three hash marks*

Comment Tags	Description
<c>	Indicates that text in a description refers to code.
<code>	Use this tag to indicate that multiple lines of comments refer to code.
<example>	Combine with the <code> tag to indicate that a comment represents example code.
<exception>	Used to specify which exceptions a class can throw.
<include>	Use <include> to refer to comments in an external file.
<list>	This tag allows you to specify a heading for a table or list. Use <listheader> and <item> to build the elements of the list or table.
<para>	Provide structure to comments by separating line text into paragraphs.
<param>	Provide reference for a named parameter.
<paramref>	Use <paramref> to indicate that a word is a parameter.
<permission>	Supports documenting the permission level for a member.
<remarks>	Use <remarks> to provide an overview of a type.
<returns>	Supports providing a description of the return type of a method.

Table 9-1 *Comment XML Document Tags for Generating HTML Documentation for Your Code*

Comment Tags	Description
<see>	Creates a cross-reference for a document item.
<seealso>	Adds an item to a See Also section of the documentation.
<summary>	<remarks> is used to provide information about a type, and <summary> is used to provide information about members of that type.
<value>	Supports providing descriptions for properties.

Table 9-1   *Comment XML Document Tags for Generating HTML Documentation for Your Code (continued)*

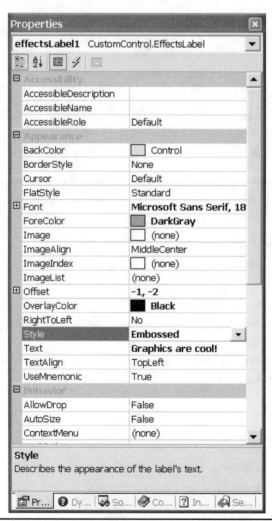

Figure 9-2   *The Properties window with the EffectsLabel properties ordered by category*

to initialize the DescriptionAttribute will be displayed at the bottom of the Properties window unless you deselect the Description context menu item.

If you apply multiple attributes, as we did in several places in Listing 9-2, then you can separate the attributes with commas. Here is an excerpt from Listing 9-2 that demonstrates two attributes applied to the DrawStyle property.

```
19:     [Description("Describes the appearance of the label's text."),
20:     Category("Appearance")]
```

Adding a Custom Bitmap for Your Control

If you want your control to have a custom bitmap, then you can apply the ToolboxBitmapAttribute to the class. This attribute can refer to an external bitmap file or use type information to request an existing icon for an existing control.

```
[ToolboxBitmap(@"c:\temp\EffectsLabel2.bmp")]
//[ToolboxBitmap(typeof(Label))]
```

The first statement demonstrates how to associate an external bitmap with our control (see Figure 9-3), and the second (commented) statement demonstrates how to request the type information for the Label control. If we use the second attribute statement, then our EffectsLabel will have the same icon as the Label control.

NOTE

Notice the use of the @ symbol in the ToolboxBitmapAttribute statement. The \ (slash character) is used for escape text sequences. (Recall that we used it to create the © symbol for our About box.) To actually get the backslash in a string, you will need to use two backslashes \\ or you can use a single one and the @ character to indicate that the string should be interpreted literally rather than as the processing escapes sequences.

To create a custom 16×16 pixel bitmap for the EffectsLabel, you can use the Project | Add New Item menu and add a Bitmap to the solution. This step will automatically open the Image editor, which will allow you to draw a custom bitmap. The Image editor works like the Paint program that is provided with Windows.

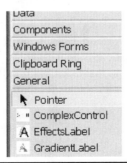

Figure 9-3   *The custom EffectLabel2.bmp—zoomed—in the Toolbox*

Testing Your Component

The next important step in the macro process is to test your custom control. You will want to contrive some unit tests that exercise all code paths for you custom control. In systems, unit testing needs to be done for every class and method within that class. For a control, a single class (or a few classes) represents the entire assembly; you will still need to test every class, but the process is shorter, as there is less to test.

An easy way to test your custom control is to add an application to the solution containing the control. If the control is a Windows Forms control, then add a Windows application to the solution. Add a project reference to the control in your Windows application, and programmatically create and invoke methods that exercise the behavior of your custom control. The code listing that follows creates the text shown in Figure 9-4.

```csharp
private void TestLabel_Load(object sender, System.EventArgs e)
{
  CustomControl.EffectsLabel effectsLabel = new
    CustomControl.EffectsLabel();
  effectsLabel.Text = "Dynamically Created!";
  effectsLabel.AutoSize = true;
  effectsLabel.Style = CustomControl.EffectsLabel.DrawStyle.Embossed;
  effectsLabel.ForeColor = Color.White;
  effectsLabel.OverlayColor = Color.Black;
  effectsLabel.Font = new Font("Times new Roman", 24);
  Controls.Add(effectsLabel);
}
```

Code to test a Windows Forms control can be placed in the Load event handler for a Form. The preceding code tests many of the code paths, but you need a good strategy for testing all code paths. There are some changes you can make to the EffectsLabel class that will facilitate this process.

Implementing a Test Function

The first change is to make the test method part of the EffectsLabel class. Implement a static method called Test and invoke that method. Because we are testing a Windows Forms control, we will need to pass in the Controls collection we want to add our control to, or we can return an instance of the custom control and make the addition to the Controls collection externally.

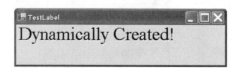

Figure 9-4   *A dynamically created instance of your custom control provides a convenient way to step through the code and test every code path.*

The following addition to the EffectsLabel class makes our custom control self-contained, including testability.

```
public static void Test(ControlCollection Controls)
{
  EffectsLabel effectsLabel = new EffectsLabel();
  effectsLabel.Text = "Dynamically Created!";
  effectsLabel.AutoSize = true;
  effectsLabel.Style = DrawStyle.Embossed;
  effectsLabel.ForeColor = Color.White;
  effectsLabel.OverlayColor = Color.Black;
  effectsLabel.Font = new Font("Times new Roman", 24);
  Controls.Add(effectsLabel);
}
```

To test our control, we simply need to invoke EffectsLabel.Test, passing the ControlCollection of the owning ContainerControl. This will usually be a Form's Controls property, but you could pass the Controls property of any derivative of the ContainerControl, like a Panel control.

Implementing Trap Behavior

President Reagan used to say "trust but verify" when referring to the Russians at the end of the Cold War. This sage advice is wise counsel for software development, too. Trust that your code works because you're smart—but verify, too. Verifying that your code works will help avoid embarrassing situations.

You can verify that all code paths work to some degree by simply exercising those paths. Exercising a path simply means that you compile and test the code, providing test data that takes all possible branches within your code. This won't test your code for all possible states, but it will help you ensure that there are no obvious, embarrassing defects. A good technique for ensuring that you have exercised all states is to implement a trap.

A *trap* is a method that is called that halts processing when a code path has been executed. You can implement a trap simply by calling the Debug.Assert method with the argument False. If you place a trap at each code branch and comment out the traps each time one is triggered, you have a record verifying that all branches have been tested. Remove all of the comments to reset the traps if you need to run the tests after your component is updated. Here is a statement that demonstrates the technique. (This statement assumes that you have included a *using* statement with the System.Diagnostics namespace in the module containing the trap.)

```
Debug.Assert(false);
```

For example, if we wanted to ensure that all of the DrawStyles yield the right visual effect, we could place a trap for each case in the DrawStyleChanged method. By visually inspecting the resultant effect of each DrawStyle and commenting out the trap when the appearance is as desired, we can ensure that all styles paint correctly. Here is the revision to the DrawStyleChanged method as described.

```
protected virtual void DrawStyleChanged()
{
  switch(style)
  {
    case DrawStyle.Shadowed:
      Debug.Assert(false);
      offset = new Point(-1, -1);
      break;
    case DrawStyle.Embossed:
      Debug.Assert(false);
      offset = new Point(-1, -2);
      break;
    case DrawStyle.Engraved:
      Debug.Assert(false);
      offset = new Point(1, 2);
      break;
    case DrawStyle.Custom:
      Debug.Assert(false);
      offset = new Point(0, 0);
      break;
    }
}
```

When each trap is thrown and you are satisfied with the result, simply comment out the trap in the source code and click the Ignore button in the Assert dialog. Because we are using the Debug.Assert method, the trap code will automatically be turned off when we compile our control assembly in release mode.

It is easier to test this kind of code before you install the control into the Toolbox. You will save time and effort by testing the control programmatically. (Of course you can add the code to the Toolbox before testing if you want to.) Ultimately, when you are satisfied with the control you will want to add it to the Toolbox. We will do that in the next section.

Adding the Component to the Toolbox

After you have created your custom control, you will want to incorporate the control into the Toolbox. This step is accomplished by selecting Tools | Customize Toolbox and browsing to the assembly containing the custom control.

You can add additional tabs to the Toolbox through the Toolbox context menu and drag your controls to their own tabs.

After you have added your control to the Toolbox, you can drag and drop instances of the control to Forms. When you add a control to your application from the Toolbox, an instance of the control is added to the Form and a reference to the assembly is added to the list of References in the solution.

If you modify your control, then you may need to Reset the Toolbox and re-add the modified assembly to the Toolbox. (If changes to the control do not seem to be reflected in your application, then remove the reference to the control's assembly and Reset the Toolbox, adding the updated list of assemblies referenced by the Toolbox.)

Creating a Merge Module

Thus far we have built and tested a custom control and installed it in our Toolbox. Suppose you want to distribute your control to other developers. To reliably distribute your control with your applications, you will need to create a Merge Module Project.

Merge Module Projects are defined as template projects in Visual Studio .NET. The recommended process is to define a Merge Module Project for every custom control and include all of the files, resources, registry entries, and setup logic necessary to install your custom control. Merge Modules contain version information for a component, ensuring that components are not removed when other application assemblies have dependencies on those components. For this reason, a new Merge Module should be created for every version of your component after a Merge Module has been added to an Installer file. Merge Modules cannot be installed directly; a Merge Module must be installed as part of a Windows Installer (.msi) file.

Follow the numbered steps provided next to add a Merge Module Project to the solution containing the Custom Control, add the output from the CustomControl project to the Merge Module, and create a Windows Installer.

1. Select File | Add Project | New Project and select the Merge Module Project template from the Add New Project dialog. (The Merge Module Project is a template in the Setup and Deployment Projects folder.)

2. Provide a meaningful name for the Merge Module and click OK. (I used CustomControls.msm for the EffectsLabel assembly.)

3. Select the Merge Module Project in the Solution Explorer, and click Project | Add | Project Output to open the Add Project Output Group dialog (shown in Figure 9-5).

4. Repeat step 1. This time, select the Setup Project template.

5. Select the Setup Project in the Solution Explorer, and select Project | Add | Merge Module. The Merge Modules explorer dialog will be displayed. Navigate to the CustomControls.msm Merge Module and click OK.

6. When the Setup Project is compiled, the Windows Installer, setup, and .ini files will be copied or created in the Setup Project folder.

The primary output from the Setup Project is the setup.msi file. This file contains the application files, registry settings, dependent files like our CustomControl.dll, and instructions for installing these files.

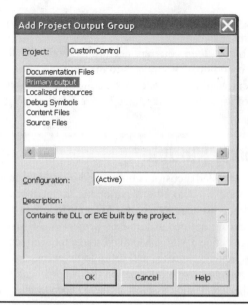

Figure 9-5   *The Add Project Output Group is used to add the output from our control assembly to the Merge Module Project.*

Secondary Topics

There are several advanced topics that facilitate creating advanced custom controls. We didn't necessarily need these capabilities for the EffectsLabel, but you will find them useful for creating a professional fit and finish. To demonstrate the topics in this section of the chapter, I have included several additional components for showing how to

- ▶ Implement the IConvertible interface for run-time type conversion and demonstrate operator overloading
- ▶ Create a Type Converter and apply the convert using the TypeConverterAttribute
- ▶ Create a custom Type Editor
- ▶ Implement the IDesigner interface

These skills will be used to create a Shape control, a gradient text label, and a control that represents a complex number. The last control was created to demonstrate a custom TypeConverter but is not especially useful as a control.

Creating a Type Converter

Type converters let data be represented in more than one logical way. For example, it makes sense to represent an integer as both a numeric value and a string value. When you want to perform arithmetic operations you need the integer, and when you want to display the value you need a string.

The Common Language Runtime provides two ways to convert types. The IConvertible interface requires that you implement methods that convert between simple data types, such as between the integer and string. The IConvertible interface is useful only at run-time, and it throws an exception if it doesn't make sense to convert between two types. (Remember, you must implement every method defined by an interface.) An example would be trying to convert the string "Hello World!" to a DateTime value.

The second way to convert between types is to derive a TypeConverter class. The TypeConverter is a bit more complex to implement but supports converting between more complex types. For example, we can use a TypeConverter to provide a suitable representation for an Image as string. This is the role of the ImageConverter defined in the System.ComponentModel namespace.

In general, the IConvertible interface is faster because you are invoking methods directly, but it is less flexible and powerful and is supported only at run time. The TypeConverter is slower because it relies on Reflection (which is slow because it relies on dynamic binding and method invocation) but supports design time and run-time conversion and is significantly more flexible than the IConvertible interface. Implement IConvertible to convert between existing .NET types. Implement a TypeConverter to convert between new types and representative types.

The two subsections that follow demonstrate how to implement the IConvertible interface and a TypeConverter.

Implementing IConvertible

Classes that implement IConvertible will let consumers convert between the type represented by the class and the types named by the IConvertible interface. IConvertible does not support converting back to the original type, because there is no way to know in advance what types might be converted from. If you define a class that implements IConvertible, then you must implement GetTypeCode, ToBoolean, ToByte, ToChar, ToDateTime, ToDecimal, ToDouble, ToInt16, ToInt32, ToInt64, ToByte, ToSingle, ToString, ToType, ToUInt16, ToUint32, and ToUInt64.

TIP

The System.Convert class implements static methods that support converting between an argument type and the type named by the method. Use the Convert class for general type conversions at run time.

To demonstrate the IConvertible interface, we implement a class that represents a complex number. A complex number is a number comprised of a real and an imaginary part. When two complex numbers are added, the real parts are added and the imaginary parts are added, yielding the new number.

Implementing a complex number will reasonably require support for converting between the values that represent the complex number and a string. We also have to implement some operators to support arithmetic operations, and we might elect to convert a complex number to an integer, simply truncating the imaginary part. We can start with a struct that implements a Complex number. We will use the struct shown in Listing 9-3 to demonstrate how to implement the IConvertible interface and alternately to demonstrate the TypeConverter.

Listing 9-3   *Defining a Complex number struct that implements the IConvertible interface.*

```
1:   public struct Complex : IConvertible
2:   {
3:     private int r;
4:     private int i;
5:
6:     public Complex( int r, int i )
7:     {
8:       this.r = r;
9:       this.i = i;
10:    }
11:
12:    public override string ToString()
13:    {
14:      return i>=0 ? string.Format("{0} + {1}i", r, i) :
15:      string.Format("{0} - {1}i", r, i * -1);
16:    }
17:
18:    private static Complex op_Add(Complex lhs, Complex rhs)
19:    {
20:      return new Complex(lhs.r + rhs.r, lhs.i + rhs.i);
21:    }
22:
23:    public static Complex operator+(Complex lhs, Complex rhs)
24:    {
25:      return op_Add(lhs, rhs);
26:    }
27:
28:    private static Complex op_Subtract(Complex lhs, Complex rhs)
29:    {
30:      return new Complex(lhs.r - rhs.r, lhs.i - rhs.i);
31:    }
32:
33:    public static Complex operator-(Complex lhs, Complex rhs)
34:    {
35:      return op_Subtract(lhs, rhs);
36:    }
37:
```

```
38:    TypeCode IConvertible.GetTypeCode()
39:    {
40:      return TypeCode.Object;
41:    }
42:
43:    private void ThrowException(string message)
44:    {
45:      throw new InvalidCastException(message);
46:    }
47:
48:    bool IConvertible.ToBoolean(IFormatProvider provider)
49:    {
50:      ThrowException("conversion to Boolean not supported");
51:      return false;
52:    }
53:
54:    byte IConvertible.ToByte(IFormatProvider provider)
55:    {
56:      ThrowException("conversion to byte not supported");
57:      return 0;
58:    }
59:
60:    char IConvertible.ToChar(IFormatProvider provider)
61:    {
62:      ThrowException("conversion to char not supported");
63:      return ' ';
64:    }
65:
66:    DateTime IConvertible.ToDateTime(IFormatProvider provider)
67:    {
68:      ThrowException("conversion to DateTime not supported");
69:      return DateTime.Now;
70:    }
71:
72:    decimal IConvertible.ToDecimal(IFormatProvider provider)
73:    {
74:      return (decimal)r;
75:    }
76:
77:    double IConvertible.ToDouble(IFormatProvider provider)
78:    {
79:      return (double)r;
80:    }
81:
82:    short IConvertible.ToInt16(IFormatProvider provider)
```

```
 83:    {
 84:      return (short)r;
 85:    }
 86:
 87:    int IConvertible.ToInt32(IFormatProvider provider)
 88:    {
 89:      return (int)r;
 90:    }
 91:
 92:    long IConvertible.ToInt64(IFormatProvider provider)
 93:    {
 94:      return (long)r;
 95:    }
 96:
 97:    sbyte IConvertible.ToSByte(IFormatProvider provider)
 98:    {
 99:       ThrowException("conversion to sbyte not supported");
100:      return (sbyte)0;
101:    }
102:
103:    float IConvertible.ToSingle(IFormatProvider provider)
104:    {
105:      return (float)r;
106:    }
107:
108:    string IConvertible.ToString(IFormatProvider provider)
109:    {
110:      return ToString();
111:    }
112:
113:    object IConvertible.ToType(Type type, IFormatProvider provider)
114:    {
115:      return this.GetType();
116:    }
117:
118:    ushort IConvertible.ToUInt16(IFormatProvider provider)
119:    {
120:      return (ushort)r;
121:    }
122:
123:    uint IConvertible.ToUInt32(IFormatProvider provider)
124:    {
125:      return (uint)r;
```

```
126:   }
127:
128:   ulong IConvertible.ToUInt64(IFormatProvider provider)
129:   {
130:     return (ulong)r;
131:   }
132:
133:   [Conditional("DEBUG")]
134:   public static void Test()
135:   {
136:     IConvertible c = new Complex(1,1);
137:     Debug.WriteLine(c.GetTypeCode().ToString());
138:       try{Debug.WriteLine(c.ToBoolean(null));}
139:       catch(InvalidCastException e){Debug.WriteLine(e.Message);}
140:       // test  each method in a try catch block
141:   }
142: }
```

The IConvertible interface defines the methods described in the first paragraph of this section. You have to provide an implementation for every interface member, but an appropriate implementation might be to throw an exception for a type we don't want to convert to. Lines 97 to 101 of Listing 9-3 demonstrate throwing an exception when a user tries to convert our Complex struct to a signed byte.

IConvertible methods are called by the System.Convert class. All of the members of Convert are static. For example, to Convert a Complex to an integer, you can write

```
Complex c = new Complex(1, 3);
Convert.ToInt32(c);
```

The Convert class will invoke the Complex method that implements IConvertible.ToInt32.

As mentioned, the methods in the IConvertible interface are only usable at run time. RAD tools like Visual Studio .NET have a design time aspect, too. To support converting types at design time, we can implement a TypeConverter. The next section uses the Complex struct to demonstrate design time type conversion.

Implementing a TypeConverter

The TypeConverter class is used to support converting between types. A common conversion is one between an object and a string representation of an object. An example we encountered earlier in the chapter is the ImageConverter that displays text in the absence of an Image for an Image property.

This section demonstrates a custom TypeConverter, how to associate the TypeConverter with a type using the TypeConverterAttribute, and how to use the TypeDescriptor class to convert between two types supported by the TypeConverter.

Defining the ComplexConverter Class

The TypeConverter base class introduces several methods that can be overloaded, depending on the kind of conversion behavior you want to support. Unlike the IConvertible interface, the TypeConverter is supported at design time and run time, and the TypeConverter supports converting back and forth between types. For instance, our converter supports converting a string to a Complex and a Complex back to a string.

Listing 9-4 demonstrates a TypeConverter for the Complex struct. After Listing 9-4, I will describe the ComplexConverter class and demonstrate how to associate a TypeConverter with a class using the TypeConverterAttribute.

Listing 9-4 *Implementing a TypeConverter for the Complex struct*

```
1:  public class ComplexConverter : TypeConverter
2:  {
3:    public override bool CanConvertFrom(ITypeDescriptorContext context,
4:      Type sourceType)
5:    {
6:       return sourceType == typeof(string) ? true :
7:         base.CanConvertFrom(context, sourceType);
8:    }
9:
10:   public override object ConvertFrom(ITypeDescriptorContext context,
11:     CultureInfo culture, object value)
12:   {
13:     if (value is string)
14:     {
15:       string[] v = ((string)value).Split(new char[] {'+', '-', 'i'});
16:         return ((string)value).IndexOf('-') > 0 ?
17:         new Complex(int.Parse(v[0]), int.Parse(v[1]) * -1) :
18:         new Complex(int.Parse(v[0]), int.Parse(v[1]));
19:     }
20:     return base.ConvertFrom(context, culture, value);
21:   }
22:
23:   public override object ConvertTo(ITypeDescriptorContext context,
24:     CultureInfo culture, object value, Type destinationType)
25:   {
26:     if (destinationType == typeof(string))
27:     {
28:       return value.ToString();
29:     }
```

```
30:        return base.ConvertTo(context, culture, value, destinationType);
31:    }
32:
33:    public override bool CanConvertTo(ITypeDescriptorContext context,
34:       Type destinationType)
35:    {
36:      return destinationType == typeof(string) ? true :
37:         base.CanConvertTo(context, destinationType);
38:    }
39: }
```

The ComplexConverter implements conversion between a string and a Complex value. (Recall that you can convert between more complex types, too, as illustrated by the ImageConverter implemented in the CLR.) ComplexConverter implements CanConvertFrom, ConvertFrom, ConvertTo, and CanConvertTo. The methods prefixed with *Can* answer the questions indicating whether a conversion for a specific type is supported. The methods without the *Can* prefix actually perform the conversions.

TIP

Line 7 of Listing 9-4 demonstrates how to invoke methods or refer to base class members by using the base keyword.

CanConvertFrom on lines 3 through 6 of Listing 9-4 performs a dynamic type evaluation. If the sourceType argument on line 4 is a string, then the method returns True; otherwise, the code passes on responsibility to the parent TypeConverter class.

Lines 10 through 21 of Listing 9-4 implement the overridden ConvertFrom method. Line 15 uses the string.Split method to determine whether the string is correctly formatted. Correctly formatted strings for the Complex type are in the following format: *number ± imaginary*i. The piece represented by *number* is the real number part, and the piece presented by *imaginary* is affixed with an *i* suffix. Lines 17 and 18 demonstrate the int.Parse method that is used to clean up the string array returned by Split and to construct a new Complex object.

Lines 23 through 31 of Listing 9-4 implement the ConvertTo method. We implemented an overridden Complex.ToString method that we can use (see line 28 to convert a Complex to a string). Finally, the CanConvertTo method implemented on lines 33 through 38 returns True if we are trying to convert to a strng representation of the Complex type.

There are additional capabilities that can be overridden in a custom TypeConvert. Refer to the Visual Studio .NET help documentation for the TypeConverter class defined in the System.ComponentModel namespace.

Using the TypeConverterAttribute

Applying a custom TypeConverter is done by associating the converter with the type it converts using the TypeConverterAttribute. To associate the ComplexConverter with the

Complex struct, add an attribute to the struct defined in Listing 9-3. The following code demonstrates the attribute immediately preceding the struct header in Listing 9-3.

```
[TypeConverter(typeof(ComplexConverter))]
public struct Complex : IConvertible
```

You will need to add a *using* statement that refers to the System.ComponentModel namespace, and the ComplexConverter class will need to be accessible to the Complex struct. Both the Complex struct and the ComplexConverter are implemented in the imaginary.cs module in the ComplexControl.csproj available for download from the **www.osborne.com** website.

TIP

*All code from this chapter will be available online at **http://www.softconcept.com/books/source** and **http://www.osborne.com**.*

Run-Time Conversion with the TypeDescriptor Class

Applying the TypeConverterAttribute to a class ensures that type conversion will occur at design time. For example, deleting an image will set an image property back to the text "(None)" because the ImageConverter is part of the CLR.

After we associated the ComplexConverter with the Complex struct, design-time support will exist for Complex properties too. If you want to perform run-time type conversion using a TypeConverter, then you need to request the TypeConverter using the TypeDescriptor class, instead of creating the generalized TypeConverter directly.

The code fragments that follow demonstrate how to dynamically request a TypeConverter for the Complex struct and perform conversions to and from a string.

```
CustomControl.Complex c = new CustomControl.Complex(2, 3);
string s = "1+1i";

if( TypeDescriptor.GetConverter(c).CanConvertTo(typeof(string)) )
  s = TypeDescriptor.GetConverter(c).ConvertToString(c);
CustomControl.Complex d =
(CustomControl.Complex)TypeDescriptor.GetConverter(c).ConvertFrom(s);
```

The first statement creates an instance of the Complex type. The second statement defines a string that is in a format consistent with a Complex number. TypeDescriptor.GetConverter returns the right kind of converter for the type passed to GetConverter. CanConvertTo returns a Boolean indicating whether the conversion is supported. We know it is in this instance, and the conversion is performed. The last statement converts the string back to a Complex struct.

TypeConverters use Reflection to perform type conversions and, as a result, will be slower than conversions performed by the IConvertible interface. Recall that the IConvertible interface will allow you to convert a type to a new type but not back again. Additionally, the TypeConverter supports design time conversion support, which is essential to implementing components that behave in an intuitive way in Visual Studio .NET, as is illustrated by the Point, Rectangle, and Image types.

Implementing a Type Editor

The previous section demonstrated the type converter. If you have been following along with the sample code, then you know that you can define the values for a Point property by entering a comma-delimited string in any property that represents a Point. The TypeConverter is one aspect of implementing professional, custom controls.

Have you gotten around to wondering how those small icons are painted next to properties in the Properties window? Or how combo boxes, color drop-down lists, or dialog-based property editors are implemented? The answer is the UITypeEditor. The UITypeEditor (for User Interface Type Editor) is the base class for implementing editors in .NET.

If you define a custom control that has properties that cannot be managed by simple string values—even if you have a TypeConverter—then you need a UITypeEditor. You need a UITypeEditor if you simply want to provide a cool way to implement editing properties at design time.

This section will demonstrate how to implement a dialog-based UITypeEditor, a drop-down editor based on the NumericUpDown control, and a UITypeEditor that demonstrates custom painting in the Properties window. We will accomplish our objectives by implementing a GradientLabel. (Our GradientLabel will be a custom control that paints the label using a gradient brush.) We will display a sample of the output from our label in the Text property by implementing a GradientEditor. And, we will use two versions of an AngleEditor to demonstrate the drop-down NumericUpDown editor and a dialog-based editor. The AngleEditor will allow us to express the angle used to describe the GradientBrush.

Creating the GradientEditor

Often it is useful to provide a visual clue demonstrating what role a property plays in a custom control. For example, if you have a Shape control, then it might be useful to describe an editor that provides a visual cue illustrating what the shape will look like. This kind of feature adds richness to the IDE and makes your controls appear more professional.

A GradientLabel control is implemented in the CustomControl.csproj class library. The control demonstrates the painting capabilities of a UITypeEditor. (The GradientEditor is difficult to see in Figure 9-6, but it is represented by the boxed-in area with the "T" printed in a green and white gradient brush. In this instance you may have to take my word for it.)

Having established the goal of our UITypeEditor—to display the effect of the LinearGradientBrush in the Properties window—I will demonstrate the code in Listing 9-5.

Listing 9-5   *The source code to implement the GradientEditor, which shows text based on a LinearGradientBrush in the Properties window*

```
1:  public class GradientEditor : UITypeEditor
2:  {
3:    public override bool GetPaintValueSupported(
4:      ITypeDescriptorContext context)
5:    {
```

```
6:      return true;
7:    }
8:
9:    public override void PaintValue(PaintValueEventArgs e)
10:   {
11:    GradientLabel label = (GradientLabel) e.Context.Instance;
12:      e.Graphics.DrawString(label.Text, label.Font,
13:      new LinearGradientBrush(e.Bounds,
14:      label.ForeColor, label.BlendColor, label.Angle),
14:      e.Bounds);
15:   }
16: }
```

You will have to add a reference to the System.Design.dll assembly to generalize the UITypeEditor (shown on line 1 of Listing 9-5). The UITypeEditor class is defined in the System.Drawing.Design namespace. Add a *using* statement at the top of the module containing the code in Listing 9-5.

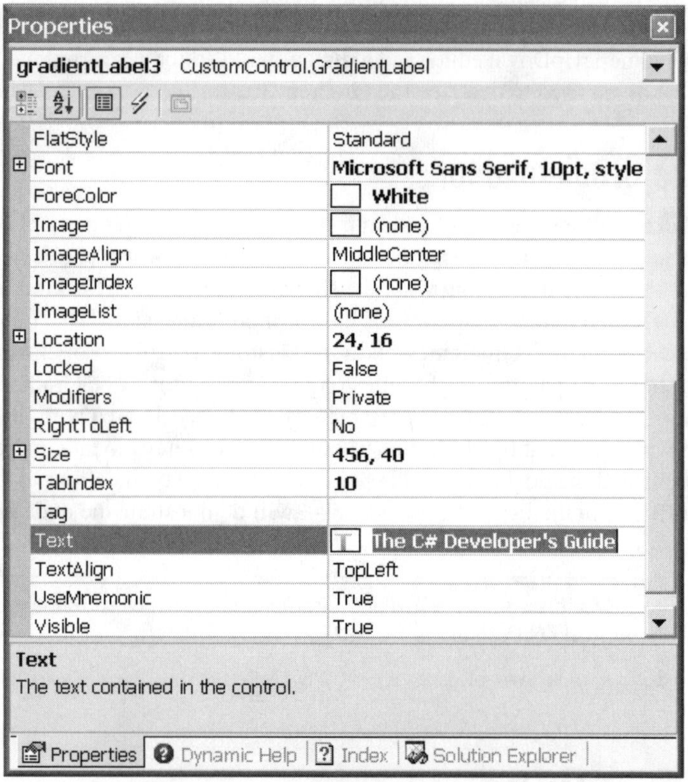

Figure 9-6   *The GradientEditor shown in the selected property*

TIP

When you draw content in the boxed-in region, use the Bounds property of the PaintValueEventArgs argument to constrain the display region.

Our objective is to create a custom editor that displays the gradient text; hence, all we have to do is override the GetPaintValueSupported and PaintValue methods inherited from UITypeEditor. GetPaintValueSupported returns False by default. By returning True, on line 6 of Listing 9-5, we are indicating that we are going to perform custom painting in the Properties window. The PaintValueEventArgs argument for the PaintValue method on line 9 represents the canvas—also referred to as hDC, DC, or Device Context—of the small boxed region in the Properties window (see Figure 9-6). The code in PaintValue—between lines 10 and 16—uses GDI+, DrawString, and a LinearGradientBrush to display a sample of the visual effect of changes in the GradientLabel.

Implementing the AngleEditor

The GradientEditor demonstrated the custom painting aspects of a UITypeEditor. The AngleEditor demonstrates how to implement methods that support editing a value. To implement the AngleEditor, we will override UITypeEditor.EditValue and UITypeEditor.GetEditStyle. GetEditStyle returns a UITypeEditorEditStyle enumerated value; the enumerated value returned describes the type of editor to display.

Listing 9-6 demonstrates the AngleEditor. A compiler directive is used to separate the code that supports both the dialog and drop-down version of the editor. If GetEditStyle returns UITypeEditorEditStyle.DropDown, then define the compiler directive DROPDOWN. To use the modal dialog version of the AngleEditor, undefine the DROPDOWN compiler directive.

Listing 9-6   *A custom UITypeEditor that demonstrates the GetEditStyle and EditValue methods of a custom editor*

```
1:  public class AngleEditor : UITypeEditor
2:  {
3:    private IWindowsFormsEditorService editorService = null;
4:    private bool IsValidContext(ITypeDescriptorContext context)
5:    {
6:      return context != null && context.Instance != null;
7:    }
8:
9:    private bool IsValidProvider(IServiceProvider provider)
10:   {
11:     return provider != null;
12:   }
13:
14:   private IWindowsFormsEditorService GetService(
```

```
15:       IServiceProvider provider)
16:    {
17:      return (IWindowsFormsEditorService)provider.GetService(
18:        typeof(IWindowsFormsEditorService));
19:    }
20:
21:    public override object EditValue(ITypeDescriptorContext context,
22:      IServiceProvider provider, object value)
23:    {
24:      if( !IsValidContext(context) || !IsValidProvider(provider))
25:        return value;
26:
27:      editorService = GetService(provider);
28:      if( editorService == null ) return value;
29:
30: #if DROPDOWN
31:
32:      NumericUpDown control = new NumericUpDown();
33:      control.Maximum = 360;
34:      control.Minimum = 0;
35:
36:      if(value is float)
37:      {
38:        control.Value = Convert.ToDecimal(value);
39:        editorService.DropDownControl(control);
40:      }
41:      return (float)control.Value;
42: #else
43:      if(value is float)
44:      {
45:        using( FormAngle form = new FormAngle())
46:        {
47:          form.Angle = (float)value;
48:          if(editorService.ShowDialog(form) == DialogResult.OK)
49:            return form.Angle;
50:        }
51:      }
52:
53:      return value;
54: #endif
55:    }
56:
57:    public override UITypeEditorEditStyle GetEditStyle(ITypeDescriptorContext
context)
58:    {
59:      return IsValidContext(context) ?
60: #if DROPDOWN
61:        UITypeEditorEditStyle.DropDown : base.GetEditStyle(context);
62: #else
63:        UITypeEditorEditStyle.Modal : base.GetEditStyle(context);
```

```
64: #endif
65:   }
66: }
```

TIP

Conditional directives must be defined first at the top of a module.

The kind of editor displayed in this particular example hinges on the conditional directive defined on line 1 of Listing 9-6. If DROPDOWN is defined, then we try to return the UITypeEditorEditStyle.DropDown enumerated value on line 61; otherwise we try to return the UITypeEditorEditStyle.Modal value on line 63. (Figure 9-7 shows the DropDown AngleEditor in the Properties window.)

The IsValidContext method invoked on line 59 of Listing 9-6 tests to determine if the context is valid. IsValidContext is implemented on lines 4 through 7. IsValidContext tests to determine if the PropertyDescriptor and the PropertyDescriptor container are not null.

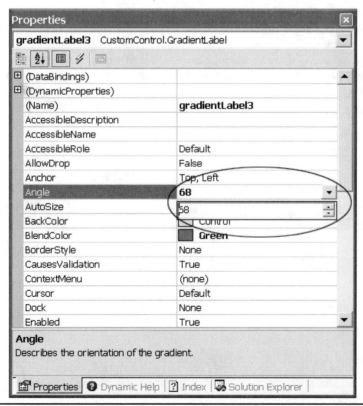

Figure 9-7   *A custom UITypeEditor using the UITypeEditorEditStyle.DropDown style*

GetEditStyle is the first key method. The second key method is EditValue, defined on lines 21 through 55 of Listing 9-6. Line 24 implements a sentry; if we don't have a valid context or provider, then the method returns the argument Value. The ITypeDescriptorContext refers to a PropertyDescriptor, most often used to perform type conversions for data, and an IServiceProvider. The IServiceProvider implements one method, GetService. The ServiceProvider we need is an IWindowsFormsEditorService. IWindowsFormsEditorService defines methods for showing a control to drop down or display as a modal dialog.

The DropDown version defined on lines 31 to 41 of Listing 9-6 creates an instance of the NumericDropDown control, setting the minimum and maximum values, and uses the IWindowsFormsEditorService to display the control. Lines 43 to 53 implement the modal dialog behavior. A *using* block on line 45 is used to create the form, and the IWindowsFormsEditorService is used to display the form within the context of Visual Studio .NET. All that's left to do is to associate the custom UITypeEditor with a property.

Applying the Custom Editor with the EditorAttribute

As with many things in this chapter, we associate a custom UITypeEditor with a control using an attribute. The EditorAttribute is defined in the System.ComponentModel namespace.

The version of the EditorAttribute we will use takes the type information of our custom type and the base type. The custom type is the AngleEditor class defined in the previous section and the type we derived it from, the UITypeEditor. We want to associate the editor with the Angle property of the GradientLabel. Combined with all of the attributes for the GradientLabel's Angle property, the property with its attributes is provided in the listing next:

```
[Description("Describes the orientation of the gradient."),
Category("Appearance"),
Editor(typeof(AngleEditor), typeof(UITypeEditor)),
DefaultValue(45)]
public float Angle
{
  get
  {
    return angle;
  }
  set
  {
    angle = value;
    Invalidate();
  }
}
```

The four attributes for the Angle property provide a description, category, default value, and custom UITypeEditor. These represent significant enhancements over the property itself, resulting in a richer user experience.

Defining a Windows Forms Designer

Programming in C# is a rewarding and fun experience. (For some fun, try the Terrarium examples in Chapter 4.) Unfortunately, however, we have to draw this chapter to a close. This means that I have to leave some things for you to discover; otherwise, by the time I finish this book, it will be time to write the second edition. I would like to close this chapter with a quick discussion of the IDesigner interface and the ControlDesigner class.

The IDesigner interface is defined in the System.ComponentModel.Design namespace. The interface defines Component and Verbs properties and DoDefaultAction and Initialize methods. An interesting application of the IDesigner interface is to define the ControlDesigner class.

ControlDesigner is defined in the System.Windows.Forms.Design (and there is one in the System.Web.UI.Design) namespace. By inheriting and extending the ControlDesigner class, you can provide extended behavior for custom controls at design time. The basic approach is quite straightforward: inherit from ControlDesigner; define a read-only Verbs property, which will become context menus for the control in Visual Studio .NET; and use the initialized reference to the Component property to update a referenced control at design time. Finally, associate the ControlDesigner with a control using the DesignerAttribute defined in the System.ComponentModel namespace.

The shape.cs module contained in the CustomControl.csproj project demonstrates a control that draws shapes. The designer displays one additional menu item, based on the implementation in Listing 9-7—an About menu item. You can refer to the code available online for the Shape control. The ShapeDesigner is provided in Listing 9-7.

Listing 9-7 *Implementing a ControlDesigner to extend design–time support for custom controls*

```
1:     public class ShapeDesigner : ControlDesigner
2:     {
3:       public override DesignerVerbCollection Verbs
4:       {
5:         get
6:         {
7:           return new DesignerVerbCollection(
8:             new DesignerVerb[]{new DesignerVerb("About",
9:             new EventHandler(OnAbout))});
10:        }
11:      }
12:
13:      private void OnAbout(object sender, System.EventArgs e)
14:      {
15:        const string About =
16:          "The C# Developer's Guide\n" +
17:          "Copyright \xA9 2002. All Rights Reserved.\n" +
18:          "Written by Paul Kimmel. pkimmel@softconcepts.com\n";
19:
```

```
20:          MessageBox.Show(About, "About", MessageBoxButtons.OK,
21:            MessageBoxIcon.Information);
22:      }
23:    }
```

OnAbout on lines 13 through 22 of Listing 9-7 implements the behavior of our designer. The OnAbout handler displays a simple About dialog to tell developers using my control about the author. (This is a perfectly valid use for a ControlDesigner, especially if you are in the developer tools business.) Lines 3 through 11 implement the overridden, read-only Verbs collection. Essentially, a verb translates to a menu item, and with menus you generally need a handler for the click event. Lines 7, 8, and 9 construct the DesignerVerbCollection, an array of DesignerVerbs, and initializes the DesignerVerb array with the menu caption and an event handler to respond when the verb is invoked by clicking the menu item.

 TIP

Several of the attributes in this chapter are initialized with type information. The reason for this is that by getting the type information of any type, Reflection can be used to dynamically access members of that type without knowing anything about the type in advance. See Chapter 2 for information about Reflection.

You can associate the ShapeDesigner with a control by initializing the DesignerAttribute with the type information of our custom ControlDesigner. The application of the attribute is demonstrated in the next code fragment:

```
[ToolboxBitmap(@"C:\temp\Shape.bmp"),
  Designer(typeof(ShapeDesigner))]
public class Shape : Control
{ // implement the class here
}
```

Summary

This chapter is one of those chapters that is fun to write. I am a toolsmith by nature. A toolsmith is someone who likes building parts of solutions, like components. Building custom controls is fun and rewarding, because it is often quick work with highly visible and reusable results and without a lot of the other things that go with developing systems, like gathering requirements and meetings.

This chapter contains significantly more than just an EffectsLabel. I have introduced you to many of the aspects that you can use over and over to build solid, professional, and rich custom controls. You learned how to create controls, ControlDesigners, and TypeEditors, and how to perform GDI+ custom painting operations. You also were shown how to use attributes defined in the ComponentModel to provide helpful metadata with your controls, and how to employ Merge Modules and type converters.

Support for building custom controls feels very rich in Visual Studio .NET and C#. The hallmark of a great tool is self-extensibility. Visual Studio .NET is very extensible in C# because the Common Language Runtime is a rich and expressive framework.

Creating
Custom Attributes

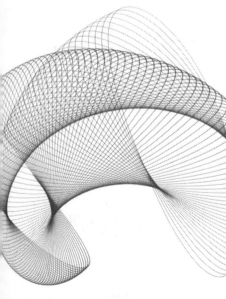

By now you have heard a lot about attributes. Attributes provide one of the means by which Microsoft has mitigated the impact of "DLL Hell." DLL Hell is caused by version problems related to registering and copying COM components for applications. In the past, the information that described the COM component was written to the registry and traveled separately from the component. Part of what attributes do is to help solve this problem by combining information that used to be written to the registry with the assembly itself. (An *assembly* is an application combined with its metadata—that is, the information added by the attributes.)

NOTE

Any user-defined type can be used as an attribute. It is assumed that most attributes will inherit from System.Attribute.

Attributes are commonly derived from the System.Attribute class, as the Attribute class was designed for this specific purpose. Attributes support adding a wide variety of information to code. Attributes are examined using Reflection and are employed for a wide range of purposes, including declarative security. Chapter 9 demonstrated how attributes are used to enhance design-time features for Windows Forms and to provide a description and categorization for controls.

NOTE

Declarative security is employed by associating security permissions using attributes. Imperative security is employed by declaring instances of security classes and invoking methods on those classes at run time.

You have had several opportunities to explore Reflection (refer to the AssemblyViewer.sln from Chapter 2) and use a variety of attributes (refer to the control examples from Chapter 9). In this chapter I will demonstrate how to combine and extend these skills by creating custom attributes.

Demonstrated Topics

The basic skills demonstrated in this chapter relate to implementing custom attributes. Refer to the "Secondary Topics" section, later in this chapter. for related additional topics covered in this chapter. The primary subject matter of this chapter demonstrates how to

- ▶ Implement a custom attribute
- ▶ Apply the AttributeUsageAttribute
- ▶ Define a constructor for your custom attribute
- ▶ Describe positional and named arguments for your custom attributes
- ▶ Apply the custom attribute

We will accomplish these objectives by building a HelpAttribute class. The HelpAttribute class will support associating an URL, an HTML target, and a description with code that the attribute is applied to. Any code can use Reflection to resolve the URL.

Defining the Custom Attribute Class

Suppose you are building tools. It is easy enough to associate context help for your user interface by using the HelpProvider and a help file. What if you want to associate help with your code? This is what developers want. You might elect to use the HelpAttribute to associate help with code. On the basis of the specific class in your tool that a customer is actively using, you could display help based on the code context.

Creating a custom attribute requires that you inherit from System.Attribute. You know how to specify an inheritance relationship in C#, so I will demonstrate the class header here without further elaboration.

```
class HelpAttribute : System.Attribute
```

If there is an existing attribute that provides some of the behaviors we need, then we can inherit from that other attribute.

Implementing an Attribute Constructor

If you have any initialization code you need to run, then you will want to implement a constructor. Additionally, where attributes are concerned, if you need initial values (recall the DescriptionAttribute from Chapter 9), you will want to define a constructor.

Arguments that must be supplied because they are arguments supplied to the constructor are referred to as *positional arguments*. Attributes support positional and named arguments. I elected to require that the user supply an URL and a description and, optionally, a target tag. On the basis of these decisions, we need to implement a constructor with two positional arguments and one named argument.

Positional Arguments

Positional arguments are constructor arguments. If I want to implement the HelpAttribute with two positional arguments, URL and description, then I need to define the constructor accordingly. Our class as described so far has evolved as follows:

```
class HelpAttribute : System.Attribute
{
  private string url;
  private string description;
```

```
public HelpAttribute( string url, string description )
{
  this.url = url;
  this.description = description;
}
}
```

As described, the attribute must be applied with a string argument for each of the constructor arguments. Here is an example:

```
[Help("http://www.softconcepts.com", "SoftConcepts Home")]
```

Named Arguments

Optional arguments that can be supplied to an attribute are referred to as *named arguments*. Named arguments are implemented as public properties in the custom attribute that have both *getters* and *setters*. This is opposed to positional arguments, which are typically exposed by public properties with getters only.

For our project, we need to implement a named argument called "target," and we need to implement public, read-only properties for the URL and Description fields. If we implement the properties, then consumers of our attribute will not be able to read the state of our custom attribute. As can be seen here, HelpAttribute has matured to adolescence with the addition of the following details:

```
class HelpAttribute : System.Attribute
{
  private string url;
  private string description;
  private string target;
  public HelpAttribute( string url, string description )
  {
    this.url = url;
    this.description = description;
  }

  public string Target
  {
    get
    {
      return target;
    }
    set
    {
      target = value;
    }
```

```
  }
  public string URL
  {
    get
    {
      return url;
    }
  }
  public string Description
  {
    get
    {
      return description;
    }
  }
}
```

The class now has two positional arguments and one named argument. With the addition of the property methods, consumers will be able to read the value of the attributes. In addition, URL and Description are not modifiable after the attribute is created. Constrained by our implementation, the attribute can now be applied with two or three arguments.

```
[Help("http://www.amazon.com", "Books Online")]
[Help("http://www.yahoo.com", "Search Engine", Target="Maps")]
```

The first example uses the required positional arguments that will be passed to the constructor. The second example demonstrates the positional arguments, which must come first, and the named argument. Note the use of the property name Target. As the *named argument* designation suggests, use the *name* when supplying a value for an attribute's named argument.

NOTE

By examining the attribute statement, you might make some inferences about how attributes are managed by .NET. The attribute statement is read only. The name of the attribute is used to request the constructor information. Reflection, the attribute named, and the arguments can be used to dynamically invoke the constructor. The property name of named arguments can be used in conjunction with Reflection to initialize the properties of the attribute. (It would be nice to have the framework source code to explore this supposition.)

Adding Other Members to Custom Attributes

Custom attributes are just classes used in a specialized way. You can add other members to your custom attributes if you need them. The basic idea is to add members that support the role your attribute will play.

Applying the AttributeUsageAttribute

The last thing we need to do before we compile our attribute into a class library is to apply the AttributeUsageAttribute to our custom attribute. The AttributeUsageAttribute is used to specify the kinds of entities that an attribute can be applied to, whether the attribute can be applied multiple times, and whether the attribute is inherited or not.

The AttributeUsageAttribute has one positional argument, an AttributeTargets enumerated value, and two named arguments, Inherited and Allow Multiple. We'll review each of the arguments for the AttributeUsageAttribute after I show you the application for the HelpAttribute. Here it is, preceding the class header.

```
[AttributeUsage(AttributeTargets.All)]
public class HelpAttribute : Attribute
```

Specifying Attribute Targets

The AttributeTargets enumeration is used as the positional argument for the AttributeUsageAttribute. If your attribute is suitable for all members, then initialize the AttributeUsageAttribute with AttributeTargets—as we did for the HelpAttribute.

If you want to limit an attribute to a specific kind of code element, then select the enumeration member that describes the element your custom attribute can be applied to. You can combine attributes with a binary or (|) operator. For example, if you define an attribute that can be applied to properties and methods, then you would apply the AttributeUsageAttribute as demonstrated next.

```
[AttributeUsage(AttributeTargets.Method | AttributeTargets.Property)]
```

Specifying If Your Attribute Is Inherited

AttributeUsageAttribute accepts two named arguments. The Inherited property is a Boolean property that you can initialize when you apply the AttributeUsageAttribute. If you initialize the AttributeUsageAttribute with Inherited = true, then classes that generalize classes that have your attribute applied to them will inherit your attribute too.

By default, the Inherited property is True. Here is an example of the AttributeUsageAttribute demonstrating the Inherited named argument.

```
[AttributeUsage(AttributeTargets.Struct, Inherited=false)]
```

The preceding statement indicates that the attribute can be applied to structs, and the attribute is not inherited.

Specifying If Your Attribute Can Be Applied Multiple Times

The AllowMultiple named argument is a Boolean value that is False by default. If AllowMultiple is True, then the attribute can be applied multiple times to the same member. Attributes where

AllowMultiple is True are referred to as multi-use attributes. When AllowMultiple is False, these attributes are referred to as single-use attributes.

```
[AttributeUsage(AttributeTargets.All, AllowMultiple=true)]
```

AllowMultiple is False by default. You would want to allow an attribute to be applied more than one time only if there is no potential for conflict by applying an attribute more than once. For example, you would not want to allow multiple security attributes to be applied and then have to worry about conflicting security permissions. (Refer to Chapter 16 for more information on security in .NET.) Listing 10-1 in the next section provides an example of a custom attribute that could reasonably allow multiples.

Reading Attributes

Chapter 2 demonstrated that information about a class can be read using Reflection. One aspect of Reflection is the ability to retrieve the custom attributes that have been applied to types. Provided with a System.Type record for a specific type, we can request the attributes applied to that type. To explore the attributes applied to the members of a type, we can request the members of the type and then request the attributes applied to each member.

Think a moment about the relationship between types and members. Attributes may be applied to classes as well as to the members of a class. Additionally, the members of a class may themselves be complex types, classes. Listing 10-1 is a method that iterates over all of the members of a class and requests the custom attribute information for the class and its members.

Listing 10-1   *Exploring all the attributes of a type using Reflection*

```
1:   ArrayList topics;
2:   [Help(@"C:\Temp\CWP13.HTM", "Constructor")]
3:   public HelpAttributeDemo()
4:   {
5:     topics = new ArrayList();
6:     topics.AddRange( GetType().GetCustomAttributes(
7:       typeof(HelpAttribute), false));
8:
9:     MemberInfo[] memberInfo = GetType().GetMembers();
10:    IEnumerator enumerator = memberInfo.GetEnumerator();
}
11:    while( enumerator.MoveNext())
12:    {
13:      topics.AddRange( ((MemberInfo)
14:        enumerator.Current).GetCustomAttributes(
15:        typeof(HelpAttribute), false));
16:    }
17: }
```

The ArrayList on line 1 in Listing 10-1 is used to store the reflected attributes. (This procedure is defined in the HelpAttributeDemo class in the HelpAttribute.sln available online. The .HTM help documents (shown in Figure 10-1) were created using the Tools, Build Comment Web Pages in Visual Studio .NET.) Line 2 applies a HelpAttribute using Web Pages generated from Visual Studio .NET. The description for the attribute explains that the method is the constructor. The ArrayList is constructed on line 5.

Line 6 in Listing 10-1 invokes GetType to get the Type information for the HelpAttributeDemo class. The Type object is used to request an array of custom attributes. By specifying the typeof(HelpAttribute) as an argument to GetCustomAttributes, GetCustomAttributes will return only the HelpAttribute attributes applied to the class.

Lines 9 through 16 in Listing 10-1 request all of the MemberInfo objects for the HelpAttributeDemo type. The memberInfo array—line 10—is used to request an enumerator, and lines 13 through 16—constituting a statement—adds all of the HelpAttribute attributes applied to all of the members of the HelpAttributeDemo to the topics ArrayList.

Returning to our scenario, once we have all of the attributes dynamically discovered, we can display the list of descriptions. When a user can pick a specific description, there will be an URL associated with the HelpAttribute owning that description. With the URL we can display the help page. The HelpAttributeDemo class and the AttribueDemo.exe application demonstrate precisely this behavior.

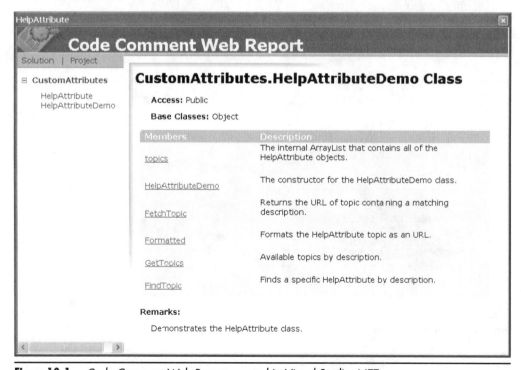

Figure 10-1 *Code Comment Web Report created in Visual Studio .NET*

TIP

Generate Comment Web Pages from the Tools menu in Visual Studio .NET.

The key to using Reflection is to request the Type information. With the Type information you can use Reflection to explore all of the members of a type, including reading attribute instances and the properties of those instances.

Secondary Topics

The previous section demonstrated a HelpAttribute that displayed dynamic HTML help using Reflection. A reasonable person might want to employ this attribute but also want an easy way to generate professional Web pages. You can use Tags for Documentation and Visual Studio .NET to generate the HTML comment pages automatically.

This section of the chapter demonstrates several topics. In addition to tags designed for generating HTML documentation for your code, this section will explore

▶ The ToolTip Component and how to implement an Extender Provider

▶ The EditorBrowsableAttribute

▶ The DesignerSerializationAttribute

Commenting Attributes

Visual Studio .Net will generate high-quality HTML documentation for your source code. You provide the comments, and Visual Studio .Net will take care of the rest.

Table 9-1 in Chapter 9 introduced the comment XML tags for commenting source code. You can use the Visual Studio .NET help documentation as a general reference. Here I will demonstrate a few of the commenting tags used to create the HTML documentation shown in Figure 10-1.

The description column shown in Figure 10-1 was created by using the <summary> tag. The Remarks section shown at the bottom of Figure 10-1 was created using the <remarks> tag, and the <param> and <returns> comments are shown in Figure 10-2. The Type, Name, and Description information for the method shown in Figure 10-2 is created by the <param> tag, and the Return information is added by the <returns> tag.

The Description for the topics element shown in Figure 10-1 was created by adding the following comment to the topics field.

```
/// <summary>
/// The internal ArrayList that contains all of the HelpAttribute objects.
/// </summary>
ArrayList topics;
```

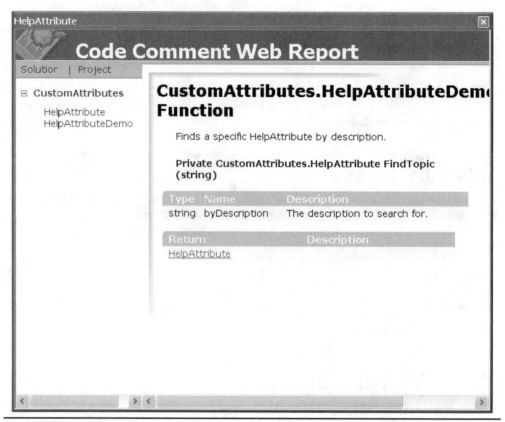

Figure 10-2 *The parameter type and name and return type of a method added to a Code Comment Web Report using the <param> and <returns> tags*

The Remarks in Figure 10-1 were created with the following comment applied to the HelpAttributeDemo class.

```
/// <remarks>
/// Demonstrates the HelpAttribute class.
/// </remarks>
[Help(@"C:\Temp\CWP11.HTM", "Class")]
public class HelpAttributeDemo
{
```

The parameter and return information was created by applying the <param> and <returns> tags, as demonstrated here.

```
/// <param name="byDescription">The description to search for.</param>
/// <returns>HelpAttribute</returns>
[Help(@"C:\Temp\CWP17.HTM", "Find Topic")]
private HelpAttribute FindTopic(string byDescription)
```

By providing text and documentation tags, you can create rich help documentation for your source code.

Implementing Extender Provider

Extender Providers provide properties to other components. Instead of every control having its own Hint property, an Extender Provider can provide a Hint—or ToolTip—property to controls dynamically. There are several existing Extender Providers, including the ComponentTray, ErrorProvider, HelpProvider, LocalizationExtenderProvider, PropertyTab, and ToolTip.

For example, the ToolTip provider can be added to the Component Tray and controls dynamically given a ToolTip control. Consumers can query Extender Providers by invoking the single method IExtenderProvider classes must implement, CanExtend. CanExtend returns a Boolean indicating whether or not a particular provider can extend that consumer. To create custom Extender Providers, define a class that inherits from Component and implements the IExtenderProvider interface.

To demonstrate the IExtenderProvider interface, we'll create a HelpProvider that extends controls by adding a HelpLink property to controls. There a few basic features of the .NET Framework that we will need to make use of to implement the HelpProvider. We will need to inherit from System.ComponentModel.Component, implement the System.ComponentModel .IExtenderProvider interface, and apply the System.ComponentModel.ProviderPropertyAttribute. We will explore each of these pieces in the subsections that follow and wrap up the chapter with the complete code listing for the provider.

Specifying the Class Header for the HelpProvider

The HelpProvider will provide links to help information. We will need a collection to store the links in. The IExtenderProvider interface and the ProviderPropertyAttribute are defined in the System.ComponentModel namespace, and we will be associating the HelpProvider with Windows Forms controls. Thus, it will be helpful to include the namespaces containing these capabilities in the module implementing the HelpProvider.

NOTE

The term generalize means to inherit from a class and the term realize means to implement an interface. These terms are synonyms. "Inherit" and "implement" are most often used in the context of a programming language, like C#, and "generalize" and "realize" are most often used in the context of a modeling language like the Unified Modeling Language (UML).

To place the HelpProvider in the Component Tray, we need to generalize the System .Windows.Forms.Component class and realize the System.ComponentModel. IExtenderProvider. The *using* statements and class header follow:

```
using System;
using System.Collections;
using System.ComponentModel;
```

```
using System.Windows.Forms;

public class HelpProvider : Component, IExtenderProvider
```

The last statement indicates that the HelpProvider inherits from Component and implements IExtenderProvider.

Applying the ProviderPropertyAttribute

The ProviderPropertyAttribute is used to provide a name for the property that a particular Extender Provider will provide. You can initialize the ProviderPropertyAttribute with the name of the property provided and the name or type of the object this provider can extend. We want our provider to extend System.Windows.Forms.Controls with a HelpLink property, which guides the ProviderPropertyAttribute statement (shown next in relation to the class header):

```
[ProvideProperty("HelpLink", typeof(Control))]
 public class HelpExtender : Component, IExtenderProvider
{
```

The ProviderPropertyAttribute indicates that our provider will be providing a property named HelpLink and can extend Control objects. (Keep in mind that every Windows Forms control inherits from Control.) An alternate form of the ProvidePropertyAttribute is initialized with the name of the property and the type of the property provided.

When the HelpProvider is added to the ComponentTray, every Control will have a HelpLink property unless that Control is specifically excluded by the CanExtend method.

Implement the IExtenderProvider Interface

IExtenderProvider defines the method CanExtend. When a class realizes an interface, that class must implement all of the members defined by the interface. You can implement an interface member explicitly, either by prefixing the member that satisfies the interface contract with the name of the interface or by declaring a public member with a signature identical to the member defined by the interface. Either of the following two method signatures will satisfy the IExtenderProvider interface:

```
public bool CanExtend(object extendee)
```

or

```
bool IExtenderProvider.CanExtend(object extendee)
```

The public method CanExtend implicitly satisfies the IExtenderProvider interface, and the second example explicitly satisfies the contract.

Suppose you have a class that implements two interfaces containing one or more identical members. You can use the second, explicit form of implementing an interface to indicate which members are implementing a specific interface.

Our control will play the role of provider to any Control; as a result, the HelpProvider .CanExtend method will return True if the type of the extendee is a Control. Here is the implementation for the CanExtend method.

```
bool IExtenderProvider.CanExtend(object extendee)
{
  return extendee is Control;
}
```

Implement the HelpProvider

The HelpProvider will provide a HelpLink property to every control that it extends. As a result, all that remains to do is to implement the methods for getting and setting the HelpLink and to provide a place to store all of the HelpLinks. Listing 10-2 provides the complete implementation of the HelpProvider.

Listing 10-2   *An implementation of an IExtenderProvider component that extends a control by providing a HelpLink*

```
1:   using System;
2:   using System.Collections;
3:   using System.ComponentModel;
4:   using System.Windows.Forms;
5:
6:   namespace HelpExtender
7:   {
8:     [ProvideProperty("HelpLink", typeof(Control))]
9:     public class HelpExtender : Component, IExtenderProvider
10:    {
11:
12:      private Hashtable links;
13:
14:      public HelpExtender()
15:      {
16:        links = new Hashtable();
17:      }
18:
19:      public string GetHelpLink(Control control)
20:      {
21:        return links[control] == null ? string.Empty
22:          : (string)links[control];
23:      }
24:
25:      public void SetHelpLink(Control control, string text)
```

```
26:      {
27:        if(text == null)
28:          links[control] = string.Empty;
29:        else
30:          links[control] = text;
31:      }
32:
33:      bool IExtenderProvider.CanExtend(object extendee)
34:      {
35:        return extendee is Control;
36:      }
37:
38:    }
39: }
```

The constructor defined on lines 14 through 17 of Listing 10-2 creates an instance of a HashTable. We will rely on the GetHashCode method that every class inherits from the Object class to provide a means of storing unique HelpLink values. GetHelpLink and SetHelpLink provide the read and write behavior for the HelpLink property.

SetHelpLink on lines 25 through 31 of Listing 10-2 uses the control to index the HashTable, storing the string value of the HelpLink for a specific control at the hash index created by the control itself. GetHelpLink performs the inverse operation. If the HashTable entry at a particular index returns null, then the value string.Empty is returned; otherwise, the hashing function returns an object (which we know to be a string), and we can return the string value as demonstrated on line 22.

Using the HelpProvider

Include the module containing the HelpProvider in a class library. Build the class library project and add the HelpProvider library to the Toolbox. (Refer to "Adding the Component to the Toolbox" in Chapter 9 for information on customizing the Toolbox in Visual Studio .NET.)

To use the HelpProvider, drag a HelpProvider from the Toolbox to a Form. The HelpProvider will be added to the Component Tray, and the form and the controls on the form will be extended with a HelpLink property (shown in Figure 10-3).

The value of a property added by an extender lives in the extender, not in the control it extends. Normally, you would read a property value by requesting the property from a specific instance of an object. For example, button1.Text provides access to the Text property of an object named button1. To access the value of a property added by an extender, request the value from the extender's Get method. The following statement demonstrates how to request the HelpLink value associated with an object named button1.

```
helpExtender1.GetHelpLink(button1)
```

In our example, the HelpLink is an URL referring to an HTML document created with the Comment Web Pages. To display the Web page, we could pass the value of the HelpLink to the Process.Start method. The HTTP:// moniker is associated with Internet Explorer

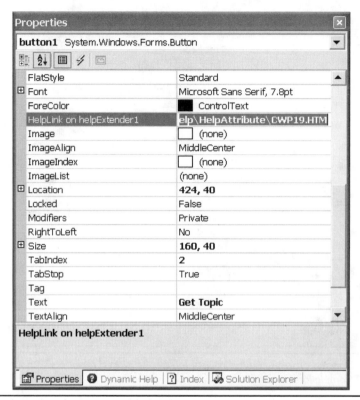

Figure 10-3   *The HelpLink property added to the Button control by the HelpProvider*

(on my machine); hence, Process.Start called with an HTTP:// address will open the document referred to in the URL.

Reviewing the EditorBrowsableAttribute

The EditorBrowsableAttribute is defined in the System.ComponentModel namespace. Initialized with an EditorBrowsableState enumerated value, the EditorBrowsableAttribute will determine whether a property or method is viewable in an editor. For example, [EditorBrowsable(EditorBrowsableState.Never)] will conceal the element it is applied to from Visual Studio .NET's Intellisense capability.

The values for EditorBrowsableState are Never, Always, and Advanced. If Hide advanced members is selected in the Options dialog (see Figure 10-4), then members that have an EditorBrowsableAttribute initialized with EditorBrowsableState.Advanced will not be displayed by Intellisense.

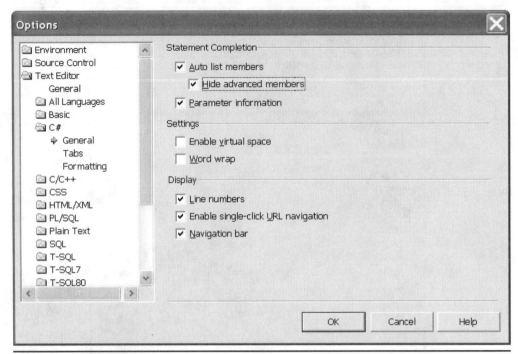

Figure 10-4   *Conceal or reveal EditorBrowsableState.Advanced members with the Statement Completion Options.*

Reviewing the DesignerSerializationVisibilityAttribute

The DesignerSerializationVisibilityAttribute (that's a mouthful) is used to describe how a property is saved by a designer. There are three enumerated values, Visible, Content, and Hidden, defined in the DesignerSerializationVisible enumeration that you can initialize this attribute with. The Visible value indicates that a designer can use the default behavior to serialize properties. Use Hidden to indicate that a property is not serialized and Content to indicate that the value of the property is serialized. For example, use Content to serialize the elements of a collection.

We can combine the EditorBrowsableAttribute, the BrowsableAttribute, and the DesignerSerializationAttribute to remedy a semantics deficit from Chapter 9. Chapter 9 introduced an EffectsLabel. The EffectsLabel inherited from Label and created a shadow effect by overriding the OnPaint behavior. The deficit was subtle. To create the shadow effect, an overlay color was combined with the existing, inherited ForeColor. The deficit was that the ForeColor actually created the background shadow effect and that the OverlayColor property actually became the ForeColor. A reasonable person might be confused by this subtle yet annoying incongruity.

To resolve this problem, we can introduce a new property called ShadowColor and hide the old property named ForeColor. As a result, the EffectsLabel has properties named

ShadowColor and OverlayColor and the role of each property is much clearer in the context of the EffectsLabel. To complete the revision, all we have to do is add the two properties shown in Listing 10-3 to the EffectsLabel control class defined in Chapter 9.

Listing 10-3   *Add the code in the listing to the EffectsLabel custom control from Chapter 9 to hide the ForeColor property and introduce a ShadowColor property that is more meaningful.*

```
1:   [Browsable(false),
2:   EditorBrowsable(EditorBrowsableState.Never),
3:   DesignerSerializationVisibility(DesignerSerializationVisibility.Hidden)]
4:   public override Color ForeColor
5:   {
6:     get
7:     {
8:       return base.ForeColor;
9:     }
10:    set
11:    {
12:      base.ForeColor = value;
13:    }
14:  }
15:
16:
17:   [Category("Appearance"),
18:   Description("The color that is used to create the shadow.")]
19:   public Color ShadowColor
20:   {
21:     get
22:     {
23:       return ForeColor;
24:     }
25:     set
26:     {
27:       ForeColor = value;
28:     }
29:   }
```

The BrowsableAttribute on line 1 of Listing 10-3 will prevent the ForeColor from being displayed in the Properties window. The EditorBrowsableAttribute as applied on line 2 will prevent Intellisense from displaying the ForeColor property in the code designer, and the DesignerSerializationVisibilityAttribute as applied will prevent the ForeColor from being serialized by the code editor.

For all intents and purposes, the EffectsLabel revised with the addition of the code in Listing 10-3 will no longer have a ForeColor property. The EffectsLabel from the perspective of the consumer will have a ShadowColor and an OverlayColor, which are much more meaningful in the context of a shadow label. Of course, you and I know (from Listing 10-3) that the ShadowColor is implemented in terms of the inherited ForeColor. We have employed a bit of sleight of hand to make the EffectsLabel easier to use.

Summary

The intent of code should be conveyed by the way you write the code. For the most part, consumers of controls and providers are going to be introduced to your code by the members you provide them with. Consumers may never see your internal comments and will most likely encounter your external documentation after exploring the code.

This chapter has demonstrated how to associate help documentation with your code by creating a custom Attribute and an Extender Provider. The last part of the chapter demonstrated how you can combine attributes to perform a bit of programmatic sleight of hand to conceal existing properties and expose new properties that convey greater meaning.

You can create custom attributes to add metadata to your code. Use Extender Providers to extend existing controls by adding new properties, and you can use existing attributes to convey additional information about your code.

Practical Reflection

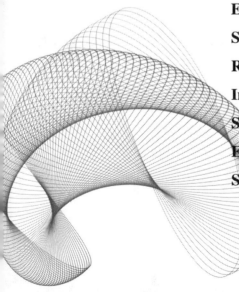

Reflection is a capability that facilitates dynamically managing assemblies. It is an evolutionary enhancement of run-time type information. With Reflection you can load and emit assemblies, you can discover and create types dynamically with compiled and running code, and you can invoke operations on or emit members with running code.

Run-time type information, or RTTI, supports dynamic type discovery. Querying COM interfaces supports dynamic interface discovery. Reflection provides support for both of these operations and significantly more. In addition to discovering information about a type or interface, Reflection allows you to discover information about fields, events, properties, methods, constructors, and attributes. An enhancement to discovering information about assemblies and types is the writing of emitters—that is, defining code generators—that write object-oriented intermediate language (IL). This chapter will demonstrate how to do all of these things.

Demonstrated Topics

This chapter demonstrates practical applications for using Reflection. There are several example programs, as well as a discussion of the Assembly Viewer 2 sample application from Chapter 5. In this chapter, you will have an opportunity to learn how to

- ▶ Dynamically discover information about types using Reflection
- ▶ Load assemblies at run time
- ▶ Explore the .NET Framework programmatically
- ▶ Emit assemblies, modules, classes, and members

The secondary topics complement core Reflection topics by demonstrating some additional uses for Reflection. In the secondary topics, I will demonstrate how to implement the metaclass—class of a class—idiom, serialize objects with XML, serialize objects to an ADO.NET DataSet, and emit compiled regular expressions.

Discovering and Using Types Dynamically

You will likely encounter several instances where you define a generic type and initialize that generic object to a specific type at run-time as opposed to compile time. Several examples in this chapter will prove useful in practical applications, such as the metaclass idiom described in "Implementing the Metaclass Idiom" near the end of this chapter. This section will demonstrate the basic concepts for discovering type information that you will use in routine programming and in creating objects from a class's Type object.

Using Type Objects

When you invoke the typeof(*object*) operation, an instance of a class's Type record is returned. Like any other class, the Type class has members. The only difference is that a Type class contains properties, fields, and methods that describe a Type. For example, if you declare a new class with the default name of Class1 and request the typeof(Class1), then you will get an instance of System.Type as the return value. Using this Type object, you can invoke operations on the Type object with the Type.InvokeMember. Here is a brief example:

```
using System;

namespace TypeofDemo
{
  class Class1
  {
    [STAThread]
    static void Main(string[] args)
    {
      Type type = typeof(Class1);
      Console.WriteLine(type.FullName);
      Console.ReadLine();
    }
  }
}
```

The typeof statement returns an instance of Class1's Type object. The FullName member returns the namespace and name of the type represented by the Type object. The example will write TypeofDemo.Class1 to the console.

Type objects contain methods about their containing assembly and the members defined by the type. There are methods to request the attributes, constructors, events, fields, properties, interfaces, methods, method parameters, nested types, containing assembly and namespace, and the access modifiers applied to the type.

A second way to request a type is to pass the full name to the Type.GetType shared method. Type.GetType("TypeofDemo.Class1") will return the Type object representing Class1, precisely as the typeof(Class1) statement did. All you need to do to explore a type or invoke operations on it is obtain an instance of its Type object.

A metaclass is the class of a class. A Type class is similar to a metaclass, but the Type class is less specific. The Type class describes all types, and a metaclass describes a single type. Because the Type class is generic to all types, the operations you will perform on Type objects are generic, requiring more information than a metaclass would. For example, invoke a constructor on a metaclass and you get the correct object. Invoke a constructor on a Type object, and you must invoke the constructor indirectly, passing the parameter as an array of objects. If you are familiar with metaclasses, the differences will be obvious. In general, think of a metaclass as a class describing a specific class and the System.Type class as describing all possible classes.

Instantiating Objects with Reflection

Unless you are invoking only static members on a type, you will need to construct an instance of a reflected type. There are three ways to create an instance using the Type object of a type. You can use the Activator.CreateInstance method. You can request a ConstructorInfo and instantiate an instance with that type, or you can call Type.InvokeMember and pass the arguments that describe a constructor. All three ways work reasonably well; using the static Activator.CreateInstance method seems to be easiest.

The three short fragments that follow demonstrate how to request a Type object from the name and create instances of that type.

```
// Using an activator
Type type = Type.GetType("TypeofDemo.Class1");
object o = Activator.CreateInstance(type);
type.InvokeMember("Test", BindingFlags.InvokeMethod,
  null, o, new object[]{});
```

This example creates an instance of Class1 using the shared method Activator.CreateInstance. Pass the Type object, and CreateInstance will invoke a default constructor. There are several overloaded forms of CreateInstance; for example, if you pass an array of arguments representing arguments to the constructor, then CreateInstance will create an instance of the type using the constructor that most closely matches the arguments' parameter.

```
// Using a ConstructorInfo
Type type = Type.GetType("TypeofDemo.Class1");
ConstructorInfo constructorInfo = type.GetConstructor(new Type[]{});
object o = constructorInfo.Invoke(new object[]{});
type.InvokeMember("Test", BindingFlags.InvokeMethod,
  null, o, new object[]{});
```

The second example obtains a ConstructorInfo object, which represents a single constructor. The ConstructorInfo object is used to create an instance of the type by passing an array of object values. The ConstructorInfo object will match the constructor with the closest matching arguments. Passing an empty array of objects will invoke the default constructor.

```
// Type.InvokeMember
Type type = Type.GetType("TypeofDemo.Class1");
object o = type.InvokeMember("Class1",
  BindingFlags.CreateInstance, null, null, new object[]{});
type.InvokeMember("Test", BindingFlags.InvokeMethod,
  null, o, new object[]{});
```

The final example treats the constructor like a method and invokes the method Class1. Recall that constructors in C# have the same name as the class, and every class has a default constructor whether you define one or not. Recall from the code for Class1 at the beginning of this section that we did not define a constructor explicitly; however, if you examine the IL in Figure 11-1, it is obvious that a default constructor has been defined.

Dynamic Member Invocation

You might have heard the phrases ".NET allows developers to be language agnostic" and "the .NET language you choose is a lifestyle choice." These are true statements for a couple of reasons. The first reason is that C# and Visual Basic .NET have equal access to the Common Language Runtime. A second reason is that there are just a few noticeable differences between C# and Visual Basic .NET (most of the differences are syntactical). One of the noticeable differences is that Visual Basic .NET supports implicit late binding, and C# does not.

NOTE

Of course, there are several .NET languages. The basic idea is that a .NET language sits on top of the CLR. As a consequence, many languages implemented for .NET will differ most significantly by syntax.

Implicit late binding is where you define a type as a generic type like Object and assign it to an instance of a specific type. Late binding in Visual Basic .NET means that you invoke operations based on a presumption of the members defined by the instantiated type. I will demonstrate what this means by example. Here is the code that uses the Activator to create an instance of Class and invoke a member named Test.

```
// Using an activator
Type type = Type.GetType("TypeofDemo.Class1");
object o = Activator.CreateInstance(type);
type.InvokeMember("Test", BindingFlags.InvokeMethod,
  null, o, new object[]{});
```

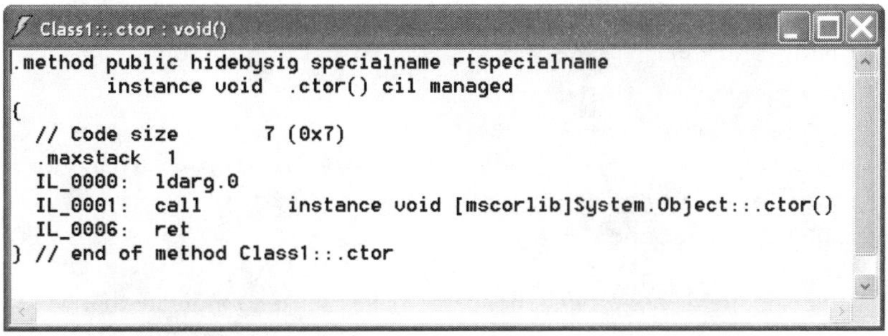

```
Class1::.ctor : void()
.method public hidebysig specialname rtspecialname
        instance void  .ctor() cil managed
{
  // Code size       7 (0x7)
  .maxstack  1
  IL_0000:  ldarg.0
  IL_0001:  call        instance void [mscorlib]System.Object::.ctor()
  IL_0006:  ret
} // end of method Class1::.ctor
```

Figure 11-1   *Classes are provided with a default constructor, as shown here by the IL.*

Here is an identical listing in Visual Basic .NET.

```
Dim type As Type = type.GetType("VBTypeofDemo.Class1")
Dim o As Object = Activator.CreateInstance(type)
o.Test()
```

Notice that we are not required to use InvokeMember to call the Test method, even though we declared *o* as an Object instance rather than a Class1 instance. This is late binding in Visual Basic .NET.

Defining the Member to Invoke

As is true with object-oriented frameworks in general, you are likely to find several overloaded methods for any method. Covering all of the variations of every method is the function of the integrated help or a reference manual. There are three versions of InvokeMember. The version I am going to demonstrate accepts five arguments and has the following method signature:

```
public object InvokeMember(string, BindingFlags, Binder, object, object[]);
```

The first argument is the name of the member to invoke. You can interact with fields, properties, events, or methods using this same—InvokeMember—method.

When you call InvokeMember, the return type is defined as an object. Of course, when you write your code, you will know what type to expect and can typecast the return type to the actual type returned. For example, if you InvokeMember on an event, then you can cast the return type to the delegate type defined by the event. (Refer to the preceding section for an example that demonstrates invoking a member method named Test.)

Specifying the BindingFlags

The second argument in the version of InvokeMember that we are reviewing is an OR'd parameter containing BindingFlags-enumerated values. The BindingFlags described the kind of member, including such things as the access modifiers. The BindingFlags values are defined in Table 11-1.

BindingFlags are OR'd together in specific combinations. Three common combinations include a flag that indicates the member type, a flag that indicates the access level, and a flag that indicates whether the member is an instance member, static member, or both. Here are some examples of BindingFlags combinations that make sense:

```
BindingFlags.GetField | BindingFlags.NonPublic |
    BindingFlags.Instance
BindingFlags.InvokeMember | BindingFlags.Public | BindingFlags.Static
BindingFlags.SetProperty | BindingFlags.Public |
    BindingFlags.Instance
```

As a general rule, fields are private; hence, it makes sense to indicate that we want a non-public instance when invoking a field operation. Generally, public methods make up the public interface, so we might want to call a public static or instance method. (The second

Member Name	Description
CreateInstance	Indicates that an instance of the invoking type should be created.
DeclaredOnly	Means skip inherited members when reflecting a member.
Default	No binding flags.
ExactBinding	Argument types must precisely match parameter types.
FlattenHierarchy	Static members are returned. (Does not include nested types.)
GetField	Used to indicate reference to a Field member
GetProperty	Used to indicate reference to a Property member.
IgnoreCase	Ignore case when reflecting a member.
IgnoreReturn	Return value can be ignored for COM Interop.
Instance	Include instance members.
InvokeMethod	Used when invoking a method.
NonPublic	Used for non-public members. ReflectionPermission is required.
OptionalParamBinding	Used for methods with default arguments and varargs.
Public	Public members are included in the search. ReflectionPermission is not required.
PutDispProperty	PROPPUT on a COM object should be invoked.
PutRefDispProperty	PROPPUTREF member on a COM object should be invoked.
SetField	Treat invoked member as a left-hand–side value.
SetProperty	Invoke property setter.
Static	Include static members in invocation.
SuppressChangeType	(Help indicates that this is not implemented.)

Table 11-1   *Combine BindingFlags Values to Describe the Type of Member to Invoke*

statement demonstrates how to invoke a public static method.) The final example invokes a public property setter method.

The code in Listing 11-1 was added to the example class Class1. The additional code implements a private field and a public property that represents the underlying field value.

Listing 11-1   *Examples of BindingFlags combinations for getting and setting fields and properties*

```
1:  private string field;
2:
3:  public string Property
4:  {
5:    get{ return field; }
6:    set{ field = value; }
```

```
7:   }
8:
9:   private static void DemoBindingFlags()
10: {
11:    Type type = Type.GetType("TypeofDemo.Class1");
12:    object o = Activator.CreateInstance(type);
13:
14:    type.InvokeMember("field",
15:      BindingFlags.SetField | BindingFlags.NonPublic |
16:      BindingFlags.Instance, null, o,
17:      new object[]{
18:      "Welcome to Valhalla Tower Material Defender!"});
19:
20:
21:    string s = (string)type.InvokeMember("Property",
22:      BindingFlags.GetProperty | BindingFlags.Public |
23:      BindingFlags.Instance, null, o,
24:      new object[]{});
25:
26:    Console.WriteLine(s);
27:    Console.ReadLine();
28:
29: }
```

Lines 1 through 7 of Listing 11-1 represent the field and property that we will be reflecting. Note that the field is private and that the property is public. (The use of the name *field* for the field member and *property* for the property member is not relevant to our discussion.) DemoBindingFlags requests the type by passing the full name to the Type.GetType method on line 11, and line 12 uses an Activator to create an instance of the type.

Lines 14 through 24 of Listing 11-1 demonstrate a combination of BindingFlags that will allow us to set the private field value, and the array of object argument takes a single argument with the same type as the field we are reflecting. The *field* field is a string; hence, we pass an array containing a single string element. Because *field* is an instance member, we need to pass an object to invoke the reflected operation on—that is, we need memory to store the field value in.

NOTE

If you are a beginning programmer, properties, public access modifiers, and instances may seem foreign. I respect your ambition in tackling this subject matter as a beginner, so here is a quick review of what you need to learn for the BindingFlags to make sense. Properties are methods that act like data and have to do with the concept of encapsulation. Public access modifiers relate to the subject of information hiding, and instantiation has to do with the concept of classes versus objects. These are fundamental OOP concepts that you will have to learn.

Lines 21 through 24 of Listing 11-1 demonstrate how to get a public property value and assign the value to a temporary variable. BindingFlags.GetProperty, BindingFlags.Public, and BindingFlags.Instance become self-explanatory in this context. If you understand the concepts of a property, public access, and an instance method, then the flags make sense. This time we are using the result of InvokeMember as a right-side value; InvokeMember is defined to return an object, but the type is really a string, so we perform the typecast on line 21. The remaining code simply displays the text "Welcome to Valhalla Tower Material Defender!"

Defining a Binder

Whether you pass a Binder to InvokeMember or not, you are using a Binder—the DefaultBinder. Binders are used to convert arguments you pass to InvokeMember to the formal argument types expected by the member. The easiest thing to do is pass the argument types that the member you are invoking expects. However, it is likely that you will encounter a situation where you want a reasonable conversion between types to work. For example, IBM's *Universal Database* has a specific format for the Timestamp data type. If you pass a valid .NET date/time value to a Timestamp function in an SQL statement, UDB will not accept it. Here is a method that I wrote to convert a .NET DateTime value to a suitable string for the UDB Timestamp data type.

```
public static string ToTimeStamp(DateTime Value)
{
  return string.Format("{0}-{1:0#}-{2:0#}-{3:0#}.{4:0#}.{5:0#}.{6:000000}",
    Value.Year, Value.Month, Value.Day,
    Value.Hour, Value.Minute, Value.Second,
    Value.Millisecond);
}
```

NOTE

It is possible that someone at IBM is aware of a workaround; however, I tested several variations and it seemed that the precise string format described for a DateTime value was needed to set a Timestamp column.

Following the string.Format method, the basic syntax for a UDB Timestamp is d-m-yy-hh:mm:ss.mils. In plain English, the format is the day, month, and year values separated by a dash, followed by a dash and the hour, minute, second, and six-digit millisecond value. It would be preferable if such highly specialized values accepted a reasonable value for the date and time and performed the conversion for me. This is the role of a Binder.

The Binder class is an abstract class. If you want to describe custom binding, then you can inherit from the Binder class and implement BindToMethod, BindToField, SelectMethod, SelectProperty, ChangeType, and ReorderArgumentArray, all inherited from the default Binder class. (The Binder class is defined in the System.Reflection namespace.) Listing 11-2 demonstrates a binder that will perform a conversion between a string and a DateTime value when resolving a DateTime property.

Listing 11-2   *This contains a simple Binder that will convert a string to a DateTime.*

```
 1:  public class DateTimeBinder : Binder
 2:  {
 3:
 4:    public override MethodBase BindToMethod(
 5:      BindingFlags bindingAttr,
 6:      MethodBase[] match,
 7:      ref object[] args,
 8:      ParameterModifier[] modifiers,
 9:      CultureInfo culture,
10:      string[] names,
11:      out object state)
12:    {
13:      state = null;
14:      return match.Length == 1 ? match[0] : null;
15:    }
16:
17:    public override FieldInfo BindToField(
18:      BindingFlags bindingAttr,
19:      FieldInfo[] match,
20:      object value,
21:      CultureInfo culture)
22:    {
23:        return null;
24:    }
25:
26:    public override MethodBase SelectMethod(
27:      BindingFlags bindingAttr,
28:      MethodBase[] match,
29:      Type[] types,
30:      ParameterModifier[] modifiers)
31:    {
32:      return null;
33:    }
34:
35:    public override PropertyInfo SelectProperty(
36:      BindingFlags bindingAttr,
37:      PropertyInfo[] match,
38:      Type returnType,
39:      Type[] indexes,
40:      ParameterModifier[] modifiers)
41:    {
```

```
42:      return null;
43:    }
44:
45:    public override object ChangeType(
46:      object value,
47:      Type type,
48:      CultureInfo culture)
49:    {
50:      if ( value.GetType() != typeof(string)) return value;
51:
52:      try
53:      {
54:        return Convert.ToDateTime(value);
55:      }
56:      catch
57:      {
58:        return value;
59:      }
60:    }
61:
62:    public override void ReorderArgumentArray(
63:      ref object[] args,
64:      object state)
65:    {}
66: }
```

Quickly scanning Listing 11-2 you can determine that most of the inherited methods are just stubbed out. All I want this converter to do is convert a string representation of a date/time to a DateTime value.

BindToMethod sets the *out* parameter—*out* parameters are not initialized by the caller but are expected to have a value when the callee returns—and the MethodBase object that we want to bind to. My implementation returns one MethodBase object if only one was found.

The MethodBase class is the base class for MethodInfo. In our example, I passed a DateTimeBinder to a reflected property request. When properties are emitted to IL, hidden methods named get_*property* and set_*property*, where *property* is the name of the property associated with these methods, are emitted to IL. When a property is reflected, the values are retrieved from these hidden methods. Hence, BindToMethod is called for a Binder even when we are reflecting properties. (Figure 11-2 shows the emitted setter (highlighted) and getter methods for Class1.DateOfBirth.)

To demonstrate the DateTimeBinder in Listing 11-2, a DateOfBirth property and a dateOfBirth field were added to the Class1 sample class. The code in Listing 11-3 demonstrates code that implicitly invokes the BindToMethod and ChangeType methods of the custom Binder.

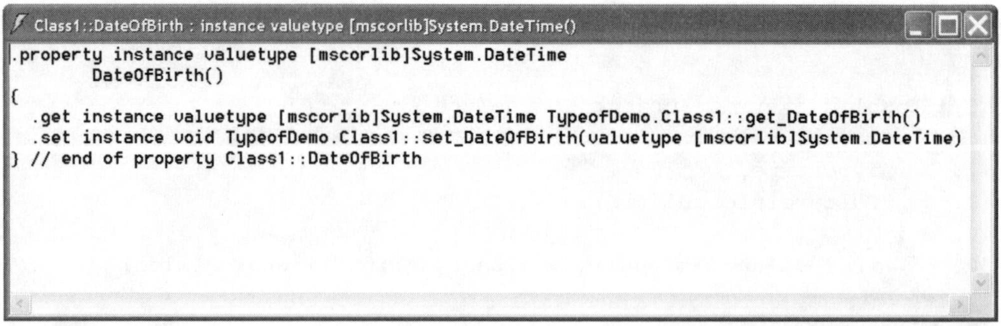

```
Class1::DateOfBirth : instance valuetype [mscorlib]System.DateTime()
.property instance valuetype [mscorlib]System.DateTime
        DateOfBirth()
{
  .get instance valuetype [mscorlib]System.DateTime TypeofDemo.Class1::get_DateOfBirth()
  .set instance void TypeofDemo.Class1::set_DateOfBirth(valuetype [mscorlib]System.DateTime)
} // end of property Class1::DateOfBirth
```

Figure 11-2   *Properties are modified by getter and setter methods in MSIL that represent the get and set block in C#.*

Listing 11-3   *Code that invokes the DateTimeBinder methods from Listing 11-2*

```
Type type = typeof(Class1);
object o = Activator.CreateInstance(type);
type.InvokeMember( "DateOfBirth",
  BindingFlags.Instance | BindingFlags.SetProperty |
  BindingFlags.Public, new DateTimeBinder(),
  o, new object[]{@"02/12/1966"});
```

The only difference from examples we have seen so far is the usage of the custom binder, DateTimeBinder, in Listing 11-3. The InvokeMember method in Listing 11-3 will use the DateTimeBinder to bind the reflected DateOfBirth invocation. Without the custom binder, the call to InvokeMember would fail because DateOfBirth is defined as a DateTime rather than string member.

Passing Parameters to InvokeMember

If you need to pass values to a reflected member, then pass the arguments as an array of heterogeneous object arguments (see Listing 11-3). You can declare this value in line, as demonstrated in Listing 11-3, or declare a temporary variable. (Try to avoid temporary variables. Avoiding temporary variables is argued in books on Refactoring.)

The DefaultBinder will use the order and type of the arguments in the object array to resolve the reflected member. If you implement a custom binder, then you can use the ReorderArgumentArray method to facilitate resolving which member was intended by the caller.

If you are invoking methods, property setters, or fields, then the array of object arguments are used as parameters to a method or as right-side values for fields and property set methods. Listing 11-4 demonstrates how to invoke an indexed property and pass multiple arguments to a reflected member. This is not at all intuitive unless you understand indexers and how they are represented.

Listing 11-4   *Reflecting an indexed property set method*

```
1:   DateTime[] dateTimes = new DateTime[10];
2:   public DateTime this[int index]
3:   {
4:     get{ return dateTimes[index]; }
5:     set{ dateTimes[index] = value;}
6:   }
7:
8:   private static void InvokeIndexedPropertyDemo()
9:   {
10:    Type type = typeof(Class1);
11:    object o = Activator.CreateInstance(type);
12:    type.InvokeMember( "Item",
13:      BindingFlags.Instance |
14:      BindingFlags.SetProperty | BindingFlags.Public,
15:      null, o, new object[]{0, new DateTime(1966, 2, 12)});
16:
17:    Console.WriteLine(((Class1)o)[0].ToString());
18:  }
```

Line 1 of Listing 11-4 declares a field as an array of DateTime values. (If you are going to declare a fixed-size array, then the property method should have some error handling, but this isn't relevant to our discussion.) Lines 2 through 6 define an indexer that supports treating the containing object as if it were an array. The indexer is named *this*. Lines 8 through 18 implement a test method that invokes the indexer.

Of special note: we refer to the indexer by the name "Item." This is not especially intuitive: you just have to know indexers can be referred to by an implied property named Item. Using a default name for an indexer makes it convenient to refer to indexers in languages that do not directly support them. For example, Visual Basic .NET does not support indexers directly; however, a Visual Basic .NET consumer of a C# class can invoke the indexer by referring to the implied Item property. Finally, note that we can pass disparate types to the array of arguments. On line 15 of Listing 11-4, we pass an integer and a DateTime value. The integer represents the indexed value, and the DateTime value will be assigned to the underlying field accessed via the property set method.

Loading Assemblies Using Reflection

An assembly contains metadata and the IL representation of an application. To use an assembly dynamically, you can invoke Load or LoadFrom static methods on the Assembly class. (In Chapter 4 you had an opportunity to learn how to use Assembly.LoadFrom, which loads an assembly from a path and an assembly file name. I won't repeat that information here; refer to Chapter 4 for examples of LoadFrom.) I will demonstrate how to load an assembly using the Assembly.Load method here.

NOTE

You can use Assembly.LoadFromPartialName to load assemblies registered in the GAC (Global Assembly Cache), but this is not a recommended practice.

The Assembly.LoadFrom method is the easiest way to load an assembly at run-time. There are seven variations of Assembly.Load. You can refer to the help documentation for information on the variations of Assembly.Load. One version of Assembly.Load accepts an AssemblyName object that describes them explicitly, including the full name of the assembly, the version, culture information, and a public key token. Listing11-5 demonstrates an example of the Assembly.LoadFrom method (for quick reference), and Listing 11-6 demonstrates Assembly.Load using an AssemblyName object, demonstrating how to construct and initialize an AssemblyName object.

Listing 11-5   *A quick reference for the Assembly.LoadFrom method*

```
Assembly assembly = Assembly.LoadFrom(
  "C:\\WINNT\\Microsoft.NET\\Framework\\" +
  "V1.0.3705\\System.Windows.Forms.dll");
  foreach( Type type in assembly.GetTypes())
  {
    Console.WriteLine(type.FullName);
  }
```

Listing 11-5 loads an assembly by providing the complete file path to the System.Windows .Forms.dll assembly. (Check Chapter 4 for more Reflection examples.) This is the easiest way to dynamically load an assembly. The *foreach* statement iterates through all of the types defined by System.Windows.Forms.

Listing 11-6   *Loading an assembly using an AssemblyName object*

```
AssemblyName assemblyName = new AssemblyName();
assemblyName.CodeBase =
  "file:///C:\\WINNT\\Microsoft.NET\\Framework\\" +
  "V1.0.3705\\System.Windows.Forms.dll";

assemblyName.Version = new Version("1.0.3300.0");
assemblyName.CultureInfo = new CultureInfo("en-US");
```

```
Assembly assembly = Assembly.Load(assemblyName);

foreach( Type type in assembly.GetTypes())
{
  Console.WriteLine(type.FullName);
}
```

The code in Listing 11-6 is equivalent to the code in Listing 11-5. We used the more verbose
Assembly.Load method, passing an instance of an AssemblyName object. We could have
initialized the AssemblyName.CodeBase argument only, as demonstrated using a file://
moniker and the path. Listing 11-6 also demonstrates how to specify the Version and
CultureInfo; both Version and CultureInfo are object properties. In the example, we loaded
the English-US version represented by the "en-US" string used to initialize the CultureInfo
object. We might use this more verbose version of the Load method to switch between
culture-specific assemblies.

Generating User Interfaces with Reflected Objects

Being able to reflect type information means that you can figure out the type and value of an
object's properties dynamically. Equate specific kinds of data to a specific control and it is
possible to create user interfaces dynamically. For example, assume you have an object with
a string property. Equate the name of the property to a Label's Text property, the data type
string to a TextBox control, and the value of the property to the value of the TextBox, and
you can add a Label and TextBox to a form. Repeat this process for other object properties,
and you have a dynamic user interface. Employ DataBinding, and the changes in the control
are automatically reflected in the object.

Listing 11-7 combines a strongly typed collection, reflected properties of the type contained
by the collection, and DataBinding to generate a user interface. Notice that the form does not
know anything about the kind of object being used to create the user interface; everything is
accomplished using Reflection.

Listing 11-7   *Code that automatically generates a user interface using Reflection*

```
1:   using System;
2:   using System.Drawing;
3:   using System.Collections;
4:   using System.ComponentModel;
5:   using System.Windows.Forms;
6:   using System.Data;
7:   using System.Reflection;
8:
9:   namespace DynamicUserInterface
10:  {
```

```
11:    public class Form1 : System.Windows.Forms.Form
12:    {
13:
14:    [Used outlining to hide auto-generated code]
15:    [Windows Form Designer generated code]
16:
17:    [STAThread]
18:    static void Main()
19:    {
20:      Application.Run(new Form1());
21:    }
22:
23:    private void menuItem7_Click(object sender, System.EventArgs e)
24:    {
25:      const string about =
26:        "Dynamic User Interface Demo\r\n" +
27:        "Written by Paul Kimmel. pkimmel@softconcepts.com\r\n" +
28:        "Copyright \xA9 2002. All Rights Reserved.\r\n" +
29:        "Published in Advanced C# Programming\r\n";
30:
31:      MessageBox.Show(about, "About",
32:        MessageBoxButtons.OK, MessageBoxIcon.Information);
33:    }
34:
35:    private void menuItem2_Click(object sender, System.EventArgs e)
36:    {
37:      Application.Exit();
38:    }
39:
40:    private void menuItem4_Click(object sender, System.EventArgs e)
41:    {
42:      CompactDiscs compactDiscs = CompactDiscs.Create();
43:      CreateUserInterface(compactDiscs, typeof(CompactDisc));
44:    }
45:
46:    private void menuItem5_Click(object sender, System.EventArgs e)
47:    {
48:      Customers customers = Customers.Create();
49:      CreateUserInterface(customers, typeof(Customer));
50:    }
51:
52:    private void ClearControls()
53:    {
54:      panel1.Controls.Clear();
55:    }
```

```
56:
57:    private object dataSource;
58:    private void CreateUserInterface(IList list, Type type)
59:    {
60:      dataSource = list;
61:      ClearControls();
62:
63:      PropertyInfo[] properties = type.GetProperties();
64:      for( int i=0; i < properties.Length; i++)
65:      {
66:        AddControl( properties[i], i, list );
67:      }
68:    }
69:
70:    private void AddControl(PropertyInfo propertyInfo, int i, IList list)
71:    {
72:      Label label = new Label();
73:      label.AutoSize = true;
74:      label.Text = propertyInfo.Name;
75:      label.Location = new Point(10, (i + 1) * 25);
76:      panel1.Controls.Add(label);
77:
78:      TextBox textBox = new TextBox();
79:      textBox.Location = new Point(250, (i + 1) * 25);
80:      textBox.Width = 250;
81:      panel1.Controls.Add(textBox);
82:      textBox.DataBindings.Add("Text", list, propertyInfo.Name);
83:    }
84:
85:
86:    private void menuItem8_Popup(object sender, System.EventArgs e)
87:    {
88:      menuItemNext.Enabled = panel1.Controls.Count > 0;
89:      menuItemPrevious.Enabled = panel1.Controls.Count > 0;
90:    }
91:
92:    private void menuItemNext_Click(object sender, System.EventArgs e)
93:    {
94:      try
95:      {
96:      panel1.BindingContext[dataSource].Position += 1;
97:      }
98:      catch{}
99:    }
100:
```

```
101:   private void menuItemPrevious_Click(object sender, System.EventArgs e)
102:   {
103:     try
104:     {
105:       panel1.BindingContext[dataSource].Position -= 1;
106:     }
107:     catch{}
108:   }
109: }
110:}
```

There a few comments I need to make before we review the code. Lines 14 and 15 of Listing 11-7 represent outlined code. This code will not run as is. Download and run the UserInterfaceDemo.sln to test the code. The outlined code represents the controls, constructor, and Dispose method, which are all generated by the View Designer.

The code that performs the work is defined in CreateUserInterface and AddControl. Pass an IList and a Type to CreateUserInterface on lines 58 through 68 of Listing 11-7. CreateUserInterface iterates through all of the properties defined by Type and invokes AddControl. AddControl on lines 70 through 83 create a Label control and set the text property to the PropertyInfo.Name value. Then, a TextBox is created, and the IList and the PropertyInfo.Name value are used to create a Binder—on line 82—to the TextBox's Text property. The menuItemNext_Click and menuItemPreviousClick event handlers use panel1's BindingContext to move forward and backward between the objects in the IList. Modify the value in a TextBox and the bound object's property is updated.

Types.cs implements two strongly typed collections containing Customer and CompactDisc objects to demonstrate the user interface generator.

What is left to create a robust solution? Well, if I were implementing this software, I would consider making the following changes:

▶ Insert spaces into the PropertyInfo.Name value to make the Label.Text property more user friendly.

▶ Perhaps right justify the Label control and make all Labels the same width as the widest text value, resulting in less whitespace between the Label and TextBox (or other control).

▶ Use the PropertyInfo.PropertyType to determine an optimal control to render, rather than defaulting to a TextBox.

▶ Dynamically assign an event handler to facilitate validation.

▶ Implement a layout manager to support dynamically changing interface styles.

▶ Separate the code-generation code into a separate class.

▶ Implement the code-generation code as an interface and realize a version for Windows Forms and Web Forms.

NOTE

I opened Pandora's box a couple of decades too soon. It is possible to generate clever user interfaces using Reflection. You can also use Reflection to emit dynamic types. My concern is that some manager will read this and think that programmer obsolescence is just around the corner. Nothing could be further from the truth. The demands of users are greater than ever. We may be able to automate some boring tasks like creating common kinds of input screens, but that will just leave time for more challenging problems. This is a pattern of evolution that all innovation seems to take. With the current evolution of object-oriented languages, I do think that we are on the cusp of some clever applications.

The preceding bulleted list describes the changes that come to mind for an actual application; there are probably some other good modifications, too. With a little imagination, it would be possible to create some reasonably advanced user interfaces.

Exploring the .NET Framework with Reflection

The AssemblyViewer.sln from Chapter 2 demonstrates code that will allow you to explore the .NET framework. If you have been reading this book from the beginning, you are sufficiently well prepared to contrive some algorithms to discover information about types using Reflection. The key to working with types using Reflection is to obtain an Assembly object, get the types defined in that Assembly, and invoke operations on the members defined in those types.

Assembly.GetTypes will return an array of System.Type objects representing all of the types defined by an assembly. From the Type object, you can obtain information about any member by requesting the *kind*Info objects. For example, to get all of the members of a single type, invoke Type.GetMembers. GetMembers returns a heterogeneous mix of MemberInfo objects, combining constructors, properties, events, fields, and methods into a single array. The ConstructorInfo, PropertyInfo, EventInfo, FieldInfo, and MethodInfo classes all inherit from the MemberInfo class. All of these classes are defined in the System.Reflection namespace.

You can request an array of a specific type by invoking the get method for that type. For example, Type.GetMethods will return an array of MethodInfo objects. Type.GetMethod will return a single MethodInfo, based on the parameters that you pass to GetMethod. It is easier to invoke operations on members when you have a specific Info object; however, you know from the "Dynamic Member Invocation" section that you can invoke operations on members directly with a Type object.

In the next section I will demonstrate some operations you are likely to want to perform in real applications relying on dynamic type interaction. We'll review Reflection examples from the AssemblyViewer.sln from Chapter 5, examples of dynamically invoked methods and parameters, and binding to events using Reflection.

Returning to the CLR Reference Application, Assembly Viewer 2

The AssemblyViewer.sln contains several examples of Reflection for fields, properties, methods, events, constructors, and types. As you may recall, the sample application from Chapter 5 allows you to load an assembly at run-time and adds all of the types and their incumbent members to a database. Refer to that application for general examples of Reflection. I will refer to the AssemblyViewer.sln occasionally in this section, as well as provide some additional new sample programs.

Requesting Type Information

An easy way to think about Reflection is as a hierarchical arrangement of entities with an assembly at the pinnacle of the hierarchy. Inside an assembly are the types, and inside each type are members, including nested types. The members might include enumerations, structures, classes, properties, methods, events, fields, and constructors. Thus, once you have loaded an assembly, the next thing you will need to do is request a Type object.

There are a couple of ways to request type objects. You can use the typeof operator, which is the easiest and most convenient way to obtain a Type object, or you can use the static method Type.GetType. Here are a couple of syntactical examples demonstrating how to obtain type information.

```
typeof(type)
Type.GetType(typename)
```

For example, typeof(Form1) will return a Type object for a class named Form1. The second example is a bit misleading. From the help documentation for Type.GetType, you might assume that you can simply express the *typename* argument as a simple name. The tricky part is that it seems that for some types you can. For example, Type.GetType("System.Int32") will return a Type object for Int32, but Type.GetType("System.Windows.Forms.Form") will return null. However, if you pass the assembly qualified name to Type.GetType then Type.GetType will work correctly. Here is an example demonstrating an assembly qualified name for the System.Windows.Forms.Form class and why you'll appreciate typeof.

```
Type.GetType("System.Windows.Forms.Form, System.Windows.Forms,
   Version=1.0.3300.0, Culture=neutral,
   PublicKeyToken=b77a5c561934e089");
```

To reflect types using the Type.GetType reliably, you will need to provide an assembly qualified name. Here is an example that loads the System.Windows.Forms.Form class by name using an assembly qualified name. Listing 11-8 provides an example of an assembly qualified name. The fragment was taken from the TypeDemo.sln available for download. (You can probably tell from the fragment that the user interface is composed of two Button controls and a TextBox on a form.)

Listing 11-8 *Reflecting Type and MemberInfo objects, including an example of an assembly qualified name*

```
1:  private void ReflectMembers(Type type)
2:  {
3:    textBox1.Clear();
4:    foreach(MemberInfo memberInfo in type.GetMembers())
5:    {
6:      textBox1.AppendText(memberInfo.Name + "\r\n");
7:    }
8:  }
9:
10: private void button1_Click(object sender, System.EventArgs e)
11: {
12:   ReflectMembers(typeof(System.Windows.Forms.Form));
13: }
14:
15: private void button2_Click(object sender, System.EventArgs e)
16: {
17:   const string assemblyQualifiedName =
18:     "System.Windows.Forms.Form, System.Windows.Forms, " +
19:     "Version=1.0.3300.0, Culture=neutral, " +
20:     "PublicKeyToken=b77a5c561934e089";
22:   ReflectMembers(Type.GetType(assemblyQualifiedName));
23: }
```

ReflectMembers, beginning on line 1 of Listing 11-8, demonstrates how to iterate all members as a homogeneous group. This is a good strategy for quick reference. The event handler on lines 10 through 13 demonstrate how to obtain type information using the typeof operator. The typeof operator will not work if you do not have a reference to the assembly. For example, if System.Windows.Forms.dll is not part of the assembly, you will not be able to obtain its type information.

The event handler on lines 15 through 23 of Listing 11-8 demonstrates how to obtain the type information for the same type as the event handler for button1—System.Windows.Forms .Form—using an assembly qualified name. The fields in the string include the type to get the Type object for, the declaring types, the version and culture information, and the public key.

A reasonable person might inquire as to how a fully qualified assembly name is obtained. The answer is that I reflected System.Windows.Forms.Form using the typeof operator and read the Type.AssemblyQualifiedName property. This isn't very convenient. Here is an example of a practical problem presented by the requirement for an assembly qualified name.

Geoff Caylor, a member of a team of programmers working on a C# project in Oregon, came up with the idea of using Reflection to generate ASP.NET user interfaces. Geoff wanted to create a CustomAttribute (refer to Chapter 10) to tag properties in our business objects with a hint describing the kind of Web control to render for a particular field. When the GUI generator read the property, the custom attribute could be read and a good control rendered. There are a couple of ways of solving this problem: a person could create a layout manager and dynamically resolve the kind of control to render; a Type object of the control to render could be associated with the property; or a string name of the control to render could be associated—for example, "CheckBox" for a Boolean property. Geoff originally chose the latter when he was prototyping because it seemed lightweight; that is, he chose to use a string. However, you cannot obtain the type information for the System.UI.Web.WebControls.CheckBox without the assembly qualified name, and tying the property to a specific assembly version will break as soon as the .NET Framework is updated. (Recall the assembly qualified name includes the version information.) There is a practical solution to the problem that probably includes a layout manager and an aspect of a control hint and dynamic control-type resolution.

My role in the project in Oregon I have mentioned was architect. The project manager asked me about a practical problem. On our project, there were contractors that were well grounded in OOP principles and main frame programmers transitioning to OOP and .NET. The project manager expressed a concern about esoteric code, like user interface generators, and the ability of less-experienced permanent employees to maintain this kind of code. I coined the term *esoterrorism,* which is applied to code that is intentionally or maliciously esoteric. (We wanted to avoid unnecessarily esoteric code.)

Our pragmatic approach was to get the project done efficiently, taking advantage of the best and most powerful aspects of .NET without making the code unmaintainable. The solution is that we provided models and written architectural overviews tied to well-documented patterns and refactorings, and tagged code that might seem esoteric to a "junior" programmer with the name of the pattern or "Refactoring." For example, when we used a factory method, we provided a reference to a book in the team's library that described factory methods. Clearly, it is the responsibility of permanent and new staff to use this information, but there is no practical alternative.

All of this was tied to the concept of a "junior" programmer. *Junior programmer* means a novice and is also a euphemism for a poorly compensated programmer. What such a person may know or be motivated to learn is a crapshoot. We could not justify ignoring Web Services, interfaces, delegates, Reflection, inheritance, or any of the things a junior programmer may not yet comprehend, because to do so would risk the primary objective, which was to deliver the application. A secondary and real goal was to acknowledge the long-term budgetary constraints of the customer. This combination of technical and human factors demonstrates why software development can be difficult, and why it is important to have both a seasoned architect and a project manager guiding application development.

Reflecting Methods and Method Parameters

To obtain method information using Reflection, you can use MemberInfo.Name and MemberInfo.MemberType or directly request the MethodInfo objects from a type. Where methods are concerned, it is not sufficient to know the method name only. You must acquire the entire signature of a method to determine how to invoke a method. Hence, after you require the MethodInfo object, you will need to require the ParameterInfo objects that describe the parameters that must be provided to the method invocation. Listing 11-9 provides an example that displays the approximate signature of the methods of a type.

Listing 11-9 *Reflecting the method signatures of a type*

```
1:  using System;
2:  using System.Reflection;
3:  using System.Text;
4:
5:  namespace InvokeMethod
6:  {
7:    class Class1
8:    {
9:      [STAThread]
10:     static void Main(string[] args)
11:     {
12:        Type type = typeof(System.Windows.Forms.MessageBox);
13:        MethodInfo[] methods = type.GetMethods();
14:
15:        foreach( MethodInfo methodInfo in methods )
16:        {
17:          ApproximateSignature( methodInfo );
18:        }
19:
20:        Console.ReadLine();
21:
22:     }
23:
24:     private static void ApproximateSignature( MethodInfo methodInfo )
25:     {
26:        // access return_type name( paramtype1 param1
27:        // [, paramtypen paramn]);
28:        const string mask = "{0} {1} {2}({3})";
29:
30:        Console.WriteLine( string.Format(mask,
31:          GetAccessModifier(methodInfo),  methodInfo.ReturnType,
```

```
32:           methodInfo.Name, GetParameterList( methodInfo )));
33:       }
34:
35:     private static string GetAccessModifier(MethodInfo methodInfo)
36:     {
37:       return methodInfo.IsPublic ? "public" : "private";
38:     }
39:
40:     private static string GetParameterModifier(
41:         ParameterInfo parameterInfo )
42:     {
43:       if( parameterInfo.IsIn ) return "[in]";
44:       if( parameterInfo.IsOut) return "[out]";
45:       return string.Empty;
46:     }
47:
48:     private static string GetParameterList(MethodInfo methodInfo)
49:     {
50:       // modifier type name
51:       const string mask = "{0} {1}";
52:       StringBuilder s = new StringBuilder();
53:       ParameterInfo[] parameters = methodInfo.GetParameters();
54:
55:       for( int i = 0; i < parameters.Length; i++ )
56:       {
57:         if( GetParameterModifier(parameters[i]) != string.Empty )
58:           s.Append( GetParameterModifier(parameters[i]) );
59:         s.Append( string.Format(mask,
60:           parameters[i].ParameterType, parameters[i].Name ));
61:         if( i < parameters.Length-1 ) s.Append(", ");
62:       }
63:       return s.ToString();
64:     }
65:   }
66: }
```

The code in Listing 11-9 will print the approximate method signatures. You can obtain a good visual picture of a method using this program, but it would be difficult to invoke methods in a purely dynamic way using this information, because the parameters could represent any type, including types that haven't been invented yet.

The code in Listing 11-9 begins in Main by requesting the method signatures of the System.Windows.Forms.MessageBox class on line 12. (The sample application for this code is InvokeMethod.sln.) ApproximateSignature displays an access modifier, a return type, name, and parameter list. Reflection distinguishes between public and non-public methods;

thus, GetAccessModifier returns only public or private, but may, in reality, be public, protected, private, internal, or protected internal. You can dynamically invoke public and non-public methods based on ReflectionPermission settings. GetParameterList provides the list of parameters, including any modifier, type, and name, as shown in lines 48 through 64.

NOTE

Technologies like Reflection, including the ability to emit dynamic code (see "Emitting Dynamic Assemblies" later in this chapter), may ultimately lead to smart programs that write their own code, but, as you may be able to glean from this section, it may be challenging to write completely dynamic code. From this section you can see that it may be difficult to invoke any method without knowing something about its signature in advance.

GetParameterModifier on lines 40 through 46 of Listing 11-9 only returns [in] and [out] modifiers. You may recall that there is a *ref* modifier for parameters, too. This is reflected as an ampersand (&) in the type signature. Hence, if a string parameter uses the *ref* modifier, then the ParameterInfo.ParameterType will return System.String&. The ampersand is actually used in C++ to represent pass-by-reference objects. (The presence of the ampersand for *ref* parameters provides a hint as to the underlying language used to create C#.)

With some innovation, you may be able to create a completely dynamic method invocation application. Reflect the MethodInfo and ParameterInfo objects for a particular method. Use the ParameterInfo to dynamically generate a user interface for input fields, obtaining parameters from a user and invoking the method by passing those parameters to the method. This is a reasonable approximation of what Web Services do with .asmx pages. (Refer to the Expressions.sln Web Service from Chapter 4 for an example of the dynamic input test page for Web Services.)

Creating the dynamic user interface and invoking the method with dynamic user inputs is left as an exercise. If you combine the user interface form code demonstrated in the earlier section "Generating User Interfaces with Reflected Objects" with examples for dynamically invoking methods provided throughout the chapter, you can derive a solution. If you are having difficulties, download the InvokeMethod.sln from the **www.osborne.com** or **www.softconcepts.com** website for an example implementation. The dynamic form is demonstrated in input.cs, and the invocation is provided in Main.cs.

TIP

If you like a challenge, try to complete the dynamic form, method and parameter reflection, and invocation of a method sample before downloading the code. Here is a hint that will help you get started: look at an .asmx page from a Web Service for inspiration. A solution is provided in InvokeMethod.sln, available for download.

Accessing Properties and Fields Dynamically

The key to accessing properties and fields using Reflection is to obtain the property and field through InvokeMember, PropertyInfo, or FieldInfo, as the case may be; cast the reference to the appropriate data type; and then simply treat the value as you would a property or field.

I implied that there are two ways to access properties and fields: InvokeMember or obtain a PropertyInfo for properties or a FieldInfo for fields. I will demonstrate using properties and fields as left-side and right-side values using both InvokeMember and the Info objects. The class used for this section is provided in Listing 11-10.

Listing 11-10 *A class used to demonstrate reflecting fields and properties*

```
public class Target
{
  private string text;

  public string Text
  {
    get{ return text; }
    set{ text = value; }
  }
}
```

The class Target is representative of any class with fields and matching properties. (Clearly, if we modify either the field or property, the related value is modified, too.) Target will be used to demonstrate reflections in the sections that follow.

Setting and Getting Fields Using InvokeMember

InvokeMember can be used to interact with any member type. The general application of InvokeMember is to name the member, provide the BindingFlags, specify a Binder or pass null to use the DefaultBinder, pass an object for non-static members, and an array of objects representing parameters to the member. Listing 11-11 provides an example of InvokeMember on the private instance field: Target.text from Listing 11-10.

Listing 11-11 *Using InvokeMember on a private instance field*

```
Type type = typeof(Target);
object o = Activator.CreateInstance(type);

// set private field using InvokeMember
type.InvokeMember("text",
  BindingFlags.SetField | BindingFlags.NonPublic |
  BindingFlags.Instance, null, o,
  new object[]{"Advanced C# Programming"});

// get private field using InvokeMember
string text = (string)type.InvokeMember("text",
  BindingFlags.GetField | BindingFlags.NonPublic |
```

```
        BindingFlags.Instance, null, o, new object[]{});
```

```
MessageBox.Show(text);
```

The first two statements obtain the Type object and create an instance of the Target type. The first use of InvokeMember indicates the field name, *text,* and specifies the BindingFlags that help pinpoint the field. We want to set the field value, so we pass BindingFlags.SetField. The field is private, so we OR—represented by the | operator—BindingFlags.NonPublic to BindingFlags.SetField; Target.text is private, which is represented by OR*ing* BindingFlags .Instance to our BindingFlags argument. We can use the Type.DefaultBinder for the text field; therefore, passing null will implicitly instruct InvokeMember to use the DefaultBinder. The *o* argument represents the instance of Target returned by the Activator.CreateInstance method, and, finally, we are setting a field, which only needs a single value. The field Target.text is assigned the string "Advanced C# Programming".

The second call to InvokeMember is used to get the Target.text field value. To invoke the set method for text, we need to make a few changes to the parameters to InvokeMember. Instead of BindingFlags.SetField, we OR BindingFlags.GetField into the BindingFlags argument. Because we are invoking what is effectively a function, we can pass an empty array to InvokeMember. Finally, cast the return value of InvokeMember to the type we are getting. The MessageBox.Show method will display "Advanced C# Programming" when the final statement executes.

Setting and Getting Fields Using a FieldInfo

Using a FieldInfo object is much simpler than using InvokeMember to perform the same operation. The reason is that when we obtain a FieldInfo object, we have set the context to fields, resulting in the need to provide less information (see Listing 11-12).

Listing 11-12   *Reflecting a field with a FieldInfo object*

```
Type type = typeof(Target);
object o = Activator.CreateInstance(type);
//set and get a field using a FieldInfo
FieldInfo field = type.GetField("text",
  BindingFlags.NonPublic | BindingFlags.Instance);
field.SetValue(o, "www.codeguru.com");
text = (string)field.GetValue(o);
```

```
MessageBox.Show(text);
```

The first two statements in Listing 11-12 create an instance of the Target object. The third statement obtains a FieldInfo for the Target.text field. Because the field is private, we need to use the BindingFlags to pinpoint the field. Notice that we do not need to use BindingFlags.GetField

BindingFlags .SetField; simply specifying the access type and whether we want an instance or static member is sufficient. The final two statements set and get the value of the field.

Setting and Getting a Property Using InvokeMember

Getting and setting a property using InvokeMember is very similar to getting and setting a field. The only noticeable difference between using InvokeMember on fields and properties is the use of BindingFlags. We need to use BindingFlags.SetProperty and BindingFlags .GetProperty, as demonstrated in Listing 11-13.

Listing 11-13   *Invoking operations on properties*

```
Type type = typeof(Target);
object o = Activator.CreateInstance(type);

// set and get a property using InvokeMember
type.InvokeMember("Text",
  BindingFlags.SetProperty | BindingFlags.Instance |
  BindingFlags.Public, null, o,
  new object[]{"Windows Developer Magazine"});

// get property using invoke member
text = (string)type.InvokeMember("Text",
  BindingFlags.GetProperty | BindingFlags.Instance |
  BindingFlags.Public, null, o, new object[]{});

MessageBox.Show(text);
```

If you are reflecting an indexed property, you will need to pass the index in the array of objects passed to InvokeMember. (Refer to the earlier section "Passing Parameters to InvokeMember" for an example of calling InvokeMember on an indexed property.)

Setting and Getting a Property Using a PropertyInfo

Setting and getting properties using a PropertyInfo object is similar to working with FieldInfo objects using Reflection, as Listing 11-14 demonstrates.

Listing 11-14   *Using PropertyInfo objects*

```
Type type = typeof(Target);
object o = Activator.CreateInstance(type);
//get and set a property using a PropertyInfo
PropertyInfo property = type.GetProperty("Text");
property.SetValue(o, "www.softconcepts.com", null);
```

```
text = (string)property.GetValue(o, null);

MessageBox.Show(text);
```

The PropertyInfo object in Listing 11-14 accounts for a possible index property by accepting a third argument on SetValue and a second argument on GetValue. PropertyInfo .GetValue, as demonstrated in Listing 11-14, passes null to GetValue, as Target.Text is not an indexed property. Pass an argument specifying the index of the value you want to modify for indexed properties.

Binding to Events Dynamically

You can bind an event handler to a dynamically reflected EventInfo. Obtain the EventInfo object by name from the Type object and invoke EventInfo.AddEventHandler to associate the event handler with an instance of the reflected object. I added a Changed event to the Target class to demonstrate this. Listing 11-15 contains the revised Target class and a fragment of code that demonstrates how to associate an event handler to the Changed event.

Listing 11-15   *Binding to a reflected event member*

```
1:  public class Target
2:  {
3:    private string text;
4:
5:    public string Text
6:    {
7:      get{ return text; }
8:      set
9:      {
10:       text = value;
11:       OnChanged();
12:     }
13:   }
14:
15:   private void OnChanged()
16:   {
17:     if( Changed != null )
18:       Changed(this, System.EventArgs.Empty);
19:   }
20:
21:   public event EventHandler Changed;
22: }
23:
```

```
24: public class Class1
25: {
26:   [STAThread]
27:   static void Main( string[] args )
28:   {
29:     Type type = typeof(Target);
30:     object o = Activator.CreateInstance(type);
31:     EventInfo eventInfo = type.GetEvent("Changed");
32:     eventInfo.AddEventHandler(o, new EventHandler(Class1.OnChanged));
33:
34:     ((Target)o).Text = "New Value";
35:   }
36:
37:
38:   private static void OnChanged(object sender , System.EventArgs e)
39:   {
40:     MessageBox.Show(((Target)sender).Text);
41:   }
42: }
```

The class Target is revised on lines 1 through 22 of Listing 11-15 and now contains an OnChanged that raises the Changed event if Changed is not null. OnChanged is called when the value of the Text property is changed on line 11.

The static method Class1.Main obtains the Type object for Target and creates an instance of Target on lines 29 and 30 of Listing 11-15. Target's Type object is used to obtain an EventInfo object that represents Target.Changed on line 31. The EventInfo.AddEventHandler method is called to associate Class1.OnChanged with the Target.OnChanged. (We don't need an instance of Class1, since we are using a static event handler.) We take a shortcut on line 34 to change Target.Text, which will raise the Changed event. The OnChanged handler on lines 38 through 41 will display the Text property of the Target object represented by the variable *o*.

The fundamental operations for using objects directly and for using reflected objects are the same. The only difference is that you have to write verbose code to specify the types and members that you want to interact with.

Emitting Dynamic Assemblies

A powerful aspect of .NET programming with a significant amount of untapped potential is the ability to use the Reflection.Emit namespace to generate code.

Microsoft .NET compiles code to MSIL (Microsoft Intermediate Language). MSIL approximates assembly language but is not tied to a specific operating system. The net effect of MSIL is that we are likely to see .NET applications running on other platforms besides

Windows- and Intel-based computers. IL code is Just-In-Time compiled (JITted) to machine language before it is executed. I suppose someone is already working on .NET for the Apple Macintosh or Unix platforms, but a benefit we have today is the ability to emit IL code to memory and disk from a running application. The System.Reflection.Emit namespace supports this capability. In this section, I will review salient aspects of the Emit namespace and demonstrate how to emit an assembly, class, and code and dynamically load and execute the assembly.

The fundamental steps required to emit an assembly and type with code are analogous to those for writing code from scratch. You have to define the same elements; the difference is that you have to write code to do the job rather than create the entities with the keyboard and editor. The basic steps for creating a dynamic assembly and dynamic types include the following:

▶   Emitting an assembly to memory and disk

▶   Emitting a module

▶   Emitting a dynamic type (a class)

▶   Emitting members, including constructors, methods, properties, and fields

▶   Saving, loading, and executing dynamic assemblies

All of the code that demonstrates the topics in this section is available for download in the Emitter.sln. The code demonstrates emitting a strongly typed collection that inherits from System.Collections.CollectionBase and a Test collected object. Between the two sample classes that emit IL there are examples of emitting fields, properties, methods, constructors, classes, modules, and assemblies. There are Reflection.Emit examples that demonstrate declaring local variables, performing type casting, applying the DefaultMemberAttribute, and creating a class indexer. Several of these topics are explored, but you are encouraged to download the Emitter.sln for the complete sample application.

There are a couple of important and easy-to-follow strategies that will help you write code that emits MSIL. If you remember that you have to perform the same kinds of things with your emitter code that you do if you were interacting with the IDE, you will be less likely to miss steps. If you keep in mind that reading a lot of code will help you write code and apply this concept to emitting MSIL, you will find writing emitters more enjoyable. Finally, remember that because you can write code in C#, compile the code, and view the MSIL with the ildasm.exe utility, you will have an excellent resource for creating, viewing, and learning MSIL from your own code.

Emitting Assemblies in Memory

One of the steps you need to perform when emitting MSIL is to create an assembly. Assemblies have names represented by the AssemblyName class and an Assembly object represented by the AssemblyBuilder class.

NOTE

Entities emitted in MSIL have analogous classes that are designed specifically for generating these entities. These classes end with the suffix Builder. Hence, to emit an assembly, you will need an AssemblyBuilder. To emit a class or structure, you will need a TypeBuilder, and so on. Look at the System.Reflection.Emit namespace for all of the Builder classes.

The code samples for this section are contained in Emitter.sln, as previously mentioned. The Emitter.sln contains a module Emitter.cs that provides an implementation of an emitter that writes a strongly typed collection derived from the CollectionBase class and also contains a sample class that can be used as a collected class. (Refer to Chapter 6 for more on strongly typed collections.) The EmitTypedCollection creates a derived class that generalizes System.Collections.CollectionBase for any type that you use to initialize an emitter. For example, if you have a Music class that represents your favorite artists and titles, you can emit a typed collection at run-time without writing any additional code.

The first step in creating our emitter is to create a dynamic assembly to contain the typed collection. EmitTypedCollection.GetClass is a static factory method that is the starting point for the emitter. GetClass returns a Type, which is, in fact, the dynamically created type. GetClass requires a string and Type argument. The string argument represents the name of the typed collection class, the module, and the assembly, and the Type argument will be the strong type stored by the dynamic class.

GetClass has two forms. The first form accepts the string and Type argument, and the second version accepts a string, Type, AppDomain, and AssemblyBuilderAccess-enumerated value. All of this information is necessary to create the AssemblyName and Assembly objects, the first objects we have to create. Listing 11-16 shows the implementation of the code that will yield a dynamic assembly, albeit an empty one at this point.

TIP

It is important to remember that the orchestration of the code is up to the individual. You certainly could consolidate the emitter code into fewer methods, but you would end up with some extremely long methods.

Listing 11-16 *Essential ingredients for emitting a dynamic assembly*

```
1:   public class EmitTypedCollection
2:   {
3:     private string name;
4:     private Type collectedType;
5:     private AssemblyName assemblyName;
6:     private AssemblyBuilder assemblyBuilder;
7:     private ModuleBuilder moduleBuilder;
8:     private TypeBuilder typeBuilder;
9:     private MethodBuilder addMethod;
10:    private PropertyBuilder indexerProperty;
11:
```

```
12:    public EmitTypedCollection(string name, Type collectedType)
13:    {
14:      this.name = name;
15:      this.collectedType = collectedType;
16:    }
17:
18:    public static Type GetClass(string name,
19:      Type collectedType )
20:    {
21:      return GetClass(name, collectedType,
22:        Thread.GetDomain(), AssemblyBuilderAccess.Run);
23:    }
24:
25:    public static Type GetClass(string name,
26:      Type collectedType, AppDomain domain,
27:      AssemblyBuilderAccess access)
28:    {
29:      EmitTypedCollection o = new EmitTypedCollection(name,
30:      collectedType);
31:
32:      return o.CreateClass(domain, access);
33:    }
34:
35:    private Type CreateClass(AppDomain domain,
36:      AssemblyBuilderAccess access)
37:    {
38:      assemblyName = CreateAssemblyName();
39:      assemblyBuilder = CreateAssemblyBuilder(domain, assemblyName, access);
40:      moduleBuilder = CreateModuleBuilder(assemblyBuilder, access);
41:      typeBuilder = CreateTypeBuilder(moduleBuilder);
42:      EmitCode(typeBuilder);
43:
44:      return typeBuilder.CreateType();
45:    }
46:
47:    private AssemblyName CreateAssemblyName()
48:    {
49:      AssemblyName aName = new AssemblyName();
50:      aName.Name = name;
51:      return aName;
52:    }
53:
54:    private AssemblyBuilder CreateAssemblyBuilder(AppDomain domain,
55:      AssemblyName assemblyName, AssemblyBuilderAccess access)
```

```
56:    {
57:      return domain.DefineDynamicAssembly(assemblyName, access);
58:    }
59:    // more code needs to be added here
60: }
```

Decomposed as demonstrated in Listing 11-16, the code should be easier to follow. Call GetClass(*name, collectedType*) to get started. The overloaded GetClass is called, adding the AppDomain and AssemblyBuilderAccess-enumerated value to the mix. AppDomains exist to provide application isolation. We will be emitting an assembly, and assemblies are isolated by an AppDomain. In the listing we use the AppDomain of the application this code runs in, Emitter.exe. AssemblyBuilderAccess has three enumerated values: Run, RunAndSave, and Save. Use Run for dynamic assemblies that won't be written to disk, use RunAndSave to run in memory and save, and use Save to write an assembly to disk but not to run in memory. (You can run a saved assembly by referencing it in an application in the usual way.)

The second GetClass creates an instance of our EmitTypedCollection class and calls CreateClass. CreateClass is the nexus of control for the emitter. Just as promised, CreateClass creates an AssemblyName, an AssemblyBuilder, a ModuleBuilder, and a TypeBuilder, and finally emits the code contained in that type. (The module, Type, and code-building code is not shown yet, intentionally.)

You know how to construct an AssemblyName; thus, the code on lines 47 through 52 of Listing 11-16 should be no surprise. Finally, the AssemblyBuilder code is quite straightforward. The call to domain.DefineDynamicAssembly(assemblyName, access) is separated into the CreateAssemblyBuilder method—on lines 54 through 59—to provide a well-named method describing what is going on. More important is the recurring pattern that is introduced here.

When you are writing code everything you do is context dependent. The same is true for emitting code. To end up with an assembly, you create a new project. Modules are added in Visual Studio .NET to the project. When you are emitting code, you emit the assembly directly, but modules still need to be added to the assembly. This contextually dependent behavior is evident when we use AppDomain.DefineDynamicAssembly on line 57. The code is understood to mean that the dynamic assembly belongs to the AppDomain. You will see this recurring pattern everywhere. AppDomains contain assemblies, which contain modules, which contain types, which contain members, which contain code.

The boldfaced code in Listing 11-16 is described in the upcoming section "Using Builder Objects to Create IL."

Saving Emitted Assemblies to File

The Assembly class contains a Save method. If you invoke AppDomain.DefineDynamic Assembly with either of the AssemblyBuilderAccess.Save or AssemblyBuilderAccess

.RunAndSave values (see Listing 11-16, line 22, for an example of AssemblyBuilderAccess .Run), you can write a dynamic assembly to disk.

The static factory method EmitTypedCollection.SaveAssembly and the private instance method EmitTypedCollection.SaveAssembly demonstrate how to emit a Test class and a strongly typed collection class containing Test objects to disk. You can load and experiment with the Test.dll application just as you would an assembly hand-crafted in the Visual Studio .NET IDE. The code used to create the typed collection is the same code defined in EmitTypeCollection, and EmitType provides an example of a simple class containing a field, a property, and a constructor.

To experiment with the Test.dll assembly, follow the numbered steps:

1. Download and run the Emitter.sln.
2. Click the Write Assembly button shown in Figure 11-3.
3. Close the application and open the Emitter.sln project.
4. Add a reference to the Test.dll assembly in the Emitter.csproj. (Test.dll should be in the same directory containing the compiled Emitter.sln).
5. Find the button3_Click event handler. This is the event handler for the Test Written button shown in Figure 11-3. Change the compiler #if conditional to True, enabling the code for testing Test.dll.
6. Run Emitter.sln again and click the Test Written button.

Following the numbered steps will allow you to try the emitted code in Test.dll. The test code will create an instance of the Test collection, add a TestData object to the collection, demonstrate the *foreach* construct, and bind the strongly typed collection to the DataGrid (shown in Figure 11-3).

If you want to modify the code that emits Test.dll, remove the reference to Test.dll, disable the conditional code, modify the EmitTypedCollection or EmitType code, and repeat the numbered steps to test your changes. Of course, you can step through the code to explore how everything works.

Using Builder Objects to Create IL

Builder objects are beneficial for emitting entities, including dynamic assemblies. Lines 40, 41, 42, and 44 of Listing 11-16 exemplify the importance of Builders. On line 40, we create a ModuleBuilder, and on line 41 a TypeBuilder. Ultimately, we want to get to our TypeBuilder, which represents the class we will be emitting. Listing 11-17 shows the CreateModuleBuilder and CreateTypeBuilder methods that I implemented. (These are part of the EmitTypedCollection class from Listing 11-16.)

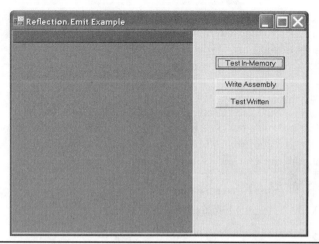

Figure 11-3 Click Write Assembly to write the Test.dll Assembly containing an emitted type and typed collection.

Listing 11-17 EmitTypedCollection methods create the ModuleBuilder and TypeBuilder, representing a dynamic module and class, respectively.

```
private ModuleBuilder CreateModuleBuilder(AssemblyBuilder assemblyBuilder,
  AssemblyBuilderAccess access)
{
  if( access == AssemblyBuilderAccess.Run)
    return assemblyBuilder.DefineDynamicModule(name);
  else
    return assemblyBuilder.DefineDynamicModule(name + ".mod",
      NameToFileName);
}

private TypeBuilder CreateTypeBuilder(ModuleBuilder moduleBuilder)
{
  TypeBuilder t = moduleBuilder.DefineType(name,
    TypeAttributes.Public | TypeAttributes.BeforeFieldInit,
    typeof(System.Collections.CollectionBase));

  Type type = typeof(DefaultMemberAttribute);
  ConstructorInfo constructorInfo =
  type.GetConstructor(new Type[]{typeof(string)});

  CustomAttributeBuilder customAttributeBuilder =
    new CustomAttributeBuilder(constructorInfo, new Object[]{"Item"});
```

```
    t.SetCustomAttribute(customAttributeBuilder);
    return t;
}
```

The code in Listing 11-17 looks more daunting than it is, but it does suggest a tendency toward complexity as we get to the emitter code that writes lines of code. CreateModuleBuilder emits a dynamic module name if we are going to run the assembly in memory or a valid assembly name and module if we are going to save the assembly and module to disk. The ".mod" extension indicates a module containing compiled executable code, like .lib files. The .mod file is an intermediate file between the compiling and linking process. The NameToFileName method was implemented by me; NameToFileName simply adds a ".dll" extension to the name passed to the emitter.

CreateTypeBuilder is defining and emitting the class for us. ModuleBuilder.DefineType creates a TypeBuilder object and emits the type code. The arguments passed to DefineType indicate that we want a public class derived from the CollectionBase class, demonstrating how to emit a subclass. TypeAttributes.BeforeFieldInit initializes the class before any static members are accessed. The default type to emit is a class, but we could have specified this by OR*ing* TypeAttributes.Class into the TypeAttributes parameter.

After we define the type, the remaining statements demonstrate how to emit an attribute with our class. Because we are emitting a typed collection, we want an indexer. By emitting the DefaultMemberAttribute, we are signifying that Item will be our default member. Emitting Item with the DefaultMemberAttribute is identical to defining a *this* indexer property. The first statement gets the Type object of the attribute we want to emit. The second statement obtains DefaultMemberAttribute's ConstructorInfo for the constructor that accepts a single string named "argument." Then, we request a CustomAttributeBuilder—another Builder that facilitates emitting entities, in this case, an attribute—by constructing the object from the ConstructorInfo. Finally, we invoke TypeBuilder.SetCustomAttribute to emit our attribute and return the TypeBuilder.

NOTE

There is approximately an order of magnitude difference in lines of code that is hand-written and lines of code that emits IL. For example, it takes me about 15 minutes and 10 lines of code to implement a strongly typed collection in C#. It took me about 30 hours and 400 hundred lines of code to write the emitter examples in Emitter.sln. (I am getting faster, though.)

At this point, we are at EmitCode on line 42 of Listing 11-16. We have an assembly with a module and a type. We are ready to emit members and lines of code. The listings can be quite long at this point.

Writing Lines of OpCodes

Writing lines of code requires that we have Builders that need lines of code. Events and fields are easier to emit than methods, since properties, fields, and events are represented by simple statements. Methods, which include property methods, can be very long and complex because you have to write C# that emits IL almost as granular as assembly language code. Hence, if you are used to writing two or three lines of C# in your methods, then you will write about 25 lines of C# code to emit IL equivalent to three lines of C#. Contrarily, if you are used to writing 25-line methods or greater, your emitting methods will be hundreds of lines long.

We can look at a run-of-the-mill typed collection to figure out what members we have to emit to IL to dynamically create a typed collection. Listing 11-18 contains a prototypical typed collection we can use as a roadmap.

Listing 11-18 *A typed collection that contains instances of a class named Prototype*

```csharp
public class PrototypeCollection : CollectionBase
{
  public PrototypeCollection(){}

  public Prototype this[int index]
  { get{ return (Prototype)List[index];}
    set{ List[index] = value; }
  }

  public int Add(Prototype value)
  {
    return List.Add(value);
  }
}
```

The 14 lines of emitted code equates to approximately 266 lines of emitter code. With some Refactoring, I am sure I could reduce this amount substantially, but at half that number, we're still talking about an order of magnitude more emitter code. The question is whether I will get at least ten times the payout. In simpler terms, will I or another developer create more than 10 typed collections. The answer is yes, so arguably it is worth writing the emitter once.

Clearly, from the code listing we can determine that we need to emit a type that inherits from CollectionBase. (We did that in Listing 11-17.) We might want to emit a constructor. Although our constructor doesn't do anything, I will demonstrate this process. We need to emit an indexer property with a set and get method. The get method is surprisingly complex because we have to emit a dynamic type case. And, if we want our typed collection to serialize correctly, we will need to emit an Add method. The following list describes the steps we still need to complete.

▶ Emit a constructor that calls our base class.

▶ Emit an index property that will be our default property.

▶ Emit the get and set methods for the indexer.

▶ Emit the Add method.

Summarizing, we need to emit one constructor, three methods, and a property. The EmitCode method in Listing 11-19 shows how I organized the remaining steps.

Listing 11-19 *The EmitCode method organizes emitting the remaining parts of our typed collection emitter.*

```
private void EmitCode(TypeBuilder typeBuilder)
{
  EmitMethod(typeBuilder);
  EmitProperty(typeBuilder);
  EmitConstructor(typeBuilder);
}
```

EmitMethod emits the Add method. EmitProperty emits the index property and the set and get methods that support it, and EmitConstructor emits our do-nothing constructor.

Emitting the Add Method

Consistent with the examples thus far, we need to obtain a Builder. Methods reside in types; as a result, we need to request a MethodBuilder from the TypeBuilder representing the type that will contain the method. Listing 11-20 contains the EmitMethod code that emits the Add method. This code demonstrates several important facets of emitting IL.

Listing 11-20 *Emitting a method*

```
1: private void EmitMethod(TypeBuilder typeBuilder)
2: {
3:   addMethod = typeBuilder.DefineMethod(
4:     "Add", MethodAttributes.Public |
5:     MethodAttributes.HideBySig, CallingConventions.HasThis,
6:     typeof(int),
7:     new Type[]{ collectedType });
8:
9:   ILGenerator generator = addMethod.GetILGenerator();
10:  generator.DeclareLocal(typeof(int));
11:
12:  generator.Emit(OpCodes.Ldarg_0);
13:  Type type = typeof(System.Collections.CollectionBase);
14:
15:  MethodInfo methodInfo = type.GetMethod("get_List",
16:    BindingFlags.InvokeMethod | BindingFlags.NonPublic |
17:    BindingFlags.Instance,
18:    null, Type.EmptyTypes, null);
```

```
19:
20:    generator.Emit(OpCodes.Call, methodInfo);
21:    generator.Emit(OpCodes.Ldarg_1);
22:
23:    type = typeof(System.Collections.IList);
24:    methodInfo = type.GetMethod("Add");
25:    generator.Emit(OpCodes.Callvirt, methodInfo);
26:    generator.Emit(OpCodes.Stloc_0);
27:    Label label = generator.DefineLabel();
28:    generator.Emit( OpCodes.Br_S, label);
29:    generator.MarkLabel(label);
30:    generator.Emit(OpCodes.Ldloc_0);
31:    generator.Emit(OpCodes.Ret);
32: }
```

The code in Listing 11-20 is part of the EmitTypedCollection class, and the line numbers were added for reference only.

Lines 3 through 7 of Listing 11-20 define a new method from the TypeBuilder.DefineMethod method. The first argument will be the method name, and the second argument will be the method attributes. The third argument indicates that we are passing a reference to the owning object, the ever-present *this* object; the fourth argument indicates that the return type is an integer; and the fifth argument indicates that a single parameter will be whatever type we will be storing in this collection. The MethodAttributes used indicate that the method will be a public method and that the method hides by name and signature, describing how information hiding is implemented.

The ILGenerator class is introduced on line 9 of Listing 11-20. When we want to write individual lines of code, we get a contextually dependent ILGenerator. Line 10 declares a local variable that is used as a temporary variable to hold the index of the item added to our collection. The MSIL for the Add method in the Test.dll is shown in Figure 11-4. Line 10 emits the .locals statement shown in Figure 11-4.

Line 12 of Listing 11-20 loads the first argument onto the evaluation stack, emitting ldarg.0. This is the silent *this* reference. Line 13 obtains the Type object for CollectionBase; we need it to get the get method—get_List—for the List property inherited from CollectionBase. (You have to understand properties and their relationships to get and set methods to get this far.) Using the MethodInfo object, we can emit the code that invokes the List property's get method, returning the List object. The reference to the List is placed on the evaluation stack on line 21. Having the List object inherited from CollectionBase, we can obtain the MethodInfo for the inherited IList.Add method on lines 23 and 24. Because we are dealing with an interface, we have to use the polymorphic call to get the Add method actually implemented by CollectionBase, occurring on line 25.

Finally, we store the return integer from Add into our local variable (line 26), define a label (the infamous *goto* alive and well in low-level code on line 27), and emit a branch statement (branching to our label on lines 28 and 29—the Br_S is the *goto* statement). We

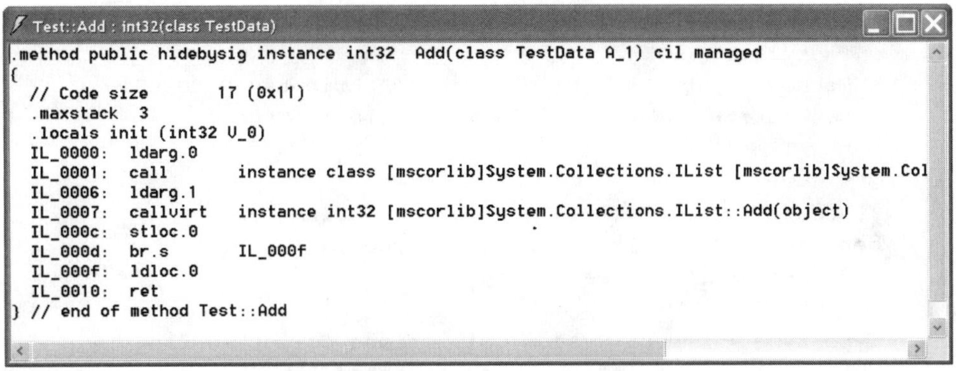

```
Test::Add : int32(class TestData)                              _ □ X
.method public hidebysig instance int32  Add(class TestData A_1) cil managed
{
  // Code size        17 (0x11)
  .maxstack  3
  .locals init (int32 V_0)
  IL_0000:  ldarg.0
  IL_0001:  call         instance class [mscorlib]System.Collections.IList [mscorlib]System.Col
  IL_0006:  ldarg.1
  IL_0007:  callvirt     instance int32 [mscorlib]System.Collections.IList::Add(object)
  IL_000c:  stloc.0
  IL_000d:  br.s         IL_000f
  IL_000f:  ldloc.0
  IL_0010:  ret
} // end of method Test::Add
```

Figure 11-4   *One instance of the MSIL emitted by the Add method described in Listing 11-20*

load the integer returned by our inherited call to add onto the stack to be obtained by the caller when the method returns—lines 30 and 31, respectively.

A significant portion of emitting code at this level is very similar: obtain an ILGenerator and write the individual lines of OpCodes that consummate your algorithm.

Emitting an Indexer Property and Property Methods

Listing 11-21 demonstrates code that will emit a property to a type. The PropertyBuilder is straightforward but is reliant on the get and set methods that actually implement the property. The get and set methods are simply methods associated with a property. You can use Listing 11-20 as an example of implementing methods, but I have included the property get method because it demonstrates dynamic typecasting via emitted code. (Refer to Emitter.cs for the set method.)

Listing 11-21   *Emitting a property and a property get method*

```
1:  private void EmitProperty(TypeBuilder typeBuilder)
2:  {
3:    indexerProperty = typeBuilder.DefineProperty("Item",
4:      PropertyAttributes.None, collectedType,
5:      new Type[]{typeof(int)});
6:
7:    indexerProperty.SetSetMethod(EmitSetter(typeBuilder));
8:    indexerProperty.SetGetMethod(EmitGetter(typeBuilder));
9:  }
10:
11: private MethodBuilder EmitGetter(TypeBuilder typeBuilder)
12: {
13:
```

```
14:    MethodBuilder getBuilder = typeBuilder.DefineMethod(
15:      "get_Item",
16:      MethodAttributes.Public | MethodAttributes.HideBySig |
17:      MethodAttributes.SpecialName, collectedType,
18:      new Type[]{typeof(int)});
19:
20:    ILGenerator generator = getBuilder.GetILGenerator();
21:    generator.DeclareLocal(collectedType);
22:    generator.Emit(OpCodes.Ldarg_0);
23:
24:    Type type = typeof(System.Collections.CollectionBase);
25:    MethodInfo methodInfo = type.GetMethod("get_List",
26:    BindingFlags.InvokeMethod | BindingFlags.NonPublic |
27:    BindingFlags.Instance,
28:    null, Type.EmptyTypes, null);
29:
30:    generator.Emit(OpCodes.Call, methodInfo);
31:    generator.Emit(OpCodes.Ldarg_1);
32:
33:    type = typeof(System.Collections.IList);
34:    methodInfo = type.GetMethod("get_Item",
35:      BindingFlags.Instance | BindingFlags.Public |
36:      BindingFlags.InvokeMethod,
37:      null, new Type[]{typeof(int)}, null);
38:
39:    generator.Emit(OpCodes.Callvirt, methodInfo);
40:    generator.Emit(OpCodes.Castclass, collectedType);
41:    generator.Emit(OpCodes.Stloc_0);
42:    Label label = generator.DefineLabel();
43:    generator.Emit(OpCodes.Br_S, label);
44:    generator.MarkLabel( label );
45:    generator.Emit(OpCodes.Ldloc_0);
46:    generator.Emit(OpCodes.Ret);
47:    return getBuilder;
48: }
```

The EmitProperty method in Listing 11-21 is easy. Request a PropertyBuilder from the TypeBuilder; if you indicate a get method only, the property is a read-only property. Include a set method, and you have a read-write property. Because we are implementing an indexed property, we need to specify a return type and a parameter type. The return type is the type of the object we are collecting, and the argument type is the indexer, an integer.

As I mentioned, get methods are simply methods. The EmitGetter method is mechanically similar to every other method: you are writing code to emit the algorithm. I will not repeat parts that are similar to the Add method, but I do want to point out a few salient points. By convention, we use get_ and set_ prefixes followed by the property name for property getters and setters, respectively, as demonstrated on line 15 of Listing 11-21. Generally, we don't make these directly available to consumers because getters and setters represent the implementation details of a property. However, I made the getter public so you could see it in the emitted object. The SpecialName method attribute signifies that we are dealing with a special-purpose method.

The final piece of new information is the type cast emitted on line 40 of Listing 11-21. Remember, one of the benefits of a strongly typed collection is that we get the strongly typed object from our indexer rather than littering our code with type casts; we do it in one place, the indexer. Line 40 demonstrates how to emit a type cast. Line 40 emits code that is equivalent to the cast part of (*type*)List[index], where *type* represents the type stored in our collection.

All of the OpCodes can be looked up in the Visual Studio .NET help documentation.

Emitting a Constructor That Calls a Base Class Constructor

Finally, we wrap things up by examining our constructor briefly. Most constructors exist to initialize fields. You know how to initialize fields from parameters because it is the same as initializing fields passed to methods. (If you need an example, download the Emitter.cs class and look at the constructor emitter for the EmitType class.) Listing 11-22 demonstrates how to invoke a base class constructor; in our example, we are calling the CollectionBase constructor explicitly.

Listing 11-22   *Emitting a constructor that calls a base class constructor*

```
1:   private void EmitConstructor(TypeBuilder typeBuilder)
2:   {
3:     ConstructorBuilder constructor =
4:       CreateConstructorBuilder(typeBuilder, new Type[]{});
5:
6:     ILGenerator generator = constructor.GetILGenerator();
7:     EmitConstructorCode(generator);
8:   }
9:
10:  private void EmitConstructorCode(ILGenerator generator)
11:  {
12:    generator.Emit(OpCodes.Ldarg_0);
13:    Type type = typeof(System.Collections.CollectionBase);
14:    ConstructorInfo parent =
15:      type.GetConstructor(BindingFlags.NonPublic | BindingFlags.Instance,
16:      null, Type.EmptyTypes, null);
17:
18:    generator.Emit(OpCodes.Call, parent);
19:    generator.Emit(OpCodes.Ret);
20:  }
```

In Listing 11-22, EmitConstructor creates a ConstructorBuilder directly by invoking its constructor. An ILGenerator is requested to create context for code emitted to our constructor, and EmitConstructorCode writes the lines of code. (This all happens on lines 1 through 8 of Listing 11-22.)

As with the code for a method, we need to emit individual lines of code that represent our algorithm. Our only stated purpose is to explicitly invoke our base class's constructor. Line 12 of Listing 11-20 loads the *this* pointer. Line 13 gets the Type object for the CollectionBase class, which can be used to get the Collection class ConstructorInfo object. We generate a call to the parent constructor on line 18 and return on line 19.

Constructors should be simple. A general rule of thumb for constructors is to call a parent constructor, store parameters into fields, and call an Initialize method if necessary. Long, complex constructors can significantly slow down an application that creates a lot of a particular type of object.

Loading and Executing Dynamic Assemblies

I provided several types of examples that demonstrate how to load assemblies and create instances of types defined in those assemblies. I won't repeat that information again here. The biggest difference between an assembly on disk and one your code has emitted to memory is that the emitted assembly is already loaded. This is what our GetClass method indicates.

When GetClass returns, we have an assembly and type already in memory. All you need to do is create an instance of it. The Emitter.sln sample application contains a form (shown in Figure 11-3). Click the Test In-Memory button to create strongly typed collection based on a simple Music type. The dynamic collection will be bound to the DataGrid (also shown in Figure 11-3).

Listing 11-23 *Creating and using an instance of the in-memory assembly containing a strongly typed Music Collection*

```
Type type = EmitTypedCollection.GetClass(
  "MusicCollection", typeof(Music));

// Test construction
IList list = (IList)Activator.CreateInstance(type);

// Test Add
list.Add(new Music("Charlie Pride", "16 Biggest Hits"));
list.Add(new Music("Ted Nugent", "Great Gonzos"));

// Test indexer
for( int i =0; i < list.Count; i++)
{
```

```
    Music m = (Music)list[i];
    Debug.WriteLine(m.Artist + ", " + m.Title);
}

// General test
dataGrid1.DataSource = list;
```

Listing 11-23 emits the type and uses an Activator to create an instance of the MusicCollection type. Because the type is created dynamically, we have to use a compatible type for the instance, IList; however, we could declare the type as a MusicCollection object if the type were emitted to disk.

A couple of Music objects are added to the collection. We use a *for* loop to test our indexer, and, finally, we bind the list to the DataGrid to demonstrate in fact that it is a strongly typed collection. (Recall from Chapter 6 that a strongly typed collection implements IList, IListSource, and IEnumerable, making typed collections very convenient to use.)

There is a lot to emitting dynamic IL. If you can imagine it as C# code, then you can probably write an emitter that will generate that code. There is support for all of the constructs that you write when you type C# code into Visual Studio .NET. This includes things that I didn't show, like exception handlers. Emitting is a huge subject that could easily fill a book all by itself. Until a comprehensive book on .NET emitting is published I hope I have provided you with a suitable way to get started.

Secondary Topics

I will wrap this chapter up by showing you a couple of neat things that you can do with Reflection and IL. I am going to keep them short because you already know the mechanics from earlier discussions, particularly in Chapter 6.

Reflection and Web Services

Reflection is used in Web Services. A Web Service serializes objects to support returning an object from a Web Method. The object returned is a flattened version of the object requested. For example, if you request that a strongly typed collection be returned from a Web Method—like the MusicCollection—what you will actually get is an array of Music objects rather than the actual MusicCollection object. This is still useful but is not as powerful as getting the fully reconstituted MusicCollection object would be. (See Chapter 12 for more on this subject.)

How does .NET return objects from a Web Service? The answer is Xml Serialization and Reflection. These two technologies combined support obtaining aggregate data from an application across a network like the Internet.

Web Services, Xml Serialization, and Reflection are three compelling reasons to switch to .NET.

Implementing the Metaclass Idiom

A metaclass is a class of a class. Or, phrased another way, a metaclass is a class that is treated as an object. .NET does not support the metaclass idiom directly. (Borland's Delphi does, for example.) However, you implement the metaclass idiom using Reflection.

To use a class like a metaclass, you can pass a class's Type object as a parameter to a method. With the type object, you can request Info objects, like MethodInfo objects. Create an instance of the class using an Activator and dynamically invoke operations using the Type.InvokeMember method and—voila!—you have a metaclass. Listing 11-24 contains an example from the Metaclass.sln sample program.

Listing 11-24 *Treating a class like an object, a metaclass*

```
private void CreateControl(Type type)
{
  Control control = (Control)Activator.CreateInstance(type);
  control.Text = "Dynamic";
  control.Location = new Point(10, 35 * (Controls.Count - 2));
  Controls.Add(control);
}

private void button1_Click(object sender, System.EventArgs e)
{
  CreateControl(typeof(CheckBox));
}

private void button2_Click(object sender, System.EventArgs e)
{
  CreateControl(typeof(TextBox));
}
```

In Listing 11-24, we are passing the Type object to CreateControl. Clearly, an observant person will see that the same result could be achieved by passing an instance of a control to CreateControl. There are two deficits we are correcting. The first is that we are eliminating the need for consumers of CreateControl to have to create an instance, which is what we would have to do if we passed a Control type. The second is presented when the consumer doesn't know which type to create.

Not knowing is especially useful when implementing the factory pattern. For example, we could implement a code generator that has a factory method capable of creating a dynamic control on demand. The caller doesn't have to know what control to create; the caller may only know about the data. The factory pattern could examine the type of the data and return an instance of a control based on the data. The caller simply accepts what it gets.

Further refining the approach, we could ask all of the possible subtypes if the data represented the kind of data the subtype is interested in. By using the metaclass idiom, we could ask the subtype without ever creating an instance of the type. How? By using InvokeMember on a static member. Instead of creating every possible subtype, we could simply use InvokeMember on a static method, passing the data. If the subtype is interested in the data, we could create an instance of the subtype. This won't work with .NET controls as they exist today, because they weren't implemented this way. However, you can write new code to play the role of metaclass.

Serializing Objects

Objects can be serialized to XML. Reflection plays a role in XML serialization because the XML serializer uses Reflection to determine the properties that need to be serialized. You can write custom serialization to serialize any data you want, but the default behavior works pretty well, too.

In the last line of Listing 11-23, we bound a strongly typed collection to a DataGrid .DataSource. What if you wanted to convert a typed collection into a DataSet and persist that data to a database? XML serialization, in conjunction with Reflection, supports this behavior. Listing 11-25 demonstrates how to serialize the MusicCollection from Listing 11-23 directly into a DataTable inside of a DataSet.

Listing 11-25   *Serializing a typed collection to an ADO.NET DataSet*

```
private void SerializeToDataSet()
{
  PrototypeCollection c = new PrototypeCollection();
  c.Add(new Prototype("Item 1"));
  c.Add(new Prototype("Item 2"));
  c.Add(new Prototype("Item 3"));

  XmlSerializer serializer =
    new XmlSerializer(typeof(PrototypeCollection));
  MemoryStream stream = new MemoryStream();
  serializer.Serialize(stream, c);
  stream.Position = 0;
  DataSet dataSet = new DataSet("Data");
  dataSet.ReadXml(stream);
  dataGrid1.DataSource = dataSet.Tables[0];
}
```

CAUTION

You can serialize a dynamic assembly as demonstrated in Listing 11-25. Write an assembly to disk, and then you can serialize objects in the assembly.

Listing 11-25 creates an instance of the PrototypeCollection and adds three elements to it. After we create the collection, we create an instance of the XmlSerializer based on the type of the PrototypeCollection. To serialize an object, a class must implement ISerializable or have the Serializable attribute applied to the class. CollectionBase has the Serializable attribute applied to it, so our derivative collections are serializable.

After we create an XmlSerializer based on the PrototypeCollection, we create a MemoryStream as a place to receive the serialized object. We invoke XmlSerlializer .Serialize, writing the serialized form of the collection to the MemoryStream. Finally, we re-position the stream, create a DataSet, and read the XML from the stream into the DataSet.

When the last line of Listing 11-25 completes, the DataSet object contains a serialized form of the PrototypeCollection. You can observe the results in the Emitter.sln sample application.

There are a couple of things you need to be aware of to get the code to work. You will need to include the System.IO namespace to use the MemoryStream. (Other streams, like the FileStream, will work, too.) You will need to include the System.Xml.Serialization namespace because it contains the XmlSerializer class, and, finally, your collected objects will need a default constructor that accepts no arguments. The reason for this last requirement is that deserialization constructs an object by invoking the default constructor and then uses the Reflection and the properties to reassign the underlying field values. Without the default constructor, the serializer cannot create a serialized copy of the object. (The code for the Prototype and PrototypeCollection classes is available for download in the Emitter.sln assembly.)

Emitting Regular Expression Assemblies

One emitter that exists and is already available for use is the emitter represented by the Regex .CompileToAssembly method. CompileToAssembly emits a DLL assembly with a class that generalizes the Regex class. The emitted regular expression class contains the initialization string that represents your regular expression.

I will demonstrate how to emit the assembly in a moment. Regular expressions have their own grammar, representing a language, albeit a terse language (see Chapters 4 and 6 for examples of regular expressions). Regular expressions are comprised of literal characters and metacharacters that make up the regular expression language. .NET regular expressions use a Nondeterministic Finite Automation engine similar to those used by Perl, Python, Emacs, and Td, and is compatible with Perl 5. You can also compile regular expressions to an assembly, resulting in a slower load time but faster execution; it takes longer to load the assembly, but, when compiled to an assembly, the regular expression is converted to .NET code and executes faster than when executed by the regular expression engine. In limited test cases, I have noticed significant speed improvements with compiled regular expressions, and the Visual Studio .NET help documentation also indicates that this is the case.

You can use the CompileToAssembly method to dynamically compile and emit a compiled regular expression to an assembly. Fortunately someone has written the emitter, making it relatively easy to use. Listing 11-26 contains part of the EmitExpressionDemo.sln that emits a compiled regular expression to an assembly. (The whole sample application supports inputting and testing regular expressions before emitting them to an assembly.)

Listing 11-26   *Code that demonstrates emitting a compiled regular expression to an assembly*

```
private string InputString
{ get{ return textBox2.Text; }}

private string Expression
{ get{ return textBox1.Text; }}

private void Compile()
{
  RegexCompilationInfo[] CompilationInfo =
    new RegexCompilationInfo[]{
      new RegexCompilationInfo(Expression,
      RegexOptions.Compiled,
      "Regex", "CompiledExpressions", true)};

  AssemblyName assemblyName = new AssemblyName();
  assemblyName.Name = "Regex";
  Regex.CompileToAssembly(CompilationInfo, assemblyName);
}
```

To create a class that generalizes the System.Text.RegularExpression.Regex class, representing an immutable regular expression, create an array of RegexCompilationInfo objects and an AssemblyName, and invoke the Regex.CompileToAssembly method. Pass the array of RegexCompilationInfo objects to CompileToAssembly. To convert the regular expression to .NET code, pass the RegexOptions.Compiled option to the RegexCompilationInfo constructor.

Summary

If Reflection were an option on a car, you might consider buying a car simply because of the rich features introduced by Reflection. Reflection is an evolution of run-time type information and is central to XML Serialization, discovering type information, dynamic binding of types and members, and emitting code at run-time. There are several examples that demonstrate these topics associated with this chapter.

One of the by-products of Reflection is the Regex class's capability to emit a regular expression to an assembly. In addition to emitters supporting Web Services and ADO.NET, I expect that there will be new cottage industry, like the component industry in the 1990s, dedicated to creating and selling .NET emitters.

Web Applications — IBUYSPY Portal

OBJECTIVES

► Learn to implement synchronous and asynchronous Web Services in C#

► Learn how to implement every aspect of the IBuySpy portal

► Learn how to create custom server and user controls

► Explore and hone your ADO.NET skills, including stored procedures

► Learn about forms and Windows authentication

► Read the introduction to code base security

CHAPTER 2

Implementing
Web Services

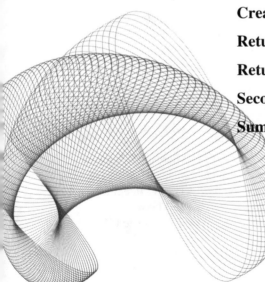

T here are several technologies that support XML Web Services. I am going to introduce these technologies in this chapter. However, if you think of Web Services in the context of all of these supporting utilities and technologies, you might think that using XML Web Services is difficult. Nothing could be further from the truth. Creating and consuming Web Services is easier because of these technologies.

You may have heard of the acronyms XML, UDDI, WSDL, DISCO, HTTP, and SOAP in conversations about XML Web Services. This plethora of tools may make Web Services seem complicated. I will talk about the role of these technologies and tools as they relate to Web Services, but it is important to know that these technologies and tools work seamlessly and, for the most part, in the background. If you and I had to master XML, UDDI, WSDL, or SOAP before we were able to create a Web Service, Web Services would be challenging. Fortunately, we do not. C# and Visual Studio .NET allow us to emphasize designing a solution and writing the code.

Demonstrated Topics

Programming XML Web Services with C# and Visual Studio .NET allows you to focus on the C# code. There are several technologies working in the background, so we'll cover those, too. In this chapter you will learn about the following:

▶ The supporting role of WSDL, DISCO, UDDI, XML, HTTP, and SOAP

▶ Creating, testing, and consuming Web Services

▶ Returning complex data types from Web Services

▶ Object serialization

Objects are serialized as XML and transported over the wire. For the most part, the XML and serialization are automatic and occur without your intercession; however, there are circumstances where you may want to take control of the tools and the serialization process. The secondary section will demonstrate how to implement the ISerializable interface and manage XML serialization yourself.

Web Services: Discovery and Description

The best description of UDDI is the one I heard from Harry Pierson from Microsoft's National Technology Team. UDDI is the Web Services' Yellow Pages. A longer explanation is derived from the initials UDDI. UDDI stands for Universal Description, Discovery, and Integration. A couple of companies host UDDI servers. Two UDDI directory hosts that I know of are Microsoft and IBM. You can browse **http://uddi.microsoft.com** for a list of hosted Web Services at Microsoft.

A convenient tool for browsing for Web Services is the Add Web Reference dialog, shown in Figure 12-1. (Notice the UDDI Directory link shown in Figure 12-1.) If you want to find a Web Service located at a specific location, type in the URL to the Web Service in the address bar. The Web Service is represented by .asmx files. For example, if you create a Web Service named WebService1, uncomment the sample code for the HelloWorld Web Method, and compile the Web Service, you would be able to browse to it at **http://localhost/WebService1/** and select the Service1.asmx file.

The .asmx page will be displayed in the Add Web Reference dialog, just as if we had browsed to it with Internet Explorer. (We can test the Web Methods in the Add Web Reference dialog.) After we have selected the .asmx file, the Add Reference button will be enabled. Click the Add Reference button (shown in Figure 12-1) to incorporate the Web Service into a project.

UDDI has made it easy to find and consume Web Services. The only real skills you need are those you would use to browse to your favorite website. (One of mine is definitely Amazon.com.)

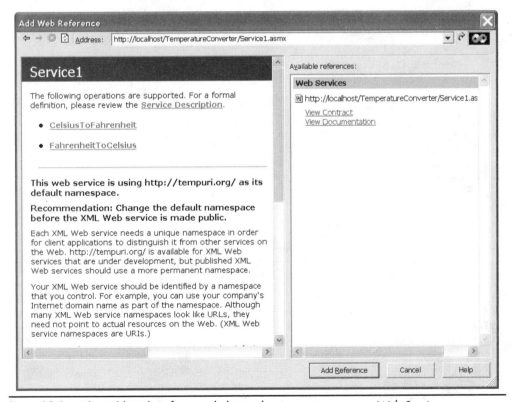

Figure 12-1   *The Add Web Reference dialog makes it easy to consume Web Services.*

DISCO Is Back

Techies *do* have a sense of humor. Disco.exe is the name of a utility that is used by the Add Web Reference dialog to create a .MAP file, a .disco file, and a .wsdl file. (You may also run the disco.exe utility from the Visual Studio .NET Command Prompt.)

TIP

Select Start | Program Files | Microsoft Visual Studio .NET | Visual Studio .NET Tools | Visual Studio .NET Command Prompt to open a command window configured to allow you ready access to .NET framework utilities.

The Reference.map contains the URL reference to the DISCO and the WSDL files. The DISCO file is the discovery file and the WSDL file describes the schema for the Web Service class. (We'll talk more about the WSDL file in a moment.) Listing 12-1 provides a listing for a Reference.map file. Listing 12-2 provides an example listing for the DISCO file for the same Web Service.

Listing 12-1   *A MAP file that contains a reference to the DISCO and WSDL files for a Web Service*

```xml
<?xml version="1.0" encoding="utf-8"?>
<DiscoveryClientResultsFile xmlns:xsd="http://www.w3.org/2001/XMLSchema"
xmlns:xsi="http://www.w3.org/2001/XMLSchema-instance">
  <Results>
    <DiscoveryClientResult
referenceType="System.Web.Services.Discovery.ContractReference"
url="http://localhost/TemperatureConverter/Service1.asmx?wsdl"
filename="Service1.wsdl" />
    <DiscoveryClientResult
referenceType="System.Web.Services.Discovery.DiscoveryDocumentReference"
url="http://localhost/TemperatureConverter/Service1.asmx?disco"
filename="Service1.disco" />
  </Results>
</DiscoveryClientResultsFile>
```

Listing 12-2   *A DISCO file that contains a reference to the Web Service contract file, the WSDL file*

```xml
<?xml version="1.0" encoding="utf-8"?>
<discovery xmlns:xsd="http://www.w3.org/2001/XMLSchema"
xmlns:xsi="http://www.w3.org/2001/XMLSchema-instance"
xmlns="http://schemas.xmlsoap.org/disco/">
  <contractRef ref="http://localhost/TemperatureConverter/Service1.asmx?wsdl"
docRef="http://localhost/TemperatureConverter/Service1.asmx"
xmlns="http://schemas.xmlsoap.org/disco/scl/" />
  <soap address="http://localhost/TemperatureConverter/Service1.asmx"
xmlns:q1="http://tempuri.org/" binding="q1:Service1Soap"
xmlns="http://schemas.xmlsoap.org/disco/soap/" />
</discovery>
```

The MAP and DISCO files are implemented in XML, demonstrating another aspect of how XML is used in .NET. Fortunately, these files are generated by the DISCO tool.

If you mentally filter the XML, you will note that the MAP file contains URLs that refer to the commands that generate the WSDL and DISCO files and the name of the DISCO and WSDL files. You can request the WSDL, for example, by entering the name of the Web Service followed by the **?WSDL** query in Internet Explorer. For example, to return the WSDL for the temperature converter, we can type **http://localhost/TemperatureConverter/Service1.asmx?wsdl**.

NOTE

*The TemperatureConverter Web Service was originally implemented for an article I wrote in the VB Tech Notes section of **www.codeguru.com**. You can find the code there. I re-implemented in C# in the next section, but there is no requirement that Web Services have to be in the same language as the one you are developing in. XML is the common language shared between Web Service producers and consumers.*

WSDL

If you write a Web Service, you will know what the methods and classes are that are defined by that Web Service. However, if you are consuming a Web Service from an external vendor, you have to have some source of information that tells you what is in the Web Service. This includes the signature of the Web Methods provided by the service and the types that are returned by those Web Methods.

WSDL (Web Services Description Language), pronounced whiz-dul, describes what is in the Web Service and provides with the information you will need to use those Web Methods. Listing 12-3 provides an implementation of a temperature converter in C# and part of the WSDL that describes the Web Method in Listing 12-4.

Listing 12-3   *A Web Method that converts temperatures from Fahrenheit to Celsius*

```
[WebMethod]
public double FahrenheitToCelsius(double temperature)
{
  return (temperature - 32) * 5 / 9;
}
```

We'll talk about the steps for creating Web Services in a moment. From Listing 12-3, you might be able to infer that one of the obvious differences between a method and a Web Method is the application of the WebMethodAttribute.

Listing 12-4   *An excerpt from the WSDL file for the FahrenheitToCelsius Web Method*

```
- <types>
- <s:schema elementFormDefault="qualified"
targetNamespace="http://tempuri.org/">
```

```
-  <s:element name="FahrenheitToCelsius">
-  <s:complexType>
-  <s:sequence>
   <s:element minOccurs="1" maxOccurs="1" name="temperature" type="s:double" />
   </s:sequence>
   </s:complexType>
   </s:element>
-  <s:element name="FahrenheitToCelsiusResponse">
-  <s:complexType>
-  <s:sequence>
   <s:element minOccurs="1" maxOccurs="1" name="FahrenheitToCelsiusResult"
type="s:double" />
   </s:sequence>
   </s:complexType>
   </s:element>
   <s:element name="double" type="s:double" />
   </s:schema>
   </types>
```

The XML indicates that there is an element named FahrenheitToCelisus that accepts a single parameter (a double) named *temperature*. The second element name tag describes the method response, named FahrenheitToCelsiusResponse. FahrenheitToCelsiusResponse has a return value named FahrenheitToCelsiusResult that is a double, too.

When we consume the Web Method in an application, we invoke it as shown in Listing 12-3. All of the XML used to describe the Web Service is concealed from us as consumers. When you add a reference to a Web Service, a proxy class is created. You can create an instance of the Web Service class and invoke the Web Methods as if the Web Service class were contained in the consuming application.

Consuming Web Services

To consume a Web Service, select Add Web Reference from the Project menu or the context menu for the Solution Explorer. Use the Add Web Reference dialog to browse to a UDDI directory service or a Web site containing the service you want to link to.

Figure 12-2 shows the ConvertTemperature Web Service added to the TestConvertTemperature.csproj (both the Web Service and test application are available for download). The name of the host is added to the Web References folder and plays the role of namespace. For example, to refer to the Web Service class, we can add a *using* statement to the module containing the Web Service or we can use the fully qualified path to the Web Service class. Listing 12-5 contains code for a console application that demonstrates how to create an instance of the ConvertTemperature Web Service.

Listing 12-5   *Consuming the ConvertTemperature Web Service*

```
using System;
using Service = TestConvertTemperature.localhost;
```

```
namespace TestConvertTemperature
{
  class Class1
  {
    [STAThread]
    static void Main(string[] args)
    {
      Service.Convert convert = new Service.Convert();
      Console.WriteLine(convert.FahrenheitToCelsius(32));
      Console.ReadLine();
    }
  }
}
```

Figure 12-2 *The Solution Explorer with a Web Reference to the ConvertTemperature Web Service*

Listing 12-5 shows how to refer to the host-derived namespace, TestConvertTemperature .localhost. However, the System namespace contains the Convert class, so we can resolve the ambiguity by declaring the Convert class using the full name. Notice that in our code it looks just as though the Convert class is defined in a local assembly.

For programmers, this is an example of the power and ease of XML Web Services. All of the technology and tools are working silently in the background to get us to the point where the Web Service looks just like any class in any assembly. Quietly, HTTP or SOAP and XML are being used in the background to marshal calls across a network. (Of course, in our example the network is my laptop.)

When you incorporate a Web Service, a proxy class is created. You don't have to worry about this when you are using Visual Studio .NET, but you can use the wsdl.exe utility to generate the proxy source code to see what it looks like. Run the wsdl.exe utility, passing the URL of the Web Service to the WSDL tool. For example, on my laptop—PCs and laptops are excellent places to test Web Services—I can generate the proxy file for the ConvertTemperature Web Service with the following command line:

```
wsdl http://localhost/ConvertTemperature/ConvertTemperature.asmx
```

The generated Convert.cs module—Convert is the name of the Web Service class that contains the Web Method from Listing 12-3—contains a class named Convert that inherits from System.Web.Services.Protocols.SoapHttpClientProtocol, a constructor, and three methods. The proxy method FahrenheitToCelsius uses a synchronous call to the SoapHttpClientProtocol.Invoke method to invoke the Web Service. The other two methods support asynchronous Web Method invocation.

Again, it is important to know that proxy classes are created using WSDL, but these things happen automatically. For the general case, you can simply add a Web reference and create an instance of the Web Service as if it were a class in an assembly referenced by your project.

Reviewing Web Services Wire Formats

There are three wire formats for Web Services. There is HTTP GET, HTTP POST, and SOAP. HTTP GET uses a name-and-value pair–encoded URL. For example, we can invoke the Web Service with an HTTP GET URL–encoded address:

```
http://localhost/converttemperature/ConvertTemperature.asmx/
FahrenheitToCelsius?temperature=32
```

HTTP POST uses name-and-value pair encoding, but the parameters are encoded in the header of the message. SOAP messages are encoded as XML. You can navigate to the command page to see samples of SOAP, HTTP GET, and HTTP POST messages and responses if you are curious.

```
http://localhost/converttemperature/ConvertTemperature.asmx?op=
FahrenheitToCelsius
```

If you send an HTTP GET message (as shown in the first example in this section) and compare the result to the HTTP GET response encoding, you will see that the response encoding describes the format of the response from the Web Service. Listing 12-6 shows the format of the HTTP GET response and an actual response from the FahrenheitToCelsius Web Service.

Listing 12-6 *The HTTP GET request and response format, taken from the .asmx page*

```
GET
/converttemperature/ConvertTemperature.asmx/FahrenheitToCelsius?temperature=
string

<?xml version="1.0" encoding="utf-8"?>
<double xmlns="http://tempuri.org/">double</double>
```

The first statement demonstrates the syntax of the HTTP GET message, and the remaining statements demonstrate the response text. An actual response will have a value in place of the word "double." Again, this is the supporting information for Web Service technology. When we are consuming the Web Service as a part of our application, message request and response formats are concealed from us.

Testing Web Services

There are several ways to test Web Services. You can test a Web Service using the integrated debugger in Visual Studio .NET. You can use the "build and browse" method, by running the Web Service application and entering data in the test page generated by browsing to the Web Service .asmx page. Or, you can browse to the Web Service outside of the IDE and use an HTTP GET–encoded URL to invoke the Web Methods. (As an alternative, you can also use an HTTP POST message in an HTML document to invoke the Web Service.)

Integrated debugging in Visual Studio .NET is the most convenient way to test the Web Service. Place a breakpoint on the code in the .asmx.cs source file containing the code that you want to test and build and run the Web Service application. When the Web Service is invoked and your breakpoint is reached, the debugger will switch the code view to Visual Studio .NET, and you can step through your code and debug as you would any other assembly. (Ultimately, a Web Service is a DLL assembly and can be tested as such.)

Creating a Simple Web Service

To create Web Services on your PC, you will need to be connected to a network with access to an IIS server or have IIS installed on your PC. Creating the project can be accomplished by selecting the ASP.NET Web Service applet in the New Project dialog. The Wizard Engine will create a Web Service project from the CSharpAddWebServiceWiz wizard templates. Table 12-1 describes the files that will be added to your Web Service and the role each of these files plays in the Web Service.

All of these files may seem a bit daunting, but you can implement a Web Service by adding public methods to the .asmx.cs file and tagging those methods with the WebMethodAttribute. You learned how to add metadata to an AssemblyInfo.cs file in Chapter 2. The Web.config can be modified to enable tracing or cookie support, and the Global.asax file can be modified to respond to application-level events.

The application level contains a Global class that inherits from System.Web.HttpApplication. HttpApplication events and methods can be explored in depth in the Visual Studio .NET help documentation.

Returning Simple Data

The easiest kind of Web Service to create is one that returns simple data, like a double, as demonstrated in the ConvertTemperature Web Service. We'll look at the process of creating

File Name/Extension	Description
.dll	The Web Service assembly compiled to a DLL
.pdb	Contains symbolic debug information
.sln	The Web Service solution file
.csproj	The Web Service project file
.csproj.webinfo	Contains the project path on the server or PC
AssemblyInfo.cs	Contains assembly metadata for the project
.asmx	Contains the Web Service processing directive; used as an entry point to the Web Service
.asmx.cs	The code-behind file for your Web Service. This is where your Web Methods are coded and paired with the .asmx and .asmx.resx files
.asmx.resx	Resource file
.vsdisco	Discovery file that describes searchable paths for Web Services
Global.asax	Contains application-level event handlers
Global.asax.cs	The code-behind page for application-level events
Web.config	Configuration information for ASP.NET applications

Table 12-1 *Project Files for an ASP.NET Web Service*

a simple Web Service, indicating a Namespace, adding a Description, and handling Web Service exceptions. Fortunately, we can return complex types from Web Services, which we'll look at in the next section.

To create a Web Service, create a new ASP.NET Web Service project in the New Project dialog. The Web Service project will be created in c:\inetpub\wwwroot*webservicename*. This directory will be located on your PC if you create the project using the localhost host name. The .asmx.cs code-behind file will contain a class named Service1 (by default) or some variation. The class will inherit from System.Web.Services.WebService. It is this inheritance that makes the solution a Web Service. To provide some behavior, you need to define a public method with the WebMethodAttribute applied.

You can have as many Web Methods and supporting methods as you need. A good model for Web Services is to implement a solution and then implement a Web Service and Web Methods that expose aspects of the solution that a consumer might want. As is true with object-oriented programming in general, if you keep the number and variety of public Web Methods to a small number, your Web Services will be easier to use. Provide too few Web Methods and your Web Services won't be compelling enough to attract attention. Happily, .NET's Web Services technology affords us the luxury of focusing on the solution without having to wrangle with the technical nuts and bolts.

The code in Listing 12-7 will determine whether a number is a prime number by using an approximation of the Sieve of Eratosthenes. The listing is provided next, followed by a summary of the code.

Listing 12-7   *Calculate prime numbers using the Sieve of Eratosthenes*

```
1:   using System;
2:   using System.Collections;
3:   using System.ComponentModel;
4:   using System.Data;
5:   using System.Diagnostics;
6:   using System.Web;
7:   using System.Web.Services;
8:
9:   namespace Primes
10:  {
11:     [WebService(Namespace="http://www.softconcepts.com",
12:     Description="Calculate primes using the Sieve of Eratosthenes")]
13:     public class Primes : System.Web.Services.WebService
14:     {
15:       public Primes()
16:       {
17:         //CODEGEN: This call is required by the
18:         //ASP.NET Web Services Designer
19:         InitializeComponent();
20:       }
21:
22:       [region Component Designer generated code]
```

```
23:
24:        [WebMethod]
25:        public long[] PrimesTo(long max)
26:        {
27:           return (new PrimeEngine(max)).Primes;
28:        }
29:
30:        [WebMethod]
31:        public bool IsPrime(long number)
32:        {
33:           return (new PrimeEngine(number)).IsPrime(number);
34:        }
35:    }
36:
37:    class PrimeEngine
38:    {
39:
40:        private ArrayList primes;
41:
42:        /// <summary>
43:        /// Calculates prime numbers up to max
44:        /// using an approximation of the 'Sieve of Eratosthenes'
45:        /// </summary>
46:
47:        public PrimeEngine(long max)
48:        {
49:           primes = new ArrayList();
50:           primes.Add(2L);
51:           BuildPrimes(max);
52:        }
53:
54:        private bool TestPrime( long number )
55:        {
56:           foreach(long l in Primes)
57:           {
58:              if( number % l == 0) return false;
59:              if( l >= Math.Sqrt(number)) return true;
60:           }
61:
62:           return true;
63:        }
64:
65:        public void BuildPrimes(long max)
66:        {
67:           if( max < 3) return;
68:
69:           for( long i=3; i<= max; i++)
70:           {
71:              if(TestPrime(i)) primes.Add((long)i);
72:           }
```

```
73:      }
74:
75:      public bool IsPrime(long number)
76:      {
77:         return primes.IndexOf(number) > -1;
78:      }
79:
80:      public long[] Primes
81:      {
82:         get{ return (long[])primes.ToArray(typeof(long)); }
83:      }
84:   }
85: }
```

NOTE

Calculating large primes is time consuming. The Sieve of Eratosthenes will be extremely slow for very large prime numbers. Because large prime numbers take time to calculate, they are excellent for encryption. The basic idea is that by the time an information thief has solved a large prime, the opportunity to exploit the data will have passed.

The WebService class Primes exposes the capabilities of the PrimeEngine. The Web Service allows the consumer to inquire whether a number is a prime and will return an array of long integers up to the max value specified. Based on the implementation in Listing 12-7, calculating very large prime numbers will be slow.

All integers are a product of primes. A prime number is a number that is divisible only by itself and 1. Eratosthenes was a respected scholar and librarian in Alexandria about twenty-two hundred years ago. Eratosthenes resolved that prime numbers could be calculated by checking to see if a number were divisible by all of the prime numbers less than the square root of the candidate number. (We only have to check numbers up to the square root because, if a number greater than the square root is a divisor, then a number less than the square root will be a divisor, too.)

If we seed the array of primes with the first prime, 2, then we can use 2 to calculate all of the primes between 2 and the candidate number. The PrimeEngine constructor seeds the array with the lowest known prime, 2, and calculates all of the primes up to max. (We don't calculate more primes than we need, since calculating large primes using Eratosthenes' algorithm will be slow for huge primes.) BuildPrimes checks all of the integers between 3 and the maximum value on lines 65 to 73. TestPrime—on lines 54 to 63 of Listing 12-7— iterates through all of the primes calculated less than the number. If the number is evenly divisible by one of the primes, then the candidate is not a prime and we return false on line 58. If we reach a number greater than or equal to the square root of the candidate number, then we have a prime number, and we can stop testing.

I prefer to implement solutions as classes. Then, if I want to expose a solution to a specific kind of consumer, I can implement the solution in terms of the existing class. For example, instead of implementing solutions in the Web Methods, I prefer to implement them in terms of a class that solves the general problem. As a result, the solution can be exposed to a variety of consumers. It is worth noting that you can add a reference to a Web Service DLL, create instances of the WebService-derived class, and invoke the methods directly. Fundamentally, a WebService is a class and can be used and treated like any other class, as long as you have access to the physical DLL.

Providing a Namespace and Description

Web Service classes must be unique. The Namespace is used to uniquely describe the Web Service. When you are testing your Web Service, you can use the default tempuri.org. Before you deploy your Web Service, you can apply the WebServiceAttribute to the Web Service class, providing named argument values for the Namespace, and a Description to let consumers know what the Web Service does. Lines 11 and 12 in Listing 12-7 demonstrate how to use the WebServiceAttribute. (For more information on named arguments and custom attributes, refer to Chapter 10.)

Handling Web Service Exceptions

You can handle or throw exceptions from Web Services. The consumer will actually receive a SoapException. The SoapException class will contain contents that indicate the underlying exception, but the class of the exception will be a SoapException. To handle exceptions thrown from Web Services, use a catch block or a catch block that specifies the SoapException. Here is a syntactic example of a *try* catch block that handles a SoapException.

```
try
{
  //invoke Web Method
}
catch(SoapException x)
{
  // handle exception
}
```

If you want to throw an exception in your Web Service code, you can throw a specific class of an exception, and it will be converted to a SoapException. For example, if a consumer passes a number less than 2 to the Primes Web Service, we could raise an ArgumentException. The following two methods can be added to the Web Service in Listing 12-7 to raise an exception for an invalid argument.

```
private void ThrowException(long number)
{
  const string error = "Number ({0}) must an integer greater than 2";
  throw new ArgumentException(string.Format(error, number));
}

private void Validate(long number)
{
```

```
    if(number < 2) ThrowException(number);
}
```

When a consumer receives a Web Service exception, you can try to convert it to a specific exception based on the contents of the SoapException, but this seems like an unnecessary exercise. Use the exception content to provide an error handler or notify the provider of the error in the Web Service.

Invoking Web Services Asynchronously

There are two ways that you can invoke Web Methods. The first way is to invoke a Web Method synchronously: invoke the Web Method and wait until the response comes back. The second way is to invoke the Web Method, do some other processing, and handle the response from the Web Method at a later time. This second way is referred to as *asynchronous processing*. .NET supports asynchronous processing for a large part of the framework, including Windows Forms, ASP.NET Web Forms, and ASP.NET Web Services, among other aspects of .NET.

When you add a reference to a Web Service, the wsdl.exe utility generates a proxy class. Inside of the proxy class are two methods, Begin*XXXX* and End*XXXX*, for each Web Method in your Web Service. For example, our IsPrime method will be represented by a synchronous method, IsPrime, and an asynchronous pair of methods, BeginIsPrime and EndIsPrime. The latter two methods are wrappers for a call to the SoapHttpClientProtocol.BeginInvoke and SoapHttpClientProtocol.EndInvoke asynchronous methods. By using the asynchronous methods, you can invoke an operation on a Web Method, perform some additional processing, and handle the result asynchronously when the data is ready. Listing 12-8 demonstrates a Console Application client that invokes the IsPrime Web Method asynchronously. In this manner, the same client can send several requests to IsPrime and display the results when they are available.

Listing 12-8   *Invoking a Web Service asynchronously*

```
1:   using System;
2:   using TestPrimes.localhost;
3:
4:   namespace TestPrimes
5:   {
6:
7:     class Class1
8:     {
9:       [STAThread]
10:      static void Main(string[] args)
11:      {
12:        TestAsynch();
13:
14:        Console.WriteLine("Press any key...");
```

```
15:          Console.ReadLine();
16:      }
17:
18:
19:      private static void TestAsynch()
20:      {
21:        while(true)
22:        {
23:          Console.WriteLine("Enter a number (Q=Quit):");
24:          string value = Console.ReadLine();
25:          if( value.ToUpper() == "Q" ) return;
26:          try
27:          {
28:            TestPrime(Convert.ToInt64(value));
29:          }
30:          catch
31:          {
32:            Console.WriteLine(value.ToString() + " is not a number");
33:          }
34:        }
35:      }
36:
37:
38:      private class Data
39:      {
40:        public long number;
41:        public DateTime dateTime;
42:
43:        public Data(long number)
44:        {
45:          this.number = number;
46:          dateTime = DateTime.Now;
47:        }
48:
49:        public TimeSpan Elapsed()
50:        {
51:          return DateTime.Now.Subtract(dateTime);
52:        }
53:      }
54:
55:      private static void TestPrime(long prime)
56:      {
57:        IAsyncResult result =
58:        p.BeginIsPrime(prime, new AsyncCallback(Class1.Callback),
59:          new Data(prime));
```

```
60:      }
61:
62:      static Primes p = new Primes();
63:      private static void Callback(IAsyncResult result)
64:      {
65:        if( result.IsCompleted )
66:           WriteResult(result);
67:      }
68:
69:      private static void WriteResult(IAsyncResult result)
70:      {
71:        WriteResult((Data)result.AsyncState, p.EndIsPrime(result));
72:      }
73:
74:      private static void WriteResult( Data data, bool isPrime)
75:      {
76:        const string mask = "{0} {1} prime";
77:        Console.WriteLine(string.Format(mask, data.number,
78:          new string[]{"is not", "is"}[Convert.ToInt16(isPrime)]));
79:        Console.WriteLine("Calculated in " + data.Elapsed());
80:      }
81:    }
82: }
```

NOTE

The use of the static modifier is not relevant to the solution. Static methods were used for convenience. The only difference is that I would have to create instances of Class1 if I didn't use static methods. Using instance methods neither adds to nor detracts from the example.

Lines 19 through 35 of Listing 12-8 implement a *while* loop representing a simple user interface. Enter a number to test for primeness or Q to quit. TestPrime is implemented on lines 55 through 60. Because TestPrime invokes the Web Method IsPrime asynchronously, by calling BeginIsPrime, it returns immediately.

Call asynchronous methods by passing an AsyncCallback delegate. The wrapper BeginIsPrime accepts the number to test, the AsyncCallback delegate, and an optional third argument used to pass data to the AsyncCallback delegate. In our example, we pass an instance of an internal class, Data. Data stores the tested number and a seeded start time. (We can use the seeded start time to calculate the elapsed time.) The Data class demonstrates the nested class idiom and how to pass complex data to asynchronous delegates.

The callback method was named Callback to make it easy to find. (We have to use the class name, Class1, simply because the callback is static.) TestPrime returns immediately. We know that the asynchronous data is ready when the delegate, Callback, is called. Callback tests the IAsyncResult argument to make sure the method completed, on line 64 of Listing 12-8. If the asynchronous call completed, then we write the result of the IsPrime method to the Console with the overloaded WriteResult method.

We could have created any user interface for the asynchronous example. The important point is that we use the wrapper methods for BeginInvoke and EndInvoke, and we use the EndInvoke method to obtain the data when the asynchronous data is ready through a delegate. This basic use of asynchronous methods is consistent, whether we are using Windows Forms or Web Forms or implementing the asynchronous Web Method with some other user interface.

You can use the IAsyncResult object returned from BeginInvoke—in our example BeginIsPrime, the wrapper for BeginInvoke—and obtain a WaitHandle through the AsyncWaitHandle property. The WaitHandle can be used to block by invoking WaitHandle.WaitOne, WaitHandle.WaitAll, or WaitHandle.WaitAny. Your code will block if you call EndInvoke, too.

Combining the techniques discussed so far, you can test IAsyncResult.IsCompleted in a loop, use a WaitHandle, or use EndInvoke—EndIsPrime in our example—to block until an asynchronous method invocation returns. For example, you could call BeginInvoke, perform some other operations, and call EndInvoke to block until the asynchronous call returns.

Returning Complex Data from a Web Service

You can return simple data from a Web Service, and, more important, you can also return complex data from a Web Service. Web Services create a proxy type for classes defined in the Web Service. The proxy type flattens the original type, converting properties to public fields and providing you with the equivalent of a data-only record containing the values of the original object.

TIP

The SOAP protocol supports returning complex data types from Web Services. If you use either the HTTP GET or HTTP POST protocol, you are limited to simple name-and-value pairs of data.

For example, suppose you have a Web Service that returns basic statistics about a professional sports team. You might store the name, city, state, and game statistics in the Web Service, as well as provide some basic operations. We can name the class "Team." The class contained in the Web Service will be a fully constituted Team object, but, when you return the Team object from the Web Service, it will look flat. Listing 12-9 contains a Web Service and the Team class. Listing 12-10 shows what the Team class will look like after the wsdl.exe utility has generated a proxy class for the Team class. (I used sproxy.exe to manually generate the Team proxy generated automatically when you add a Web reference.)

Listing 12-9   *A Web Service and a class defined in a Web Service representing information about sports teams*

```
1:  using System;
2:  using System.Collections;
```

```
3:    using System.ComponentModel;
4:    using System.Data;
5:    using System.Diagnostics;
6:    using System.Web;
7:    using System.Web.Services;
8:
9:    namespace ComplexDataDemo
10:   {
11:     public class Service1 : System.Web.Services.WebService
12:     {
13:       public Service1()
14:       {
15:         //CODEGEN: Required by the ASP.NET Web Services Designer
16:         InitializeComponent();
17:       }
18:
19:       [Component Designer generated code]
20:
21:
22:       [WebMethod]
23:       public Team CreateTeam(string name)
24:       {
25:         return new Team(name);
26:       }
27:
28:     }
29:
30:     public class Team
31:     {
32:       private string name;
33:       private string city;
34:       private string state;
35:       private bool isProfessional;
36:       private string sport;
37:       private int season;
38:       private int wins;
39:       private int losses;
40:       private int ties;
41:
42:       public Team(){}
43:       public Team(string name)
44:       {
45:         this.name = name;
46:       }
```

```
47:
48:     public string Name
49:     {
50:       get{ return name; }
51:       set{ name = value; }
52:     }
53:
54:     public string City
55:     {
56:       get{ return city; }
57:       set{ city = value; }
58:     }
59:
60:     public string State
61:     {
62:       get{ return state; }
63:       set{ state = value; }
64:     }
65:
66:     public bool IsProfessional
67:     {
68:       get{ return isProfessional; }
69:       set{ isProfessional = value; }
70:     }
71:
72:     public string Sport
73:     {
74:       get{ return sport; }
75:       set{ sport = value; }
76:     }
77:
78:     public int Season
79:     {
80:       get{ return season; }
81:       set{ season = value; }
82:     }
83:
84:     public int Wins
85:     {
86:       get{ return wins; }
87:       set{ wins = value; }
88:     }
89:
```

```
90:        public int Losses
91:        {
92:          get{ return losses; }
93:          set{ losses = value; }
94:        }
95:
96:        public int Ties
97:        {
98:          get{ return ties; }
99:          set{ ties = value; }
100:       }
101:
102:       public override string ToString()
103:       {
104:         const string mask =
105:          "Name: {0}\r\n" +
106:          "City/State: {1}, {2}\r\n" +
107:          "Sport: {3}\r\n" +
108:          "IsProfessional: {4}\r\n";
109:
110:         return string.Format(mask,
111:           name, city, state, sport, isProfessional);
112:       }
113:    }
114: }
```

The WebMethod in line 23 of Listing 12-9 creates and returns an instance of Team. The Team class—lines 30 through 113—contains several fields, properties, and a method, ToString, representing a capability of the Team class. It is valuable to return aggregate data from a Web Service—you do need to know that the Team object in the assembly containing the Web Service will not be the same Team object that the client receives.

When you add a reference to the Web Service shown in Listing 12-9, you will get a flattened team object. Listing 12-10 contains the Team class that a client will get from the Web Service.

Listing 12-10   *Complex types returned from Web Services do not contain methods but have fields that mirror public properties.*

```
/// <remarks/>
[System.Xml.Serialization.XmlTypeAttribute(Namespace="http://tempuri.org/")]
public class Team {
  /// <remarks/>
```

```
    public string Name;

    /// <remarks/>
    public string City;

    /// <remarks/>
    public string State;

    /// <remarks/>
    public bool IsProfessional;

    /// <remarks/>
    public string Sport;

    /// <remarks/>
    public int Season;

    /// <remarks/>
    public int Wins;

    /// <remarks/>
    public int Losses;

    /// <remarks/>
    public int Ties;
}
```

Notice in Listing 12-10 that the fields have been removed and the properties have been replaced by public fields. There is no sign of our ToString method.

XML serialization is used to convert complex data into an XML representation of objects returned from Web Services.

Returning a DataSet from a Web Service

An excellent way to return data from a Web Service is to return a DataSet. On both sides of a Web Service—the Service and the client—the DataSet is a complete object. This means you can return a DataSet that contains multiple tables, table relations, and mapping relationships. Chapter 5 discusses ADO.NET and the DataSet; how to return a DataSet from a Web Service is demonstrated in the Chapter 5 section "Returning a DataSet from a Web Service." Chapter 11, in the section "Serializing Objects," demonstrates how to serialize objects into a DataSet. Both of these sections provide additional Web Service examples.

The DataSet was coded by Microsoft to support being consumable by Web Services without intervention from the programmer. The DataSet uses a DiffGram to serialize the original and current row values of a DataSet. Web Service consumers don't have to worry about serialization and deserialization of DataSets; DataSets are fully reconstituted across Web Service boundaries.

Web Services can consume a DataSet. In simple terms, this means that if you pass a DataSet to a Web Service or return a DataSet from a Web Service, then you get a System.Data.DataSet object. If you consume a custom class in a Web Service, then you get a flattened class (see Listing 12-9 and Listing 12-10). For example, the Team class in Listing 12-9 was flattened to the Team class in Listing 12-10 when it was returned from the Web Service.

Interestingly, if I add a reference to the Web Service in Listing 12-9, I can modify the reference.cs proxy file. By removing the flattened version of the Team class in Listing 12-10 and adding a *using* statement referencing an assembly that contains the real Team, the Web Service returns a completely initialized version of Team, methods included.

I don't know the answer, but it does seem that DataSets are consumable as objects simply because of the reference to System.Data in the Reference.cs wsdl-generated file. Unfortunately, changing the Reference.cs file manually—in the example, removing the generated Team class and adding a *using* statement and a reference to a Teams.dll assembly—is not very extensible because the Reference.cs file is regenerated any time the Web Reference is updated.

Secondary Topics

Objects can be serialized as XML documents or in a binary or SOAP format. You can use the XmlSerializer class to convert an object to an Xml document, or you can use the Serializable attribute to support serializing to a binary or SOAP format. You can also implement the System.Runtime.Serialization.ISerializable interface to control the serialization process when using a SOAP or binary formatter.

Chapter 11, in the section "Serializing Objects," demonstrates how to use the XmlSerializer. In this section, I will demonstrate how to use the SoapFormatter to serialize an object and how to implement the ISerializable interface to allow you to manually control how the BinaryFormatter and SoapFormatter serialize an object.

Using the SoapFormatter

The SoapFormatter will format an object as a Soap document. The SoapFormatter class implements the System.Runtime.Remoting.Messaging.IRemotingFormatter. We can declare the SoapFormatter as an IRemotingFormatter and serialize an object much as we did with the XmlSerializer in Chapter 11. Listing 12-11 demonstrates how to serialize the Team class to a Soap document.

Listing 12-11   *Serializing an object to a Soap document*

```
// include these additional namespaces
using System.Runtime.Remoting.Messaging;
```

```
using System.Runtime.Serialization.Formatters.Soap;
using System.IO;

public void SerializeToSoap()
{
  Teams.Team team = new Teams.Team("Red Wings");
  team.IsProfessional = true;
  team.City = "Detroit";
  team.State = "Michigan";
  team.Sport = "Hockey";

  IRemotingFormatter formatter = new SoapFormatter();
  MemoryStream stream = new MemoryStream();
  formatter.Serialize(stream, team);
  stream.Position = 0;
  textBox1.Text =
    System.Text.ASCIIEncoding.ASCII.GetString(stream.ToArray());
}
```

(The example in Listing 12-11 can be found in the ComplexDataDemo.csproj sample program.) Here we create an instance of the Team class directly (found in the Teams.csproj project). We create an instance of the SoapFormatter and a MemoryStream. (The MemoryStream is defined in System.IO.) We instruct the formatter to Serialize to the object to the stream, reposition the stream, and use the System.Text.ASCIIEncoding.ASCII.GetString method to convert the stream to a string.

We can invoke stream.ToArray to return an array of bytes (byte[ ]), and the ASCII.GetString method can convert the bytes to an ASCII string. When the last statement runs, the object will appear as a SOAP message, as shown in Figure 12-3.

The System.SerializableAttribute applied to the Team class is what allows the SoapFormatter and BinaryFormatter to serialize the Team class. (This is the original Team class, not the Team class returned by the Web Service.) If you want to manually control the serialization process, you can implement the ISerializable interface in conjunction with the Serializable attribute.

Implementing the ISerializable Interface

System.Runtime.Serialization.ISerializable requires that you implement a GetObjectData method to support serializing an object using the BinaryFormatter or the SoapFormatter and that you implement a protected constructor, taking the same arguments as GetObjectData, to support deserializing an object using the BinaryFormatter and SoapFormatter.

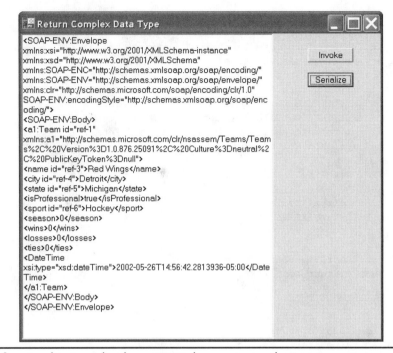

Figure 12-3   *An object serialized as a SOAP document using the SoapFormatter*

The modifications shown in Listing 12-12 demonstrate how to implement ISerializable for the Team class defined in Teams.csproj. The balance of the Team code is shown in Listing 12-9.

Listing 12-12   *Implementing ISerializable to support SOAP and binary serialization*

```csharp
using System;
using System.Runtime.Serialization;
using System.Diagnostics;

namespace Teams
{
  [Serializable]
  public class Team : ISerializable
  {
    // Original code from listing 12-9 goes here.
    protected Team(SerializationInfo info,
      StreamingContext context)
```

```
    {
      name = (string)info.GetValue("name", typeof(string));
      city = (string)info.GetValue("city", typeof(string));
      state = (string)info.GetValue("state", typeof(string));
      isProfessional = (bool)info.GetValue("isProfessional", typeof(bool));
      sport = (string)info.GetValue("sport", typeof(string));
      season = (int)info.GetValue("season", typeof(int));
      wins = (int)info.GetValue("wins", typeof(int));
      losses = (int)info.GetValue("losses", typeof(int));
      ties = (int)info.GetValue("ties", typeof(int));

      DateTime dateTime = (DateTime)info.GetValue("DateTime",
        typeof(DateTime));
      Debug.WriteLine("Serialized at: " + dateTime.ToString());
      Debug.WriteLine("Deserialized at: " + DateTime.Now.ToString());
    }

    public void GetObjectData(SerializationInfo info,
      StreamingContext context)
    {
      info.AddValue("name", name);
      info.AddValue("city", city);
      info.AddValue("state", state);
      info.AddValue("isProfessional", isProfessional);
      info.AddValue("sport", sport);
      info.AddValue("season", season);
      info.AddValue("wins", wins);
      info.AddValue("losses", losses);
      info.AddValue("ties", ties);
      info.AddValue("DateTime", DateTime.Now);
      Debug.WriteLine("Serialized at: " + DateTime.Now.ToString());
    }
  }
}
```

The basic implementation of ISerializable will invoke GetObjectData when you call SoapFormatter.Serialize or BinaryFormatter.Serialize. GetObjectData writes the field values you want to serialize to the SerializationInfo object. The constructor allows a caller to initialize an instance of the object—in this case, Team—with a SerializationInfo object.

If you are only going to write the members represented by public properties, you don't need to implement ISerializable. To demonstrate, our implementation of ISerializable adds a DateTime value indicating when the object was serialized and deserialized. Practical use of ISerializable would be to serialize data that makes up an object's state and that may be stored in private fields having no associated public properties.

The StreamingContext object contains information about the source or destination of the transmitted data. For example, you can poll context.State == StreamingContextStates .CrossMachine to determine whether the context is a different computer.

For more information on using the SoapFormatter or BinaryFormatter, explore the Visual Studio .NET help documentation for information about .NET Remoting. Remoting is another way that .NET supports communications between different operating system processes, on the same or different computers, and is a non-proprietary replacement for Microsoft's DCOM technology.

Summary

I have read at least one article and at least one book that suggests that Microsoft's Web Services are "not quite ready for prime time" or that there is a lot of noise surrounding Web Services without substance. Nothing could be further from the truth.

In this chapter, I demonstrated how to return simple and complex data from Web Services. Clearly, the open standards of XML and SOAP imply that this is not a Microsoft-only technology, and, also clearly, we can make requests that Web Services can satisfy, as well as obtain advanced data types. These operations can be performed both synchronously and asynchronously.

The only difficulty I have found so far is returning what I refer to as a completely reconstituted object. When a custom object is returned, the default behavior is to flatten the object into a fields-only shallow image of the actual object residing in the Web Service. (In a note earlier in the chapter, I described one way of getting around even this modest limitation—although it is questionable whether this behavior represents a limitation or a necessity. When a type is returned from a Web Service, there is clearly no guarantee that the type or any of its sub-types exist on the client machine.) My suspicion is that perceived limitations and the perception of over-hype may be caused by limitations in understanding of some of the core technologies that support Web Services. There is a lot to .NET, and it may be a while before there is both a broad and deep understanding across a broad population of developers.

I do believe that open standards (XML and SOAP) are better than a proprietary standard (DCOM) and that XML Web Services represent a powerful and compelling means of sharing data between systems and across networks.

IBuySpy and Dynamic User Interfaces in ASP.NET

This section of the book is significant because the next four chapters contain examples taken by express permission from the IBuySpy portal sample application implemented by Microsoft.

IBuySpy.com (see the following logo) is an online Web storefront application that sells humorous and fictitious spy goods. More important, it is a complete working Web application that employs Microsoft's ASP.NET and demonstrates Visual Basic .NET, C#, security, and Microsoft's Mobile Internet Toolkit, thereby blazing a trail for developers. You can download, visually customize (using the Administration tools), or programmatically customize the portal application, borrowing from practical examples and best practices demonstrated in production-quality code.

The entire IBuySpy portal can be downloaded from **www.ibuyspy.com**. This includes the application, database, documentation, and source code. You may install and configure the IBuySpy portal to run on your PC or Intranet, and Microsoft extends permission to you to use any of the code and many of the figures as aids in building your own portal application. This chapter and the three that follow, which are made possible courtesy of Microsoft, will help you work with the IBuySpy portal code as well as build your own ASP.NET applications.

To download and run the IBuySpy Portal on your PC, you will need

▶   Windows 2000 or Windows XP server or professional

▶   SQL Server or MSDE 2000 or higher

▶   .NET Framework SDK or Visual Studio .NET

▶   Microsoft Internet Explorer 5.5 or higher

To install the portal, you will need to download the IBuySpy portal from **www.ibuyspy.com** (PortalCS_VS_0204.exe) and run the self-extracting archive. Ensure that you have the requisite configuration in your target environment and follow the instructions for the portal setup and configuration.

Demonstrated Topics

The IBuySpy portal demonstrates everything you need to know to build a Web portal application. IBuySpy includes dynamic Web pages, an SQL Server database, security, pages for mobile devices, code-behind, stored procedures, dynamic content, administration, and much more.

This chapter emphasizes the way in which ASP.NET, custom UserControls, and code were combined to implement an environment with a dynamic user interface. In the first section of the chapter, we will explore

- ▶ How to create a cascading style sheet
- ▶ How to implement the IBuySpy portal banner
- ▶ Portal modules and the dynamic nature of the portal
- ▶ The stored procedures used to support the dynamic interface design
- ▶ Roles-based security for the portal

Consistent with the rest of the book, the "Secondary Topics" section will provide supplemental material relevant to the "Demonstrated Topics" and the IBuySpy portal, including discussions of how to administer the portal and debug the IBuySpy portal application, and an introduction to Microsoft's Mobile Internet Toolkit.

Creating a Cascading Style Sheet

Cascading styles sheets (CSS files) have been around awhile. Cascading style sheets allow you to describe the appearance of HTML and ASP.NET Web pages in named styles and in a single location and to apply those styles to your content. The result is that it becomes easier to manage the *appearance* of the content separately from the *actual* content. The IBuySpy portal has a distinctive appearance (see Figure 13-1), which is controlled primarily by the portal.css cascading style sheet.

NOTE

The view in Figure 13-1 shows the IBuySpy portal application before a user has been authenticated. End users will have access to features, and administrative users will have an additional Admin tab and links that allow dynamic content management of the portal.

Almost everything you see in Figure 13-1 is dynamic content represented by UserControls or the portal style sheet. You can create a style sheet by selecting File | New | File and selecting the Style Sheet applet from the New File dialog (see Figure 13-2). The portal.css style sheet already exists, and we can explore and customize it by selecting the portal.css file from the solution explorer.

Navigating Style Sheets

As is true with many aspects of Visual Studio .NET, the view you are presented with is related to the context in which you are working. When you open a .css file to modify it, you will get the text that is the style sheet and the CSS Outline—the document outline describing the content of the style sheet (see Figure 13-3).

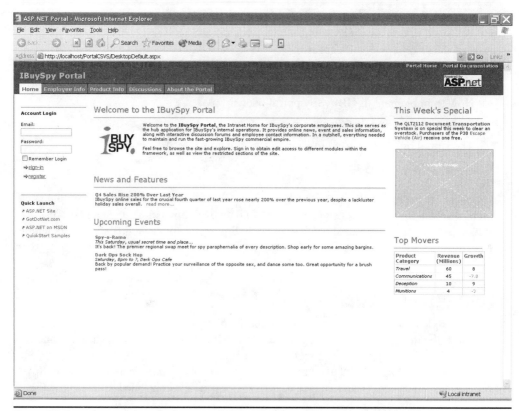

Figure 13-1 *The visual result shown in the IBuySpy portal application is controlled by the centralized values described in the portal.css cascading style sheet.*

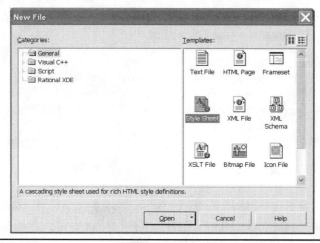

Figure 13-2 *Add a cascading style sheet to an ASP.NET project by selecting File | New | File and picking the Style Sheet applet from the New File dialog.*

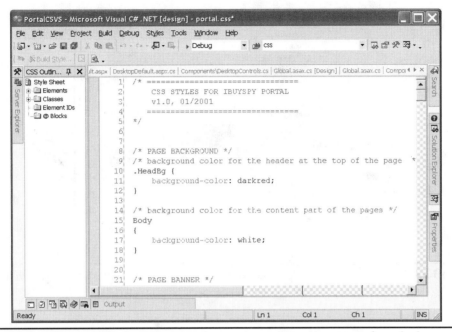

Figure 13-3   *The Visual Studio .NET view when you are editing the content of a style sheet*

TIP

You can also open a Document Outline for the content of an ASP.NET page by selecting the .aspx file and choosing View | Other Windows | Document Outline.

The CSS outline, as well as any outline view, helps you quickly navigate the style sheet document without having to scroll over every line of text. To navigate to a specific element, expand the folder containing that element and click the element name in the CSS Outline. Items in the Elements folder include things like styles for Horizontal Rules <HR>, links, and lists <LI>. Items in the Classes folder include styles for named classes that you create.

You can add, edit, or build styles by using the context menu in the CSS Outline view or by manually editing the text in the actual style sheet document. The Style Builder (see Figure 13-4) provides a categorized way to manage styles, and the .css document itself employs Intellisense to make it easier to add attributes to style elements correctly (see Figure 13-5).

TIP

You can press CTRL+SPACEBAR to display the list of available attributes for an element or begin typing an attribute name.

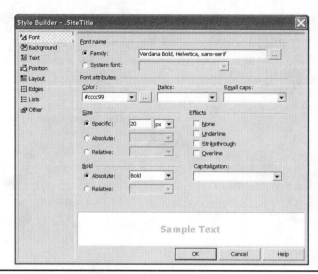

Figure 13-4 *The Style Builder dialog opened from the CSS Outline context menu item Build Style with the SiteTitle style focused*

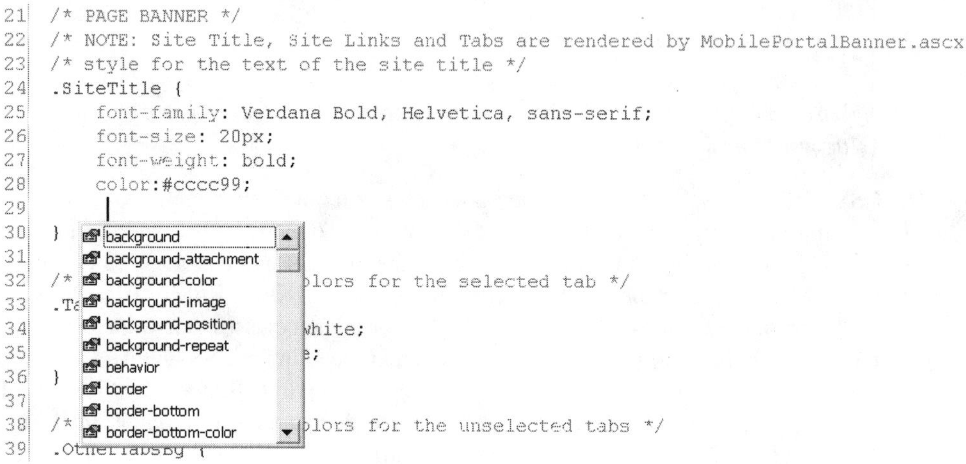

```
21   /* PAGE BANNER */
22   /* NOTE: Site Title, Site Links and Tabs are rendered by MobilePortalBanner.ascx
23   /* style for the text of the site title */
24   .SiteTitle {
25       font-family: Verdana Bold, Helvetica, sans-serif;
26       font-size: 20px;
27       font-weight: bold;
28       color:#cccc99;
29       |
30   }    background
31        background-attachment
32   /*   background-color          olors for the selected tab */
33   .Ta  background-image
34        background-position        white;
35        background-repeat          ;
36   }    behavior
37        border
38   /*   border-bottom              olors for the unselected tabs */
39   .OtherTabsBg {  border-bottom-color
```

Figure 13-5 *Intellisense showing a list of available style items for the SiteTitle style*

Defining Elements

Elements like the horizontal rule tag have a default appearance. You can modify the default appearance adding a style rule for the <HR> element. The following steps describe the visual process for adding an element style rule for the horizontal rule element.

1. In the CSS Outline, right-click the Elements folder and select Add Style Rule from the context menu. (The Add Style Rule dialog will be displayed, as shown in Figure 13-6.)
2. Select the Element radio button and pick the HR element.
3. Click OK to add the style rule to the .css document.

If you selected the HR element, you will see the following text in the style sheet document:

```
HR
{
}
```

The example is referred to as a *style block*. By adding declarations to the style block, you can control how that style will look throughout the pages that use the style sheet containing the style block.

After you have added the style block, you can manually enter the declarations in the style block or use the Style Builder mentioned earlier to define the style. The horizontal rule for the IBuySpy portal is defined as follows:

```
HR {
  color: dimgrey;
  height:1pt;
  text-align:left
}
```

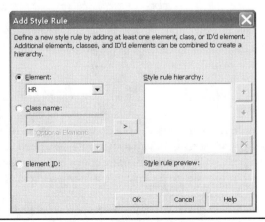

Figure 13-6   *You can use the Add Style Rule dialog to define new styles.*

The style indicates that the horizontal rule will be dimgrey in color and be 1 point high, with text left-aligned. Examples of the horizontal rule can be seen in Figure 13-2, which shows the main page of the IBuySpy portal. Change the color declaration to color: red and build and run the portal, and you will see that all instances of horizontal rules will now be red. This is significantly more convenient than performing a global search-and-replace in every .aspx and .ascx page.

Defining Classes

Classes are added and defined similarly to elements. A class defines a new style rule that you will associate with controls in your Web pages. To add a new class, right-click the Classes folder in the CSS Outline view and select Add Style Rule. This time, choose the Class name radio button and type the name of the class. For example, if you want to create the style rule for the portal site, you might name the class SiteTitle. Click OK, and the SiteTitle style block will be added to the .css document.

You can use the Build Style dialog to visually describe the style or enter the declarations manually, using Intellisense to guide you. The Build Style dialog is especially helpful when selecting items like color. If you pick an RGB color, it may be easier to pick a visual color (see Figure 13-7) in the Style Builder rather than guessing. Here is the style block for the SiteTitle.

```
.SiteTitle {
    font-family: Verdana Bold, Helvetica, sans-serif;
    font-size: 20px;
    font-weight: bold;
    color:#cccc99;
}
```

TIP

I added the semicolon for the last—color—declaration, but you don't need a semicolon for the last declaration in a style rule.

Experiment with the Elements and Classes in the portal.css style sheet to see the effect these changes have on the portal pages.

Using Elements and Classes

When you add style rules for elements like the horizontal rule, these rules are applied whenever you use that element. If you want to associate a style rule described by a class, you will have to associate that class with a CssClass property of a control or by manually editing the HTML that describes the control; it is easier to modify the properties in the Properties window than it is to modify the HTML directly.

The SiteTitle was actually applied only once in the portal application. The SiteTitle is applied to the DesktopPortalBanner.ascx (UserControl). The banner control contains a label with the "IBuySpy Portal" text. The ASP that sets the CssClass attribute for the title label is

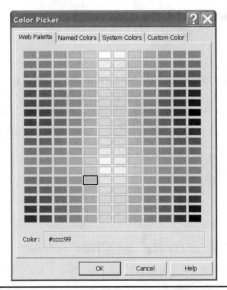

Figure 13-7   *Visually picking some declaration values is much easier using the Build Style dialog, as demonstrated here by the Color Picker dialog.*

shown next. The Properties window containing the modified CssClass property for the Label is shown in Figure 13-8.

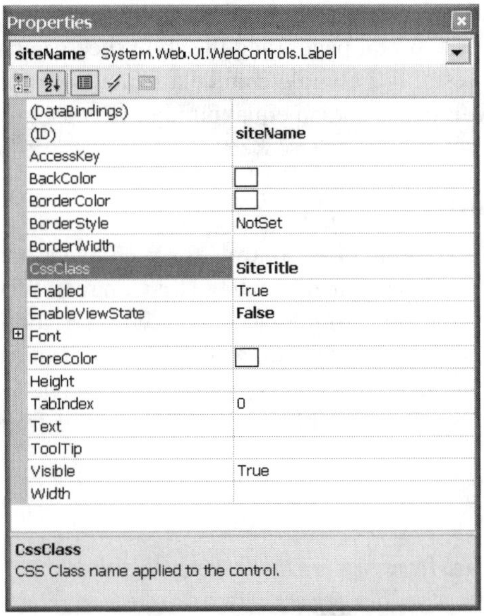

Figure 13-8   *The CssClass property for the Label control demonstrates an instance of applying a style rule from the portal.css style sheet.*

```
<asp:label id="siteName" CssClass="SiteTitle" EnableViewState="false"
runat="server" />
```

Whenever you want to apply a class in the style sheet to a control, you will need to define the style rule, find the CssClass property for that object, and type the name of the style rule in the Properties window (or directly in the HTML text). Several controls, like the DataList, have nested properties that also contain a CssClass property. That is, you can apply different styles for different elements of the control. For example, the DataList control has a CssClass property, as well as the nested properties EditItemStyle.CssClass, FooterStyle.CssClass, HeaderStyle.CssClass, ItemStyle.CssClass, SelectedItemStyle.CssClass, and the SeparatorStyle .CssClass properties. Each can have their own style rule or will inherit the rule applied to the control itself.

Implementing the Portal Banner

ASP.NET UserControls are heavily used in the IBuySpy portal. The benefit of UserControls is clearly reuse. It is much easier to describe a general layout and plug in a UserControl than it is to hardwire every aspect of the user interface. For example, creating one banner means that every page simply needs to *refer* to the banner in order to display the banner. Even if you use only a piece of a page one time, it is still beneficial to create UserControls, because a UserControl can easily be reused. Figure 13-9 shows the DesktopPortalBanner.ascx UserControl before it is rendered, and Figure 13-1 (at the top) shows the dramatic difference after the control has been rendered in a Web page.

The basic approach followed throughout the IBuySpy portal is that the page and controls define the basic layout of the portal pages, and the style sheets and code determine which elements to display. The result is a complete and elaborate Web application with a relatively small number of .aspx Web pages and an equal number of reusable UserControls.

Designing User Controls

The fundamental steps for creating UserControls for Web pages are similar to those outlined in Chapter 8, which introduced the topic of creating UserControls. When you create a Web UserControl you will be inheriting from System.Web.UI.UserControl instead of System .Windows .Forms.UserControl. You can add a Web UserControl to a project by selecting the Web UserControl applet from the Add New Item dialog. The DesktopPortalBanner already exists, so we will commence with the description of its implementation (shown in Figure 13-9).

TIP

You can convert a Web Forms page to a UserControl by removing the <html>, <body>, and <form> elements from the page and changing any @Page directive to an @Control directive. Make sure you remove @Page attributes that are not applicable to @Control directives.

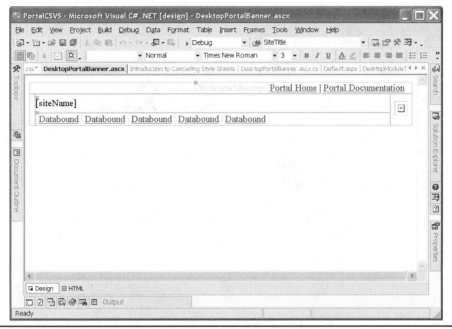

Figure 13-9   *The DesktopPortalBanner.ascx UserControl before rendering*

From Figure 13-9, it is clear that the design-time effort spent on the DesktopPortalBanner was minimal. The control layout is described by a <table>, and there are a couple of Label controls, HTML links, and a DataList. We will explore the various aspects of implementing the DesktopPortalBanner.ascx UserControl in the sections that follow.

Working with the Design View

After we have added a Web UserControl to the project, we can use the designer or the HTML editor to create the control layout. The ASP and HTML that implement the DesktopPortalBanner is shown in Listing 13-1 for reference. (It is difficult to format HTML both in this text and the HTML designer, which is one reason why it is beneficial to use the Document Outline to navigate the text.)

Listing 13-1   *The HTML that implements the DesktopPortalBanner.ascx UserControl*

```
1:  <%@ Control CodeBehind="DesktopPortalBanner.ascx.cs"
2:  Language="c#" AutoEventWireup="false"
3:  Inherits="ASPNetPortal.DesktopPortalBanner" %>
4:  <%@ Import Namespace="ASPNetPortal" %>
```

```
 5:  <%--
 6:
 7:     The DesktopPortalBanner User Control is responsible for
 8:     displaying the standard Portal
 9:     banner at the top of each .aspx page.
10:
11:     The DesktopPortalBanner uses the Portal Configuration
12:     System to obtain a list of the portal's sitename and
13:     tab settings. It then renders this content into the page.
14:
15:  --%>
16:  <table width="100%" cellspacing="0" class="HeadBg" border="0">
17:    <tr valign="top">
18:    <td colspan="3" class="SiteLink"
19:    background="<%= Request.ApplicationPath %>/images/bars.gif"
20:    align="right">
21:    <asp:label id="WelcomeMessage" forecolor="#eeeeee" runat="server" />
22:    <a href="<%= Request.ApplicationPath %>"
23:    class="SiteLink">Portal Home</a>
24:    <span class="Accent">
25:                    |</span>
26:    <a href="<%= Request.ApplicationPath %>/Docs/Docs.htm"
27:      target="_blank" class="SiteLink">
28:      Portal Documentation</a>
29:    <%= LogoffLink %>
30:         
31:    </td>
32:    </tr>
33:    <tr>
34:      <td width="10" rowspan="2">
35:          
36:      </td>
37:      <td height="40">
38:        <asp:label id="siteName" CssClass="SiteTitle"
39:        EnableViewState="false" runat="server" />
40:      </td>
41:      <td align="middle" rowspan="2">
42:        <a href="http://www.asp.net"><img id="logo"
43:        src="<%=Request.ApplicationPath%>/images/poweredby_simple.gif"
44:        border="0"></a>
45:      </td>
46:    </tr>
47:    <tr>
```

```
48:      <td>
49:        <asp:datalist id="tabs" cssclass="OtherTabsBg"
50:        repeatdirection="horizontal" ItemStyle-Height="25"
51:        SelectedItemStyle-CssClass="TabBg"
52:        ItemStyle-BorderWidth="1" EnableViewState="false" runat="server">
53:          <ItemTemplate>
54:             <a href='<%= Request.ApplicationPath
%>/DesktopDefault.aspx?tabindex=<%# Container.ItemIndex %>&tabid=<%#
((TabStripDetails) Container.DataItem).TabId %>' class="OtherTabs"><%#
((TabStripDetails) Container.DataItem).TabName %></a> 
55:          </ItemTemplate>
56:          <SelectedItemTemplate>
57:             <span class="SelectedTab"><%# ((TabStripDetails)
Container.DataItem).TabName %></span> 
58:          </SelectedItemTemplate>
59:        </asp:datalist>
60:      </td>
61:    </tr>
62: </table>
```

A UserControl has many of the same HTML elements as a Web page. From the previous section, we know that a UserControl does not have the <form>, <html>, and <body> elements, and the code-behind is associated with the control using an @Control directive instead of an @Page directive.

Using an HTML Table to Manage Layout

An excellent and lightweight way to manage the layout of a UserControl (and a page) is to add an HTML table to the control in order to subdivide the real estate of the control using rows and data cells. The <table> in Listing 13-1 extends from line 16 to line 62, intertwined with the controls added to that table. The Document Outline view is the best way to navigate individual elements of the table, like the three row elements <tr>, and you can use the context menu to add rows and cells to a table. To create very elaborate layouts, you can also nest HTML <table> elements.

To create a <table> element that has a layout similar to the DesktopPortalBanner, follow these steps:

1. Create a new Web UserControl.

2. Select the HTML tab in the toolbox and drag the Table control to the UserControl designer. (By default, there are three columns and rows rendered in an HTML table; we will modify the default number.)

3. Right-click the top right cell and select Delete | Cells from the context menu. Repeat this step again, deleting the middle data cell.

4. Press F4 to display the Properties window and change the colspan property of the <TD> (data cell) element to 3. This step will create a top row like that used to display the Portal Home and Portal Documentation links shown in Figure 13-1.

5. To create the bottom two rows of the DesktopPortalBanner, delete two cells from the bottom row using the context menu again.

6. Select the middle-left data cell and change the rowspan property to 2.

7. Repeat step 6 for the middle-right cell.

8. Move the mouse over one vertical edge of either of the center data cells, and drag the mouse until the second and third row middle cells consume most of the horizontal space for the control.

9. Finally, select the two-rowspan rightmost data cell, and press F4 to open the Properties window. Change the cell width to about 50.

The result of the previous nine steps creates the table layout shown in Figure 13-10 and the code shown in Listing 13-2.

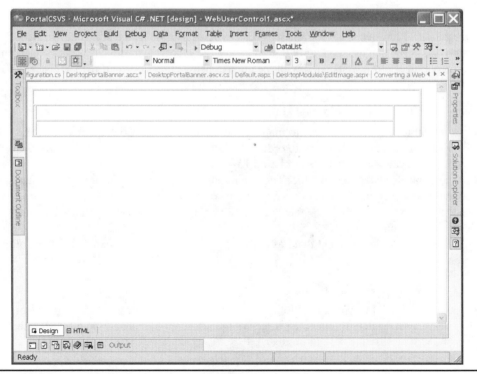

Figure 13-10   *A table layout that approximates the layout of the DesktopPortalBanner UserControl*

Listing 13-2   *An HTML table control that is similar to the layout for the DesktopPortalBanner*

```
<%@ Control Language="c#" AutoEventWireup="false"
Codebehind="WebUserControl1.ascx.cs"
Inherits="ASPNetPortal.WebUserControl1"
TargetSchema="http://schemas.microsoft.com/intellisense/ie3-2nav3-0"%>
<TABLE id="Table1" height="96"
cellSpacing="1" cellPadding="1" width="784" border="1">
  <TR>
    <TD colSpan="3"></TD>
  </TR>
  <TR>
    <TD rowSpan="2"></TD>
    <TD width="739"></TD>
    <TD width="50" rowSpan="2"></TD>
  </TR>
  <TR>
    <TD width="739"></TD>
  </TR>
</TABLE>
```

A strategy I employ when using a table to manage layout is to leave the border value greater than 0, so I can see the cell boundaries as I am adding controls to the layout. To complete the DesktopPortalBanner, we need to add some controls that act as placeholders for the data.

Adding Controls to the Table

Now that we have the data cells, we can add controls to create the UserControl design by dragging and dropping controls onto the UserControl cells. For example, the vertical bars are created by adding a background image to the <TD> element. This is demonstrated by line 19 of Listing 13-1; notice the use of the function invocation to Request.ApplicationPath appended to the relative path /images/bars.gif.

Using the server-side script block allows you to insert script inline. The Request .ApplicationPath call will be replaced with the actual application path. (Using the server-side script makes it possible to easily move the portal application to your PC or deploy it.) The top row of the banner contains a label that will be replaced with a welcome message when you log in. There are two hyperlinks that allow the user to navigate to the portal home page or portal documentation and the server-side script to display the LoggoffLink field. Again, when you log in, the LogoffLink field will return HTML that renders the Logoff link in the Page Load event if the user is authenticated. Here is the DesktopPortalBanner.ascx.cs code-behind file that initializes the LogoffLink field.

```
if (Context.User.Identity.AuthenticationType == "Forms")
{
  LogoffLink =
```

```
   "<" + "span class=\"Accent\">|</span>\n" + "<" +
   "a href=" + Request.ApplicationPath + "/Admin/Logoff.aspx class=SiteLink>
   Logoff" + "<" + "/a>";
}
```

The LogoffLink string creates the following HTML text:

```
<span class="Accent">|</span>
<a href=/PortalCSVS/Admin/Logoff.aspx class=SiteLink> Logoff</a>
```

If you view the pages and UserControls in the IBuySpy portal, you will see server-side script used frequently to create a dynamic relationship between the content displayed and the code that manages the content.

Adding a DataList to Implement the Navigation Tabs

The DataList control is added from the Web Forms tab of the toolbox and can be bound to the same kinds of objects that you would bind a DataGrid to, for example, an ArrayList or DataSet. The DataList is a data-bound template-derived control that supports viewing, updating, and deleting data in the list. Cleverly, the data list is used to bind tab names to display available tabs for the IBuySpy portal based on the authentication state of the portal; there are more items displayed for administrative users and fewer tab items for end users.

The DataList can be edited from the Edit Template context menu item. There are several templates you can modify to create the desired result for a DataList, including: Header and Footer Templates, Item Templates, and a Separator Template. The Item Templates include the ItemTemplate, AlternatingItemTemplate, SelectedItemTemplate, and EditItemTemplate. The Header and Footer templates describe the appearance of the header and footer, and the Separator template describes the content between DataList items. The Item Templates describe the appearance of the data-bound content of the DataList. The ItemTemplate describes all items in the DataList. The AlternatingItemTemplate describes the appearance of every other item in the DataList. The SelectedItemTemplate describes the appearance of the DataList item that is selected, and the EditItemTemplate describes the element that is being edited in the list. Define each of these template items if you want to customize the appearance of the DataList in any particular state.

If you open the Item Templates editor for the DataList for the DesktopPortalBanner, it may be difficult to tell which templates were employed and how they were defined, so we will turn to the code. (Of course, you can modify the DataList and other ASP.NET controls by turning directly to the HTML editor or the Properties window, too.) Listing 13-3 contains the ASP.NET code that describes the DataList for the banner.

Listing 13-3   *The ASP.NET code that describes the DataList used to create the navigation tabs for the IBuySpy portal*

```
1:   <asp:datalist id="tabs" runat="server"
2:   EnableViewState="false" ItemStyle-BorderWidth="1"
3:   SelectedItemStyle-CssClass="TabBg"
4:   ItemStyle-Height="25" repeatdirection="horizontal"
```

```
 5:   cssclass="OtherTabsBg">
 6:     <ItemTemplate>
 7:         <a href='<%= Request.ApplicationPath
%>/DesktopDefault.aspx?tabindex=<%# Container.ItemIndex %>&tabid=<%#
((TabStripDetails) Container.DataItem).TabId %>'
 8:       class="OtherTabs">
 9:       <%# ((TabStripDetails) Container.DataItem).TabName %>
10:       </a> 
11:     </ItemTemplate>
12:     <SelectedItemTemplate>
13:        <span class="SelectedTab"><%# ((TabStripDetails)
Container.DataItem).TabName %>
14:     </span> 
15:     </SelectedItemTemplate>
16:  </asp:datalist>
```

(ASP.NET contains some very long text. Instead of arbitrarily breaking the statements into formattable chunks, I elected to display the code that describes the DataList roughly as it will appear in the HTML editor, and the line numbers were added for reference.)

The DataList itself is defined by the <asp:datalist> and </asp:datalist> tags. Basically, ASP.NET controls are rendered as text, which supports building ASP.NET pages in any text editor. (I wouldn't do this now, but ASP.NET was released before Visual Studio .NET and this is how early beta developers may have demonstrated building Web pages.) Lines 1 through 5 describe the DataList. The runat attribute indicates that the DataList code is to be processed on the server. The EnableViewState="false" attribute indicates that the view state information for the DataList will not be stored on the page. (View state information looks like garbage text but is actually encrypted state information stored in the clear.) The SelectedItemStyle-CssClass represents the DataList.SelectedItemStyle.CssClass property and is assigned the rule TabBg defined in the portal.css cascading style sheet. The ItemStyle-Height is 25; the items will be displayed horizontally; and the general style rule for the DataList is the OtherTabsBg style. (You can examine the portal.css to see the styles defined by these rules. You'll find that the styles define the background color, which is suggested by the Bg suffix used in the style name.)

The   (non-breaking space) is used to force a space between the DataBound elements in the DataList. This tag is used at the left and right sides of the DataBound elements in both the ItemTemplate and SelectedItemTemplate to produce a uniform spacing between elements.

Again, the DataList is using the server-side script tags. The DataList tab items are obtained programmatically in the code-behind page, which we will discuss in a moment. The DataList in the DesktopPortalBanner demonstrates how to programmatically bind data at run-time, resulting in the tabs shown in Figure 13-1.

Programming in the Code-Behind Module

A convenient way to demonstrate the code-behind module is to describe how the tabs—DataList in the DesktopPortalBanner—are generated in the portal application.

ASP.NET is more challenging a tool than Windows Forms for creating graphical user interfaces because there are more ways to create the interface. In Windows Forms, we have the Form designer and the code-behind. In ASP.NET, we have the Page designer, HTML editor, and the code. Fortunately, the code-behind page does make it easier to associate code with ASP.NET Web pages in a manner that is more consistent with how we have been implementing non-Web applications since Alan Cooper invented Visual Basic.

You can press F7 to switch from the Page designer view to the code-behind view and SHIFT+F7 to switch back to the Page designer view. By convention, the ASP.NET page has an .aspx extension, and the code-behind file has the .aspx.cs extension, but the association happens in the Codebehind attribute of the @Page and @Control statements (see Listing 13-2 for an example.)

You might assume that the code-behind code runs first, but this isn't necessarily the case. The code in the Global.asax page is executed first. I will describe the order of execution beginning with the Global.asax page and ending with data being bound to the DataList control named tabs.

Implementing Event Handlers in the Global.asax Module

The Global.asax module inherits from HttpApplication and provides you with a convenient place to add event handlers for responding to application level events. The Global.asax file cannot be requested directly by a user, but the code in it is run when an application-level event is requested. In the IBuySpy portal application, the Global.asax file implements two event handlers: BeginRequest and AuthenticateRequest. (There are about a dozen event handlers you can implement; writing any code in the application file is optional.)

In the Portal, BeginRequest uses the TabIndex and TabId in the URL-encoded message string to build the PortalSettings object each time a request is made. The AuthenticateRequest event handler is implemented to determine whether the user has been authenticated and what roles that person has been assigned. Listing 13-4 contains the code for the Application_BeginRequest event handler (you can refer to Chapter 16 for more information on roles-based security).

Listing 13-4   *The BeginRequest event handler is used to initialize the PortalSettings based on the URL-encoded request.*

```
1:   protected void Application_BeginRequest(Object sender, EventArgs e)
2:   {
3:      int tabIndex = 0;
4:      int tabId = 0;
5:
6:      // Get TabIndex from querystring
7:
8:      if (Request.Params["tabindex"] != null) {
9:         tabIndex = Int32.Parse(Request.Params["tabindex"]);
10:     }
11:
```

```
12:    // Get TabID from querystring
13:
14:    if (Request.Params["tabid"] != null) {
15:      tabId = Int32.Parse(Request.Params["tabid"]);
16:    }
17:
18:    Context.Items.Add("PortalSettings", new PortalSettings(tabIndex,
tabId));
19: }
```

When you select an item in the tab navigator, the hyperlink in the ItemTemplate creates a URL-encoded request string, such as the one demonstrated here:

http://localhost/PortalCSVS/DesktopDefault.aspx?tabindex=1&tabid=2

The parameters in the request can be read from the Request.Params property, using the parameter name as an indexer, as demonstrated on lines 9 and 15 of Listing 13-4. The parameters *tabindex* and *tabid* are used as arguments to the constructor for the PortalSettings. Each time a request is made, the PortalSettings object is re-created. The PortalSettings object is essential in the IBuySpy portal, providing information about the presentation of the Web application. The PortalSettings are stored in the application's Context object, which is accessible anywhere in the application during the life of a single request.

Reading the Portal Settings from the Database

The PortalSettings class is defined in the configuration.cs module. The PortalSettings are read from the portal database using the *tabindex* and *tabid* parameters as arguments to the GetPortalSettings stored procedure. In this section, we will look at the constructor for the PortalSettings class, including how to create, invoke, and obtain information from stored procedures using ADO.NET.

Implementing a Stored Procedure   The PortalSettings class is initialized from the stored procedure shown in Listing 13-5. When you create the portal, the script PortalDB.sql is run to create the portal database. One of the steps the script takes is to generate the GetPortalSettings stored procedure, and the procedure shown in Listing 13-5 modifies that stored procedure slightly and then retrieves specific portal setting values from the database in the PortalSettings constructor.

Listing 13-5   *A stored procedure that changes slightly based on portal context and is used to retrieve portal settings*

```
1:    ALTER PROCEDURE dbo.GetPortalSettings
2:    (
3:        @PortalAlias    nvarchar(50),
4:        @TabID          int,
```

```
 5:      @PortalID        int OUTPUT,
 6:      @PortalName      nvarchar(128) OUTPUT,
 7:      @AlwaysShowEditButton bit OUTPUT,
 8:      @TabName         nvarchar (50)  OUTPUT,
 9:      @TabOrder        int OUTPUT,
10:      @MobileTabName nvarchar (50)  OUTPUT,
11:      @AuthRoles       nvarchar (256) OUTPUT,
12:      @ShowMobile      bit OUTPUT
13: )
14: AS
15:
16: /* First, get Out Params */
17: IF @TabID = 0
18:     SELECT TOP 1
19:         @PortalID       = Portals.PortalID,
20:         @PortalName     = Portals.PortalName,
21:         @AlwaysShowEditButton = Portals.AlwaysShowEditButton,
22:         @TabID          = Tabs.TabID,
23:         @TabOrder       = Tabs.TabOrder,
24:         @TabName        = Tabs.TabName,
25:         @MobileTabName = Tabs.MobileTabName,
26:         @AuthRoles      = Tabs.AuthorizedRoles,
27:         @ShowMobile     = Tabs.ShowMobile
28:
29:     FROM
30:         Tabs
31:     INNER JOIN
32:         Portals ON Tabs.PortalID = Portals.PortalID
33:
34:     WHERE
35:         PortalAlias=@PortalAlias
36:
37:     ORDER BY
38:         TabOrder
39:
40: ELSE
41:     SELECT
42:         @PortalID       = Portals.PortalID,
43:         @PortalName     = Portals.PortalName,
44:         @AlwaysShowEditButton = Portals.AlwaysShowEditButton,
45:         @TabName        = Tabs.TabName,
46:         @TabOrder       = Tabs.TabOrder,
47:         @MobileTabName = Tabs.MobileTabName,
48:         @AuthRoles      = Tabs.AuthorizedRoles,
49:         @ShowMobile     = Tabs.ShowMobile
```

```
50:
51:      FROM
52:          Tabs
53:      INNER JOIN
54:          Portals ON Tabs.PortalID = Portals.PortalID
55:
56:      WHERE
57:          TabID=@TabID
58:
59: /* Get Tabs list */
60: SELECT
61:      TabName,
62:      AuthorizedRoles,
63:      TabID,
64:      TabOrder
65:
66: FROM
67:      Tabs
68:
69: WHERE
70:      PortalID = @PortalID
71:
72: ORDER BY
73:      TabOrder
74:
75: /* Get Mobile Tabs list */
76: SELECT
77:      MobileTabName,
78:      AuthorizedRoles,
79:      TabID,
80:      ShowMobile
81:
82: FROM
83:      Tabs
84:
85: WHERE
86:      PortalID = @PortalID
87:   AND
88:      ShowMobile = 1
89:
90: ORDER BY
91:      TabOrder
92:
93: /* Then, get the DataTable of module info */
94: SELECT
```

```
 95:      *
 96:
 97: FROM
 98:      Modules
 99:    INNER JOIN
100:      ModuleDefinitions ON Modules.ModuleDefID =
ModuleDefinitions.ModuleDefID
101:
102: WHERE
103:      TabID = @TabID
104:
105: ORDER BY
106:      ModuleOrder
```

We can't fit a stored procedure tutorial in the space available. A good SQL Server programmer's guide, such as *SQL Server 2000 Developer's Guide* by Michael Otey and Paul Conty (McGraw-Hill/Osborne), is an essential part of every database developer's toolkit. In addition, there are a couple of dozen stored procedures in the IBuySpy portal that you can borrow or learn from. I will provide you with a brief overview explaining how the stored procedures work and how they were used in the portal.

Stored procedures accept up to 2,100 parameters and can return parameters. Microsoft SQL Server's stored procedures can contain any number of T-SQL statements. The result is that you can package a large request for many bits of related data into a stored procedure, which, in turn, are all run in one group on the server and selectively return the data in the form of the output parameters that you are interested in. ALTER PROCEDURE dbo.GetPortalSettings defines two input parameters and eight output parameters—that is, we are getting eight pieces of data from the database from this one stored procedure.

The stored procedure in Listing 13-5 modifies GetPortalSettings based on the *TabId* passed in the URL-encoded request that I mentioned earlier in "Implementing Event Handlers in the Global.asax Module." A SELECT statement is added to the stored procedure based on the T-SQL If Else test on lines 17 through 58. Lines 59 through 73 obtain the tabs list. Lines 75 through 91 obtain the tabs list for the mobile device pages, and lines 93 through 106 obtain the module information.

Defining Input and Output Parameters for Stored Procedures   GetPortalSettings and other stored procedures represent a kind of encapsulation as a general strategy for enhancing performance. The stored procedure encapsulates several SELECT statements into a single, simpler package, and all of the SELECT queries run on the database server as a single request from the portal application. This reduces frequency of requests between the portal application and the database server, resulting in a tuned performance.

Now that we know the portal is using stored procedures to simplify programming and improve performance, we need to know how to invoke stored procedures using ADO.NET. (See Chapter 5 for an introduction to ADO.NET.) Listing 13-6 shows the constructor for the

PortalSettings class, which is initialized by invoking the GetPortalSettings stored procedure from Listing 13-5.

Listing 13-6   *The PortalSettings constructor demonstrates how stored procedures are used in the IBuySpy portal.*

```
1:  //**********************************************************************
2:  //
3:  // PortalSettings Constructor
4:  //
5:  // The PortalSettings Constructor encapsulates all of the logic
6:  // necessary to obtain configuration settings necessary to render
7:  // a Portal Tab view for a given request.
8:  //
9:  // These Portal Settings are stored within a SQL database, and are
10: // fetched below by calling the "GetPortalSettings" stored procedure.
11: // This stored procedure returns values as SPROC output parameters,
12: // and using three result sets.
13: //
14: //**********************************************************************
15:
16: public PortalSettings(int tabIndex, int tabId) {
17:
18:     // Create Instance of Connection and Command Object
19:     SqlConnection myConnection = new SqlConnection(
20:       ConfigurationSettings.AppSettings["connectionString"]);
21:     SqlCommand myCommand = new SqlCommand("GetPortalSettings", myConnection);
22:
23:     // Mark the Command as a SPROC
24:       myCommand.CommandType = CommandType.StoredProcedure;
25:
26:     // Add Parameters to SPROC
27:     SqlParameter parameterPortalAlias =
28:       new SqlParameter("@PortalAlias", SqlDbType.NVarChar, 50);
29:     parameterPortalAlias.Value = "p_default";
30:     myCommand.Parameters.Add(parameterPortalAlias);
31:
32:     SqlParameter parameterTabId =
33:       new SqlParameter("@TabId", SqlDbType.Int, 4);
34:     parameterTabId.Value = tabId;
35:     myCommand.Parameters.Add(parameterTabId);
```

```
36:
37:    // Add out parameters to Sproc
38:    SqlParameter parameterPortalID =
39:      new SqlParameter("@PortalID", SqlDbType.Int, 4);
40:    parameterPortalID.Direction = ParameterDirection.Output;
41:    myCommand.Parameters.Add(parameterPortalID);
42:
43:    SqlParameter parameterPortalName =
44:      new SqlParameter("@PortalName", SqlDbType.NVarChar, 128);
45:    parameterPortalName.Direction = ParameterDirection.Output;
46:    myCommand.Parameters.Add(parameterPortalName);
47:
48:    SqlParameter parameterEditButton =
49:      new SqlParameter("@AlwaysShowEditButton", SqlDbType.Bit, 1);
50:    parameterEditButton.Direction = ParameterDirection.Output;
51:    myCommand.Parameters.Add(parameterEditButton);
52:
53:    SqlParameter parameterTabName =
54:      new SqlParameter("@TabName", SqlDbType.NVarChar, 50);
55:    parameterTabName.Direction = ParameterDirection.Output;
56:    myCommand.Parameters.Add(parameterTabName);
57:
58:    SqlParameter parameterTabOrder =
59:      new SqlParameter("@TabOrder", SqlDbType.Int, 4);
60:    parameterTabOrder.Direction = ParameterDirection.Output;
61:    myCommand.Parameters.Add(parameterTabOrder);
62:
63:    SqlParameter parameterMobileTabName =
64:      new SqlParameter("@MobileTabName", SqlDbType.NVarChar, 50);
65:    parameterMobileTabName.Direction = ParameterDirection.Output;
66:    myCommand.Parameters.Add(parameterMobileTabName);
67:
68:    SqlParameter parameterAuthRoles =
69:      new SqlParameter("@AuthRoles", SqlDbType.NVarChar, 256);
70:    parameterAuthRoles.Direction = ParameterDirection.Output;
71:    myCommand.Parameters.Add(parameterAuthRoles);
72:
73:    SqlParameter parameterShowMobile =
74:      new SqlParameter("@ShowMobile", SqlDbType.Bit, 1);
75:    parameterShowMobile.Direction = ParameterDirection.Output;
76:    myCommand.Parameters.Add(parameterShowMobile);
77:
```

```
78:    // Open the database connection and execute the command
79:    myConnection.Open();
80:    SqlDataReader result = myCommand.ExecuteReader();
81:
82:    // Read the first resultset -- Desktop Tab Information
83:    while(result.Read()) {
84:
85:      TabStripDetails tabDetails = new TabStripDetails();
86:      tabDetails.TabId = (int) result["TabId"];
87:      tabDetails.TabName = (String) result["TabName"];
88:      tabDetails.TabOrder = (int) result["TabOrder"];
89:      tabDetails.AuthorizedRoles =
90:        (String) result["AuthorizedRoles"];
91:
92:      this.DesktopTabs.Add(tabDetails);
93:    }
94:
95:    if (this.ActiveTab.TabId == 0) {
96:      this.ActiveTab.TabId =
97:        ((TabStripDetails) this.DesktopTabs[0]).TabId;
98:    }
99:
100:   // Read the second result --  Mobile Tab Information
101:   result.NextResult();
102:
103:   while(result.Read()) {
104:
105:     TabStripDetails tabDetails = new TabStripDetails();
106:     tabDetails.TabId = (int) result["TabId"];
107:     tabDetails.TabName = (String) result["MobileTabName"];
108:     tabDetails.AuthorizedRoles =
109:       (String) result["AuthorizedRoles"];
110:
111:     this.MobileTabs.Add(tabDetails);
112:   }
113:
114:   // Read the third result --  Module Tab Information
115:   result.NextResult();
116:
117:   while(result.Read()) {
```

```
118:
119:    ModuleSettings m = new ModuleSettings();
120:    m.ModuleId = (int) result["ModuleID"];
121:    m.ModuleDefId = (int) result["ModuleDefID"];
122:    m.TabId = (int) result["TabID"];
123:    m.PaneName = (String) result["PaneName"];
124:    m.ModuleTitle = (String) result["ModuleTitle"];
125:    m.AuthorizedEditRoles = (String) result["AuthorizedEditRoles"];
126:    m.CacheTime = (int) result["CacheTime"];
127:    m.ModuleOrder = (int) result["ModuleOrder"];
128:    m.ShowMobile = (bool) result["ShowMobile"];
129:    m.DesktopSrc = (String) result["DesktopSrc"];
130:    m.MobileSrc = (String) result["MobileSrc"];
131:
132:    this.ActiveTab.Modules.Add(m);
133: }
134:
135: // Now read Portal out params
136: result.NextResult();
137:
138: this.PortalId = (int) parameterPortalID.Value;
139: this.PortalName = (String) parameterPortalName.Value;
140: this.AlwaysShowEditButton = (bool) parameterEditButton.Value;
141: this.ActiveTab.TabIndex = tabIndex;
142: this.ActiveTab.TabId = tabId;
143: this.ActiveTab.TabOrder = (int) parameterTabOrder.Value;
144: this.ActiveTab.MobileTabName = (String) parameterMobileTabName.Value;
145: this.ActiveTab.AuthorizedRoles = (String) parameterAuthRoles.Value;
146: this.ActiveTab.TabName = (String) parameterTabName.Value;
147: this.ActiveTab.ShowMobile = (bool) parameterShowMobile.Value;
148:
149: myConnection.Close();
150:}
```

NOTE

The code in Chapters 13, 14, 15, and 16 is provided by permission from Microsoft Corporation and is listed as it actually occurs in the IBuySpy portal, with only very modest changes for pagination purposes. The style reflects that of the author of the portal code, and the format and content was left intact to prevent unintentional modification. I will be referring to the PortalSettings Constructor in Listing 13-6 in this section and the next.

In Chapter 5 you learned about creating a connection object. The PortalSettings constructor creates an SQL provider connection object on lines 19 and 20 of Listing 13-6. One difference from Chapter 5 is the way in which the portal stores application information. The connection string is stored in the web.config file (see Listing 13-7). The ConfigurationSettings class's shared property AppSettings allows you to store and retrieve application settings from the <appSettings> element of the web.config file.

Listing 13-7 *The appSettings portion of the web.config file for the IBuySpy portal, accessible via the ConfigurationSettings class*

```
<!-- application specific settings -->
<appSettings>
<add key="ConnectionString"
value="server=localhost;Trusted_Connection=true;database=Portal" />
</appSettings>
```

Next, the constructor creates an SqlCommand object used to represent the stored procedure (see line 21 of Listing 13-6). On line 24, we indicate that the command type will be a stored procedure—CommandType.StoredProcedure. These first couple of steps are consistent with recurring behavior for executing stored procedures in general. The next general step is to express the in and out parameters for the stored procedure, followed by executing the stored procedure and retrieving any output values. (We'll look at running the stored procedure and retrieving output parameters in the next section.)

Parameters for stored procedures, like everything else in the .NET framework, are expressed as instances of classes. To create and send a parameter to a stored procedure, we need to create an instance of the SqlParameter (OleDbParameter for OLEDB providers) class and add the parameter object to the SqlCommand object's Parameters collection. Lines 26 through 30 of Listing 13-6 demonstrate an input parameter, the *PortalAlias*, and lines 38 through 40 demonstrate an output parameter. (There are several examples of both kinds of parameters in Listing 13-6.)

The SqlParameter constructor shown on line 28 of Listing 13-6 is initialized with the parameter name, data type, and size. (There are six overloaded constructors for the SqlParameter class.) Line 29 provides an input value for the *PortalAlias* input parameter, and line 30 adds the parameter to the SqlCommand.Parameters collection.

Output parameters are initialized similarly. Instead of providing a SqlCommand.Value representing the input argument for output parameters, we modify the SqlParameter.Direction value to be ParameterDirection.Output. An example of the difference between an input and an output parameter is shown on line 40 of Listing 13-6. When we have all of the input and output parameters expressed, we can invoke the stored procedure.

Invoking the GetPortalSettings Stored Procedure   After creating the connection, command, and parameter objects, we are ready to connect to the Portal, the default name of the IBuySpy database, and retrieve the results. Line 79 of Listing 13-6 opens the connection, and we use the SqlCommand object to execute the stored procedure. As we are only reading data, we can use an SqlDataReader to retrieve the output parameters. The SqlDataReader is returned from the SqlCommand.ExecuteReader method (line 80); then an SqlDataReader is a unidirectional, read-only cursor and yields a better performance than a DataSet.

Consistent with the order of the SELECT statements, we retrieve the result data by executing the Read to retrieve all of the desktop tab information. When all of the TabDetail objects are initialized from the resultset—lines 83 through 93, we move onto the next resultset by invoking SqlDataReader.NextResult, as demonstrated on line 101. This sequence of events is repeated until we have read all of the resultsets, and we wrap up the constructor by closing the connection (see line 150).

Notice that where there were possibly many rows of data returned in an individual resultset, we used a *while* loop and SqlDataReader.Read to retrieve all rows, and the output parameters were read using the parameter objects on lines 138, 139, 140, 143, 144, 145, 146, and 147. (The values tabIndex and tabId—lines 141 and 142—were passed into our constructor; we just store them in the PortalSettings.ActiveTab object.)

Debugging, Creating, and Modifying Stored Procedures Using stored procedures and ADO.NET represents a strategy you will see used consistently and repeatedly in the IBuySpy portal. Stored procedures are an optimal way to manage data and the disconnected ADO.NET model supports tremendous scalability. Understanding how one object is instantiated using stored procedures will allow you to work with all objects in the portal and any other application that employs this strategy. For more examples of classes that use this strategy in the portal, refer to the .cs source code files in the Components folder of the portal.

The final thing you need to know how to do is to write, modify, and debug stored procedures. The Visual Studio .NET IDE supports creating, modifying, and debugging stored procedures through the Server Explorer window (see Figure 13-11).

To create a new stored procedure, right-click the Stored Procedures node (see Figure 13-11) or any of the individual stored procedures, and select New Stored Procedure from the context menu. This step will create a template-stored procedure if you have the SQL Server Enterprise Manager installed. (The menu item will not be displayed if the Enterprise Manager is not installed on your workstation.)

To edit an existing stored procedure, select the stored procedure you want to edit and pick Edit Stored Procedure from the right-click context menu. You can also run or step into a particular stored procedure from the same menu. You might get an error (see Figure 13-12) if you try to debug a stored procedure and don't have adequate permissions to do so. Contact your administrator or click the Help button, shown in Figure 13-12, for instructions on resolving this problem. When you are stepping into a stored procedure, you can use breakpoints and watch values just as you would for debugging C# code.

Implementing the Page Load Init Handler

After the BeginRequest event is handled, the Page_Init event (followed by Page_Load) event is raised. The portal uses the Page_Init event handler to initialize the portal settings read from the stored procedure and stored in the HttpContext object at the end of the BeginRequest event. The Page_Init event handler for the DesktopDefault.aspx Web page is shown in Listing 13-8.

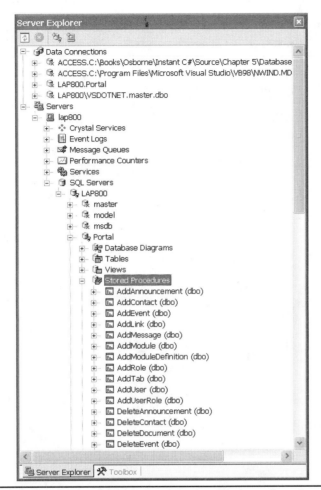

Figure 13-11   *The Server Explorer expanded to show the alphabetically ordered Stored Procedures for the IBuySpy portal*

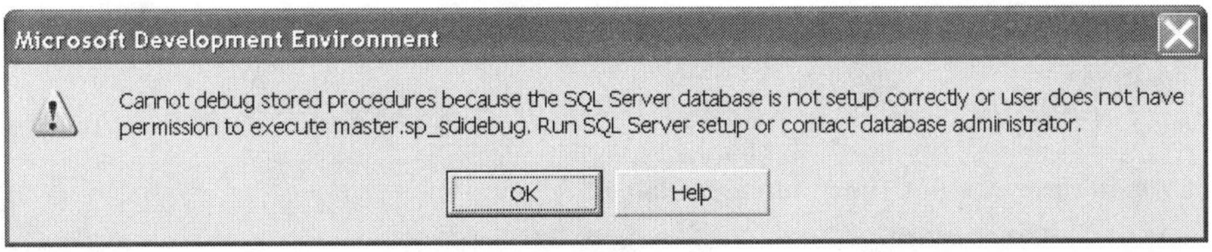

Figure 13-12   *Trying to debug a stored procedure from the Server Explorer without adequate permissions*

Listing 13-8 *The Page_Init event handler for the DesktopDefault.aspx Web page uses the PortalSettings object to initialize the page dynamically.*

```
1:   private void Page_Init(object sender, EventArgs e) {
2:       //
3:       // CODEGEN: This call is required by the ASP.NET Web
4:       // Form Designer.
5:       //
6:       InitializeComponent();
7:
8:       //********************************************************************
9:       //
10:      // Page_Init Event Handler
11:      //
12:      // The Page_Init event handler executes at the very beginning
13:      // of each page request (immediately before Page_Load).
14:      //
15:      // The Page_Init event handler below determines the tab
16:      //  index of the currently
17:      // requested portal view, and then calls the
18:      // PopulatePortalSection utility
19:      // method to dynamically populate the left,
20:      // center and right hand sections of the portal tab.
21:      //
22:      //********************************************************************
23:
24:      // Obtain PortalSettings from Current Context
25:      PortalSettings portalSettings =
26:       (PortalSettings) HttpContext.Current.Items["PortalSettings"];
27:
28:      // Ensure that the visiting user has access to the current page
29:      if (PortalSecurity.IsInRoles(
30:        portalSettings.ActiveTab.AuthorizedRoles) == false) {
31:        Response.Redirect("~/Admin/AccessDenied.aspx");
32:      }
33:
34:      // Dynamically inject a signin login module into the top
35:      // left-hand corner of the home page if the
36:      // client is not yet authenticated
37:      if ((Request.IsAuthenticated == false)
38:        && (portalSettings.ActiveTab.TabIndex == 0)) {
39:        LeftPane.Controls.Add(
40:          Page.LoadControl("~/DesktopModules/SignIn.ascx"));
41:        LeftPane.Visible = true;
42:      }
43:
```

```
44:    // Dynamically Populate the Left, Center and Right
45:    // pane sections of the portal page
46:    if (portalSettings.ActiveTab.Modules.Count > 0) {
47:
48:      // Loop through each entry in the configuration system for this tab
49:      foreach (ModuleSettings _moduleSettings in
50:        portalSettings.ActiveTab.Modules) {
51:
52:        Control parent = Page.FindControl(_moduleSettings.PaneName);
53:
54:        // If no caching is specified, create the user control
55:        // instance and dynamically
56:        // inject it into the page.  Otherwise, create a cached
57:        // module instance that
58:        // may or may not optionally inject the module into the tree
59:
60:        if ((_moduleSettings.CacheTime) == 0) {
61:
62:          PortalModuleControl portalModule =
63:            (PortalModuleControl) Page.LoadControl(
64:            _moduleSettings.DesktopSrc);
65:
66:          portalModule.PortalId = portalSettings.PortalId;
67:          portalModule.ModuleConfiguration = _moduleSettings;
68:
69:          parent.Controls.Add(portalModule);
70:        }
71:        else {
72:
73:          CachedPortalModuleControl portalModule =
74:            new CachedPortalModuleControl();
75:
76:          portalModule.PortalId = portalSettings.PortalId;
77:          portalModule.ModuleConfiguration = _moduleSettings;
78:
79:          parent.Controls.Add(portalModule);
80:        }
81:
82:        // Dynamically inject separator break between portal modules
82:        parent.Controls.Add(new LiteralControl("<" + "br" + ">"));
83:        parent.Visible = true;
84:      }
85:    }
86: }
```

The default Web page, DesktopDefault.aspx, has a very simple visual design, as shown in Figure 13-13. Essentially, the DesktopDefault.aspx Web page is composed of an instance of the DesktopPortalBanner.ascx UserControl and an HTML table. The rest of what you see (refer to Figure 13-1) in the portal is incorporated dynamically in the Page_Init event handler. (In fact, Listing 13-8 comprises all of the user-defined code for the DesktopDefault.aspx page, too.) Simplicity of design and flexibility of employing UserControls dynamically are benefits of programming with ASP.NET.

The user-defined code starts on lines 25 and 26 of Listing 13-8. Lines 25 and 26 obtain a local copy of the PortalSettings object we created in the BeginRequest event handler in the global.asax file. Lines 29 through 32 employ role-based security to determine whether we have permission to view the page indicated as the ActiveTab. If we don't, we are redirected to the AccessDenied.aspx page on line 31. (The tilde (~) indicates that the URL is relative to the root of the application. If you look in the admin folder in the project, you can view the design of the AccessDenied page.)

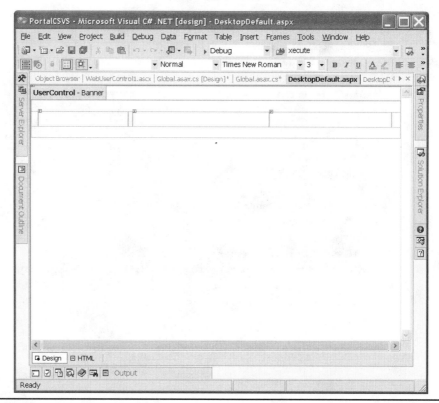

Figure 13-13   *The main page of the IBuySpy portal has a very basic design that includes a UserControl and an HTML table.*

If the user has not been authenticated, the SignIn.ascx control is added to the top-left pane (LeftPane) of the HTML table, as shown in Figure 13-1. Because of the way the portal is designed, The SignIn control will show up every time the DesktopDefault.aspx page is shown and we have not signed in.

Finally, the remainder of the code on lines 46 through 86 of Listing 13-8 iterates through all of the modules—these are dynamic controls associated with each tab, read from the database—and places these modules on the various data cells (called *panes* in the application). The PaneName is stored in the PortalSettings.ActiveTab.Modules collection—see line 49, and the ModuleSettings object has the PaneName property. Page.FindControl (ModuleSettings .PaneName) is used to locate a specific User Control on one of the HTML data cells on the page (see line 52).

TIP

Keep in mind that "module" is a term local to the IBuySpy portal. The portal uses "module" when referring to UserControls that make up the portal dynamic interface.

The pane name is resolved on line 52 of Listing 13-8. If the module has not been cached— line 60—then we dynamically load the module with Page.LoadControl, set the PortalId and ModuleSettings, and finish up by adding the module to the page's Controls collection. (These steps occur on lines 62 through 69.)

If the module has been cached, then an instance of the portal-defined CachedPortalModule Control is created, initialized, and added to the page's Controls collection. For more information on caching, refer to Chapter 15.

After each module is added, a line separator—the <BR> tag—is inserted into the page dynamically. Line 82 of Listing 13-8 demonstrates how to dynamically insert a LiteralControl into a Web page. (Refer to Chapter 14 for more information on creating custom server controls.) The loop continues until all modules have been added to the dynamic page. The result of dynamic page creation for the Home tab can be seen in Figure 13-1.

Reviewing the Portal Design

Clearly, there is a lot more going on in the portal than the simple design of the DesktopDefault.aspx page and the code in Listing 13-8. Knowing this is essential to understanding the elegance of the portal design.

The are a relatively few number of IBuySpy pages, yet the user experience is very rich. The key is that the Web pages are fairly generic, and it is the UserControls, referred to as modules, that make up the rich and dynamic nature of the IBuySpy portal. This is as it should be. Essentially, the developers of the portal are demonstrating best practices that are consistent with good OOP practices; that is, make the individual elements self-responsible through the class idiom. For example, the Sign-In module is an independent class that knows about accepting user names and passwords and authentication. Consequently, the modules can be plugged in anywhere they are needed—in effect, reused.

A significant amount of what you see in the portal is a combination of UserControls and cascading styles. Refer to Chapter 14 for more information on creating the UserControls that make up the rich and dynamic client experience.

Secondary Topics

The IBuySpy is a diverse playground for exploring .NET technologies. We have demonstrated many of the facets of .NET used to create this rich Web portal application, and I would like to take this opportunity to showcase some of the supporting cast of features that you can incorporate into your own projects or that will make your interaction with the portal a successful experience.

Administrating the Portal

The IBuySpy portal supports dynamic administration. As shown in Figure 13-1, the portal supports user authentication. The kind of security exemplified is role-based security managed by the portal itself. You can add new users with the sign-in module or log in with user=guest and password=guest. (Refer to Chapter 16 for more information on portal and .NET security.)

If you sign in with the default administrative password, "guest," or any other administrative password, the portal will display an Admin tab and additional administrative links. The Admin tab and administrative links allow non-programmers to customize the portal (see Figure 13-14). More important, these features provide a clear path (with some exploration) that demonstrates how you can implement a Web application that supports management and extensibility by a remote user, even non-programmers.

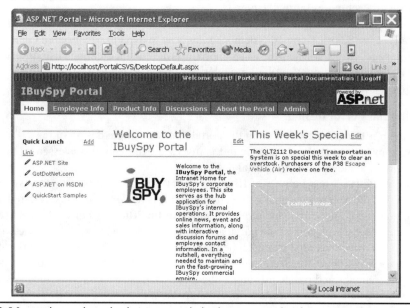

Figure 13-14   *Admin tab and administrative links that support the dynamic and remote customizations*

TIP

Remember that the IBuySpy portal represents an intranet application for corporate employees.

For example, notice that the portal shown in Figure 13-14 contains an Example Image: this week's special, the Document Transport System. Knowing that there was a significant surplus of Night Vision goggles, a portal administrative user elects to make the surplus goggles this week's special. By logging in as an administrator and clicking the Edit link by "This Week's Special" (see Figure 13-14), the administrative user can quickly update the weekly special reminder directly from the portal.

To modify the portal, click the aforementioned edit link. Modify the text and <img src> tag to refer to the content representing a new promotion for Night Vision Goggles. (See Figure 13-15 for an example of the Administrative management facilities demonstrated in IBuySpy.) Click the Update link when you have finished, and the revisions will be made. If you look at the initial page content and the revised content in Figure 13-15, you will notice that I updated some of the text content and the image link. (Being a conscientious manager, I would, of course, go look up the productID, too.)

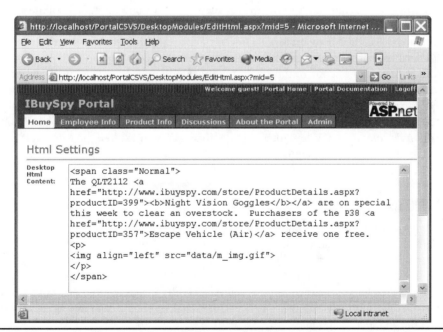

Figure 13-15   *Update the portal dynamically using the built-in administrative capabilities.*

Debugging the IBUYSPY Portal

When you download the Portal, you will not be immediately able to step through the application. The portal code online was modified slightly to support a product-ready state. The portal installs and sets up very smoothly, but you will need to make one additional change to debug the portal.

To debug the IBuySpy portal code in Visual Studio .NET, you will need to open the web.config file, find the <compilation debug=false> tag, and change the value to True. (The new value will be <compilation debug=true>.) After the change, you will be able to easily explore and debug all of the portal code.

Introducing Mobile Modules

The IBuySpy portal demonstrates how to use Microsoft's Mobile Internet Toolkit to leverage the same core code for Web-enabled mobile devices like WAP phones and PDAs. If you download and install the Microsoft Mobile Internet Toolkit (MMIT) from **www.microsoft.com**, you will be able to experiment with the pages for mobile devices that ship with the portal code.

MMIT is beyond the scope of this book, but it is worth repeating that a well-architected application will allow you to leverage the same basic object-oriented code for mobile devices with .NET. Separate the business objects from the interface and the mobile toolkit will allow you to reuse the same code for your mobile application development. (My book *.NET Mobile Application Development* (Wiley), due out later this year, will explore the Microsoft Mobile Internet Toolkit and .NET in depth.)

Summary

The IBuySpy portal is an excellent resource for developers trying to get the most out of ASP.NET and C# as early as possible. Microsoft has provided this portal application and made the code available for learning or outright use by developers.

In addition to gaining an understanding of aspects of .NET by exploring the IBuySpy portal, in this chapter you learned more about ADO.NET, T-SQL, stored procedures, creating dynamic user interfaces, cascading style sheets, the DataList control, and managing application events in the global.asax module.

Chapters 14, 15, and 16 explore Web UserControls, caching, and security as they are employed in the IBuySpy portal. Borrowing from the best practices made available to us by Microsoft and Susan Warren, you will be building scalable, dynamic enterprise applications in ASP.NET and C# right out of the gate.

CHAPTER
14

Creating Custom Web Controls

IN THIS CHAPTER:

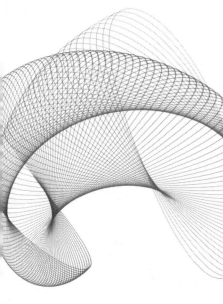

C ontrols are simply classes with a visual aspect. From this perspective, a control is at least as powerful as a class, and their visual representation makes controls more powerful than the average class. As powerful as visual classes are, it is just as important to design your application in an object-oriented way when designing the business objects as well as the graphical user interface. This is the approach the IBuySpy portal takes.

In the IBuySpy portal, controls are central to the implementation of the portal. The IBuySpy portal implements a common UserControl that is the base class for many of the modules in the portal application. This chapter will explore the user controls—referred to as "modules"—in the IBuySpy portal and demonstrate how to extend the portal application consistent with the architectural strategy used to build the IBuySpy portal.

Demonstrated Topics

This chapter zooms in on the IBuySpy portal controls and the .NET classes used to implement these controls. There are seven basic modules that ship with the Portal example, affording a wide variety of dynamically generated Web pages. This chapter will describe inheriting from and implementing a custom UserControl and will demonstrate how to

► Render controls dynamically using an HtmlWriter

► Generalize the PortalModuleControl

► Bind data to the DataList control

► Create the links module

► Use an XSL transform to format XML data, separating the data from the appearance of the data

The "Secondary Topics" section explores the HttpServerUtility class and introduces the Repeater control. The Repeater control aids us in presenting read-only data on a Web page.

Rendering Controls Dynamically

The Render method is roughly the equivalent of a Window's Form Paint method. Instead of a GDI+ Graphics object, you get an HtmlTextWriter. The HtmlTextWriter represents the output stream for a server control as it is being rendered to a Web page. You can override the Render method in a custom server control to enhance the appearance of server controls or add content as the control is being rendered.

The portal uses a Render method in a couple of distinct places. We'll look at the portal's usage of the Render method after we spend a moment exploring how to create custom server controls.

Creating a Custom Server Control

You can create a custom server control by creating a new class library and defining a new class that inherits from System.Web.UI.Control. Override the Render method inherited from Control, and you have a custom server control.

> **NOTE**
>
> Creating a custom server control from the Control class is the last thing you want to do. The reason is simple. You want to reuse as much code as possible and do the job of creating the control as efficiently as possible. Consequently, you will want to start with the control that provides as much of the functionality as possible already. If you need to create a compositional control, then the best starting place is the User Control. Susan Warren at Microsoft said that a control derived from the User Control is almost always the best choice. This perspective is reflected in the IBuySpy portal.

Listing 14-1 implements a custom user control that has one Text property and simply displays the value of the Text property. The HelloWorld control is a server control because it inherits from System.Web.UI.Control, and is a simple approximation of a Label.

Listing 14-1   *A basic custom server control inherits from System.Web.UI.Control and overrides the Render method.*

```
1:   using System;
2:   using System.Web;
3:   using System.Web.UI;
4:
5:   namespace ServerControl
6:   {
7:     public class HelloWorld : Control
8:     {
9:       private string text;
10:      public string Text
11:      {
12:        get{ return text; }
13:        set{ text=value; }
14:      }
15:
16:      protected override void Render(HtmlTextWriter writer)
17:      {
18:        writer.RenderBeginTag("i");
19:        writer.Write(Text);
20:        writer.RenderEndTag();
21:      }
```

```
22:   }
23: }
```

Lines 2 and 3 of Listing 14-1 add *using* statements for namespaces containing code we are likely to need for any server control. Line 5 provides a namespace for the control, which we'll need in a moment to register our user control. Line 7 demonstrates inheritance from System.Web.UI.Control, making this simple class a server control. Lines 9 through 14 introduce the single additional field and related property, and lines 16 through 21 implement the overridden Render method.

Render receives a single HtmlTextWriter, representing our IO stream of HTML content. As the page is rendered, the various controls are processed. This is our chance to describe our control as HTML. The HtmlTextWriter.RenderBeginTag writes the tag brackets for us. For example, **writer.RenderBeginTag("i")** will add the italicize tag, <i>, to the stream. The Write method on line 19 of Listing 14-1 sends the literal text to the HTML stream, and line 20 closes the previously opened tag. Assigning the HelloWorld.Text property the literal "Hello, World!", the rendered HTML is <i>Hello, World!</i>, and the rendered output is *Hello, World!*

You could employ variations on the Render method. For example, you could write the entire literal content to the stream as follows:

```
writer.Write("<i>Hello, World!</i>");
```

For very simple output this approach works well, but the number of tags and variety of attributes can be difficult to manage as literal text.

There are a couple of dozen methods defined by the HtmlTextWriter for rendering HTML. You can render simple or complex compositional controls by defining a custom server control. You will find that it is much easier to create compositional controls using the User Control, and new controls can more easily be contrived from an existing control than by starting from scratch.

Incorporating the Custom Server Control into a Web Page

In the preceding section, we defined a custom control as a class defined in a DLL assembly. To incorporate the control into an ASP.NET application, we will need to reference the DLL, register the assembly, and include the control in the <body> of our ASP.NET Web page.

I created the HelloWorld control in the ServerControl.csproj, which is available for download at **www.osborne.com** (or **www.softconcepts.com**). I also created the ConsumeServerControl.csproj. ConsumeServerControl is a Web application containing a single page that demonstrates how to register the control and add an instance of the server control to the page. Listing 14-2 provides a complete sample Web page, providing an example of the HTML that shows the additional steps necessary to consume the custom control.

TIP

The Register statement is case sensitive.

Listing 14-2   *Registering the custom control and adding a single instance to the otherwise blank Web page*

```
1:   <%@ Page language="c#" Codebehind="WebForm1.aspx.cs"
AutoEventWireup="false" Inherits="ConsumerServerControl.WebForm1" %>
2:   <%@ Register TagPrefix="ACSP" Namespace="ServerControl"
Assembly="ServerControl"%>
3:   <!DOCTYPE HTML PUBLIC "-//W3C//DTD HTML 4.0 Transitional//EN" >
4:   <HTML>
5:     <HEAD>
6:       <title>WebForm1</title>
7:       <meta content="Microsoft Visual Studio 7.0" name="GENERATOR">
8:       <meta content="C#" name="CODE_LANGUAGE">
9:       <meta content="JavaScript" name="vs_defaultClientScript">
10:      <meta content="http://schemas.microsoft.com/intellisense/ie5"
name="vs_targetSchema">
11:    </HEAD>
12:    <body MS_POSITIONING="GridLayout">
13:      <ACSP:HelloWorld runat="server" id="HelloWorld1" Text="Hello,
World!" />
14:    </body>
15: </HTML>
```

The boldfaced statements indicate the part of the code that I added. Line 2 of Listing 14-2 implements the @Register statement. The @Register statement associates the alias with an actual namespace. In the example, the alias ACSP (*Advanced C# Programming*) is associated with the namespace ServerControl. TagPrefix defines the alias. Namespace provides the complete real namespace name, and Assembly provides the name of the assembly containing the namespace. (If you recall, when we create a class library, by default the assembly and namespace names are identical.)

Line 13 of Listing 14-2 demonstrates how to add an instance of the control to the page. The runat attribute indicates that this control should be processed on the server. The id attribute provides a unique name for the control. If we wanted to refer to this control in the code-behind page, we would need to add a field in the code-behind page with the same name as the one indicated in the id attribute. The Text attribute sets the value of the Text property. Listing 14-3 shows an example of a code-behind page that defines the HelloWorld1 field, allowing us to programmatically modify the HelloWorld control.

Listing 14-3   *Adding a matching field in the code-behind page allows us to programmatically interact with the custom control.*

```
1:   using System;
2:   using System.Collections;
3:   using System.ComponentModel;
```

```
4:  using System.Data;
5:  using System.Drawing;
6:  using System.Web;
7:  using System.Web.SessionState;
8:  using System.Web.UI;
9:  using System.Web.UI.WebControls;
10: using System.Web.UI.HtmlControls;
11:
12: namespace ConsumerServerControl
13: {
14:    /// <summary>
15:    /// Summary description for WebForm1.
16:    /// </summary>
17:    public class WebForm1 : System.Web.UI.Page
18:    {
19:
20:        protected ServerControl.HelloWorld HelloWorld1;
21:        private void Page_Load(object sender, System.EventArgs e)
22:        {
23:           // Put user code to initialize the page here
24:        }
25:
26:        [Web Form Designer generated code]
27:
28:        private void WebForm1_Init(object sender, System.EventArgs e)
29:        {
30:           HelloWorld1.Text = "Hello, World!";
31:        }
32:    }
33: }
```

The boldfaced case statement on line 20 of Listing 14-3 contains the field statement I added to facilitate referring to the HelloWorld1 control programmatically. For example, line 30 initializes the HelloWorld1.Text property each time the page is initialized.

As defined, our control will always be initialized to have the "Hello, World!" text. This behavior is consistent with a static text Label control. What if we wanted to create a control that was modified by the user and maintain its value when we post the control back to the server? We would have to code behavior to allow a custom server control to save state information between post-backs.

Saving Control State

For a custom control to maintain state between page posts, we need to implement the IPostBackDataHandler in the custom control class. IPostBackDataHandler requires that we implement LoadPostData and RaisePostDataChangedEvent methods. LoadPostData will let us read the value from the ViewState, and RaisePostDataChangedEvent gives us an opportunity to raise a changed event.

Retaining Control Value Between Form Posts

Sometimes you will want to retain state information between form posts and other times not. For example, you would more than likely want to save state information for the user name portion of a login control, but not for the password information. That is, you would not want to populate the password field on post-back and thereby possibly allow someone else to borrow another user's password.

To support this dynamic relationship, we could implement a custom server control that displays and supports post-backs for the user name but not the password. Combining static text with an <input> tag in a base control, we can implement the basic behavior that displays a prompt and an input box. Listing 14-4 provides an implementation of a custom control and a generalized version of the custom control that implements the password behavior. (Remember the password does not support the post-back behavior.)

Listing 14-4   *A base class that renders a prompt and input control, and a subclass that implements the password control*

```
1:   using System;
2:   using System.Web;
3:   using System.Web.UI;
4:   using System.Web.UI.WebControls;
5:   using System.Collections.Specialized;
6:
7:   namespace ServerControl
8:   {
9:     public class InputBox : Control
10:    {
11:      private string fieldValue;
12:      private string prompt;
13:      private string type;
14:
15:      public string FieldValue
16:      {
17:        get{ return fieldValue; }
18:        set{ fieldValue = value; }
19:      }
20:
21:      public string Prompt
22:      {
23:        get{ return prompt; }
24:        set{ prompt = value; }
```

```
25:     }
26:
27:     public string Type
28:     {
29:       get{ return type; }
30:       set{ type = value; }
31:     }
32:
33:     protected override void Render(HtmlTextWriter writer)
34:     {
35:       writer.AddStyleAttribute("width", "125");
36:       writer.RenderBeginTag("b");
37:       writer.Write(prompt);
38:       writer.RenderEndTag();
39:       writer.AddAttribute("type", type);
40:       writer.AddAttribute("value", fieldValue);
41:       writer.AddAttribute("Name", UniqueID);
42:       writer.AddStyleAttribute("width", "125");
43:       writer.RenderBeginTag("input");
44:       writer.RenderEndTag();
45:     }
46:   }
47:
48:   public class PasswordText: InputBox
49:   {
50:     public PasswordText() : base()
51:     {
52:       Prompt = "Password: ";
53:       Type = "password";
54:     }
55:   }
56: }
```

Lines 9 through 46 of Listing 14-4 implement the base class, InputBox. InputBox allows the user to express the text value of the prompt and the type of the input tag. The Prompt property will be the value displayed in the label, and the type will be used as a Type attribute for the <input> tag. (Initialize Type with "text" and we get a basic HTML text box. Initialize Type with "password" and we get a basic password textbox, which masks the input characters.)

Lines 48 through 54 of Listing 14-4 implement the PasswordText custom control. PasswordText provides a simple constructor that initializes the control to have a prompt and <input> tag type of "password"—all suitable for a control used to enter passwords. With the PasswordText control, we don't want to post the value of the PasswordText control back to the form. On the other hand, it would be appropriate to post back a non-password value, like a user name.

Posting Form Data

Listing 14-5 demonstrates how to implement the IPostBackEventHandler. The IPostBackEventHandler interface is used to implement the UserNameText control. UserNameText generalizes InputBox and realizes the IPostBackDataHandler.

Listing 14-5   *Supporting form post-back state retention*

```
1:   public class UserNameText: InputBox, IPostBackDataHandler
2:   {
3:     public UserNameText() : base()
4:     {
5:       Prompt = "User Name: ";
6:       Type = "text";
7:     }
8:
9:     public virtual bool LoadPostData(string key,
10:       NameValueCollection values)
11:    {
12:      if (FieldValue == null || !FieldValue.Equals(values[key]))
13:      {
14:        FieldValue = values[key];
15:        return true;
16:      }
17:      return false;
18:    }
19:
20:    public virtual void RaisePostDataChangedEvent(){}
21:  }
```

Listing 14-5 implements the IPostBackDataHandler.LoadPostData method. The NameValueCollection class is defined in the System.Collections.Specialized namespace. The NameValueCollection represents all of the incoming names and associated values when a page is posted back. The code on lines 9 through 18 obtains this value and assigns it to the FieldValue property if the form's value is different from the object's value.

The RaisePostDataChangedEvent can be used to call a method that raises an event indicating that the value has changed. If you need to use this aspect of the IPostBackDataHandler, add an event statement to the class and implement a method with an On prefix that raises the event, for example, OnDataChanged. Then, call OnDataChanged from the RaisePostDataChangedEvent method, calling the event handler through the event added to the control class.

Creating a Composite Custom Control

A composite control is a custom control composed of multiple child controls. An excellent way to build composite controls is to inherit from and add controls to the UserControl class. However, you can create a composite control programmatically by inheriting from the System.Web.UI.Control class, realizing the INamingContainer interface and overriding the CreateChildControls method.

The INamingContainer interface does not require you to implement any members. What it does for you is ensure that child controls have unique names on a page, even if you use more than one instance of the composite control on the same page.

The CreateChildControls method adds all of the child controls that make up the composite to the custom control's Controls collection. To demonstrate a composite control we can make a new custom control from the UserNameText and PasswordText custom controls. Because both of these controls already know how to render themselves, our composite control does not need to implement a Render method. Listing 14-6 implements the custom server control that I named SignIn.

Listing 14-6 *Creating a composite custom server control, SignIn, comprised of two nested child controls*

```
1:   public class SignIn : Control, INamingContainer
2:   {
3:     private UserNameText GetUserNameTextBox()
4:     {
5:       return (UserNameText)Controls[1];
6:     }
7:
8:     private PasswordText GetPasswordText()
9:     {
10:      return (PasswordText)Controls[3];
11:    }
12:
13:    public string UserName
14:    {
15:      get{ return GetUserNameTextBox().FieldValue; }
16:      set{ GetUserNameTextBox().FieldValue = value; }
17:    }
18:
19:    public string Password
20:    {
21:      get{ return GetPasswordText().FieldValue; }
22:      set{ GetPasswordText().FieldValue = value; }
23:    }
```

```
24:
25:    protected override void CreateChildControls()
26:    {
27:      Controls.Add(new LiteralControl("<hr>"));
28:      Controls.Add(new UserNameText());
29:      Controls.Add(new LiteralControl("<br>"));
30:      Controls.Add(new PasswordText());
31:    }
32: }
```

As far as classes go, SignIn is not very complex. Inheriting from System.Web.UI.Control and overriding CreateChildControl makes it a custom server control, and adding more than one child control makes it a composite control. Throwing in the INamingContainer interface manages unique names for the child controls. Figure 14-1 shows the SignIn control rendered on a Web page.

The composite control is incorporated in the Web page in the same way as every other custom control. Add a Register directive at the top of the page and include the tag reference to the composite control. (Refer to Listing 14-2 for a syntactical example, demonstrating how to add custom controls.)

The composite custom server control SignIn exemplifies an important strategic way to program. By slowly building up controls—beginning with the InputBox—the composite control was very easy to create. The same strategy is used to create a beautiful finish on furniture or compose complex symphonies. Several light applications yield a finish on furniture that appears to have depth. Complex symphonies begin with a few simple notes,

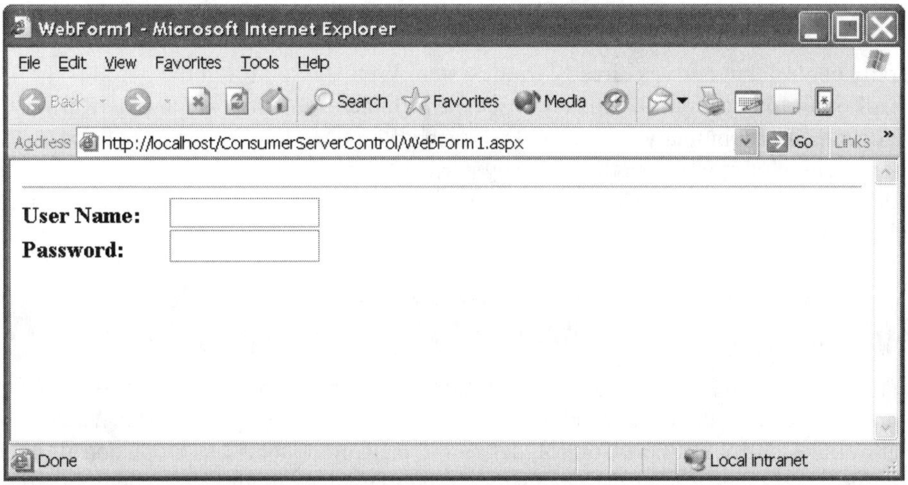

Figure 14-1   *The rendered custom server control, SignIn*

layering in complexity and instruments as the piece progresses. The same is true of software. Layering in complexity and adding changes in small increments is simpler than trying to manage code created in monolithic leaps and bounds.

Using the WebControl Library Project Template

The System.Web.UI.WebControls.WebControl class is a good starting place for creating custom server controls. The WebControl class contains properties for managing the appearance of a server control, public events for responding to interaction with the control, and methods that you might expect to find in a server control. For example, WebControl introduces a DataBind method that can be called to bind a server control to a data source. You will find that many Web controls are derived from the WebControl class, which extracts out the behavior common to most Web controls.

If you want to customize the rendering behavior of a control derived from the WebControl, then override the RenderContent method.

When you want to create a custom server control, create a new class library containing a class that inherits from the WebControl class. You can easily accomplish this by selecting the Web Control Library template from the New Project dialog. In general, consider these guidelines when creating new Web controls:

- ▶ Implement a new Web control by inheriting from the UserControl. (This approach should work in most cases.)
- ▶ If you need a finer degree of control, consider using the WebControl.
- ▶ If you want to start from scratch, inherit from the Control class.

Reviewing Custom Controls in the Portal

The only control that derives directly from System.Web.UI.Control in the portal is the CachedPortalModuleControl. This is consistent with the idea that you can inherit from a less-general control in many instances. The CachedPortalModuleControl is defined to support caching of modules in the IBuySpy portal. As this control emphasizes caching, we will defer exploration of the CachedPortalModuleControl until the thorough treatment of caching in Chapter 15.

Reviewing the PortalModuleControl Base Control

The specific use of the term "module" in reference to IBuySpy refers to UserControls that are derived from the PortalModuleControl, defined in the IBuySpy portal. The PortalModuleControl is a UserControl, defined in the Components\DesktopControls.cs file, that defines portal-specific properties that are used to manage module presentation.

Exploring Base Control Properties

The PortalModuleControl introduces five public properties that every module will inherit. These properties are ModuleId, PortalId, IsEditable, ModuleConfiguration, and Settings. The ModuleId is a key value that is central to navigating the data in the Portal database. The PortalId is used to identify specific instances of the portal. The IsEditable property is used to determine whether modules can be modified. The ModuleConfiguration property returns a ModuleSettings object that defines detailed information for a specific tab. The Settings property returns a Hashtable containing specific module settings based on the ModuleId. The module settings are retrieved from PortalSettings.GetModuleSettings, which invokes the GetModuleSettings stored procedure. The GetModuleSettings stored procedure returns information from the ModuleSettings table. For example, the ModuleSettings table contains setting names and values that point to external information, such as the image for "This Week's Special" found in the ImageModule.ascx control.

The benefit of sharing these properties in a base class is that they act as a common stringer that provides the infrastructure for orchestrating existing and new modules on a Web page added to the portal application. We'll return to these properties in the upcoming section "Creating a Custom Portal Module."

Using Control Attributes

The PortalModuleControl applies two attributes to every property defined by the custom UserControl: they are the BrowsableAttribute and the DesignerSerializationVisibilityAttribute. The BrowsableAttribute prevents a property from showing up in the Properties window. The DesignerSerializationVisibilityAttribute is used to describe how a property is serialized. You can read more about these attributes in Chapter 10.

NOTE

In spoken languages, we support the notion of people specializing in linguistics. I consider myself an object-oriented linguist. By exploring common idioms in various languages, I have discovered that it helps to understand how aspects of language work by finding related idioms in other languages. Borland has an excellent language, Delphi. The Delphi language introduces the concept of the published access modifier. Properties marked as published in Delphi show up in Delphi's properties window. C# does not support a published access modifier; instead, C# uses attributes to accomplish the same thing. Public properties will show in the Properties window of Visual Studio .NET unless the Browsable Attribute is initialized with False.

Binding the Tabs Data

The DesktopPortalBanner module uses a DataList to display the tabs for the portal. The DataList.DataSource property can be bound to any object that implements the System .Collections.IEnumerable interface.

The DesktopPortalBanner iterates over the PortalSettings.DesktopTabs and determines whether a specific tab is supported by the user's role. If the tab has features supported by the user's role, the object representing the tab details are added to an ArrayList. The ArrayList containing the tab details is assigned to the DataList.DataSource property, and the DataList.DataBind method is called. This aspect of the IBuySpy portal can be explored in the Page_Load event for the DesktopPortalBanner module (see Listing 14-7).

Listing 14-7   *An example that binds an ArrayList to a DataList control, dynamically creating the DesktopPortalBanner tabs*

```
1:   private void Page_Load(object sender, System.EventArgs e)
2:   {
3:     // Obtain PortalSettings from Current Context
4:     PortalSettings portalSettings = (PortalSettings)
5:       HttpContext.Current.Items["PortalSettings"];
6:
7:     // Dynamically Populate the Portal Site Name
8:     siteName.Text = portalSettings.PortalName;
9:
10:    // If user logged in, customize welcome message
11:    if (Request.IsAuthenticated == true) {
12:
13:      WelcomeMessage.Text = "Welcome " +
14:        Context.User.Identity.Name + "! <"
15:        + "span class=Accent" + ">|<" + "/span" + ">";
16:
17:      // if authentication mode is Cookie, provide a logoff link
18:      if (Context.User.Identity.AuthenticationType == "Forms") {
19:        LogoffLink = "<" + "span class=\"Accent\">|</span>\n" +
20:        "<" + "a href=" + Request.ApplicationPath
21:        + "/Admin/Logoff.aspx class=SiteLink> Logoff" + "<" + "/a>";
22:      }
23:    }
24:
25:    // Dynamically render portal tab strip
23:    if (ShowTabs == true) {
24:      tabIndex = portalSettings.ActiveTab.TabIndex;
25:
26:      // Build list of tabs to be shown to user
27:      ArrayList authorizedTabs = new ArrayList();
28:      int addedTabs = 0;
29:
30:      for (int i=0; i < portalSettings.DesktopTabs.Count; i++) {
31:        TabStripDetails tab =
32:          (TabStripDetails)portalSettings.DesktopTabs[i];
```

```
33:
34:        if (PortalSecurity.IsInRoles(tab.AuthorizedRoles)) {
35:          authorizedTabs.Add(tab);
36:        }
37:
38:        if (addedTabs == tabIndex) {
39:          tabs.SelectedIndex = addedTabs;
40:        }
41:
42:        addedTabs++;
43:      }
44:
45:      // Populate Tab List at Top of the Page with authorized tabs
47:      tabs.DataSource = authorizedTabs;
48:      tabs.DataBind();
49:    }
50: }
```

The PortalSettings are retrieved from the HttpContext on lines 4 and 5 of Listing 14-7. If the user is authenticated—lines 11 through 23—then a welcome message and a Logoff link is displayed. Lines 23 through 43 iterate through the possible tabs, examining the role associated with the tab and the role of the current user; if the tab and user roles coincide, then the tab is added to the ArrayList, authorizedTabs. Finally, authorizedTabs is assigned to the DataList's DataSource property, and the DataBind method is called.

The DesktopPortalBanner demonstrates how you can use controls and control binding to bind to collections of objects that are not part of ADO.NET. This means you can take advantage of ease-of-use ADO.NET without trying to force all objects to look like database objects. (We'll discuss the role-based security strategy employed in Listing 14-7 and the portal in Chapter 16.)

Visually Designing the SignIn Module

All modules in the IBuySpy portal use a basic approach to design. The controls and layout are quite simple (see Figure 14-2). The fit and finish is created by applying the portal.css cascading style sheet and adding programmatic customizations.

The SignIn control is made up of three spans, two TextBox controls, one CheckBox control, an HTML table, and two images. Account Login, Email, and Password are defined using the <span> tag. The <span> tag allows you to select a region of an HTML document and wrap it in the tag. You may then apply attributes or a style sheet class to the controls or text contained within the span. For example, the Account Login text is wrapped in the following <span> tag.

```
<span class="SubSubHead" style="HEIGHT: 20px">Account Login</span>
```

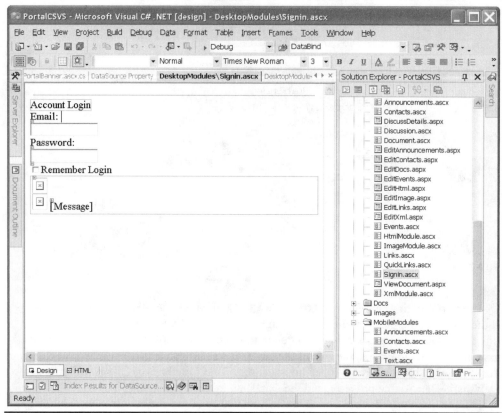

Figure 14-2   *The design-time view of the SignIn.ascx module*

The cascading style sheet class is SubSubHead, and the height of the span is 20 pixels. You can look in the portal.css for the style rule for the SubSubHead class.

NOTE

The Insert | Span menu item will not be enabled if the document's targetSchema is set to Internet Explorer 3.02/Navigator 3.0 in the Properties window. However, you can enter the <span> tag manually into the HTML text. You will get a warning indicating that it is not supported by the current schema.

The TextBox and CheckBox controls are ASP.NET Web Controls, and the sign-in and register links are actually images that are associated with a hyperlink. The rendered SignIn.ascx control is shown in Figure 14-3. The code for the Signin.ascx module is relatively short, demonstrating forms authentication and using cookies. We'll defer a discussion on these topics until Chapter 16.

Account Login

Email:

Password:

☐ Remember Login

➡ sign-in

➡ register

Figure 14-3   *The rendered SignIn.ascx module*

Creating the Image Module

Custom controls do not have to be complex to be useful. Keeping custom controls short and sweet will actually allow greater reuse and create fewer defects. The ImageModule.ascx module exemplifies this notion. This very simple module is composed of the DesktopModuleTitle .ascx control added to a second user control with an ASP.NET image control. (The image control is defined in the System.Web.UI.WebControls namespace.)

Recall that in administration mode you can dynamically change the image referred to by this module. This humble module will eliminate the need to implement the layout of an image and related text more than just one time. Figure 14-4 shows the rendered ImageModule displaying the title Night Vision and the related image. Listing 14-8 shows the Page_Load event handler, which is responsible for managing the width and height of the image.

This Week's Special

The QLT2112 **Night Vision Goggles** are on special this week to clear an overstock. Purchasers of the P38 Escape Vehicle (Air) receive one free.

Night Vision

Figure 14-4   *The ImageModule manages a simple image and title and an edit link in administration mode (not shown).*

Listing 14-8   *Code that manages the ImageModule's image height and width*

```
private void Page_Load(object sender, System.EventArgs e) {

  String imageSrc = (String) Settings["src"];
  String imageHeight = (String) Settings["height"];
  String imageWidth = (String) Settings["width"];

  // Set Image Source, Width and Height Properties
  if ((imageSrc != null) && (imageSrc != "")) {
    Image1.ImageUrl = imageSrc;
  }

  if ((imageWidth != null) && (imageWidth != "")) {
    Image1.Width = Int32.Parse(imageWidth);
  }

  if ((imageHeight != null) && (imageHeight != "")) {
    Image1.Height = Int32.Parse(imageHeight);
  }
}
```

The dynamic image path, height, and width are read from the inherited Settings property. (We discussed the Settings property in the earlier section "Exploring Base Control Properties.") The Settings property is initialized by calling the PortalSettings.GetModuleSettings method. The PortalSettings.GetModuleSettings method calls a stored procedure named GetModuleSettings, which reads the module settings, including the image source from the ModuleSettings table. In the default installation, there were no values for the height and width properties.

Creating the Links Module

The Links.ascx module is another example of a control that uses the DataList control. The Links module provides the hyperlinks, similar to those used to create the Quick Launch portion shown on the home page of the portal. (The Quick Launch section is actually supported by a simpler control named QuickLinks.ascx.) The Links module provides us with another module that uses a DataList. This time, we'll examine how we can describe the presentation of the DataList data from the perspective of the DataBinder and script blocks in the HTML source.

NOTE

This section describes the Links.ascx control and code. The actual control used by default in the IBuySpy portal is the QuickLinks.ascx control. The two controls produce a similar result using slightly different design and coding techniques. You swap out the QuickLinks.ascx control with the Links.ascx control by modifying the Modules table. Change the ModuleDefID to 7 from 8 where Modules.ModuleID is 1. I picked the Links.ascx module because it demonstrated more code than the revised QuickLinks.ascx module.

Coding Script Blocks in the HTML Code

The DataList control, like the Repeater and DataGrid, is a template control. The presentation of the control is described by templates. Indicate the way a single element on the control appears as a template tag, and all items displayed will be defined visually by the template. You can define these templates by writing the script by hand in the HTML editor, or you can use the template editor in the designer. In this section, I will describe the ASP that defines the template for the Links.ascx module, and the next section will demonstrate how to use the template editor. The ASP code for the Links.ascx module DataList is shown in Listing 14-9.

Listing 14-9   *The DataList is described by providing ASP.NET code that describes how elements will be displayed, as shown in the listing from the Links.ascx module.*

```
1:   <asp:DataList id="myDataList" CellPadding="4" Width="100%"
runat="server">
2:      <ItemTemplate>
3:        <SPAN class="Normal">
4:          <asp:HyperLink id=editLink runat="server"
5:          NavigateUrl='<%# "~/DesktopModules/EditLinks.aspx?ItemID=" +
DataBinder.Eval(Container.DataItem,"ItemID") + "&amp;mid=" + ModuleId
%>'
6:          ImageUrl="<%# linkImage %>">
7:          </asp:HyperLink>
8:          <asp:HyperLink id=HyperLink1 runat="server" NavigateUrl='<%#
DataBinder.Eval(Container.DataItem,"Url") %>'
9:          Target="_new" ToolTip='<%#
DataBinder.Eval(Container.DataItem,"Description") %>'
10:         Text='<%# DataBinder.Eval(Container.DataItem,"Title") %>'>
11:         </asp:HyperLink>
12:       </SPAN>
13:    </ItemTemplate>
14: </asp:DataList>
```

When you paint a DataList control from the Web Forms tab of the toolbox onto a User Control of Web Form, you get the code shown on lines 1 through 14 of Listing 14-9. The <asp:DataList> tag describes the DataList. The description of the template is defined between lines 2 and 13. The Links.ascx module defines an ItemTemplate only. You can define separator, header, and footer templates in a manner similar to how the ItemTemplate is defined. (We'll come back to this in a moment.)

The first thing that happens in the ItemTemplate is the inclusion of a <span>. Recall that span can be used as a convenient means of applying a cascading style sheet. The Normal class from the portal.css file is applied to the elements between the span on lines 3 and 12. The remaining code on lines 4 through 11 define one element in the DataList.

The controls used to describe the appearance of a DataList element include two hyperlinks. The first HyperLink control is defined by lines 4 through 7, and the second is defined by lines 8 through 11. The first link represents a link for editing the link itself, and the second actually will navigate the user to the described location.

Using NavigateUrl

Line 5 of Listing 14-9 introduces the NavigateUrl property of the HyperLink control. All of the code on line 5 creates an URL-encoded path. Recall that the first hyperlink refers to a location that will allow an administrative-role user to edit the link itself. All of the code on line 5 simply describes this path dynamically.

```
NavigateUrl='<%# "~/DesktopModules/EditLinks.aspx?ItemID=" +
DataBinder.Eval(Container.DataItem,"ItemID") + "&amp;mid=" + ModuleId
%>'
```

The NavigateUrl will be ~/DesktopModules/EditLinks.aspx?ItemID=*value*&mid=*value*. The tilde (~) is the root-relative indicator, which means that DesktopModules is a folder relative to the root of the Web site. EditLinks.aspx is an ASP.NET Web page, and ItemID and mid are names in the URL-encoded string. The actual ItemID is dynamically read from the DataSource associated with the DataList, and ModuleId is inherited from the PortalModuleControl class.

The second HyperLink control uses a similar technique to dynamically associate an URL with the HyperLink.NavigateUrl property. The first link navigates to the dynamic URL representing an edit page for this control if the logged-in user is an administrator, or an error page, if the user has not been authenticated. The second link navigates to the dynamically associated Web address.

Using Block Script

The dynamic code is defined in script blocks denoted by <% and %>. For example, the first HyperLink control is visually represented by the value linkImage defined in the script block for the HyperLink.ImageUrl property. From line 6 of Listing 14-9,

```
ImageUrl="<%# linkImage %>">
```

we set the ImageUrl of the first HyperLink to one of ~/images/edit.gif or ~/images/ navlink .gif, depending on whether the PortalModuleControl.IsEditable inherited property is True or False. This logic occurs in the Page_Load event for the Links.ascx module, which modifies the linkImage field.

The second HyperLink control displays a Tooltip and a Text value for the link. (The first link is named editLink, and the second link is named HyperLink1—lines 4 and 8 of Listing 14-9, respectively.) The second HyperLink control navigates to the value for the Url field of the DataSource. Outside of the script block for the second HyperLink, we find the Target attribute _new on line 9, indicating that a new page will be opened. The second script block for the second HyperLink begins on line 9. This script block reads a Description from the DataSource, assigning this value to the HyperLink.ToolTip property; and the final script block, beginning on line 10, assigns the DataSource's Title value to the HyperLink.Text property. The last script block represents the display value of the HyperLink.

When combined, the two HyperLinks will create a blue arrow image, which navigates to an error message screen, for non-authenticated users, or creates a pencil that navigates to an edit screen, for authenticated administrators. The second part of the link will display a title for the link and an actual target URL. For example, when you aren't signed in, you will see a blue arrow graphic and the text "ASP.NET Site." Click the ASP.NET Site text and your browser will attempt to navigate to the **www.asp.net** website.

Employing the DataBinder

The DataBinder class is used to evaluate and parse data binding expressions. The static method DataBinder.Eval (shown in Listing 14-9) is used to dynamically bind to fields in the DataList.DataSource property. There are two versions of the static Eval method. The first version of Eval allows you to express the source of the data and the field name of the data. For example, Container.DataItem represents the DataList.DataListItem in the DataList, and ItemID indicates the ItemID field.

The second form of DataBinder.Eval is a string representing a formatting expression. For example, if we were displaying values that represented dollar amounts, we might write

```
DataBinder(Container.DataItem, "Amount", "{0:c}")
```

where "Amount" is the name of a field in the DataSource and "{0:c}" is the actual format string for displaying values as currency. You can try the following statement in a Console application to experiment with formatting strings:

```
Console.WriteLine("{0:c}", 13567);
```

The preceding statement will write $13,567.00 to the console. You can use the same formatting expressions in DataBinder.Eval statements that you would use for Windows or Console applications.

If you encounter a DataBinder statement in script, then you can expect to find a related DataSource and field in the code-behind module. You can find the DataSource code for the Links.ascx module in the Page_Load event handler in the code-behind module. The next fragment shows the code that provides the dynamic DataSource for the Links.ascx module's DataList.

```
ASPNetPortal.LinkDB links = new ASPNetPortal.LinkDB();
myDataList.DataSource = links.GetLinks(ModuleId);
myDataList.DataBind();
```

The LinksDB class is referred to as a façade pattern. The façade pattern provides a simplified interface for performing operations that constitute part of the business rules of an application. You can find the code for the Links.ascx module in LinksDB.cs. LinkDB.GetLinks returns a SQLDataReader, which can be bound directly to the DataList, as demonstrated.

Creating Script Blocks Using the Template Editor

An alternate way to modify the templates of a DataList is to use the Template Editor in the designer. The Template Editor allows you to drag and drop controls directly into the designer, as shown in Figure 14-5, and to visually modify the appearance of the controls that make up the template by changing values in the Properties window.

To modify a template visually, right-click over the control and select Edit Template and the particular template region you wish to modify. When you have finished, display the context menu again and select End Template Editing. For example, you could add a horizontal rule between DataList elements by editing the SeparatorTemplate and dragging the horizontal rule control into the field representing the SeparatorTemplate template. The visual appearance of the SeparatorTemplate is controlled by the SeparatorTemplateStyle tag. (You can modify this value in the HTML editor or the Properties window.)

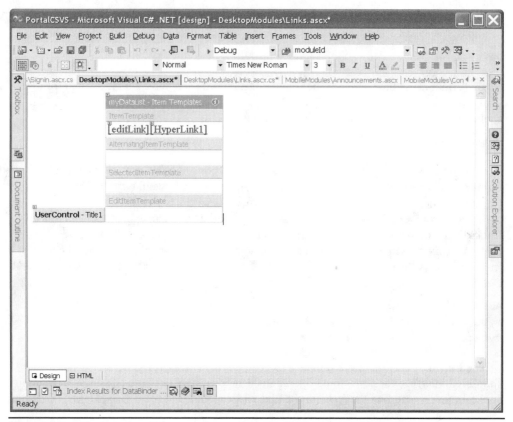

Figure 14-5 *The Template Editor can be used to visually design control templates.*

Implementing the XML/XSL Transform Module

XML contains self-describing data. You can apply an XSL/T transform style sheet, separating data from the format. By changing the XSL/T sheet, you can change the appearance of the data without changing the data in the XML document. XSL/T (or XSLT) is a practical alternative to using cascading style sheets.

The IBuySpy portal demonstrates XML and XSLT in the XmlModule control. One example demonstrating the XmlModule can be found by default in the lower-right corner of the home page containing the title Top Movers. The XmlModule module is created using the DesktopModuleTitle.ascx control and the Xml control found on the Web Forms tab of the toolbox.

The Xml control makes it easy to indicate an XML document and an XSLT document. Specify the Xml.DocumentSource property and the Xml control will display the contents of the XML document. Include an XSL/T file for the Xml.TransformSource property and the XML document will be displayed in the formatted style consistent with the transform described in the .xsl file. Listing 14-10 contains the sample XML file for the Top Movers data, and Listing 14-11 contains the XSL transform file applied to create the layout shown in Figure 14-6.

Reviewing the XML Document

Listing 14-10 contains the XML document representing revenue trends for the IBuySpy.com store. I will review the format of an XML file, which is pretty straightforward, after Listing 14-10.

Figure 14-6   *The Top Movers section created using an XML document containing data and an XSL/T document describing the appearance*

Listing 14-10   *The sales.xml document, representing revenue trends in the IBuySpy.com store*

```
 1:   <?xml version='1.0'?>
 2:   <sales xmlns:HTML="http://www.w3.org/Profiles/XHTML-transitional">
 3:       <product id='Travel'>
 4:           <revenue>60</revenue>
 5:           <growth>8</growth>
 6:       </product>
 7:       <product id='Communications'>
 8:           <revenue>45</revenue>
 9:           <growth>-7.8</growth>
10:       </product>
11:       <product id='Deception'>
12:           <revenue>10</revenue>
13:           <growth>9</growth>
14:       </product>
15:       <product id='Munitions'>
16:           <revenue>4</revenue>
17:           <growth>-3</growth>
18:       </product>
19:   </sales>
```

The XML document is consistent with data that might be returned by a Web Service, for example. The first statement on line 1 of Listing 14-10 is the XML declaration. It contains a mandatory version number and optional character encoding information. The second statement on line 2 defines a namespace, uniquely identifying the sales element with an xmlns (XML namespace) statement. The namespace tag uniquely identifies the sales tag in the event that another sales tag existed but was intended to convey some other meaning. The rest of the document in Listing 14-10 describes named product objects containing revenue and growth values. Each product tag represents one product object.

This data formatted as XML could have originated from a DataSet or a collection or array of product objects. We could use a text editor to create such a document or any tool or program that is capable of exporting to an XML document.

XML is used as the underlying framework for persisting data, including data represented by ADO.NET objects. For this reason, non-traditional kinds of data can be used as data sources. ADO.NET or user-defined objects can be serialized to and from XML. For example, you can save the *view* state information of an object by using an XmlSerializer and reassembling the object from XML. (Refer to the Emitter.sln in Chapter 11 for an example that demonstrates building a DataSet from an XML document.)

Note that I did not make any mention of the presentation of the XML defined in Listing 14-10. That is the role of the XSL/T document.

Reviewing the XSL Document

The XSL/T document supports separating document data from data presentation. The XML document contains the data, and the XSL/T document contains the transform describing how the data should be selected and presented. Listing 14-11 contains the sales.xsl document for the XmlModule.ascx control, followed by a brief synopsis.

Listing 14-11   *The sales.xsl XSL/T document describes the presentation of the sales.xml data, separating content from presentation.*

```
1:    <xsl:stylesheet version='1.0'
2:    xmlns:xsl='http://www.w3.org/1999/XSL/Transform'>

3:    <xsl:template match="/">
4:    <table width="210" border="1pt" cellspacing="0" cellpadding="3"
5:      bordercolor="#dddddd" style="border-collapse:collapse;">
6:        <tr>
7:          <th align="left">Product <br/>Category</th>
8:          <th>Revenue (Millions)</th>
9:          <th>Growth</th>
10:       </tr>
11:       <xsl:for-each select='sales/product'>
12:       <tr>
13:         <td class="Normal" width="100">
14:           <i><xsl:value-of select='@id'/></i>
15:         </td>
16:         <td class="Normal">
17:           <CENTER>
18:             <xsl:value-of select='revenue'/>
19:           </CENTER>
20:         </td>
21:         <td class="Normal">
22:           <xsl:if test='growth &lt; 0'>
23:           <xsl:attribute name='style'>
24:           <xsl:text>color:red</xsl:text>
25:           </xsl:attribute>
26:           </xsl:if>
27:           <CENTER>
28:             <xsl:value-of select='growth'/>
29:           </CENTER>
30:         </td>
31:       </tr>
32:       </xsl:for-each>
33:     </table>
34:  </xsl:template>
35:  </xsl:stylesheet>
```

NOTE

*XML and XSL are complete technologies incorporated in, yet independent of, .NET. You are encouraged to acquire at least one whole book on XML and XSL/T if you will be creating custom documents extensively. The XSLT Developer's Guide in the Visual Studio .NET at **ms-help://MS.VSCC/MS.MSDNVS/xmlsdk30/ htm/xmconxsldevelopersguide.htm** is a good starter resource for Microsoft XML 3.0.*

The XSL/T document creates a new XML tree independent of the XML data. Many of the tags used in our document are recognizable HTML tags, such as <table>, <th>, and <td>. Other elements are unique to XSL/T documents. For example, the *for-each select* beginning on line 11 and ending on line 32 of Listing 14-11 indicates that all of the rows in the XML document representing product objects—where sales/product represents the namespace sales and product represents the product items—should be returned. The values selected are the revenue and growth values, as indicated on lines 18 and 28, respectively. And, if the growth number is negative—represented by the if test on line 22—then the text will be displayed using a red font.

As with any language, simple elements of XSL/T like *for-each select* and *if test* statements help provide tremendous power and flexibility. For this reason, you are encouraged to acquire a book that that will serve as a reference source for XML. McGraw-Hill/ Osborne has an excellent book, *XML: The Complete Reference* by Heather Williamson. We can perform a couple of additional transforms on the XML document, which I will briefly describe next.

Sorting XML

We can apply a sort transform to order our XML data. Adding the following XSL/T to sales.xsl shown in Listing 14-11 after line 11 will sort based on the growth value.

```
<xsl:sort select='growth' data-type='number' order='descending' />
```

By default, the value is treated as a string. By adding the data-type='number' attribute, the growth value will be treated as a numeric type, yielding the correct result. The select='growth' attribute indicates the column we are sorting on, and the order attribute indicates the order. Replace 'descending' with 'ascending' to reverse the sort order.

Selecting Data Conditionally

Another option we might be interested in is to select only a specific number of elements or those that pass a set of minimum criteria. For example, we may only be interested in positive growth when presenting to investors, but the sales people should still also know what needs improvement. We could modify the sales.xsl document, inserting <xsl:if test='growth > 0'> after line 11 and </xsl:if> before line 32 of Listing 14-11. The end result is that we would get only the positive top movers displayed without changing the sales.xml file.

Loading the XML and XSL Documents with the Xml Control

The XmlModule.ascx control is initialized in the Page_Load handler. Both the values for the .xml and .xsl files are read from the PortalModuleControl.Settings inherited property. The

PortalModuleControl.Settings property returns a Hashtable. The Settings Hashtable is initialized by the PortalSettings.GetModuleSettings method. The actual XML and XSL documents are read by invoking the GetModuleSettings stored procedure, which reads the values from the ModuleSettings table.

The SettingName column contains xmlsrc and xslsrc in two separate rows and the relative path to the two data files in the SettingValue column. For example, the first statement in the XmlModule.Page_Load handler passes the indexer "xmlsrc" to the Settings property, which is used as a lookup value into the ModuleSettings table. Here is the statement:

```
String xmlsrc = (String) Settings["xmlsrc"];
```

This statement initially runs the GetModuleSettings stored procedure, returning the value ~/data/sales.xml from the database. The HttpServerUtility object inherited by the UserControl class contains a method MapPath, which takes the relative path and maps it to a physical path. If the document exists, it is loaded. The same technique is used to load the XSL file. Listing 14-12 shows the code used to safely load the XML document. (An identical technique was used to load the XSL document.)

Listing 14-12   *Safely loading a relative path document*

```
1:   String xmlsrc = (String) Settings["xmlsrc"];
2:   if ((xmlsrc != null) && (xmlsrc != "")) {
3:     if  (File.Exists(Server.MapPath(xmlsrc))) {
4:        xml1.DocumentSource = xmlsrc;
5:     }
6:     else {
7:        Controls.Add(new LiteralControl("<" + "br" + "><" + "span
8:          class=NormalRed" + ">" + "File " + xmlsrc +
9:          " not found.<" + "br" + ">"));
10:    }
11: }
```

The first statement demonstrates a string indexer in use. The consumer of the Settings property does not need to know that this Hashtable is originally initialized from a stored procedure. It is a good practice to hide these details precisely as demonstrated in the portal. The code on line 3 of Listing 14-12 maps a relative path to a physical path, using the HttpServerUtility represented by the Server object. The result is that the portal can be physically relocated without breaking code, while allowing for reasonable validation such as file existence checks. If the file exists, the Xml.DocumentSource property is assigned the relative path value. (File.Exists does not work with URL relative path strings.) If the file was not found, a dynamically created Literal control is created instead. If you examine the Page_Load event, you will find almost identical code for the XSL file.

TIP

The block for loading the XML and XSL files could be refactored into a single method inside the XmlModule.ascx file, passing the string indexer to a method containing the code in common.

Creating a Custom Portal Module

With most software, the greatest cost will be incurred when you try to grow the software. Employees and contractors are more likely to be asked to maintain an existing program than to write a new program from scratch. In fact, I personally have worked for many companies where the applications are "made available" rather than "released." Instead of getting to go on to the next big thing, the developers immediately begin a maintenance cycle that involves moving bugs around that everyone knew were in the software when it was made available. (Generally, these environments aren't very fun to work in.)

NOTE

All except the most trivial applications should have UML models, written architectural overviews, a documented convention, and preferably an evolution plan, describing the best way to grow the software. The alternative is that software decays much more quickly relative to the number of hands that modify it. The basic idea is that the greater your employee turnover, the faster your company's software will decay into spaghetti code and become unmaintainable — unless you have the artifacts described in the first sentence.

Regardless of the reason for working on existing software, one of the first things to do is figure out how it was implemented and how to extend the software. After the software was originally hacked together, usually more hacking occurs, resulting in software that is never really quite done. Having an architecture, using UML models and written architectural overviews, and following an established set of best practices constitute the best ways to slow the decay of software quality. For example, the IBuySpy portal provides accessible explanations in writing—which is not the same thing as inferring from the code—that describe how to modify and maintain the portal, and it adheres to best practices that Microsoft is promoting with respect to the architecture of .NET. As a result, we can adhere to the style demonstrated by the portal and follow the published documentation, resulting in a seamless integration of our customizations.

Creating a Custom Portal Module

All programmers have heard or used the word "extensible." An extensible system is one that encourages and promotes consistent enhancement. If you have to use a crowbar to wedge revisions in, the software is not extensible.

The IBuySpy is very extensible. You can create a custom portal module and integrate the customization in the portal by following these steps.

1. With the portal solution open in Visual Studio .NET, find the DesktopModules folder in the Solution Explorer.

2. Right-click the DesktopModules folder and select Add | Add Web User Control from the context menu.

3. In the Name field in the Add New Item dialog, enter a file name for your custom module. (I named the example module CustomModule.ascx.)

4. Click Open. This will close the dialog, adding CustomModule.ascx to your copy of the IBuySpy portal.

5. Double-click the new module and switch to the Code Designer view. Change the class header to inherit from ASPNetportal.PortalModuleControl and save the file.

6. Using SHIFT+F7, switch back to the Form Designer view. Click the HTML tab at the bottom to switch to the HTML editor. Define a <span> and add the class attribute to the span, indicating that you want to use the Normal style class for your control. The span statement follows:

```
<span class="Normal"></span>
```

7. Click the Design tab to switch back to the Designer view. Drag the DesktopModuleTitle.ascx control from the Server Explorer to the Designer view of the new control. (This will allow an administrator to name the module when it is added as a page.)

8. Finally, add some controls, text, or HTML to define the appearance of the custom control.

I planned to use the new control to announce book releases. To make the control truly flexible, we could use a DataList and read the book release from the database. (You can use other controls like the Links.ascx or QuickLinks.ascx controls to make the control use data from the Portal database.) To finish up, I simply added some literal text announcing the release of this book.

The final step is to incorporate the custom control into the portal. We could create a new tab and page or incorporate the CustomModule.ascx control into an existing tab. I chose the latter. The next section walks you through incorporating the CustomModule.ascx control into the Home page of the IBuySpy portal.

Integrating the Custom Module into the IBuySpy Portal

To incorporate a control into the IBuySpy portal, log in using an administrative password. The default administrative Email and password are both "guest." After you log in as guest, the Admin tab of the portal will be displayed. Navigate to the Admin tab and you can incorporate the new control without writing any additional code. Follow the steps to complete the process, using the referenced images as a graphical guide.

1. Ensure that you are logged in with an administrative role. (Email equals *guest* and Password equals *guest* for the default administrative login.) Also, make sure you are on the Admin tab (shown in Figure 14-7).

2. Click Add New Module Type at the bottom-right of the Admin page (also shown in Figure 14-7). The Module Type Definition view will open.

3. Specify a Friendly Name and Desktop Source for the new module. (You can use Figure 14-8 as a visual guide. The module name is the relative path and file name of the file containing the new User Control.)

4. Click Update to save the changes.

5. Again, on the Admin tab, in the Tabs section, select the Home tab and click the icon graphic of the pencil to edit the Tab definition for the Home tab.

6. Modify the Tab Name and Layout view, using Figure 14-9 as a visual guide. Select the Custom Portal Module (or whatever Friendly Name you used in step 3). For the Module Type, provide a Module Name, which will be displayed in the DesktopTitleModule.ascx control, and click the Add to "Organize Modules" Below link.

7. By default, the module will be added to the Content Pane. You can use the blue directional arrows to move the module to an alternate pane. (I stuck with the ContentPane.)

8. Click the Apply Changes link when you are satisfied and navigate to the Home tab to view the new module.

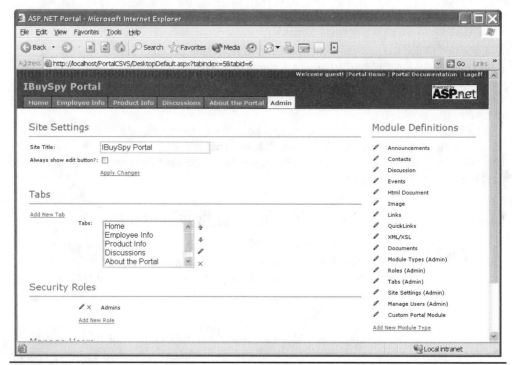

Figure 14-7   *Select Add New Module Type on the Admin tab to incorporate a new module into the IBuySpy.*

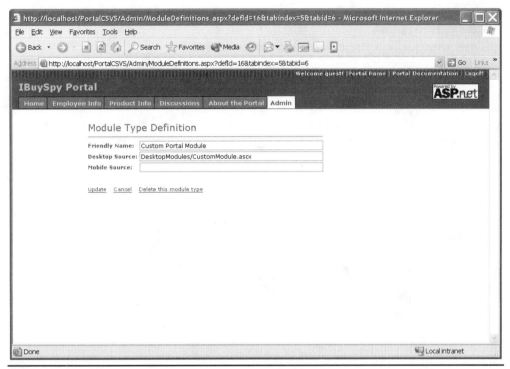

Figure 14-8   *Provide a Module Type Definition, where the Friendly Name will be the name you refer to when administrating the portal and the Desktop Source is the relative User Control file path.*

In eight fairly simple steps, we customized the IBuySpy portal in a very non-technical way. We certainly could have opened up the database tables and tried to figure out which columns and rows to change, but the administrative tool is a significant improvement over that. The method of managing a website using plug-and-play controls and an administrative front end is very maintainable and extensible.

Secondary Topics

Chapters on C# and the .NET Framework could go on interminably, as evidenced by the hundred or so books that have been published already. I have mixed feelings about every chapter. There is more I would have liked to share, but in each it is necessary to draw to a close if the book is ever to get to press.

I mentioned a couple of things that are part of the IBuySpy portal that I would like to explore a little more before we wrap up this chapter. Specifically, I'd like to explore the HttpServerUtility class a bit more and offer an example that demonstrates the Repeater control.

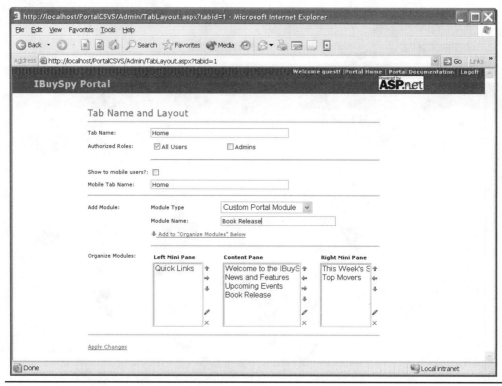

Figure 14-9 *The CustomModule.ascx control added to the IBuySpy portal*

Using the HttpServerUtility

The HttpServerUtility provides support services. This class is represented by the Server object, which is a property of the System.Web.UI.Page control. The Server object can be used to complete tasks like requesting the machine name of the server, transferring control to a new page, or mapping the relative path of a page to a physical file path. (Listing 14-12 demonstrates how mapping a relative to a physical path can be used to ensure that files exist, by invoking the HttpServerUtility.MapPath method.) You can obtain the machine name by accessing the HttpServerUtility.MachineName property, and the HttpServerUtility.Transfer method stops the execution of the current page and transfers execution to a page passed to the Transfer method.

TIP

The HttpServerUtility.Transfer method can be used as a substitute for the Response.Redirect method. Response.Redirect occurs on the client, and the HttpServerUtility.Transfer method occurs on the server.

Using the Repeater Control

The Repeater control is a data-bound, template control that provides no default layout or style information but does allow you to split tags across templates. For example, a <table> tag can start in the <ItemTemplate> and end in the <FooterTemplate>, spanning <AlternatingItem> and <SeparatorTemplate> tags in between. However, you must specify an ItemTemplate at a minimum to display data in the DataSource. Listing 14-13 shows the <table> tag, spanning both the <ItemTemplate> and <AlternatingItemTemplate>, and the <TR> tag, crossing both templates, resulting in a red and black checkerboard pattern.

Listing 14-13 *Tags spanning templates in the Repeater control*

```
<asp:Repeater id="Repeater1">
<table>
<ItemTemplate>
<tr>
  <td bgcolor=black>
     
  </td>
</ItemTemplate>
<AlternatingItemTemplate>
  <td bgcolor=red>
     
  </td>
</tr>
</AlternatingItemTemplate>
</table>
</asp:Repeater>
```

The <table> tag wraps the <ItemTemplate> and the <AlternatingItemTemplate>. Notice that the <tr> (row) tag spans both the <ItemTemplate> and the <AlternatingItemTemplate>. Listing 14-13 results in a checkerboard pattern where alternating DataSource items are actually displayed in the same row.

Unfortunately, you may get a smattering of errors in the Task List, indicating that the active schema does not support a particular element, for example, the <AternatingItemTemplate>. The error report may be inaccurate or only partially correct. With a little experimentation, you can produce some creative presentations with the Repeater control.

Summary

The IBuySpy portal is maintained through the administrative pages and can be extended by creating modules—UserControls—that are easily plugged into the portal using the administrative pages.

This chapter expands on what you already learned from Chapter 8, demonstrating how to build UserControls for the Web. This is a developer's guide, so I showed you how to create UserControls that fit into a specific application, the IBuySpy portal. Clearly, you don't have to inherit from the PortalModuleControl for any other application than the IBuySpy portal. Rather, the portal application provides you with an implicit best practice: define the basic infrastructure of your application and "genericize" that aspect, allowing all participants in development to integrate their code seamlessly.

The IBuySpy portal was implemented by Microsoft to blaze a trail for developers. ADO.NET and stored procedures can be used to organize and retrieve data efficiently, and the UserControl is an excellent way to create a dynamic presentation layer. As a combined strategy, the stored procedure and the UserControl allow you to focus on the business rules, the middle tier.

Output Caching and Persisting State Information

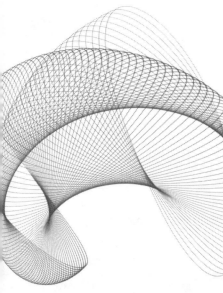

If you compare a Web application to a Windows application, you are likely to detect a noticeable sluggishness in the Web application relative to the Windows application. Web applications are hosted in a browser and have to make trips between the client and server, with the greatest part of the code residing on the server. Anything you can do to enhance performance and responsiveness should be considered.

In terms of strategy, one of the best things you can do is a little process re-engineering before you begin developing your application. Consider the flow of your application from the perspective of how the user will complete tasks and minimize trips to the Web server. After you have resolved ways in which you can simplify task completion, you can minimize the number of times pages have to be rendered and data has to be retrieved from a database. (For our purposes, we are assuming there will be a database, although the data repository could be something else.)

This chapter is about enhancing the performance of your Web applications by relying on strategies that reduce the frequency that code has to run to render pages and the frequency that databases must be accessed. This information is covered with the IBuySpy portal as the backdrop. However, every application will not use all techniques; hence, I will be showing you useful techniques that are used not only by the portal but also by others.

Demonstrated Topics

There are several kinds of caching that we can take advantage of to optimize the performance of our Web applications. These are not the same kinds of optimizations that we refer to when we talk about optimizing code; that kind of optimization has to occur, too. As a reminder, tune your code after your application is working correctly. And, you can treat the material presented in this chapter as tuning and optimizing strategies or you can implement these strategies when you initially write the code. In this chapter I will demonstrate

▶   How to cache entire pages to reduce the number of times a page is rendered, including how to use declarative and programmatic caching

▶   How to use UserControls to cache partial pages

▶   The various ways that you can cache data, as an alternative to caching pages

▶   How to administer the expiration policy

One way in which you can cache data is to use the Session cache. There are two general ways in which data is cached. There is the default in-process memory cache and the out-of-process caches. The in-process cache is fast but does not maintain state if the server is restarted, and there are two out-of-process caches that maintain cache data between server restarts, and as a result, they are more robust. If you plan to deploy a Web farm, you will need to use an out-of-process cache server. The "Secondary Topics" section will demonstrate how to configure and use out-of-process caching.

Output Caching Pages

When you request a page, the page is Just-In-Time compiled on the server and the code-behind is executed to render the page. All of this takes time. If the content of a page doesn't change very often, you can cache the page. Subsequent requests for the page will be read from the cache, avoiding the overhead of JITting and rendering the page for each request.

You can cache pages declaratively or programmatically. Declarative caching, using the @ OutputCache directive, will work in most circumstances, but you can obtain a finer degree of control using programmatic page caching. Let's take a look at declarative page caching as it is used in the IBuySpy portal, and we'll explore programmatic caching that results in the same behavior.

Using Declarative Caching

The @ OutputCache directive is added directly to the HTML text when you define a Web page. You need to specify a duration attribute and a value for the VaryByParam attribute at a minimum. There are variations on these attributes that we will talk about in a minute. The basic declarative output caching statement will appear in the HTML text, as in the following:

```
<%@ OutputCache Duration="60" VaryByParam="None" %>
```

The directive is OutputCache. Duration expresses the amount of time to hold the cached page in seconds. Duration="60" means that the page should be held for 60 seconds. The *VaryByParam* parameter is required even if the value is "None". The basic directive will cause the whole page to be cached.

Consider the page shown in Figure 15-1, which is based on the Xml control and the IBuySpy portal's sales.xml and sales.xsl files. Without caching, the page is compiled and run each time a user requests the page. (The Submit button represents a page request.) Click the Submit button and the page is posted to the server. The date and time stamp will change, reflecting the fact that the page code has been run.

NOTE

A quick test is to add a breakpoint in the code-behind page or observe the date and time stamp at the bottom of the page as you click the Submit button. You will see that the breakpoint is reached (and the date and time stamp value changes) almost every time you click the Submit button.

If we examine the sales.xml and sales.xsl, we quickly realize that this is static data. So, what is the benefit of regenerating the page for every query? The answer is that there is no benefit. After the first request, every page will contain the same data and our users will pay for unnecessary CPU cycles. This is a perfect opportunity to enhance the performance of the Web site vis-à-vis this page by caching the rendered sales data. Adding the OutputCache directive to the HTML text—declaratively, using page caching—will inhibit the page from rendering for every requestor.

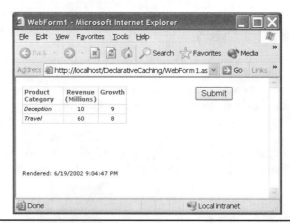

Figure 15-1   *A simple page that shows some data from an XML file each time the page is requested*

Add the basic OutputCache directive demonstrated and the page will be rendered once approximately every 60 seconds, and all users will simply be served the cached version of the page. Consider the case of dozens or hundreds of requestors in 60 seconds, and you will realize performance savings scaled by the number of requestors who don't need to wait for the page to render. Add the OutputCache directive, as shown in boldface in Listing 15-1, and re-run the DeclarativeCaching.sln Web application. You will see that the date and time stamp is updated after every minute or so. (You can open and close the Web browser to simulate multiple users.)

Listing 15-1   *The HTML text for the WebForm1.aspx page in the DeclarativeCaching.sln*

```
<%@ Page language="c#" Codebehind="WebForm1.aspx.cs" AutoEventWireup="false"
Inherits="DeclarativeCaching.WebForm1" %>
<%@ OutputCache Duration="60" VaryByParam="None"  %>
<!DOCTYPE HTML PUBLIC "-//W3C//DTD HTML 4.0 Transitional//EN" >
<HTML>
  <HEAD>
    <title>WebForm1</title>
    <meta name="GENERATOR" Content="Microsoft Visual Studio 7.0">
    <meta name="CODE_LANGUAGE" Content="C#">
    <meta name="vs_defaultClientScript" content="JavaScript">
    <meta name="vs_targetSchema"
content="http://schemas.microsoft.com/intellisense/ie5">
    <link href="portal.css" type="text/css" rel="stylesheet">
  </HEAD>
```

```
<body MS_POSITIONING="GridLayout">
  <form id="Form1" method="post" runat="server">
    <table class="Normal" height="100%" width="100%" align="left">
      <tr>
        <td valign="top" style="WIDTH: 343px; HEIGHT: 166px">
          <asp:Xml id="Xml1" runat="server"></asp:Xml>
        </td>
        <td style="HEIGHT: 166px" vAlign="top">
          <asp:Button id="Button1" runat="server"
Text="Submit"></asp:Button>
        </td>
      </tr>
      <tr>
        <td valign="top" colspan="2">
          <asp:Label id="Label1" style="Z-INDEX: 101"
runat="server">Label</asp:Label>
        </td>
      </tr>
    </table>
  </form>
  <P></P>
</body>
</HTML>
```

A reasonable person might want to see some evidence that page caching has provided some performance improvements before committing resources to optimizing pages with output caching. If you have to convince other developers or managers, then visuals might help. Before we continue our discussion of the OutputCache directive, let's explore a means of evaluating performance improvements by taking a quick tour of Microsoft's Application Center Test (ACT).

Examining Performance Heuristics

Microsoft Visual Studio .NET Enterprise and Enterprise Architect ship with Microsoft Application Center Test (ACT). ACT is an excellent tool for simulating multiple, simultaneous client connections.

ACT allows you to record or write a custom VBScript that interacts with your ASP.NET application. After you have defined one or more tests, you can configure the tests, including the number of users, and ACT will spin up that number of HTTP connections to the Web server.

ACT is completely configurable and provides you with visual and textual feedback during the test run and after the test has completed. To demonstrate ACT, I will show you how to record, configure, and run a test that can be used to compare the differences in DeclarativeCaching.sln with and without the @ OutputCache directive.

Recording the Test   To record a test, start ACT by selecting Start | Program Files | Microsoft Visual Studio .NET | Visual Studio .NET Enterprise Features | Microsoft Application Center Test. Follow the numbered steps to record a test script for the DeclarativeCaching.sln.

1. In ACT, select File | New Project to create a new test project. The sample test project is named test.act and is available for download.

2. After you have created the test project, you can add one or more tests to the project by selecting Actions | New test. The New Test Wizard starts, which we will use to record a script.

3. After the introduction screen, select Record A New Test.

4. Select the script language (VBScript) and click Next; the Browser Record step in the wizard will let you start recording. Click the Start recording button.

5. When you start recording, the browser will be opened to a blank page. Everything you do in the browser from this point until you click Stop Recording will be recorded as VBScript.

6. Navigate the browser to **http://localhost/declarativecaching/webform1.aspx** and click the Submit button several times. (This step assumes that you are running the sample Web application on your PC or on the same computer you are running ACT on.) The first time you click the Submit button, you should see the date and time stamp change, if you have added the @ OutputCache directive to the page.

7. After you have clicked the Submit button a couple of times, close the browser.

8. Click the Stop Recording button in the wizard and click through the remaining steps in the ACT wizard. (One of the steps is to provide a name for the test. I named the test I created Submit.)

After you have finished recording the test, you can select it from the navigator window in ACT, shown in Figure 15-2. You can create as many tests as you want to in a similar manner.

Configuring the Test   After recording the test, we can configure the test run. To configure the test, we can select a specific test from the navigator window and select Actions | Submit Properties (see Figure 15-3). In the Submit Properties window, you can indicate the number of simultaneous connections, warm-up time, and run-time. You can also specify how users are generated and add performance counters to measure. (You can read more about performance counters in Chapter 7.)

For the test I created, I selected 10 simultaneous browser connections, a warm-up period of 20 seconds, and test duration of 5 minutes. (These settings are shown in Figure 15-3 on the General tab of the Properties window.) I let ACT automatically generate users, and I picked the Interrupt Time and Disk Read Time performance counters (see Figure 15-4). The Interrupt Time counter tracks the time the processor spends servicing hardware interrupts, and the Disk Read Time is the amount of time the drive spends performing reads.

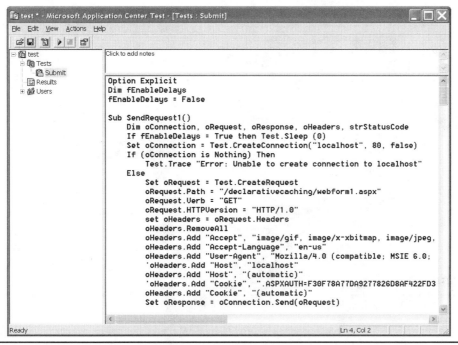

Figure 15-2   *ACT showing the VBScript created after recording an interaction with the DeclarativeCacing.sln*

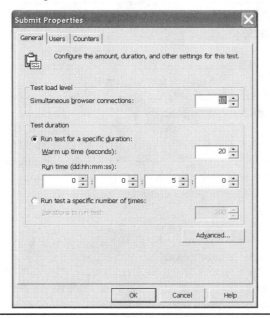

Figure 15-3   *The Submit Properties window is used to configure the test.*

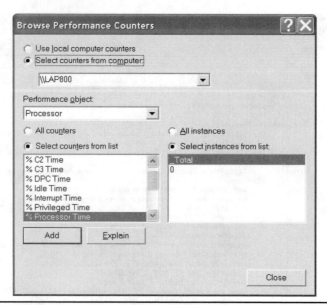

Figure 15-4   *The Browse Performance Counters dialog*

TIP

Click the Explain button in the Browse Performance Counters dialog for a description of each performance counter.

Running the Test   After we have configured the test, we are ready to run. Select the test and Actions | Start Test to begin running the test. ACT will display the test status as the test is running (see Figure 15-5). You can observe test performance during execution and view all of the results after the test has completed.

When the test has completed, you can click the Results folder in the navigator and view a wide variety of test results. The Summary results (shown in Figure 15-6) in our test show how much time was spent retrieving the portal.css style sheet and the Web page. You can compare the results between tests run with and without page caching and tune the Web application to enhance the performance characteristics you are interested in.

Caching by Parameter

After our brief detour, we are back to caching. The simplest way to cache a page is to express a duration and the VaryByParam="None" attribute. You can also express literal parameter names for the VaryByParam name. If the page request includes parameters, you can use this attribute to indicate that a new page needs to be rendered if the value of the parameters have changed, even if the page requested hasn't changed.

Express the parameters between quotes in a semicolon-delimited list. Our example doesn't use parameters; however, we could have implemented the page so that the user could indicate

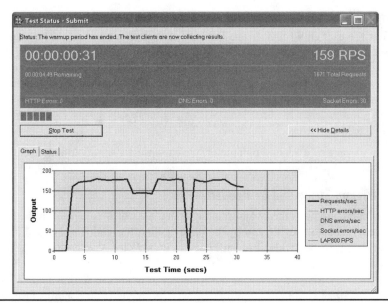

Figure 15-5   *The Submit test in progress with details showing*

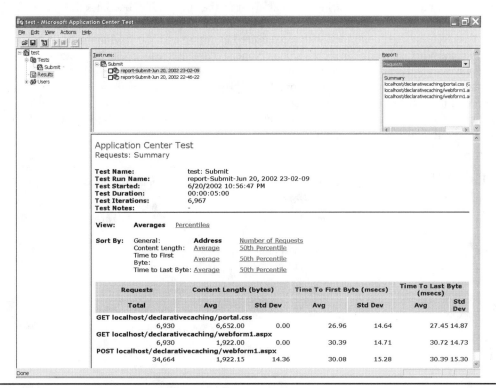

Figure 15-6   *The Request Summary report for the Submit test*

the XML file to view. For example, we could have used a parameter file and listed all of the available files the user could pick from. The URL-encoded request might be **http://localhost/ DeclarativeCaching/webform1.aspx?file=sales.xml**. On the initial request, the page would be cached by the value of the *file* parameter, and for each unique value of *file* a different version of the page would be cached. The @ OutputCache directive expressing that we want to vary by the value of the *file* parameter would be added to the HTML, as demonstrated next:

```
<%@ OutputCache Duration="60" VaryByParam="file" %>
```

If we want to vary by a second parameter, we can insert a semicolon after the word "file" and insert additional parameter names.

Caching by Custom String and by Header

Declaratively, there are two other ways to indicate that a cached page needs to be regenerated. We can cache by a custom string and by the page header; these attributes are VaryByCustom and VaryByHeader, respectively. You still have to include the VaryByParam attribute even if you set its value to None.

Caching by Custom String   Suppose you implement a Web page that contains browser-specific capabilities. You can cache by a custom string—VaryByCustom—and a new page will be rendered if the value of that string changes. That is, the string value becomes the cache determinator.

VaryByCustom is combined with the required Duration and VaryByParam attributes, even if the VaryByParam attribute value is None. To declaratively cache by custom string, add the VaryByParam attribute and a unique string. This string can be compared to an argument passed to the HttpApplication.GetVaryByCustomString method, which you must override to work with the VaryByCustom attribute. Listing 15-2 shows the @ OutputCache directive with the VaryByCustom attribute, and Listing 15-3 shows the GetVaryByCustomString method implemented in the global.asax file.

Listing 15-2   *An @ OutputCache directive with the VaryByCustom attribute shown in the first few lines of an aspx page*

```
<%@ Page language="c#" Codebehind="WebForm1.aspx.cs" AutoEventWireup="false"
Inherits="DeclarativeCaching.WebForm1" %>
<%@ OutputCache Duration="360" VaryByParam="None" VaryByCustom="cookies"%>
<!DOCTYPE HTML PUBLIC "-//W3C//DTD HTML 4.0 Transitional//EN" >
<HTML>
  <HEAD>
    <title>WebForm1</title>
    <meta name="GENERATOR" Content="Microsoft Visual Studio 7.0">
    <meta name="CODE_LANGUAGE" Content="C#">
```

The string we will compare to in the Global.asax file is the value of the VaryByCustom attribute "cookies". Listing 15-3 shows a complete Global.asax file with the overridden GetVaryByCustomString method.

Listing 15-3 *Implement the GetVaryByCustomString method to manage page caching by a string value.*

```
1:   using System;
2:   using System.Collections;
3:   using System.ComponentModel;
4:   using System.Web;
5:   using System.Web.SessionState;
6:
7:   namespace DeclarativeCaching
8:   {
9:     /// <summary>
10:    /// Summary description for Global.
11:    /// </summary>
12:    public class Global : System.Web.HttpApplication
13:    {
14:      public Global()
15:      {
16:        InitializeComponent();
17:      }
18:
19:    protected void Application_Start(Object sender, EventArgs e)
20:    {
21:
22:    }
23:
24:    protected void Session_Start(Object sender, EventArgs e)
25:    {
26:
27:    }
28:
29:    protected void Application_BeginRequest(Object sender, EventArgs e)
30:    {
31:
32:    }
33:
```

```
34:    protected void Application_EndRequest(Object sender, EventArgs e)
35:    {
36:
37:    }
38:
39:    protected void Application_AuthenticateRequest(Object sender,
40:      EventArgs e)
41:    {
42:    }
43:
44:    protected void Application_Error(Object sender, EventArgs e)
45:    {
46:
47:    }
48:
49:    protected void Session_End(Object sender, EventArgs e)
50:    {
51:
52:    }
53:
54:    protected void Application_End(Object sender, EventArgs e)
55:    {
56:
57:    }
58:
59:    public override string GetVaryByCustomString(HttpContext context,
60:      string arg
61:    {
62:      return arg == "cookies" ?
63:        context.Request.Browser.Cookies.ToString() : string.Empty;
64:    }
65:
66:    #region Web Form Designer generated code
67:    /// <summary>
68:    /// Required method for Designer support - do not modify
69:    /// the contents of this method with the code editor.
70:    /// </summary>
71:    private void InitializeComponent()
72:    {
73:    }
```

```
74:    #endregion
75:    }
76: }
```

The Global.asax file contains application-level and session-level event handlers that you can implement. (Refer to Chapter 13, the section "Implementing Event Handlers in the Global.asax Module," for more information.) We provided an overridden implementation of the HttpApplication.GetVaryByCustomString method on lines 59 to 64 of Listing 15-3. The code uses a ternary operator to evaluate the string argument arg. Reading the ternary operator, we understand lines 62 and 63 to mean *if arg is equal to the literal string "cookies" then return the string value of the HttpBrowserCapabilities.Cookies property.* If the current browser supports cookies, then the string text "true" will be used as the custom string that decides whether the page is cached. Caching with "true" and a subsequent test that returns "false" will cause a new page to be rendered. This is in addition to the timeout expressed in the @ OutputCache Duration attribute in Listing 15-2.

Unlike the VaryByParam attribute, VaryByCustom uses only one string value. For example, VaryByCustom="cookies;frames" does not treat cookies as one string and frames as another.

Caching by Header   HTTP requests send header information that describes the client-browser, supported languages, host information, and a bevy of other details about the HTTP request. You can cache based on any single key, combination of keys, or all keys in the HTTP header.

To cache based on HTTP header information adds the VaryByHeader attribute, passing the name of the header key. If you want to cache based on multiple keys, then you can separate header keys by a semicolon or use the asterisk to cache based on all header keys. Here are three declarative @ OutputCache directives that demonstrate caching on a single value in the header, multiple values, and all values.

```
<%@ OutputCache Duration="10" VaryByParam="None" VaryByCustom="cookies"
VaryByHeader="user-agent"%>
<%@ OutputCache Duration="10" VaryByParam="None" VaryByCustom="cookies"
VaryByHeader="user-agent;host"%>
<%@ OutputCache Duration="10" VaryByParam="None" VaryByCustom="cookies"
VaryByHeader="*"%>
```

The first statement caches the page for 10 seconds, ignores URL-encoded parameters, and will render the request if made by a client that switches between cookie support and no cookie support or if the user-agent changes. The second @ OutputCache directive differs only by the VaryByHeader attribute—it takes the host into account. The last directive will vary if any of the header values differs. Varying by all headers—or any large variety of caching configurations—will cause your Web server to cache a version of the page based on each variation attribute until the page expires.

Caching Examples in the IBuySpy Portal

The IBuySpy portal uses declarative caching in pages that will not change significantly between requests. Specifically, the portal caches pages that convey error information to a user.

TIP

*A version of grep ships with rotor. To search all of the files in the portal, change directories to the PortalCSVS directory and enter the following text at a command prompt: **grep −i −d OutputCache *.aspx**. The −i switch means a case-insensitive search, and −d indicates that subfolders should be searched.*

If you perform a *grep*—a source file text search—on the source files in the portal, you will see that the AccessDenied.aspx, EditAccessDenied.aspx, and the NotImplemented.aspx pages use declarative caching. Here is the OutputCache directive for the AccessDenied.aspx page.

```
<%@ OutputCache Duration="36000" VaryByParam="none" %>
```

According to the Duration attribute, this page won't expire for ten hours. You can experiment with Duration settings in the DurationDemo.sln available for download. EditAccessDenied.aspx uses OutputCache settings identical to AccessDenied.aspx. NotImplemented.aspx demonstrates a shorter duration and an argument for VaryByParam.

NOTE

*The beta version of ASP.NET had a five-minute cache limitation. The deployed version no longer has this limitation. Set the duration for longer than 5 minutes, and the page will be cached for a greater period of time. You can download and try the DurationDemo.sln available at **www.osborne.com** to experiment.*

NotImplemented.aspx is displayed when you select an option that is not completed. (This is an excellent strategy for Windows and Web applications.) The OutputCache directive for the NotImplemented.aspx page is implemented as follows:

```
<%@ OutputCache Duration="600" VaryByParam="title" %>
```

The NotImplemented.aspx page will be compiled and run when the ten-minute duration period expires and for each title parameter. That is, every time the URL-encoded value of "title" changes, a new page will be cached. The NotImplemented.aspx page exists for links that are not part of the sample data for the portal.

Using Programmatic Caching

Programmatic page caching provides features identical to declarative caching. For everyday use, declarative caching should work fine. If you want slightly more control or need to change caching policies at run-time, then you can manage page caching programmatically through the HttpCachePolicy.

An HttpCachePolicy object is accessible through the HttpResponse.Cache property; an HttpResponse object is, in turn, accessible through the Page.Response property. Page .Response.Cache will provide you access to a page's HttpCachePolicy. The portal doesn't use programmatic output page caching, so we'll take a little detour and examine programmatic caching that is analogous to the declarative caching used by the portal.

Specifying a Cache Expiration

The OutputCache Duration attribute specifies how long the page will be cached. The equivalent programmatic command is HttpCachePolicy.SetExpires. Pass the time that the cached page will expire. For example, you can invoke the DateTime.Now property and add a number of seconds, minutes, or hours to the current time. Here is an example taken from the ProgrammaticCacheDemo.sln.

```
Page.Response.Cache.SetExpires(DateTime.Now.AddSeconds(30));
```

(The Page object is not required, since you are in the Page when this code is executed.) DateTime.Now returns the current date and time, and AddSeconds(30) adds 30 seconds to the current time. That is, the page will expire 30 seconds from the time this code is executed.

You need more than just the SetExpires method to use programmatic output caching. From online sources and books, you might be led to believe that you only need SetExpires and SetCacheability. Unfortunately, this information seems to be incomplete. To cache a page programmatically, you need to supply several pieces of information; Listing 15-4 provides you with an example that programmatically caches a page.

Listing 15-4   *Programmatically caching a page*

```
Page.Response.Cache.SetExpires(DateTime.Now.AddSeconds(30));
Page.Response.Cache.VaryByParams["None"] = true;
Page.Response.Cache.SetCacheability(HttpCacheability.Public);
Page.Response.Cache.SetValidUntilExpires(true);
```

The preceding example indicates when the cached page will expire. In the example, the page will expire 30 seconds after the statement is executed. With the @ OutputCache directive, we need to specify VaryByParams["None"] = true. I didn't find any mention of this in the help documentation, but you can try it. Without a VaryByParams statement, the page will not cache. The SetCacheability statement sets the Cache-Control header (see Table 15-1), and

Value	Description
NoCache	Sets the Cache-Control header to *no cache*. The page will not be cached.
Private	The default value sets the Cache-Control header to *private*, indicating that the page is cached on the client.
Public	Sets the Cache-Control header to *public,* indicating the page is cached by clients and proxy caches.
Server	The page is cached on the server.

Table 15-1   *HttpCacheability-Enumerated Values for Programmatic Caching*

SetValidUntilExpires(true) instructs the ASP.NET to ignore HTTP Cache-Control headers that invalidate the cache. SetValidUntilExpires is implicitly set to true when you use the @ OutputCache directive. If you don't use SetValidUntilExpires(true), then the browser may send header information that causes the cache to be invalidated. The four statements in conjunction seem to work most reliably and consistently with the @ OutputCache directive that expresses a Duration and a VaryByParam equal to "None".

Caching by Parameters

Use the VaryByParams property to express the URL-encoded parameters that control page caching. Express the name of the parameter in the subscript operator and the value on the right side of the equals-sign operator. For example, to vary by the title parameter programmatically—which is what the portal does declaratively—place the word "title" in quotes in the subscript operator and assign it the value true.

```
Page.Response.Cache.VaryByParams["title"] = true;
```

If you want to ignore parameters, then run this code:

```
Page.Response.Cache.VaryByParams.IgnoreParams = true;
```

As you can determine, it takes a little extra effort to cache pages programmatically, but doing so will allow you to dynamically change page caching behavior after the code is compiled and deployed. Generally, you can use declarative caching and revert to programmatic caching if cache behavior is dynamic.

- ▶ Response.Cache.SetExpires(DateTime.Now.AddSeconds(60))
- ▶ Response.Cache.SetCacheability(HttpCacheability.Public)
- ▶ Response.Cache.SetValidUntilExpires(True)

Caching Partial Pages

Partial page caching—also known as fragment caching—is managed via user controls. You can cache part of a page by adding the @ OutputCache directive to the user control, as you would for an entire page, or you can apply the PartialCachingAttribute to the class in the code-behind page. You already saw how to use the @ OutputCache directive in the preceding section; let's focus on the just-introduced PartialCachingAttribute.

CAUTION

If you enable output caching on a user control, you will not be able to refer to that user control in code.

System.Web.UI contains the definition for the PartialCachingAttribute. The concepts for partially caching a user control are similar to those for caching a page. The biggest differences are syntactical, and you can vary caching based on the properties of constituent controls defined on the user control.

There are two forms of the PartialCachingAttribute. The first accepts a duration expressing how long to hold the control cached in memory. The second version of the constructor takes four arguments. The first is the duration, followed by a semicolon-delimited list of parameters to vary by, followed by a semicolon-delimited list of constituent control properties and a value equivalent to the declarative VaryByCustom attribute. (If you use the VaryByCustom argument, you will need to override GetVaryByCustomString, as demonstrated in the earlier section "Caching by Custom String and by Header.")

The PartialPageCachingDemo.sln provides an example that demonstrates using the PartialCachingAttribute (see Listing 15-5). The solution implements a UserControl that has the PartialCachingAttribute applied to the user control. When you create an instance of a UserControl that uses the PartialCachingAttribute, the type of the actual object created will be PartialCachingControl, not the specific user control you defined. The PartialCachingControl does not have a public Controls collection. As a result, you cannot refer to constituent controls on the UserControl. This makes sense, because what you may be seeing on the client is likely to be the cached UserControl, rather than the actual object.

Listing 15-5   *The UserControl that uses the PartialCachingAttribute*

```
 1:   namespace PartialPageCachingDemo
 2:   {
 3:     using System;
 4:     using System.Data;
 5:     using System.Drawing;
 6:     using System.Web;
 7:     using System.Web.Caching;
 8:     using System.Web.UI;
 9:     using System.Web.UI.WebControls;
10:     using System.Web.UI.HtmlControls;
11:
12:     [PartialCaching(36000)]
13:     public abstract class CachedControl : System.Web.UI.UserControl
14:     {
15:       protected System.Web.UI.WebControls.Label Label1;
16:       protected System.Web.UI.WebControls.Button Button1;
17:       protected System.Web.UI.HtmlControls.HtmlGenericControl P1;
18:       protected System.Web.UI.WebControls.Xml Xml1;
19:
20:       private void Page_Load(object sender, System.EventArgs e)
21:       {
22:         Label1.Text = "Control updated: " + DateTime.Now.ToString();
23:         if( !IsPostBack )
24:           Initialize();
25:       }
```

```
26:
27:     private void Initialize()
28:     {
29:       SetData("sales.xml", "sales.xsl");
30:     }
31:
32:     public void SetData( string document, string transform)
33:     {
34:       Xml1.DocumentSource = document;
35:       Xml1.TransformSource = transform;
36:     }
37:
38:     [Web Form Designer generated code]
39:
40:   }
41: }
```

NOTE

We can't simply add the PartialCachingAttribute to the XmlModule.ascx control in the IBuySpy portal. The reason this particular revision wouldn't work in the portal is that the XmlModule.ascx inherits from the PortalModuleControl, which is a UserControl. A weird side effect of the PartialCachingAttribute is that the UserControl is wrapped inside of the PartialCachingControl class, which does not inherit from UserControl or the PortalModuleControl. When the portal dynamically loads the control, it attempts to cast it to PortalModuleControl on line 72 of the DesktopDefault.aspx page. This cast is invalid because the loaded control is actually a PartialCachingControl.

The PartialCachingAttribute on line 12 of Listing 15-5 indicates that the page will be cached for 36,000 seconds, or 10 hours. The rest of the code is plain-vanilla UserControl code. This code, which is similar to the XmlModule.ascx in the IBuySpy portal, displays the contents of the sales.xml XML document, formatted using the sales.xsl XSL transform document.

Caching Data

Thus far, I have demonstrated how to cache whole pages and fragments of pages. Sometimes it is the data you want to cache instead of the page. For example, data that is read from a database and is used across multiple pages can be cached in the Cache property of a Page. (The Cache class is defined in System.Web.Caching if you are interested in exploring the help documentation.)

The classic example of using a cache for storing data is storing a user's shopping cart as the user travels around the Web site. The IBuySpy portal uses the Cache for a different purpose. The portal caches the user controls that make up various pages in the portal application.

The IBuySpy defines a custom control, CachedPortalModuleControl. The CachedPortal ModuleControl represents the data that a portal module is composed of. If you set the

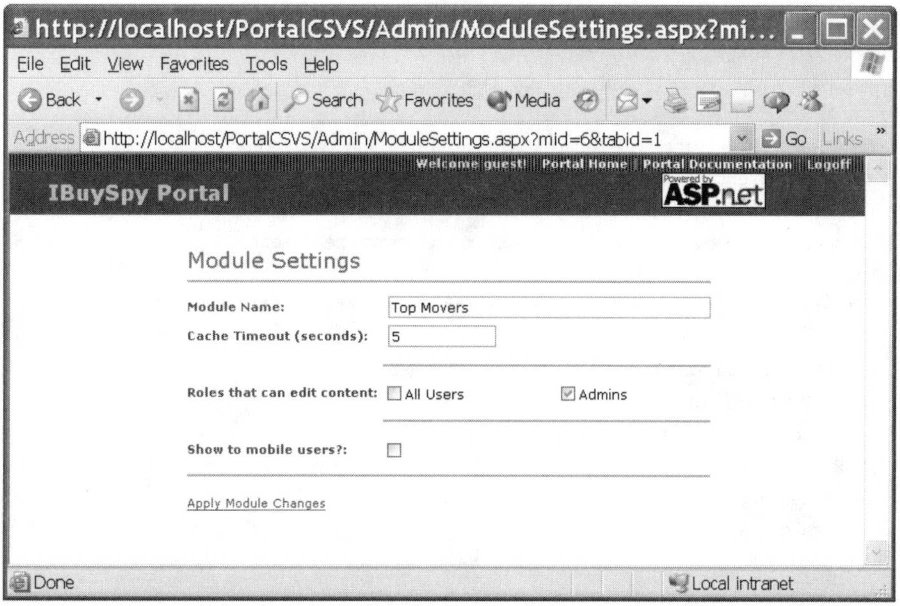

Figure 15-7   *Use the Module Settings page in the portal to indicate that a page should be cached.*

Modules table, CacheTime column—either directly in the database or in the Module Settings administration page in the portal (see Figure 15-7)—then the portal will use the Cache. Pages will be cached and subsequent requests for the same page will be created out of the Cache.

Portal Caching

The election to load a new control or create one from the Cache occurs in the Page_Init method for the IBuySpy portal shown in Listing 15-6.

Listing 15-6   *The portal will load a new page or use cached pages depending on the Modules.CacheTime column in the portal database.*

```
1:  private void Page_Init(object sender, EventArgs e) {
2:    //
3:    // CODEGEN: This call is required by the ASP.NET Web Form Designer.
4:    //
5:    InitializeComponent();
6:
7:  //*********************************************************************
8:    //
9:    // Page_Init Event Handler
```

```
10: //
11: // The Page_Init event handler executes at the very beginning
12: // of each page request (immediately before Page_Load).
13: //
14: // The Page_Init event handler below determines the tab index
15: // of the currently requested portal view, and then calls the
16: // PopulatePortalSection utility method to
17: // dynamically populate the left, center and right hand sections
18: // of the portal tab.
19: //*********************************************************************
20:
21:    // Obtain PortalSettings from Current Context
22:    PortalSettings portalSettings = (PortalSettings)
23:      HttpContext.Current.Items["PortalSettings"];
24:    // Ensure that the visiting user has access to the current page
25:    if PortalSecurity.IsInRoles(portalSettings.ActiveTab.AuthorizedRoles)
26:      == false) {
27:      Response.Redirect("~/Admin/AccessDenied.aspx");
28:    }
29:    // Dynamically inject a signin login module into the top left-hand
30:    // corner of the home page if the client is not yet authenticated
31:    if ((Request.IsAuthenticated == false) && (portalSettings.ActiveTab.TabIndex == 0)) {
32:      LeftPane.Controls.Add(
33:        Page.LoadControl("~/DesktopModules/SignIn.ascx"));
34:      LeftPane.Visible = true;
35:    }
36:    // Dynamically Populate the Left, Center and Right pane sections
37:    if (portalSettings.ActiveTab.Modules.Count > 0) {
38:
39:      // Loop through each entry in the configuration system for this tab
40:      foreach (ModuleSettings _moduleSettings in
41:        portalSettings.ActiveTab.Modules) {
42:        Control parent = Page.FindControl(_moduleSettings.PaneName);
43:
44:        // If no caching is specified, create the user control instance
45:        // and dynamically inject it into the page.  Otherwise, create a
46:        // cached module instance that may or may not optionally
47:        // inject the module
48:        if ((_moduleSettings.CacheTime) == 0) {
49:          PortalModuleControl portalModule =
50:            (PortalModuleControl)
51:            Page.LoadControl(_moduleSettings.DesktopSrc);
52:          portalModule.PortalId = portalSettings.PortalId;
```

```
53:          portalModule.ModuleConfiguration = _moduleSettings;
54:
55:        parent.Controls.Add(portalModule);
56:      }
57:      else {
58:        CachedPortalModuleControl portalModule = new
59:          CachedPortalModuleControl();
60:
61:        portalModule.PortalId = portalSettings.PortalId;
62:        portalModule.ModuleConfiguration = _moduleSettings;
63:
64:        parent.Controls.Add(portalModule);
65:      }
66:
67:        // Dynamically inject separator break between portal modules
68:        parent.Controls.Add(new LiteralControl("<" + "br" + ">"));
69:        parent.Visible = true;
70:    }
71:  }
72: }
```

If Modules.CacheTime is 0, then we create a new instance of a PortalModuleControl by
loading a page that inherits from that UserControl. This occurs in the single statement spanning
lines 49, 50, and 51 of Listing 15-6. However, the *else* condition kicks in—boldfaced on lines
57 through 65—if the CacheTime is greater than 0. That is, if the control is cached, we will
create a control by constructing an instance of the CachedPortalModuleControl wrapper.

The CachedPortalModuleControl determines whether the requested control has actually
been cached. If it has not, then CachedPortalModuleControl loads the page in the same
manner as shown on lines 49, 50, and 51 of Listing 15-6. However, if the control is cached,
then the control is created from the cache. The CachedPortalModuleControl is provided in
Listing 15-7. (Both the PortalModuleControl and the CachedPortalModuleControl are
defined in DesktopControls.cs.)

Listing 15-7   *The CachedPortalModuleControl acts as a wrapper for cached portal modules,
loading the control if it hasn't been cached yet.*

```
1:  public class CachedPortalModuleControl : Control {
2:
3:    // Private field variables
4:
5:    private ModuleSettings   _moduleConfiguration;
6:    private String           _cachedOutput = "";
7:    private int              _portalId = 0;
8:
```

```
 9:
10:     // Public property accessors
11:
12:     public ModuleSettings ModuleConfiguration {
13:
14:       get {
15:         return _moduleConfiguration;
16:       }
17:       set {
18:         _moduleConfiguration = value;
19:       }
20:     }
21:
22:     public int ModuleId {
23:
24:       get {
25:         return _moduleConfiguration.ModuleId;
26:       }
27:     }
28:
29:     public int PortalId {
30:
31:       get {
32:         return _portalId;
33:       }
34:       set {
35:         _portalId = value;
36:       }
37:     }
38:
39:     //*******************************************************************
40:     //
41:     // CacheKey Property
42:     //
43:     // The CacheKey property is used to calculate a "unique" cache key
44:     // entry to be used to store/retrieve the portal module's content
45:     // from the ASP.NET Cache.
46:     //
47:     //*******************************************************************
48:
49:     public String CacheKey {
50:
51:       get {
52:         return "Key:" + this.GetType().ToString() +
```

```
53:       this.ModuleId + PortalSecurity.IsInRoles(
54:         _moduleConfiguration.AuthorizedEditRoles);
55:     }
56:   }
57:
58:   //********************************************************************
59:   //
60:   // CreateChildControls Method
61:   //
62:   // The CreateChildControls method is called when the ASP.NET Page
63:   // Framework determines that it is time to instantiate a
64:   // server control.
65:   // The CachedPortalModuleControl control overrides this method
66:   // and attempts to resolve any previously cached
67:   // output of the portal module from the ASP.NET cache.
68:   //
69:   // If it doesn't find cached output from a previous request, then the
70:   // CachedPortalModuleControl will instantiate and add the portal
71:   // module's User Control instance into the page tree.
72:   //
73:   //********************************************************************
74:
75:   protected override void CreateChildControls() {
76:
77:     // Attempt to resolve previously cached content
78:     // from the ASP.NET Cache
79:     if (_moduleConfiguration.CacheTime > 0) {
80:       _cachedOutput = (String) Context.Cache[CacheKey];
81:     }
82:
83:     // If no cached content is found, then instantiate and add
84:     // the portal module user control into the portal's
85:     // page server control tree
86:     if (_cachedOutput == null) {
87:
88:       base.CreateChildControls();
89:
90:       PortalModuleControl module = (PortalModuleControl)
91:       Page.LoadControl(_moduleConfiguration.DesktopSrc);
92:
93:       module.ModuleConfiguration = this.ModuleConfiguration;
94:       module.PortalId = this.PortalId;
95:
96:       this.Controls.Add(module);
```

```
 97:     }
 98:  }
 99:
100:  //**********************************************************************
101:  //
102:  // Render Method
103:  //
104:  // The Render method is called when the ASP.NET Page Framework
105:  // determines that it is time to render content into the page
106:  // output stream.
107:  // The CachedPortalModuleControl control overrides this method
108:  // and captures the output generated by the portal module user
109:  // control. It then adds this content into the
110:  // ASP.NET Cache for future requests.
111:  //**********************************************************************
112:
113:  protected override void Render(HtmlTextWriter output) {
114:
115:     // If no caching is specified, render the child tree and return
116:
117:     if (_moduleConfiguration.CacheTime == 0) {
118:       base.Render(output);
119:       return;
120:     }
121:
122:     // If no cached output was found from a previous request, render
123:     // child controls into a TextWriter, and then cache the results
124:     // in the ASP.NET Cache for future requests.
125:
126:     if (_cachedOutput == null) {
127:
128:       TextWriter tempWriter = new StringWriter();
129:       base.Render(new HtmlTextWriter(tempWriter));
130:       _cachedOutput = tempWriter.ToString();
131:
132:       Context.Cache.Insert(CacheKey, _cachedOutput,
133:         null, DateTime.Now.AddSeconds(_moduleConfiguration.CacheTime),
134:         TimeSpan.Zero);
135:     }
136:     // Output the user control's content
137:
138:     output.Write(_cachedOutput);
139:  }
140:}
```

In Listing 15-7, the two methods that implement the CachedControlPortalModuleControl are the overridden CreateChildControls and Render methods. CreateChildControls—lines 75 through 98 of Listing 15-7—is responsible for reading the cache and loading the control module if the module has not been cached once already. Subsequent requests will come from the cache because the Render method of the control is added to the cache as a text stream (using the StringWriter class on line 128. Line 132) actually stuffs the HTML representing the UserControl into the Cache. If you examine the value of the Cache, you will see that the value placed in the Cache is the literal HTML text that makes up the page.

It is the HTML text representing our control that is the data we are interested in caching. This data could just as easily be an ADO.NET DataSet or some other data. The manner in which we express how it is stored in the Cache is the same.

Adding Data to the Cache

The reference to the Context object on line 132 of Listing 15-7 represents an HttpContext object (or the objectification of a single HTTP request). Context.Cache returns an instance of the Cache object. Line 132 demonstrates the basic step for inserting an object into the Cache. There are four overloaded versions of Cache.Insert that you can reference in the help document for Visual Studio .NET. The example used in the portal is one of the more complex, including everything except a priority and a callback delegate for notification when cached items are removed.

The first argument, as demonstrated in Listing 15-7, is the key name that will be used to identify the object. The second argument is the object to cache. This argument is typed as an object. The third argument—null, in the example—is a cache dependency, which we will talk about in a moment. The fourth argument is the absolute expiration time, and the final argument is the sliding expiration interval. In the example, the sliding expiration is TimeSpan.Zero. This means that the items are not cached on a sliding expiration; as a result, the cached item will be purged after the absolute expiration period has passed. Had we expressed a non-zero TimeSpan, then the cached item would be removed after an interval equal to the last access time plus the TimeSpan. For example, if TimeSpan were equal to 10 minutes, then the object would be removed from the cache after the expiration period plus the sliding expiration period had elapsed.

Creating a File Dependency

You can create a CacheDependency on cached items. For example, you could cache data read from an external file and create a dependency on that file. If the file is modified, the Cache would be updated. The portal does not employ the CacheDependency object, so we will return to our PartialPageCachingDemo.sln to demonstrate.

The DependentControl.ascx UserControl implements caching using a dependency based on a file. If any of the external files used to create the dependency change, then the cached item associated with the dependency is dumped. The way the code is written in Listing 15-8, if either the XSL/T or XML documents change, the cache will be flushed.

Listing 15-8 *Cache dependencies based on an external file*

```
1:   private void Page_Load(object sender, System.EventArgs e)
2:   {
3:     Label1.Text = "CacheDependency: " + DateTime.Now.ToString();
4:
5:
6:     if( Context.Cache["transform"] == null )
7:     {
8:       XslTransform transform = new  XslTransform();
9:       transform.Load(Server.MapPath("sales.xsl"));
10:      Xml1.Transform = transform;
11:      Context.Cache.Insert("transform", Xml1.Transform,
12:         new CacheDependency(Server.MapPath("sales.xsl")));
13:    }
14:    else
15:      Xml1.Transform = (XslTransform)Cache["transform"];
16:
17:    if(Context.Cache["document"] == null)
18:    {
19:      Xml1.DocumentSource= "sales.xml";
20:      Context.Cache.Insert("document", Xml1.Document,
21:        new CacheDependency(Server.MapPath("sales.xml")));
22:
23:    }
24:    else
25:      Xml1.Document = (XmlDocument)Cache["document"];
26: }
```

In Listing 15-8, there are two cached items that are associated with a CacheDependency. The first is an XslTransform object and the second is an XmlDocument. The first time this code is run, an XslTransform (line 8 of Listing 15-8) and an XmlDocument (line 19) are created. The XslTransform is created explicitly on lines 8 and 9 and cached on line 11. The XmlDocument is created implicitly when we provide an Xml.DocumentSource on line 19. (It is necessary to map a file name to a physical server path, as demonstrated on lines 12 and 21.) Both objects are added to the Cache employing a CacheDependency based on the existence of the respective files. As long as the files remain the same, the cached objects are valid. If we edit either sales.xml or sales.xsl, the cached object is dumped and the *if* part of the conditional statement will run.

Try the PartialPageCachingDemo.sln. You will see that the UserControl that uses the PartialCachingAttribute will be out of date if you change the sales.xml file, but the DependentControl UserControl will automatically update the data when the page is submitted.

Each approach to caching has its uses. Choose between output, partial, or data caching according to what would suit your needs. Cached pages, partial pages, and data are not specifically tied to individual users or pages. This data is shared across all requests. If you want to cache data relative to a user, you can use the Session cache.

Using the Session Cache

Every user connection is represented by a session. You can cache data associated with individual user sessions by storing objects in the Session cache. The Session cache works in two modes. A cookie containing a unique session identifier is stored on the client's machine. The session identifier uniquely identifies the client between trips to the server. This is the default mode. In some situations, cookies may be disabled, and devices such as cell phones that do not support cookies will have to rely on cookieless sessions. Cookieless sessions work by embedding the session identifier into the URL; the session identifier is parsed out of the URL when it is submitted.

NOTE

I am going to demonstrate session caching that relies on cookies. You convert to cookieless session states by setting the <sessionState> tag's cookieless attribute to true in the web.config file. Try experimenting with this mode to see the session identifier mixed in with the URL. (Refer to Figure 15-8 for an example of a cookieless session URL. The Web page is from the SessionDemo.sln.)

![WebForm1 - Microsoft Internet Explorer window. Address: http://localhost/SessionDemo/(bmyqwwzabyvy5dyjlachsn55)/WebForm1.aspx. A text field contains "If you've got the grits, serve 'em!" with a Store button. Below is "Item Number:" with a field containing "0" and a Retrieve button.]

Figure 15-8   *The session identifier passed as part of the URL in a cookieless session*

By default, items cached in the Session are associated with a single session and are cached in memory. When the session ends or the server restarts, the session information is lost. In-process session management is fast, since it runs in memory, but it is not scalable, because the session information does not survive a server reboot and cannot be used in Web farms. Fortunately, there are two other ways to store session information, using an external session server and the SQL Server database. These other methods will survive IIS server restarts and, because they work well in Web farms, are very scalable. I will talk about configuring out-of-process state management in the sections "Configuring the Session State Server" and "Configuring the SQL Server for Session Management." For now, I will demonstrate how to use the Session cache in general, regardless of whether the information is cached in or out of process.

Caching Data in the Session

Caching data in the Session cache is simply a matter of indexing the Session argument with a unique name for the datum and assigning the data to the Session object. The data can be retrieved from the Session cache by placing the name-indexed Session object on the right side of an assignment, casting the return value to the known type.

For example, we can store the Text property of a TextBox control in the Session object and retrieve that data at some other point during the same session. Storing some text in the Session object can be accomplished by assigning a literal string, as demonstrated here:

```
Session["text"] = "If you've got the grits, serve 'em.";
```

The same data can be retrieved and assigned to the Text property of a control named TextBox1. Here is an example that reads the data out of the Session cache.

```
TextBox1.Text = (string)Session["text"];
```

There is no point in storing the information in a control using the Session, because you can accomplish the same thing much more easily by enabling the *view* state. For example, TextBox1.EnableViewState = true will instruct the page to store the value of TextBox1 in a hidden field within the page. Listing 15-9 shows the *view* state information in boldface for the Web page in the SessionDemo.sln.

Listing 15-9 *ViewState information stored in the page in a hidden field*

```
<!DOCTYPE HTML PUBLIC "-//W3C//DTD HTML 4.0 Transitional//EN" >
<HTML>
<HEAD>
<title>WebForm1</title>
  <meta name="GENERATOR" Content="Microsoft Visual Studio 7.0">
  <meta name="CODE_LANGUAGE" Content="C#">
  <meta name="vs_defaultClientScript" content="JavaScript">
  <meta name="vs_targetSchema"
```

```
content="http://schemas.microsoft.com/intellisense/ie5">
  </HEAD>
  <body MS_POSITIONING="GridLayout">
  <form name="Form1" method="post" action="WebForm1.aspx" id="Form1">
  <input type="hidden" name="__VIEWSTATE"
    value="dDwtNDM5MzM1ODM2Ozs+kKb/ejZfdsDgE9O7OiAWcI8CLro=" />


  <input type="submit" name="Button1" value="Store" id="Button1"
   style="width:86px;Z-INDEX: 101; LEFT: 458px; POSITION: absolute; TOP:
   43px" />
  <input name="TextBox1" type="text" value="If you've got the grits, serve
    'em!" id="TextBox1" style="width:397px;Z-INDEX: 102; LEFT: 36px;
    POSITION: absolute; TOP: 41px" />
  <input type="submit" name="Button2" value="Retrieve" id="Button2"
    style="Z-INDEX: 103; LEFT: 458px; POSITION: absolute; TOP: 84px" />
  </form>
</body>
</HTML>
```

However, if you want to pass information from one page to the next, then *view* state won't help you. Stuff the information in the Session.

An example of when you might elect to use the Session cache is illustrated on a Web site like that of Federal Express. Shipping a document spans a couple of pages. You select your shipping information to create a shipment. After you have created the shipment, you can elect to schedule a courier. The courier information is on a separate page, but when scheduling a courier, FedEx needs to know who is shipping what. You could use Session state to track an object representing a user's shipment, and that information would be available when the user navigated from creating a shipment to scheduling a pickup.

Of course, the implication here is that you can put complex objects into the Session cache—and, in fact, you can. You can put custom objects or objects like an ADO.NET DataSet into the Session, making it easier to maintain complex information between round trips to the server or even in the stateless world of the Web.

Caching Objects in the Session Cache

When your application is on one page, you might be gathering information about a user, such as information that describes a service request. When the page is submitted to the server, you could post the information to a database and track the user by a cookie on the user's workstation. Moving to the next step, you could retrieve the information back from the database—remember, object-oriented code runs on the server to render the page and then disappears—and use that information to continue servicing the user's request. A scenario using the FedEx example would be to create a shipment and schedule a shipment pickup. The result is that there is a lot of back and forth between the IIS server and the database.

As an alternative, you could store the user's information in the Session cache, and then you wouldn't have to make all of those expensive extra trips to the database server. When the user has finished, you could update the database all at one time. The end result is that objects representing what your users are doing are in memory rather than in the database.

A reasonable person might surmise that objects representing a user's interaction don't sound very robust. Recall, though, that we can use the default in-process Session server or a more robust out-of-process server that can withstand IIS restarts. As a result, we can use multiple Web servers, and the Session information can withstand IIS restarts needing code to constantly write pieces of information to the application's database. (Refer to the "Secondary Topics" section for more information.)

You can add and remove objects in the Session cache in precisely the same way as you add and remove simple data from the Session cache. Refer to the Session cache property, index it with a unique string identifier, and use object assignment. Listing 15-10 demonstrates code that stores an ArrayList of strings into the Session cache. The ArrayList could just as easily be a DataSet.

Listing 15-10   *Storing a complex object in the Session cache*

```
1:  using System;
2:  using System.Collections;
3:  using System.ComponentModel;
4:  using System.Data;
5:  using System.Drawing;
6:  using System.Web;
7:  using System.Web.SessionState;
8:  using System.Web.UI;
9:  using System.Web.UI.WebControls;
10: using System.Web.UI.HtmlControls;
11:
12: namespace SessionDemo
13: {
14:   /// <summary>
15:   /// Summary description for WebForm1.
16:   /// </summary>
17:   public class WebForm1 : System.Web.UI.Page
18:   {
19:     protected System.Web.UI.WebControls.Button Button1;
20:     protected System.Web.UI.WebControls.TextBox TextBox1;
21:     protected System.Web.UI.WebControls.TextBox TextBox2;
22:     protected System.Web.UI.WebControls.Label Label1;
23:     protected System.Web.UI.WebControls.Button Button2;
24:
25:     const string name = "text";
26:
```

```
27:      [ Web Form Designer generated code]
28:
29:      private ArrayList Text
30:      {
31:        get
32:        {
33:          if( Session[name] == null )
34:            Session[name] = new ArrayList();
35:          return (ArrayList)Session[name];
36:        }
37:      }
38:
39:      private void Button1_Click(object sender, System.EventArgs e)
40:      {
41:        Text.Add(TextBox1.Text);
42:      }
43:
44:      private void Button2_Click(object sender, System.EventArgs e)
45:      {
46:        try
47:        {
48:          TextBox1.Text = (string)Text[Int32.Parse(TextBox2.Text)];
49:        }
50:        catch
51:        {
52:          TextBox1.Text = "Not found, enter a valid number less than " +
53:            Text.Count.ToString();
54:        }
55:      }
56:    }
57: }
```

If you examine the code in Listing 15-10, you might have to look twice before it is obvious that this is code-behind for an ASP.NET Web page. It is. This is one of the beauties of .NET. The code-behind for building Web applications is fairly similar to the code in Windows or Console applications.

A style I prefer is to hide the Session indexing code in one place, localizing Session initialization and references in case I want to modify something related to the Session object. Additionally, referring to a property named Text makes the code more readable than having Session[name] and conditional code that checks for null all over the place.

Lines 29 through 37 of Listing 15-10 use lazy instantiation to create the ArrayList on demand and localize all references to the Session cache to that single location in the page. The rest of the code is very manageable.

Managing the Session Cache

The Session object is an instance of the HttpSessionState class. There are several methods for managing the Session state. You can determine the number of items in the Session cache through the Count property. You can request the SessionID, obtain a list of all Keys, Abandon the current session, or Clear all items in the cache. Refer to the help documentation on the HttpSessionState class for a complete reference.

Using the Application Cache

The Application cache works syntactically just like the Session cache. You can store simple data or complex objects in the Application cache. The question is: when would you put something in the Application cache? The answer: when you want to cache some data that is shared at the application level, that is, by all users.

An enterprise application I worked on had a commissary feature. Every consumer could purchase items from a small commissary that was available to everyone. Instead of reading the commissary items for every user, we read the commissary items when the application started Global.asax Application_Start event. The items were always available without further hits on the database.

Another option might have been to render the page and use output caching to store the rendered page, also avoiding additional database hits. However, we actually picked items from the commissary list and used those items to create orders. Hence, instead of static data, we needed dynamic objects, and we resolved on the Application cache. To demonstrate using the Application cache, replace Application with Session on lines 33, 34, and 35 of Listing 15-10. Open two or more Web pages, and you will see that all pages—representing sessions—can see all of the strings in the ArrayList. Switch back to Session, and each page will be able to see only the strings entered for that session.

Use the Session cache when the data is relevant to a single user represented by a single session, and use the Application cache when the data is relevant all users.

Secondary Topics

Every application will not need to use all of the capabilities of .NET. It is valuable to know as much as possible about what is available in .NET and selectively use those features.

The IBuySpy portal demonstrates how to use cookies, output page caching, and the Cache object. However, the portal does not use Session or Application caching; yet, with a little experimentation, you can quickly determine that the portal is a powerful, maintainable, and extensible Web application. (Keep in mind that portal code is available as a starting point for your Web applications.)

We talked about the Session and Application caches even though they are not in the portal. I want to wrap up this chapter by demonstrating how to configure the out-of-process state servers. These two states servers operate more slowly than the in-process state management but are more robust and support optimal Web scalability. That is, you can use one of the out-of-process state servers in a Web farm, and they are capable of maintaining state even if IIS restarts.

All three state servers have the Web.config file in common. You can modify the <sessionState> tag to indicate which session state server you will be using and then configure the server accordingly. Listing 15-11 contains a default <sessionState> tag taken from the Web.config file for the SessionDemo.sln.

Listing 15-11   *An example Web.config file's <sessionState> tag*

```
<sessionState mode="InProc"
  stateConnectionString="tcpip=127.0.0.1:42424"
  sqlConnectionString="data source=127.0.0.1;user id=sa;password="
  cookieless="false"
  timeout="20"
/>
```

In Listing 15-11, the mode attribute indicates the session state server that will be used. The four possible values are InProc, Off, SQLServer, and StateServer. InProc is the in-process server used by default. Off indicates that session state is disabled. SQLServer indicates that you will be using SQL Server out-of-process to manage state, and StateServer is the ASP.NET State Server represented by the asponet_state.exe Windows service application.

If you specify SQLServer for mode, the sqlConnectionString will be used to connect to that state server. If you specify StateServer for mode, the stateConnectionString will be used on the loopback IP 127.0.0.1 on port 42424 to talk to the aspnet_state.exe service. The cookieless attribute is false, indicating that the session identifier is stored as a cookie; change it to true to pass the session identifier in the URL. The last value, timeout, indicates the number of minutes the session can remain idle before the session information is abandoned.

The InProc and Off mode state configurations require no extra steps. Read the remaining two sections for instructions on how to configure the two out-of-process state servers.

Configuring the Session State Server

The ASP.NET State Server ships with the .NET framework and is installed automatically when the .NET framework is installed. You can configure any server to manage session state using the ASP.NET State Server. Complete the numbered steps to use the out-of-process state server.

1. Modify the Web.config file for the application that will be using the aspnet_state.exe Windows service.

2. Change mode to StateServer and the tcpip value of the stateConnectionString to the IP address of the server running the ASP.NET State Service. You can leave the default value if the Web application and the aspnet_state.exe service are running on the same machine. (The service listens on port 42424, so be sure to leave this value.)

3. Open a command window (or the Services console) and start the aspnet_state.exe service. To start the service from the command prompt, enter **net start aspnet_state**.

TIP

*You can stop and start any Windows service with **net stop** servicename and **net start** servicename, respectively, if you know the name of the service application.*

You can start and stop the service from the Services console, shown in Figure 15-9, or use the net start and net stop commands. To stop the service from a command prompt, type **net stop aspnet_state**.

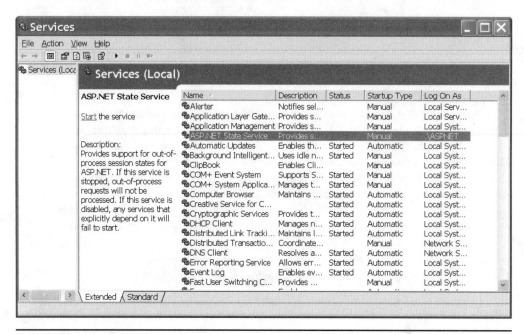

Figure 15-9 *The Services console, used to start and stop Windows services, focused here on the ASP.NET State Service application*

Configuring the SQL Server for Session Management

Using SQL Server to manage state is the most robust form of state management. SQL Server runs out of process, providing for support of Web farms; you can also cluster multiple instances of SQL Server together. If one SQL Server instance goes down, other servers pick up the slack. Follow the numbered steps to set up a single SQL Server instance to manage the session state.

1. Modify the Web.config file mode attribute to SQLServer, leaving everything else as is.

2. Run Microsoft's SQL Server Query Analyzer and run the InstallSqlState.sql script (shown in Figure 15-10). This script will create the SQL Server Session state database. (The InstalSqlState.sql script is installed with the .NET framework by default in the Winnt\Microsoft.Net\Framework*version*\ directory, where version is the latest version of the framework.)

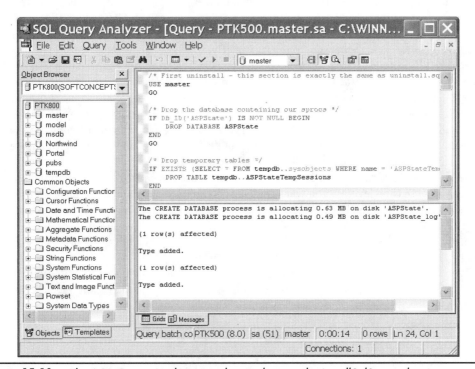

Figure 15-10   *The SQL Query Analyzer can be used to run the InstallSqlState.sql script, which builds the ASPState database.*

3. Run the InstallSqlState.sql script logged in with SQL Server authentication and the same account. The script will create an SQL Server Instance named ASPState on the machine you logged into and ran the InstallSqlState.sql script against.

That's all there is to it.

Summary

There are several ways to manage state information in ASP.NET. Some of them are used in the IBuySpy portal application, and all of them are available for C# and ASP.NET developers. Let's wrap up the chapter by reviewing the basic ways we can store state information in ASP.NET.

You can use cookies for small pieces of information up to 4K. Cookies are used for session identifiers if you are using Session caching, and are commonly used to store information such as an authenticated user identifier. *View* state is supported in Web forms controls. You can enable *view* state information if you will be recreating a page, or disable it if not. If you enable *view* state, then controls will maintain their individual values between round trips to the server, and you won't need to cache this information. *View* state is maintained in an encrypted hidden field that is sent to the server. If you will be rendering a specific page each time, then disable *view* state to avoid the extra work of restoring information that will be overwritten with new data. You also have the option of passing state information in an URL-encoded request as parameters. Output page caching and partial page output caching can be employed to save an entire page or individual UserControls on a page. The Cache can be used to cache data that is accessible to everyone. Output page and data caching are good ways to optimize your application by eliminating the need for JITting and rendering pages or data that are redundant across sessions.

Finally, the Application and Session caches can be used to cache data at the application or individual session level. If you want any user running your application to have access to shared data, then you can stuff objects into the Application cache, reserving the Session cache for data relevant to a single session. Cache information can be stored in-process for single-server ASP.NET applications with optimal responsiveness, or out-of-process caching can be configured for maximum scalability and robustness.

Web applications are stateless by nature, but it is clear that we do need to track information about the users and the state of an application—and there are a lot of possibilities to choose from in ASP.NET.

CHAPTER
16

Security and Authentication

IN THIS CHAPTER:

Demonstrated Topics

Using Windows NTLM Authentication

**Implementing Forms Authentication
with Cookies**

Implementing the SignIn Module

Administering Users

Secondary Topics

Implementing Code Access Security

Summary

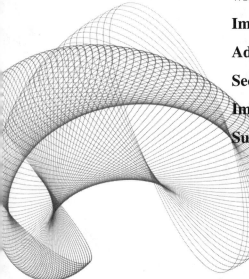

T here are two kinds of general security that we will talk about in this chapter. There is the security associated with a user and role, and there is the security associated with code. The first form of security is used in the IBuySpy portal and is manifested as *roles-based* security (or Windows security). Another kind of security is referred to as *Code Access Security* and is new in .NET. The portal uses the former kind of security; hence, we will talk about roles-based security in the "Demonstrated Topics" section and Code Access Security in the "Secondary Topics" section.

Roles-based security is the kind of security that you are probably most familiar with. Define a role, assign user names and passwords to users, and allow them to perform some operations based on their authenticated role. For Web applications running behind a firewall—intranets—we can use Windows authentication. For extranets and the Internet, we can employ roles-based authentication with cookies. The IBuySpy portal is capable of allowing you to use Windows authentication if you are running the portal as an intranet application or Forms authentication if not.

The second kind of security, Code Access Security, is new in .NET. Code Access Security is not designed to be used instead of the roles-based or Windows security. Code Access Security was designed to complement traditional security models. Roles-based or Windows security authenticates the user, and Code Access Security authenticates the code, as it were.

The key is not to choose one over the other. Nor is it necessary to use both all of the time. Instead, you can use roles-based and Windows authentication for many kinds of applications and rely on the extra security provided for managed code—.NET applications—by default with Code Access Security. The default configurations are pretty good. Where Code Access Security needs extra scrutiny is on the World Wide Web. If you are running applications that are interchanging data across the Web, then you will need to more closely scrutinize the Code Access Security model, in conjunction with traditional security steps.

Demonstrated Topics

The IBuySpy portal supports Windows and Forms authentication, using cookies to store an authenticated user name and password. This chapter will demonstrate how to use cookies, modify the Web.config file for Windows and Forms authentication, implement the SignIn module, and administer the IBuySpy portal.

All of these skills are valid for intranet, extranet, and Internet ASP.NET application development. This section will show you how to

- ▶ Implement the SignIn module and authenticate portal users

- ▶ Modify a Web.config file for Windows and Forms authentication

- ▶ Program with cookies

- ▶ Administer IBuySpy portal users

The "Secondary Topics" section will introduce the Code Access Security model, new with .NET. These topics include programming with imperative and declarative Code Access

Security and how to administer the Code Access Security policy. When you combine traditional roles-based or Windows security with the complementary Code Access Security, you can diminish the security threat from the riskiest avenue of attack, the Web.

Using Windows NTLM Authentication

You can build ASP.NET applications using simple Windows NT Lan Manager (NTLM) authentication. Relying on internal network Windows user accounts is a pretty reasonable model for ASP.NET intranet applications.

As a reminder, intranet applications are internal network applications that run on a browser over a TCP/IP network. However, they reside behind your firewall, so only authenticated users and PCs wired into your network should have access to these sites. The portal supports this mode of operation.

NOTE

The Web.config file is not served by IIS. As a result, users cannot request the Web.config file and modify the application settings contained in it.

You can modify the IBuySpy portal's Web.config file (or any ASP.NET application's), setting the user security authentication model by changing the attributes for the <authentication> tag. The IBuySpy portal is a teaching tool and conveniently has this metadata commented out inside of the Web.config file. All we have to do is modify the Web.config file.

Modifying the Web.config File for Windows Authentication

By default, the IBuySpy portal uses Forms authentication. We have to comment out the tags that set the authentication mode to Forms and uncomment the code that switches to Windows authentication. Listing 16-1 shows the default authentication settings for the portal. (We will come back to Forms authentication in a moment.)

Listing 16-1   *An excerpt from the Web.config file that defines the authentication mode for the IBuySpy portal*

```
<!--IBuySpy Portal supports either Forms authentication (Internet)
    or Windows authentication (for intranets).  Forms Authentication is
    the default.  To change to Windows authentication, comment the
    <authentication mode="Forms"> section below, and uncomment the
    <authentication mode="Windows"> section. -->

    <authentication mode="Forms">
    <forms name=".ASPXAUTH" protection="All" timeout="60" />
    </authentication>
```

```
<!--<authentication mode="Windows" />
<authorization>
<deny users="?" />
</authorization>-->
```

TIP

The <!- - begins a comment block in HTML and XML, and the - -> ends the comment block.

Uncomment the <authentication> and <authorization> tags in boldface and comment the <authentication> tag, setting the default mode to Forms. When you run the portal application with Windows authentication, you will n see the SignIotn module.

The authentication tag with attribute mode="Windows" instructs the application to use the Windows user name and password to authenticate the user. If you are logged into your computer, then you are logged into the application. The portal will still authenticate your user name against the users and roles configuration data in the portal database, but this happens automatically without your having to specifically log into the portal. (The portal authenticates the user the same way internally, regardless of the authentication mode in the Web.config file. We'll explore the authentication code in the next section, "Implementing Forms Authentication with Cookies.")

The <authorization> tag supports two subtags, <deny> and <allow>, which each have two attributes. Let's look next at the purpose of <deny> and <allow>.

Denying and Allowing Authorization

The Windows authentication mode in the portal uses the <deny> tag. The <deny> tag has two attributes: Users and Roles. We can deny specific users or roles by providing a comma-delimited list of users or roles or use one of two wildcard values, * or ?.

The asterisk (*) refers to all users and the question mark (?) refers to anonymous users. For example, if you use

```
<deny users="?" />
```

then anonymous users will not be allowed to access the Web site. A comma-delimited list of roles or the ? or * wildcard can be used for the <allow> tag too.

When the Web application runs, the <deny> and <allow> tags are read from top to bottom until it finds the first access rule that is relevant to a user. For example, if you have

```
<authorization>
<allow Roles="Admins" />
<deny Users="*" />
</authorization>
```

then users in the administrative role will be allowed access, and all other users will be denied access to the Web application. (Refer to the AuthenticationDemo.sln available for download from **www.osborne.com**.)

TIP

The Machine.config file is installed in the C:\WINNT\Microsoft.NET\ Framework\ [version]\ CONFIG\ machine.config folder by default.

The top-level .config file is the Machine.config file. By default, Machine.config uses the <Allow Users="*" /> tag, providing access to all users on the machine. This is the default configuration. You can implement one or more Web.config files for each directory in your Web application. The Web.config file will be examined before access to files in that directory are allowed access, and the authorization rule will be examined before allowing access to users. Thus, you can subdivide your Web application by folders, providing different levels of access for different areas of your Web application.

Implementing Forms Authentication with Cookies

The IBuySpy portal authenticates users regardless of the form of authentication that you use. In this section, we will begin by looking at the configuration settings for Forms authentication and then walk through the code that is used to authenticate users for both Windows and Forms authentication.

Modifying the Web.config File for Forms Authentication

The IBuySpy portal defaults to Forms authentication. The default Web.config settings for the portal are provided in Listing 16-2.

Listing 16-2   *The Forms authentication configuration settings*

```
<authentication mode="Forms">
  <forms name=".ASPXAUTH" protection="All" timeout="60" />
</authentication>
```

The four possible values for the <authentication> tag's mode attribute are Windows, Forms, Passport, and None. Windows mode authenticates the user based on the authentication information supplied to log into Windows. Forms authentication means that you will supply a login form to authenticate the user, and the Passport mode means that a Passport authentication server will be used to authenticate the user. (None simply means that no authentication will take place.) The portal defaults to Forms authentication, so we'll explore the Web.config file and the IBuySpy authentication code in that context.

The <forms> subtag allows you to supply Name, loginUrl, Protection, Timeout, and Path attributes. IBuySpy uses Name, Protection, and Timeout. (We'll look at the other attributes in the upcoming section, "Defining Forms Attributes.")

The Name attribute is the HTTP cookie name to use for authentication. By default, the name of this cookie is .ASPXAUTH. The Protection attribute supports four possible values, including All, None, Encryption, and Validation. The All Protection attribute indicates that the cookie is protected by encryption and data validation. The Timeout attribute indicates the number of minutes until the cookie will expire. A portal login expires after 60 minutes by default.

Defining Forms Attributes

The two attributes not used in the portal authentication element are the loginUrl and the Path attribute. The Path attribute indicates the path for cookies used by the application. The Path attribute defaults to the root—equivalent to a slash (/)—so we don't need to supply that Path attribute unless we want to use a path other than the root.

The loginUrl will let you provide the URL of a login page. If an unauthenticated user attempts to browse to a page that requires authentication, then the user will be redirected to the page indicated in the loginUrl. The portal displays the login form as a UserControl on the Home page and redirects the user to the AccessDenied.aspx administration page if an attempt is made to navigate to a page that requires authentication. For this reason, the loginUrl is not supplied. However, the portal could redirect the user to the Home page if such an attempt were made.

TIP

If no loginUrl attribute is provided, the default value is default.aspx.

The AuthenticationDemo.sln provides a simple login screen and Web.config file designed to use Forms authentication. The two Web pages are Main.aspx and BrowseToMe.aspx. If you attempt to browse directly to BrowseToMe.aspx, you will be redirected to the page indicated in the loginUrl attribute. The redirected URL will be approximately **http:// localhost/AuthenticationDemo/Main.aspx?ReturnUrl=%2fauthenticationDemo%2fBro wseToMe.aspx**. After the user has been authenticated, the *ReturnUrl* parameter can be used to redirect the user back to the originally requested page.

CAUTION

When users sign out after having been authenticated, they may still be able to browse to pages that require authentication. They will need to close their browser to sign all the way out. For example, you could log in as an IBuySpy administrator, log out, and still return to the Admin page until the browser is closed.

Supplying User Credentials

The <forms> tag accepts a <credentials> tag. The <credentials> tag enables you to supply user name and password credentials in the Web.config file. You can supply these values using an encryption scheme or in the clear. Listing 16-3 puts the <authentication> tag all together, providing you with an example of the <forms> and <credentials> tags. (The listing is taken from the AuthenticationDemo.sln sample application.)

Listing 16-3 *A complete authentication example from the AuthenticationDemo.sln's Web.config file*

```
<authentication mode="Forms">
  <forms name=".ASPXAUTH"
    protection="Encryption"
    loginUrl="Main.aspx"
    path="/">

    <credentials passwordFormat="Clear">
      <user name="DThoreau" password="Walden" />
    </credentials>
  </forms>
</authentication>
```

Listing 16-3 demonstrates how to express Forms authentication using the default cookie name, .ASPXAUTH. The authentication cookie will be encrypted. The loginUrl is Main.aspx, which means the user will be redirected to Main.aspx until authenticated and the default cookie path is expressed. A set of credentials is provided in the clear, expressed by the passwordFormat attribute "Clear".

When a user requests a Web page, the HttpApplication.AuthenticateRequest event is raised. (The handler for this event is defined in the Global.asax file.) At this point, you have an opportunity to provide custom authentication behavior, which is exactly what the IBuySpy portal does.

Authenticating Users

Regardless of whether you are running the portal with Windows or Forms authentication, the portal takes over in the Global.asax's HttpApplication.AuthenticateRequest event handler to provide custom authentication.

If a request from any user is authenticated, the portal replaces the intrinsic User role with an IPrincipal security object that permits the portal to compare the user to roles that are relevant to the application. The AuthenticateRequest event handler is provided in Listing 16-4, followed by a synopsis.

Listing 16-4 *The HttpApplication.AuthenticateRequest event permits you to provide custom IPrincipal security roles.*

```
1:  protected void Application_AuthenticateRequest(Object sender,
2:    EventArgs e)
```

```
3:   {
4:     if (Request.IsAuthenticated == true) {
5:       String[] roles;
6:
7:       // Create the roles cookie if it doesn't exist for this session.
8:       if ((Request.Cookies["portalroles"] == null) ||
9:           (Request.Cookies["portalroles"].Value == "")) {
10:        // Get roles from UserRoles table, and add to cookie
11:        UsersDB user = new UsersDB();
12:        roles = user.GetRoles(User.Identity.Name);
13:
14:        // Create a string to persist the roles
15:        String roleStr = "";
16:        foreach (String role in roles) {
17:          roleStr += role;
18:          roleStr += ";";
19:        }
20:
21:        // Create a cookie authentication ticket.
22:        FormsAuthenticationTicket ticket = new FormsAuthenticationTicket(
23:          1,                             // version
24:          Context.User.Identity.Name,    // user name
25:          DateTime.Now,                  // issue time
26:          DateTime.Now.AddHours(1),      // expires every hour
27:          false,                         // don't persist cookie
28:          roleStr                        // roles
29:        );
30:
31:        // Encrypt the ticket
32:        String cookieStr = FormsAuthentication.Encrypt(ticket);
33:
34:        // Send the cookie to the client
35:        Response.Cookies["portalroles"].Value = cookieStr;
36:        Response.Cookies["portalroles"].Path = "/";
37:        Response.Cookies["portalroles"].Expires =
38:          DateTime.Now.AddMinutes(1);
39:      } else {
40:
41:        // Get roles from roles cookie
42:        FormsAuthenticationTicket ticket =
43:        FormsAuthentication.Decrypt(
44:          Context.Request.Cookies["portalroles"].Value);
45:        //convert the role into a string array
```

```
46:        ArrayList userRoles = new ArrayList();
47:        foreach(String role in ticket.UserData.Split( new char[] {';'} ))
48:        {
49:          userRoles.Add(role);
50:        }
51:        roles = (String[]) userRoles.ToArray(typeof(String));
52:      }
53:
54:      // Add our own custom principal to the request containing the roles
55:      Context.User = new GenericPrincipal(Context.User.Identity, roles);
56:    }
57: }
```

Listing 16-4 contains the AuthenticateRequest event handler defined in the portal's Global.asax file. The event handler contains a sentinel: if (Request.IsAuthenticated == true). If the user is not authenticated then the event handler simply exits.

NOTE

Sentinel is a cute name for a conditional check that simply bars entry to the code if it fails. A positive sentinel is: if condition is true, then do something. I prefer to write the negative sentinel: if condition is false, let's get out of Dodge. Revising Listing 16-4 to use a negative sentinel, Line 4 would be rewritten as if (!Request.IsAuthenticated) return; It would then be immediately apparent to the reader that if the condition were not met, the method needs no further evaluation. This is especially useful when reading code or debugging. By using a positive sentinel — if (Request.IsAuthenticated == true) — we have to read the rest of the method to make sure some other code isn't running later on. The sentinel permits us to take a shortcut when the negative condition is true.

From Listing 16-4 we can determine two things. The first is that nothing happens unless the user is authenticated, and the second is that no matter how the user is authenticated, the code runs. The user may be authenticated in two ways: Windows authentication could be used (the user is authenticated when he or she logged into Windows), or the user could provide an e-mail address (which serves as the user name in the portal) and a password, which can be authenticated against the Users table in the portal database. If the user is authenticated in either of these ways, the Request.IsAuthenticated will evaluate to True.

NOTE

When Windows authentication is employed, Windows will provide the authentication. When we are using Forms authentication, the user is authenticated (or not) when he or she signs in or registers with the portal. A user is considered authenticated by invoking FormsAuthentication.SetAuthCookie. This step stores an authentication cookie that represents the user as having been authenticated. Refer to "Implementing the SignIn Module" later in this chapter for the specifics.

If the request made by the user is authenticated, the AuthenticateRequest event handler converts general authentication into user roles that are relevant to the IBuySpy portal. This occurs on lines 5 through 55 of Listing 16-4.

The conversion between authentication and portal roles occurs in one of two ways. If the "portalroles" cookie has not been saved—see lines 8 and 9 of Listing 16-4—then we read the roles out of the database using the UsersDB class, storing the roles in the array of strings named "roles." Each role is read and added to a semicolon-delimited string (lines 16 through 19). The string of roles is stored in a FormsAuthentication ticket object, encrypted as a string, and stuffed into the "portalroles" cookie. (Next time a request is made, assuming the cookie hasn't expired, the *else* condition code is run.)

If the "portalroles" cookie has already been saved, then the FormsAuthenticationTicket is reconstituted by decrypting the stored cookie (see lines 43 and 44 of Listing 16-4). The semicolon-delimited list of roles is split apart on lines 46 through 50 and assigned to the String[ ] roles on line 51. In either case, we end up with an array of the String class by the time we reach line 55.

Line 55 of Listing 16-4 uses the array of string-roles to construct a GenericPrincipal object. GenericPrincipal is initialized with the identity of the user and the roles. GenericPrincipal also implements the IPrincipal interface, which allows the portal to use the roles' information to perform checks to determine whether a user is in a certain role.

After we have created the object that realizes the IPrincipal interface, GenericPrincipal, and associated that object with the Context.User property, we can perform simple tests to determine whether a user is in a role such as the Admins role. Checks for user roles are centralized in the Security.cs module.

Security.cs implements the static methods PortalSecurity.IsInRole and PortalSecurity .IsInRoles, which accept a single, string argument. The string is used as an argument to the HttpContext.Current.User.IsInRole method, returning a Boolean value that indicates whether the user is in a particular role represented by the argument string. If you perform a grep—or an equivalent search—you will see that PortalSecurity.IsInRoles is used to quickly determine how the portal should be configured relative to a request. For example, the DesktopPortalBanner .ascx control uses PortalSecurity.IsInRoles to determine which tabs to display.

Programming with the FormsAuthentication Class

The FormsAuthentication class provides functions for managing a *ticket*. Tickets represent the authentication information stored in a cookie. By exploring Listing 16-4, we can examine how the FormsAuthentication class is used in the portal.

Line 22 of Listing 16-4 creates an instance of the authentication ticket indicating the user's identity on line 24, the time the ticket was issued on line 25, when the ticket expires on line 26, whether the cookie is persisted on line 27, and a string representing the user roles on line 28. After the ticket is created, the static method FormsAuthentication.Encrypt is invoked to encrypt the cookie to a string, and the cookie is written to the client. Lines 35 through 38 store the cookie. (Cookies are stored as strings. Refer to the upcoming section "Programming with Cookies" for more information.)

Whether the portal is caching the roles information for the first time—when Request .IsAuthenticated == true—or the cookie already exists—the *else* condition beginning on line 39 of Listing 16-4—the array of string-roles is populated, indicating the user roles. The roles information is used to create an IPrincipal object, which permits us to perform tests to determine whether the user has permissions to participate in a particular facet of the portal.

The basic idea is that if the user is authenticated, whether via Windows or Forms authentication, the user's roles are stored in a cookie. The cookie is retrieved when the user's roles need to be evaluated. The roles are stored in an IPrincipal object, which exists to provide a convenient way to examine those roles.

Programming with the IPrinicpal Interface

The IPrincipal interface defines a property, Identity, and a method, IsInRole. Classes that implement IPrincipal can be examined to determine the identity and roles of the user. The Identity property implements the IIdentity interface. Classes that implement IIdentity include FormsIdentity, GenericIdentity, PassportIdentity, and WindowsIdentity. Each of these classes contains members that realize the IIdentity interface, in addition to members essential to a specific kind of identification type.

IIdentity classes must define the AuthenticationType, IsAuthenticated, and Name properties. AuthenticationType is a string indicating the kind of authentication used. IsAuthenticated is a Boolean that indicates whether the user has been authenticated or not, and Name is the string name of the user. IIdentity classes let us know if and how a user was authenticated and who that user is.

Once we know the user is allowed to do something, IPrincipal classes tell us what the user is specifically allowed to do. The IsInRoles method is defined to accept a string and return a Boolean. The portal uses the GenericPrincipal, which realizes IPrincipal and implements the Identity property and IsInRoles method for us. Thus, we can pass any string data to IsInRoles to evaluate whether or not that particular string represents a valid role in the application, getting a Boolean result. The IBuySpy portal encapsulates the IPrincipal interaction in the Security.cs module's PortalSecurity class. An excerpt from the PortalSecurity class is provided in Listing 16-5.

Listing 16-5 *The PortalSecurity class uses the IPrincipal interface implemented by the Context.User property to test whether a user is in a specific role.*

```
1:   public static bool IsInRole(String role) {
2:       return HttpContext.Current.User.IsInRole(role);
3:   }
4:
5:   public static bool IsInRoles(String roles) {
6:
7:       HttpContext context = HttpContext.Current;
8:
9:       foreach (String role in roles.Split( new char[] {';'} )) {
10:
11:          if (role != "" && role != null && ((role == "All Users") ||
12:          (context.User.IsInRole(role))))) {
```

```
13:        return true;
14:      }
15:    }
16:    return false;
17: }
```

In Listing 16-5, PortalSecurity implements IsInRole in terms of the IPrincipal.IsInRole method. The HttpContext.User property represents the object that implements IPrincipal. (This assignment was made on line 55 of Listing 16-4.) GenericPrincipal is queried to determine whether the user is defined as a member in a specific role on line 2 and in the *Or* predicate on line 12 of listing 16-5.

The fundamental design of the portal relies on the premise that when a user is authenticated, and as the user navigates through the portal, the user's IPrincipal information assigned to the HttpContext.User property can be examined to determine what the user is allowed to do.

Programming with Cookies

I have mentioned cookies several times with the assumption that you have heard about them and that the concept is not completely foreign to you. Let's take a moment to explore what cookies are and how they are used, and, more important, what are appropriate uses for cookies.

Cookies are small pieces of information that are stored in memory while the browser is open or in text files on the client workstation. Cookies are useful for storing bits of information on the client's computer. Cookies are easy to use, as you will see in a moment, but they present a few minor stumbling blocks that you should be aware of.

Cookies can store only up to 4KB of information and, as a result, cannot be used to store objects like a DataSet. While most browsers support Cookies, the end user can delete cookie files (see Figure 16-1) or disable cookies (see Figure 16-2). With all of the security concerns these days, it is likely that Internet users may have disabled cookies from the browsers.

What practical use is left for cookies then? Well, you can use cookies to store small pieces of information that will make the user's interaction with your Web application a bit easier without making it critical that cookies be enabled. For example, you can store user authentication information, so that when a user returns to your Web site, you can acknowledge the user's return visit. What you shouldn't do is store critical information like credit card information, social security numbers, or other private information that adds to the general concern about using cookies. Cookies are reasonably secure because they are sent only to the originating computer, and the information is not stored as clear text in the cookie file.

The IBuySpy portal uses cookies to store information that authenticates the user. If you create an account in the portal, you can tell the portal to remember your account information. The account information is stored as a cookie on the PC until you explicitly log off. (Closing the browser does not delete the cookie.) Each time you return to the portal, you are authenticated using the cookie information (if the cookie exists). If you click the Logoff link in the portal, the cookie is deleted (see Figure 16-3).

Figure 16-1   *Internet Explorer 6.0 allows you to delete cookies via the browser's Internet Options dialog.*

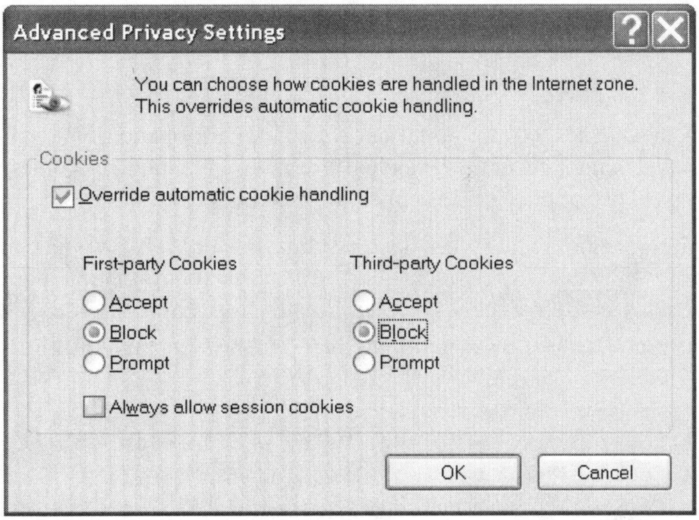

Figure 16-2   *Internet Explorer 6.0 allows you to disable cookies via the Advanced Privacy Settings dialog.*

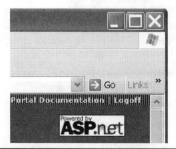

Figure 16-3   *The Logoff link will log you out of the portal application and delete a cookie used to authenticate you.*

Managing Cookies

Cookies are represented by the System.Net.Cookie class in .NET. You can manage cookies through the HttpResponse.Cookies property. The HttpResponse.Cookies property is read-only and is in an HttpCookieCollection derived from NameObjectCollectionBase. The Cookies property supports adding and removing cookies from the collection and indexing cookies with a string, representing the cookie key, or an integer value.

To store or retrieve a cookie, use the name of the cookie in parentheses as an argument to the Response.Cookies property. For example, Response.Cookies["portalroles"] will create or access an existing cookie if used as an l-value, and Request.Cookies["portalroles"] will return the "portalroles" HttpCookie that will be sent to the server when used as an r-value. When you have indexed a cookie, you can perform operations that are provided by the System.Net .Cookie class. These include providing comments and setting the expiration date and time, as well as a name, port, path, and value.

Using Cookies in the Portal

The portal uses the cookies to store portal-encrypted role information. This information is stored and retrieved to implement the IPrincipal object. From Listing 16-4, lines 35 through 38, we can see a typical use of the Cookies collection (see Listing 16-6).

Listing 16-6   *An excerpt from Listing 16-4, focusing on the use of cookies in the portal*

```
32: String cookieStr = FormsAuthentication.Encrypt(ticket);
33:
34: // Send the cookie to the client
35: Response.Cookies["portalroles"].Value = cookieStr;
36: Response.Cookies["portalroles"].Path = "/";
37: Response.Cookies["portalroles"].Expires = DateTime.Now.AddMinutes(1);
```

Line 32 of Listing 16-6 uses the static method to encrypt the cookie represented by the ticket to a string. Line 35 adds the cookie to the Cookies collection. The cookie will be referred to as "portalroles." The encrypted value of the cookie is assigned to the Cookie.Value property on line 35; the Cookie path is set to the root, indicating the URI on the server that this cookie applies to; and the cookie is set to expire in one minute from the time the cookie is added to the collection.

TIP

If the cookie path — see Listing 16-6, line 36 — were set to a specific path, then the cookie would be available only in requests to that path.

NOTE

If you don't express an expiration time for the cookie, then it will not be written to disk and will disappear when the browser is closed. Cookies without an expiration date and time are referred to as session cookies. Cookies with an expiration date and time are referred to as persistent cookies (they are "persisted" to disk).

The Logoff.aspx page contains code that responds to the user logging off and demonstrates how to sign the user out and clear a cookie. Listing 16-7 contains the Page_Load event handler from Logoff.aspx. (A user logs off by clicking the Logoff link, shown in Figure 16-3.)

Listing 16-7   *The Logoff.aspx code that runs when the user logs off*

```
1:    private void Page_Load(object sender, System.EventArgs e)
2:    {
3:
4:      // Log User Off from Cookie Authentication System
5:      FormsAuthentication.SignOut();
6:
7:      // Invalidate roles token
8:      Response.Cookies["portalroles"].Value = null;
9:      Response.Cookies["portalroles"].Expires =
10:       new System.DateTime(1999, 10, 12);
11:     Response.Cookies["portalroles"].Path = "/";
12:
13:     // Redirect user back to the Portal Home Page
14:     Response.Redirect(Request.ApplicationPath);
15:    }
```

The static method FormsAuthentication.SignOut logs the user out of the cookie authentication system on line 5 of Listing 16-7. Line 8 sets the "portalroles" cookie value to null, and setting the expiration to some time in the past ensures that the cookie is expired. After logging off, the user is redirected to the default home page (line 14). (You can download an experiment with the CookieDemo.sln, available at **www.osborne.com**, to practice reading and writing cookies.)

Implementing the SignIn Module

Signing out of the portal is managed by the Logoff.aspx page. Logging in is handled by the SignIn.ascx module. We have talked about the SignIn.ascx control relative to the visual design; now, let's take a few minutes to explore the SignIn.ascx code, which demonstrates how authentication cookies are created. Listing 16-8 contains the code for the SignIn.ascx control.

Listing 16-8	This code implements the SignIn.ascx control, which authenticates a user and creates an authentication ticket.

```
1:  using System;
2:  using System.Collections;
3:  using System.ComponentModel;
4:  using System.Data;
5:  using System.Drawing;
6:  using System.Web;
7:  using System.Web.UI;
8:  using System.Web.UI.WebControls;
9:  using System.Web.UI.HtmlControls;
10: using System.Web.Security;
11:
12: namespace ASPNetPortal {
13:
14:   public abstract class Signin : ASPNetPortal.PortalModuleControl {
15:     protected System.Web.UI.WebControls.TextBox email;
16:     protected System.Web.UI.WebControls.TextBox password;
17:     protected System.Web.UI.WebControls.CheckBox RememberCheckbox;
18:     protected System.Web.UI.WebControls.ImageButton SigninBtn;
19:     protected System.Web.UI.WebControls.Label Message;
20:
21:
22:     private void LoginBtn_Click(Object sender, ImageClickEventArgs e) {
23:
24:       // Attempt to Validate User Credentials using UsersDB
25:       UsersDB accountSystem = new UsersDB();
26:       String userId = accountSystem.Login(email.Text, password.Text);
27:
28:       if ((userId != null) && (userId != "")) {
29:         // Use security system to set the UserID within a client-side
30:         // Cookie
```

```
31:          FormsAuthentication.SetAuthCookie(email.Text,
32:            RememberCheckbox.Checked);
33:          // Redirect browser back to originating page
34:          Response.Redirect(Request.ApplicationPath);
35:        }
36:      else {
37:        Message.Text =
38:          "<" + "br" + ">Login Failed!" + "<" + "br" + ">";
39:        }
40:      }
41:    public Signin() {
42:      this.Init += new System.EventHandler(Page_Init);
43:    }
44:
45:    private void Page_Init(object sender, EventArgs e) {
46:      //
47:      // CODEGEN: This call is required by the ASP.NET Web Form
48:      // Designer.
49:      InitializeComponent();
50:    }
51:
52:    [Web Form Designer generated code]
53:    }
54: }
```

The portal roles-based security works by authenticating the user from the Portal database's User table. The User table is encapsulated in the UserDB class created on line 25 of Listing 16-8. The user name, represented by the TextBox control named e-mail, and the password are sent to the UserDB.Login method on line 26. If the user is authenticated by the portal and the User table, a UserID is returned. This constitutes roles-based authentication.

To indicate that the user has been authenticated—in this case, against the User table—the FormsAuthentication.SetAuthCookie method is invoked to create a cookie indicating that this specific user has already been authenticated. The Global.asax page uses this data when Request.IsAuthenticated is called; IsAuthenticated is True when SetAuthCookie has been invoked. Finally, the authenticated user is redirected to the home page.

If the user does not exist in the portal, the *else* condition displays the text "Login Failed!" at the bottom of the SignIn.ascx module.

Administering Users

The portal is user friendly from an administrative perspective. New users can register by clicking the register link in the SignIn module. The register link will redirect the user to the Admin/Register.aspx page and create a new row in the User table in the Portal database.

Administrative users—sign in with e-mail=guest and password=guest, by default—can create new roles, add users to roles, modify page and module views, edit permissions, create tabs, and manage tab permissions.

To manage the portal, log in as a user who is in an Admin role and navigate to the Admin tab. The portal has pretty good instructions for managing the portal and represents a good model for a Web application that has a lightweight extensibility model.

Secondary Topics

There as yet has been no mention of Code Access Security. The reason is that the portal doesn't use Code Access Security. I don't want to diminish the importance of Code Access Security for the obvious reason that it is important in .NET, and especially because Microsoft thinks it is important. What I do want is to provide some perspective.

Clearly, we have been building Web applications for several years without Code Access Security, and the IBuySpy portal is a great Web application that doesn't use Code Access Security—so what is it and why is it important?

Traditionally, applications have provided security at the user level. If a user was authenticated, that user could perform the functions assigned to the role of the user. Code Access Security is complementary. Code Access Security is designed to authenticate the code. Putting it in perspective, though, you do not have to use Code Access Security in every application to program in .NET: unmanaged code—non-.NET applications—don't use Code Access Security, and the Code Access Security policy that is configured by default is pretty good. The riskiest point of access for applications vis-à-vis malicious users is the Internet, and the other risky possibility is that an internal user accidentally performs an operation that wreaks havoc on a system. The upshot is that you can focus your attention on code that could possibly cause problems if misused or accessed by an unauthorized user. These are big problems if you are writing code that is or can be used by other developers—specifically, class libraries that provide services for other developers.

If you are not writing libraries for general consumption or code that can be accessed from the Internet, then you can expend less energy on Code Access Security. The reason that Code Access Security is so important is that many very considerable enterprises are writing libraries that are mission-critical and applications that can be accessed from the Web. For example, in our enterprise application in Oregon, if we allow users to indiscriminately delete records, then inmates—much to their pleasure—will be released early from prison. Almost as bad, if we release them too late, then the financial liability could be tremendous. To accommodate these risky possibilities, we use Code Access Security to tighten up access to operations.

Let's take a look at how Code Access Security is employed in .NET. I encourage you to pick up a copy of the comprehensive book *.NET Framework Security*, by Brian A. LaMacchia, et al., (Addison-Wesley).

Implementing Code Access Security

Code Access Security is employed by adding metadata in the form of attributes or security code directly to your application. Whether you use attributes, referred to as "declarative security," or code, referred to as "imperative security," you are basically using the same classes defined in the .NET framework.

The security permissions are added to the code, and they stipulate what the code is capable of doing or would like to be granted permissions to be able to do. Security covers just about everything imaginable.

Whether the code will actually be granted permission to perform a specific operation depends on the security policy established by an administrator. (For example, if you are the administrator on your PC, you can set the security policy.) The security policy can be set with the command-line tool caspol.exe or the Microsoft .NET Framework Configuration applet in the Administrative Tools folder. Refer to Figure 16-4 to see where the Microsoft .NET Framework Configuration applet is and Figure 16-5 for the Runtime Security Policy folder in the .NET Framework Configuration view.

Figure 16-4   *The Microsoft .NET Framework Configuration applet provides access to the security policy management capabilities of .NET.*

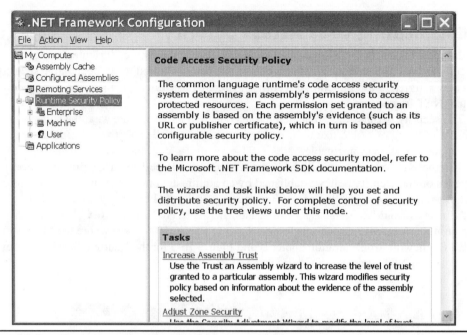

Figure 16-5   *The Runtime Security Policy folder permits administrators to set enterprise, machine, and user security permissions.*

Remember that the default security permissions are pretty good. It is a good idea to have an outcome-based plan before modifying security permissions. I would treat changing the security policy with the same deference you give to modifying the registry. Change the wrong permissions and your applications, even Visual Studio .NET, may stop functioning correctly. Fortunately, the last task in the tasks list (shown in Figure 16-5) enables you to reset all security policy levels.

Each node in the Runtime Security Policy equates to a different level of security. As the names suggest, the Enterprise node refers to enterprise security policy and is the highest level, while User is the lowest. Each node contains code groups, permission sets, and Policy Assemblies.

Code Groups refer to the code that falls under the specific policy. The default code group is All_Code. The Permission Sets provide specific levels of access to resources based on which set a specific assembly belongs to. The Permission Sets contain the following sets: FullTrust, SkipVerification, Execution, Nothing, LocalIntranet, Internet, and Everything. If you examine the permissions for each set, you will see that permissions are the most restricted for the Internet set. That is, code that falls under control of the Internet permission set has the most restrictive permissions. (Click Enterprise | Permission Sets | Internet and select View Permissions to see the permissions given to code that originates from the Internet.) The Policy Assemblies node refers to assemblies that are used to evaluate the security policy. If you create custom permissions, you will associate the assembly that implements the custom permission with the list of Policy Assemblies.

As developers, we can use .NET framework security declaratively by adding attributes to our assembly or imperatively by writing code. The next two sections provide a couple of examples of each. Because security is implemented as part of the framework, you can extend and customize security in .NET through inheritance. However, you should thoroughly explore the comprehensive existing security capabilities before customizing security.

Declarative Security

Declarative security is implemented in .NET by adding an attribute to a code element. The attribute will be the name of a specific security attribute class constructor with the necessary positional or named arguments required to construct the security object.

Suppose your code needs File IO permissions to function correctly. You can request File IO permissions with an assembly-level attribute to indicate that the assembly must have File IO permissions to function correctly. This doesn't mean that your assembly will be given File IO permissions, but when it doesn't function correctly, an administrator can diagnose the problem and determine whether File IO should be granted or not (see Listing 16-9).

Listing 16-9   *Declaratively requesting File IO permissions at the assembly level*

```
[assembly: System.Security.Permissions.FileIOPermission(
  System.Security.Permissions.SecurityAction.RequestMinimum,
  Unrestricted=true)]
```

The enumerated value SecurityAction.RequestMinimum is a position argument to the attribute FileIOPermissionAttribute, and Unrestricted is a named argument. This attribute indicates that the assembly will need unrestricted File IO permissions at a minimum to function correctly.

When the attribute is applied declaratively—as is the case in Listing 16-9—the assembly can be evaluated. If it will not be given the minimum requested permissions, the assembly will not run. You can also request SecurityAction.RequestOptional and SecurityAction .RequestRefuse. RequestOptional will allow the code to run even if it will not be granted the permissions, and RequestRefuse indicates that the code should not be granted the permission— in this case, File IO—even if the security policy would have normally granted it.

There are several security classes that can be explored in the System.Security namespace.

Imperative Security

Declarative security can be examined by the .NET framework before an assembly is allowed to execute. Imperative security works by creating instances of the security classes in code and invoking operations on those security objects. The assembly will load and run, but a specific section of code may not be able to run if it isn't granted that permission. For example, Listing 16-10 demonstrates how to demand File IO permissions imperatively at run-time.

Listing 16-10 *Imperative security demand for File IO*

```
1:  using System;
2:  using System.IO;
3:  using System.Security.Permissions;
4:  using System.Diagnostics;
5:
6:  namespace FileServices
7:  {
8:    public class MyFile
9:    {
10:     public MyFile(){}
11:
12:     public static void Delete(string FileName)
13:     {
14:       if( !File.Exists(FileName)) return;
15:
16:     (new FileIOPermission(
17:       FileIOPermissionAccess.NoAccess, @"C:\WINNT\")).Demand();
18:       // Simulate deleting the file
19:       Debug.WriteLine(string.Format("Deleting file {0}", FileName));
20:       //File.Delete(FileName);
21:     }
22:
23:   }
24: }
```

The FileServices.MyFile class is contained in a class library that provides a single service: it deletes files. (This class is representative of a part of a system File IO service.) Lines 16 and 17 of Listing 16-10 create an instance of the FileIOPermission class (not the attribute) in line with FileIOPermissionAccess.NoAccess and the path to the C:\WINNT directory. The FileIOPermission object is created, and the Demand method is invoked. This code is understood to mean that all callers in the call stack must have FileIOPermission to access files in the WINNT directory. If a stack walk reveals that the caller does not have permission, a SecurityException is raised, like the one in Figure 16-6.

The consumer ImperativeFileSecurityDemo.csproj and FileServices.csproj actually resided on the same machine, so I had to manipulate the security permissions for the

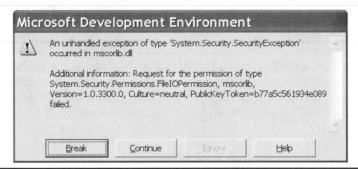

Figure 16-6   *A System.Security.Security exception because the consumer application calling MyFile.Delete did not have FileIOPermission to perform the requested operation*

ImperativeFileSecurityDemo.csproj application (the consumer). Listing 16-11 demonstrates the assembly-level attribute used to disable FileIOPermissions for the C:\WINNT directory for the consumer application.

Listing 16-11   *Refuse FileIOPermission for the C:\WINNT directory for the assembly that contains this attribute*

```
[assembly: FileIOPermission(SecurityAction.RequestRefuse, All=@"C:\WINNT")]
```

You have a tremendous amount of control in .NET. The security policy manager and Code Access Security permissions, in conjunction with more traditional approaches, will permit you to maintain tight access control over users and code in .NET.

Summary

This chapter demonstrated how roles-based security is used in the IBuySpy portal. You learned how to use the FormsAuthentication class, create principals to manage users, and store information in cookies.

Roles-based security is just one possibility in .NET. In the "Secondary Topics" section, you were also introduced to both declarative and imperative Code Access Security. From the perspective of management, this is probably the topic that will cause the most concern.

What you now know is that basic security capabilities are better in .NET than in any other platform prior. However, the greatest control over your network requires a holistic approach.

Limiting physical access to computers, updating operating systems with security patches, maintaining proper network administration, employing roles-based and Windows user authentication, and using Code Access Security are all part of the whole. Ignore one of these facets and some unscrupulous person is liable to take advantage of your code or resources. This is a big job, but .NET security now provides you with better control than ever before. As a programmer, you can use existing good practices and combine Code Access Security where appropriate and beneficial, working with your network administrator to obtain optimal security.

Index

Q

R

S

U

X

INTERNATIONAL CONTACT INFORMATION

AUSTRALIA
McGraw-Hill Book Company Australia Pty. Ltd.
TEL +61-2-9415-9899
FAX +61-2-9415-5687
http://www.mcgraw-hill.com.au
books-it_sydney@mcgraw-hill.com

CANADA
McGraw-Hill Ryerson Ltd.
TEL +905-430-5000
FAX +905-430-5020
http://www.mcgrawhill.ca

**GREECE, MIDDLE EAST,
NORTHERN AFRICA**
McGraw-Hill Hellas
TEL +30-1-656-0990-3-4
FAX +30-1-654-5525

MEXICO (Also serving Latin America)
McGraw-Hill Interamericana Editores S.A. de C.V.
TEL +525-117-1583
FAX +525-117-1589
http://www.mcgraw-hill.com.mx
fernando_castellanos@mcgraw-hill.com

SINGAPORE (Serving Asia)
McGraw-Hill Book Company
TEL +65-863-1580
FAX +65-862-3354
http://www.mcgraw-hill.com.sg
mghasia@mcgraw-hill.com

SOUTH AFRICA
McGraw-Hill South Africa
TEL +27-11-622-7512
FAX +27-11-622-9045
robyn_swanepoel@mcgraw-hill.com

**UNITED KINGDOM & EUROPE
(Excluding Southern Europe)**
McGraw-Hill Education Europe
TEL +44-1-628-502500
FAX +44-1-628-770224
http://www.mcgraw-hill.co.uk
computing_neurope@mcgraw-hill.com

ALL OTHER INQUIRIES Contact:
Osborne/McGraw-Hill
TEL +1-510-549-6600
FAX +1-510-883-7600
http://www.osborne.com
omg_international@mcgraw-hill.com